THE ROUTLEDGE HANDBOOK OF THE PHILOSOPHY AND SCIENCE OF PUNISHMENT

Philosophers, legal scholars, criminologists, psychiatrists, and psychologists have long asked important questions about punishment: What is its purpose? What theories help us better understand its nature? Is punishment just? Are there effective alternatives to punishment? How can empirical data from the sciences help us better understand punishment? What are the relationships between punishment and our biology, psychology, and social environment? How is punishment understood and administered differently in different societies? *The Routledge Handbook of the Philosophy and Science of Punishment* is the first major reference work to address these and other important questions in detail, offering 31 chapters from an international and interdisciplinary team of experts in a single, comprehensive volume. It covers the major theoretical approaches to punishment and its alternatives; emerging research from biology, psychology, and social neuroscience; and important special issues like the side-effects of punishment and solitary confinement, racism and stigmatization, the risk and protective factors for antisocial behavior, and victims' rights and needs.

The *Handbook* is conveniently organized into four sections:

I. Theories of Punishment and Contemporary Perspectives
II. Philosophical Perspectives on Punishment
III. Sciences, Prevention, and Punishment
IV. Alternatives to Current Punishment Practices

A volume introduction and a comprehensive index help make *The Routledge Handbook of the Philosophy and Science of Punishment* essential reading for upper-undergraduate and postgraduate students in disciplines such as philosophy, law, criminology, psychology, and forensic psychiatry, and highly relevant to a variety of other disciplines such as political and social sciences, behavioral and neurosciences, and global ethics. It is also an ideal resource for anyone interested in current theories, research, and programs dealing with the problem of punishment.

Farah Focquaert is Professor of Philosophical Anthropology at Ghent University in Belgium. She is one of the Directors of the international Justice Without Retribution Network and the Founder and Co-Chair of the Ethics Committee at The Forensic Psychiatric Centers Ghent/Antwerp in Belgium.

Elizabeth Shaw is Senior Lecturer in the School of Law at the University of Aberdeen, UK. She is the Founder and one of the Directors of the international Justice Without Retribution Network. Her research interests are interdisciplinary, involving criminal law, philosophy, and neuroethics.

Bruce N. Waller is Professor of Philosophy at Youngstown State University, Ohio, USA. Among his recent books are *Against Moral Responsibility* (2011), *The Stubborn System of Moral Responsibility* (2015), *Restorative Free Will* (2015), and *The Injustice of Punishment* (2018).

ROUTLEDGE HANDBOOKS IN PHILOSOPHY

Routledge Handbooks in Philosophy are state-of-the-art surveys of emerging, newly refreshed, and important fields in philosophy, providing accessible yet thorough assessments of key problems, themes, thinkers, and recent developments in research.

All chapters for each volume are specially commissioned, and written by leading scholars in the field. Carefully edited and organized, *Routledge Handbooks in Philosophy* provide indispensable reference tools for students and researchers seeking a comprehensive overview of new and exciting topics in philosophy. They are also valuable teaching resources as accompaniments to textbooks, anthologies, and research-orientated publications.

Also available:

The Routledge Handbook of Philosophy of Humility
Edited by Mark Alfano, Michael P. Lynch and Alessandra Tanesini

The Routledge Handbook of Metaphysics
Edited by Ricki Bliss and JTM Miller

The Routledge Handbook of Philosophy of Skill and Expertise
Edited by Ellen Fridland and Carlotta Pavese

The Routledge Handbook of Phenomenology and Phenomenological Philosophy
Edited by Daniele De Santis, Burt Hopkins and Claudio Majolino

The Routledge Handbook of the Philosophy and Science of Punishment
Edited by Farah Focquaert, Elizabeth Shaw and Bruce N. Waller

The Routledge Handbook of Phenomenology of Agency
Edited by Christopher Erhard and Tobias Keiling

For more information about this series, please visit: https://www.routledge.com/Routledge-Handbooks-in-Philosophy/book-series/RHP

THE ROUTLEDGE HANDBOOK OF THE PHILOSOPHY AND SCIENCE OF PUNISHMENT

Edited by Farah Focquaert, Elizabeth Shaw, and Bruce N. Waller

Routledge
Taylor & Francis Group
NEW YORK AND LONDON

First published 2021
by Routledge
605 Third Avenue, New York, NY 10017

and by Routledge
2 Park Square, Milton Park, Abingdon, Oxon, OX14 4RN

First issued in paperback 2022

Routledge is an imprint of the Taylor & Francis Group, an informa business

Publisher's Note
The publisher has gone to great lengths to ensure the quality of this reprint but points out that some imperfections in the original copies may be apparent.

Library of Congress Cataloging-in-Publication Data
A catalog record for this title has been requested

ISBN 13: 978-0-367-55365-4 (pbk)
ISBN 13: 978-1-138-58062-6 (hbk)
ISBN 13: 978-0-429-50721-2 (ebk)

DOI: 10.4324/9780429507212

Typeset in Bembo
by Newgen Publishing UK

CONTENTS

CONTRIBUTORS

Natalie Aga is Lecturer and Researcher at the Thomas More University College of Applied Sciences, Antwerp, Belgium. Her research concerns the recovery process of people labeled "*Not Criminally Responsible*."

Eyal Aharoni is Assistant Professor of Psychology, Philosophy, and Neuroscience at Georgia State University, USA.

Peter A. Alces is Rita Anne Rollins Professor of Law at The College of William & Mary School of Law, USA. He is the author, most recently, of *The Moral Conflict of Law and Neuroscience* (2018) and *The Law and Neuroscience Dialectic* (2022).

Corey H. Allen is a doctoral candidate in the Neuroscience Institute at Georgia State University, USA, with a particular interest in neuroethics.

Mirko Bagaric is Dean of the Swinburne University Law School, Melbourne, Australia, and Director of the Evidence-Based Sentencing and Criminal Justice Project. He is the author or co-author of over 30 books and 150 articles which have been published in leading international journals. While his main work is in the area of punishment and sentencing, he has also written extensively in migration and refugee law and human rights law.

Ekaterina Bagreeva has been teaching criminology for more than 10 years at Plekhanov University, Moscow, Russia. She has also worked at the National Research Institute of the Penal system of the Russian Federation, and been a research fellow on several international projects at Euroacademia, Council of Nordic Countries. She is a practicing graphologist.

Arielle Baskin-Sommers is a licensed clinical psychologist and Associate Professor of Psychology at Yale University, USA. She studies the neurocognitive mechanisms underlying disinhibited behavior across antisocial populations.

Colleen M. Berryessa is Assistant Professor in the School of Criminal Justice, Rutgers University, Newark, USA. Her research examines discretion in the criminal justice system, focusing on social contexts and societal attitudes toward mental disorders and biological research on behavior, and how they may affect the legal process and justice system.

Eva Blomme is an academic assistant and doctoral researcher at the Institute for Research on Crime and Criminal Policy at Ghent University, Belgium.

Thom Brooks is Dean of Durham Law School and Professor of Law and Government at Durham University, UK. His books include *Hegel's Political Philosophy* (2007), *Punishment* (2012) and, edited with Martha C. Nussbaum, *Rawls's Political Liberalism* (2015).

Robert Canton is Professor in Community and Criminal Justice at De Montfort University, Leicester, UK. He has worked extensively on the theories and practices of probation. His most recent book is *Why Punish? An Introduction to the Philosophy of Punishment* (2017).

Gregg D. Caruso is Professor of Philosophy at SUNY Corning, New York, USA, and Honorary Professor of Philosophy at Macquarie University, Sydney, Australia. He is also Co-Director of the *Justice Without Retribution Network* (JWRN) at the School of Law, University of Aberdeen, UK. His books include *Rejecting Retributivism: Free Will, Punishment, and Criminal Justice* (forthcoming), *Free Will and Consciousness: A Determinist Account of the Illusion of Free Will* (2012), *Exploring the Illusion of Free Will and Moral Responsibility* (2013).

Shou-An Ariel Chang is a third year PhD student at Yale University, USA, examining how socio-cognitive processing may differ in individuals from disadvantaged backgrounds, and how that, in turn, may impact antisocial behaviors.

Olivia Choy is Assistant Professor in the Department of Psychology at Nanyang Technological University, Singapore.

Charlotte Colman is Assistant Professor of Criminology at the Institute for Research on Crime and Criminal Policy at Ghent University, Belgium.

Federica Coppola is Presidential Scholar in Society & Neuroscience and a lecturer in Criminal Law & Neuroscience at Columbia University, USA. She studies the implications of social and affective neuroscience for substantive criminal law and criminal justice. Her first book *The Emotional Brain and the Guilty Mind: A Novel Paradigm of Criminal Culpability* is forthcoming.

Michael Louis Corrado is Arch Allen Distinguished Professor of Law, Emeritus, at the University of North Carolina Law School, USA. He has published articles on criminal responsibility and free will skepticism. His books include *Presumed Dangerous: Punishment, Responsibility, and Preventive Detention in American Jurisprudence* (2013), and *Comparative Constitutional Review: A Casebook* (2004).

Michele Cotton is Associate Professor of Legal Studies at the University of Baltimore College of Arts and Sciences in Baltimore, Maryland, USA. Her work includes publications in American law journals on the law of criminal punishment and its philosophical and scientific context.

Tom Daems is Associate Professor of Criminology at the Leuven Institute of Criminology (LINC), KU Leuven, Belgium. His recent publications include *Electronic Monitoring: Tagging Offenders in a Culture of Surveillance* (2020), *Privatising Punishment in Europe?* (2018, with Tom Vander Beken) and *Europe in Prisons* (2017, with Luc Robert).

Antony Duff is Professor Emeritus in Philosophy at the University of Stirling, UK. He works in the philosophy of criminal law. His books include *Answering for Crime (*2007*)* and *The Realm of Criminal Law* (2018).

David P. Farrington is Emeritus Professor of Psychological Criminology at Cambridge University, UK. His major research interest is in developmental criminology, and he is Director of the Cambridge Study in Delinquent Development, which is a prospective longitudinal survey of over 400 London males from age 8 to age 61.

Seena Fazel is Professor of Forensic Psychiatry at the University of Oxford, UK, and holds a Wellcome Trust Senior Research Fellowship in Clinical Science. He researches the relationship between mental illness and violence and violence risk assessment, and is the co-editor of *International Perspectives in Violence Risk Assessment* (2016).

Chad Flanders is Professor of Law at Saint Louis University School of Law in Saint Louis, Missouri, USA. He writes primarily in the areas of criminal law and philosophy of law and is the editor (with Zachary Hoskins) of *The New Philosophy of Criminal Law* (2015).

James Gilligan is a Clinical Professor of Psychiatry and Law at New York University, USA, after teaching for 30 years at Harvard Medical School. He is the author of *Violence* (1996*)*, *Preventing Violence* (2001), and *Why Some Politicians Are More Dangerous than Others* (2011).

Dorothee Horstkötter is Assistant Professor in the Department of Health, Ethics and Society at Maastricht University in the Netherlands. Her research covers ethical and conceptual questions in neuroscience and mental health. Together with K. Hens and D. Cutas she is the co-editor of *Parental Responsibility in the Context of Neuroscience and Genetics* (Springer, 2017) and has published in *The American Journal of Bioethics Neuroscience, Bioethics, BioSocieties, International Journal of Law and Psychiatry, Neuroethics, Theory and Psychology*, and various national journals.

Zachary Hoskins is Assistant Professor of Philosophy at the University of Nottingham, UK. He writes on moral, political, and legal theory, and he is the author of *Beyond Punishment? A Normative Account of the Collateral Consequences of Convictions* (2019).

Gerry Johnstone is Professor of Law at the University of Hull, UK. He is the author of *Restorative Justice: Ideas, Values, Debates* (2011) and *Building Bridges: Prisoners, Crime Victims and Restorative Justice* (2018, with Iain Brennan).

Erin I. Kelly is Professor of Philosophy at Tufts University, USA. She is author of *The Limits of Blame: Rethinking Punishment and Responsibility* (2018), which criticizes the role of blame in popular theories of criminal justice.

William R. Kelly is Professor of Sociology at the University of Texas at Austin, USA. His research focuses on criminology and criminal justice. He is the author of four recent books on criminal justice reform.

Youngjae Lee is Professor of Law and Associate Dean for Research at Fordham University School of Law, New York, USA. His recent publications include: "The Criminal Jury, Moral Judgments, and Political Representation" (2018) in *University of Illinois Law Review* 1255 and "Multiple Offenders and the Question of Desert," in *Sentencing Multiple Crimes* (2017).

Mike C. Materni earned his doctorate from Harvard Law School, USA, where his research focused on criminal and constitutional law. He works as a litigator in New York City.

Allan McCay teaches at the University of Sydney Foundation Program, and is Affiliate Member of the Centre for Agency, Values, and Ethics at Macquarie University in Australia. His research interests include neurolaw, free will and punishment, and the doctrinal and ethical challenges to law resulting from emerging technologies. He co-edited *Free Will and the Law: New Perspectives* (2019).

Arne Kvernvik Nilsen spent 15 years (in Norway and the UK) in pastoral and social work, prison chaplaincy, and developing and managing institutions, before joining the Norwegian Correctional services. He worked as a Chief Probation officer and Governor at Bastøy human ecological prison, as well as several years in the Department of Correctional Services, Ministry of Justice, in Norway. He has also worked as an international expert in Georgia, as well as with project and dialogue cooperation in a number of countries as a coach and adviser, including developing a human ecological prison unit in Romania. He is a practicing Gestalt psychotherapist.

Justine Olderman is Executive Director of The Bronx Defenders, a public defender nonprofit in New York, USA, where she has spent over 18 years as a skilled trial lawyer, representing clients in criminal matters. She authored "Fixing New York's Broken Bail System," published in *CUNY Law Review*. She has also taught courses at Fordham and Seton Hall Law School, and been a guest lecturer at NYU School of Law, USA.

Derk Pereboom is Susan Linn Sage Professor of Philosophy at the Sage School of Philosophy and Senior Associate Dean for the Arts and Humanities, both at Cornell University, USA. His books include *Living Without Free Will* (2001); *Consciousness and Prospects of Physicalism* (2011); *Free Will, Agency, and Meaning in Life* (2014); and *Free Will Skepticism in Law and Society* (2019, co-edited with Elizabeth Shaw and Gregg Caruso).

Howard Ryland is Forensic Psychiatrist and NIHR Doctoral Research Fellow at the University of Oxford, UK. His research focuses on outcome measurement in forensic mental health services.

Ivana Sekol is Lecturer in the Department of Criminology and Social Sciences, University of Derby, UK. Her main research and professional interests include the emergence and evidence-based prevention of bullying and peer violence in secure settings, (children's homes and correctional facilities for young people); risk and protective factors relating to anti-social and delinquent behavior; and early crime prevention. As a consultant she has been actively involved in the process of de-institutionalization and improving the lives of young people in care in Croatia.

Christopher Slobogin is Milton Underwood Chair at the Vanderbilt University Law School in Nashville, Tennessee, USA. He is the author of *Advanced Introduction to Criminal Procedure* (2020) and a co-author of *Juveniles at Risk: A Plea for Preventive Justice* (2011).

Scott Tillem is a fifth year PhD candidate studying the neurocognitive mechanisms underlying psychopathy at Yale University, USA. His most recent work titled "Psychopathy is associated with shifts in the organization of neural networks in a large incarcerated male sample" explored how psychopathy may fundamentally alter the organization of the brain.

Freya Vander Laenen is Associate Professor in the Department of Criminology at Ghent University, Belgium. Her research focuses on people with mental illness who offend, drug policy, and recovery and addiction.

Wouter Vanderplasschen is Associate Professor in the Department of Special Needs Education of Ghent University, Belgium.

Daniel Whiting is a Forensic Psychiatrist and NIHR Doctoral Research Fellow at the University of Oxford, UK. His research focuses on violence risk assessment and intervention in psychosis.

Izabela Zych is Associate Professor at the Department of Psychology in the University of Cordoba, Spain, member of the LAECOVI research team, and visiting scholar at the Institute of Criminology at Cambridge University, UK.

INTRODUCTION

Farah Focquaert, Elizabeth Shaw, and Bruce N. Waller

Punishment is at a critical crossroads. In the first three-quarters of the 20th century there was broad movement away from the retributive model of punishment, with many alternatives proposed and a significant number implemented. Starting around 1974 the "nothing works" movement became dominant in the United States, and it joined forces with retributivism, populist punitivism, and "selective incapacitation" to promote mass incarceration. The "nothing works" movement involved a popular meme claiming that no treatment program could ever be successful in rehabilitating offenders and thereby reducing recidivism. It basically assumed that prisoners cannot be rehabilitated. Although the criminological findings at the time suggested that many existing prison-based treatment programs did not lead to any appreciable reductions in recidivism, a variety of community-based programs had already demonstrated their effectiveness in reducing recidivism, and later programs have also proved their worth. Unfortunately, the "nothing works" meme lead to the further delusion that the more "hellish" one's time spent in prison is, the more likely it will function as a deterrent. In 1974 the US prison population was approximately 200,000; by 2006, it exceeded 1,500,000. The "prison-industrial complex" – including private for-profit prisons – had become a major growth industry, and "supermax" prisons (relying heavily on solitary confinement) had proliferated. By the early 21st century, the harms of mass incarceration had become obvious: enormous costs, high recidivism rates, psychological damage to prisoners, disruption of social structure in communities from which inmates were taken, hundreds of false convictions, and no evidence of reducing criminal behavior. In fact, incarceration may be criminogenic rather than rehabilitative for many individuals. Incarceration often causes and exacerbates physical and mental health problems in offenders, leads to significant post-incarceration harms due to stigmatization and socio-economic isolation, and involves long-term, secondary harms to offenders' family members and communities. Prisons pose a huge cost to society in terms of buildings, staff, care, and consequential costs such as the risk of disease spread upon reentry into society. The US system – with its high incarceration rate, harsh conditions, and high rate of recidivism – was in stark contrast with the policies in most of Europe, where dramatically lower imprisonment rates were accompanied by much lower crime rates. Nevertheless, many European prisons and forensic psychiatric institutions are similarly prone to human rights violations. At present, populist demands for punitive approaches to criminal behavior are voiced in several European countries and non-retributive proposals to crime reduction and prevention are often easily dismissed. In addition, existing non-retributive alternative programs to address criminal behavior often lack the necessary resources to be long-term effective.

At the same time that problems with retributivism and mass incarceration became increasingly obvious, the scientific study of crime and criminology and corrections was taking an enormous leap. Sociologists brought more rigorous methods of cultural investigation to the study of crime and corrections; psychologists studied the social and environmental factors contributing to crime and crime prevention; biologists and neuroscientists examined the complex biopsychosocial factors related to crime. Decades of research on criminal behavior has shown that a multitude of environmental factors contribute to criminal behavior. In addition, a growing body of research suggests that, on average, individuals who engage in violent, antisocial behavior show differences in brain structure and functioning, and hormone and neurotransmitter levels. Behavioral genetics studies also indicate that about 40–60% of the variance in criminal behavior is due to genetic influences. The environmental and biological factors that increase an individual's risk for criminal behavior are highly connected. Biological risk and protective factors influence the ways in which individuals react to the environment. In turn, environmental factors can affect gene expression, hormone and neurotransmitter levels, and ultimately brain structure and functioning. It is important to keep in mind that identifying neurobiological risk factors for criminal behavior does not imply that criminal behavior is "hard-wired" in the brain or that some individuals are irreversibly destined for a life of crime. There is no one-to-one relationship among biological factors and crime. Many individuals with biological risk factors will not go on to commit crimes and some individuals who do not exhibit a specific risk factor may proceed to commit a crime. All complex human behavior, not just criminal behavior, is caused by the interplay between our biology, psychology and environment. The main focus of biopsychosocial studies on criminal behavior is to achieve new ways to prevent crime through increased knowledge of the risk and protective factors that impact desistance. In addition to the biopsychosocial studies investigating the multitude of risk and protective factors related to crime and desistance, corrections officials (especially in Scandinavia, Canada and New Zealand) worked on new methods of reducing the recidivism rate; and the courts (and legal scholars) explored new possibilities for the criminal justice system. Retributivism remains popular, especially in the United States and the UK; however, it no longer dominates to such an extent that it blocks serious consideration of alternatives.

This Handbook presents research and theoretical analysis from a variety of disciplines and perspectives. It is a resource for researchers and scholars who wish to become familiar with complementary research from other disciplines and cultures. The essays consider a wide range of empirical studies, explore the challenges these pose for various theoretical models, and link theoretical views with contemporary research.

The first section, "Theories of Punishment and Contemporary Perspectives," explores major contemporary theories of punishment, including retributivism, utilitarianism, hybrid theories, and restorative justice.

The second section, "Philosophical Perspectives on Punishment," examines a wide range of important philosophical issues raised by the question of punishment, together with the implications of contemporary psychological research for our theories and practices of criminal punishment.

The third section, "Sciences, Prevention, and Punishment," looks at contemporary research in psychology, neuroscience, biosocial studies, and biopsychosocial criminology and its importance in restructuring our institutions and practices of criminal punishment.

The final section, "Alternatives to Current Punishment Practices," proposes and examines radical alternatives to current practices as well as critically important possibilities for modifications of the present system (such as the elimination of the bail bond system).

PART I

Theories of Punishment and Contemporary Perspectives

1
THEORIES OF PUNISHMENT

Robert Canton

Introduction: What Is a Theory of Punishment?

This chapter begins by asking what a theory of punishment might be and proposes two kinds of theoretical inquiry. The first of these seeks to understand why punishment takes place at all and why it takes the forms that it does at particular times and places. This, at least in principle, involves empirical investigations. The second project is a normative inquiry, asking about the morality of punishment. The chapter concludes with some reflections on the connection between these two projects of inquiry. Looking through a wider lens than some other contributions to this volume, this chapter does not look to defend any particular account; the attempt rather is to clarify some questions and to uncover some of the assumptions underlying these debates.

What, then, is a "theory of punishment"? The job of any theory is to explain or at least to illuminate something that is incompletely understood. What is to be expected of a theory of punishment is therefore likely to depend on what is found to be problematic or puzzling about it and, since the practices of punishment in any society constitute a complex social institution (Garland 1990), there are puzzles in abundance. Nor are these merely abstract or scholarly concerns: the attempt to understand punishment is also often prompted by practical concerns about crime and about justice.

Forms of punishment vary across time and place. Among the any number of ways in which societies have punished wrongdoers are the death penalty, corporal punishments (tortures, mutilations, brandings, whippings), banishment (exile or transportation), enslavement, shackling and other restraints, imprisonment, confiscations, fines and other financial deprivations. These most obviously constitute the "hard treatment" (Feinberg 1965) that are part of almost all definitions of punishment. But account must also be taken of several other types of sanction, including probation, community service/unpaid work, requirements to participate in various kinds of treatment programme, exclusion from specified places, disqualifications, curfews and electronic monitoring. We should also think of cautions, warnings, formal reprimands, conditional and suspended sentences. To come to understand why some of these responses to wrongdoing are favoured or rejected at particular times and in certain places, an empirical investigation is required, calling for the skills of the social sciences – especially psychology, sociology and anthropology.

Yet punishment also raises complex moral problems. The imposition of hard treatment is not normally what is expected of the state, which is supposed to defend and uphold the liberties of its citizens and others under its authority. How the moral dimensions of punishment are to be appraised, then, is our second inquiry – a normative exploration, requiring the methods of analysis and the perspectives of moral philosophy. Yet while the distinction between these two inquiries is useful for exposition, we shall see that there are important connections between the projects: most theories of punishment include both empirical and normative claims, even though these are not always made explicit.

Why Punish? An Empirical Inquiry

Perhaps the prior question is why we punish at all. In a study looking for values that might be common to all human societies (as a possible basis for international human rights standards that transcend different cultures), Alison Dundes Renteln (1990) found that, almost always and everywhere, people recognise and often act in accordance with the feeling that wrongs call for a retributive response, an urge to return harm for harm. There may be other countervailing sentiments, as we shall see, but retributive emotions are ubiquitous and maybe universal. These sentiments are – and once again almost always and everywhere – accompanied by a conviction that the punishment should be in proportion to the offence. The wrong has thrown a balance out of kilter and this must be redressed: the scales of justice are a widespread motif, found in many cultures (Atwood 2008).

Yet what counts as proportionate punishment and what it takes to restore the balance vary across time and place, with any number of cultural variations. One of the best known guiding principles is often referred to as the *lex talionis*, most familiar from the Book of Exodus:

> … and if any mischief follow, then thou shalt give life for life, eye for eye, tooth for tooth, hand for hand, foot for foot, burning for burning, wound for wound, stripe for stripe.
>
> *(Exodus 21: 23–25, King James Version)*

The principle is to be found in one of the earliest legal texts, the (Babylonian) Code of Hammurabi, although there are aspects here to the idea of just punishment that are strikingly at odds with modern conceptions of proportion. For example:

> If a builder build a house for someone, and does not construct it properly, and the house which he built fall in and kill its owner, then that builder shall be put to death. If it kill the son of the owner, the son of that builder shall be put to death.
>
> *(Code of Hammurabi, 229–230)*

Even if there is a sense in which we can recognise that the exact same pain (the death of a son) is being imposed on the offender, that the son of the builder should be put to death for the mistakes of his father is deeply offensive to modern sensibilities, including ideas of retributive justice. The Code reveals something important not only about conceptions of justice, but also about status and power. Throughout the Code there are examples of offences where the specified punishment depends on the standing of the offender and the victim: social status, freeman or slave, age and gender may all make a difference to the stipulated response.

Conceptions of proportion, then, may vary, even if insistence upon this as a principle of justice is widespread. Reflecting on the ubiquity of retribution tied to proportion, Margaret Atwood remarks that "... the older a recognisable pattern of behaviour is – the longer it's demonstrably been with us – the more integral it must be to our human-ness and the more cultural variations on it will be in evidence" (2008: 11). Renteln argues that proportionate retribution limits violence: a cycle of retaliation, vendetta or feud is otherwise probable. The state therefore seeks to establish a monopoly in imposing punishment for the most serious wrongdoings. It is not that societies necessarily deliberate about this; rather, those societies that find regulated and orderly ways of responding to wrongs can avoid the destructive effects of feuding and blood revenge and, to this extent, are more likely to prosper. As Pinker has put it, "the disinterested justice of a decent Leviathan induces citizens to curb their impulse for revenge before it spirals into a destructive cycle" (Pinker 2011: 541). It is to be noted, though, that the urge for retribution persists and people feel let down if the state does not vindicate wrongs against them, even if this is now formalised and managed by an impartial authority.

The temptation to say that this effect of limiting violence is in some sense "the purpose" of punishment should be resisted. Punishment does not and could not have a purpose over and above the several (and often conflicting) purposes that people set for it. The term "function" can also mislead, importing unwanted connotations of deliberate design or intention. Many penal practices and institutions are not designed: rather they evolve and, like evolution in the natural world, are shaped by their history and by the need to adapt to changing circumstances. "Function" is also associated with a particular way of understanding society, where institutions and practices work harmoniously to sustain the well-being of the whole, like the organs in a healthy body. But societies are marked by relationships of power as well as cooperation, and may be riven by differences of interest and conflicts. These tensions may be reflected in the practices of punishment. Punishment indeed has several effects or consequences, but only some of them (and just to some extent) are part of anybody's design or intent. As we shall see, some ethical defences of punishment rest on assumptions about its effects, but not only are these effects not always as supposed, but other consequences may be ignored.

Quite as ubiquitous as retributive responses are efforts to reconcile after wrongdoing, to repair broken relationships, to extend and to accept apology, to explore ways in which amends can be made or to bring about changes in the wrongdoer's behaviour or attitudes (McCullough 2008). It seems that both retribution and reconciliation – and indeed the tensions between them – are essential to social cooperation (Fehr and Gächter 2002; McCullough 2008; Greene 2013). Often the institutions and practices of punishment may manifest this ambivalence (Duncan 1996). Some penal practices can represent both hard treatment and an attempt to change people for the better. The prison is the most obvious example. Although there is room for scepticism about the possibility of improving people in the oppressive and squalid conditions that characterise so many prisons, the ambition to design regimes and programmes to facilitate personal change is a persistent aspiration throughout the history of the prison (Morris and Rothman 1995).

What Shapes the Practices of Punishment?

Even if we are content to conclude that retributive emotions are "integral … to our human-ness", there remain questions about why the punishments they are taken to call for vary in form and "weight". Some of the most instructive attempts to fathom these complex matters are discussed by David Garland in his magisterial *Punishment and Modern Society* (1980). Garland's exposition involves a critical summary of the works of many of the most influential thinkers about punishment – some of whom have addressed the matter directly and explicitly; some paying less attention to criminal justice specifically but offering a broader understanding of the social order that has inspired others to apply their perspective to punishment. Emile Durkheim, for example, understood punishment as an emotional reaction to the violation of a community's shared values represented by the crime. Forms and amounts of punishment will be determined by characteristics of the wider society, the complexity of the social order, the associated aspects of divisions of labour and "solidarity", and by cultural conceptions of what is fitting (for an overview, see Lukes and Scull 2013).

Norbert Elias emphasised changes in manners and customs generally. In the domain of punishment, corporal and capital punishments gradually, though variably and unevenly, came to be unacceptable to public sensibilities. In England, for example, after the excesses of the eighteenth (and indeed early nineteenth) century, most capital statutes were repealed by 1837. The hanging of murderers in public was abandoned in 1868. Subsequently the bloody code, prescribing the death penalty for a wide range of offences, was remembered as something remote and dreadful, its rejection taken as a sign of moral progress (Gatrell 1994). In general, the ways in which cultural and emotional sensibilities influence penal change are illuminatingly discussed by Philip Smith (2008). Among his insights is the thought that:

> Punishment … is only partly about program efficiency, inky statutes, or the armatures of power for it is also a form of expressive, communicative, ritualistic activity whose reach and grasp are shaped in decisive ways by *meaning*.
>
> *(Smith 2008: 169; my emphasis)*

The development of modern, bureaucratic institutions constitute another influence. Garland draws on Weber to show how professionalisation, bureaucratisation, centralisation, and a move towards uniformity did not just represent attempts to enhance efficiency, but altered the *cultural meaning* of sanctions: the penal system came to stand between the offender and the expression of public sentiment, so that punishment ceased to be social and became technical and professional instead.

The Marxist tradition emphasises the economic order and the relationships of *power* that will shape the criminal law and the forms that punishment is likely to take. While this tradition draws particular attention to social class, gender, race and other dimensions of difference also affect punishment. Oppressed and disadvantaged groups are always strongly over-represented in penal populations and there are times and places where the criminal law (and/or its practices of enforcement) ignore the wrongdoings of the rich and powerful in their preoccupation with the misbehaviour of the powerless and the poor (Muller and Wildeman 2013; Reiman and Leighton 2013)

The contribution of Michel Foucault has been especially influential in recent discussions of punishment. *Discipline and Punish* (Foucault 1977) begins with a description of the crude and gory efforts to execute the would-be regicide Robert-François Damiens in Paris in 1757. This is juxtaposed with a description of the meticulously ordered disciplines of the regime at Pentonville in London at the time of its opening in 1842. Foucault proposes that this should not be understood as a move towards greater humanity – to punish less – but as part of a project to "punish better". The aspiration was no longer to inflict bodily suffering, but to manage the body in order to change the mind.

At the centre of Foucault's work is an examination of how the human sciences – for example, medicine, psychiatry, criminology – and the social institutions with which they are deeply interdependent – hospitals, asylums, prisons – contribute to the control and "discipline" of modern societies. Apart from those who are altogether intractable, offenders should be "normalised".

> The normal child, the healthy body, the stable mind, the good citizen, the perfect wife and the proper man – such concepts haunt our ideas about ourselves, and are reproduced and legitimated through the practices of teachers, social workers, doctors, judges, policemen and administrators.
>
> *(Philp 1985: 67)*

At the same time, the area of deviance is demarcated and becomes a subject for "investigation, surveillance and treatment" (*ibid.*). Indeed Foucault saw the penitentiary as a laboratory for developing techniques to set and inculcate these standards of normality across wider society.

Cohen (1985), developing Foucault, writes of a "great transformation". Punishment had been shaming, public and local (think, perhaps, of the pillory or the stocks). In the nineteenth century, increasing involvement of the state in deviancy control and the development of a centralised bureaucratic apparatus transformed punishment from a local to a national enterprise; the segregation of people in various places of confinement within walls (asylums, prisons) made punishment more private than public; increased differentiation and classification by accredited experts made punishment more of a technical than a moral undertaking – which is not to say that punishment's moralising and shaming effects have disappeared, or indeed ever could.

The "grand theories" we have been considering have enriched our understanding of why punishment takes the forms that it does. They are best understood less as rival accounts than as "reciprocal commentaries, mutually deepening" (Garland 1990: 279, borrowing this elegant expression from Clifford Geertz.) Culture, power relations and the economic order – none reducible to another – all properly enter into a rounded understanding of punishment. At the same time, these high-level theories have their limitations and their hazards. They are often vague (and may be inaccurate) on historical detail – an allegation that has sometimes been levelled at Foucault. They may overgeneralise, implicitly assuming that the experiences of some countries are somehow representative if not typical of all and drawing more general conclusions than their limited study sample would warrant. They are also rarely "couched in terms that respect the motivations and actions of the actors and agencies involved" (Garland 2001: 104). They are incomplete to the extent that they usually fail to explain how broad social characteristics and influences are specifically "translated into the folkways of the [penal] field" (*id.* 2001: 24). Above all, perhaps, the error made by many theorists is to discover a partial truth about the influences on punishment and then to mistake it for the whole.

Other efforts to understand what shapes punishment have recourse not to historical accounts or to the ideal-typical societies envisaged by Marx or Durkheim, but to international comparative studies, inquiring what makes some countries so different from some others. Attempts have been made to try to map penal institutions and practices against broader socio-economic, political and cultural characteristics (see Cavadino and Dignan 2006; Tonry 2007). Such comparative investigations tends to show that punishment practice is *local* (Tonry 2007) – strikingly different attitudes, policies and practices can be found in countries in very similar social and economic situations.

Rather than looking for causal factors, an illuminating metaphor is that of an *ecological niche* (see Hacking 1999). A diverse, interacting and often conflicting set of influences, shaped by a broad range of social, economic, political and cultural factors, collectively constitute a milieu in which institutions and practices emerge, operate and develop. These include the framework of law, political agendas (well beyond penal policy), the political economy (emphasised by Cavadino and Dignan 2006), national wealth, criminal justice institutions and practices (whose momentum or inertia always influence the pace and indeed direction of change), technology, commerce (notably when the private sector becomes involved – see especially Christie 2000), borrowings from other countries through policy transfer (Canton 2014) or impositions (for example, through colonialism), research findings, public opinion (including anxieties about crime), media and pressure groups, the ethical environment (for instance, a commitment to human rights) and a wide range of cultural constraints (on which generally see Smith 2008). These vectors, which of course influence each other too, constitute the "niche" and changes in them can mould the character of penal practice and institutions. The indefinitely many ways in which these factors interact will account for local variation and idiosyncrasy, as well as making the development of penal policy and practice inherently hard to predict (see also Lacey, Soskice and Hope 2018).

A further consideration arises from the relationship between policy and practice, between what Cohen (1985) called the "stories" that institutions tell about themselves and the lived realities of practice. Policies are the principal source for the study of punishment, but these written accounts are aspirational and stand for what the policymakers wish to accomplish and to present. The extent to which these ambitions are achieved in practice is another matter. Practitioners (for example, prison staff, probation officers) have to receive their instruction, but then must find ways of putting it into practice – ways that are likely to include attempts to accommodate policy to their own values and interests, the occupational culture and their own understanding of what it takes to get the job done. This is Garland's warning: our accounts of punishment must "respect the motivations and actions of the actors and agencies involved" (Garland 2001: 104). Further, these "actors" include those subject to punishment. The meanings with which the punishers and the punished invest their experiences are hard to access and may not be assumed to align with the intentions of legislators, courts and senior managers – intentions that are themselves complex. Yet these meanings are critical to a fuller understanding of punishment.

Punishment has been described as a "relatively autonomous" domain (Garland 2001) – autonomous because it has its own independent trajectories and dynamics, but only relatively so because it is also and inevitably shaped and channelled by the social, legal, economic, political and cultural influences just discussed. Reciprocally, the institutions and transactions of punishment not only reflect a culture and socio-economic order, but lend authoritative endorsement to many social practices and exercise an influence of their own. One implication of this is that a study of punishment can illuminate the character of a society, its values, relationships and structures of power, in instructive and sometimes surprising ways. So it can be said that:

> What appears on the surface to be merely a means of dealing with offenders so that the rest of us can lead our lives untroubled by them, is in fact a social institution which helps define the nature of society, the kinds of relationships which compose it, and the kinds of lives it is possible and desirable to lead there.
>
> *(Garland 1990: 287)*

The Morality of Punishment: A Normative Inquiry

At the very beginning of an excellent book Linda Radzik remarks, "Our moral theories should tell us not just what is right and what is wrong but also how to deal with wrongdoing once it occurs" (Radzik 2009: 3) Punishment may be at least part of how we should deal with wrongdoing and many moral philosophers have accordingly considered its ethical dimensions (for a broad overview, see Bean 1981). These debates have often been conducted under the heading "the justification(s) of punishment". The reason why punishment needs justification is because it involves – and on most definitions necessarily involves – a deliberate imposition of pain or deprivations or constraints upon freedom. The state normally defends its citizens and other members of its communities against such intrusions. Philosophers have therefore investigated "the justifications of punishment" to see how it is that a state may – or even must – impose such hardships when criminal offences have taken place.

Many of the chapters in this book explore candidate justifications in detail. Most accounts find a justification on the basis of one or other of these claims:

- punishment, by one mechanism or another, reduces crime and so makes for a safer society;
- punishment gives the offender what they deserve;
- punishment expresses solidarity with victim(s) and compassion for the harms they have suffered.

These claims may enter into a justification, but as they stand they are more aptly characterised as aims or purposes. Each claim sets out something that punishment should aim to do, with the implication that punishment can indeed achieve these objectives. To justify something, however, is to show that it is morally required or morally permissible or at least morally better than alternatives. And to set a purpose is not *of itself* an assurance that either the purpose or the means by which it is pursued is morally justifiable.

In this case, even so, the purposes seem morally unassailable: society should be made safer; wrongdoing should be vindicated in proportion to desert with the responsibility of the wrongdoer suitably respected; and victims should find support and compassion. Nevertheless other questions arise. There may, for example, be moral considerations that have been insufficiently taken into account as the justifications have been explored. Or perhaps there are other and better ways of accomplishing these aims. For that matter, if "ought" implies "can", it may not be simply assumed that these purposes can be achieved by punishment. Again, there are questions about the forms that punishment should take – for example, some forms of punishment may fail to respect the wrongdoer's responsibility or neglect the victim altogether. This chapter goes on to make some general remarks about these identified aims and the extent to which they do or could amount to a justification. Other chapters will scrutinise these accounts in much more detail.

Safer Society – Reductivism

The main mechanisms that are conventionally considered to reduce offending (or reoffending) are deterrence, rehabilitation and incapacitation (for example, Canton 2017). Very roughly, deterrence supposes that the prospect of a punishment will deter (frighten off) potential offenders. Rehabilitation is a complex concept (McNeill 2012), but broadly aspires to bring about or enable changes such that people can find ways of living in which offending has no place. Incapacitation involves physical constraint and is normally associated with some form of secure detention, although a level of incapacitation can be achieved by vigilant supervision in the community. (Other reductive means could include the prevention of private reprisal, as we have already seen, or the exhortative effects of the affirmation of communal values that Durkheim emphasised. More generally, Jean Hampton (1984) drew attention to the educative effects of well-administered and principled punishment on all members of a society.)

Each candidate justification raises distinctive ethical questions. Fear and threat (deterrence) seem ethically dubious as means to induce law-abiding behaviour in a liberal democracy. Punishing people more than they deserve to achieve a wider good (for instance, through exemplary sentences to show people that the courts really mean business) looks very like using people as a device of social engineering. Even if this was argued to be for the greater good, there is more to ethics than calculation and people have rights that must be respected. Punishment must be concerned with the proper dispensation of justice and not mere social control.

Rehabilitation has often been impugned on ethical grounds (Canton 2017: Chapter 6), although McNeill (2012) has shown this is levelled at just one (narrow and insufficient) conception: rehabilitation should be understood as much more than psychological correctionalism. Even within those limited terms, Bennett (2010) has pointed out that the word may refer to any of a very wide range of interventions and convincingly argued that there are differences of method and objective that determine the ethical value of rehabilitative endeavours. To the extent that incapacitation involves a sentence beyond desert to prevent future offending, it looks perilously close to punishing people for something they haven't (yet?) done and, if the sanction is sufficient and well-administered, never will do. Even if those objections can be overcome, there is wide agreement that this is a principle that applies just to the riskiest offenders and cannot justify the punishment of the great majority of those who have committed criminal offences.

It has been insisted that setting an aim does not constitute a justification. But on the other hand if it were to turn out that punishment does not and perhaps could not achieve the purposes set for it, any justification that rested on such a claim would be fatally undermined. The case to show the reductive effectiveness of penal measures is not strong. With regard to deterrence, a distinction can be made between "certainty" (of being caught) and "severity" (of punishment) (Bottoms and von Hirsch 2010). The weight of research evidence suggests that perceptions of certainty do have some effect, while the prospect and severity of the punishment seem to form little or no part of offenders' decision making (*ibid.*). Nor is the formal punishment always the most feared of the consequences of being caught. The effectiveness of rehabilitation is contested, to a significant extent because the term can refer to such a wide and disparate range of activities. The success of some methods can be plausibly claimed, although changes to the individual's attitudes and motives are unlikely to be sufficient without a fair opportunity to gain the "social capital" needed to live a law-abiding life (Canton 2017: Chapter 6 and references there cited). Incapacitation can reduce offending for some people, but merely postpone it for others. Prolonged detention can be crime-causing (criminogenic), aggravating the problems associated with the original offending and/or frustrating desistance (stopping offending) by blocking pathways out of crime. It can be too readily assumed, then, that these mechanisms of reduction "work", but there is a weight of evidence to show a much more complex state of affairs and to invite a degree of scepticism about the capacity of punishment to reduce crimes, with troubling implications for any ethical defence that rests on that foundation.

Punishing According to Desert – Retributivism

The idea that wrongdoers should be punished according to what they deserve (and in ways that respect the individual's responsibility) is compelling and is not vulnerable to the misgivings that can be expressed about reductivism. From a moral point of view, what all reductive defences of punishment are at risk of losing is a clear and tight connection between the crime and the weight and form of the punishment. And it is this that is most strongly affirmed by retributive accounts. At the heart of this connection between crime and punishment is the idea of desert – the persuasive and widespread notion that people should be punished because and just to the extent that they deserve. It is precisely this that warrants the claim that we have a system of criminal *justice* as opposed to a system of crime management.

Yet how are the form and weight of a just punishment to be determined? Desert-based or retributive accounts suppose that this is to be decided by reference to the harm done by the crime and the individual's culpability for that crime. Both of these turn out to be much more complex constructs than first appears, however. It can be agreed that in theory the punishment should in some sense "fit" the crime and this chimes with our intuitions. The *lex talionis* seems to offer one way in which this might be done, but in the gravest cases its implications can seem brutal and no less morally problematic than the original offence. It has also been pointed out that, on these principles,

> it is hard to see what punishment one should inflict on a blackmailer, a forger, a dope peddler, a multiple murderer, a smuggler, or "a toothless fiend who has knocked somebody else's tooth out" (Kleinig 1973, p. 120).
>
> *(Ryberg and Peterson 2014: 4067)*

The appeal to justice remains compelling. The first half of this chapter, however, drew attention to those critiques that insist that both the criminal law and its enforcement are influenced by the interests of the powerful: some harms are not criminalised in the first place and others are weakly enforced. Can "justice" be hermetically sealed within the courtroom without regard to the processes that have brought this person to punishment, while another who has offended more harmfully and just as culpably gets away with it? These are not random processes, it is argued, but systematically represent and reproduce the interests of the powerful (Reiman and Leighton 2013).

Ideas of culpability are no more straightforward. Some people's life circumstances have been so disadvantaged, their choices so limited, that they justly merit a "hardship defence" (Hudson 1999). More fundamentally, some argue (see this volume, Chapter 12) that the very idea of culpability is challenged by advances in our understanding of the neurophysiological influences on our development and character. We do not choose our genetic inheritance nor the way in which our parents or others bring us up in our formative years. Since our behaviour is, if not determined, at least powerfully constrained by these influences, can we be held responsible for what we do?

Nor should the impact of the punishment be overlooked. Sentencing according to desert implies that the same crime should meet the same punishment. Variations in harm and culpability complicate the question of when crimes could be said to be the same, while "the same punishment" can have very different effects on people. Michael Tonry makes the point sharply:

> … two years' imprisonment in a single setting will have very different meanings to different offenders who have committed the same crime. Two years' imprisonment in a maximum

> security prison may be a rite of passage for a Los Angeles gang member. For a … twenty-year-old, it may mean the terror of repeated sexual victimization. For a forty-year-old head of household, it may mean the loss of a job and a home and a family. For an unhealthy seventy-five- year-old, it may be a death sentence.
>
> *(Tonry 1996: 19)*

All these considerations make problematic the concept of proportionality which is at the heart of retributive justifications. Here an initial distinction must be made between absolute or cardinal proportionality (the punishment in some sense fitting the crime) and relative proportionality (worse crimes should receive weightier punishments) (for an insightful discussion of this, see Matravers 2011). There is broad agreement about which crimes are most serious (Ashworth 2010: Chapter 4), and (questions of impact notwithstanding) there is probably sufficient consensus about the weight of punishments for a tariff of relative proportionality to be constructed. There remains, however, the question of where to fix the "anchor points" of such a tariff. The worst crime should be awarded the most serious punishment, but how much is that and what form should it take? In practice, this seems a matter of custom and practice in different jurisdictions and few argue that there is a specific and exact punishment that is uniquely suitable for a particular crime (although some supporters of the death penalty might attempt that argument). While it will always be relevant to object that this punishment is too severe (or too lenient) for this offence, a relative proportionality is probably the most that can be achieved. For all its (almost universal) recognition, however, the concept of proportionality may turn out to be unable to check penal excess to the extent that its proponents might hope (Lacey and Pickard 2015).

Censure theory has become influential in many contemporary accounts of punishment (du Bois-Pedain and Bottoms 2019; see Chapter 3 this volume). A punishment should make a communication; it should be declaratory. Yet there are several "audiences" – the offender, the victim, everybody else – and it may not be assumed that all will understand the message in the same way or that all (or indeed any) of them will receive the message as intended, even if there is a straightforward and single message to be conveyed. With regard to the offender in particular, it is not only the pronouncement of the punishment (in the sentence of the court), but the manner of its implementation that will "send the message". Walgrave (2003: 65) has referred to the "communicative aridity" of retributive punishment, arguing that restorative processes are much more fertile ground for effective communication. Again, censure is more than self-righteous scolding. It attempts to enhance awareness of the wrong and indeed to induce remorse, including the sincere wish not to offend again (one component of sincere remorse) (Maslen 2015). Some forms of punishment may instead provoke defiance or resentment and inhibit the purposes of fitting censure. If censure is at the heart of any ethical defence of retribution, then, the shortcomings of retributive punishment as communication represent a substantial critique.

Solidarity with and Compassion For Victims

A third account is that punishment is morally justifiable because it is the best (perhaps the only) way to demonstrate compassion for victims and vindicate their experience. Punishment is a commonly accepted form of vindication for victims so that a failure to punish (or to punish sufficiently) may be taken by victims and their supporters as a slight, an inadequate recognition of the distress the offence brought about. Yet sometimes, perhaps often, stern punishment fails to bring victims the satisfaction they had anticipated (Carlsmith, Wilson and Gilbert 2008; though see also Funk, McGeer and Gollwitzer 2014). Martha Nussbaum (2017) argues for a tight conceptual connection between a retributive wish for payback and *anger*. It is typically anger that leads to the urge for retributive payback, but for victims and their supporters anger is destructive and "especially poisonous when people use it to deflect attention from real problems that they feel powerless to solve." The focus on payback, she argues, brings a sense of control against the overwhelming helplessness induced by grief, but this sense is illusory and blocks the grieving that needs to take place in the gravest cases whatever punishment befalls the offender. It should also be remarked that, in political debate, some self-proclaimed champions of victims have urged severe punishment and then turned their back on the needs, rights and indeed the wishes of victims. Even if victims are entitled to weighty punishment of those who have committed a crime against them, this is by no means all that they need, especially in the most serious cases.

Even to raise the question about what victims need is to expose the probability that their needs will be diverse, depending on the nature of the crime, the support that they can receive from families and friends, and other considerations. Sometimes material compensation is the least and the most required to make good the harm that has been done; in other circumstances, the offer of (usually) a financial payment can be interpreted as further insult (see Moon 2013). This is because, as Duff (2001) insists, victims have not only been harmed but *wronged*. Harms can be compensated, but how can the wrong be made good? Restorative justice (see Chapter 7, this volume) holds out this prospect.

In political (and indeed sometimes in scholarly) debate, the interests of offenders and victims are presented in stark opposition. Restorative justice tries to go beyond the assumption that the interests of victims and offenders are inherently opposed and looks for resolutions that meet the legitimate interests of both. It rejects any notion that a vindication of the victim's experience is best achieved by the imposition of hard treatment, coercion, exclusion or denunciation of the offender, as opposed to the proper and proportionate censure of their conduct in committing the offence. There is an increasing weight of evidence to show that well-managed restorative meetings are much more likely than a conventional criminal justice process with a retributive focus to lead to a resolution that brings a degree of satisfaction to the victim and indeed to the offender (Sherman and Strang 2011; Shapland, Robinson and Sorsby 2011).

Yet while some commentators draw a sharp distinction between punishment and restorative justice, regarding them as different and indeed incompatible conceptions of justice (for references and discussion, see Roche 2013; Zedner 1994), Duff argues that restorative and retributive justice are better understood as two sides of a coin. He concludes that we should "recognise criminal mediation and reparation as punitive, indeed as a paradigm of retributive punishment" (Duff 2003: 53). Once again, however, the *form* of the punishment has to be taken into account. For while some punishments may succeed in achieving actual or symbolic redress as part of a reparative process, others may fail completely in that respect. Imprisonment of the offender, notably, brings nothing to a victim beyond the doubtful satisfaction of contemplating the hardships visited on the wrongdoer and perhaps the (sometimes specious) assurance that they are no longer in a position to cause harm.

Punishment may bring some benefit to victims, then, but with much less value than has sometimes been supposed. As Nussbaum has argued in detail (2016, 2017), the passion for punishment can divert attention not only from the crucial matter of crime reduction, but also from the needs and legitimate interests of victims. Nor must we overlook those many victims whose offenders are not brought to justice (for example because never identified). Their need for compassion and vindication is no less, but cannot be met by the sentence of the court.

It has been argued that none of the main accounts that set out to justify punishment is compelling. Reductive accounts are exposed not only to ethical criticism, but rest on a wholly exaggerated confidence in the capacity of punishment to reduce offending. Arguments that invoke justice typically fail to offer much guidance about the form and weight of punishments. They must also address the challenge of whether retributive justice can be achieved in any society that is scarred by social injustice. Our zeal for punishment in the name of the victim rarely brings the anticipated satisfaction or sense of closure and indeed distracts from important questions about victims' true interests and rights. Even so, each account seems to capture something about the character of punishment which eludes the others and some have been encouraged accordingly to think about using these theories in complementary ways – in some form of "hybrid" theory. How this might be accomplished and the extent to which any such attempt might be persuasive is considered by Hoskins (Chapter 4, this volume).

Finally, in appraising the moral arguments, it could be remarked that each account is incomplete, usually failing to go beyond the pronouncement of the punishment (the sentence of the court) to go on to consider the form the punishment should take or the manner of its implementation, which could undermine the most ethically defensible sentence. A more complete ethical account of punishment, moreover, should also have regard to "the end state of cases of wrongdoing – some point at which we can describe the wrongful act as having been successfully resolved" (Radzik 2009: 112; Canton, with Padfield 2019). We cannot stop with the pronouncement of the punishment but must address the question of how the (ex-) offender can be reinstated to a full and proper civic status once the punishment has been served. Any justification of punishment must look not only to its beginning, as it were, but also to its end.

Concluding Remarks

Theories of punishment (in every sense of the word "theory") are worth studying for their own sake, but many of those who study these matters are inspired by a belief that it should be possible to make changes and improvements to the policies, institutions and practices of punishment. Moral philosophy should have an application: it should be able to guide us in our policies and in our decisions. Reflecting on the philosophy of punishment, however, David Garland observed that:

> … at present we lack a detailed appreciation of the nature of punishment, of its character as a social institution, and of its role in social life. … [The image on which philosophies of punishment are typically based, then,] is an impoverished one, and fails to capture the full dimensions and complexities of punishment, [so that] the solutions offered by philosophy are unlikely to match up to the problems of the institution.
>
> *(Garland 1990: 9)*

Few moral philosophers have responded to the challenges in this remark with the result that many accounts make assumptions about the nature, meaning and significance of punishment, as well as about its effects. These assumptions need to be exposed and put to test. The failure to do this means that arguments in the philosophy of punishment often seem remote from practice and with little to offer to policymakers, judges and penal practitioners who are trying to do things better.

The study of the dynamics of punishment should also be put to use. A deeper understanding of why punishments take the form that they do is intellectually engaging in its own right, but if these insights are to be deployed to inform penal policy there must be regard to ethics. Without the wisdom of moral philosophy it might be possible to devise arrangements to control crime, but this would not be a criminal justice system.

For the purposes of exposition, the empirical inquiry into the social and cultural factors that influence the form and weight of punishment in a society and the ethical inquiry into the moral parameters of punishment have been sketched here as discrete undertakings. But to a significant extent they are complementary projects in the cause of penal reform. Such reform needs a moral inquiry to determine the direction of reform (what would "better punishment" be like) and a deeper understanding (through empirical inquiry) of how and indeed whether such changes can be brought about. In this way, the inquiries we have distinguished here are mutually dependent and must be used in synergy.

References

Ashworth, A. (2010) *Sentencing and Criminal Justice*, (5th edition), Cambridge: Cambridge University Press.

Atwood, M. (2008) *Payback: Debt and the Shadow Side of Wealth*, London: Bloomsbury.

Bean, P. (1981) *Punishment*, Oxford: Martin Robertson.

Bennett, C. (2010) "Punishment and rehabilitation", in J. Ryberg and J. Angelo Corlett (eds.), *Punishment and Ethics: New Perspectives*, Basingstoke: Palgrave Macmillan.

Bottoms, A. and von Hirsch, A. (2010) "The crime-preventive impact of penal sanctions" in Kane, P. and Kritzer, H. (eds.) *The Oxford Handbook of Empirical Legal Research*, Oxford: Oxford University Press.

Canton, R. (2014) "Transfer of policies and practices to other countries" in G. Bruinsma, and D. Weisburd, (eds.) *Encyclopedia of Criminology and Criminal Justice*, Springer: 2623–2632.

Canton, R. (2017) *Why Punish? An Introduction to the Philosophy of Punishment*, London: Palgrave Macmillan.

Canton, R. with Padfield, N. (2019) "Why punish?" *Howard Journal of Crime and Justice*, **58** (4), 535–553. https://onlinelibrary.wiley.com/doi/abs/10.1111/hojo.12342

Carlsmith, K., Wilson, T. and Gilbert, D. (2008) "The paradoxical consequences of revenge", *Journal of Personality and Social Psychology*, **95** (6): 1316–1324.

Cavadino, M. and Dignan, J. (2006) *Penal Systems: A Comparative Approach*, London: Sage.

Christie, N. (2000) *Crime Control as Industry: Towards Gulags, Western Style* (3rd edition), London: Routledge

Code of Hammurabi Translated by L.W. King. Available online at http://www.general-intelligence.com/library/hr.pdf (accessed October 2018).

Cohen, S. (1985) *Visions of Social Control*, Cambridge: Polity Press

du Bois-Pedain, A. and Bottoms, A. (eds.) (2019) *Penal Censure: Engagements Within and Beyond Desert Theory*, Oxford: Hart.

Duff, A. (2001) *Punishment, Communication and Community*, Oxford: Oxford University Press.

Duff, A. (2003) "Restoration and retribution" in A. von Hirsch, J. Roberts, A. Bottoms, K. Roach and M. Scheff (eds.) *Restorative Justice and Criminal Justice: Competing or Reconcilable Paradigms*, Oxford: Hart.

Duncan, M.G. (1996) *Romantic Outlaws, Beloved Prisons*, New York: New York University Press.

Fehr, E. and Gächter, S. (2002) "Altruistic punishment in humans", *Nature*, **415** (6868): 137–140.

Feinberg, J. (1965) "The expressive function of punishment", *The Monist*: 397–423.

Foucault, M. (1977) *Discipline and Punish: The Birth of the Prison*, Harmondsworth: Penguin.

Funk, F., McGeer, V. and Gollwitzer, M. (2014) "Get the message: punishment is satisfying if the transgressor responds to its communicative intent", *Personality and Social Psychology Bulletin*, **40** (8): 986–997.

Garland, D. (1990) *Punishment and Modern Society: A Study in Social Theory*, Oxford: Oxford University Press.

Garland, D. (2001) *The Culture of Control: Crime and Social Order in Contemporary Society*, Oxford: Oxford University Press.

Gatrell, V. (1994) *The Hanging Tree: Execution and the English People 1770–1868*, Oxford: Oxford University Press.

Greene, J. (2013) *Moral Tribes: Emotion, Reason and the Gap Between Us and Them*, New York: Penguin.

Hacking, I. (1999) *Mad Travellers: Reflections on the Reality of Transient Mental Illnesses*, London: Free Association Books.

Hampton, J. (1984) "The moral education theory of punishment", *Philosophy & Public Affairs*, **13** (3): 208–238.

Hudson, B. (1999) "Punishment, poverty and responsibility: the case for a hardship defence", *Social and Legal Studies*, **8** (4): 583–592.

Kleinig, J. (1973) *Punishment and Desert*, The Hague: Martinus Nijhoff.

Lacey, N. and Pickard, H. (2015) "The chimera of proportionality: institutionalising limits on punishment in contemporary social and political systems", *The Modern Law Review*, **78** (2): 216–240.

Lacey, N., Soskice, D. and Hope, D. (2018) "Understanding the determinants of penal policy: crime, culture, and comparative political economy", *Annual Review of Criminology*, **1**: 195–217. Available online at https://tinyurl.com/y947vn4t (accessed October 2018)

Lukes, S. and Scull, A. (eds.) (2013) *Durkheim and the Law* (2nd edition), Basingstoke: Palgrave Macmillan.

Maslen, H. (2015) *Remorse, Penal Theory and Sentencing*, Oxford: Hart.

Matravers, M. (2011) "Is Twenty-first century punishment post-desert?" in M. Tonry (ed.) *Retributivism Has a Past Has it a Future?*, New York: Oxford University Press.

McCullough, M. (2008) *Beyond Revenge: The Evolution of the Forgiveness Instinct*, San Francisco: John Wiley.

McNeill, F. (2012) "Four forms of "offender" rehabilitation: towards an interdisciplinary perspective", *Legal and Criminological Psychology*, **17** (1) 18–36.

Moon, C. (2013) "Money as the measure of man: values and value in the politics of reparation" in M. Cowburn, M. Duggan, A. Robinson and P. Senior (eds.) *Values in Criminology and Community Justice*, Bristol: Policy Press.

Morris, N. and Rothman, D. (eds.) (1995) *The Oxford History of the Prison: The Practice of Punishment in Western Society*, New York: Oxford University Press.

Muller, C. and Wildeman, C. (2013) "Punishment and inequality" in J. Simon and R. Sparks (eds.) *The Sage Handbook of Punishment and Society*, London: Sage.

Nussbaum, M.C. (2016) *Anger and Forgiveness: Resentment, Generosity, Justice*, New York: Oxford University Press.

Nussbaum, M.C. (2017) *Powerlessness and the Politics of Blame,* The Jefferson Lecture in the Humanities, May 2017. https://www.law.uchicago.edu/news/martha-c-nussbaums-jefferson-lecture-powerlessness-and-politics-blame. Accessed October 2018.

Philp, M. (1985) "Michel Foucault" in Quentin Skinner (ed.) *The Return of Grand Theory in the Human Sciences*, Cambridge: Cambridge University Press

Pinker, S. (2011) *The Better Angels of Our Nature: The Decline of Violence in History and its Causes*, London: Allen Lane.

Radzik, L. (2009) *Making Amends: Atonement in Morality, Law and Politics*, New York: Oxford University Press.

Reiman, J. and Leighton, P. (2013) *The Rich Get Richer And The Poor Get Prison: Ideology, Class and Criminal Justice* (10th edition), New York: Pearson.

Renteln, A. Dundes (1990) *International Human Rights: Universalism versus Relativism*, Newbury Park CA: Sage.

Roche, D. (2013) "Retribution and Restorative Justice" in Gerry Johnstone and Daniel Van Ness (eds.) *Handbook of Restorative Justice*, London: Routledge.

Ryberg, J. and Petersen, T. (2014) "Proportionality" in G. Bruinsma, and D. Weisburd, (eds.) *Encyclopedia of Criminology and Criminal Justice*, Springer: 2623–2632.

Shapland, J., Robinson, G. and Sorsby, A. (2011) *Restorative Justice in Practice: Evaluating What Works for Victims and Offenders*, Cullompton: Willan

Sherman, L. and Strang, H. (2011) "Empathy for the devil: the nature and nurture of revenge" in S. Karstedt, I. Loader and H. Strang (eds.) *Emotions, Crime and Justice*, Oxford: Hart.

Smith, P. (2008) *Punishment and Culture*, Chicago: University Of Chicago Press.

Tonry, M. (1996) *Sentencing Matters,* New York: Oxford University Press.

Tonry, M. (2007) "Determinants of penal policies", *Crime and Justice*, **36** (1): 1–48

Walgrave, L. (2003) "Imposing restoration instead of inflicting pain: Reflections on the judicial reaction to crime", in Andrew von Hirsch, Julian Roberts, Anthony Bottoms, Kent Roach and Mara Schiff (eds.) *Restorative Justice and Criminal Justice: Competing or Reconcilable Paradigms?*, Oxford: Hart.

Zedner, L. (1994) "Reparation and retribution: are they reconcilable?", *The Modern Law Review*, **57** (2): 228–250.

2

RETRIBUTION

Thom Brooks

Introduction

Retribution is probably the most familiar theory of punishment.[1] Retributivists argue that an offender must deserve punishment in order to be punished. Yet retributivists differ widely on the issue of what it means to deserve punishment. They also disagree on the relation, if any, between how deserving an offender is and how severe his or her punishment should be. This chapter will begin by explaining how retribution has been understood traditionally and then consider the many variations of retributivist theories of punishment that have been developed since. The overarching aim is to provide a critical overview of retribution as a diversity of views under the shared tent of desert.

Classic, Or Positive, Retribution

Perhaps the original view of retribution is as *positive retribution*, or simply "classic" retribution (as opposed to more contemporary conceptions). This view defines retribution in this way: an offender *deserves* punishment *in proportion to* his or her crime. This classic understanding of retribution holds that it is both necessary and sufficient to punish a criminal if that person deserves it. Desert informs us as to whether someone can be subjected to punishment and how punishment can be distributed justifiably. In other words, this concept provides both a justification and indicates its amount.

This view of desert is an important limit on punishment. Someone cannot be punished because he or she was only unpopular or to make an example in pursuit of some other social policy. Retributivists cannot justify the punishment of the innocent on the grounds that they do not deserve it. Someone must have, in fact, deserved punishment in order to be punished. Desert plays a gamekeeper-like role in who can or cannot be subjected to punishment.

It also plays a second, concurrent role of a sliding scale. Desert is not only present or absent, but if present then desert can be more or less. Not everyone who deserves punishment will deserve the same amount of it. This is because desert comes in degrees. Where zero, then no punishment is deserved – but where someone has much desert, then a more severe punishment is warranted.

An example is the *lex talionis* of "an eye for an eye". This saying can be seen by contemporary standards to make retribution seem extreme: few, if any, would argue that someone could be punished by having an eye removed whatever the crime committed. However, an eye for an eye – if seen from within its historical perspective over two millennia ago – exemplifies classic retributivism. First, someone must have committed an offence for any such action to be justified. It is not a view that such a harsh punishment can happen to anyone. Secondly, "an eye for an eye" sets a clear upper boundary for punishing: only an eye for an eye is to be lost, not one's limbs or life.

A more modern version of classic retributivism is found in Immanuel Kant's theory of punishment (Kant 1996; Brooks 2003).

Retribution Is Not Vengeance

It can be helpful to grasp retribution partly through what it rejects. Retributivism is sometimes thought to be synonymous with vengeance. This connection is rejected fundamentally by retributivists. The reasons are several. An act of vengeance is one where I take matters into my own hands. I restrain or cause injury to another because I alone feel it is warranted. I might be mistaken about whether I was wronged – or, if I was wronged, I may be mistaken about the identity of the wrongdoer. In acting against another, there is no guarantee that I will treat like cases alike. Vengeance is a kind of atomistic anarchy where the individual acts as judge, jury and executioner following his or her own sense of when a line has been crossed.

This is not retribution. For example, Michael Moore says:

> But retributivism goes further. As a theory of a kind of justice, it *obligates* us to seek retribution through the punishment of the guilty. This means that officials have a duty to punish deserving offenders and that citizens have a duty to set up and support institutions that achieve punishments.
>
> *(1993: 15)*

Whether or not someone deserves punishment is not a matter of a single person's guess, but an objective fact about an offender's guilt and corresponding desert. Retribution is about not private morality, but public justice. However, this requires much further elaboration about how retributivists determine desert and its amount – and it is from here that we begin to see a diversity of views emerge.

Desert Is a Kind of Moral Responsibility

Retributivists attach specific meaning to their central concept of desert. An individual has or lacks desert through a conscious act or omission. Desert is not a property that somebody has by accident. The offender comes to possess desert because of his or her *responsibility* for committing a crime.

An offender has desert when that person is morally – and not merely causally – responsible for some act or omission. The bare fact that Adam is injured by a sharp stick belonging to Brenda does not entail that Brenda deserves punishment. For example, Adam might have self-harmed with the stick before handing it to Brenda. Or perhaps Brenda did harm Adam, but in self-defence. For retributivists, these cases do not merit desert. Causal responsibility is insufficient.

An important consequence is that most retributivists reject the use of so-called *strict liability offences.* These are crimes where moral responsibility is not a factor. Such illustrations include the bare fact of possessing banned drugs or driving a car faster than a set speed limit. These actions are *mala prohibita*, or wrong because they are unlawful. I might be unaware that the envelope in my bag contains a banned substance or, if I were a Formula One race driver, my driving a few miles above a set speed limit might not actually pose any genuine risk to others on account of my car driving abilities.

Mala prohibita crimes pose an important test case and challenge for retributivists. They are an important test case insofar as, if there are crimes which lack moral responsibility, they would be desert-free and would seem to fall outside punishable offences that could be justified by retributivists. It is perhaps little surprise that these crimes are usually punished more leniently than most other crimes. However, the challenge for retributivists is that these crimes can make up a significant portion of the criminal law.[2] Some retributivists try to argue that no such crimes exist to escape this problem.

They argue that there is some moral justification to the overall legal system and so to breach any part of it is to necessarily break some morally justified law (Duff 2001).

Instead, what matters is *moral* responsibility for immoral acts or omissions.[3] It is not sufficient to know merely that Brenda's sharp stick has stabbed Adam, but whether she is responsible for doing a wrong to him. Moral responsibility is the measure of punishable desert (Brooks 2012: 20). The responsibility for wrongness is at the heart of retribution – and at the same time its Achilles' heel.

Problems with Knowing Intentions

The moral responsibility of an offender is essential to determining whether he or she has desert. This adds a kind of moral magic that can transform a non-criminal situation to a crime. Suppose Brenda stands over Adam who has been stabbed by a sharp stick in her hands. Whether or not Brenda is morally responsible can be the difference between her having desert or not, for example.

The problem is that we might have to gain some insight into the intentions of another to determine his or her moral responsibility. But, of course, we are unable to read each other's minds and so any precise certainty about desert can be elusive. This is spelled out well by Kant:

> The real morality of actions, their merit or guilt, even that of our own conduct, thus remains entirely hidden from us. Our imputations can refer only to the empirical character. How much of this character is ascribable to the pure effect of freedom, how much to mere nature, that is, to faults of temperament for which there is no responsibility, or to its happy constitution, can *never* be determined, and upon it therefore *no perfectly just judgements* can be passed.
> *(1963: 475)*

Kant's points are that we can make no error-free judgement about another's moral responsibility, including their guilt. All we can do is manage an educated guess based on the available evidence. Someone confessing to a crime does not mean they did it, as there can be secret motives – such as police pressure or a desire to be put in custody – that are actually in play.

This fact that we cannot know with certainty another's guilt has repercussions. The first is the prevalence of standards for securing convictions in court. These are commonly of *beyond reasonable doubt* – and not beyond any doubt. We cannot render a perfect judgement every time and nor does the criminal justice system make such an impossible demand on us. Mistakes are inevitable and will happen over time.

A second repercussion concerns the retributivist justification of practices, specifically, the death penalty. If criminals deserve punishment to the degree they have done wrong, then retributivists justify the harshest sanction for murderers. But the fallibility of our knowing the desert of another is a major problem for any retributivist wanting to support capital punishment. This is captured well by Judge Jed Rakoff in *US v Quinones*:

> What DNA testing has proved, beyond cavil, is the remarkable degree of fallibility in the basic fact-finding processes on which we rely in criminal cases. In each of the 12 cases of DNA-exoneration of death row inmates referenced in *Quinones*, the defendant had been found guilty by a unanimous jury that concluded there was proof of his guilt beyond a reasonable doubt; and in each of the 12 cases the conviction had been affirmed on appeal, and collateral challenges rejected, by numerous courts that had carefully scrutinized the evidence and the manner of conviction. Yet, for all this alleged "due process", the result, in each and every one of these cases was the conviction of an innocent person who, because of the death penalty, would shortly have been executed (some came within days of being so) were it not for the fortuitous development of a new scientific technique that happened to be applicable to their particular cases.[4]

The argument is that the decision as to whether to execute an individual is not one that can be undone. Mistakes cannot be corrected insofar as the condemned cannot be brought back to life. Despite unanimous jury verdicts, affirmed appeals and due process, it is very possible to be found conclusively innocent through scientific breakthroughs in confirming evidence.

As a general rule, we can be mistaken notwithstanding all compelling evidence to the contrary. Retributivists might support the execution of murderers in principle, but they cannot in practice. This is because of the centrality of desert for retributivism. We may only hold others accountable beyond a reasonable doubt, but must always leave the door open for errors which the death penalty makes it impossible to rectify.

One objection is raised by the British Conservative Member of Parliament, David Davis. He argues that capital punishment should be reintroduced in the United Kingdom only for those convicted of two or more murders. His position is that perhaps there may be doubt – or, indeed, innocence – where someone is convicted only once. However, he surmises that any such chance of being innocent of committing a murder will be close to nil the more convictions that someone has. But in response, it is unclear that the procedures we follow for one or many convictions will necessarily always guarantee that a murderer is guilty with no chance of any error. Therefore, this objection does not overcome the problem of justifying the death penalty facing retributivists (Brooks 2011). While *Quinones* was later overruled, this retributivist argument against capital punishment has been developed and gained traction.[5] The problem of knowing intentions with sufficient certainty puts limits on the severity of punishments that retribution could justify.

Problems with Desert

A criminal must possess desert if punishment is to be justified. This raises interesting issues about how this might be done. Kant provides an illuminating example:

> Whatever undeserved evil you inflict upon another within the people, you inflict upon yourself. If you insult him, you insult yourself; if you steal from him, you steal from yourself; if you strike him, you strike yourself; if you kill him, you kill yourself.
>
> *(1996: 106)*

Punishment is deserved when someone is morally responsible for committing some act that is evil. Insulting, stealing, hitting and killing are all evil acts, but not all evil acts are equally evil. Some are more so than others. But how much?

For Kant, there is a universal moral law. We must only act in such a way that everyone could so act at the same time. When we choose to act differently, we become responsible for breaking this moral law and deserving punishment, on his view. The thief fails to recognise universal rights of property ownership and instead sees herself as being an exception. It is clear that Kant's equivalency between crime and punishment is an equivalency of value – he elsewhere rejects treating inhumanely those who perform inhumane acts. But if all criminal acts are those that contradict the universality of the moral law, what does it mean to say breaking the moral law for inconsistent behaviour concerning property is less bad that any other inconsistent behaviour? For Kant, the answer lies in the value of the thing harmed. So murder will be punished more severely because, for Kant, human beings have infinite worth. We punish murderers by capital punishment on this view not because we must follow an eye for an eye, but because the infinite value of what is lost in murdering someone can only be equivalent to the loss of the murderer's own life of infinite value.

This view – like virtually all retributivist views – presupposes a specific moral theory. If retributivism is about punishing deserving offenders for their moral responsibility for committing an evil, then we must clarify which moral standard is to count for determining what is evil. Kant's view is only one of many contested moral standards. Punishing evil requires having a compelling theory about evil – and such a fundamental part of retributivism is too often assumed and unstated. Thus retributivists can support very different outcomes for the same crime depending on which moral theory they rely on as a standard.

This position has consequences. For example, if we are only to punish those responsible for committing acts of evil in some degree, this informs not only how we punish but what we criminalise. Retributivism requires the crimes it punishes to be some kind of immoral wrongdoing. A problem is that it is far from clear whether all acts we might want to criminalise are immoral wrongdoings. This speaks to the distinction between crimes that are wrong because they are unlawful (*mala prohibita*) versus crimes that are wrongs in themselves (*mala in se*). Many violent crimes fall into the latter category for most theorists ranging from assault to murder, but the former category produces difficulties.

Some potential candidates for a mala prohibita crime might include drug use or prostitution. While many moral theories may lead their adherents to find these acts immoral, this is contested and other moral views might support a different view. There may be reasons for rendering each unlawful on grounds of public health or safeguarding that might be non-retributive at its core.

Traffic offences are a less controversial case. There is no clear universal moral norm about which direction a one-way road must follow or why illegal parking must be criminal. The different status of traffic offences is partly recognised in places like the United States where convictions must be listed on most job applications, unless it is only one motoring offence. No other such type of criminal offence is routinely downgraded.

Traffic offences matter. These are the crimes that most people actually commit. Any theory of crime and punishment really should be able to speak to their justification. Yet it is far from clear how retributivists could do so. The best example is as follows. Suppose there is a driver with a broken speedometer. She believes that she is driving at 75 mph, but is actually at the speed limit of 55 mph. Larry Alexander (1994: 29) argues that "in the absence of a good reason for driving unsafely, [the driver] is reckless with respect to lives, bodies and properties" despite the fact that he is actually driving at "a safe speed". This view is mistaken. It errs in assuming the lowering of the speed limit on American highways to 55 mph was justified with respect to safety. In fact, federal highways changed their speed limit because this would have the urgently needed effect of lowering public consumption of oil during an oil shortage crisis. The speed limit was not set to ensure public safety – as it had been approved for much higher speeds. Moreover, even if this reasoning about consumption rather than safety is faulty, the motorist is in fact driving at a safe speed of 55 mph even if falsely believing she is going much faster. Such behaviour is neither criminal nor punishable: the driver may have moral responsibility for what they do, but they are not actually engaged in any immoral wrongdoing.

If retributivists only punish crimes that are immoral wrongdoings, then this requires that an offender is responsible for what she has done and that what is done is immoral. Yet whether an act is or is not immoral may depend on which moral theory we find most compelling. And if we could agree on which moral theory provides the best standard, it is unclear how it might grapple with including acts – like traffic offences and perhaps many others – that we might want to find unlawful but which do not easily cohere with all such moral theories.

To summarise: retributivists traditionally understand desert in terms of an offender's moral responsibility for immoral wrongdoing. This view presupposes there is a universal moral standard that we can appeal to in order to determine what is criminal or lawful. Furthermore, this standard can assist us in linking the amount of punishment to the degree of immoral wrongdoing. Retributivists may come to different views about what is criminal and how much crimes should be punished when appealing on different moral standards – but such moral standards are assumed and play a fundamental role. So one issue is that such standards are contested, but a second issue is that not all acts we might want the criminal law to punish are clearly illegal because they are immoral. And if retributivists then choose to only include what is immoral, this would potentially leave out large swathes of what is in the criminal law, such as traffic offences, that then create large gaps.

Making Punishment Fit the Crime

There are other ways in which retributivists claim criminals must deserve punishment and be punished to the degree they deserve. One way is to follow Kant and claim a strict equality in value between the amount of evil in an act and the amount of punishment this act deserves, as already noted above. A problem with this view is that such a precise determination is very difficult to discern and yet, for strict equality to hold, any amount slightly too much or too little is an injustice. For example, someone stole my bicycle when I was a young teenager from my house. What is the strict equality view of retributivist punishment for this – to steal that person's bicycle at some point in future? Or how many days of hard treatment is strictly equal to the loss of a teenager's bicycle? These questions do not admit of easy answers.

A second way of understanding how the punishment might fit the crime is to say the offender "pays back" in being punished. This view derives from the Latin roots, *re* and *tribuo*, meaning "to pay back" (Cottingham 1979: 238). The problem with this position is that it is difficult to discern who precisely is paid back. Who does a criminal pay back in serving six months' imprisonment for a victimless crime? It is difficult to see how all punishments might serve as a kind of repayment for what is owed.

A third view is to say the offender enjoys an unfair advantage. When the thief steals property, he has acquired holdings – and so is enjoying an advantage he would not otherwise enjoy – and done so in an unfair way through illegality. In short, the thief derives a benefit from unlawfulness. Retributivist punishment, on this view, says that he should get what is deserved and remove the unfair advantage he unlawfully enjoys. However, the problem with this view is that it is unclear that criminals are advantaged through unlawfulness. For example, we would not want to say that the rapist or murderer is enjoying an advantage over others. Instead, we would claim that they harm themselves in harming others like this by choosing evil and damaging their character.

A fourth view is that punishment should seek to annul crimes. This view is often attributed to Hegel, although it is very questionable whether he in fact holds it (see Brooks 2004; Brooks 2017). Hegel does say: "The cancellation of crime is *retribution* in so far as the latter, by its concept, is an infringement of an infringement" (Hegel 1991: 127). The argument is that retributivist punishment is not merely a response to crime, but a cancellation of crime. The idea is that an offender's crime challenges the existence of the law unless this challenge's existence is annulled. For Hegel, our punishing an individual for an act of theft or murder would reassert the existence of a right to property or life and so "cancel", or "annul", those crimes.

The problem with this view is that it seems impossible to enact. Perhaps a thief who steals a purse might be forced to return it intact and undamaged to its rightful owner. But any such talk of cancelling the crime is more metaphorical than real. The clock cannot be turned back and restarted – nor can the dead be brought back to life. Perhaps we can heal or forgive, but it is much less clear how we can annul, hence there are no modern defenders of this specific view of retributivism today.

A fifth view is proportional retributivism, itself a kind of limiting retributivism. This is best articulated by Jeffrey Reiman:

> Proportional retributivism, then, in requiring that the worst crime be punished by the society's worst punishment and so on, could be understood as translating the offender's just deserts into its nearest equivalent in the society's table of morally acceptable punishments.
>
> *(1985: 129)*

Reiman is attempting to address the issue of how retributivists can avoid justifying punishments that appear overly harsh. His solution is to create two lists. The first list contains all the crimes we wish to punish ranked from most to least wrong. The second list is the full range of acceptable punishments.

We then match the most wrong crime with the most severe punishment we are willing to accept – and so on until we cover all crimes. The benefit of this procedure is that, if we find the death penalty or corporal punishment objectionable, we can still punish crimes proportionately but without disagreeable severity. The problem is that this disconnects the moral link between making punishment proportionately fit the crime that is so important for all varieties of retributivism. The point is not that retributivists must be open to accepting the death penalty, but that the link between crime and punishment cannot simply be a somewhat random connection of the first, second and third worst crimes with whatever happens to be thought separately to be the first, second and third most severe acceptable punishments. The amount of punishment is connected to the amount of desert – and this gets lost in this view.

A final, sixth view is of negative retributivism. Until this point, the retributivist views considered have broadly been part of the family of so-called positive retributivism. This is the view that desert is necessary and sufficient to justify punishment: all criminals must deserve punishment and their punishment must be in proportion to the amount they deserve.

Negative retributivism sees things differently. They claim desert is necessary, but not sufficient for justifying punishment. They first ask if an offender has desert – and, if so, they then look to other non-retributivist goals such as deterrence or rehabilitation in setting the amount of punishment to be given to an offender. This is an important break from traditional retributivism where "the consequences of punishment are irrelevant" (Easton and Piper 2005: 49). Negative retributivists would never punish an innocent person, but would also not necessarily punish a guilty person to the degree of their immoral wrongdoing. Instead, when someone has been found guilty there would then be a second question: how should this guilty person be treated in order to bring about the best consequences, including non-retributivist consequential goals such as deterrence and rehabilitation. The attraction of this view is its attempt at trying to incorporate being both backward-looking in accounting for desert while also being forward-looking in considering future consequences.

The problem is that this view is not integrated well, nor is it retributivist in more than name. If an offender's having desert is critically important enough that it makes all the difference between those that can or cannot be punished, it is difficult to grasp why it carries no weight at all in determining the amount of punishment that someone might receive. And if desert does not have importance for setting the amount, then it is unclear how the goals to be achieved can link to the desert of an offender. For example, someone who commits a minor crime in light of immoral wrongdoing could potentially be subjected to a disproportionately severe punishment if a deterrent were needed. Perhaps it is compelling that our punishments should be set in light of future consequences, but it is unclear how a view like negative retributivism – that awkwardly mixes retribution and non-retributivist elements – can bring these elements together in a coherent, unified way.[6]

Conclusion

Chin Liew Ten (1987: 38) claims that "there is no complete agreement about what sorts of theories are retributive except that all such theories try to establish an essential link between punishment and moral wrongdoing." This chapter has attempted to survey the terrain in a philosophically engaging way. Retribution is perhaps the oldest and best known of penal theories, but it is also one of the most varied and largest tents of all penal theories. Varieties of retributivism are many. They have a common core centred on the fundamental importance of desert as a kind of moral responsibility for immoral wrongdoing, but disagree on how this is understood and implemented. Strict equality, to pay back, an unfair advantage, an annulment, proportional or limiting retributivism and negative retributivism all have their attractions and defenders, but also their shortcomings. This chapter leaves to the reader which of these positions is most compelling while acknowledging the theoretical limitations of each view. The passing of time has only seen the varieties of retributivism grow and it can be expected that more will continue to develop.

Notes

1 For a broad overview of retributivism and its place in theories of punishment, see Brooks 2012 and White 2011.
2 Part of the reason for this is that strict liability offences are easier to prosecute. Only bare, observable facts about what was found in possession or how fast a car was driven need be known for conviction. However, for offences requiring some element of moral responsibility, there are thornier issues about what was intended when someone acted.
3 Brudner (2009) calls these species of retributivism "moral retributivism" to distinguish from his more legalistic variant.
4 *US v Quinones*, 205 F. Supp. 2d. 256, 264 (2002).
5 See Brooks (2012:158–62) and *State v Santiago (Santiago II)*, 318 Conn. 1, 105 (2015).
6 Elsewhere, I develop a "unified theory" of punishment that attempts to do just this (Brooks 2012: 123–48).

References

Alexander, L. (1994) "Crime and Culpability," *Journal of Contemporary Legal Issues* 1–30.
Brooks, T. (2003) "Kant's Theory of Punishment," *Utilitas* 15. 206–24.
Brooks, T. (2004) "Is Hegel a Retributivist?" *Bulletin of the Hegel Society of Great Britain* 49/50: 113–26.
Brooks, T. (2011) "Retribution and Capital Punishment" in Mark D. White (ed.), *Retributivism: Essays on Theory and Practice*. Oxford: Oxford University Press, pp. 232–45.
Brooks, T. (2012) *Punishment*. London: Routledge.
Brooks, T. (2017) "Hegel on Crime and Punishment" in Thom Brooks and Sebastian Stein (eds), *Hegel's Political Philosophy: On the Normative Significance of Method and System*. Oxford: Oxford University Press, pp. 202–21.
Brudner, A. (2009) *Punishment and Freedom: A Liberal Theory of Penal Justice*. Oxford: Oxford University Press.
Cottingham, J. (1979) "Varieties of Retribution," *Philosophical Quarterly* 29: 238–46.
Duff, A. (2001) *Punishment, Communication, and Community*. Oxford: Oxford University Press.
Easton, S. and Piper, C. (2005) *Sentencing and Punishment: The Quest for Justice*. Oxford: Oxford University Press.
Hegel, G.W.F. (1991) *Elements of the Philosophy of Right*, ed. A.W. Wood. Cambridge: Cambridge University Press.
Kant, I. (1963) *Critique of Pure Reason*, trans. N. K. Smith. London: Macmillan.
Kant, I. (1996) *The Metaphysics of Morals*, trans. Mary Gregor. Cambridge: Cambridge University Press.
Moore, M.S. (1993) "Justifying Retribution," *Israeli Law Review* 27: 15–49.
Reiman, J.H. (1985) "Justice, Civilization, and the Death Penalty: Answering van den Haag," *Philosophy and Public Affairs* 14: 115–48.
State v Santiago (Santiago II), 318 Conn. 1 (2015).
Ten, C.L. (1987) *Crime, Guilt, and Punishment*. Oxford: Clarendon Press.
US v Quinones, 205 F. Supp. 2d. 256 (2002).
White, M.D. (2011) *Retributivism: Essays on Theory and Policy*. Oxford: Oxford University Press.

3

OFFENDERS AS CITIZENS

Antony Duff

Citizens and Enemies

Günther Jakobs notoriously distinguished "*Bürgerstrafrecht*" (citizen criminal law) from "*Feindstrafrecht*" (enemy criminal law).[1] *Bürgerstrafrecht* is criminal law for citizens: law appropriate to the law-respecting members of a political community, who can generally be trusted to refrain from crime and to respect others' rights. They might still commit crimes – they are not angels – but their crimes do not reveal a law-flouting disposition, or a disdain for the values that the law embodies. *Feindstrafrecht*, by contrast, is appropriate for those whose criminal conduct shows them to be enemies of the polity, who cannot be trusted to act as law-abiding citizens. Those who thus constitute themselves as enemies lose their civic status: they lose their entitlement to the rights and respect that citizens can expect from each other and from the state (though Jakobs insisted that it must be possible to regain that status by showing that one's attitude had changed).

A crude version of this distinction between "citizens" and "enemies" can be seen in penal practice and rhetoric (and theory) in both the USA and Britain, especially in the treatment of those who commit imprisonable crimes. A contrast is drawn between "law-abiding citizens" whom the criminal law must protect, and the "criminals" against whom they need protection; and although the class of "criminals" is not taken to include *all* those who commit crimes, it does include those who commit the kinds of crime (especially attacks on the person) that are perceived as most serious, or who persist in criminal conduct. These are the enemies against whom the "war on crime" must be fought: they can be excluded (since they have excluded themselves) from the community of law-abiding citizens, and can no longer claim the rights and benefits of citizenship.

This conception of "criminals" as enemies is displayed most dramatically in such penal provisions as "life without prospect of parole" (Ogletree and Sarat 2012), and "three strikes and you're out" (a third felony conviction brings mandatory life imprisonment; Zimring et al 2001): the commission of the relevant type of crime brings permanent exclusion from the polity behind the walls of a prison. But it is also shown in our readiness to use imprisonment, forcible exclusion from "normal" life, as the sanction for a wide range of crimes; in the denial of the vote to those in prison (and sometimes to those who have left prison; Tripkovic 2019); and in the exclusions from the normal rights and benefits of civic life to which "ex-offenders" may be subjected (Hoskins 2019).

Such a conception of "criminals," those who (persistently) commit very serious crimes, might seem to flow from familiar ways of understanding the political community from which criminals are excluded. If we understand political community in contractualist terms, we can see minor crimes as breaches of the terms of the social contract that trigger a penalty clause: if the offender pays the penalty, the contract remains in force. More serious crimes, however, strike at the heart of that contract, so that it is no longer binding as between the criminal and his fellows: by violating the basic terms of the contract, he renders it void – he can no longer claim its protection. If we instead understand political community in communitarian terms, we can see it as an association whose members are bound together by a shared commitment to live together in the light of certain values: although, in a human community, continued membership must be consistent with occasional violations of those values, those who flout them persistently or flagrantly cannot remain as members; they exclude themselves by renouncing the bonds of community, and cannot expect their fellows still to treat them as members of the community.

Such an exclusionary conception of "criminals" is too often realised in our penal practices (see e.g. Alexander 2010; Lerman and Weaver 2014); it is also sometimes supported by penal theorists (e.g. Goldman 1982; Morris 1991) – but is it inevitable? Or could we articulate a more inclusionary penal theory, which treats those who commit even persistent and serious crimes not as enemies who must be excluded from civic community, but as citizens who must still be seen, and treated, as fellow members of that community? I will argue that we can and should do this, though I will not say much about the "should" in what follows. Apart from the pragmatic point that most of those who are punished for crimes will return to "normal" life, and will be more likely to do so successfully if they have not been excluded as enemies while being punished, we should take seriously the demands of human and civic solidarity. We do not choose our fellow citizens, but find ourselves bound with them as members of a polity;[2] given the importance of citizenship to a good human life, and given the human fallibility that we should recognise in ourselves as in our fellows, we should be very slow – much slower than our penal systems often are – to exclude wrongdoers from civic community.

In what follows I describe one route by which we might articulate a more inclusionary conception of offenders. That route involves taking seriously the idea that the criminal law should be our law as citizens, and that we should therefore be ready to play various civic roles within the practice of criminal law; understanding "offender" and "convicted offender" as civic roles with their own sets of rights and responsibilities; and appealing to a conception of criminal punishment as a communicative enterprise. I should, however, note two issues that I cannot discuss here.

First, there is another category of offenders who do not fit into Jakobs' schema of citizens and enemies: many who appear in our criminal courts are neither citizens, nor plausibly portrayed as enemies; they are non-citizens who are in our country as tourists, as temporary or long-term workers, as refugees or asylum seekers, and so on. Even if an account of the aims of criminal law and punishment focuses initially on the law's relationship to the polity's citizens, it must also say something about its relationship to non-citizens who come within its jurisdiction; but we cannot pursue that topic here, beyond flagging the suggestion that they should be seen as having the distinctive normative status of guests (Duff 2018: ch. 3.3).

Second, a radical inclusionary claim would be that citizenship is irrevocable: although one should be able to resign citizenship, it may never be taken away – no crime could justify its deprivation. Anyone making that claim would need to say something about self-declared terrorists who precisely define themselves as enemies of the polity they attack – perhaps they have resigned their citizenship; but I do not rule out the possibility that some non-terrorist crimes or criminal careers are so radically destructive of civil community that presumptively permanent exclusion from that community is the only tenable response (only presumptively permanent, because there must be a way back into community even for perpetrators of the most terrible crimes). I offer here only the more modest claim that we should seek an account of crime and punishment according to which the vast majority of offenders must still be seen and treated as citizens – full members of the political community; and that we should strive so to reform our penal practices that they reflect such an understanding.

Civic Roles and a Common Law

The criminal law, indeed law in general, is often portrayed as something that is owned – created, interpreted, applied, enforced – by officials; as a law in relation to which lay citizens are subjects, whose role is to obey its requirements. On this view law, in particular criminal law, is an external imposition, by a sovereign (which might be a body rather than a single person) on its subjects. That is no doubt often how the law is experienced by those who are subjected to its coercive attentions, but it is not how the law should function in a democratic polity of self-governing citizens. In such a polity, the law should be a "common" law (see Cotterrell 1995: ch. 11). It should be our law as citizens: a law that we make for ourselves, a law through which we address each other in terms of the values that define our shared civic life. It should therefore be a law in relation to which we are active rather than merely passive, agents rather than mere subjects: if we are to engage in the enterprise of democratic self-governance, we must be actively involved in the law that partly structures that enterprise.

The question of what forms that active involvement should take is a central question for democratic theory; I focus here on how citizens may be involved in the distinctive enterprise of criminal law. One set of issues concerns citizens' involvement in the process of criminal legislation, but I will focus on the ways in which citizens might actively relate to criminal law that already exists, ways that can be clarified by looking at some of the distinctive civic roles that citizens can play in this context.

Some of those roles are professional and official (police officers, prosecutors, defence counsel, judges and court officials, correctional officers): those who fill them are employed by the polity to do so, and are meant to bring professional skills to the job. Other roles carry formal legal authority, but are filled by lay citizens: obvious examples are those of juror and lay magistrate. A third kind of role is acquired by citizens who have a relevant connection to a particular crime: examples are those of victim, witness, suspect, and defendant. If I become the victim of a crime, or witness a crime, or face investigation and questioning as a suspect, or am summoned to face trial on a criminal charge, I acquire distinctive new responsibilities and rights: I can expect, as a matter of right, certain kinds of support and protection from the state; and I can be expected, as a matter of civic responsibility, to assist the criminal law's enterprise – for instance by reporting the crime, by testifying in court, by cooperating with legitimate police inquiries, by appearing in court and answering the charge that I face. There is much to be said about such roles: about what a polity should expect of victims, witnesses, and suspects – what their responsibilities, civic or legal, should be; about what they should be able to expect from their fellow citizens to support them in discharging those responsibilities and protect them against oppressive treatment ("due process" values figure here). I cannot discuss them further here (see Marshall 2014; Duff and Marshall 2016); nor can I discuss the role of the defendant in a criminal trial, as someone who is called to answer to a charge of criminal wrongdoing, and to answer for that wrongdoing if it is proved against him (see Duff et al 2007). All I can say here is that to understand what these roles should involve, we must have a conception of the character and aims of the criminal law as a distinctive kind of practice – as, I would argue (Duff 2018), a practice that functions to provide an appropriate response to "public" wrongs. Given such a conception, and a related conception of citizenship as a set of distinctive civic responsibilities and rights, we can ask what contributions to those aims a polity should be able to expect from its citizens, and what they should be able to expect from it.

It is worth saying a word about offenders who know that they have committed a crime, since this brings us closer to the role of convicted offender on which I want to focus. It might seem inappropriate to count "offender" as a civic role: one who commits a crime is precisely failing to discharge her civic responsibilities (unless she is engaged in civil disobedience; see Brownlee 2012). But we can see "offender" as a context-specific determination of the role of citizen. Role-definitions typically make provision for what should be done when things go wrong, in particular when the role-holder misconducts herself – what is to be done not just by others, but by the agent herself. A doctor, or teacher, or parent, might engage in medical, or pedagogical, or parental misconduct: by doing so she acquires new medical, pedagogical, or parental responsibilities, to take appropriate steps to repair or make up for that misconduct. Analogously, a citizen who engages in civic misconduct, who commits a crime, can be said to acquire new responsibilities by doing so – those that attach to being an offender.

What are those responsibilities? They include, of course, ordinary moral responsibilities to apologise or make reparations to my victim (when there was one). But they arguably also include distinctive civic responsibilities in relation to the criminal law – a responsibility, in particular, not merely to cooperate with the police if they investigate the crime, but to come forward to confess my crime, and (if prosecuted) to plead "Guilty" at my trial. For, first, as a citizen, I have a responsibility to assist the criminal law's enterprise, including the enterprise of calling criminal wrongdoers to public account. Second, I should recognize my crime as a wrong, which is *inter alia* to recognize it as something for which I should answer, to those whose business it is. As a public wrong, a crime is the business of the whole polity, and the criminal trial is the public forum in which criminal wrongdoers are formally called to answer to the polity; so I have a civic responsibility to answer for my crime in that forum. (However, first, such a responsibility depends on the justice of the criminal process and punishment that I will face if I give myself up; and, second, to portray this as an offender's civic responsibility is not to say that it should be a legally enforceable duty. Indeed, given the radical imbalance in power between offender and state, and the dangers of oppressive policing and mistaken identifications of offenders, we should insist on the kinds of protection that "due process" provides, including protection against being compelled to incriminate oneself.)

We cannot discuss the civic responsibilities of not-yet-convicted offenders further here, important though they are as aspects of the active citizenship that a democratic criminal law requires. Instead, I turn to the distinct but related role of convicted offender – the role of one who has been convicted of a crime, and now faces criminal punishment. In discussing this role, we will also be discussing the proper aims of criminal punishment, and how it could be (or become) something that citizens could impose on each other whilst still treating each other with the respect and concern due to citizens – how criminal punishment could be or become a genuinely civic enterprise.

Punishment is typically portrayed as a one-way enterprise, as the infliction of a punitive burden by the state on an offender whose role in the affair is essentially passive: if we ask what responsibilities the convicted offender has, the answer seems to be simply that he must accept his punishment – he should not resist it. Rarely do theorists ask whether a conviction (or the commission of the offence itself) might bring any positive responsibilities – whether the offender should be an active participant in the penal process (but see Adler 1992, Tadros 2011). However, if we are to see punishment as a civic enterprise, in which those punished are engaged as citizens, we must attend not just to the question of what "we" may or should do to "them" (convicted offenders), but what they should do – how a citizen should respond to his own conviction and sentence.

Civic Punishment

Criminal punishment is, of course, imposed, not chosen: the convicted offender does not get to choose whether to be punished, or what her punishment will be; the court determines whether and how she will be punished. (We could, however, imagine a more "participatory" sentencing process in which the offender was expected to propose a punishment appropriate to her crime, or to discuss possible sentences with those affected by the crime. Although any proposed sentence would need approval from the court, and although sentences would still be imposed if the offender refused to propose one or could not agree on one, this would give convicted offenders an active role in determining their punishment; Duff 2001: 158–63.) However, that a sentence is imposed does not mean that it is simply inflicted on an offender whose role is passively to undergo or suffer punishment.

The first point to notice is that most punishments in fact require the offender to be active: punishments must be undertaken, not simply undergone. This is most obviously true of non-custodial punishments. Even a fine is something that the offender is required to pay (although it may be exacted if he fails to do so); other modes of punishment demand more in the way of activity. Someone sentenced to Community Payback is required to undertake a specified type of work (www.communitypayback.com). Someone sentenced to probation is also required to be active: to report to a probation officer, to undertake programmes that address her offending. Imprisonment looks like a striking exception to this claim, to be discussed shortly, but it is worth beginning with non-custodial punishments, the most common sentences even in the most enthusiastically carceral systems, which can be portrayed as – in the familiar rhetoric – a debt that the offender owes the polity, and that it is (initially) up to him to pay.

But in what spirit could convicted offenders be expected to undertake their punishments? No doubt many in fact undertake them only under duress, because they realise that a refusal will simply result in the coercive infliction either of the punishment itself (as when an unpaid fine is taken from my wages), or of an inflictable alternative (such as imprisonment). This is indeed the most that we could reasonably expect from many of those who are sentenced in our courts: given the often oppressively dehumanising character of existing punishments, and the exclusionary spirit in which they are often imposed, we cannot honestly say that offenders should willingly undertake their punishments. But if we ask what punishment could be like in a decent system of law, and what responsibilities the citizens of such a system could be taken to incur in being convicted of a crime, we can see how punishment could be something that convicted offenders ought to undertake, rather than merely undergo – and ought to undertake as a matter of civic duty rather than merely as a matter of prudence. Such a penal system, in which offenders could legitimately be required to undertake their punishments as a matter of civic duty, would be an inclusionary system in which convicted offenders were still treated as citizens who had an active role to play in the enterprise of criminal law. They would not be enemies, on whom "we" are entitled simply to impose penal burdens; they would be fellow members of the community who are expected to play their part, as citizens, in this civic enterprise – including their part as convicted offenders who must now pay for their crimes.

How far criminal punishment can be portrayed as an active civic duty that is required of the convicted offender depends on how we understand punishment and its aims. If we see it, for instance, simply as deterrence or incapacitation aimed at reducing the incidence of future crimes or harms, we will not give offenders an essentially active role. It is easier to operate a penal system if offenders cooperate, but incapacitation and deterrence are measures that we inflict upon people, not enterprises to which their own active cooperation could be integral. (This might not be true of accounts according to which punishment should aim to reform or rehabilitate: whilst reform and rehabilitation can be portrayed as one-way exercises of power, as something done *to* offenders, we could instead suggest that punishment should aim to persuade, and help, offenders to reform and rehabilitate themselves. To see punishment in this way, however, we must abandon the strictly consequentialist framework within which ideas of reform and rehabilitation are often set, in favour of a framework within which we ask what we owe to offenders as responsible agents. This would lead us towards a communicative account of this kind sketched below.)[3]

The same is true of those versions of retributivism that portray punishment as a matter of inflicting a quantum of deserved suffering on offenders:[4] offenders are again portrayed as the passive recipients of punishment. Such retributivists can argue that offenders should cooperate in their punishment: they should recognize that the punishment is justified and for that reason cooperate in its imposition. But there is nothing about the aims or meaning of punishment, on such accounts, that requires cooperation: non-cooperation does not undermine punishment's legitimacy, or frustrate its aims. However, if we are to portray punishment as an active civic duty, we must portray it as something that ideally requires the offender's active participation: the paradigm of the sentence must be not "This is what we will do to you," but "This is what you must do." Offenders who refuse to undertake their punishment will not thereby escape it; punishment will be imposed if it is not undertaken. But punishment that is merely imposed is on this view imperfect precisely as punishment: it is not something the offender undertakes as a citizen.

We can make better sense of the idea that criminal punishment should seek the offender's active participation, and thus of a fully inclusionary conception of criminal law, by portraying punishment as a communicative enterprise – not just as a one-way process in which the polity communicates to offenders the censure that their crimes deserve, but as a two-way process in which offenders are also supposed to communicate to the polity, by undertaking their punishment.

A conception of punishment as a one-way process of communication is familiar, though theorists differ over the precise content and aims of the communication (see Feinberg 1970). Consequentialists can find a place for communicative punishments, insofar as they can assist the aims (most obviously that of preventing future crime) of the penal system (see e.g. Lacey 1988; Braithwaite and Pettit 1990). However, the idea of punishment as communication is appealed to more often by theorists seeking to make sense of retributivism – of the claim that the core justification of criminal punishment must consist in showing, not that its contingent future effects are sufficiently beneficial to outweigh its undoubted costs, but that it constitutes an appropriate kind of response to past crimes. What makes such a response appropriate is now not (as cruder versions of retributivism hold) that it inflicts a quantum of deserved suffering on offenders; it is rather that punishment communicates to offenders the censure that they deserve for their crimes (see recently Maslen 2015; du Bois-Pedain and Bottoms 2019).

An obvious question for such accounts is why the communication of deserved censure should take the materially burdensome form that criminal punishments take.[5] For we can communicate censure by words, and can give such communication emphasis and formal weight by some suitable ceremony (or by "punishments" that are purely symbolic in the sense that they are burdensome only in virtue of their censorial meaning). An offender's conviction at her trial itself communicates censure: it declares her to be guilty of a criminal wrong, and that declaration can be given further emphasis by the judge's comments after conviction. If the aim is to communicate censure, why should we also then impose a material punishment on the offender? Such punishments *can* communicate censure (if imposed in the right context and spirit), but if we are to justify a system of criminal punishment, we need to show not merely that such impositions *can* communicate an appropriate message, but that they are *necessary*.

One kind of answer to this question admits that the need to communicate censure cannot itself justify using materially burdensome punishments as the vehicle for that communication, and justifies the use of that vehicle in deterrent terms: we should impose such burdens not merely to communicate censure, but because they also provide some prudential incentive that might deter from crime those who are not sufficiently motivated by the law's censorial voice. A purely censorial response to crimes makes a moral appeal: we should refrain from such actions because they are wrong, and the censure imposed on those who commit crimes is meant to remind them, and us, of that wrongfulness. But since we are morally fallible beings, who are not always appropriately motivated by moral values, such appeals will too often be ineffective; so we seek to give them more persuasive force by adding the deterrent element provided by materially burdensome punishment (see von Hirsch 1993).

Another kind of response seeks to justify materially burdensome punishment in terms of what is needed for effective communication: mere words, or purely symbolic punishments, will predictably not be forceful enough to get through to the offender, or to make sure that he hears and understands the law's censorial message; but by giving that message a materially burdensome form, we can hope that it will get through (see e.g. Falls 1987; Kleinig 1991). If this kind of answer is to be plausible, it must explain just how giving punishment a materially burdensome form assists its communicative aims. If the answer is that it is a way of forcing the offender's attention onto his crime, and thus helping him to recognise it as a wrong that he must now repent (see Duff 1986), it will be objected that such attempts to force a moral response from the offender are of dubious legitimacy, since they seek to break into "the inner citadels of his soul" (Lucas 1968 [1969]: 215); and of dubious efficacy, since the intended message is likely to be radically distorted in its transmission or its reception (see e.g. Mathiesen 1990: 58–73).

We cannot pursue these responses, or the objections to them, here;[6] instead, I will sketch an alternative way to develop the idea of punishment as a communicative enterprise, one that gives the offender a more active role by arguing that punishment should aim to be a two-way process. If we take seriously the slogan that punishment is a "debt" that the offender owes to the polity, we can see it as something that the offender ought to *do*. Even if debts that I owe can sometimes (depending on what is owed) be extracted from me without my participation, as when money that I owe can be garnished from my wages if I fail to pay it, such extraction must be a last resort. If you owe me something, I am entitled to demand it from you, but I owe it to you (out of respect for your agency) to demand it rather than taking it forcibly – to give you the opportunity (even if I am sure that you will not take it) to pay the debt yourself. I can justifiably extract it if you refuse to pay, but only if I first gave you a chance to pay.

What then does the offender owe her fellow citizens? It might seem that this is not what we should be asking – that the real question ought to be what the offender owes her victim, if the crime was a victimising one (though sometimes, of course, the only victims are her fellow citizens collectively, as in cases of tax evasion, or environmental crime). That is true of tort law, when one who has suffered wrongful harm sues the person who (she alleges) wrongfully harmed her; and there are questions to be asked, which we cannot pursue here, about the role of victims in the criminal process (see Zedner 1997). But a criminal case is brought by the polity, not by an individual victim; and whilst, in the case of victimising crimes, it must focus on the wrong that was done to this victim, the punishment imposed on the offender cannot be seen as a debt owed to that victim (a debt whose payment the victim could then forgive). Rather, that punishment must be understood as being owed to the polity as a whole.

The idea of a penal debt that is owed to the community is made explicit in "Community Payback" as a sentence, but what is being paid? The punishment involves some materially burdensome kind of work, which might indeed involve making good the kind of material damage that the offender's crime caused: someone convicted of vandalism might be required to clean up the effects of vandalism (although probably not his own vandalism). But crimes do not often involve the kind of material harm that could be thus repaired, and criminal law is anyway focused on wrongs rather than merely on such harms as the crime might cause, so we must ask what kind of debt the commission of a wrong incurs. The obvious answer is that a wrongdoer owes those whom she wronged an apology: an avowal that she recognises the wrong she has committed, is sorry for it, and seeks to repair the relationship that her wrong threatened to damage.

Now apologies are typically verbal but, in this as in other contexts, mere words might not be enough to convey a recognition of the seriousness and implications of the wrong. So the apology can be given material form in the undertaking of some burdensome task – as a kind of secular penance. Just as I can pay the debt of gratitude I owe to those who helped me not merely by thanking them in words, but by giving my thanks material form – and thus greater communicative force – in a gift or service to them, so I can express my apologetic recognition of the wrong I have done, and my desire to make up for it, by undertaking a suitable penitential burden (see Duff 2001; Bennett 2008).

What must be emphasised, however, is that criminal punishment (in liberal societies like our own) should have an essentially formal, even ritualistic, character. In our personal moral dealings with those close to us, apologies and moral reparations are of value only if sincere, but the criminal law is concerned with our more formal, public relationships as citizens – our relationships with fellow citizens with whom we might have no personal acquaintance. In this context, and given a liberal reluctance to allow the law to inquire into our inner thoughts and feelings, what matters is the public enactment of appropriate civic attitudes, and a necessarily formal ritual of reparation. This, the court says in passing sentence, is what you must do to make reparation for your wrong: the "this" must be a punishment that carries the appropriate, conventional public meaning; and so long as the offender completes the punishment, we (and the law) must treat him as one who has apologised, and made appropriate reparation, without inquiring into whether he meant it – whether he did sincerely repent his crime (any more than we inquire into the sincerity of those undertaking other kinds of public ritual).

If we can understand criminal punishment in these terms, we can see it as an essentially civic enterprise, in which citizens engage with each other as citizens. For to call a person to account for her wrongdoing (as a criminal trial calls the offender to account), and to require her to undertake apologetic penal reparation for that wrongdoing, is precisely to treat her as a member of the political community: a citizen who has done wrong, who therefore owes it to her fellow citizens to make reparation for that wrong, and who can restore or sustain her relationship with her fellows by undertaking the reparation that a court requires her to make. Punishment does not, on this view, exclude the offender from community, or treat or portray her as anything other or less than a full member of the polity. Rather, her punishment treats her as a citizen who has acquired a new civic duty – to undertake this punishment – in virtue of her criminal wrongdoing.

Civic Punishment and its Appropriate Modes

More precisely, on this view punishment *could* be an inclusionary civic enterprise, *if* it is of the right kind, and administered in the right spirit and in the kind of social-political context that makes it possible for it to be understood in this way – a context of social and political justice, in which we can rightly say that those who commit crimes have violated the values of a political community to which they belong, within which they are treated as full and equal members. I owe apologetic reparation to my fellow citizens only if they are indeed my fellow citizens; only if, that is, they have treated me as a fellow member of the polity. If, however, I have not been treated as a citizen, if I and the group to which I belong have been subjected to systematic injustices that excluded us from many of the ordinary rights and benefits of civic membership, it is hard to say that I owe my "fellow citizens" such apologetic reparation for the crimes I commit. This point requires us to confront the vexed question of whether we can do penal justice in contexts of grave social injustice: can the privileged majority justly punish members of an unjustly disadvantaged minority for their crimes? We cannot pursue that issue here (but see Heffernan and Kleinig 2000; Holroyd 2010; Howard 2013; Duff 2019); instead, I should comment briefly on the first of the two conditions noted above, concerning modes of punishment.

What modes of punishment can citizens properly demand of or impose on each other? What modes are consistent with a recognition of citizenship? This question concerns not just the material or psychological impact of punishment, but its meaning: what does each mode of punishment say about the offender or the crime? We cannot discuss all the different modes of punishment here, save to note that if punishment is to be a civic duty that the offender should undertake, the punishments must not degrade those who undertake them (see Braithwaite 1989; Kahan 1996; Garvey 1998). Punishment must be something offenders can undertake without humiliating themselves, while retaining the respect of their fellow citizens.

That still leaves the question of imprisonment, which does not seem amenable to such an account. Surely imprisonment must mean exclusion from ordinary civic life and fellowship; and it is simply imposed on offenders – it is not a sentence that they are required to undertake as active participants in the enterprise of criminal law. But if we cannot portray imprisonment as a punishment that citizens can properly require of each other, talk of criminal punishment as a civic duty will seem hollow: it cannot capture this most serious mode of punishment (leaving capital punishment aside). If we cannot show imprisonment to be a sentence that the offender could properly be required to undertake, or to be consistent with a recognition of the offender as our fellow citizen, we must argue either that imprisonment cannot be justified in a democratic republic; or that some crimes or criminal careers are such that those who engage in them can no longer be seen as citizens – that they can be excluded as wrongdoers whose citizenship is forfeited; or that imprisonment is an injustice that the necessity of preserving society forces us to commit.

Now it is certainly true that we can and should use imprisonment much less than we do in societies such as Britain and the United States (see e.g. Allen 2012; Ashworth 2013; British Academy 2014). But while some do indeed argue that we should aim to abolish imprisonment altogether (see e.g. Mathiesen 1990, 2015; McLeod 2015), it is hard to render such a radical view plausible. This is not just because of public safety concerns – the fear that if those who commit various kinds of serious predatory crimes are left at liberty, they will continue to prey on others; it is also because a punishment that allows the offender to continue an ordinary life among his fellow citizens seems inadequate to address, to do justice to, the character and the community-destroying implications of the most serious crimes. Surely we must sometimes say that we cannot, for a time, continue to live in ordinary civic fellowship with one who has committed such a crime; and surely an offender who recognises the seriousness of the wrong he has done should also feel that he cannot, at least for a time, continue to live his ordinary civic life. If we understand some crimes in this light, we will see reason to use imprisonment as a punishment, to mark the way in which such crimes make ordinary civic community impossible.[7] But is this to say that to punish such serious crimes we must exclude offenders from the civic community – that punishment must now be exclusionary? Or could we argue that imprisonment can still be understood as a kind of moral reparation that offenders ought to undertake for themselves, as a species of – we might say – seclusion within the community rather than outright exclusion from it? It would be absurd to think that we could in this way justify imprisonment as it is currently practised in too many American and British prisons: that is not a punishment that treats those subjected to it as citizens, or that an offender could undertake as a mode of punitive reparation in which he retains his dignity as a citizen (see e.g. Cover 1986; McLeod 2015). But prisons need not be like that, and we can ask how far they could become sites of genuine civic punishment.

Imprisonment can be actively undertaken. Suppose an offender is sentenced to N months in prison, and is instructed (as happens in some systems) to report to a specified prison on a specified date to serve his term; suppose the prison is an open prison with no walls to prevent prisoners walking out. Imprisonment is then something that is required of the offender, as a duty that he must undertake. However, a system of imprisonment will have to rely, to some extent, on secure closed prisons: could this be justified as an inclusionary civic punishment that citizens could legitimately be expected to undertake?

Imprisonment in a closed prison can be undertaken, not merely undergone, if the prisoner approaches it in the appropriate spirit. Those in prison can be active rather than passive, if the prison is minimally decent: they may be able to make the prison regime their own, rather than merely an alien order that they must obey; to engage in productive work, and in educational programs. However, if prisoners should have towards the prison regime the kind of respect that citizens should have for the law (for the prison regime is an aspect of the law), prisoners must be enabled and ready to take a respectfully critical stance towards it: they must be ready to object to what they see as oppressive or unjust; the prison must make such dissent possible, not merely as an ineffective letting off of steam, but as a way in which change can be sought, and achieved (see McLeod 2012–3; Mathiesen 2015).

We can thus try to rethink prison regimes so as to make prisons possible sites of civic punishment. We can rethink prison architecture, prison living conditions and regimes, how prison staff address and treat prisoners, what kinds of work or activity are available, what kind of control they have over their daily lives (see Lippke 2007; Ugelvik and Dullum 2011; Pratt and Eriksson 2012). We can think about how porous prison walls could be – what kinds of connection or engagement with the civic world outside the prison can be enabled (the right to vote, and to participate in political life, are symbolically important here).

Whatever such changes can be made, however, the brute fact of prison walls remains: the walls might be more porous, but they will still be there. Can we honestly say to an offender that he is required, given his crime, to seclude himself from his ordinary personal and civic life for a specified time? If we can say that, we can see the prison walls as more like the locks we put on our houses: a method of preventing the offender from doing what he has a duty not to do – leaving the prison. And we could then justify imprisonment as a civic punishment for the limited range of crimes whose seriousness can be adequately marked only by the offender entering the kind of temporary, partial seclusion that prison provides; this could become a civic punishment that offenders could be expected to undertake as citizens.

Notes

1 See e.g. Jakobs 1985, 2004. I will not be concerned here with the details or evolution of Jakobs' views: see Ohana 2014.

2 I rely here on an account of political obligation as a matter of "associative" duties: see Dworkin 1986; Horton 2006, 2007.

3 In this paragraph I take a dogmatically oversimplified view of consequentialist theories of punishment. For more nuanced discussions, see Canton and Bagaric in this volume, Chapters 1 and 6 respectively.

4 For the clearest contemporary version of this kind of view, see Moore 1997: chs 2–4; also Brooks in this volume, Chapter 2.

5 The question is usually put as one about "hard treatment" (Feinberg 1970), but that label unhelpfully implies that punishment is necessarily harshly oppressive; it would be odd to describe the payment of a fine, or the performance of 100 hours of community work, as "hard treatment"—but they are punishments. It is better to say that criminal punishment involves a materially burdensome imposition or requirement.

6 Apart from the items already cited in the text, see Boonin 2008: 171–80; Hanna 2008; Tasioulas 2006; von Hirsch and Ashworth 2005: ch. 7.

7 We cannot discuss here two other uses of imprisonment—to detain those awaiting trial, and as a final backup sanction against those who persist in violating the requirements of non-custodial sentences.

References

Adler, J. (1992) *The Urgings of Conscience*, Philadelphia: Temple University Press.

Alexander, M. (2010) *The New Jim Crow: Mass Incarceration in the Age of Colorblindness*, New York: New Press.

Allen, R. (2012) *Reducing the Use of Imprisonment: What can We Learn from Europe?*, London: Criminal Justice Alliance.

Ashworth, A.J. (2013) *What if Imprisonment were Abolished for Property Offences?* London: Howard League.

Bennett, C.J. (2008) *The Apology Ritual: A Philosophical Theory of Punishment*, Cambridge: Cambridge University Press.

Boonin, D. (2008) *The Problem of Punishment*, New York: Cambridge University Press.

Braithwaite, J. (1989) *Crime, Shame and Reintegration*, Cambridge: Cambridge University Press.

Braithwaite, J., and Pettit, P. (1990) *Not Just Deserts*, Oxford: Oxford University Press.

British Academy (2014) *A Presumption against Imprisonment: Social Order and Social Values*, London: British Academy.

Brownlee, K. (2012) *Conscience and Conviction: The Case for Civil Disobedience*, Oxford: Oxford University Press.

Cotterrell, R. (1995) *Law's Community*, Oxford: Oxford University Press.

Cover, R.M. (1986) "Violence and the Word," *Yale Law Journal* 95: 1601–30.

du Bois-Pedain, A. and Bottoms, A. (eds) (2019) *Penal Censure: Engagements Within and Beyond Desert Theory*, Oxford: Hart Publishing.

Duff, R.A. (1986) *Trials and Punishments*, Cambridge: Cambridge University Press.

Duff, R.A. (2001) *Punishment, Communication, and Community*, New York: Oxford University Press.

Duff, R.A. (2018) *The Realm of Criminal Law*, Oxford: Oxford University Press.

Duff, R.A. (2019) "Moral and Criminal Responsibility: Answering and Refusing to Answer," in D. Justin Coates and Neal A. Tognazzini (eds), *Oxford Studies in Agency and Responsibility Vol.5: Themes from the Philosophy of Gary Watson*, Oxford: Oxford University Press: 165–90

Duff, R.A., Farmer, L., Marshall, S.E., and Tadros, V. (2007) *The Trial on Trial (3): Towards a Normative Theory of the Criminal Trial*, Oxford: Hart Publishing.

Duff, R.A., and Marshall, S.E. (2016) "Civic Punishment," in A. Dzur et al (eds), *Democratic Theory and Mass Incarceration*, Oxford: Oxford University Press: 33–59

Dworkin, R.M. (1986) *Law's Empire*, London: Fontana.

Falls, M.M. (1987) "Retribution, Reciprocity, and Respect for Persons," *Law and Philosophy* 6: 25–51.

Feinberg, J. (1970) "The Expressive Function of Punishment," in his *Doing and Deserving*, Princeton, NJ: Princeton University Press: 95–118.

Garvey, S.P. (1998) "Can Shaming Punishments Educate?," *University of Chicago Law Review* 65: 733–94.

Goldman, A. (1982) "Toward a New Theory of Punishment," *Law and Philosophy* 1: 57–76.

Hanna, N. (2008) "Say What? A Critique of Expressive Retributivism," *Law and Philosophy*, 27: 123–150.

Heffernan, W.C., and Kleinig, J. (eds) (2000) *From Social Justice to Criminal* Justice, New York: Oxford University Press.

Holroyd, J. (2010) "Punishment and Justice," *Social Theory and Practice* 36: 78–111.

Horton, J. (2006) "In Defense of Associative Political Obligations – I," *Political Studies* 54: 427–43.

Horton, J. (2007) "In Defense of Associative Political Obligations – II," *Political Studies* 55: 1–19.

Hoskins, Z. (2019) *Beyond Punishment? A Normative Account of Collateral Restrictions on Offenders*, Oxford: Oxford University Press.

Howard, J. (2013) "Punishment, Socially Deprived Offenders, and Democratic Community," *Criminal Law and Philosophy* 7: 121–36.

Jakobs, G. (1985) "Kriminalisierung im Vorfeld einer Rechtsgutsverletzung," *Zeitschrift für die gesamte Strafrechtswissenschaft* 97: 751–85.

Jakobs, G. (2004) "Bürgerstrafrecht und Feindstrafrecht," *Höchstrichterliche Rechtsprechung Strafrecht* 5: 88–102.

Kahan, D.M. (1996) "What Do Alternative Sanctions Mean?," *University of Chicago Law Review* 63: 591–653.

Kleinig, J. (1991) "Punishment and Moral Seriousness," *Israel Law Review* 25: 401–21.

Lacey, N. (1988) *State Punishment: Political Principles and Community Values*, London: Routledge.

Lerman, A., and Weaver, V. (2014) *Arresting Citizenship: The Democratic Consequences of American Crime Control*, Chicago: University of Chicago Press.

Lippke, R.L. (2007) *Rethinking Imprisonment*, Oxford: Oxford University Press.

Lucas, J.R. (1968 [1969]) "Or Else," *Proceedings of the Aristotelian Society* 69: 207–22.

Marshall, S.E. (2014) "'It Isn't Just About You': Victims of Crime, Their Associated Duties, and Public Wrongs," in R.A. Duff et al. (eds), *Criminalization: The Political Morality of the Criminal Law*, Oxford: Oxford University Press: 291–306.

Maslen, H. (2015) *Remorse, Penal Theory and Sentencing*, Oxford: Hart Pubishing.

Mathiesen, T. (1990) *Prison on Trial*, London: Sage.

Mathiesen, T. (2015) *The Politics of Abolition Revisited*, London: Routledge.

McLeod, A.M. (2012–3) "Confronting Criminal Law's Violence: The Possibilities of Unfinished Alternatives," *Unbound: Harvard Journal of the Legal Left* 8:109–32.

McLeod, A.M. (2015) "Prison Abolition and Grounded Justice," *UCLA Law Review* 62: 1156–1239.

Moore, M.S. (1997) *Placing Blame: A Theory of Criminal Law*, Oxford: Oxford University Press.

Morris, C. (1991) "Punishment and Loss of Moral Standing," *Canadian Journal of Philosophy* 21: 53–79

Ogletree, C., and Sarat, A. (eds) (2012) *Life without Parole: America's New Death Penalty?* New York: New York University Press.

Ohana, D. (2014) "Günther Jakobs's Feindstrafrecht: A Dispassionate Account," in M. D. Dubber (ed.), *Foundational Texts in Modern Criminal Law*, Oxford: Oxford University Press: 353–71.

Pratt, J., and Eriksson, A. (2012) *Contrasts in Punishment*, London: Routledge.

Tadros, V. (2011) *The Ends of Harm: The Moral Foundations of Criminal Law*, Oxford: Oxford University Press.

Tasioulas, J. (2006) "Punishment and Repentance," *Philosophy* 81: 279–322.

Tripkovic, M. (2019) *Punishment and Citizenship: A Theory of Criminal Disenfranchisement*, Oxford: Oxford University Press.

Ugelvik, T., and Dullum J. (eds) (2011) *Penal Exceptionalism? Nordic Prison Policy and Practice*, London: Routledge.

von Hirsch, A. (1993) *Censure and Sanctions*, Oxford: Oxford University Press.

von Hirsch, A., and Ashworth, A.J. (2005) *Proportionate Sentencing*, Oxford: Oxford University Press.

Zedner, L. (1997) "Victims," in M Maguire et al (eds), Oxford Handbook of Criminology, Oxford: Oxford University Press: 577–612.

Zimring, F.E., Hawkins, G., and Kamin, S. (2001) *Punishment and Democracy: Three Strikes and You're Out in California*, Oxford: Oxford University Press.

4
HYBRID THEORIES OF PUNISHMENT

Zachary Hoskins

Historically, normative theories of punishment have tended to fall into one of two broad camps. Consequentialist accounts construe punishment as justified instrumentally, in virtue of some supposedly valuable states of affairs to which punishment contributes. The end at which punishment aims on such accounts is standardly crime reduction (either through deterrence, rehabilitation, or incapacitation). By contrast, retributivists contend that punishment is an intrinsically appropriate, because deserved, response to crime. The debate between consequentialists and retributivists has traditionally gone this way: consequentialists charge that retributivist theories of punishment, because they do not justify the practice in terms of some valuable consequences, struggle to explain why we should want an institution of punishment, especially given the massive investment of time and money required to maintain the institution and the burdens it inflicts on those subject to it. To consequentialists, retributive punishment looks like little more than gratuitous inflictions of suffering. Retributivists, however, charge that consequentialist theories lack the resources to ground in-principle prohibitions on punishment of the innocent or disproportionate punishment of the guilty, and that consequentialist punishment runs afoul of the Kantian proscription on treating people as mere means to some end.

A half century ago, H.L.A. Hart wrote that this "confusing shadow-fighting" between consequentialists and retributivists about punishment could be resolved by recognizing that the question of punishment's justification was not a single question but many, and that these distinct questions could be answered by appeal to distinct moral considerations (Hart 1960: 9). Hart wrote:

> [W]hat is most needed is *not* the simple admission that instead of a single value or aim (Deterrence, Retribution, Reform or any other) a plurality of different values and aims should be given as a conjunctive answer to some *single* question concerning the justification of punishment. What is needed is the realization that different principles … are relevant at different points in any morally acceptable account of punishment.
>
> *(Ibid: 3)*

Distinguishing the question of punishment's rationale from the question of what considerations should constrain its implementation allows us to answer the rationale question by appeal to crime reduction or other valuable consequences that punishment ostensibly promotes, and also to endorse retributivist prohibitions on punishment of the innocent or disproportionate punishment of the guilty as at least part of the answer to the constraints question. Such an approach looks appealing insofar as it allows us to avoid the objections traditionally raised against pure consequentialist or pure retributivist theories. For a number of years after Hart's observation, this strategy of appealing to different values or principles to answer distinct questions of punishment's justification constituted arguably the dominant strategy in punishment theory (see also, e.g. Ten 1987; Lacey 1988; Scheid 1997).

In recent decades, however, hybrid accounts such as Hart's have fallen out of favor. Critics have charged, variously, that the attempt to identify distinct levels of justification is ad hoc, muddled, and unsustainable; that such accounts relegate retributivism to too minor a role; and relatedly, that they fail to respect offenders as moral agents (see, e.g. Kaufman 2008: 45–49; Lippke 2006: 280–83; Wood 2002: 304–07; Duff 2001: 13–14). As a result, many theorists have largely given up on hybrid justifications, aiming instead to defend univocal accounts of one form or another. As one critic writes, "it is now evident that the triumphant claims [of hybrid theorists] to have solved the problem of punishment were unwarranted" (Kaufman 2008: 38). Instead, much recent work in the philosophy of punishment has involved attempts to defend one or another univocal account, especially versions of retributivism (see, e.g. Duff 1986 and 2001; Bennett 2008; Moore 2010).

Dismissing hybrid accounts of punishment is, in my view, a mistake. This chapter thus aims to help resuscitate scholarly interest in hybrid approaches. In what follows, I first discuss the diversity of ways in which different moral considerations might be brought together into at least *prima facie* plausible hybrid views. Objections to certain prominent examples of hybrid views, such as Hart's, have led some critics to dismiss the hybrid strategy altogether. But this is too quick, as even if one believes accounts such as Hart's are flawed in various ways, other hybrid accounts may be more promising. Then, in the remainder of the chapter, I address three general lines of objection to hybrid strategies. The first claims that in standard hybrid accounts, retributivism is relegated to too minor a role. The second contends that crime reductive and retributivist perspectives yield incompatible pictures of those subjected to punishment. And the third raises concerns about the strategy itself of disaggregating the problem of punishment's justification into multiple questions. I contend that none of these objections gives us good reason to abandon the hybrid approach to justifying punishment.

Varieties of Hybrid Account

Hart's key insight is that the question of punishment's justification is not a single question at all, but multiple distinct questions. As he put it: "in relation to any social institution, after stating what general aim or value its maintenance fosters we should enquire whether there are any and if so what principles limiting the unqualified pursuit of that aim or value" (Hart 1960: 9–10). With punishment, as with any social institution, we can ask what compelling rationale exists to maintain the institution, and we can also ask what principles should constrain whether and how we pursue it. Hart offered a consequentialist answer to the question of what aim or values are fostered by the institution of punishment, and a nonconsequentialist answer (though not precisely a retributivist one) to the question of what principles should limit the pursuit of those values.

Accepting the distinction between the question of punishment's rationale and the question of how particular impositions of punishment should be constrained does not itself commit us to endorsing a hybrid justification of punishment. Even univocal theories, insofar as they are at all plausible, will entail (whether implicitly or explicitly) answers to the question about the rationale for punishment and to the question about what considerations should constrain how punishment is meted out. Whatever rationale we endorse will itself entail certain constraints on punishment. For example, if we hold that the rationale for punishment is to deter potential wrongdoers, then this aim itself generates certain constraints: punishment that has no deterrent effects or, worse, that tends to exacerbate crime rates would be ruled out. Alternatively, for retributivists who believe the appropriate rationale for punishment is to mete out deserved suffering for wrongdoing, it will follow that punishment should be inflicted only on those who deserve it, and only to an extent commensurate with their desert.

What distinguishes univocal and hybrid theories, however, is whether the constraining considerations *all* flow from the rationale for punishment. Unlike univocal theories, hybrid accounts may incorporate other constraining considerations that are not entailed by the rationale itself. Thus a hybrid theorist who endorsed deterrence as the rationale for punishment might also endorse – in addition to the constraints (mentioned above) entailed by the deterrent rationale itself – additional *side*-constraints on punishment. For example, she might endorse the principles that only the guilty deserve punishment and that they deserve punishment only of a severity that is proportionate to the seriousness of their wrongdoing. And importantly, she might endorse these principles not because she believes they promote the best overall consequences (as some philosophers have suggested), but because she believes justice demands them. This would count as a hybrid view insofar as at least some of the constraints on how punishment may be inflicted do not derive from its rationale.

Notice that, as Hart pointed out, we can distinguish these questions of rationales and constraints for social institutions generally. Consider, as another example, taxation. The standard rationale for taxation is to generate funding to subsidize public goods. This rationale itself generates some constraints on the implementation of taxation: namely, taxation levels shouldn't be so low as to be inadequate for funding the desired public goods, or higher than is needed to subsidize those goods. But other questions are also relevant to how a taxation scheme should be implemented, such as whether taxation should be proportionate to income, to wealth, to spending, or a flat rate, or something else. The rationale of taxation does not itself supply answers to these questions. Thus we can ask what compelling rationale there is to tax the citizenry, and also what considerations should constrain the implementation of the tax scheme, and we should not be surprised if some of the constraining considerations do not flow from the rationale. Just as it is with taxation, so it is with punishment.

The uniting feature of hybrid theories of punishment is that they incorporate distinct values, principles, aims, or other considerations in their answers to the different questions relevant to punishment's overall justification.[1] This characterization makes clear that Hart's own account, on which a utilitarian "general justifying aim" was constrained by the prohibitions against punishing the innocent or disproportionately punishing the guilty, is only one of many ways in which a hybrid theory might be constructed. First, one might differ from Hart about the answers to the rationale and constraints questions. One might, for example, defend a theory on which the compelling rationale for punishment is to mete out retribution, but the constraints implied by this rationale (e.g. no punishment of the innocent, no disproportionate punishment of the guilty) do not exhaust the principles constraining the implementation of punishment. Other constraining principles might be derived on consequentialist grounds, such as that punishment should not tend to contribute to increased levels of crime, or undermine offenders' prospects of reform, etc. One might even endorse a hybrid view that does not include retributivism as either a rationale or a constraint: perhaps punishment has a consequentialist rationale that is to be constrained by deontological but not retributive considerations, such as human rights. Alternatively, one might endorse a hybrid view that incorporates only various deontological considerations, and no consequentialist ones.[2]

Alternatively, one might disagree with Hart about the nature or number of distinct questions to be answered. For example, rights forfeiture theorists insist that in addition to questions of punishment's rationale and appropriate constraints, there is a normatively prior third question that must be addressed: namely, does punishment violate an offender's rights (see, e.g. Wellman 2012)? Forfeiture theorists generally do not claim that their view implies a particular answer to the rationale claim. Rather, they contend that unless it can be demonstrated that (and why) punishment does not violate the rights of offenders, the practice will be unjustified no matter how compelling its rationale. Similarly, forfeiture theorists do not typically claim that considerations relating to rights forfeiture need exhaust the considerations relevant to constraining inflictions of punishment. Rights forfeiture accounts are thus best understood not as complete justificatory theories of punishment, but as candidate elements of a hybrid theory.

Hybrid theories might differ from Hart's, then, about what questions are in need of answers, or about the correct answers to those questions, or both. A hybrid view might even diverge from Hart's theory by offering pluralistic answers to one or more of the disaggregated questions themselves. For example, one might maintain that the rationale for punishment is both to reduce crime and to mete out retribution. David Wood considers (but ultimately rejects) such an account, which he calls "integrated dualism":

> The guiding thought behind integrated dualism is that, even though retribution does not by itself offer a sufficient justification of punishment as a social institution, it does once reductivist benefits are taken into account – such benefits compensate for the shortfall in the justificatory force of retribution.
>
> *(Wood 2002: 307)*

Wood's discussion of the integrated dualist account implicitly collapses the rationale-constraints distinction, as he writes of retribution and crime reduction as both featuring in the answer to the question of punishment's function, or purpose, and also as both doing work to constrain particular inflictions of punishment. But the rationale-constraints distinction is still useful even on this sort of integrated dualist view, for at least two reasons: First, it leaves room for the possibility that reductivist and retributivist considerations may be integrated *differently* at the level of punishment's rationale from their integration at the level of punishment's constraints. Second, attending to the rationale-constraints distinction allows for the possibility that *additional* considerations might be relevant for one of these questions without also being relevant for the other. For example, an integrated dualist might hold that reductivist and retributivist claims exhaust the relevant considerations in establishing punishment's rationale, but that there are additional considerations relevant to constraining how punishment should be implemented that are not reducible to crime reduction or retribution: considerations related to, say, human rights, offender reform, or racial justice.

Hart would have regarded the integrated dualist approach as unhelpful insofar as it appears to stumble back into the thicket from which he intended his hybrid account to extricate punishment theory. In his view, as we saw above, we should not seek to integrate multiple distinct (namely, consequentialist and retributivist) considerations into the answer to a single question, but should instead appeal to distinct considerations in answering different questions. My aim here is not to evaluate whether an integrated dualist approach could be successful; rather, I raise the example as a further illustration of the diversity of hybrid accounts available.

In this section, I have tried to highlight the diverse range of possible hybrid theories that are available. This suggests that critics who have rejected hybrid theorizing based on the perceived inadequacies of Hart's particular view may be overlooking opportunities for fruitful development of other hybrid views. In the remainder of the paper, I consider three lines of objection raised against hybrid accounts. I contend that none of these objections ultimately succeeds.

Relegating Retributivism

One prominent objection raised against hybrid views such as Hart's is that they relegate retributivism to a minor role in the overall justification of punishment. David Wood writes that by restricting retributivism "to grounding constraints on the pursuit of utilitarian or reductivist goals, [hybrid theorists] do not treat it seriously enough. Rather than merely being another crime reductivist institution or practice, punishment is special in having retribution as its pivotal notion" (Wood 2002: 305). Similarly, D.J. Galligan writes: "[t]o many people there is a deeply embedded intuition that part at least of the general purpose of criminal justice is the correction of wrongs, quite apart from any consequential contribution to crime control" (Galligan 1981, 151). Moreover, Wood writes that there seems to be no way to accommodate this intuition with Hart's hybrid view, which he calls a two-level view. "Having separate levels requires keeping the materials to the questions at each level separate, and this means confining retributivist considerations to the second level, and so giving them (according to the criticism) a lesser role" (Wood 2002: 306).

I offer two responses to this line of objection. First, whether Hart's theory is inadequate in not incorporating retributivism into punishment's rationale is an open question. In my view, the compelling rationale for an institution of punishment is to help reduce crime (see Hoskins 2011). If our best evidence indicated that this institution had no effect on crime levels, then I do not believe that we could justify the state's inflicting intentionally burdensome, condemnatory treatment on those who commit crimes, and at such an expense to taxpayers. That is, absent some crime reductive effect, I don't believe there is a compelling rationale for state punishment.[3] But this is consistent with maintaining that there are appropriate and inappropriate ways of pursuing crime reduction, and that if we are going to pursue it through a system of intentionally burdensome, condemnatory treatment, we should ensure that this treatment is deserved.

But suppose one believes Hart's view is inadequate insofar as it relegates retribution to too limited a role within the theory. My second response is that there is nothing about the hybrid strategy generally that precludes acknowledging other questions, in addition to the rationale and constraints questions, as relevant to a complete justification of punishment. Earlier we discussed the rights forfeiture view's claim that a normatively prior question to the rationale and constraints questions is whether punishment violates an offender's rights. There is some disagreement among punishment theorists about whether to cast forfeiture theorists' answer to this question as a species of retributivism.[4] But at any rate, one might endorse a more straightforwardly retributivist answer to this question, according to which in virtue of committing a crime, an offender comes to deserve punishment, and the state does not violate a person's rights when it gives her what she deserves. On this sort of view, retributivist considerations would be relevant in answering this normatively prior question of punishment's in-principle permissibility as well as grounding certain constraints on how punishment is imposed. Thus the role of retributivist considerations in the overall hybrid theory would be greater than appears to be the case on Hart's view.

Necessary Characteristics of the Punished

A second line of objection to hybrid views such as Hart's holds that punishment aimed at crime reduction and retributive punishment are grounded in different assumptions about the necessary characteristics of people liable to punishment. Richard Lippke writes that retributivism is centrally concerned with conveying blame for prior wrongdoing, and thus it requires that those subject to punishment be the sorts of individual for whom blame would be appropriate (Lippke 2006: 274).

> Such blame is properly levied only against beings capable of understanding moral considerations and incorporating them into their conduct. By contrast, beings capable of acting solely on considerations of self-interest can be threatened with legal punishment and such prudential incentives may induce them to refrain from offending. But such agents are unresponsive to moral reasons for action and thus incapable of self-restraint based on an understanding and appreciation of the moral reasons against many criminal acts.
>
> *(Ibid.)*

The tension Lippke highlights for hybrid accounts involves whether those who are not sufficiently "capable of grasping and acting on the moral reasons against a wide array of criminal offenses" are appropriate subjects of punishment. From the perspective of the consequentialist rationale of crime reduction, Lippke believes there is no necessity that those punished have the capacity of responsiveness to moral reasons that retributivist constraints on punishment would require. After all, nonmoral agents can still be deterred or incapacitated in the interests of crime reduction. Lippke concludes that the diversity of offenders in terms of their responsiveness to moral reasons may make any resolution of the tensions between crime reduction and retribution within a single hybrid theory elusive (ibid.: 292).

I agree with Lippke that there is a fundamental tension between what characteristics a person would have to possess to be a proper subject of deterrence or incapacitation and what characteristics she would need to have to be a proper subject of retributive blame. We can acknowledge this tension, however, without despairing about whether it can be resolved. I contend that we should give normative priority to the retributivist constraint that punishment is only appropriate when the person punished is adequately capable of responding to moral reasons. For those who are responsive only to nonmoral, self-interested reasons, or those who lack the capacity of responsiveness to reasons at all, punishment would be inappropriate even if it would (by helping to deter or incapacitate these individuals) serve the aim of crime reduction.

The basis for elevating retributivist considerations above crime reductive ones in this context has to do with the distinctive nature of punishment as what Lippke calls "a form of institutionalized blame" (ibid.: 274). The state might seek to reduce crime in different ways: it might invest more money in early childhood education (which empirical research suggests has a significant crime-reductive effect), or devote its efforts to decreasing unemployment (which studies show correlates with crime), or employ other measures. But punishment is distinctive as a crime-reductive tool in that it conveys the society's blame; it condemns an offender for her offense. This means that this particular tool for reducing crime is not appropriately employed against people who are not proper objects of blame, and standardly it is held that beings not sufficiently capable of understanding and acting on moral considerations are not proper subjects of blame. Thus, as punishment is distinctively a blaming institution, individuals without sufficient moral responsiveness would not be proper subjects of punishment.

Lippke argues that those interested in crime reduction will be unmotivated by this prohibition on punishment of offenders who are not rational moral agents "up to the level required by retributivism's assumption that punishment functions as a type of institutionalized moral blame" (ibid.: 278). He writes:

> Would legislators focused on reducing crime balk at crafting institutions that convicted and punished such offenders? It is hard to believe that they would. Such offenders might be more dangerous than those whose capacities for morally responsible conduct were intact. Again, not only are some offenders deficiently responsive to moral considerations, some may not be capable of reliably acting in their own long-term self-interest. The latter might be especially dangerous and, as such, would surely demand attention from legislators seeking to reduce crime
>
> *(Ibid.: 278–79)*

Lippke is correct that the state will have an interest, even an obligation, in responding to the threats posed by amoral (or even irrational) offenders. But it does not follow from this that *punishment* is an appropriate response. Again, punishment is distinctive in that it conveys societal condemnation, or blame, of an offender for her offense. To say that it is inappropriate to convey such blame of those who, though perhaps dangerous, do not have sufficient capacity for responsiveness to moral reasons, is not to say that the state may not respond at all. The state might impose various preventive legal measures aimed at keeping the public safe from such individuals. But it would not be justified in punishing them.

Within an account of punishment, then, I believe the tension Lippke cites may be relieved by acknowledging the retributivist principle that punishment is appropriate only of those with the capacity to receive its blaming message (and that the sentence should be proportionate to the deserved degree of blame), and recognizing that this principle constrains how the state may pursue the crime-reductive rationale that drives punishment.

An Unsupported Distinction

Finally, I want to consider a cluster of objections that cut to the heart of the hybrid strategy itself. Whitley Kaufman, for example, accuses Hart of being unclear about whether his distinction of the question of punishment's general justifying aim from the question of punishment's distribution is a logical, conceptual, sociological, pragmatic, or moral distinction (Kaufman 2008: 48). Kaufman also objects that the distinction "violates common sense," as consequentialism and retributivism "each claim to provide us with a positive goal and a limiting principle" (ibid.). Another critic of hybrid accounts, David Wood, writes that they are not sufficiently integrated into a coherent theory:

> If one cannot account for the relation between the two types of considerations, the role each is to play, one has only a bifurcated theory, or worse still, two half theories. ... If we accept the principles are separate, we have to explain how they relate to each other.
>
> *(Wood 2002: 317)*

Evident in Kaufman's and Wood's objections is the idea that hybrid theories are ad hoc solutions, and that the strategy of distinguishing different questions is undertheorized and unsustainable. What might be said in response to these charges?

To Kaufman's question about the nature of the distinction, I think the answer is reasonably straightforward. Given that Hart's focus is on the moral justification of punishment, I read him as invoking a moral distinction: there are multiple questions relevant to punishment's moral justification, and these questions may be answered by appeal to different moral considerations.

What about Kaufman's objection that the distinction violates common sense, as both consequentialist and retributivist views purport to provide both a rationale and constraining principles for punishment? Some consequentialists may be confident, of course, that their account has the resources to ground all the needed principles to govern how punishment may be imposed, including prohibitions on punishment of the innocent or disproportionate punishment of the guilty. By contrast, retributivists may deny that crime reduction or similar ends are proper ends of punishment; they may insist that a sufficient rationale for punishment is that it constitutes a deserved response to wrongdoers. For those who are entirely uncompelled by the standardly raised objections to their respective views, a hybrid account will obviously seem to be something of a solution in search of a problem. But many of us find compelling both the intuition that if punishment is justified, it must be in some substantial measure because of its role in helping to reduce crime, and the intuition that particular impositions of punishment should be intrinsically appropriate responses to the corresponding crimes. We may thus be reluctant to surrender either of these intuitions.[5]

Part of Kaufman's objection to Hart's strategy of drawing the distinction between punishment's rationale and its constraining principles is that whatever rationale we endorse will itself imply certain constraints on the implementation of punishment. He writes that it is "inaccurate to separate the utilitarian goal from the distributive principle, as utilitarianism already contains within it a principle of distribution" (Kaufman 2008: 48, citing Lacey 1988). The same is true of retributivism. Thus, he writes, "Hart's claim cannot be that a General Justifying Aim can never entail a principle of distribution" (ibid.).

Kaufman is right about this, and indeed this is not Hart's claim. In fact, Hart recognized that punishment's rationale will imply certain constraints on how the institution is implemented. He writes, for example, that a general justifying aim of retribution would entail retribution in its distribution (Hart 1960: 9). He does not elaborate on this point, which is unfortunate in that doing so might have clarified that he was not arguing that punishment's rationale has no implications for how it may be implemented. Rather, his point was that, as discussed earlier, whatever values or principles we take to provide the compelling rationale (or general justifying aim, in his terms) of punishment, we should not expect these to *exhaust* the considerations relevant to whether and how the institution may be implemented. Again, a pure consequentialist or pure retributivist might deny this claim, and insist that the aim of crime reduction or the rationale of meting out deserved suffering or censure both provide the compelling rationale for the institution of punishment and exhaust the relevant constraints on its implementation. But it is precisely the often cited intuitive inadequacies of either of these sorts of univocal approaches to justifying punishment that have motivated Hart and others to develop a mixed account.

What about Wood's objection that hybrid accounts are not sufficiently integrated, that the relationship between the considerations relevant to the rationale question and the considerations relevant to the constraints question is not adequately explained? In one sense, Wood is asking for more than a hybrid account can (or aims to) deliver, in that the basic insight of such accounts is that the rationale question and the constraints question may be answered by appeal to distinct, unrelated considerations. But perhaps Wood's point is that we need an account of how the considerations will interact within the structure of the hybrid theory – in particular, how potential tensions between the considerations will be resolved. Hybrid theories look messy in this regard, as admitting of distinct considerations into the theory raises the prospect of tensions between these considerations. Thus Antony Duff asks, "[S]hould we … recognize that we can never achieve more than an unstable compromise – that we will always face conflicts, which cannot be confidently or readily resolved, between the demands of justice and those of crime prevention?" (Duff 1996: 8). Perhaps we should prefer univocal theories insofar as they avoid these sorts of tension.

In my view, however, virtually any plausible theory of punishment will incorporate constraints grounded in considerations that do not derive from punishment's rationale; thus they will have to cope with potential tensions between distinct considerations that are not reducible to one another. In the remainder of this section, I focus on accounts that endorse a retributivist rationale for punishment, as it is these accounts that are most prominently offered as univocal (and therefore superior) alternatives to hybrid theories.

Retributivism holds that punishment is deserved not because of some valuable consequences it promotes, but as an intrinsically appropriate, because deserved, response to criminal wrongdoing. Some, more traditional retributivist views focus on the burdensomeness of punishment: these accounts justify punishment as the infliction of deserved suffering. Other, more recent retributivist accounts focus instead on punishment's expressive or communicative function: they contend that punishment is justified as the expression or communication of deserved blame, or censure.[6] Central to either variety of retributivism, however, is the claim that the suffering or censure is justified insofar as it is a deserved response to the prior offense.

But this is not the only sense of desert relevant in punishment. Margaret Falls provides a useful analysis of the claim "Person *P* deserves *X*." The claim, she explains, is "(1) an assessment or acknowledgement of *P*'s worth (2) relative to a given role or capacity (3) based upon what already is or has been true of *P*'s characteristics, abilities, and/or acts" (Falls 1987: 38).[7] If we say, for example, that Rafael Nadal deserves to be regarded as the best tennis player in the world, we are making a claim that Nadal is worthy of certain regard, relative to his role as a tennis player, in virtue of his accomplishments in competitive tournaments in recent years.

Central to Falls's account, however, is the Kantian idea that all of us, simply as moral persons, deserve (or are worthy of) certain treatment simply in virtue of those features that make us moral persons (ibid.: 39).[8] That is, we may deserve certain treatment not only in virtue of *what we have done* but also in virtue of *who we are*. Falls characterizes this latter sort of desert as *unearned* desert: for example, as a moral person, we deserve not to be lied to merely for others' convenience, or to be killed for sport (ibid.: 39–40). She distinguishes this from *earned* desert, the sort of desert we come to merit in virtue of our previous conduct. Retributivism is grounded in the notion of earned desert: it is ultimately concerned with what offenders deserve (whether in absolute terms or relative to other offenders) in virtue of their previous culpable wrongdoing.

Some would reject the notion of unearned desert as a contradiction in terms (see, e.g. Rachels 1978: 150–63). But whatever terms we prefer, Falls highlights an important and, I believe, intuitively plausible distinction between treatment to which we are entitled, or have a right, or deserve, in virtue of our prior conduct, and treatment to which we are entitled, or have a right, or deserve, in virtue of our status as moral persons. Recognizing this distinction helps to highlight that the two senses of desert may come to be in tension with each other: we may deserve *as earned desert* certain treatment based on our previous behavior that conflicts with what we deserve *as unearned desert* simply in virtue of our status as moral persons.

My claim is that many prominent accounts typically labeled "retributivist" are in fact committed to what Falls calls *unearned* desert as well as *earned* desert. But the notion of unearned desert does not derive from retributivism. Thus these accounts are in fact best characterized as hybrid views.

Consider perhaps the most famous supposed retributivist, Immanuel Kant. Some have argued that Kant's is a hybrid view because it allows that deterrent or reformist aims may be pursued via punishment as long as the person punished has first been proved guilty of a crime (see Byrd 1989; Hill 2000). Rather than revisit these arguments, though, I want to focus on another sense in which Kant's view appears to be a hybrid one. Kant famously appealed to *lex talionis* to ground his argument for capital punishment of murderers. He wrote:

> whatever undeserved evil you inflict upon another within the people, that you inflict upon yourself. If you insult him, you insult yourself; if you steal from him, you steal from yourself; if you strike him, you strike yourself; if you kill him, you kill yourself.
>
> *(Kant [1785]1996: 473)*

Kant claimed, however, that in some cases, exceptions to the strict like-for-like response would be warranted. For instance, for the crime of rape, he prescribed not that the perpetrator likewise be raped, but rather that he be castrated. But castration is not a like-for-like response to rape. The physical damage of castration is not particularly similar to that of rape, nor is it clear that the two are similar in their emotional impact (also, this punishment is inapplicable in cases of rape by a female). Still, Kant wrote that this punishment respects *lex talionis* "if not in terms of its letter at least in terms of its spirit" (ibid.: 498). But why not respect the letter of *lex* as well as its spirit by imposing the strict like-for-like punishment in rape cases? The most plausible answer, in my view, is that Kant was committed to *lex* as a principle of earned desert but also recognized that like-for-like treatment may come into tension with what sort of treatment people deserve simply as moral persons, and that when it does, our unearned desert constrains what may be done to us as earned desert. This is essentially the interpretation of Kant that Falls defends (Falls 1987: 38–48). She contends that Kant's retributivism, grounded in *lex talionis*, "is solely about earned moral desert, and according to it, torture, death, whatever, can be the earned moral desert of the most wicked" (ibid.: 47). But Kant's categorical imperative – which instructs us to treat humanity always as an end in itself, never as a mere means to some ends – grounds a principle (based on unearned desert) that constrains how severely the state may mete out retribution.

More recently, J. Angelo Corlett describes his view as "retributivist" and also "mixed," in that, "though desert is what serves as the primary justification of punishment, considerations of social utility may serve as secondary reasons to punish" (Corlett 2001: 78). Corlett's theory is a hybrid view in another respect, as well, although it is less clear whether he recognizes this second respect. He endorses what is often called "negative retributivism," which he describes as the view that the guilty "should never be punished at any level higher than approximate proportionality permits, though sometimes the guilty need not be punished at all, or may be punished at a level significantly lower than proportionality dictates" (ibid.). What neither Corlett nor others who endorse "negative retributivism" make clear is how retributivism can be thought to ground this asymmetrical stance regarding upward and downward variations from retributivist proportionality. The only plausible answer, in my view, is that punishing less severely than is deserved may sometimes be warranted according to unearned desert or other considerations that are not derivable from retributivism itself and may sometimes override retributivist requirements. In general, then, I suggest that so-called "negative retributivist" accounts are not pure retributivist accounts at all, but rather hybrid theories that contain a prominent retributivist element.

Many more so-called retributivist accounts have been offered, of course, but what unites these accounts is the rationale that punishment is deserved (in the sense of earned moral desert) for the offender's prior wrongdoing. As we have seen, however, earned moral desert does not tell the full story of what treatment a person deserves, all things considered. Other considerations (such as unearned desert) are relevant, as well. Similarly, theories that posit a consequentialist rationale for punishment, insofar as they are plausible, will also incorporate certain nonconsequentialist constraints on its imposition. The lesson here is that virtually all plausible accounts of punishment will be hybrid accounts insofar as the considerations they endorse as governing the implementation of punishment will not derive entirely from the rationale for the institution of punishment. This matters because, as we have seen, adherents to supposedly unified theories of punishment, especially retributivists, often criticize hybrid theories as being unstable in that they incorporate distinct moral considerations that may come into tension with each other. But in fact, virtually any plausible account will draw on distinct moral considerations, and thus there will be potential tensions in need of resolution within the account. In my view, it is better to be up front in acknowledging these potential tensions from the outset. Morality may just be messy, and as W.D. Ross put it, "it is more important that our theory fit the facts than that it be simple" (Ross 1930: 19).

Conclusion

In conclusion, I contend that Hart was essentially correct in his insight that the question of punishment's justification is in fact multiple questions, which admit of answers that appeal to distinct moral considerations. We might disagree with the particular ways that Hart answered the questions of punishment's compelling rationale and the appropriate constraints. We might even argue that there are additional salient questions, such as whether pursuing this rationale, constrained in whatever ways, violates offenders' rights. But these are all essentially intramural questions within hybrid theorizing. My aim in this chapter has just been to contend that, for those who believe a satisfactory justification of punishment will need to incorporate crime-reductive as well as retributivist considerations, there is no reason to despair that these can be plausibly incorporated into a pluralistic account.

Acknowledgements

I presented previous drafts of this paper in workshops at University College London, the London School of Economics, and at the 35th International Social Philosophy Conference. I am grateful to those in the audience at each of these events for their questions and comments. Thanks also to the editors of this volume for useful feedback.

Notes

1 This articulation of hybrid views highlights that John Rawls's (1955) theory of punishment, often cited alongside Hart's as a paradigmatic expression of a hybrid theory, is not a hybrid view after all. The view Rawls developed was in fact (and ironically, given his later writings) a version of rule utilitarianism, according to which utilitarian considerations justify implementing a system of punishment governed by retributivist prohibitions on punishment of the innocent or disproportionate punishment of the guilty. On Rawls's account, the rule (the institution of punishment incorporating the retributivist constraints) is

justified insofar as it generates more overall net utility than available alternatives, and the individual actions (inflictions of punishment governed by the retributivist constraints) are justified insofar as they conform to the rule. In my view, Hare's (1981: 161–63) account is similarly not best regarded as a hybrid theory, for roughly the same reasons.

2 Thanks to Farah Focquaert for discussion on this point.

3 Although crime reduction is the most commonly endorsed consequentialist rationale, others have been offered. For example, theorists have cited offender moral education (see, e.g. Hampton 1984) or victim restitution and restoration (see Callender 2018) as goals that punishment can help to achieve. I am skeptical, for different reasons, of each of these accounts, but engaging with them is beyond the scope of this chapter.

4 David Boonin (2008: 103–18), for example, describes the forfeiture view as a version of retributivism, whereas Christopher Heath Wellman (2012: 372) claims that the forfeiture view is not a retributivist theory.

5 Even critics of the hybrid view have acknowledged discomfort with simply endorsing a pure consequentialist or pure retributivist account. See Kaufman 2008: 39; Lippke 2006: 292.

6 On the distinction between expression and communication in this context, see Duff 2001: 79–80.

7 Falls builds on analyses of desert by Feinberg (1970) and Kleinig (1971).

8 Accounts differ about specifically what these features are, although most cite some version of autonomy or moral agency.

References

Bennett, C. (2008) *The Apology Ritual: A Philosophical Theory of Punishment*, Cambridge: Cambridge University Press.

Boonin, D. (2008) *The Problem of Punishment*, New York: Cambridge University Press.

Byrd, B.S. (1989) "Kant's Theory of Punishment: Deterrence in Its Threat, Retribution in Its Execution," *Law and Philosophy* 8(2): 151–200.

Callender, J.S. (2018) "Justice, Reciprocity, and the Internalisation of Punishment in Victims of Crime," *Neuroethics* online first: 1–12. Available at https://doi.org/10.1007/s12152-018-9367-6.

Corlett, J.A. (2001) "Making Sense of Retributivism," *Philosophy* 76(295): 77–110.

Duff, R.A. (1986) *Trials and Punishments*, Cambridge: Cambridge University Press.

Duff, R.A. (1996) "Penal Communications: Recent Work in the Philosophy of Punishment," *Crime and Justice* 20: 1–97.

Duff, R.A. (2001) *Punishment, Communication, and Community*, Oxford: Oxford University Press.

Falls, M.M. (1987) "Retribution, Reciprocity, and Respect for Persons," *Law and Philosophy* 6(1): 25–51.

Feinberg, J. (1970) *Doing and Deserving: Essays in the Theory of Responsibility*, Princeton: Princeton University Press.

Galligan, D.J. (1981) "The Return to Retribution in Penal Theory," in C.F.H. Tapper (ed.) *Crime, Proof and Punishment: Essays in Memory of Rupert Cross*, London: Butterworths.

Hampton, J. (1984) "The Moral Education Theory of Punishment," *Philosophy and Public Affairs* 13(3): 208–38.

Hare, R.M. (1981) *Moral Thinking*, Oxford: Oxford University Pres.

Hart, H.L.A. (1960) "Prolegomenon to the Principles of Punishment," *Proceedings of the Aristotelian Society* 60: 1–26.

Hill, T.E. (2000) "Kant on Punishment: A Coherent Mix of Deterrence and Retribution?" in *Respect, Pluralism, and Justice: Kantian Perspectives*, Oxford: Oxford University Press.

Hoskins, Z. (2011) "Deterrent Punishment and Respect for Persons," *Ohio State Journal of Criminal Law* 8(2): 369–84.

Kant, I. ([1785]1996) *Metaphysics of Morals*, in Mary J. Gregor (trans. and ed.) *The Cambridge Edition of the Works of Immanuel Kant, Practical Philosophy*, Cambridge: Cambridge University Press.

Kaufman, W. (2008) "The Rise and Fall of the Mixed Theory of Punishment," *International Journal of Applied Philosophy* 22(1): 37–57.

Kleinig, J. (1971) "The Concept of Desert," *The American Philosophical Review* 8: 71–78.

Lacey, N. (1988) *State Punishment: Political Principles and Community Values*, London: Routledge.

Lippke, R.L. (2006) "Mixed Theories of Punishment and Mixed Offenders: Some Unresolved Tensions," *The Southern Journal of Philosophy* 44: 273–95.

Moore, M. (2010) *Placing Blame: A Theory of Criminal Law*, Oxford. Oxford University Press.

Rachels, J. (1978) "What People Deserve," in John Arthur and William Shaw (eds.) *Justice and Economic Distribution*, Englewood Cliffs, N.J: Prentice Hall, pp. 150–63.

Rawls, J. (1955) "Two Concepts of Rules," *The Philosophical Review* 64(1): 3–32.

Ross, W.D. (1930) *The Right and the Good*, Oxford: Oxford University Press.

Scheid, D.E. (1997) "Constructing a Theory of Punishment, Desert, and the Distribution of Punishments," *Canadian Journal of Law and Jurisprudence* 10: 441–506.
Ten, C.L. (1987) *Crime, Guilt, and Punishment*, Oxford: Oxford University Press.
Wellman, C.H. (2012) "The Rights Forfeiture Theory of Punishment," *Ethics* 122(2): 371–93.
Wood, D. (2002) "Retribution, Crime Reduction, and the Justification of Punishment," *Oxford Journal of Legal Studies* 22(2): 301–21.

5

LIMITING RETRIBUTIVISM AND INDIVIDUAL PREVENTION

Christopher Slobogin

Limiting Retributivism

Limiting retributivism, also known as modified desert theory, is a "mixed theory" of punishment that posits that retributive principles should set the outer bounds of a sentence, while the precise nature and duration of disposition should be designed to implement one or more independent criminal justice system goals. Those goals could include general deterrence, prevention of additional crime by the offender, cost containment, efficient allocation of correctional capacity, elimination of racial disparities, or any combination of these objectives. So defined, limiting retributivism has many manifestations.

This chapter will focus on a particular version of limiting retributivism. Specifically, it will examine the advantages and disadvantages of a sentencing regime it calls "preventive justice." A preventive justice regime adopts sentence ranges consistent with the offender's desert and then relies on expert parole boards to determine the nature and duration of sentence within this range based on consideration of individual prevention goals (i.e. incapacitation, specific deterrence and rehabilitation). The analysis of this chapter suggests that a system of relatively wide sentence ranges derived from retributive principles, in combination with short minimum sentences that are enhanced under limited circumstances by statistically driven risk assessment and management, can alleviate many of the inherent tensions between desert and prevention, between deontology and political reality, and between the desire for community input and the allure of expertise. If done properly, it should also significantly reduce prison populations.

Types of Limiting Retributivism

Virtually every modern criminal law scholar believes that, if criminal punishment is to occur, it must be cabined by retributive considerations. In particular, there is general consensus that an offender should never be punished more than he or she deserves (Armstrong 1969: 155; Morris 1974: 60; Tonry 2018: 9). But most scholars, and every modern sentencing regime, also endorse a punishment scheme that mixes this desert-premise with utilitarian considerations such as prevention of crime through deterrence, incapacitation and treatment (Frase 2004: 84). One very popular mixed theory is limiting retributivism.

The progenitor of limiting retributivism as an organizing concept is often said to be Norval Morris, who almost a half century ago wrote *The Future of Imprisonment* (1974). In that book, Morris proposed that retributivism should play a "negative" role at sentencing (73). In other words, a person's desert or blameworthiness should act as a constraint on sentencing, but not as a determinant of a particular sentence. As a practical matter, this meant that desert would determine the range of the sentence for particular crimes, but not the disposition in a particular case. Rather, Morris argued, the specific sentence should depend on other considerations such as general deterrence and, rarely, the risk posed by the offender (79). It would also be guided by what Morris called the "parsimony principle" – the idea, endorsed both before and since by many commentators, that punishment should be no more severe than necessary to carry out the state's punishment purposes (Morris 1974: 60–62; Bentham 1789; Frase 2013: 32–33).

Morris' work was in some respects a reaction to the prevailing mode of sentencing, often called indeterminate, in which the legislature sets broad sentencing ranges (e.g. one year to 30 years, or one year to life), and a parole board determines the offender's release date after considering culpability, risk of reoffending and other factors (for a description of indeterminate sentencing, see Reitz 2012: 274). Other commentators also criticized indeterminate sentencing but, in contrast to Morris' scheme, proposed in its place what has been called a "positive" retributivist regime that is based entirely on desert and rejects consideration of utilitarian factors such as risk (e.g. von Hirsch 1976). Given its divergence from this latter approach, Morris' limiting retributivism has often been called a "hybrid" approach that attempts to reconcile, or at least marry, deontologically driven desert theory with the consequentialist goals of protecting the public and conserving public resources.

While Morris contributed the limiting retributivism label and fleshed out its rationale, the practice it describes existed in various forms long before he wrote his book and continues to be popular in both US and European jurisdictions. Even some versions of "indeterminate" sentencing are consistent with limiting retributivism, in that they rely on desert-based sentence boundaries, albeit usually very large ones. For instance, the original Model Penal Code (MPC), promulgated in 1962, mandated three broad sentencing ranges – for first-degree felonies, one year up to life in prison (or up to 20 years, depending on which version of the Code was adopted); for second-degree felonies, one to ten years; and for third-degree felonies one to five years (American Law Institute 1962: § 6.06). However, there remains a key difference between Morris's version of limiting retributivism and indeterminate regimes like the original MPC. Whereas under Morris' approach the length of sentence is set at the front end, in regimes like that endorsed in the original MPC the sentence served depends on a back-end decision by a parole board, and thus is truly indeterminate at the time of sentencing (American Law Institute 1962: § 6.10).

Even within those limiting retributive systems that set sentences at the time of adjudication, significant variation can occur in terms of (1) sentence scope, (2) the sentencing factors considered, and (3) sentencing procedures. With respect to the scope issue, Morris himself believed that measuring desert is a very imprecise task and thus he was not particularly attentive to proportionality concerns (Morris 1974: 74). In contrast, most modern systems rely on guidelines that establish narrower ranges, in the belief that desert can be gauged at least in a comparative sense (e.g. murder is worse than robbery), and in the hope that this method will reduce disparity between sentences for the same crime. For example, the revisions to the MPC, adopted in 2016, not only reject the original Code's back-end decision-making scheme, but also call for more numerous sentencing categories with much smaller ranges than the original Code (American Law Institute 2016: § 6.06).

Minnesota's sentencing guidelines, which are often cited as a good example of modern limiting retributivism, illustrate a number of these features (Minnesota Sentencing Guidelines 2018). The guidelines have 11 categories of sentences, which provide fairly narrow ranges (about 20 months) for lower level felonies, but fairly broad ranges (about 120 months) for higher level felonies. The lower end of the most punitive category approximates the higher end of the next most punitive category, the lower end of the second most punitive category abuts the higher end of the next category, and so on. Most lower-level felonies result in imposition of sentences that are then suspended, at least for first-time offenders.

Richard Frase has proposed perhaps the most detailed limiting retributivism proposal in the scholarly literature, modeled in several ways on the Minnesota system (Frase 2013). He calls his approach "definite" limiting retributivism, not only to emphasize the need for clear upper limits but also to signal that sentence ranges should represent a desert-based hierarchy, in the way Minnesota's categories do, rather than significantly overlap, as Morris seemed to prefer. Further, Frase advocates an "asymmetric" approach to sentencing: while the maximum end of the range is definite, the lower limits of the range are meant to be very flexible, and might often consist of suspended sentences (25–26).

In addition to different approaches to setting the retributive scope or range, limiting retributivism approaches can vary in the factors that determine where within a given range a particular sentence falls. In arriving at a precise sentence, Morris distrusted assessments of risk and treatment potential, but he was willing to permit consideration of criminal history, which he believed was relevant to both culpability and risk (Morris 1974: 65–66). He also thought general deterrence could play a role in sentencing (79). Other scholars who are more wedded to retributivism argue that criminal history is irrelevant, given that the offender has already been punished for his or her past crime, and also reject general deterrence as a consideration in fashioning a particular sentence, on the ground that it improperly exploits the individual for societal ends or that its effect in individual cases is incalculable (see, e.g. Moore 1997).

However, most modern systems, including the revised MPC, permit consideration of all of these factors (see MPC 2016: § 1.02(2) & commentary). Criminal history is relevant in all of them and often predominates, to such an extent that in several systems it is the only legitimate reason for departing above the usual maximum for a given crime (see, e.g. Minnesota Sentencing Guidelines 2018). In other states, judges are also allowed to consider offender risk beyond what might be deduced from criminal history, as well as the offender's amenability to treatment (Hyatt, Chanenson and Berstrom 2011). Frase too is willing to contemplate risk as a determinant of sentence within the retributive range, so that a low risk offender might receive probation while a higher risk offender convicted of the same crime might go to prison (Frase 2013: 26).

Additionally, in setting sentences (as well as sentence ranges) Frase would require "ends-benefits proportionality" analysis. Illustrative of the flexible nature of limiting retributivism, this principle would require decision-makers to consider

> not just the harms caused by different crimes but also the enforcement costs, private burdens of the penalty, and the collateral costs of arrest, conviction, and punishment (including the tendency of harsh criminal penalties to reduce offenders' future employability and other life changes).
>
> *(Frase 2013: 33)*

The third variable that is important in delineating how limiting retributivism works has to do with the implementing procedural framework, rather than the substance of the sentences. The most popular procedural mechanism in most limiting retributivism jurisdictions is the sentencing commission, which is an administrative body, populated by experts, that is charged with creating guidelines like those in Minnesota (Barkow and O'Neill 2006). As a means of reducing disparity, appellate review of the sentence is also generally available, at least when the judge departs above or below the guidelines range (Mitchell 2017: 35). Good time credits – designed to incentivize good conduct in prison – range from 15% to 50% of the sentence, depending on the crime and the jurisdiction (American Law Institute 2009: 99–104). Parole is abolished or severely curtailed in many of these states. In those states where it has been retained, the parole decision-making process is generally very informal compared to a trial, and is generally not subject to appellate review (Jacobi, Richardson and Barr: 2014).

Limiting Retributivism and Risk Assessment

As noted above, a number of limiting retributivist sentencing schemes contemplate that the precise sentence imposed within the retributive range can be based on assessments of risk. While Morris distrusted such assessments, that distrust was based in part on the belief that predictions about reoffending were not reliable (Morris 1974: 66–73). The more recent movement toward "evidence-based sentencing," which relies on statistically derived algorithms to assess risk, has inspired somewhat more optimism about combining risk assessment with limiting retributivism (Klingele 2016).

For instance, the revised MPC and Frase tentatively endorse use of the "newer actuarial risk prediction tools" to determine, at the front end, the appropriate sentence within the offense-driven range (American Law Institute 2017: §6.03; Frase 2013: 35). Both schemes focus on use of these tools as a means of reducing sentence. Additionally, however, under both schemes an extensive criminal history, or a "high" risk assessment based on a prediction tool, could move a sentence toward the high end of the retributively designated range. If an offender ends up in prison, the release date in these risk-based regimes is determined at sentencing; parole boards have no impact on sentence duration, but rather are relegated to monitoring offenders after release, which in Frase's system would never occur until 85% of the sentence has been served, minus good time credit; the 15% remainder would be reserved as incentive for the offenders to adhere to post-release conditions (Frase 2013: 69–70).

In contrast, Rhine, Petersilia and Reitz have proposed an approach to limiting retributivism that continues to rely on parole boards as back-end decision-makers (Rhine, Petersilia and Reitz 2017). However, unlike the traditional parole board, which is usually composed of political appointees, their proposed board would consist of people recommended by a non-partisan panel and include expert criminologists and professionals versed in risk assessment. Further, rather than the usual wide-ranging power granted such boards, the entity proposed by Rhine et al. would be significantly constrained by the judge's sentence which, consistent with limiting retributivism, would stay within a desert-driven range. Prisoners would be entitled to a presumption of release when the judicially imposed sentence expired. Only if the board judged an offender to pose a "credible risk of serious crime" could the sentence be extended, and even then only up to an amount equal to 25–30% of the maximum allowable sentence for the offense, the upper end of the relevant guidelines range, or 15 years, whichever comes first (282). As do Frase and the revised MPC, Rhine et al. tentatively endorse the use of risk assessment instruments in determining whether an offender is a "credible risk," and state that "paroling authorities should be required to validate their instruments on their local offender populations and consider how actuarial predictions of recidivism are inexorably connected to race and social class" (282).

Another variation of a risk-based limiting retributivism regime is found in Virginia, which engages in a relatively aggressive use of risk assessment. In 1994, the Virginia legislature abolished parole and adopted a determinate sentencing regime (Virginia Code 1994: § 17.2–805). However, anticipating that the increase in prison terms mandated by the statute would lead to a fiscal "collapse" of the state's prison system, the legislature also directed the newly formed Virginia Criminal Sentencing Commission (VCSC) to develop an empirically based risk-assessment instrument that would enable judges to divert 25% of the "lowest-risk, incarceration-bound, drug and property offenders" from prison to alternative sanctions such as jail, release, probation, community service, outpatient substance-abuse treatment, or electronic monitoring (Kern and Farrar-Owens, 2004). The Non-Violent Risk Assessment instrument (NVRA) was adopted statewide in July 2002, for all felony larceny, fraud, and drug cases. While the score from this instrument is to be considered in every such case, the decision as to whether an offender found to be low risk is diverted is left up to individual judges. A study of sentencing outcomes in 2016 found that only 42.2% of those who received a low risk score received such an alternative sentence, while 23.4% of those designated high risk received alternative sentences (Garrett, Jakubow and Monahan, 2019). Although the same study found that about 75% of the judges surveyed stated that they "always," "almost always," or "usually" consulted the NVRA score, judges obviously took full advantage of their discretion. The same types of findings occurred in connection with Virginia's sex offender risk assessment instrument, which permits within-range *enhancement* of sentences for those found to be high risk.

This sampling provides some sense of the many possible variations of limiting retributivism, particularly those variations that focus on the role of risk assessments in such a regime. The remainder of this chapter fleshes out how a particular version of limiting retributivism, which will be called "preventive justice," might be integrated with the goals of protecting the public and efficiently allocating resources through use of risk assessment technology.

Determining Sentencing Ranges

The first goal in any limiting retributivism regime, whether or not mixed with risk assessment, is to set the sentence range for each type of crime. At one end of the spectrum are scholars like von Hirsch and Ashworth, who believe that "parity" in sentencing is crucial, and thus call for very narrow ranges based entirely on "the degree of harmfulness of the conduct and the extent of the actor's culpability" (von Hirsch and Ashworth 2012: 144). They would allow "limited variations ... say, in the range of 5–10 per cent" to permit non-prison alternatives and "back-up sanctions" for offenders who violate probation or parole conditions, but argue that preventive aims should never be grounds for deviation (162). At the other end of the spectrum is Morris, who apparently found acceptable very wide ranges, akin to those associated with indeterminate regimes. At least in his early writings, Morris held to the position that blameworthiness is such a capacious construct that a given crime could be associated with a large variety of sanctions that are, as he put it, "not undeserved" (Morris 1982: 151). In between are writers like Frase, who speaks in positive terms of Minnesota's system of moderately broad ranges. Frase thinks Morris was too casual in his attitude toward desert, but he also rejects the narrow ranges proposed by von Hirsch and Ashworth, not only because he is willing to differentiate between high and low risk offenders but because he believes broader ranges are necessary to encourage offender cooperation and to provide leeway in meeting correctional priorities (Frase 2013: 30).

The position taken in this chapter is that the wide ranges preferred by Morris make the most sense. As Morris recognized, assessing blameworthiness is a difficult task. Von Hirsch and Ashworth admit as much, conceding that "[t]here seems to be no crime for which one can readily perceive a specific quantum of punishment as the uniquely deserved one" (von Hirsch and Ashworth 2012: 142). Nonetheless, they claim that a degree of precision is still possible because consensus can at least be reached about the "ordinal" ranking of crimes. Thus, they argue, once the maximum "anchor" point (for instance, life without parole) has been set, punishments can be assigned according to their ranking, with the anchor point providing the upper limit on punishment for the most serious crime and lesser punishments assigned to lesser crimes (142).

Von Hirsch and Ashworth's claim that widespread agreement is possible with respect to the ordinal rankings of crimes is at least partially supported by the research of Paul Robinson and others (Robinson and Kurzban 2007). But outside the core crimes such as homicide, rape, robbery, and theft, consensus about ordinal ranking disappears (1890–92). Further, of course, disagreement over the all-important maximum anchor point can be significant; for instance, some might favor the death penalty for murder, while others might prefer a maximum sentence of 15 years for such a crime. Finally, the "spacing" between crimes on the ordinal scale can also be a matter of serious dispute.

Von Hirsch and Ashworth respond that the ordinal ranking and spacing questions can be addressed through analyzing the impact of a given crime on the victim's "standard of living," a concept they develop at some length (von Hirsch and Ashworth 2012: 143–46). As they acknowledge, however, "the impact of a crime on the living standard is itself very much a matter of factual and normative judgement" and in any event "is designed mainly to address crimes directly affecting natural persons, rather than crimes involving collective interests" (146). Furthermore, the standard of living metric addresses only the actus reus of the crime. Von Hirsch and Ashworth suggest that the mental state component, which can be an extremely important factor in determining desert for many crimes, instead "can be gauged with the aid of clues from substantive criminal law doctrine" (144). But as should be obvious to anyone who has studied the many controversies over such doctrine – dealing with subjects such as inchoate and accomplice liability, mistakes of fact and law, and the role of reasonableness in defining mens rea and the defenses – the parameters of an offender's blameworthiness are highly debatable. And even if the relevant criteria are agreed upon, research calls into serious doubt the legal system's ability to discern the relevant mental "facts" (what was actually going through the defendant's mind at the time of the crime?) and the jury's ability to correctly label them (did he or she act purposefully, knowingly, recklessly or negligently?) (see Slobogin 2007: 43–46).

While these difficulties do not mean we should not try to reach conclusions about these matters, they do suggest that any answers arrived at have a wide margin of error, which should be reflected in sentencing ranges. In fact, as indicated above, actual limiting retributivist sentencing schemes like Minnesota's do have relatively wide ranges, especially for more serious crimes (although in part that is to permit enhancements based on criminal history, a topic dealt with in the penultimate section of this chapter). If community views are taken into account, even these ranges are probably too constrained. My own research indicates that even when people are given relatively simple factual scenarios providing facts relevant only to actus reus and mens rea, and even when the respondents who give outlier responses are weeded out, the punishment chosen varies widely, by as much as four years for minor crimes and from 15 years to the death penalty for the most serious offenses (Slobogin and Brinkley-Rubinstein 2013: 95).

Thus, the original Model Penal Code – with its three broad ranges based on the degree of felony – may come closer to capturing both community sentiment and a more realistic view of the capaciousness of desert. To reflect the fact that consensus on the ordinal ranking of a significant number of crimes exists, greater nuance could be provided, perhaps by creating more than the original MPC's three categories for felonies (as described below). But the difficulty of determining, in any non-arbitrary way, the anchoring and spacing thresholds based on desert argues for the types of significant differentials between minima and maxima that the original MPC proposed and that Morris seemed to accept.

One can anticipate at least two objections to this regime, even from those limiting retributivists who are willing to contemplate significant flexibility in gauging desert. First, recall that minimum sentences in the original MPC were all one year, regardless of how serious the crime is. That outcome is too flexible if one takes ordinal desert and the goal of differentiating the worst from the least crimes seriously, and it is drastic enough that it could significantly undermine the general deterrent impact of specific sentences, to the extent there is any. Additionally, as Robinson argues from a consequentialist perspective, a punishment system that departs too far from community sentiment may well lose legitimacy and produce a populace willing to take the law into its own hands or to become non-compliant in other ways (Robinson 1997; Robinson, Goodwin and Reisig 2010). Although I have argued that Robinson overstates the need for adhering strictly to societal views on punishment (Slobogin and Brinkley-Rubinstein 2013), a drastic departure from community views – for instance, a default sentence of one year for a crime such as aggravated murder – might well trigger the type of de-legitimization he describes (Slobogin and Brinkley-Rubinstein 2013: 114).

Taking these considerations into account and adding two categories for the reasons described earlier, a limiting retributivist regime might adopt ranges like the following: ten to 30 years for very serious crimes (such as, and perhaps only for, aggravated murder), followed by four additional tiers of felonies, with ranges of three to ten years (for lesser forms of intentional killing, rape and armed robbery), one to five years (for crimes like aggravated assault), one to three years in prison (for crimes like burglary) and one month to one year (for, e.g. the typical low-level drug sale crime). My guess is that many readers will quibble over these ranges and examples, which should bring home the fact that desert is highly malleable; obviously, legislatures or sentencing commissions that find these choices either too harsh or too lenient could modify them accordingly.

In any event, this type of adjustment to the minima and the addition of two categories should alleviate the most significant concerns about disproportionality if the earlier points about the breadth and amorphousness of the culpability inquiry are accepted. These steps would not be responsive, however, to the aforementioned disparity objection, made most forcefully by von Hirsch and Ashworth, but also a significant concern for those like Frase who are not as wedded to precise desert determinations. Von Hirsch and Ashworth contend that wide sentencing ranges permit, and perhaps even encourage, unequal treatment of offenders (von Hirsch and Ashworth 2012: 138–140). For instance, in the sentencing scheme laid out above, the overlap in ranges in the three lowest categories might result in an offender in the lowest category receiving the same sentence as an offender in higher categories, and within any of the ranges individuals convicted of precisely the same felony might nonetheless receive very different sentences. But this objection assumes both that the desert of two different offenders can be rigorously measured and that desert is the relevant metric for gauging parity. If instead it is taken as a given that measuring desert for a specific crime is an abstruse exercise (consider, for instance, the many possible variations of "armed robbery" and the people who commit it) and that the whole point of limiting retributivism is to recognize that other criminal justice considerations besides desert may legitimately be considered in fashioning sentences (both assumptions which Morris and Frase, at least, are willing to countenance), this concern is appreciably diminished.

That is not to say that parity is not an important goal. For instance, if, as proposed here, an offender's risk is relevant to determining the precise sentence, offenders with similar risk levels should be treated similarly (Slobogin 2006: 143–150). Nor should sentences vary depending upon invidious factors like race (although, as discussed in more detail below, certain factors, like age and gender, should not automatically be anathema to risk assessments). More generally, the existence of wide sentence ranges and specific sentences based on non-desert considerations should not lead to the conclusion that sentencing can be "lawless," the term Judge Frankel famously affixed to indeterminate regimes (Frankel 1972). As developed in the next section, several principles, some of them arguably of constitutional status, should govern a preventive justice version of limiting retributivism.

Principles of Preventive Justice

The first principle of a preventive justice version of limiting retributivism would focus on its desert component rather than the prevention component, and would be straightforward: to satisfy the retributive goal, the minimum sentence required by desert must be served. For most misdemeanors and many lower-level felonies (at the least, those in the final three of the five categories proposed above), this sentence could consist of non-incarcerative restrictions in the community, such as community service and restitution; here, attention should be paid to the fact that some types of community restrictions can have as much "punitive bite" as short prison sentences (Harlow, Darley and Robinson 1995). Frase argues, as did Henry Hart before him, that the censure associated with a criminal conviction and these types of disposition can satisfy desert demands at the lower end of the criminal scale (Frase 2013: 31; Hart 1958: 427). Several other commentators, including von Hirsch and Ashworth, have recognized that retributive goals can be achieved through non-incarcerative alternatives (von Hirsch and Ashworth 2012: 156–59).

However, for more serious crimes (associated with the first two categories described above), probably no community-based condition would satisfy desert, in which case the presumptive sentence should be a prison term consistent with the minimum set by the relevant sentencing range. In contrast, Frase argues in favor of the practice in many states of making the default sentence the middle of the range, so that judges can depart upward or downward and still stay within desert-based bounds (Frase 2013: 52). But if, as we are assuming, any sentence within the range satisfies desert, the parsimony principle – which writers like Morris, Tonry, and Frase himself all endorse (as does the revised

Model Penal Code) – dictates that the minimum sentence is the place to start. Then, as suggested by Rhine, Petersilia and Reitz (2017), risk assessments, carried out by an expert parole board, would determine whether the offender should continue to be imprisoned, released subject to supervision, or released entirely.

The parsimony principle, reinforced by constitutional doctrine, would also govern the role of risk assessment and risk management. Almost 50 years ago, the Supreme Court decided *Jackson v. Indiana* (1972), involving a challenge to the prolonged detention of an individual who had been found permanently incompetent to stand trial. In concluding that Jackson's detention was unconstitutional, the Court declared that the due process clause requires that the "nature and duration of commitment bear some reasonable relationship to its purpose" (738). This pronouncement, repeated in several subsequent Supreme Court rulings (*Youngberg v. Romeo* 1982: 324; *Foucha v. Louisiana* 1992: 79; *Seling v. Young* 2001: 265), has several implications for any sentence based on a prevention rationale of the type at issue here.

First, *Jackson* can be read to require, consistent with the parsimony principle, that any government deprivation of liberty in the name of prevention be the last drastic means of achieving the state's preventive aim (Slobogin 2011: 1138–39). That would mean, for instance, that once the desert minimum has been met, community-based programs should be the presumptive disposition unless they cannot adequately protect the public. It further suggests that the state should be willing to experiment with different dispositional approaches.

Second, *Jackson* means that the government *must* provide rehabilitative services if they will reduce the length of the intervention, because otherwise the confinement is not the least restrictive way of accomplishing the state's aim (Janus and Logan 2003: 358–59). In other words, whether or not a state provides such services during the phase of punishment that is designed to meet the desert-based minimum, *Jackson* mandates a right to ameliorative treatment if a sentence is prolonged past the minimum because of a risk assessment. As developed more fully below, risk management research has identified a number of factors such as substance abuse, impulsivity, and cognitive deficiencies that, if subject to treatment, can reduce an offender's risk level.

Finally, *Jackson's* reasonable relationship requirement means that any confinement that occurs should be proportionate to the risk, and that the longer the intervention extends the greater the proof of risk that must be shown (a precept that could be called risk proportionality, analogous to desert proportionality) (Slobogin 2006: 143–150). Individuals considered low risk or at risk of committing only minor crimes should never be detained for preventive purposes (see Ashworth and Zedner: 2014: 260). Even individuals considered to be high risk could not be confined for prolonged periods of time without increasingly higher showings of risk (and again, no one could be detained beyond the retributively determined maximum sentence). Thus, as Rhine, Petersilia and Reitz (2017) propose and as developed further below, a high risk of serious crime is necessary to prolong the sentence for any amount of time.

However, in contrast to the Rhine et al. proposal, a preventive justice approach would not set a definite sentence at the time of the initial risk assessment. The risk an individual poses can easily change over time, especially if risk management is successful. Thus, risk would have to be reassessed periodically. One reason Morris was reticent about allowing risk assessment to influence sentences was his legitimate concern that assessing a person's risk while in prison may not reflect his or her risk outside of it (Morris 1974: 35–36). But risk assessment done correctly would rely not just on within-prison conduct but also on pre-prison information. Moreover, individuals who are not high risk or who can be managed in the community despite their high risk can obviously be evaluated outside the prison setting; in particular, conditional release programs can facilitate efforts to assess risk within community settings.

The important point here is that, unlike desert, risk is not a static variable. Setting a determinate, unchangeable sentence, whether at the front-end or at the expiration of the minimum sentence, is inconsistent with the concept of risk. Within the desert-based maximum, the outer boundary of a particular sentence in a preventive justice regime would be determined by periodic assessments of an offender's risk, risk which, because of the parsimony principle, would need to be increasingly more serious to authorize prolonging the intervention.

Proving Risk

As the foregoing discussion should have made clear, in a preventive justice regime risk assessment and risk management are crucial components. In contrast to the voluminous literature on the meaning of desert and how it might affect sentencing, little attention has been paid either to the principles that should govern risk assessment (discussed in the previous section) or the practical aspects of proving risk (discussed here). On the latter score, preventive justice requires concrete rules defining both when a person is "high risk," and how that risk is to be proven.

American courts have abdicated their obligations in both respects. There is virtually no jurisprudence on the standard of proof the state must meet in proving risk at sentencing nor any regulation of the methods the state may use to prove it, despite the fact that significant deprivations of liberty can ride on such determinations (see, e.g. Hopkinson 2018: 730–31). In the related civil commitment context, the Supreme Court has held that danger to others must be proven with "clear and convincing evidence" (*Addington v. Texas* 1979). Most states also define danger in that context to mean a "substantial likelihood" that the person will cause serious bodily harm to another within the foreseeable future (Melton et al. 2018: 326–27). Further, in a closely related context, the Court has held that such determinations should be subject to periodic review (*Kansas v. Hendricks* 1997: 368). If mere hospitalization mandates these requirements, imprisonment certainly should.

Translated to the sentencing context, these precepts would prohibit a high risk finding except upon clear and convincing proof that the individual is likely to commit a serious crime (at least some sort of felony) within, say, a two-year period, after which another assessment should occur. Note the combination of the standard of proof (clear and convincing evidence) with the legal standard (likelihood of reoffending). Given the state of the predictive art, proving that a person will reoffend beyond a reasonable doubt or even by clear and convincing evidence (the latter a standard often quantified at about 75%) is probably impossible. But proving that a person is *likely* to reoffend by clear and convincing evidence is not (Monahan and Wexler 1978: 40). At the same time, this hybrid standard of proof remains a high threshold that only a minority of offenders will cross; together with the requirement that the predicted reoffending involve serious crime within a two-year period, it will be difficult to meet. If it is not met, release on conditions or complete release after the retributive minimum is served should be the preferred option.

The second often-ignored question with respect to proving risk has to do with the proper method of doing so. Although there are several such methods, they can be divided into clinical and actuarial techniques (see Slobogin 2007: 101–104). Until relatively recently, risk determinations were made through the clinical method, which involves an assessment of a person's criminal, family, and social history by a probation officer or mental health professional. The alternative, actuarial assessment, relies instead on a statistically derived algorithm composed of risk factors shown to be associated with reoffending, ideally through validation on large samples. A simple algorithm, popular in several state jurisdictions for many years, consists entirely of a score based on previous convictions, or on previous arrests and convictions (see generally, Roberts 2014). More recently, "risk assessment instruments" (RAIs) have become prevalent. RAIs consist of both static (historical) factors and dynamic (changeable) factors that are statistically shown to be either positively or negatively correlated to reoffending (Viljoen, Cochrane and Jonnson 2018). These are the types of instrument that both Frase and Rhine et al. tentatively endorse.

The courts have allowed both clinical and actuarial risk assessment (see Faigman et al. 2018: § 9:1). However, at least in theory, actuarial prediction should be preferred over clinical prediction, for several reasons. First, actuarial prediction of serious crime has consistently been shown to be more accurate than clinical judgment (Hilton, Harris and Rice 2006: 402–03). Second, whereas clinical evaluators, if honest, can at most state whether a person poses a high, moderate or low risk, actuarial assessments can provide quantified risk levels (e.g. a 50% probability of committing serious crime within the next two years) that directly address whether the state has met the required burden of proof (see Scurich, 2018). Third, actuarial prediction is more transparent and thus more easily scrutinized, because, in contrast to clinical risk assessment, the factors to be considered are clear from the face of the instrument. Fourth, relevant to the parity goal, actuarial prediction provides more consistent results, assuming the same instrument is used within the jurisdiction and that judges adhere to it.

In practice, however, not all actuarial prediction can boast these benefits. Some instruments are much better than others at distinguishing high from low risk offenders, some are normed on populations that are of questionable relevance to the offender's background, some use irrelevant outcome measures (e.g. misdemeanor arrests, long-term outcome measures), and some, especially those that are privately developed, are not transparent for proprietary reasons (see generally, Slobogin 2018). Further, as the Virginia experience illustrates, judges routinely adjust the risk calculation based on clinical judgement, thus raising the probability that bias will infect the judgment.

To correct for these inadequacies, several steps should be taken. Most importantly, the legal system should insist on disclosure of the algorithms underlying RAIs and must monitor their psychometric properties (in the US, perhaps using "*Daubert* analysis") to ensure the best possible risk assessment is obtained (see Hopkinson 2018). If these requisites are met, RAIs should dominate the sentence determination. Of course, offenders should be able to introduce evidence of protective factors that were not considered in the development of the RAI, such as treatment successes, recent changes in circumstances, cooperation with the government that suggests diminished risk, or aspects of criminal history – like a wrongful arrest – that undercut the factual basis for the RAI score. But, in contrast to the apparent practice in Virginia, the presumption should be that RAI-derived risk scores drive the ultimate conclusion on risk. Otherwise, there is no scientific reason to use them.

A second overarching set of concerns about risk assessment using RAIs is that the risk factors on which they rely, even if comparatively accurate statements of reality, may be suspect for a variety of practical, ethical or legal reasons: the factors may be predominately static (e.g., criminal history), thus making a change in risk score impossible; they may be unrelated to blameworthy conduct and thus antithetical to a desert-based system (e.g. employment or marital status, or neighborhood of residence); or they may not be related to conduct at all (e.g. diagnosis, gender, age or race) (Starr 2014; Sidhu 2015). These are all legitimate worries. The US Supreme Court recently held, in *Buck v. Davis* (2017), that race may never form the basis for a sentence, and went on to state that "a basic premise of our criminal justice system [is that it] punishes people for what they do, not who they are" (778). Taken literally, the latter sentiment would prohibit reliance not only on race, but also on risk factors such as gender and age, and probably on factors such as current mental state (e.g. diagnosis, lack of insight) as well, since none of these variables involves conduct.

At the same time, on several occasions the Supreme Court has upheld even death sentences imposed on the ground that the offender is "dangerous" (*Jurek v. Texas* 1976), including when dangerousness was predicated on a diagnosis (*Barefoot v. Estelle* 1983: 919–20). Thus, the *Davis* decision is probably more accurately described as a prohibition on the use of race in sentencing, rather than as a wholesale rejection of punishment based on status. If consideration of factors such as gender and age substantially contribute to achieving the compelling state interest of protecting its citizens, it should be permitted, especially since failing to do so might inaccurately assign high risk scores to groupings that are thereby left out of the analysis, such as women and the elderly (see *Wisconsin v. Loomis* 2016: 761). Note also that subjective clinical risk assessments undoubtedly rely on the same sorts of factor, just more opaquely so; if required to be transparent, RAIs at least allow courts and opposing experts to dissect their logic, correct for racial or other biased inputs, and determine the extent to which a given risk factor contributes to the result.

Based on these types of observation, I have argued that objections to particular risk factors ought to be balanced against their incremental validity (Slobogin 2018: 592–93). Courts should prohibit use of non-criminal static risk factors that do not add appreciably to the risk score. That might mean, for instance, that gender and age would be retained in such instruments, despite their static nature, because of their heightened usefulness in distinguishing high and low risk offenders, while factors like marital status, which are only minimally predictive, would not be. I have also argued that courts should encourage inclusion of as many dynamic factors as possible, because of their usefulness in devising risk management plans. When periodic reviews occur, the impact of any completed or proposed interventions aimed at dynamic factors such as diagnosis, impulsivity, and employability that have been shown to reduce risk should be a paramount consideration, and might well supersede the admittedly highly predictive impact of criminal history, or at least support an argument for a non-incarcerative disposition.

Finally, it is important to note that, in a preventive justice regime, criminal history would be relevant at sentencing *solely* on the issue of risk. Much has been written about whether sentence enhancements based on such history can be justified on desert grounds. In particular, scholars have argued over whether recidivists deserve higher sentences (or, conversely, first-time offenders deserve lower sentences) and whether multiple crimes committed in bulk are different, in retributive terms, from multiple crimes committed over, or separated by, long periods of time (see Ryberg, Roberts and de Keijser 2018; Frase 2013: 181–87). These debates might be relevant in setting the sentence ranges in a preventive justice regime. But they would be irrelevant in setting particular sentences.

Conclusion

Limiting retributivism is a well-recognized and popular mixed theory of punishment. This chapter has described one version of limiting retributivism – preventive justice – in which sentences are constrained by inevitably broad conceptions of desert, and are otherwise based on scientifically vetted assessments of risk and periodic reviews of how well risk has been managed. This type of regime can incorporate attractive elements of both retributive and consequential theories of punishment.

This chapter's defense of this theory of punishment has been entirely conceptual. But the primary reason for venturing such a defense in the first instance is the assumption that a preventive justice system brings more benefits than other punishment schemes, particularly in terms of reducing prison populations, which in the United States are currently enormous, hugely costly, racially disproportionate, and probably criminogenic. If a sentencing regime enforced desert-based ranges similar to those proposed in this chapter, and if the risk assessment principles this chapter describes are followed, significant reductions in the incarcerated population are possible, with minimal risk to the public.

References

Addington v. Texas (1979) 441 U.S. 418.

American Law Institute (2017) Model Penal Code, www.ali.org/publications/show/sentencing/.

American Law Institute (2009) Model Penal Code Sentencing Revisions, Preliminary Draft No. 7.

American Law Institute (1962) Model Penal Code and commentaries, www.ali.org/publications/show/ model-penal-code/.

Armstrong, K.G. (1969) "The Retributivist Hits Back," in H.B. Acton *The Philosophy of Punishment: A Collection of Papers*, London: MacMillan.

Ashworth, A. and Zedner, L. (2014) *Preventive Justice*, Oxford: Oxford University Press.

Barefoot v. Estelle (1983) 463 U.S. 880.

Barkow, R.E. and O'Neill K.M. (2006) "Delegating Punitive Power: The Political Economy of Sentencing Commission and Guideline Formation," *Texas Law Review* 84: 1973–2022.

Bentham, J. (1789) *Theory of Legislation*, 4th ed. 1882, Trubner & Co. (R. Hildreth trans.).

Buck v. Davis (2017) 137 S.Ct. 759.

Faigman, D., Edward, K.C., Mnookin, J.L., Murphy, E.E., Sanders, J. and Slobogin, C. (2018) *Modern Scientific Evidence: The Law and Science of Expert Testimony*, Vol. 2, Danvers, Mass.: Thomson Reuters.

Foucha v. Louisiana (1992) 504 U.S. 71.
Frankel, M. (1972) "Lawlessness in Sentencing," *Cincinnati Law Review* 41: 1–28.
Frase, R. (2013) *Just Sentencing: Principles and Procedures for a Workable System*, Oxford: Oxford University Press.
Frase, R. (2004). "Limiting Retributivism," in Tonry, M. (Ed.) *The Future of Imprisonment.*
Garrett, B., Jakubow A. and Monahan, J. (2019) "Judicial Reliance on Risk Assessment of Drug and Property Offenders: A Test of the Treatment Resource Hypothesis," *Criminal Justice & Behavior* 46: 799–810.
Harlow, R.E., Darley, J.M. and Robinson, P.H. (1995) "The Severity of Intermediate Penal Sanctions: A Psychophysical Scaling Approach to Obtaining Community Perceptions," *Journal of Quantitative Criminology* 11: 71–95.
Hart, H. (1958) "The Aims of the Criminal Law," *Law and Contemporary Problems* 23: 401–441.
Hilton, N.Z., Harris, G.T. and Rice M.E. (2006) "Sixty-Six Years of Research on the Clinical Versus Actuarial Prediction ofViolence," *Counseling Psychologist* 34: 400–409.
Hopkinson, C. (2018) "Using *Daubert* to Evaluate Evidence-Based Sentencing," *Cornell Law Review* 103: 723–755.
Hyatt, J.M., Chanenson, S.L. and Bergstrom, M.H. (2011) "Reform in Motion: The Promise and Perils of Incorporating Risk Assessment and Cost-Benefit Analysis into Pennsylvania Sentencing," *Duquesne Law Review* 49: 707–749.
Jacobi, T., Richardson, S. and Barr, G. (2014) "The Attrition of Rights Under Parole," *California Law Review* 87: 887–976.
Jackson v. Indiana (1972) 406 U.S. 715.
Janus, E.S. and Logan, W.A. (2003) "Substantive Due Process and the Involuntary Confinement of Sexually Violent Predators," *Connecticut Law Review* 35: 319–384.
Jurek v. Texas (1976) 428 U.S. 262.
Kansas v. Hendricks (1997) 521 U.S. 346.
Kern, R.P. and Farrar-Owens, M. (2004) "Sentencing Guidelines with Integrated Offender Risk Assessment," *Federal Sentencing Reporter* 16: 165–169.
Klingele, C. (2016) "The Promises and Perils of Evidence-Based Corrections," Notre Dame Law Review 91: 537–584.
Melton, G., Petrila, J., Poythress, N., Slobogin, C., Otto, R., Mossman, D. and Condie L. (2018). *Psychological Evaluations for the Courts: A Handbook for Mental Health Professionals and Lawyers*, New York: Guilford Press.
Minnesota Sentencing Guidelines (2018) Standard Grid, http://mn.gov/msgc-stat/documents/ NewGuidelines/ 2018/StandardGrid.pdf.
Mitchell, K.L. (2017) "State Sentencing Guidelines: A Garden Full ofVariety," *Federal Probation* 81: 28–36.
Monahan, J. and Wexler, D. (1978) "A Definite Maybe:" Proof of Probability, *Civil Commitment, Law & Human Behavior* 2: 37–42.Moore, M. (1997) *Place Blame: A Theory of Criminal Law*, Oxford: Clarendon Press.
Morris, N. (1982) *Madness and the Criminal Law*, Chicago: University of Chicago Press.
Morris, N. (1974) *The Future of Imprisonment*, Chicago: University of Chicago Press.
Reitz, K. (2012) "The "Traditional" Indeterminate Sentencing Model," in *The Oxford Handbook of Sentencing and Corrections*, Oxford: Oxford University Press.
Rhine, E.E., Petersilia, J. and Reitz K.R. (2017) "The Future of Parole Release," *Crime & Justice* 46: 279–329.
Roberts, J. (2014) "Revisiting Prior Record Enhancement Provisions in State Sentencing Guidelines," *Federal Sentencing Reporter* 16: 177–186.
Robinson, P.H., Goodwin, G.P. and Reisig, M.D. (2010) "The Disutility of Desert," *New York University Law Review* 85: 1940–2033.
Robinson, P.H. and Kurzban, R. (2007) "Concordance and Conflict in Intuitions of Justice," *Minnesota Law Review* 91: 1829–1907.
Robinson, P.H. (1997) "The Utility of Desert," *Northwestern Law Review* 91: 453–499.
Ryberg, J., Roberts, J.V. and de Keijser, J.W. (2018) *Sentencing Multiple Crimes*, Oxford: Oxford University Press.
Scurich, N. (2018). "The Case Against Categorical Risk Assessments," *Behavioral Sciences & the Law* 36: 554–564.
Seling v. Young (2001) 531 U.S. 250.
Sidhu, D.S. (2015) "Moneyball Sentencing," *Boston College Law Review* 56: 671–731.
Slobogin, C. (2018) "Principles of Risk Assessment," *Ohio State Journal of Criminal Law* 15: 583–596.
Slobogin, C. (2011) "Prevention as the Primary Goal of Sentencing," *San Diego Law Review* 48: 1127–1171.
Slobogin, C. (2007) *Proving the Unprovable: The Role of Law, Science and Speculation in Adjudicating Culpability and Dangerousness*. Oxford: Oxford University Press.
Slobogin, C. (2006) *Minding Justice: Laws that Deprive People with Mental Disability of Life and Liberty*, Cambridge: Harvard University Press.
Slobogin, C. and Brinkley-Rubinstein, L. (2013) "Putting Desert in Its Place," *Stanford Law Review* 65: 77–136.
Starr, S. (2014) "Evidence-Based Sentencing and the Scientific Rationalization of Discrimination," *Stanford Law Review* 66: 803–872.

Tonry, M. (2018) "Punishment and Human Dignity: Sentencing Principles for the 21st Century," *Crime and Justice* 47: 119–157.
Viljoen, J.L., Cochrane, D.M. and Jonnson, M.R. (2018) "Do Risk Assessment Tools Help Manage and Reduce Risk of Violence and Reoffending: A Systematic Review," *Law & Human Behavior* 42: 181–205.
Virginia Code Annotated (1994).
Von Hirsch, A. (1976) *Doing Justice: The Choice of Punishments*, New York: Hill & Wang.
Von Hirsch, A. and Ashworth, A. (2012) *Proportionate Sentencing*, Oxford: Oxford University Press.
Wisconsin v Loomis (2016) 881 N.W.2d 749.
Youngberg v. Romeo (1982) 457 U.S. 307.

6

THE CONTOURS OF A UTILITARIAN THEORY OF PUNISHMENT IN LIGHT OF CONTEMPORARY EMPIRICAL KNOWLEDGE ABOUT THE ATTAINMENT OF TRADITIONAL SENTENCING OBJECTIVES

Mirko Bagaric

Introduction

In this chapter, I examine the manner in which a purely utilitarian theory of punishment would be structured if it was not distorted by political considerations or the pursuit of other penal aims. This is, of course, a somewhat ambitious project. Sentencing is the sharp end of the criminal justice system and in most countries it is a socially and politically sensitive area, and hence decisions in this realm are often influenced by populist sentiment.

There is no better illustration of this than the United States, which has been captive to a tough on crime rhetoric for at least the past five decades. The punitive attitudes have been fuelled by a number of considerations, including antipathy towards minority groups; a crime wave during the period 1960 to 1980; considerable economic instability in the past three decades; and the privatisation of aspects of criminal justice policy and practice, including the establishment of private prisons (Bagaric, Fischer and Wolf 2017). These considerations have resulted in a fundamental gap between sentencing knowledge and sentencing practice.

The discord is so significant that sentencing is the area of social practice where there is the greatest gap between practice and what knowledge tells us can be achieved (Bagaric, Fischer and Wolf 2017). In the United States this has resulted in a mass incarceration crisis. The massive financial toll associated with imprisoning more than 2 million of its citizens has caused lawmakers in many parts of the United States to attempt to implement policies aimed at reducing prison numbers (Eisen and Chettiar 2018). These reforms have been piecemeal and are not wide-ranging, but at least they demonstrate a willingness to reform the sentencing system in a manner which takes into account empirical learning regarding the objectives that can be achieved through a state-imposed system of inflicting punishment. This chapter provides an overview of the core structural aspects of a rational, evidence-based sentencing system with a view to influencing the manner in which sentencing practices should be reformed.

Most sentencing systems comprise a mix of utilitarian and retributive goals. The key goals that influence sentencing are community safety (or incapacitation), general deterrence, specific deterrence, rehabilitation, denunciation and retribution. All of these except for the last two have a clear utilitarian foundation and hence an examination of the validity of the utilitarian goals of sentencing is a study which is a highly relevant inquiry in the context of the overall design of most sentencing systems.

Thus, we see that traditionally it has been postulated that there are numerous objectives that justify a utilitarian theory of punishment. For Jeremy Bentham, general deterrence was the primary good consequence of punishment. According to Bentham:

> General prevention ought to be the chief end of punishment, as it is its real justification ... [W]hen we consider that an unpunished crime leaves the path of crime open, not only to the same delinquent, but also to all those who may have the same motives and opportunities for entering upon it, we perceive that the punishment inflicted on the individual becomes a source of security to all. That punishment which, considered in itself, appeared base and repugnant to all generous sentiments, *is elevated to the first rank of benefits, when it is regarded not as an act of wrath or of vengeance against a guilty or unfortunate individual who has given way to mischievous inclinations, but as an indispensable sacrifice to the common safety.*
>
> *(Bentham 1843: 365, 396; emphasis added)*[1]

Other key aims of a utilitarian theory of punishment, which for Bentham were subsidiary to deterrence, are rehabilitation and incapacitation. The empirical data that has amassed over the last few decades from a large number of natural and controlled social and scientific experiments sheds considerable light on the efficacy of a state-imposed system of punishment to achieve these objectives. These findings have significant implications for the design and structure that a utilitarian system of punishment should assume. In short, the findings establish that the main good consequences stemming from a state-imposed system of punishment are (i) general deterrence (but only in the form of absolute general deterrence as opposed to marginal deterrence); (ii) incapacitation, but only in relation to serious sexual and violent offenders; and (iii) rehabilitation for certain categories of offenders. In terms of setting the amount of punishment, there is no clear mechanism for this. However, a tenable argument can be mounted that the proportionality principle should be the guiding determinant. Overall, a pure utilitarian theory of punishment designed with reference to current learnings relating to the efficacy of a state-imposed system of punishment to achieve the traditional aims of sentencing would result in sentences that are significantly less severe than in most developed countries, especially for offenders who do not cause serious harm to victims, and would see more criminal justice resources being allocated to measures which detect and prevent crime.

In the next part of the chapter, I examine whether the theories of general deterrence and specific deterrence are supported by the weight of the scientific evidence relating to the capacity of criminal sanctions to deter crime. This is followed by a discussion of incapacitation and rehabilitation. Finally, I discuss the role of the principle of proportionality in the utilitarian theory of punishment.

Deterrence

General Deterrence

There are two main forms of general deterrence. *Marginal* general deterrence is the theory that severe penalties reduce crime. This assumes that people make rational cost-benefit decisions relating to criminal activity and will be motivated to desist from crime if the potential consequences of this, in the form of harsh criminal sanctions, are undesirable. *Absolute* general deterrence is a less ambitious version of this theory and is the claim that there is a link between the existence of criminal sanctions and crime. It does not suggest that there is a nexus between higher sanctions and lower crime rates; merely that if criminal conduct was not likely to be met with undesirable consequences that there would be an increase in crime. I first examine the validity of marginal general deterrence.

Logically, marginal general deterrence appears to be a persuasive theory given that humans are rational agents and seek to avoid undesirable consequences, including hardships such as the deprivation of liberty. The more severe the hardship, so the theory runs, the greater should be the human inclination to avoid being subjected to the deprivation. Research sometimes debunks common sense assumptions. This is the case in relation to marginal deterrence. A large number of empirical studies strongly suggest that there is at best a weak link between the severity of criminal sanctions and the crime rate.

The United States over the past 40 years has seen massive changes to its crime and sentencing landscape. Broadly, over this period there has been a considerable decrease in the crime rate and a four-fold increase in the imprisonment rate (Lauritsen and Rezey 2003). Hence, the United States provides an ideal setting to examine the efficacy of sentencing to achieve several important objectives.

Evidence suggests that while there has been a decrease in the crime rate over this period, this was not causally related to increases in penalty severity for many crimes (Walker 1969; Cochran, Chamlin and Seth 1994; Cloninger and Marchesini 2001; Dölling et al. 2009; Doob and Webster 2003; Levitt 2004). The reduction in the commission of offences was more likely to have been attributable to an expansion in police numbers and thus the greater probability (both perceived and actual) of detection of crime (Levitt 2004: 163, 177),[2] as well as other socio-political and economic factors (Levitt 2004; Ellison 1999), and the fact that more offenders were incapacitated and thus prevented from committing offences.

Having analysed studies of the connection between harsh criminal sanctions (other than capital punishment) and the crime rate, a 2014 report of the National Research Council of the National Academies noted:

> Ludwig and Raphael (2003) find no deterrent effect of enhanced sentences for gun crimes; Lee and McCrary (2009) and Hjalmarsson (2009) find no evidence that the more severe penalties that attend moving from the juvenile to the adult justice system deter offending; and Helland and Tabarrok (2007) find only a small deterrent effect of the third strike of California's three strikes law. As a consequence, the deterrent return to increasing already long sentences is modest at best.
>
> *(Travis and Western 2014: 139)*

Other studies have found that even the prospect of capital punishment does not affect homicide rates (Hood 1996: 211–2; Walker 1969: 60–1, 191; Berk 2005: 303, 313, 328; Cochran, Chamlin and Seth 1994: 107, 129; Dölling et al. 2009: 201, 220). There is no obvious explanation regarding the failure of marginal general deterrence theory. However, some insight into a plausible explanation stems from research findings relating to absolute general deterrence, in relation to which empirical findings are far more positive. As alluded to above, the near universal trend relating to the reduced crime rate in the United States supports the view that more police, and hence the greater actual and perceived likelihood of detection, has greatly contributed to the reduction in crime (Eck and Maguire 2000).

It has been noted that the greatest reduction in crime numbers occurs where police are highly visible. This accords with the ostensible success of "zero tolerance"[3] policing in locations such as New York City, which saw the greatest number of extra police employed and the sharpest decline in crime (Zimring 2007) In a period of only several years following the introduction of zero tolerance policing, the rates of violent and property crime fell by approximately 35% (Grabosky 1998: 1–2).[4]

After evaluating the large number of surveys analysing the connection between more police and the crime rate, Raymond Paternoster concludes:

> What we are left with, then, is that clearly police presence deters crime, but it is probably very difficult to say with any degree of precision how much it deters. Let us take Levitt's estimate as a reasonable guess, that increasing the size of the police force by 10% will reduce crime by about 4% or 5%.
>
> *(Paternoster 2010: 765, 799)*

The link between lower crime rates and higher perceptions of being caught supports the theory of absolute general deterrence, because the reason why the likelihood of being detected acts as a retardant to crime is the underlying assumption that *if* caught some hardship awaits. In order for absolute general deterrence to be effective, it is necessary that the consequence of apprehension is undesirable. To this end, the sanction does not need to be especially harsh; it is sufficient that it is something that people would seek to avoid. Thus, as far as absolute general deterrence is concerned there would not seem to be a meaningful difference between a short prison term or a very long one. Thus, the objective of absolute general deterrence is valid and can justify inflicting punishment on offenders, but the theory does not provide meaningful guidance regarding the appropriate nature of the sanction that should be imposed. It is not clear why deterrence is only effective in the form of absolute general deterrence, but it appears that when most people make a decision regarding whether to commit a crime, the cost-benefit analysis relates to an assessment of whether they are likely to be detected if they proceed, and does not traverse to the next step of the likely consequences if they are detected.

Specific Deterrence

Specific deterrence focuses on the impact of criminal sanctions on specific offenders, unlike general deterrence which looks at the wider community (Nagin, Cullen and Jonson 2009: 115). Specific deterrence is the theory that offenders will be encouraged to desist from crime if they experience the hardship of a criminal sanction (Ritchie 2011: 159; Bagaric and Alexander 2012:159). Specific deterrence is especially apposite to recidivists, with the view being that, if an offender has not desisted from crime after an experience with the criminal justice system, it is necessary to impose even sterner sanctions to give him or her a stronger pragmatic reason to not commit crime in the future. The theory of specific deterrence has not stood up to empirical assessment. The weight of scientific research suggests that offenders who are subjected to harsh criminal sanctions are not less likely to commit crime in the future and in fact on balance are slightly more likely to commit crime in the future.

The studies that establish the inability of sentencing to deter specific offenders have been undertaken over several decades and across a wide range of jurisdictions and different time periods (Ritchie 2011:159; Bagaric and Alexander 2012: 159). Daniel Nagin, Francis T. Cullen and Cheryl L. Jonson provide the most recent extensive literature review regarding specific deterrence (Nagin, Cullen and Jonson 2009: 115; see also Ritchie 2011). They reviewed the impact of custodial sanctions versus non-custodial sanctions, and the effect of sentence length on reoffending. The review examined: six experimental studies where custodial versus non-custodial sentences were randomly assigned; 11 studies which involved matched pairs; 31 studies which were regression-based; and seven other studies which did not neatly fit into any of the three previous categories, and included naturally occurring social experiments which allowed inferences to be drawn regarding the capacity of imprisonment to deter offenders.

Nagin et al. suggest that offenders who are sentenced to imprisonment do not have a lower rate of recidivism than those who receive a non-custodial penalty and, in fact, that some studies show the rate of recidivism among offenders sentenced to imprisonment to be higher. They conclude that:

> Taken as a whole, it is our judgment that the experimental studies point more toward a criminogenic [that is, the possible corrupting effects of punishment] rather than preventive effect of custodial sanctions. The evidence for this conclusion, however, is weak because it is based on only a small number of studies, and many of them point to estimates that are not statistically significant.
>
> *(Nagin, Cullen and Jonson 2009: 115, 145)*

A report of the Executive Office of the United States President published in 2016 reviewed research that suggests that imprisoning individuals can even increase the probability that they will reoffend (White House Council of Economic Advisers 2016: 23). It observes as follows:

> [A] growing body of work has found that incarceration increases recidivism.... For instance, one recent study that uses highly detailed data from Texas ... finds that although initial incarceration prevents crime through incapacitation, each additional sentence year causes an increase in future offending that eventually outweighs the incapacitation benefit. Each additional sentence year leads to a 4 to 7 percentage point increase in recidivism after release.
>
> *(White House Council of Economic Advisers 2016: 39)*

Thus, there is no basis for increasing penalties, let alone the frequency of imprisonment, in a bid to pursue the goal of specific deterrence – in fact, the objective of specific deterrence should be abolished as a goal of sentencing.

Incapacitation

Incapacitation is a means of disabling offenders from committing further crime, and is the most common means of pursuing the objective of community protection. The most effective means of achieving of this is by capital punishment. The United States and Japan are the only developed nations which execute offenders, and even in those countries this sanction is rarely used. Thus, the most common sanction used to ensure that offenders do not reoffend is imprisonment. The splendour of imprisonment is that the community can be certain (absent the rare event of an escape) that for the duration of the prison term the offender will not commit further offences in the community. However, the effectiveness and appeal of incarceration is reduced by a number of considerations.

The success of incapacitation cannot be measured solely by the height of the prison wall. Incapacitation is only effective if the offender would have reoffended during the term of the prison sentence. Further, incapacitation has an admittedly crude cost-benefit aspect. It is self-defeating to imprison offenders in order to prevent them from committing minor or trivial offences, whose cost clearly exceeds the damage from their crimes.

There are no established models for determining with a high degree of accuracy offenders who will reoffend.[5] To the extent that sound predictions can be made about reoffending, this is in relation to relatively minor (especially property) offences. However, the cost of imprisoning these offenders normally outweighs the seriousness of the offence (Bagaric and Alexander 2012). In addition, as noted above, research has demonstrated that incarceration might have "criminogenic" effects (Vieraitis, Kovandzic and Marvell 2007: 589, 593). Lower level offenders interact with more serious criminals in prison and tend to commit graver crimes upon release.

It is essentially for these two reasons that the benefits of incapacitation appear to have been minor. The United States National Academy of Sciences notes:

> The increase in incarceration [in the United States over the past four decades] may have caused a decrease in crime, but the magnitude of the reduction is highly uncertain and the results of most studies suggest it was unlikely to have been large.
>
> *(Travis and Western 2014: 4)*

In a similar vein, a recent report by the Brennan Centre based upon an analysis of state imprisonment data between 1980 and 2013 concluded that:

> [i]ncarceration has been declining in effectiveness as a crime control tactic since before 1980. Since 2000, the effect on the crime rate of increasing incarceration ... has been essentially zero. Increased incarceration accounted for approximately 6 percent of the reduction in property crime in the 1990s (this could vary statistically from 0 to 12 percent), and accounted for *less than 1 percent* of the decline in property crime this century. Increased incarceration has had little effect on the drop in violent crime in the past 24 years. In fact, large states such as California, Michigan, New Jersey, New York, and Texas have all reduced their prison populations while crime has continued to fall.
>
> *(Roeder, Eisen and Bowling 2015: 15)*

The Brennan Centre report elaborates that the ineffectiveness of incarceration as a crime-fighting tool might be due to the fact that a large percentage of

> the increase in incarceration was driven by the imprisonment of nonviolent and drug offenders. Today, half of state prisoners in the United States are serving time for nonviolent crimes and almost half of federal prisoners are in prison for drug crimes.
>
> *(Roeder, Eisen and Bowling 2015: 25)*

While serious sexual and violent offenders do not reoffend at manifestly high rates, it transpires that individuals with previous convictions for serious offences (Bagaric 2014a: 343) commit crime at a greater frequency than the rest of the criminal population. Further, offenders with prior convictions for serious sexual and violent offences reoffend more frequently than first-time offenders.[6] Thus, to the extent that incapacitation can be effective, there is some theoretical basis for imposing harsher penalties on recidivist serious offenders. To this end, it seems that while incapacitation does not justify additional prison time for minor offenders it can support a recidivist loading in the order of 20% to 50% for serious sexual and violent offenders.[7]

Rehabilitation

Rehabilitation is the theory that the criminal justice system can implement measures to positively change the value system of offenders so that they are less likely in the future to commit crime. The rehabilitation ideal was a prominent aim of sentencing in many developed countries in the mid part of the 20th century. However, it became less popular as disillusionment grew about the capacity to reform offenders. Following research conducted between 1960 and 1974, Robert Martinson, in an influential paper, concluded that empirical studies had not established that any rehabilitative programs had worked in reducing recidivism (Martinson 1974: 22, 25). The Panel of the National Research Council in the United States, several years after this work, also noted that there were no significant differences between the subsequent recidivism rates of offenders, regardless of the form of punishment. As they stated, "[t]his suggests that neither rehabilitative nor criminogenic effects operate very strongly" (Blumstein, Cohen and Nagin 1978: 66).

In recent decades, however, more promising data has emerged regarding the efficacy of criminal sanctions to elicit positive attitudinal reform in offenders. A relatively recent wide-ranging study by Karen Heseltine, Andrew Day and Rick Sarre (2011) summarised studies into the effectiveness of certain rehabilitation programs. It noted that while there were mixed results, there were some programs that reported positive outcomes. This was especially the case in relation to sexual offender programs, where some studies showed that the recidivism rate of offenders completing the program was less than half of that of other offenders (Heseltine, Day and Sarre 2011: 14). The results of programs directed towards violent offenders were less positive, but a wide-ranging review of studies focusing on United Kingdom programs noted that reductions in offending for violent offences by around 7% to 8% had occurred.

This assessment is consistent with the findings of Ojmarrh Mitchell, David B. Wilson and Doris L. MacKenzie who undertook a major analysis of studies into the effectiveness of drug treatment programs in prison (2006). The studies they focused on related to drug users and compared reoffending patterns of offenders between the years 1980 and 2004 who completed a drug rehabilitation program with those who did not complete a program, or completed only a minimum program. They analysed 66 studies in total. The report concluded that "[o]verall, this meta-analytic synthesis of evaluations of incarceration based drug treatment programs found that such programs are modestly effective in reducing recidivism" (Mitchell, Wilson and MacKenzie 2006: 17) The above overview of research into the efficacy of rehabilitation paints a relatively positive picture about the capacity for programs to reform prisoners (Hatcher et al. 2008: 525–6). It is, however, important to note that a considerable degree of progress needs to occur with respect to the development of rehabilitative measures for offenders. While some rehabilitation programs reduce reoffending, others appear to have been ineffective and certain programs have led to increased recidivism, such as the main sex offender rehabilitation program in the United Kingdom at present; a slightly higher number of the offenders who undertook the "Core Sex Offender Treatment Programme (SOTP)" committed at least one sexual offence during the follow-up period than matched offenders who did not complete the program (10% compared to 8%) (Casciani 2017).

Thus, there is some support for the view that criminal punishment can assist to reform a portion of offenders who have committed certain offence categories, although there is no firm evidence showing that it cannot work for the majority of offenders.

Proportionality

The above account suggests that utilitarianism can justify a state-imposed system of punishment. This is principally on the basis that if crime were not met with at least the threat of criminal sanctions, absolute general deterrence theory establishes that the crime rate would increase considerably. However, the above analysis does not provide meaningful guidance on the nature and severity of criminal sanctions. As was seen, incapacitation supports imprisoning serious and violent offenders, but the optimum duration of this cannot be set by incapacitative considerations. Rehabilitation favours the implementation of measures which can induce positive attitudinal reform, but it is not clear whether this occurs within the context of harsh sanctions, such as imprisonment. Thus, guidance relating to the nature and severity of sanctions must come from other principles.

The most obvious principle which can provide guidance regarding penalty type and severity is proportionality. This principle is most commonly associated with a retributive ideal. While the notion of proportionality may appear to be incompatible with utilitarian theories of punishment, proportionality need not be regarded as wholly inconsistent with utilitarian objectives of punishment. Jeremy Bentham argued in favour of the proportionality principle on the basis that if crimes are to be committed, it is preferable that offenders commit less serious rather than more serious ones (Burns and Hart 1970: 165; see also Frase 2008: 44–6). In his view, sanctions should be graduated commensurate with the seriousness of the offence so that those disposed to crime will opt for less serious offences. In the absence of proportionality, potential offenders would not be deterred from committing serious offences any more than minor ones, and hence would just as readily commit them. This argument, however, has been persuasively criticised by Andrew von Hirsch. He points out that there is no evidence that offenders make comparisons regarding the level of punishment for various offences (1987: 32). And as we have seen, the weight of empirical evidence suggests that the theory of marginal general deterrence is flawed. There is virtually no link between higher penalties and lower crime. Yet, there is an alternative basis for injecting proportionality into utilitarianism.

It has been contended that proportionality is necessary to ensure that the criminal justice system is not placed into disrepute. Disproportionate sentences would, so the argument runs, offend the principle that privileges and hardships ought to be distributed roughly in accordance with the degree of merit or blame attributable to each individual.[8] Violations of this principle lead to antipathy towards institutions or practices which condone such outcomes. Christopher Harding and Richard Ireland, for example, believe:

> Proportion in punishment ... is a widely found and deeply rooted principle in many penal contexts. It is ... integral to many conceptions of justice and as such the principle of proportion in punishment seen generally acts to annul, rather than to exacerbate, social dysfunction.
>
> *(Harding and Ireland 1989: 205)*

Empirical evidence offers some support to this sentiment. After a 1984 study of approximately 1500 people who lived in Chicago regarding their contact with legal authorities, scholars noted that normative issues are linked with compliance with the law (Tyler 1990: 107). From this study, there is some evidence to support the argument that people do not merely obey the law because it is in their self-interest to do so; they also obey the law because they believe it is proper to do so. The judgment that it is appropriate to obey the law is not only affected by the internal content of the law, but by the attitude of the community towards those who enforce the law. Thus, the perception that the content of the law is fair and legitimate can make it more likely that laws will be observed.

Accordingly, there is a utilitarian foundation for proportionality *if* the proportionalist ideal is so inherently ingrained in the human psyche that non-observance of the doctrine will disincline individuals from complying with legal norms.[9] In light of the above discussion, there is theoretical merit and some evidence in support of this argument.

However, proportionality suffers from a number of other potential shortcomings. While proportionality is a widely endorsed and embraced principle, it has been contended that the principle is a vacuous concept: it exists in the abstract only, devoid of even the sparsest of content. The most obscure and problematic aspect of proportionality is that there is no stable and clear manner in which the hardship of the punishment can be matched to the severity of the crime. Jesper Ryberg observes that one of the key criticisms of proportionality is that it "presupposes something which is not there, namely, some objective measure of appropriateness between crime and punishment" (Ryberg 2004: 184) He further notes that to give content to the theory, it is necessary to rank crimes, rank punishments and anchor the scales (Ryberg 2004: 185).

Despite infirmities with proportionality theories, it may yet be tenable to shore up the proportionality principle and inject it with concrete meaning. To do so requires a fundamental re-assessment of the principle. The starting point is to identify its constituent features. Broken down to its core elements, proportionality has two limbs: the seriousness of the crime and the harshness of the sanction. Further, the principle has a quantitative component – the two limbs must be matched. In order for the principle to be satisfied, the seriousness of the crime must be equal to the harshness of the penalty.

To this end, there is one criterion which should be used to measure offence severity and the hardship of a sanction: individual well-being, which is in effect a proxy for happiness.[10] The type and degree of punishment imposed on offenders should cause them to have their well-being set back by an amount equal to that which the crime set back the well-being of the victim.

The main difficulty with this approach relates to mapping and calculating the notion of well-being. There is admittedly a degree of approximation involved in such an assessment. However, the level of accuracy in making such determinations is increasing. The concept of well-being is becoming so mainstream that, in some contexts, it is replacing or complementing conventional and widely accepted economic indicia for evaluating human progress and achievement. The Organisation for Economic Co-operation and Development (OECD) has developed a "Better Life Index," which attempts to set out and prioritise the matters that are most essential for human "well-being."[11] The index lists 11 criteria for measuring life quality (*Create Your Better Life Index*, n.d.). From most to least important the criteria are: life satisfaction, health, education, work-life balance, environment, jobs, safety, housing, community, income, and civic engagement (Bagaric 2014b: 76, 90). In order to attain life satisfaction, key interests are the right to life, physical integrity, liberty, and the right to property.[12]

While relevant studies have not been conducted with a view to providing insight into calculations of offence seriousness or sanction severity, nevertheless, two tentative conclusions can be made regarding the relevance of the studies to the concept of proportionality. First, property offences – which deprive victims of wealth as opposed to diminishing their personal security – are over-rated in terms of their seriousness. Wealth has a far smaller impact on personal happiness than a range of other factors (*Money Can't Buy Happiness* 2011) and hence, the criminal justice system should view these offences less seriously. The second conclusion that follows from the above analysis is that offences that imperil a person's sense of security, or otherwise negatively affect a person's health and capacity to lead a free and autonomous life, should be punished severely.

These conclusions are supported by studies that assess the impact of different forms of crime on victims. The available data suggest that victims of violent crime and sexual crime have their well-being more significantly set back than for other types of crime (Hanson et al. 2010: 189). For example, one study showed that victims of violent crime, sexual crime in particular, have difficulty being involved in intimate relationships(Hanson et al. 2010: 189, 191–2), higher divorce rates (Hanson et al. 2010: 189, 191–2), diminished parenting skills (although this finding was not universal) (Hanson et al. 2010: 189, 191), lower levels of success in the employment setting (Hanson et al. 2010: 189, 192; see also Dixon et al. 2006: 26), and much higher levels of unemployment (Hanson et al. 2010: 189, 192). Victims of property crimes likewise suffer reduced levels of well-being, but at generally less pronounced rates than victims of sexual and violent crime (Denkers and Winkel 1998: 155–6).

The other side of the proportionality equation – measuring punishment severity – is less contentious. Ryberg contends that this is because of the underlying belief that the "answer is pretty straightforward" as imprisonment is clearly the harshest disposition (Ryberg 2004:102). As Ryberg notes, the answer would seem to rest on the "negative impact on the well-being of the punished" (2004: 102–3). To this end, it is clear that imprisonment is the harshest commonly applied sanction because it has a severe impact on the well-being of offenders.

The final problem regarding proportionality is how to match the severity of the punishment with the seriousness of the offence. In light of the above discussion, this is, theoretically, relatively straightforward. The type and degree of punishment imposed on offenders should set their well-being back in an amount equal to that which the crime set back the well-being of the victim.[13]

Thus, there is a tenable basis for injecting content into the proportionality principle and moreover it sits most neatly within a utilitarian construct. The above approach assesses both the hardship of punishment and the severity of crime as they relate to well-being. This enables at least a crude match to be made, which stems from a number of premises. First, the crimes which have the most serious adverse consequences for victims are assault and sexual offences. Secondly, the adverse effects of imprisonment seem to have been greatly undervalued. In light of this, a reasonable starting point is that, generally, imprisonment should be imposed only for sexual and violent offences and most prison terms should be reduced compared to those currently imposed.[14]

Conclusion

Sentencing is the area of social practice which has arguably proven to be the most resistant to progress and improvement through empirical learning. The reason for this is because of the strong feelings that crime often involves in the community and hence the politicisation of the practice. There is now, however, a large amount of knowledge regarding the efficacy of sentencing to achieve many core aims which have been promulgated in most jurisdictions. Many of these aims were traditionally associated with a utilitarian theory of punishment. Hence an understanding of what a modern utilitarian theory of punishment would look like provides an important insight into the type of sentencing system that rational communities should be moving towards.

As we have seen, the current state of knowledge suggests that most traditional utilitarian objectives of punishment are largely unattainable, either in their entirety or in relation to certain cohorts of offenders or types of offenders. Thus, punishment is justified by the goal of absolute general deterrence, but specific and marginal general deterrence should be discarded as sentencing objectives. Incapacitation, in the form of imprisonment, should only be pursued in relation to serious sexual and violent offenders, while rehabilitation needs further research and for the moment should be pursued regarding a relatively small cohort of offenders.

In broad terms, this would lead to a bifurcated sentencing system which would seek prison reserved only for serious sexual and violent offences, with other offenders being dealt with by means of less severe sanctions, such as fines. These reforms would considerably reduce the incarceration rate without diminishing community safety and save the community an enormous amount of money due to reduced prison expenditure.

Notes

1 For Bentham, specific deterrence and rehabilitation were second order objectives after general deterrence.

2 Estimating the increase in police numbers to be about 14%. For further discussion, see Eck and Maguire 2000: 207, 248; and Paternoster 2010: 765, 799.

3 Zero tolerance policing is founded on "broken windows" theory which provides that strict enforcement of minor crime and restoring physical damage and decay, such as broken windows and graffiti, would prevent the fostering of an environment which was conducive to more serious offences being committed; see Kelling and Wilson 1982: 29. The reduction in the New York crime rate has been largely attributed to this policy (Austin and Jacobson 2013).

4 Grabosky 1998: 1, 2. Grabosky notes that zero tolerance policing is not solely responsible for the drop in crime. He suggests that there are numerous contributing factors, including sustained economic growth; a reduction in the use of crack cocaine; the aging of the baby-boomer generation beyond the crime-prone years; restricting the access of teenagers to firearms; and longer sentences for violent criminals.

5 Hence, the theory of selective incapacitation is flawed. See McSherry and Keyzer 2009: 104; Black 2011: 317, 323–4. See generally McSherry and Keyzer 2011: 3. Most recently it has been suggested that habitual criminals and serious offenders have a different brain anatomy compared to other people. Neuroimaging of the brain showed that such offenders have less brain activity in certain areas of the brain, including the ventromedial prefrontal cortex and the dorsolateral prefrontal cortex, which are associated with self-awareness, learning from past experiences and emotions. See Raine 2013: 373.

6 See NSW Sentencing Council 2012: 20–25. Beyond this, there is no basis for more accurately predicting future serious offending. See McSherry and Keyzer 2009: 4–5, 23–4; Black 2011: 317.

7 See Bagaric 2014a: 343, 408–11 (arguing that this is consistent with the rate of reoffending of these offenders).

8 This is similar to the concept of desert. However, unlike retributivist theories, it is based on forward-looking considerations.

9 There is some scientific support for an intrinsic desire to punish. See Bagaric 2005: 98

10 Bagaric 2013: 411. The approach has some similarity with the majority opinion of Justice Powell in *Solem v Helm*, who stated that the seriousness of the offence is determined by harm caused and the defendant's degree of culpability: 463 US 277, 293–4 (1983); see also Frase 2008: 39, 58. However, lacking in this analysis is the criteria by which harm is to be determined.

11 *Create Your Better Life Index*. These measures are designed to be more informative than economic statistics, especially in the form of Gross Domestic Product (GDP).

12 This is the trend of information emerging from the following works and extensive research data in these works. See, e.g., Argyle et al. 1989: 189; Myers 1992; Kasser 2002; Seligman and Csikszentmilhayi 2000: 5; Seligman 2002. The results of these studies are summarised in Bagaric and McConvill 2005. For related readings, see this same edition of the Deakin Law Review, which is a thematic edition regarding the link between law and happiness research.

13 This is in keeping with the approach of some other theorists. Von Hirsch asserts that an interests analysis, similar to the living standard analysis he adopts for gauging crime seriousness, should be used to estimate the severity of penalties (von Hirsch and Jareborg 1991: 1, 34–5). Ashworth (1995) states that proportionality at the outer limits "excludes punishments which impose far greater hardships on the offender than does the crime on victims and society in general."

14 I suggest that most offences should be dealt with in a manner which does not involve a term of imprisonment and that imprisonment should be mainly reserved for serious sexual and violent offences.

References

Argyle, M. et al. (1989) "Happiness as a Function of Personality and Social Encounters" in J. P. Forgas and J. M. Innes (eds), *Recent Advances in Social Psychology: An International Perspective*. Amsterdam: Elsevier, pp. 189–203.

Ashworth, A. (1995) *Sentencing and Criminal Justice*, 2nd ed. Butterworths: Durban.

Austin, J. and Jacobson, M. (2013) *How New York City Reduced Mass Incarceration: A Model for Change?* New York: Brennan Center for Justice.

Bagaric, M. (2005) "Scientific Proof that Humans Enjoy Punishing Wrongdoers: The Implications for Punishment and Sentencing," *International Journal of Punishment and Sentencing* 1: 98–110.

Bagaric, M. (2013) "Injecting Content into the Mirage that is Proportionality in Sentencing," *New Zealand Universities Law Review* 25: 411–41.

Bagaric, M. (2014a) "The Punishment Should Fit the Crime – Not the Prior Convictions of the Person that Committed the Crime: An Argument for Less Impact Being Accorded to Previous Convictions in Sentencing," *San Diego Law Review* 51: 343–418.

Bagaric, M. (2014b) "Proportionality in Sentencing: The Need to Factor in Community Experience, Not Public Opinion" in J. Ryberg and J. V. Roberts (eds), *Popular Punishment: On the Normative Significance of Public Opinion*. New York: Oxford University Press, pp. 76–100.

Bagaric, M. and Alexander, T. (2012) "The Capacity of Criminal Sanctions to Shape the Behaviour of Offenders: Specific Deterrence Doesn't Work, Rehabilitation Might and the Implications for Sentencing," *Criminal Law Journal* 36: 159–72.

Bagaric, M., Fischer, N. and Wolf, G. (2017) "Bringing Sentencing into the 21st Century: Closing the Gap Between Practice and Knowledge by Introducing Expertise into Sentencing Law," *Hofstra Law Review* 45: 785–850.

Bagaric, M. and McConvill, J. (2005) "Goodbye Justice, Hello Happiness: Welcoming Positive Psychology to the Law," *Deakin Law Review* 10.

Bentham, J. (1843) "The Principles of Penal Law" in J Bowring (ed.), *The Works of Jeremy Bentham*. Edinburgh: William Tait, pp. 365–614.

Berk, R. (2005) "New Claims About Executions and General Deterrence: Déjà Vu All over Again?" *Journal of Empirical Legal Studies* 2: 303–30.

Black, J. (2011) "Is the Preventive Detention of Dangerous Offenders Justifiable?" *Journal of Applied Security Research* 6: 317–38.

Blumstein, A., Cohen, J. and Nagin, D. (eds) (1978) *Deterrence and Incapacitation: Estimating the Effects of Criminal Sanctions on Crime Rates*. Washington, D.C.: National Academy of Sciences.

Burns, J.H. and Hart, H.L.A. (eds) (1970) *The Collected Works of Jeremy Bentham, An Introduction to the Principles of Morals and Legislation*. Oxford: Oxford University Press. First published 1789.

Casciani, D. (2017) *Sex Offender Treatment in Prison Led to More Offending*. Television program, BBC News, London, 30 June. www.bbc.com/news/uk-40460637

Cloninger, D.O. and Marchesini, R. (2001) "Execution and Deterrence: A Quasi-Controlled Group Experiment," *Applied Economics* 33: 569–76.

Cochran, J.K., Chamlin, M.B. and Seth, M. (1994) "Deterrence or Brutalization? An Impact Assessment of Oklahoma's Return to Capital Punishment," *Criminology* 32: 107–34

Create Your Better Life Index OECD Better Life Index (n.d.) www.oecdbetterlifeindex.org/#/11111111111

Denkers, A.J.M. and Winkel, F.W. (1998) "Crime Victims' Well-Being and Fear in a Prospective and Longitudinal Study," *International Review of Victimology* 5: 141–62.

Dixon, M. et al. (2006) *Crime Share:* The Unequal Impact of Crime. London: Institute for Public Policy Research. www.ippr.org/files/images/media/files/publication/2011/05/crimeshare_1500.pdf?noredirect=1>.

Dölling, D. et al. (2009) "Is Deterrence Effective? Results of Meta-Analysis of Punishment," *European Journal of Criminal Policy Research* 15: 201–24.

Doob, A.N. and Webster, C.M. (2003) "Sentence Severity and Crime: Accepting the Null Hypothesis," *Crime and Justice* 30: 143–95.

Eck, J.E. and Maguire, E.R. (2000) "Have Changes in Policing Reduced Violent Crime? An Assessment of the Evidence," in A. Blumstein and J. Wallman (eds), *The Crime Drop in America*. Cambridge: Cambridge University Press, pp. 207–65.

Eisen, L.B. and Chettiar, I.M. (2018) *Criminal Justice: An Election Agenda for Candidates, Activists, and Legislators, Executive Summary*. 22 March, Brennan Center for Justice at New York University Law School www.brennancenter.org/publication/criminal-justice-election-agenda-candidates-activists-and-legislators#Exec%20summary

Ellison, M. (1999) 'Abortion Cuts Crime Says Study', 9 August, *The Guardian* www.theguardian.com/world/1999/aug/10/michaelellison>.

Frase, R.S. (2008) "Limiting Excessive Prison Sentences Under Federal and State Constitutions," *Journal of Constitutional Law* 11: 39–72.

Grabosky, P. (1998) "Zero Tolerance Policing," Trends & issues in crime and criminal justice 102. Canberra: Australian Institute of Criminology. https://aic.gov.au/publications/tandi/tandi102

Hanson, R.F. et al. (2010) "The Impact of Crime Victimization on Quality of Life," *Journal of Traumatic Stress* 23: 189–97.

Harding, C. and Ireland, R.W. (1989) *Punishment: Rhetoric, Rule, and Practice*. London: Routledge.

Hatcher, R.M. et al. (2008) "Aggression Replacement Training with Adult Male Offenders within Community Settings: A Reconviction Analysis," *Journal of Forensic Psychiatry and Psychology* 19: 517–32.

Heseltine, K., Day, A. and Sarre, R. (2011) "Prison-based Correctional Offender Rehabilitation Programs: The 2009 National Picture in Australia." Canberra: Australian Institute of Criminology. <https://aic.gov.au/publications/rpp/rpp112>.

Helland, E. and Tabarrok, A. (2007) "Does Three Strike Deter? A Nonparametric Estimation," *The Journal of Human Resources* 42: 309–30.

Hjalmarsson, R. (2009) "Juvenile Jails: A Path to the Straight and Narrow or to Hardened Criminality?" *The Journal of Law & Economics* 52: 779–809.

Hood, R. (1996) *The Death Penalty: A World-Wide Perspective* (2nd revised ed.) New York: Oxford University Press.

Kasser, T. (2002). *The High Price of Materialism*. Cambridge, MA: MIT Press.

Kelling, G. and Wilson, J.Q. (1982) "Broken Windows" *The Atlantic Monthly* 29.

Lauritsen, J.L. and Rexey, M.L. (2003) *Technical Report: Measuring the Prevalence of Crime with the National Crime Victimization Survey*. Washington, DC: Bureau of Justice Statistics, US Department of Justice. www.bjs.gov/content/pub/pdf/mpcncvs.pdf

Lee, D. and McCrary, J. (2009) "The Deterrence Effect of Prison: Dynamic Theory and Evidence," https://eml.berkeley.edu/~jmccrary/lee_and_mccrary2009.pdf

Levitt, S.D. (2004) "Understanding Why Crime Fell in the 1990s: Four Factors that Explain the Decline and Six that Do Not," *Journal of Economic Perspectives* 18: 163–90.

Ludwig, J. and Raphael, S. (2003) "Do Prison Sentence Enhancements Reduce Gun Crime? The Case of Project Exile." In J. Ludwig and P.J. Cook (eds), *Evaluating Gun Policy*. Washington, DC: Brookings Institution Press, pp. 251–86.

Martinson, R.M. (1974) "What Works? Questions and Answers about Prison Reform." *Public Interest* 35: 22–54.

McSherry, B. and Keyzer, P. (2009) *Sex Offenders and Preventive Detention: Politics, Policy and Practice*. Leichhardt, NSW: Federation Press.

McSherry, B. and Keyzer, P. (2011) "'Dangerous' People: An Overview" in B. McSherry and P. Keyzer (eds), *Dangerous People: Policy, Prediction, and Practice*. New York: Routledge, pp. 3–12.

Mitchell, O., Wilson, D.B. and MacKenzie, D.L. (2006) "The Effectiveness of Incarceration-Based Drug Treatment on Criminal Behaviour," Systematic Review, The Campbell Collaboration, 18 September. <www.campbellcollaboration.org/lib/download/98/>.

Money Can't Buy Happiness (2011) American Psychological Association, 14 June. <www.apa.org/news/press/releases/2011/06/buy-happiness.aspx>.

Myers, D.G. (1992) *The Pursuit of Happiness: Who is Happy and Why*. New York: William Morrow.

NSW Sentencing Council (2012) *High-Risk Violent Offenders: Sentencing and Post-Custody Management Options*. Sydney: New South Wales Sentencing Council.

Nagin, D.S., Cullen, F.T. and Jonson, C.L. (2009) "Imprisonment and Reoffending" *Crime and Justice* 38: 115–200.

Paternoster, R. (2010) "How Much Do We Really Know About Criminal Deterrence?" *Journal of Criminal Law and Criminology* 100: 765–823.

Raine, A. (2013) *The Anatomy of Violence: The Biological Roots of Crime*. London: Allen Lane.

Ritchie, D. (2011) "Does Imprisonment Deter? A Review of the Evidence." Victoria: Sentencing Advisory Council.

Roeder, O., Eisen, L.B. and Bowling, J. (2015) *What Caused the Crime Decline?* New York: Brennan Center for Justice.
Ryberg, J. (2004) *The Ethics of Proportionate Punishment: A Critical Investigation*. Dordrecht: Kluwer Academic Publishers.
Seligman, M.E.P. (2002). *Authentic Happiness*. London: Nicholas Brealey.
Seligman, M.E.P. and Csikszentmilhayi, M. (2000) "Positive Psychology: An Introduction," *American Psychologist* 55: 5–14.
Travis, J. and Western, B. (eds), (2014) *The Growth of Incarceration in the United States: Exploring Causes and Consequences*. Washington, DC: National Academies Press.
Tyler, T. (1990) *Why People Obey the Law*. New Haven, CN: Yale University Press.
Vieraitis, L.M., Kovandzic, T.V. and Marvell, T.B. (2007) "The Criminogenic Effects of Imprisonment: Evidence from State Panel Data, 1974–2002," *Criminology and Public Policy* 6: 589–622.
Von Hirsch, A. (1987) *Past or Future Crimes: Deservedness and Dangerousness in the Sentencing of Criminals*. New Brunswick, NJ: Rutgers University Press.
Von Hirsch, A. and Jareborg, N. (1991) "Gauging Criminal Harm: A Living-Standard Analysis," *Oxford Journal of Legal Studies* 11: 1–38.
Walker, N. (1969) *Sentencing in a Rational Society*. London: Allen Lane.
White House Council of Economic Advisers, Executive Office of the President (2016) Economic Perspectives on Incarceration and the Criminal Justice System. https://obamawhitehouse.archives.gov/sites/whitehouse.gov/files/documents/CEA%2BCriminal%2BJustice%2BReport.pdf
Zimring, F.E. (2007) *The Great American Crime Decline*. New York: Oxford University Press.

7

THE RESTORATIVE JUSTICE MOVEMENT

Questioning the Rationale of Contemporary Criminal Justice

Gerry Johnstone

Introduction

During the 1960s and 1970s, in north America and Europe, various experiments with alternative ways of dealing with criminal lawbreakers took place within and outside criminal justice systems. These included victim-offender reconciliation projects, neighbourhood "courts", community justice schemes, and arrangements for handling "crime" through civil law concepts and solutions.[1] The social movement for restorative justice emerged when, in the 1980s and 1990s, some of those involved in developing these alternatives began to disseminate the idea that they were the surface of something deeper that was happening (e.g. Zehr 1986 [2013], 1990; Van Ness and Strong 1993; Wright 1991; see also Barnett 1977 [2013]). They argued that the modern paradigm of crime and justice was in crisis. The established pattern of thinking about what crime is and how it should be handled, at the heart of which is the idea of crime as a public wrong for which the natural response is punishment of the perpetrators by the authorities, was no longer meeting society's needs. The systems of penal intervention constructed upon this pattern of thinking not only failed to reform offenders; they tended to further damage their capacity for constructive citizenship. They also failed to provide members of communities in which crimes occurred with a sense that something meaningful was being done in response. Above all, they did little to meet the needs of crime victims for justice and healing; indeed, they tended to exacerbate the injuries suffered by these victims.

Advocates of restorative justice suggested that, whilst there had been many attempts to address these failings by reforming penal systems, most of these reforms – because they were based upon the same fundamental pattern of thinking about crime and justice – tended to make little difference. It was suggested, however, that some of the alternatives emerging, such as victim-offender reconciliation projects, were different. They arose from a different pattern of thinking. They pointed towards an emerging new paradigm – albeit one founded upon various indigenous traditions of justice and peace-making – in which the long neglected interpersonal dimensions of crime would be foregrounded, and the preferred response would be one organised around ideas of informal justice, resolving conflicts through peaceful dialogue, and healing. The embryonic restorative justice movement gave a name to this new paradigm, developed its practices and concepts, and sought to push along the process of paradigm change.

Today, as the restorative justice movement enters its second generation (Zehr 2019), there is a huge body of literature discussing the practices of restorative justice and their rationales; evaluating the effectiveness of these practices in achieving certain outcomes such as victim satisfaction and offender reformation; developing restorative justice concepts, theories and jurisprudence; and discussing the difficulties and dangers of restorative justice.[2] This chapter, intended for readers who are perhaps not so interested in the details but do want to understand what is significant about restorative justice, takes a step back and revisits the challenges presented by the restorative justice movement to the pattern of thinking that undergirds practices of criminal justice and crime control in contemporary societies. It discusses, to borrow the language of Foucault, three central aspects of the system of thought that supports contemporary criminal justice (Foucault 1984: 383). It then explains the challenges which the restorative justice movement presents to these three aspects of the rationale of contemporary criminal justice. Along the way, it teases out a number of ambivalences of the restorative justice movement, concerning the relationship between restorative justice and other ways of thinking about and acting upon problems of crime.

Restorative Justice As a New Paradigm of Crime and Justice

To set the scene, we start with a brief account of a landmark work in articulating the key ideas of the restorative justice movement: *Changing Lenses* (1990) by Howard Zehr (often referred to as the grandfather of restorative justice).[3] The first part of Zehr's book contains some powerful accounts of how victims and offenders experience crime and subsequent criminal justice proceedings. Zehr argues that the criminal justice process not only fails to meet the needs of either party, but often compounds the injuries of crime victims and further damages the capacity of offenders to become productive citizens. He acknowledges that many others have reached the same conclusion and have tried to reform the process. But, he argues, these attempts at reform tend to go astray. The reason for this, he suggests, is that the failings of the criminal justice process are rooted in our fundamental understandings of what crime and justice are all about. Unless we question these assumptions, Zehr argues, any changes we make to the justice system will make little difference.

Zehr refers to the set of assumptions he has in mind as the paradigm of "retributive justice". This terminology, which has become common within the restorative justice movement, has caused some confusion as Zehr is not referring specifically to the retributive theory of punishment. Rather, he uses the term "retributive justice" as a shorthand for a broader set of assumptions which he sees as embodied in the criminal justice systems of Western societies. In brief, the assumptions are that in the aftermath of a crime: guilt must be assigned; the guilty must get their "just deserts"; this requires the infliction of pain; justice is measured by the process;[4] the breaking of the law defines the offence; the state is the real victim of crime; and the process of dealing with crime must be monopolised by the state. Zehr goes on to suggest that these assumptions are largely inherited and seldom questioned; we take them to be common sense. His central argument is that these assumptions need to be questioned and replaced if we are to respond to crimes in a way that meets the real needs of those involved in and affected by them. In short, the concern of his work is to expose the limitations of the "retributive" paradigm of crime and justice and to show that other paradigms are both conceivable and may lead to better ways of understanding and responding to the situations we call crime.

After exposing the limitations and difficulties of the "retributive" paradigm, Zehr goes on to introduce two alternatives: the historical and the biblical. He calls the historical paradigm "community justice". The key point in his account of it is that what we today call crimes – and think of and handle as offences against society to be met with punishment – were once regarded as interpersonal conflicts arising from acts of harm, to be settled in a community setting through acts of restitution. Zehr calls the biblical paradigm "covenant justice". Here, he shows that in the Bible the requirements of justice were conceived much more broadly than we might imagine. Whilst "justice" in the Bible certainly seems to be associated with the punishment of guilt, it also has other – much richer and more complex – meanings and requirements. Biblical justice, Zehr suggests, is more holistic and relational than modern retributive justice. It requires us to live in "right relationship" with each other. This idea of justice as right relationship disturbs many modern distinctions – that we take to be common sense – such as the distinction between corrective and social justice, between justice on the one hand and mercy and love on the other, and between doing justice and meeting people's needs for well-being.

Zehr does not, of course, suppose that the assumptions underpinning historical community justice or biblical covenant justice can be simply adopted as a basis for handling crime in contemporary society. Rather, his claim is that the paradigms of community and covenant justice are important for two reasons. First, they demonstrate that the retributive paradigm of justice is not natural or inevitable; throughout history other ways of seeing crime and imagining justice in its aftermath have been more common. Second, they provide us with different understandings which we might draw upon in efforts to start constructing an alternative paradigm of crime and justice suitable to our contemporary predicament. Drawing upon them, as well as upon ideas embodied in experiments with victim-offender reconciliation programmes (VORPs) started by Mennonite probation workers and volunteers in the 1970s, Zehr sketches a new restorative paradigm of crime and justice. He is careful to present this, not as a full-fledged paradigm, but as a signpost towards a new way of thinking about what crime means and what ought to happen in the aftermath of crime. It is intended simply as a starting point for experimentation with and exploration of alternative visions of crime and justice. In Zehr's account, the features of the new paradigm are quite complicated. Over three tables, he presents no fewer than 53 points of contrast between the "retributive" and the restorative paradigms of crime and justice. Any attempt to summarise these in a few lines risks distortion and over-simplification. But, to give some flavour of the account, in the restorative paradigm there is: (i) a new understanding of crime: crime is defined not as a violation of legal rules declared by the state, but as a concrete act of harm to people and relationships; (ii) a new understanding of accountability for crime: rather than paying for this harm by undergoing punishment, offenders will atone through acts of repentance and reparation of the harm they have caused; and (iii) a new understanding of justice: justice is achieved, not when a penal sentence prescribed by the law is imposed upon the offender through a legal procedure, but when "right relationships" have been re-established.

The Logic of Modern Criminal Justice

Moving on, let us now look more closely at three key elements of the system of thought embodied within modern criminal justice which are challenged by the restorative justice movement: crime as a public wrong; offenders must be punished; and the state is responsible for punishing offenders. The first of these three will be discussed at some length. This is because, as I will later suggest, the whole concept of restorative justice rests upon a challenge to the notion of crime as a public wrong.

Crime As a Public Wrong

The institution of criminal law assumes a distinction between two different types of wrongdoing with which the law is concerned: private wrongs and public wrongs (Lamond 2007; Lee 2015). According to this distinction, some wrongs are classified by the law as simply infringing the rights of other individuals. Where this is the case, i.e. where the wrong is classified as a private wrong, if the individual whose rights are infringed desires legal redress they need to initiate legal action against the perpetrator. However, there is of course no obligation to take legal action. For a whole variety of reasons (from desire to avoid the costs of taking legal action, through being satisfied with compensation received, to simply not caring much about the wrong done to them) the individual may decide to refrain from seeking legal redress. Moreover, if they initiate legal proceedings, they can decide to stop them at any time, again for a variety of reasons. If the legal action against the wrongdoer reaches its conclusion and is successful, the redress provided by the law will typically be non-punitive. For instance, a court might order the wrongdoer to pay compensation to the injured party for the damage they have suffered. Or, in some cases, a court might order the wrongdoer to do, or not to do, certain things in the future (such as publish an apology or stop doing something in the case of wrongful conduct which persists over a period of time). So, although the state provides legal mechanisms whereby those who suffer a private wrong can seek and obtain redress, there is a strong sense in which the wrong that has been done might be said to "belong" to the injured party. But, by the same token, the injured party has to bear more or less the full burden of seeking legal redress.

There are some wrongs, however, which are classified by the law as public wrongs or crimes. These include some wrongs which are clearly wrongs committed against a large and difficult to define group of people – the public or a section of it – rather than a specific individual or a small and well-defined group of people. For example, if a person deliberately dumps their rubbish in a public place, a great many individuals may be affected. However, no specific individual (or small group) may have a right to legal redress through a private action. Moreover, no specific individual is likely to have the incentive to undertake the costs and burdens of seeking legal redress. In such cases, the wrongdoing is likely to be defined as an offence against the public. Public authorities will then have the right to take legal action against the wrongdoer. They may also have a duty to take legal action where it is possible and reasonable to do so. Usually, legal action will take the form of a criminal prosecution. If the prosecution is successful, the wrongdoer is liable to judicial punishment: the state will deliberately impose a burdensome liability on the convicted wrongdoer in order to censure their conduct.[5]

Many criminal offences are public wrongs in the above sense. For instance, this category includes a huge number of motoring offences, public order offences, and violations of various regulatory codes. Whilst one might reasonably question whether punishment is the best or most appropriate method of dealing with such wrongdoing, there seems no reasonable case for questioning their classification as public wrongs.

However, many wrongs are classified as crimes which are not public wrongs in the obvious sense. Moreover, this includes wrongs which are conventionally considered the most serious crimes, and indeed the wrongs that most people think of when they think about what a crime is: wrongful acts such as theft, rape, murder, burglary, and assault. These wrongful acts clearly do infringe the rights of specific individuals. However, if the individual whose rights are infringed by an act declared to be criminal desires legal redress, they can obtain it without taking legal action against the perpetrator. If somebody (and not necessarily the injured party) reports the crime to the appropriate public authorities (usually the police), the authorities are empowered to initiate legal action, in the same way as they can for an act which is more obviously a public wrong. That is, the authorities can prosecute the alleged wrongdoer, and if the prosecution is successful the wrongdoer is liable to judicial punishment.

But, whilst direct victims of criminal wrongdoing are relieved of the burden of seeking redress through private legal action, they pay a price for this: they no longer have the same "ownership" of the wrong as they have over wrongs which are classified as purely private. There are a number of aspects to this. First, the injured party does not have a right to prevent the legal action from proceeding (even if it was the injured party which brought the alleged offence to the attention of the authorities in the first place). For example, if "A" commits an act of assault against the "B", and A apologises and gives B compensation, and B is satisfied with the apology and compensation and does not want criminal action taken against A, the public authorities can ignore A's wishes and proceed with criminal prosecution. And, they are likely to proceed if they deem it is in the *public* interest to do so. Moreover, the authorities can usually compel B to co-operate with the criminal process by giving evidence in a trial. If the case does go to court, the injured party will not be a party to the proceedings. The parties to the case are the public authority, on the one hand, and the alleged offender, on the other. So, if Smith assaults Jones, the criminal case against Smith will be designated (in England and Wales) *R v Smith*, with the R standing for Regina (i.e. the Queen). Elsewhere, a case might be designated *The People v Smith*. In some countries, following a successful prosecution, the convicted person might be ordered to pay compensation to their direct victim. However, their ability to pay such compensation might be affected by the penal sentence imposed upon them. In many countries (especially "common law" countries such as England and Wales) there is not even this provision. Rather, the injured party who desires compensation, in addition to knowing that the person who infringed their rights has been punished, has to pursue this in a separate legal action against the wrongdoer or through what are usually quite limited schemes of public compensation for victims of certain criminal offences (see Johnstone 2011: Chapter 4; Shapland 1984). Moreover, once a process of public prosecution has commenced, the injured party is generally not allowed to pursue private legal action until the criminal proceedings are concluded.

So, what is the rationale for treating some wrongs, which are clearly wrongs against individuals or small, clearly defined groups, primarily as public wrongs? In a survey of this issue Lamond (2007) distinguishes two different rationales that have been proposed. The first, attributed to Nozick (1974) and Becker (1974), stresses the interests affected by the wrongful act. Some wrongful acts, it suggests, cause harm to a much wider group of people than the immediate victims. In particular, intentional violations of the rights of other people harm others either by causing widespread fear in the community or by compelling other people to adjust their conduct in order to defend themselves from such harm. The second approach, developed in particular by Marshall and Duff (1998), suggests that some wrongs are, at the same time, a wrong to an individual victim and a wrong to a wider group of people who identify and associate themselves with the individual victim. On this view, for example, a racially motivated attack upon a member of a racial minority is a wrong, not just upon the specific individual(s) attacked, but upon all members of the racial minority (or perhaps upon all members of the community who despise racism). Lamond finds problems with both of these rationales and proposes a third. He suggests that the better way to understand the idea of crimes as public wrongs is to understand them not as wrongs done to the wider community, but as wrongs which the wider community is responsible for punishing. At the risk of over-simplification, the argument is that the state is responsible for supporting certain values; so, when those values are seriously violated, the state is responsible for taking action against the violator.

Offenders Must Be Punished

A second assumption embodied in contemporary criminal justice, which is challenged by the restorative justice movement, is that offenders, i.e. those convicted of public wrongs, ought to be punished. The appropriate response to criminal wrongdoing, on this assumption, is to inflict something unpleasant upon the offender which, in some way, reflects the unpleasantness of the crime to its victims and the community (Moberly 1968: 35). This, of course, reflects a much broader cultural assumption that wrongdoers ought to be punished; an assumption that underpins reactions to wrongdoing in families, schools, workplaces, competitive games, and so on. In all of these contexts there are, of course, perpetual debates about matters such as what justifies punishment, whether there is an obligation (as well as a right) to punish wrongdoers, the ends to which punishment should be directed, the most suitable methods of punishment, how severe or lenient penal regimes should be, and about whether punishment should be accompanied by other non-punitive interventions. Those who adhere to a certain position within these debates will often seek to reform systems of punishment to bring them more into line with the position they deem to be correct. But these debates revolve around the seldom questioned assumption that it is appropriate to punish wrongdoers.

The State Is Responsible for Punishing Criminal Wrongdoers

A third assumption is that, when to comes to public wrongs or crimes, it is the state in charge of the territory in which the crime is committed that is responsible for punishing offenders. Certain tasks may be delegated to non-state actors. But, the state is expected to maintain control over the process and to accept ultimate responsibility for punishing criminal wrongdoing.

There are a number of dimensions to this assumption. First, the state is generally regarded as a having a duty to punish criminal wrongdoing which occurs within its jurisdiction. Whilst the state may, for various reasons, refrain from punishing many specific acts of criminal wrongdoing, a state which simply decided not to enforce a criminal law would be regarded as failing to perform one if its central functions. Hence, if a state no longer wishes to take action against a particular form of wrongdoing, it will generally seek to de-criminalise the conduct, i.e. to have it reclassified as non-criminal. A second dimension is that the state has the *exclusive* right to punish criminal wrongdoers. So, if a non-state actor desires to "punish" a person for a breach of the criminal law, it is not allowed to do so. To act on that desire is itself likely to be criminal offence. Of course, in most societies, all sorts of unpleasant things are done to those convicted (or even simply suspected) of committing crimes by non-state actors (they may be shunned, publicly humiliated, sacked from their job, etc.). But, such actions are officially deemed to be not a part of the offender's punishment.

The Restorative Justice Challenge

Crime As a Violation of a Person

The most fundamental claim of the restorative justice movement is that crime should not be handled primarily as a public wrong; rather, in defining, talking about, and handling crime the emphasis should be upon its private dimensions. Zehr states: "Crime … is at its core a violation of a person by another person … It is the violation of the just relationship that should exist between individuals" (Zehr 2015: 185). He is clearly aware of the arguments we have seen above: that some violations of a person by another person also cause harm to wider communities, and that this wider harm needs to be considered in the response to crime. Yet, he insists that these public dimensions of crime should be regarded as secondary:

> There is also a larger social dimension to crime. Indeed, the effects of crime ripple out, touching many others. Society too has a stake in the outcome and a role to play. Still, these public dimensions should not be the starting point. Crime is not first an offense against society, much less against the state. Crime is first an offense against people, and it is here that we should start.
>
> *(Zehr 2015: 185)*

This claim is fundamental because, if the assumption that crime is a public wrong is undermined, the entire pattern of thought underlying contemporary criminal justice also fragments. If what we refer to and handle as crimes are treated first and foremost as private wrongs, then the ideas that such wrongs need to be corrected by punishment rather than restitution, and that the state must assume "ownership" of the process of correcting these wrongs, also lose their support (see de Lagasnerie 2018: 159–171).

But what, precisely, is meant by the claim that crime is at its core a violation of a person by another person? To obtain some clarity, it might be useful to compare the position of the restorative justice movement to some related positions: (i) abolition of the concept of crime; (ii) virtual abolition of criminal law and the absorption of "crimes" into civil law; and (iii) giving victims of crime more of a say in how "their" offenders are punished.

Abolition of The Concept of Crime

The penal abolitionist Louk Hulsman (1986) endorses many of the criticisms of penal systems made by proponents of restorative justice and other "critical" criminologists. He also argues, in a manner similar to many proponents of restorative justice, that rather than trying to reform these systems, they need to be abolished.[6] But crucially, for Hulsman, this requires rejection of the very concept of crime. Hulsman argues for the systematic decriminalisation of most of the conduct which the law classifies as "crime" and the replacement of the concept with an alternative such as "problematic situations". Instead of attaching stigmatic labels such as "criminal" to one of the parties involved in a problematic situation, and inflicting punishment upon them, he suggests that the conflict between this party and those whom they have injured should be handled through a "reconciliation" procedure. The primary emphasis of such a procedure should be indemnification of those injured. Judicial intervention should be reserved, as a last resort, for very few cases.

This is in large part what the restorative justice movement aspires to. Indeed, many advocates and practitioners of restorative justice try to avoid, as much as possible, using the vocabularies of crime and criminal justice. Like Christie (2013: 17), they tend to regard terms such as "offender" as "dangerous terms". In their practice, they show a preference for the language of "harm" and "conflict". They also have a preference for referring to the parties involved in "conflicts" through less stigmatic, albeit somewhat awkward, terms such as "the person who caused harm" and "the person harmed".

Yet, most have stopped short of endorsing the radical position of Hulsman. The reasons for this hesitancy are again stated, candidly, by Zehr:

> *Problematic situations* feels vague and, for serious harms, may seem to minimise the dimensions of the hurt. Certainly it is difficult to imagine *problematic situations* taking the place of *crime* in ordinary discussion!
>
> An alternative term would be helpful, but so far I have not found an acceptable replacement. So for now I'll stick to crime, keeping in mind its inadequacies.
>
> (*Zehr, 2015: 186, italics in original*)

This ambivalence over the concept of crime is, I suggest, a central feature of the restorative justice movement. It is highly critical of the way contemporary criminal justice systems define and treat violations of other people as public wrongs. Yet, it does not pursue this theme to what is arguably the logical conclusion reached by Hulsman: that the concept of crime itself should be rejected. So, the restorative justice movement does not reject in its entirety a key component of the pattern of thought which supports contemporary criminal justice systems. Rather, it seems ambivalent, and perhaps even confused, about this component. This perhaps reflects a wider ambivalence about the attitude of the movement towards criminal justice systems.

Virtual Abolition of Criminal Law and the Absorption of "Crimes" into Civil Law

We saw in the previous section that Hulsman proposes the virtual abolition of criminal law. However, this does not imply that all the "problematic situations" we currently handle through criminal law should be dealt with in the same way as the law now deals with private wrongs or torts (cf. Barnett 1977 [2013]). That is, the suggestion is not that the only process provided by the state, whereby those harmed by another's violating act could obtain redress, would be a civil law action. Rather, what is envisaged is the provision of another procedure: one in which conflicts are resolved less formally through methods similar to those used in mediation. This is the position of the restorative justice movement. Much of its energy has been devoted to the creation and development of procedures in which the goal is to enable the parties to a conflict to reach agreement on what should be done about it, with an emphasis on ensuring that persons who cause harm to others make amends in a constructive way and that the needs of their victims for healing and justice are met. Importantly, however, as Pavlich (2005) amongst others has emphasised, the restorative justice movement has tended to create such processes under the auspices of criminal law. This leads to all sorts of uncertainty and concern about the status of such processes and the uses to which they might be put.

Giving Victims of Crime More of a Say in How "Their" Offenders Are Punished

Alongside the restorative justice movement, an influential victims' movement has emerged over the last few decades (see Johnstone 2011: 58–60; 2017). One aim of this movement has been to ensure that criminal justice agencies and personnel provide crime victims with better facilities and treat them more respectfully. In the UK, this campaign led to the government publishing a *Victims Charter* (Home Office 1996). At a European level, the European Parliament and Council have issued a directive, which came into force in 2015, establishing minimum standards on the rights, support and protection of victims of crime (Pavlich and Thorlakson 2017). A second aim is to secure rights for victims to have their voice heard within the criminal justice process and to participate in decision-making about matters such as what sentence is imposed upon "their offender".

In certain respects, such aims are aligned with those of the restorative justice movement. Restorative justice proponents, inspired by Christie's celebrated essay "Conflicts as Property" (1977), often insist that modern criminal justice is founded upon an act of theft: the state has stolen conflicts which belong to others and especially to crime victims.[7] Within a restorative criminal justice system, they suggest, the conflict will be returned to its rightful owners, and this clearly includes the victim of a crime. Instead of treating victims as non-parties to a criminal case arising out of a crime committed against them, within a restorative criminal justice system, victims will be treated as primary stakeholders in the case.

However, advocates of restorative justice are at pains to point to some fundamental differences between their aims and those of the victims movement. Whilst they welcome reforms which are designed to provide victims with better services from criminal justice systems, they insist that, as they do nothing to alter the structural position of victims in the criminal justice process, they are unlikely to solve the fundamental problems (Wright 1999). And, proponents of restorative justice tend to be unenthusiastic about reforms – such as the introduction of victim impact statements – which seem to give victims more influence over decisions about the prosecution and punishment of those who harmed them. Whilst welcoming anything that gives victims the opportunity to explain, in a public forum, how they have been harmed by a crime committed against them, advocates of restorative justice argue that this needs to take place in a different context (ibid; see also van Dijk 1988). What is required, they suggest, is the creation of a non-confrontational process aimed at achieving a restorative solution to the problematic situation.

An Obligation To Repair Harm Rather Than To Undergo Punishment

A central concern of the restorative justice movement is to question the assumption that punishment is the proper response to crime. John Braithwaite (1999) – the leading thinker of the restorative justice movement – suggests that punishment can and should be pushed to the margins of social life. If we take seriously the idea that what we are dealing with when one person violates the rights of another is a "problematic situation", then the right question to ask, suggests Braithwaite, is not the usual one – i.e. "what is the proper punishment of the crime?" – but rather, "what is the best solution to the problem?" (Braithwaite 1999: 1728). Once we shift our pattern of thinking and start with this question, Braithwaite contends, we will rarely come to the conclusion that the best solution to the problem is to punish the violator. He argues that nobody familiar with evidence about the failures of punishment to achieve the things we suppose it will achieve (a sense of justice and security, deterrence, reform of the offender, etc.), and about the harm punishment causes (not just to those punished, but to the wider social fabric), is likely to think of punishment as a solution.

For its proponents, restorative justice offers a much more effective and appealing solution: a reparative solution. In brief, the nature of this solution is as follows.[8] Offenders are encouraged to enter into a facilitated dialogue, with those affected by their harmful conduct, about the impact of their harmful behaviour upon others. Through such dialogue, they are likely to come to understand, and acknowledge, that their behaviour was wrong; not because it is an offence against an abstract entity such as society, but because it causes tangible harm to other people with whom they can empathise. Once they come to this understanding, they are likely to want to repair they harm they have done. Through the restorative process, this desire will be reinforced as they realise that they will be supported in their efforts to repair harm and that, once they make these efforts, they are likely to be welcomed back into the community.

Victims who participate in such processes will have the opportunity to have many of their needs met. Unlike in conventional criminal justice, they will be treated as central parties to the "case". They will have opportunities to obtain things which are essential to recovery from the trauma of crime. They will have the opportunity to obtain answers to question they may want to ask of the offender. They will be able to express how they feel about what happened to them in a situation where such expressions (of pain, anger, bewilderment, etc.) will be acknowledged and treated respectfully. They will be able to obtain symbolic reparation (in the form of an apology) and sometimes material reparation to make up for the harm they have suffered. And, crucially, they will have the opportunity to have their voice heard on the question of what the offender needs to do to repair the harm they have caused; unlike in a conventional criminal justice process, where it is state officials who decide what the offender should do to pay for their crime.

Away From Statist Solutions: Restorative Justice and Civil Society

A key part of the established pattern of thinking about criminal justice is that it is the state's responsibility. Hence, most reform proposals involve efforts to get the state to do something different (e.g. to punish offenders differently). Restorative justice advocates, however, seek to remind us that the policing, prosecution and punishment of offenders were not always monopolised by the state to the extent that they are today. Rather, in the past, private individuals and communities had much more responsibility for, and control over, the handling of "crime" (see Johnstone and Ward 2010: 24–46).

An important theme in the discourse of restorative justice is that, before the state took charge of criminal justice, individuals and communities did not always respond to crimes committed against them through acts of violent revenge. Rather, such "conflicts" were often dealt with through negotiated settlements involving restitution to the injured party (Weitekamp 2003). The restorative justice movement urges us, once again, to explore non-statist solutions to the problematic situations we label as crimes. Justice, it suggests, "can be administered by ordinary citizens in everyday locations such as homes, neighbourhoods and workplaces" (Roche 2003: i) And, crime can be controlled most effectively, argues Braithwaite (1989), when communities, instead of wholly delegating the task of crime control to the state, take responsibility for gossiping about misconduct, shaming wrongdoing, and reintegrating offenders who have made amends into their communities.

But, whilst some proponents envisage restorative justice emerging purely from grassroots initiatives and remaining completely within civil society,[9] most acknowledge that, in contemporary society, a shift from "retributive" to restorative justice will require state action and support. O'Mahoney and Doak observe:

> Notwithstanding the spurt of innovative, bottom-up community led programmes in recent years, the majority of schemes which have developed in western criminal justice systems have been devised, funded, overseen and managed by state agencies.
>
> *(O'Mahony and Doak 2017: 39)*

This creates one of the major dilemmas facing the restorative justice movement. One the one hand, the dream of a future in which punishment is marginalised, and restorative justice is the presumptive response to crime, seems unlikely to come true in contemporary societies unless states agencies play a major role in the development of restorative justice. On the other hand, as O'Mahony and Doak point out, many fear that, the more restorative justice becomes state-controlled, the less likely it is to be "restorative justice".

Conclusion

This chapter has attempted to explain two things about the restorative justice movement that should be of interest to anybody concerned about crime, justice, control and punishment. First, it shows that the restorative justice movement is interesting because it sensitises us to, and may lead us to question, assumptions which are deeply embodied in the criminal justice systems of contemporary societies. The movement urges us think about the origins, validity, usefulness, and implications of the idea that some wrongs committed against individuals are public wrongs or "crimes". It provokes us to wonder, not just about the flaws of this or that penal practice, but about the very idea that the appropriate response to crime should be punishment-based. And, it invites us to question the assumption that, when it comes to handling crime, the state should take charge.

However, what is also interesting about the restorative justice movement is that it illustrates just how difficult it is to avoid these assumptions once one starts constructing an alternative approach to crime and justice. It is one thing to show that these assumptions are not inevitable; that many societies – most in the past, but also some small societies today –. think along entirely different lines about crime and justice. It is quite another thing to suggest that, in contemporary societies, we can avoid these assumptions once we embark upon the task of actually intervening into situations where one person violates another through an act that we currently designate as criminal. Then, as restorative justice advocates and practitioners will testify, it is necessary to work through people and institutions within whom/which the established pattern of thinking about crime and justice is deeply engrained. It is hard, as we saw with Zehr, simply to avoid the language of crime and criminal justice; and that language carries a range of assumptions with it. It is difficult to intervene in the aftermath of crime without working in and through institutions which exist in order to punish crimes. And, there is the inevitable dilemma of seeking to establish non-state solutions to the problematic situations we call crime without the sponsorship, support – and, inevitably, control – of state agencies.

In the light of these difficulties, many in the restorative justice movement are focusing their energies on more immediate and "practical" matters: creating, developing and gaining political and public support for high-quality programmes of intervention shaped by the idea of restorative justice. The idea of a paradigm change still hangs around, of course, but more and more as a distant aspiration rather than the central focus of the movement. Perhaps that too is inevitable. But, if the movement takes that direction, it is difficult to imagine how restorative justice can avoid the fate which the founders of the movement were so keen to avoid: becoming just another penal reform.

Notes

1 Part 3 of Cayley (1998) provides a useful survey. These experiments can be understood as forming part of what Cohen (1985) calls the "destructuring impulse" in the control system.
2 *The International Journal of Restorative Justice* (published by Eleven International Publishing) is a leading outlet for this literature. For a useful recent anthology of writing on restorative justice see Gavrielides (2019). On restorative justice jurisprudence, see Foley (2014).
3 For a lengthier precis, from which this is drawn, see Johnstone (2015).
4 What he means is that, provided the correct legal rules and processes are followed, we regard an outcome as just: "procedure overshadows substance" (Zehr, 2015: 81).
5 Here I am using the definition of punishment suggested by Lamond 2007: 621. There are of course many alternatives (see, for instance, Moberly 1968: 35–6).

6 Achutti 2017 is a useful discussion of the links, and differences, between the restorative justice and penal abolitionist movements.
7 See Johnstone 2019 for an account.
8 See Johnstone 2011 for a fuller account.
9 For discussions, see the edited collection *Restorative Justice and Civil Society* (Strang and Braithwaite, 2001).

References

Achutti, D. (2017) 'Is a Critical Model of Restorative Justice Possible? A Penal Abolitionist Approach', in Aertsen, I. and Pali, B. (eds.) *Critical Restorative Justice*. Oxford: Hart.

Barnett, R. (1977 [2013]) 'Restitution: A New Paradigm of Criminal Justice', in Johnstone, G. (ed.) *A Restorative Justice Reader, second edition*. London: Routledge, pp. 47–56.

Becker, L. (1974) 'Criminal Attempts and the Theory of the Law of Crimes', *Philosophy and Public Affairs*, 3:3, 262–294.

Braithwaite, J. (1989) *Crime, Shame and Reintegration*. Cambridge: Cambridge University Press.

Braithwaite, J. (1999) 'A Future Where Punishment is Marginalized: Realistic or Utopian?', *UCLA Law Review*, 46, pp. 1727–50.

Cayley, D. (1998) *The Expanding Prison: The Crisis in Crime and Punishment and the Search for Alternatives*. Cleveland, OH: Pilgrim Press.

Christie, N. (1977). Conflicts as Property. *British Journal of Criminology*, 17(1), 1–15.

Christie, N. (2013) 'Words on Words', *Restorative Justice: An International Journal*, 1:1, 15–19.

Cohen, S. (1985) *Visions of Social Control: Crime, Punishment and Classification*. Cambridge: Polity.

De Lagasnerie, G. (2018) *Judge and Punish: The Penal State on Trial*. (translated from the French by Vergnaud, L.) Stanford, CA; Stanford University Press.

Foley, T. (2014) *Developing Restorative Justice Jurisprudence*. Farnham: Ashgate.

Foucault, M. (1984) 'What is called "Punishing"', pp. 382–393 in Faubion, J. (ed.) *Power: Essential Works of Foucault 1954–1984*. London: Penguin.

Gavrielides, T. (ed.) (2019) *Routledge International Handbook of Restorative Justice*. London: Routledge.

Home Office (1996) *The Victim's Charter : a Statement of Service Standards for Victims of Crime*. London: Home Office.

Hulsman, L. (1986) 'Critical Criminology and the Concept of Crime', *Contemporary Crises*, 10:1, pp. 63–80.

Johnstone, G. (2011) *Restorative Justice: Ideas, Values, Debates, 2nd edition*. London: Routledge.

Johnstone, G. (2015) 'Twenty-five Years of Changing Lenses – a Symposium', *Restorative Justice: An International Journal*, 3:3, 419–424.

Johnstone, G. (2017) 'Restorative justice for victims: inherent limits?' *Restorative Justice: An International Journal*, 5:3, 382–395.

Johnstone, G. (2019) 'Restorative Justice and the Therapeutic Tradition: Looking into the Future', pp. 395–408 in Gavrielides, T. (ed.) *Routledge International Handbook of Restorative Justice*. London: Routledge.

Johnstone, G. and Ward, T. (2010) *Law and Crime*. London: Sage.

Lamond, G. (2007) 'What is a Crime?', *Oxford Journal of Legal Studies*, 27:4, 609–632.

Lee, A. (2015) 'Public Wrongs and the Criminal Law', *Criminal Law and Philosophy*, 9:1, 155–170.

Marshall, S. and Duff, R. (1998) 'Criminalization and Sharing Wrongs', *Canadian Journal of Law and Jurisprudence*, 11:1, 7–22.

Moberly, W. (1968) *The Ethics of Punishment*. London: Faber and Faber.

Nozick, R. (1974) *Anarchy, State, and Utopia*. Oxford: Blackwell.

O'Mahony, D. and Doak, J. (2017) *Reimagining Restorative Justice: Agency and Accountability in the Criminal Process*. Oxford: Hart.

Pavlich, G. (2005). *Governing Paradoxes of Restorative Justice*. London: Glasshouse Press.

Pavlich, G. and Thorlakson, L. (2017) 'Recalibrating Victimhood in the European Union and Canada', *Restorative Justice: An International Journal*, 5:3, 345–351.

Roche, D. (2003) *Accountability in Restorative Justice*. Oxford: Oxford University Press.

Shapland, J. (1984) 'Victims, the Criminal Justice System and Compensation', *British Journal of Criminology*, 24:2, pp. 131–249.

Strang, H. and Braithwaite, J. (eds.) (2001) *Restorative Justice and Civil Society*. Cambridge: Cambridge University Press.

van Dijk, J. (1988) 'Ideological Trends within the Victims Movement: an International Perspective', in Maguire, M. and Pointing, J. (eds) *Victims of Crime: A New Deal?*. Milton Keynes. Open University Press.

Van Ness, D. and Strong, K. (1993) *Restoring Justice: An Introduction to Restorative Justice*. Cincinnati, OH: Anderson.

Weitekamp, E. (2003) 'The History of Restorative Justice' in G. Johnstone (ed.) *A Restorative Justice Reader, first edition*. Cullompton: Willan.

Wright, M. (1991) *Justice for Victims and Offenders: A Restorative Response to Crime.* Milton Keynes: Open University Press.

Wright, M. (1999) *Restoring Respect for Justice.* Winchester: Waterside Press.

Zehr, H. (1986 [2013]) 'Retributive Justice, Restorative Justice', in in Johnstone, G. (ed.) *A Restorative Justice Reader, second edition*. London: Routledge, pp. 23–35.

Zehr, H. (1990) *Changing Lenses: A New Focus for Crime and Justice*. Scottdale, PA: Herald Press.

Zehr, H. (2015). *Changing Lenses: Restorative Justice for our Times (25th anniversary edition).* Harrisonburg: Herald Press.

Zehr, H. (2019) 'Foreword', in Gavrielides, T. (ed.) *Routledge International Handbook of Restorative Justice.* London: Routledge.

PART II

Philosophical Perspectives on Punishment

8
DEFAMILIARIZING PUNISHMENT

Tom Daems

Introduction

At first sight it may seem as if moral and theoretical reflection on punishment is somewhat unnecessary: every modern democracy has a criminal justice system that includes a criminal code with a long list of criminalized behavior, a panoply of forms of punishment, various procedures and specialized institutions (prisons, probation, courts, etc.), an army of penal professionals that staffs and runs the system, etc. This seems self-evident and beyond questioning: indeed, the right to punish has long since been perceived and celebrated as the cornerstone of modern liberal democracies. Against this background punishment hardly raises any questions. Moreover, in popular understandings of punishment it is often assumed that punishment simply follows from crime and, therefore, it does not need any further reflection. Crime triggers punishment and it is therefore the former that needs to be explained and addressed, not the latter. Or as the late Nils Christie (1993: 32) once put it: "If the criminal starts it, and all the authorities can do is react, then, naturally, the volume of prisoners is caused by crime and reflects the crime situation. It becomes destiny, not choice".

However, this self-evidence becomes shaky and untenable when we look at punishment from a historical and comparative perspective. Throughout history humans have displayed an immense creativity when it comes to punishing their fellow human beings. In his famous essay on the two laws of penal evolution Emile Durkheim (1899 [1900]) discusses how humans have, throughout history, put people to death, mentioning practices as bizarre as being crushed to death by an elephant or having boiling oil poured into one's ears and mouth. The Belgian sociologist Lieven Vandekerckhove (2000) devoted a remarkable study to the Old-European practice of punishing suicidal behavior, which included the postmortem mutilation and display of dead bodies of suicide victims. Prisons are nowadays widely perceived as evident parts of modern societies but such carceral institutions designed for punishment have a history as well that goes back, depending on the source, to the eighteenth (Foucault 1977), sixteenth (Spierenburg 1984) or thirteenth centuries (Geltner 2008). Moreover, deprivation of liberty is nowadays used in widely varying proportions across the globe (with US "mass imprisonment" as an outlier, see Garland 2001b) and it coexists with monetary fines, community sanctions, probation, mediation, electronic monitoring, death penalty, etc. Crossing boundaries of time and place enables us, therefore, to compile a seemingly endless list of penal practices.

This wide diversity in the form, intensity and use of punishment cannot be solely or primarily explained by crime. Indeed, the common-sense assumption which tells us that crime and punishment form an inseparable couplet has been proven false by decades of penological research: crime and punishment are not tied together as Siamese twins whereby any surgical attempt to separate the one from the other is loaded with life-threatening risks (Daems 2008). This crime-punishment nexus is most powerfully problematized in the following sentences from the 1939 study *Punishment and Social Structure*:

> Punishment is neither a simple consequence of crime, nor the reverse side of crime, nor a mere means which is determined by the end to be achieved. Punishment must be understood as a social phenomenon freed from both its juristic and its social ends.
>
> *(Rusche & Kirchheimer 1968 [1939]: 5)*

Here Rusche and Kirchheimer suggest that the relationship between crime and punishment needs to be problematized in two directions: on the one hand, crime does not naturally "lead" to punishment; on the other hand, the meaning of punishment cannot be fully captured if it is merely treated as a means-to-a-certain-end. The Italian criminologist Dario Melossi therefore argues that understanding punishment implies rejecting the so-called "legal syllogism":

> ...the commonsensical idea, originating in the classical school of criminal law, that punishment is simply the consequence of crime and that, therefore, if there is a need for sociological explanation, such explanation concerns criminal behavior and not the punishment of this behavior. In this view, the latter was not conceivable independently of crime: social structure explains crime and crime explains punishment.
>
> *(Melossi 1989: 311)*

And he adds: "This is the way lawyers and judges and most of those who are in contact with the criminal justice system, tend to think. This is the way the general public tends to think too" (Ibid.).

In this chapter we will introduce and address three questions which can help readers to defamiliarize some common-sense ideas about punishment and introduce them to some major debates in contemporary studies of punishment; we will try to provoke questions that "...make evident things into puzzles" (Bauman 1990: 15). These three questions concern the quantity of punishment: do we punish too much or too little?; the goals and functions of punishment: is punishment a success or a failure?; and the central features of punishment: is punishment Apollonian or Dionysian?

Too Little Or Too Much?

Our first question deals with the quantity of punishment: do we punish too much or too little? When one observes the functioning of any criminal justice system more closely it could be tempting to conclude that we punish too little (Daems 2007a). Of all inter-human conflicts and transgressions of criminal law only a very small number is eventually defined and treated as "crime". A focus on state punishment obscures the multiple ways of responding to conflicts and undesirable behavior without the use of legal categories and procedures. Indeed, societies can avail themselves of a broad range of intervention strategies, such as self-help, avoidance, regulation, mediation, compensation, surveillance, therapy, education, etc. (see e.g., Law Commission of Canada 2003) – and, of course, often no intervention follows at all. Punitive responses are therefore only one set of responses amongst many others and, arguably, not even the most important ones.

Criminologists tend to depict the functioning of the criminal justice system as a funnel that becomes smaller the further we proceed in the system. In most cases there will be no punishment at all because of reasons and decisions related to detection, reporting, cautioning, diversion, prosecution, sentencing, etc. Formal state punishment only comes at the very end of a long, highly complex, multi-staged process with numerous (unpredictable) exit doors and (more predictable) exit scenarios. The fact that punishment is more an exception than the norm should not surprise us given the inherent limitations of modern criminal justice systems: the available means and human resources are inevitably insufficient to punish every transgression of criminal law. These limitations have, moreover, become more visible and pronounced in so-called "late modern" societies which tend to develop high crime rates as a by-product of wider transformations. David Garland (2001a) argues that policy makers nowadays are confronted with a nagging predicament: high crime rates have become a normal "social fact"; the limits and failure of the criminal justice system are increasingly acknowledged; and the myth of the sovereign state and its monopoly of crime control has eroded irreversibly (see also Daems 2008).

Such observations on the (inevitably) limited role punishment can play in modern (or late modern) democracies bring some to conclude that we punish too little – and that we should therefore invest in more punishment. It is from such a perspective that we need to understand various calls to expand capacity, build new prisons and increase criminal justice personnel in order to fight "impunity", to make the justice system more "credible", or to restore "truth in sentencing" (Beyens et al. 2013). It is often suggested that this is also what the public wants. This is sometimes referred to as the "democracy at work" thesis, as expressed by Cullen et al. 1985:

> This logic suggests that rising crime rates in the 1960s and beyond precipitated a commensurate increase in the public's fear of and concern over crime. In turn, this led to the public's call for tougher handling of criminals, a call to which politicians responded by passing stringent laws and allocating funds to build more cages for the wicked.
>
> *(Cullen et al. 1985: 19)*

For Hans Boutellier (2019) this combination of limited resources and increasing demand has resulted in a "criminal justice paradox":

> A social climate has developed, in which the significance attributed to criminal justice in general – and punishment in particular – cannot be realized. …In the shadow of the perceived urgency regarding the security issue, there has been a sharp rise in the demand for criminal justice. In fact, more is expected of criminal justice than it can ever deliver.
>
> *(Boutellier 2019: 71–72)*

However, others would disagree and argue that we are not observing a "bottom-up" call for more or harsher punishment followed by a genuine response from political leaders to the *vox populi*. Rather we are witnessing a process of "populist punitiveness", a term coined by Anthony Bottoms which is "… intended to convey the notion of politicians tapping into, and using for their own purposes, what they believe to be the public's generally punitive stance" (Bottoms 1995: 40; see also Sparks 2003; Salas 2005; Daems 2007b; Pratt 2007). According to John Pratt, politicians who engage in penal populism are playing with fire:

> The consequences of penal populism are …more far reaching than politicians simply "tapping" into the public mood as and when it suits them. It is not something they can simply turn off at will ….they may be just as likely to lose control of it as to be able to manipulate it for their own purposes
>
> *(Pratt 2007: 3–4)*

Interestingly, whereas debate in TV studios or in internet fora often gives the impression that people are worried that we punish too little, others seem to be troubled about the opposite, that is, that we punish too much. Over the past decades prison populations have been increasing in most Western societies and most dramatically in the US where the rate of imprisonment has more than quadrupled since the early 1970s, reaching a population exceeding 2.2 million inmates in the 21st century (National Research Council 2014). At the same time the net of social control has widened and the penal apparatus grown with the introduction and expansion of various alternative or intermediate sanctions such as probation, electronic monitoring, community service orders, etc. (Austin & Krisberg 1981; Cohen 1985; Robinson 2016; McNeill 2019). In 2003, Jock Young suggested that the "rise in punishment" had become "the new problematic of criminology" in the final decade of the 20th century. Criminology attempted to come to terms with three related questions: "(1) Why the vast increase in the correctional population – the punitive turn? (2) Why the proliferation of agencies dealing with crime and incivilities? (3) Why the contradictory nature of these responses?" (Young 2003: 99). And, indeed, questions of punitiveness and how to make sense of recent penal developments have increasingly moved to the center of research and scholarly debate (Daems 2008). There is now a vast and burgeoning literature on the causes and consequences of mass incarceration (Garland 2001b; National Research Council 2014), mass supervision (McNeill 2019; McNeill & Beyens 2013) and mass probation (Phelps 2017). From this perspective, we are not confronted with the limits or failure of criminal justice systems to deliver punishment but rather with a transformation of how we punish and what we expect from punishment, also captured in phrases such as "the new punitiveness" (Pratt et al. 2005), "Neue Lust auf Strafen" (Hassemer 2000; Rode et al. 2005), "neopunitivismo" (Pastor 2006), "punitive turn" (Frost 2006), "penal regressions" (Radzinowicz 1991), "volonté de punir" (Salas 2005), "pénalisation du social" (Mary 2003), etc. (see Daems 2008).

Studies on the increasing use of punishment and penal change have also revived the debate on the proper "limits to pain" (Christie 1981) and renewed interest in older ideas of decarceration and penal abolition. From such a perspective, punitive responses are perceived to be selective, harmful and stigmatizing: they create and exacerbate problems instead of solving them. Prisons (and, according to some, crime as a concept or criminal law *tout court* – see e.g., Hulsman 1986a, 1986b) should therefore be abolished (for discussions, see e.g., Duff & Garland 1994; Ruggiero 2012; Carrier & Piché 2015). Such ideas were particularly popular in the 1970s and early 1980s but in recent years we have witnessed their remarkable revival, in particular within the ambit of the European Group for the Study of Deviance and Social Control and the bi-annual international conferences on penal abolition (ICOPA) (see e.g., Moore et al. 2014; Scott 2016). Less radical, but also aimed at problematizing and addressing the current over-use of punishment, are various proposals for "penal moderation" (Loader 2010), "parsimony" (Braithwaite & Pettit 1990) or "restorative justice" (Aertsen et al. 2006; Bolivar 2019; Strang 2002; Walgrave 2007). Moreover, eminent research institutions such as the British Academy (2014) and the National Research Council (2014) have in recent reports, based on a review of the evidence and written by experts after ample discussion, argued that imprisonment is being used way too often and should be substantially reduced.

Such discussions on limiting or even abolishing state punishment have, in turn, invited critical reflection on what may get lost if we turn too quickly away from criminal law. In a critical paper on restorative justice Serge Gutwirth and Paul De Hert, for example, suggest that at least three processes particular to criminal law are being disregarded: "…first, the defining of an 'offence'; second, the criminal procedure by which this offence is attributed to a person; and, third, the denunciatory and symbolic character of the subsequent criminal sentencing" (Gutwirth & De Hert 2013: 291). Scholars studying developments in the privatization of security have voiced similar concerns: a victim-centered, instrumental and cost-effective way of dealing with conflicts and (financial) losses tends to replace the public and symbolic dimensions of criminal law (see e.g., Shearing & Stenning 1983; Piret 2005).

Failure or Success?

Our second question deals with the purposes and functions of punishment: is punishment a failure or a success? The answer to this question depends on what criteria we use to measure success – and what we consider to be a failure. If we explore the effectiveness of punishment – that is, whether the stated goals of punishment are being achieved – then history does not give us much reason for optimism. Historians of crime and punishment have highlighted that the scaffold often failed to deter watchers of the spectacle: cases of pickpocketing were often reported during executions demonstrating how little effect capital punishment had on such perpetrators (Bennett 2018). The history of the modern prison reads as a long story of great expectations but poor results. In his elaborate study of the history of imprisonment in the Netherlands, Dutch criminologist Herman Franke wrote tellingly in terms of the "trauma of cellular confinement": the hope that solitary confinement and isolation would lead to moral reformation turned out to be a sour illusion; instead of converting convicts into law-abiding citizens prisoners went mad or committed suicide (Franke 1990, 1995). Indeed, the damaging consequences of solitary confinement or regimes of isolation have been documented at length in historical studies of the prison across the globe. Against that background it is significant to note that prison law in Europe nowadays pays special attention to harm reduction. For example, Article 6, para 2 of the Belgian prison Law of 12 January 2005 turns the reduction of the harm caused by imprisonment into the central objective of the execution of prison sentences. This is a U turn compared to the hopes invested in the prison in the early days of the modern penitentiary: avoiding or reducing the harmful consequences of imprisonment for inmates and his or her relatives needs to guide 21st century prison practice instead of expecting some beneficial consequences in terms of reforming or rehabilitating prisoners.

In his book *Prison on Trial* Thomas Mathiesen concluded his critical review of the multiple ways in which the prison has been, and still is, claimed to work (that is, rehabilitation, incapacitation, individual deterrence and general prevention) with the words: "…the prison is a fiasco in terms of its own purposes" (Mathiesen 1990: 137). Many would agree with Mathiesen. Over the past decades several reviews of the available empirical literature have concluded that the evidence that punishment in general and imprisonment in particular "works" – by way of deterrence, incapacitation, rehabilitation, sentence severity, and so forth – is thin indeed (see e.g., Zimring & Hawkins 1995; von Hirsch et al. 1999; Doob & Webster 2003; Kury et al. 2003).

However, the idea that state punishment is an (or: the) effective means to the desired end of "less crime" is difficult to eradicate. There are at least two reasons why the available evidence does not always trickle down (Daems 2007a). First, the idea that punishment "works" feels right and seems self-evident because this is how most people tend to experience punishment in their daily lives. As Henry (2003) observes:

> The empirical question of the effectiveness of punishment is considerably clouded by the commonsense view of the efficacy of punishment. Most people believe punishment works because they use it in their everyday life, with their children, their co-workers and their pets, and, are themselves subject to it.
>
> *(Henry 2003: 2)*

If an occasional spanking "works" for naughty boys or barking dogs, why should a lengthy prison sentence not "work" for a rapist? Such false intuitions invite discussion on the role that evidence and expert opinion can or should play in debate and policy-making to challenge commonsense ideas and in "revealing complexities", "questioning certitudes" and "puncturing the false hope of simple solutions" (Zedner 2003: 234). It seems unlikely that Europe would have become a death penalty-free zone if it were not for political leadership (Hood & Hoyle 2015). Indeed, abolishing the death penalty required leading instead of following public opinion. Many commentators on "populist punitiveness" (see above) argue that the toughening of penal policy can be explained by slavishly responding to opinion polls and a failure or unwillingness to dispel myths about punishment. Interestingly, from such a perspective, penal bureaucracies are no longer perceived to be the impersonal people-processing machineries of yore but rather welcomed as shields against "decivilizing" forces:

> The less the bureaucratic organizations of punishment have been pushed to one side in the new axis of penal power, the less the influence of populist punitiveness is likely to be and the more likely that there will still be significant voices that worry about prison levels and insist on "civilized" conditions within the prisons.
>
> *(Pratt 2002: 187)*

Or, as Michael Tonry (2004) puts it in his book on punishment in the US, where he pleads for a de-politicization and de-emotionalization of penal policy:

> We need to learn to restrain our collective emotions in public life, to change governmental institutions to provide greater insulation from the passions of the moment, and to devise structural arrangements that will force greater reflectiveness on policy makers.
>
> *(Tonry 2004: 199)*

Second, this common-sense conviction about punishment's effectiveness is actively fueled by a (semi-)scientific literature that relies heavily (if not exclusively) upon economic rational-choice models to explain human behavior (Daems 2007a). These approaches depart, as Beyens (2007: 88) pointed out, from a "social fiction" – the underlying assumption that human beings are utilitarian creatures, constantly making cost-benefit analyses is a fundamentally impoverished one. Yet, its inherent simplicity paves the way for clear-cut solutions, such as the "prison works" argument. In a 1997 paper Charles Murray suggested that the "American experiment" with imprisonment had been highly successful. Murray presented two graphs contrasting England and Wales with the United States: in the first a decline in imprisonment risk seemed to go hand in hand with a rise in crime (England and Wales, 1950–1995); in the second, a steeply rising imprisonment rate increases the risk of imprisonment and is joined with a stabilized crime rate (United States, 1950–1993). With the help of these figures Murray aimed to demonstrate that the crime rate is an inverse function of the chances of going to prison. By embarking upon the "American experiment" policy makers in the United States seemed to have understood this and, therefore, had made the right choice.

Murray attracted a number of criticisms: identifying a correlation is not the same as establishing a cause; cross-national data (derived from other nations than the ones Murray included in his essay) demonstrate that the relationship between crime rates and imprisonment levels is much more complex; the figures ignored the inter-state differences within the United States; the paper neglected the racial focus of the "American experiment"; and so forth (see e.g., Young 1999: 140–147; Henry 2003; Frost 2006: 2–7). More fundamentally, Murray's critics shared a deep aversion to this highly simplistic way of modeling the relationship between crime and imprisonment which made a mockery of the complexity of social reality. Yet, these simplified ways of picturing the social world are highly appealing: indeed, despite the sharp critique levelled at Murray, his hypothesis was "tested" and "corroborated" a few years later in Australia (Saunders & Billante 2002). And, unsurprisingly, the enthusiastic and uncritical reception of the "prison works" idea by Saunders and Billante also met with a sharp response (Ore & Birgden 2003).

It is to be expected that these (and similar) debates will be with us for a long time to come. Inevitably, in public debates on the sense and non-sense of punishment, social scientists and moral philosophers vie with others who cherish other opinions and who appeal (often with much more success) to commonsensical or ideological intuitions. One of the conclusions of a review study of the impact of severe punishment upon crime captures this well: "Simplistic solutions to complex phenomena may suffice politically but not practically" (Kury et al. 2003: 133).

There are three more observations that we want to make at this point (Daems 2007a). First, in discussions on the effectiveness of punishment one sometimes tends to forget that far from reducing crime, punishment itself may contribute to further increases, for example, by reducing life chances, disrupting social and family networks, damaging career and labor prospects, and so forth. In fact, these "collateral consequences" of punitive practices point in the opposite direction to what the instrumentalist idea behind punishment makes us believe (see e.g., Mauer & Chesney-Lind 2002; Condry 2007). Second, while punishment undoubtedly "works" at times, one should ask whether other (preventive or reactive) approaches to crime are more efficient in reducing crime. Arguably, in policy discussions about crime control the most appropriate response can hardly be state punishment; other ways of responding to crime have proven to be much more efficient. Introducing steering column locks to reduce the incidence of car crime may be much more effective that increasing penalties for car thieves (see e.g., Mayhew et al. 1976). In 2006 Andrew Coyle formulated this, at the occasion of the "Alternatives to Prison Conference" in Edinburgh, in the following words:

> I have been asked to consider the question "Does custodial sentencing work?" It occurs to me that this is rather like asking "Is war an appropriate method of resolving international disputes?" The short answer to both questions is, "Yes, but only in extreme situations, when all other possibilities have proved unsuccessful and when the harm which would otherwise be done is likely to be greater than the harm done by imprisonment/war.
>
> *(Coyle 2006: 1)*

Third, while punishment may often fail in terms of crime control, there may be other ways in which it, in fact, succeeds. Indeed, punishment sends messages and, in doing so, communicates about what citizens of a particular political community (are supposed to) value (and what not); punishment may succeed in showing that action is taken and in suggesting that those in charge of crime control are still winning the fight against crime; punishment may satisfy feelings of revenge and reinforce social cohesion; punishment may be instrumental in constituting groups of in- and outsiders within a given society; punishment may divert attention away from certain issues by acting as a scapegoat mechanism; and so forth. However, in perceiving punishment like this, we are leaving the restricted domain of the self-proclaimed goals of punishment and penal sanctions (such as deterrence, reform, rehabilitation, incapacitation) and we enter the domain of the sociology of punishment, that is, we then move from an evaluation of instrumentalist thinking about punishment, to an exploration of the functions it fulfils, the effects it produces and the meanings it communicates. For Emile Durkheim this proved to be a much more interesting and fruitful way to understand punishment:

> Although it [punishment] proceeds from a quite mechanical reaction, from movements which are passionate and in great part non-reflective, it does play a useful role. Only this role is not where we ordinarily look for it. It does not serve, or else only serves quite secondarily, in correcting the culpable or in intimidating possible followers. From this point of view, its efficacy is justly doubtful and, in any case, mediocre. Its true function is to maintain social cohesion intact, while maintaining all its vitality in the common conscience.
>
> *(Durkheim 1933 [1893]: 108)*

Apollonian or Dionysian?

As we have just seen, Durkheim argued that we should not focus too much on the goals of punishment but rather we should explore its functions and unveil how it is embedded in society; in other words, we should embark on "a social analysis of penality" (Garland & Young 1983). This brings us to our final question: is punishment about rationality, power, risk, managerialism? Or is it rather about feelings and emotions such as passion, rage, anger? In short, is punishment Apollonian or Dionysian? Such questions are typically addressed in the sociology of punishment, "...that body of thought which explores the relations between punishment and society, its purpose being to understand legal punishment as a social phenomenon and thus trace its role in social life" (Garland 1990a: 10). The relation goes from society to punishment, as was already suggested by Edwin Sutherland, in his theory of "cultural consistency": "The societal reactions to law-breaking and the methods used to implement or express those reactions show a general tendency to be consistent with other ways of behaving of the society" (Sutherland & Cressey 1970: 337). However, it also goes in the other direction, from punishment to society. As James Whitman remarked in *Harsh Justice*, it is wrong "...to analyze punishment solely by considering its effect on the person punished; acts of punishment can also profoundly affect the person, or the society, doing the punishing" (Whitman 2003: 24). Authors such as Emile Durkheim or Michel Foucault have drawn attention to the "positive" effects (not to be understood in evaluative sense) of punishment: punishment *reinforces* social solidarity (Durkheim), it *produces* docile bodies (Foucault). Moreover, punishment communicates about what we (are supposed to) value, who we should fear (and who not), how we should respond to certain acts, and ultimately, about who we are: "...the ways in which we punish, and the ways in which we represent that action to ourselves, makes a difference to the way we are" (Garland 1990a: 276). These "positive" effects of punishment escape from our attention if we restrict ourselves to addressing questions related to its sheer negativity, that is, the philosophical question of how the state's deliberate infliction of suffering can be justified (Garland 1983).

According to Richard Sparks (2003: 21) punishment has two faces: it is Janus-faced "...in its capacity simultaneously to invoke antique forms of rage and desire and to spin novel techniques and managerial styles". The Apollonian and Dionysian features of punishment therefore seem to go hand in hand:

> ...punishment is both a severely *practical* matter and a thoroughly *expressive* one. It is used in attempts to intervene in and to control many forms of undesired behavior. In punishing we threaten, detain, deprive, immobilize, supervise, watch, guard, enjoin, entreat, cajole, and educate. Yet we also, in punishing, act out anger, voice pain, exclude, reject, tell stories, vindicate the authority of law, defend the state from external threat or internal subversion – real or imagined, invoke the divine, cherish, and occasionally forgive.
>
> *(Sparks 2003: 21)*

Inspiration to flesh out the emotional energy that drives punishment has been derived primarily from classical Durkheiman work (Garland 1990a; 2013) and, more recently, neo-Durkheimian cultural sociology (Smith 2008). For Durkheim, as we have seen, the essence of punishment is not rationality or instrumental control, it is "...irrational, unthinking emotion fixed by a sense of the sacred and its violation. Passion lies at the heart of punishment" (Garland 1990a: 32). The feelings and sensibilities that accompany or are provoked by punishment – and how these have come to be tamed over time (Spierenburg 1984) or unleashed more recently (Pratt 2002) – are at the centre of Elias-inspired studies on the civilization and decivilization of punishment (Daems 2008). Aspects of control, repression and managerialism have been studied within the political economy of punishment (for an overview, see De Giorgi 2013) and, later, Foucauldian work on punishment and discipline and, more recently, risk and governmentality (Pratt 1997; Hudson 1998). In recent reflections on penal developments managerialism has been singled out as an important (see e.g., Bottoms 1995), or even a defining, feature of penal practice (on the "new penology", see e.g., Feeley & Simon 1992).

These different perspectives on punishment have led to different ways of thinking about reform and progress in penal history. One of the central features of critical or revisionist scholarship focusing on power and repression is to question explanations of penal change in terms of reform, progress, humanitarianism or benevolence. The idea that mankind had progressed from the barbaric dark ages (the cruelty and bloodshed on the scaffold) to a civilized penal enlightenment (with the modern prison as exemplary punishment) was firmly rejected (Daems 2011). Indeed, as Cohen and Scull indicate, the newer, revisionist studies (inspired by Rusche and Kirchheimer, Foucault and others) started from a different position:

> …scepticism about the professed aims, beliefs and intentions of the reformers; concern with the analysis of power and its effects; curiosity about the relationship between intentions and consequences; determination to locate the reform enterprise in the social, economic and political contexts of the period. The problem of maintaining the social order ...becomes dominant.
>
> *(Cohen & Scull 1983: 2)*

This "hermeneutics of suspicion" in the study of punishment (Garland 1990b) came to be challenged, however, from the early 1980s onwards. Michael Ignatieff, author of a revisionist study on the rise of the modern penitentiary (Ignatieff 1978), revised his own position in a lengthy essay of 1981 where he reflected upon Foucault, Rothman and his own work. What is needed, so he argued, is:

> …a model of historical explanation which accounts for institutional change without imputing conspiratorial rationality to a ruling class, without reducing institutional development to a formless ad hoc adjustment to contingent crisis, and without assuming a hyper-idealist, all triumphant humanitarian crusade.
>
> *(Ignatieff 1981: 157)*

Some years later the Dutch historian Pieter Spierenburg, who has always been deeply inspired by Norbert Elias (see Spierenburg 2013; Daems & van Swaaningen 2019), pointed out how quickly, in scholarly debate on the history of punishment, the benevolent endeavours of humanitarian reformers and "good guys" make way for the "bad guys" who now are "…indifferent to the fate of convicts and bent on creating opportunities for economic gain" (Spierenburg 1987: 439).

Developments in the field of human rights in relation to punishment have in recent years also been met with mixed feelings. The growing role of the European Court of Human Rights (ECtHR) in protecting prisoners' rights and holding states to account on the one hand, and the preventive role of bodies such as the European Committee for the Prevention of Torture and Inhuman or Degrading Treatment or Punishment (CPT) on the other, have captured the attention from scholars interested in European penology (see e.g., van Zyl Smit & Snacken 2009; Daems et al. 2013; Cliquennois & de Suremain 2017; Daems & Robert 2017). At times these developments are perceived as a "story of progress" (Murdoch 2006) or a bulwark that helps resist punitive tendencies throughout Europe (Snacken 2010). However, at the same time the impact of all of this has been questioned. Over the past decades European penal discourse has come to be permeated with notions of human dignity: bodily pain and degradation are to be eliminated or minimized as far as possible. And, yet, it has been observed time and again that these are still part of daily reality. This ambivalence in attitudes to punishment in the West has come to be scrutinized more closely: why are findings of the ECtHR contested and recommendations of the CPT neglected? What strategies do state authorities deploy when they deal with information that is felt to be annoying, troubling or threatening? How are such bodily and degradatory features of punishment concealed, masked, denied? (Daems 2017)

References

Aertsen, I., Daems, T. & Robert, L. (eds.) (2006). *Institutionalizing Restorative Justice*. Cullompton: Willan Publishing.

Austin, J. & Krisberg, B. (1981). Wider, stronger and different nets: the dialectics of criminal justice reform. *Journal of Research in Crime and Delinquency*, 18(1), 165–196.

Bauman, Z. (1990). *Thinking Sociologically*. Oxford: Basil Blackwell.

Bennett, R.E. (2018). *Capital Punishment and the Criminal Corpse in Scotland,* 1740–1834. Basingstoke: Palgrave Macmillan.

Beyens, K. (2007). Over de beperkte diepgang van de rationele keuzetheorie. *Tijdschrift voor Criminologie,* 49(1), 87–92.

Beyens, K., Snacken, S. & van Zyl Smit, D. (2013). Truth in (the implementation of) sentencing: Belgium and elsewhere. In: T. Daems, D. van Zyl Smit & S. Snacken (eds.), *European Penology?* Oxford: Hart Publishing, 271–291.

Bottoms, A. (1995). The philosophy and politics of punishment and sentencing. In: C. Clarkson & R. Morgan (eds.), *The Politics of Sentencing Reform.* Oxford: Clarendon Press, 17–49.

Bolivar, D. (2019). *Restoring Harm: A Psychosocial Approach to Victims and Restorative Justice.* London: Routledge.

Boutellier, H. (2019). *A Criminology of Moral Order.* Bristol: Bristol University Press.

Braithwaite, J. & Pettit, P. (1990). *Not Just Deserts. A Republican Theory of Criminal Justice.* Oxford: Oxford University Press.

British Academy (2014). *A Presumption Against Imprisonment: Social Order and Social Values.* London: British Academy.

Cliquennois, G. & de Suremain, H. (eds.) (2017). *Monitoring Penal Policy in Europe.* Abingdon: Routledge.

Cohen, S. (1985). *Visions of Social Control.* Cambridge: Polity Press.

Cohen, S. & Scull, A. (1983). Introduction: Social control in history and sociology. In: S. Cohen & A. Scull (eds), *Social Control and the State. Historical and Comparative Essays.* Oxford: Martin Robertson.

Condry, R. (2007). *Families Shamed. The Consequences of Crime for Relatives of Serious Offenders.* Cullompton: Willan Publishing.

Carrier, N. & Piché, J. (eds.) (2015). Dossier: Abolitionnisme. Champ Pénal, 7. https://champpenal.revues.org/9008 (accessed: 4 March 2019).

Christie, N. (1981). *Limits to Pain. The Role of Punishment in Penal Policy.* Oslo: Universitetsforlaget.

Christie, N. (1993). *Crime Control as Industry. Towards Gulags, Western Style?* London: Routledge.

Coyle, A. (2006). *Does custodial sentencing work?* Paper presented at the "Alternatives to Prison Conference", The Royal Society of Edinburgh, 8 December.

Cullen, F.T., Clark, G.A. & Wozniak, J.F. (1985). Explaining the Get Tough movement: Can the public be blamed? *Federal Probation,* 49(2), 16–24.

Daems, T. (2007a). Punishment, Victimization and Society. Unpublished PhD thesis (Criminology). KU Leuven.

Daems, T. (2007b). Engaging with penal populism: the case of France. *Punishment & Society,* 9(3), 319–324.

Daems, T. (2008). *Making Sense of Penal Change.* Oxford: Oxford University Press.

Daems, T. (2011). A peculiar sociology of punishment. *Oxford Journal of Legal Studies,* 31(4), 805–823.

Daems, T. (2017). Slaves and statues: Torture prevention in contemporary Europe. *British Journal of Criminology,* 57(3), 627–643.

Daems, T., van Zyl Smit, D. & Snacken, S. (eds.) (2013). *European Penology?* Oxford: Hart Publishing.

Daems, T. & Robert, L. (eds.) (2017). *Europe in Prisons.* Basingstoke: Palgrave Macmillan.

Daems, T. & van Swaaningen, R. (2019). "In ben een beunhaas in de criminologie": in gesprek met Pieter Spierenburg. *Tijdschrift over Cultuur & Criminaliteit,* 9(1), 16–30.

De Giorgi, A. (2013). Punishment and political economy. In: J. Simon & R. Sparks (eds.), *The SAGE Handbook of Punishment and Society.* London: Sage, 40–59.

Doob, A.N. & Webster, C.M. (2003). Sentence severity and crime: Accepting the null hypothesis. *Crime and Justice: A Review of Research,* 30, 143–195.

Duff, R.A. & Garland, D. (eds.) (1994). *A Reader on Punishment.* Oxford: Oxford University Press.

Durkheim, E. (1899/1900). Deux lois de l'évolution pénale. *L'Année sociologique,* 4, 65–95.

Durkheim, E. (1933). *The Division of Labor in Society.* Illinois: The Free Press of Glencoe.

Feeley, M.M. & Simon, J. (1992). The new penology: Notes on the emerging strategy of corrections and its implications. *Criminology,* 30(4), 449–474.

Foucault, M. (1977). *Discipline and Punish. The Birth of the Prison.* New York: Pantheon Books.

Franke, H. (1990). *Twee eeuwen gevangen. Misdaad en straf in Nederland.* Utrecht: Het Spectrum.

Franke, H. (1995). *The Emancipation of Prisoners. A Socio-Historical Analysis of the Dutch Prison Experience.* Edinburgh: Edinburgh University Press.

Frost, N.A. (2006). *The Punitive State. Crime, Punishment, and Imprisonment across the United States.* New York: LFB Scholarly Publishing LLC.

Garland, D. (1983). Philosophical argument and ideological effect: an essay review. *Contemporary Crises,* 7, 79–85.

Garland, D. (1990a). *Punishment and Modern Society: A Study in Social Theory.* Oxford: Oxford University Press.

Garland, D. (1990b). Frameworks of Inquiry in the Sociology of Punishment. *British Journal of Sociology,* 41(1), 1–15.

Garland, D. (2001a). *The Culture of Control.* Oxford: Oxford University Press.

Garland, D. (ed.) (2001b). *Mass Imprisonment. Social Causes and Consequences*. London: Sage.
Garland, D. (2013). Punishment and Social Solidarity. In: J. Simon & R. Sparks (eds.), *The SAGE Handbook of Punishment and Society*. London: Sage, 23–39.
Garland, D. & Young, P. (1983). Towards a social analysis of penality. In: D. Garland & P. Young (eds.), *The Power to Punish*. London: Heinemann, 1–36.
Geltner, G. (2008). *The Medieval Prison: A Social History*. Princeton: Princeton University Press.
Gutwirth, S. & De Hert, P. (2013). To punish or to restore? A false alternative. In: D. Cornwell, J. Blad & M. Wright (eds.), *Civilising Criminal Justice. An International Restorative Agenda for Penal Reform*. London: Waterside Press, 387–411.
Hassemer, W. (2000). Die neue Lust auf Strafe. *Frankfurter Rundschau*, 20 December.
Henry, S. (2003) *On the Effectiveness of Prison as Punishment*. Paper presented at the Conference "Incarceration Nation: The Warehousing of America's Poor' October 24, Ivy Tech State College, South Bend, Indiana, http://behaviorworks.org/files/offshoots/Prison%20as%20Punishment.pdf (accessed: 4 March 2019)
Hood, R. & Hoyle, C. (2015). T*he Death Penalty: A Worldwide Perspective (5th edition)*. Oxford: Oxford University Press.
Hudson, B. (1998). Punishment and Governance. *Social & Legal Studies*, 7(4), 553–559.
Hulsman, L.H.C. (1986a). *Afscheid van het strafrecht. Een pleidooi voor zelfregulering (Met medewerking van Jacqueline Bernat de Celis en Hans Smits)*. Houten: Het Wereldvenster.
Hulsman, L.H.C. (1986b). Critical criminology and the concept of crime. *Contemporary Crises*, 10, 63–80.
Ignatieff, M. (1978). *A Just Measure of Pain: The Penitentiary in the Industrial Revolution, 1750–1850*. New York: Pantheon Books.
Ignatieff, M. (1981). State, civil society, and total institutions: A Critique of recent social histories of punishment. *Crime and Justice: A Review of Research*, 3, 153–192.
Kury, H., Ferdinand, T.N. & Obergfell-Fuchs, J. (2003). Does severe punishment mean less criminality? *International Criminal Justice Review*, 13, 110–148.
Law Commission of Canada (2003). *What is a Crime? Challenges and Alternatives*. http://epe.lac-bac.gc.ca/100/206/301/law_commission_of_canada-ef/2006-10-20/www.lcc.gc.ca/pdf/what_is_a_crime_dp.pdf (Accessed: 4 March 2019).
Loader, I. (2010). For penal moderation. Notes towards a public philosophy of punishment. *Theoretical Criminology*, 14(3), 349–367.
Mary, P. (2003). *Insécurité et pénalisation du social*. Brussels: Éditions Labor.
Mathiesen, T. (1990). *Prison on Trial. A Critical Assessment*. London: Sage.
Mayhew, P., Clarke, R.V.G., Sturman, A. & Hough, J.M. (1976). *Crime as Opportunity*. Home Office Research Study no 34. London: Her Majesty's Stationery Office.
Melossi, D. (1989). An introduction: Fifty years later, punishment and social structure in comparative analysis. *Contemporary Crises*, 13(4), 311–326.
Mauer, M. & Chesney-Lind, M. (2002). *Invisible Punishment: The Collateral Consequences of Mass Imprisonment*. New York: The New Press.
McNeill, F. (2019). *Pervasive Punishment: Making Sense of Mass Supervision*. Bingley: Emerald.
McNeill, F. & Beyens, K. (eds.) (2013). *Offender Supervision in Europe*. Basingstoke: Palgrave Macmillan.
Moore, J.M., Rolston, B., Scott, D. & Tomlinson, M. (eds.) (2014). *Beyond Criminal Justice: An Anthology of Abolitionist Papers presented to conferences of the European Group for the Study of Deviance and Social Control*. Weston-Super-Mare: European Group for the Study of Deviance and Social Control.
Murdoch, J. (2006). Tackling ill-treatment in places of detention: The work of the Council of Europe's "Torture Committee". *European Journal on Criminal Policy and Research*, 12(2), 121–142.
Murray, C. (1997). Does prison work? In: C. Murray (ed.), *Does Prison Work?* London: The IEA Health and Welfare Unit, 1–28.
National Research Council (2014). *The Growth of Incarceration in the United States. Exploring Causes and Consequences*. Washington: The National Academies Press.
Ore, T. & Birgden, A. (2003). Does prison work? A view from criminology. *Policy*, 19(2), 62–63.
Pastor, D.R. (2006). La deriva neopunitivista de organismos y activistas como causa del desprestigio actual de los derechos humanos. *Jura Gentium. Revista de filosofía del derecho internacional y de la polica global*, 2(1). www.juragentium.org/topics/latina/es/pastor.htm (accessed: 4 March 2019).
Phelps, M.S. (2017). Mass probation: Toward a more robust theory of state variation in punishment. *Punishment and Society*, 19(1) 53–73.
Piret, J. M. (2005). Privatisering van veiligheid: ideologische en rechtsstatelijke aspecten. In: L.C. Winkel, J.J.M. Jansen, H.O. Kerkmeester, R.J.P. Kottenhagen en V. Mul (eds.), *Privatisering van veiligheid*. Den Haag: Boom Juridische uitgevers, 39–54.
Pratt, J. (1997). *Governing the Dangerous*. Annandale: The Federation Press.
Pratt, J. (2002). *Punishment and Civilization. Penal Tolerance and Intolerance in Modern Society*. London: Sage.

Pratt, J. (2007). *Penal Populism*. London: Routledge.

Pratt, J., Brown, D., Brown, M. Hallsworth, S. & Morrison, W. (eds.) (2005). *The New Punitiveness. Trends, theories, perspectives*. Cullompton: Willan Publishing

Radzinowicz, L. (1991). Penal regressions. *Cambridge Law Journal*, 50(3), 422–444.

Robinson, G. (2016). The Cinderella complex: Punishment, society and community sanctions. *Punishment & Society*, 18(1), 95–112.

Rode, I., Kammeier, H. & Leipert, M. (eds.) (2005). *Neue Lust auf Strafen*. Münster: LIT Verlag.

Ruggiero, V. (2012). *Penal Abolitionism*. Oxford: Oxford University Press.

Rusche, G. & Kirchheimer, O. (1968 [1939]). *Punishment and Social Structure*. New York: Russell and Russell.

Salas, D. (2005). *La volonté de punir. Essai sur le populisme pénal*. Paris: Hachette Littératures.

Saunders, P. & Billante, N. (2002). Does prison work? *Policy*, 18(4), 3–8.

Saunders, P. & Billante, N. (2003). Does prison work? A view from sociology. *Policy*, 19(2), 63–64.

Scott, D. (2016). *Emancipatory Politics and Praxis: Essays written for the European Group for the Study of Deviance and Social Control*. London: EG Press.

Shearing, C.D. & Stenning, P.C. (1983). Private security: implications for social control. *Social Problems*, 30(5), 493–506.

Smith, P. (2008). *Punishment and Culture*. Chicago: Chicago University Press.

Snacken, S. (2010). Resisting punitiveness in Europe? *Theoretical Criminology*, 14(3), 273–292.

Sparks, R. (2003). State punishment in advanced capitalist countries. In: T.G. Blomberg & S. Cohen (eds.), *Punishment and Social Control (Enlarged Second Edition)*. New York: Aldine de Gruyter.

Spierenburg, P. (1984). *The Spectacle of Suffering. Executions and the evolution of repression: from a preindustrial metropolis to the European experience*. Cambridge: Cambridge University Press.

Spierenburg, P. (1987). From Amsterdam to Auburn: An explanation for the rise of the prison in seventeenth-century Holland and nineteenth-century America. *Journal of Social History*. 20(3), 439–461.

Spierenburg, P. (2013). *Violence and Punishment*. Cambridge: Polity Press.

Strang, H. (2002). *Repair or Revenge. Victims and Restorative Justice*. Oxford: Oxford University Press.

Sutherland, E.H. & Cressey, D.R. (1970). *Criminology (8th Edition)*. Philadelphia: J.B. Lippincott Company.

Tonry, M. (2004). *Thinking about Crime. Sense and Sensibility in American Penal Culture*. New York: Oxford University Press.

Vandekerckhove, L. (2000). *On Punishment. The Confrontation of Suicide in Old-Europe*. Leuven: Leuven University Press.

Van Zyl Smit, D. & Snacken, S. (2009). *Principles of European Prison Law and Policy*. Oxford: Oxford University Press.

Von Hirsch, A., Bottoms, A.E., Burney E. & Wikström, P.-O. (1999). *Criminal Deterrence and Sentence Severity: An Analysis of Recent Research*. Oxford: Hart Publishing.

Walgrave, L. (2007). *Restorative Justice, Self-interest and Responsible Citizenship*. Cullompton: Willan Publishing.

Whitman, J.Q. (2003). *Harsh Justice*. New York: Oxford University Press.

Young, J. (1999). *The Exclusive Society*. London: Sage.

Young, J. (2003). In praise of dangerous thoughts. *Punishment & Society*, 5(1), 97–107.

Zedner, L. (2003). Useful knowledge? Debating the role of criminology in postwar Britain. In: L. Zedner & A. Ashworth (eds.), *The Criminological Foundations of Penal Policy: Essays in Honour of Roger Hood*. Oxford: Oxford University Press.

Zimring, F.E. & Hawkins, G. (1995). *Incapacitation. Penal Confinement and the Restraint of Crime*. New York: Oxford University Press.

9
THE RETRIBUTIVE SENTIMENTS

Erin I. Kelly

The most popular philosophy of criminal punishment today, the one that seems to enthrall moral philosophers, legal theorists, and the American public alike, is based on the idea that justice has not been done until the criminally guilty get the punishment they deserve. Justice demands retribution. Retribution is achieved when morally culpable wrongdoers suffer in proportion to their culpable wrongdoing, or so it is claimed. Punishment is ugly, but crime makes it necessary. Retribution is *morally fitting*.

Retributive theories of criminal punishment bear a natural affinity to popular philosophies of moral blame. Many moral philosophers who write about moral responsibility endorse one or another version of the retributive theory, because the retributive sentiments are central to their account of morality. By the retributive sentiments I am referring to moralized anger, resentment, and indignation – certain negative emotions that are intertwined with moral judgments. These emotive responses have both cognitive and emotive content. They are sentiments that are allegedly warranted by evidence of a wrongdoer's moral faults, as those faults are displayed by the wrongdoer's wrongful actions. They combine an appraisal of the wrongdoer's personal faults with an emotive reaction to them.

A focus on the retributive sentiments is central to P.F. Strawson's famous article, "Freedom and Resentment." Strawson's idea is that the practice of blame is organized by the retributive sentiments and is a core element of our moral practices. The retributive sentiments display moral engagement with a wrongdoer; the alternative, claims Strawson, is a disengaged "objective" standpoint of clinical diagnosis or social control. Because the perspective of diagnosis and social control is antithetical to morally engaged relationships, and a lack of response to wrongdoing is unacceptable, our blaming responses cannot be eliminated without damaging morality. Moreover, their importance to us defeats the relevance of skeptical challenges to free will.

In this way, Strawson finesses the free will debate. He emphasizes that we need not endorse either compatibilism or incompatibilism about free will. We are compelled to set the matter aside, for moral reasons. Strawson puts it this way:

> The human commitment to participation in ordinary inter-personal relationships is, I think, too thoroughgoing and deeply rooted for us to take seriously the thought that a general theoretical conviction might so change our world that, in it, there were no longer any such things as inter-personal relationships as we normally understand them; and being involved in inter-personal relationships as we normally understand them precisely is being exposed to the range of reactive attitudes and feelings that is in question.
>
> *(Strawson 2003: section 1)*

The importance of the "reactive attitudes" – and, in particular, the retributive sentiments – to social life is, he says, part of "the general framework of human life" (Strawson 2003: section 4). As members of a moral community, we cannot step outside of that framework, much less give it up.

Strawson's argument has been highly influential in analytic moral philosophy, and many current discussions of moral responsibility build upon it. In fact, there is a veritable cottage industry of blame philosophies indebted to Strawson. But Strawson's argument is unconvincing. I am skeptical about the centrality of the retributive sentiments to morality and about Strawson's "solution" to the problem of free will. I think the importance of the retributive sentiments is exaggerated by moral philosophers and that the reactive attitudes Strawson highlights are not, in fact, required by morality. Morality will not fall apart if we refuse the retributive sentiments.

In what follows I challenge the idea that moral wrongdoing calls for the retributive sentiments. I will make the argument that neither the retributive sentiments nor the practice of blame they support are morally required responses to wrongdoing.[1] My motivation for this is partly a concern about the social implications of retributive thinking, specifically regarding criminal punishment. I am concerned that the retributive sentiments help to drive the problem of overpunishment and that they decrease sensitivity to the personhood of people who have been convicted of crimes.

I understand blame to involve the moral condemnation of wrongdoers. Blame reaches beyond an assessment of wrongdoing to a personal appraisal of wrongdoers in view of their actions. The most prominent philosophical accounts of blame, including Strawson's, focus on *the quality of a wrongdoer's will* – largely apart from psychological or social context, and with little attention to a wrongdoer's personal history. Such accounts ask whether an individual's actions demonstrate *ill will,* and they suppose that ill will provides insight into a person's character and values. The quality of an agent's motives and attitudes, and the sort of person they reveal her to be, are taken to rationalize retributive reactions. We are instructed to focus on whether a wrongdoer acted for bad reasons, reasons we should reject, and whether in so doing, she has expressed disregard for the rights or moral standing of other people. If a person has *bad attitudes,* according to this philosophy, a moralized response is called for, a response that is organized by the retributive sentiments.

Blame's defenders typically are interested in a condemnatory response that expresses what moral philosophers describe as appraisals of *moral worth* – a kind of moral ranking of persons. Blame is a performance of this personal assessment. It involves feeling, thinking, and acting toward the wrongdoer in ways that reflect the disapproval deemed to be a morally appropriate response to an agent's faults. Blaming involves enacting the moral responses a wrongdoer *deserves*; there is an intimate connection between the practice of blame and evaluations of moral desert.

As I have suggested, Strawson's understanding of the practice of blame emphasizes the retributive sentiments. Retributive punishment – which ensures that a culpable wrongdoer experiences a corresponding loss – is presented as a natural extension of blame. Strawson is explicit about this. He connects the moral "reactive attitudes" with a retributive notion of justice, by linking morally reactive attitudes with our disposition to inflict harm on wrongdoers. Punitive thoughts and actions, he believes, are fitting responses to ill will. Furthermore, he thinks the value of retribution would ideally be accepted by wrongdoers themselves; judgments of moral desert that support the practice of punishment are properly internalized.[2] He argues that all parties who are sensitive to the demands of morality would naturally affirm the appropriateness of inflicting injury upon wrongdoers.

So understood, retributive punishment is a kind of public blame. Its expression is understood as deserved by criminal lawbreakers who commit the sort of heinous wrongs that earn broad and severe condemnation. The point is that blame – moral condemnation directed at the criminal actor – is called for when a person has committed a criminal wrong and displays bad intentions, motives, and attitudes. Criminal punishment serves as a justified expression of outrage that affirms the moral inferiority of criminal wrongdoers and inflicts deserved injury on them.

It should be noted that not all philosophies of blame are retributive in nature. For example, T.M. Scanlon rejects the retributive notion that the point of blaming responses is to impose a loss on culpable wrongdoers (Scanlon 2010: 128–9; see also Scanlon 2013: 104). Even though blame often has negative consequences for persons who are rightfully blamed, Scanlon thinks it is not morally important that we guarantee that it does. He argues that certain moral judgments, emotive reactions, and sanctioning behavior are warranted by virtue of a wrongdoer's personal qualities, and the wrongdoer deserves these responses, whether or not they in fact injure her. For instance, we may have reasons to mistrust, disapprove of, and distance ourselves from someone who has wronged us. These are fitting responses, and may in fact harm the wrongdoer, even though morality does not require us to impose that harm as a matter of retribution.

There is a meaningful difference between Scanlon's view and a retributive philosophy, but I will not concern myself with it. My rejection of punishment as blame applies to nonretributive as well as retributive accounts of moral blame. It applies to any account of blame that is *required* by morality or justice as a response to culpable wrongdoing. In what follows, my criticisms of the retributive theory extend to nonretributive justifications of punishment as moral blame.

I now turn to the nature and shortcomings of an understanding of punishment as blame. The idea that the public function of punishment is to blame criminal wrongdoers fits the practice of criminal justice, at least in the United States. Moral condemnation is tightly associated with criminal punishment. It is expressed through the stigma and deprivations that accompany punishment. The humiliation and indignity of punishment, as it is currently practiced, impose a serious social stigma on people who have been convicted, especially those who are or have been incarcerated. Furthermore, the stigma of criminality, when it is formally imposed through conviction and sentencing in a court of law, is accompanied by the retraction, often permanent, of important entitlements and rights in addition to basic liberty. In many US states, for example, the right to vote is withdrawn, as is eligibility for public assistance and student loans, even after a convicted person's sentence has been served. Many job applications require disclosure of felony convictions, however minor the crime or long ago it was committed. It is not illegal to discriminate against felons who apply for housing, employment, mortgages, or admission to college. Many states deny certification to ex-felons in professions like automotive repair, construction, and plumbing. These measures deepen the stigma of criminality by extending its reach in social and political space and over time. As the legal scholar Michelle Alexander has argued, felons become second-class citizens for the rest of their lives (Alexander 2010; Jacobs 2015).

The stigma of criminality expresses a moral conclusion about the criminally guilty in view of their criminal behavior: they are morally blameworthy because they are legally guilty. Yet the basis of criminal conviction is often morally inadequate to produce this assessment. Social and psychological factors that may shape our moral evaluation of people have little or no bearing on criminal liability. The influence of mental illness or racial injustice, for instance, has little to no relevance to determinations of criminal guilt. In most cases, mental illness functions as an excuse only when it fits the legal definition of insanity, a highly specialized notion that does not include bipolar disorder, autism, or many other forms of mental illness. And courts have thrown out racial discrimination as a basis for challenging criminal conviction and sentencing – for the perverse reason that such discrimination is too common.[3] A person facing a statistically higher likelihood of a harsher sentence because of his race cannot use that unfairness as a legal basis for objecting to his sentence.

Let me elaborate. In prison you are not likely to find psychologically healthy people who were leading promising lives. Instead, you meet people who had hard lives before landing in prison. Many incarcerated people struggle with mental illness, including sociopathy, schizophrenia, and bipolar disorder. Others have suffered abuse or neglect as children, mistreatment that harms emotional development. According to a report by the US Department of Justice, over half of all prison inmates have a mental health disorder (James and Glaze 2006). It is difficult to believe that *these* are the people who *deserve* the hard treatment they get.

Consider some cases that you might read about in law textbooks. Eric Clark shot and killed a police officer. American society demands the harshest penalties for crimes like his. Eric Clark was convicted of first-degree murder and received a life sentence. In 2006, the US Supreme Court heard his appeal.[4] Why? Because when Eric Clark pulled the trigger, it was a desperate effort to defeat a dangerous space alien. The Court acknowledged Clark's delusional schizophrenia but affirmed his conviction and life sentence. It ruled that his psychosis was irrelevant to determining whether he intended to kill a human being.

Now consider Sharon Patterson's case.[5] She was caring for a two year old boy who was not her son. When he wet his bed, she decided to stop giving him water in the evening. He also sometimes refused solid foods and, to get him to eat, she decided to restrict his water during the day as well. Withholding water from a child is a dangerous thing to do and, as a result, the boy died. Sharon Patterson was charged with criminally negligent homicide, found guilty, and given ten years in prison.

It is also the case, and presumably morally relevant, that Sharon Patterson is intellectually disabled. She didn't understand the harm she was doing. She thought she was helping. The court recognized that she did not understand the danger of her actions, but it upheld her conviction on the basis that a reasonable person would have recognized it.

What about a person who steals to support a drug addiction? Over 2 million people are afflicted by an opioid disorder in the United States today. But addiction does not mitigate punishment for any crime. Or consider the thousands of cases, in the United States, of people sentenced to life in prison for crimes they committed as juveniles (Rovner 2017). The state of Pennsylvania alone has more than 480 people serving life sentences they received as juveniles. Studies show that childhood abuse and neglect increase criminal delinquency by at least 40% (Widom 1992; see also Widom 1989). That truth, however, mitigates neither guilt nor punishment.

The American legal system has decreed that people such as these are legally culpable. Though the personal hardships of mental illness, trauma, and addiction represent problems that would be difficult for most people to manage well, none of them mitigates the law's assessment of criminal culpability, or not much. The same holds for the limitations of intellectual disability and immaturity. Short of the extremes of mental illness that qualify as legal "insanity," the vast majority of mentally ill, intellectually disabled, traumatized, addicted, and immature people are ruled criminally guilty when it has been established that they have committed criminal acts. It is hard to make *ethical* sense of these *legal* results. At the very least, they pose a serious challenge to the notion that moral retribution fits the law.

Of course, it might be objected that the American criminal justice system does not *now* deliver just deserts, but it *could*, were we to mitigate the sentences of teenagers, people afflicted with mental illness or addiction, and those who are intellectually disabled. Actually, the courts have expressed some sympathy with this idea, at least when it comes to the very harshest penalties, specifically, the death penalty and life without parole. They have ruled that the death penalty is unconstitutional when applied to juveniles or the mentally ill, and that juveniles cannot receive mandatory sentences of life without parole.[6]

It might also be thought that we should also go easier on people with substance addictions. The devastating opioid epidemic in the United States has increased public sympathy for a less punitive approach to the crimes of addiction. Now that addiction is no longer imagined to afflict only the ghetto poor, it has become a cause of public outcry. For example, the attorney general of the state of Massachusetts is currently suing the corporate pushers of prescription painkillers on behalf of the public.[7]

So it might be thought that by punishing less, and more selectively, we still have a chance to deliver retributive justice. But some disturbing facts would remain. American prisons are filled with people who are poor. Data from the Bureau of Justice Statistics indicates that incarcerated people across all race and ethnicity groups earned about 40% less before going to prison than their non-incarcerated peers (Rabuy and Kopf 2015: 1; Bureau of Justice Statistics 2004). These are the poorest of the poor. They are also, disproportionately, people who have suffered racial harassment, discrimination, and other forms of racialized mistreatment (The Sentencing Project 2018). For example, aggressive policing tactics in inner city neighborhoods influence the arrest rate. Although blacks are not more likely to use drugs than whites, they are more likely to be arrested and incarcerated for drug use (Edwards, Bunting and Garcia 2013).

Socioeconomic disadvantage also influences the crime rate in poor, inner-city neighborhoods – racially segregated neighborhoods with failing schools and few jobs. More crimes are committed in disadvantaged neighborhoods. Socioeconomic deprivation is not, however, a factor that mitigates a criminal offender's "just deserts." An impoverished person has no legal excuse or justification for selling illegal drugs to sustain a living. Nor does lack of police protection provide a legal excuse for the crime of gang affiliation, or the illegal possession of a weapon, whether or not a person who lives in gang territory would otherwise fear for his personal safety. Furthermore, the seriously unjust condition of the racialized ghetto does not mitigate criminal guilt for a person's oppositional use of violence.

These facts pose a serious problem for the retributivist and, more broadly, for blaming approaches to the justification of punishment. The focus of these philosophies is the idea that punitive responses to wrongdoing are *deserved* because of what a wrongdoer is like as a person. A conclusion about moral desert is grounded in an assessment of what a person's criminal behavior tells us about what she is like. That evaluation is largely insensitive to the causes and context of a person's criminal choice, except when it blocks ordinary inferences from wrongful action to bad will, for example, because a person is coerced or deceived. Granted, it might be argued that there are moral reasons to expand legally recognized excusing conditions. But, even if we do, it would still be the case, on blaming accounts of punishment, that when a wrongdoer actually displays morally faulty values and character, the social conditions that trigger a person's wrongful behavior or have influenced the person to become the way she is are beside the point of criminal justice. Morally culpable wrongdoing calls for punishment. To that extent, measures of social disadvantage rightfully drop out of the criminal process.

This way of thinking is not entirely misguided. Some actions – including robbery, assault, rape, and murder – are wrong under *any* circumstances, however difficult those circumstances may be. A criminal justice system must hold people accountable for committing such wrongs, in this sense: we owe it to victims and to law-abiding citizens to dissuade all people from committing wrongs like these and to protect ourselves from criminal wrongdoers, sometimes by removing them from society. A morally legitimate criminal justice system will protect our basic rights from wrongful violations by other people, however disadvantageous the circumstances may be that incline a wrongdoer to violate another person's rights.

A "rights protecting" approach to criminal justice is morally defensible, but it does not support blaming theories of punishment. The essence of blaming theories is that we are obligated to mark a criminal offender as *bad* – someone who is morally inferior, defective, and unworthy – and deserving of punishment on that basis. So understood, the practice of punishment invests in an inference from the wrongfulness of the criminal act to the badness of the criminal wrongdoer. It purports to license a condemnatory personal judgment and the negative sentiments that often accompany it – moralized anger, disgust, hatred, and a desire to punish. Its conclusion that punishment is deserved and required by justice depends on the importance of these "retributive sentiments" to morality.

The problem is that judgments about personal badness are hard to contain. "Badness" extends beyond the criminal wrongdoer. It goes to the circumstances under which a person commits a crime. It encompasses struggling neighborhoods, childhood exposure to violence and abuse, lack of critical resources and opportunities, weak social structures, peer pressure, lack of personal security, and psychiatric emergencies. These are powerfully bad things. In fact, the more a person's troublesome psychological and social circumstances affect our understanding of a person's morally faulty choices, the harder it is to make sense of where a person's responsibility begins and ends. We cannot thoughtfully or honestly keep our focus on what a person deserves. When a person's individual "badness" begins to seem, in context, even somewhat understandable, our evaluations of moral desert lose their grip (Indermaur et al. 2012). People may deeply disagree about what counts as a wrongdoer's "just deserts," and reasonably so.

Without solid evaluations of moral desert, there is no stable public basis for retributive punishment or, more broadly, a blaming conception of punishment. Moral evaluation in this domain is insecure. In what follows I will analyze and elaborate this point. The upshot is that we should give up a commitment to punishment as blame. If we are justified in deploying measures to incapacitate and to deter people from committing crimes, it should not be on grounds of retributive justice or moral desert.

Now if Strawson is right, the idea that wrongdoing necessitates the retributive sentiments – namely, the notion that the retributive sentiments play a critical role in the "general framework of human life" – is an obstacle to relinquishing blaming theories of punishment. Yet the possibilities Strawson envisages for understanding and responding to wrongdoing are too narrow. Evaluating an agent's will in connection with its context and causes broadens our moral options for nonblaming responses. It shows how evaluating an agent's ill will can lead to empathy rather than blame. Through our understanding we may come to acknowledge the moral significance of difficulties that beset a person, whether psychological or social. Our emotive response might be compassionate, even when the wrongdoer's unfortunate personal history has led the wrongdoer to acquire qualities we justifiably criticize. Compassion reflects our understanding of how and why a person is morally damaged, insensitive, rash, or otherwise misguided. Rejecting morally undesirable characteristics and the wrongful behavior that results from them is compatible with a compassionate response to the wrongdoer. Compassion is also consistent with acknowledging harm done to victims. A nonblaming response can acknowledge the reality and personal impact of wrongdoing and, more generally, the significance of a wrongdoer's moral flaws.

A morally sensitive person is free to choose from a range of reasonable moral responses to another person in view of her wrongdoing. Though a person whose rights have been violated might not feel morally free to choose a response, since reactions can be reflexive and highly emotional, a number of responses remain morally possible. Responses might be unforgiving or merciful, angry or detached, sorrowful or withdrawn.[8] Each in a variety of moral positions has different personal and interpersonal meaning and consequences, and the moral enactment of a response implicates the responder in ways that are significant but not morally required. At a personal level, judging a wrongdoer blameworthy and engaging in blame closes off some relationship possibilities by, for example, solidifying feelings of mistrust, diminishing interest in friendship or intimacy, and prompting feelings of anger and resentment or a desire to meet injury with injury. The exercise of a prerogative to blame might also deepen relationships by insisting that the wrongdoer answer for her wrong by providing an account of it, a meaningful apology, the expression of good intentions going forward, and so on. On the other hand, contemplating hardships that mitigate blame might open up other avenues for engagement: greater psychological understanding, feelings of compassion, empathy, and the painful yet binding intimacy of confronting a moral misdeed together.

The personal dynamics of blame and its alternatives extend to people who do not know one another. Anger, retributive sentiments, and a desire to secure an apology are common responses to wrongdoing between strangers. A desire to understand is also familiar, and feelings of empathy might well follow an effort to understand. My point is that blame is not required – we have no grounds for criticizing a victim who does not blame – when compassion is a morally reasonable option, and that this is the case more often than most blame theorists suggest. In particular, it is the case when it comes to assessing criminal behavior, since much criminal behavior is causally related to significant hardships faced by the agent. The moral relevance of, for example, trauma, illness, or social injustice is incompatible with an obligation to blame criminals for their unlawful actions, and we demonstrate respect for victims by permitting them room to decide how to manage their own moral response to the crimes they have suffered. Many moral philosophers fail to see this because their account of the ethics of blame is grounded in a categorical assessment of the moral meaning of wrongdoing: wrongdoing that is not offset by defective moral agency on the part of the wrongdoer demands blame. We should reject this view – it is too uncompromising, too rigid.

When we consider the full range of morally engaged relationships, not all of which involve blame, we should conclude that criminal law institutions should not be in the business of blame. There are morally reasonable responses to wrongdoing that do not force us to choose between blaming and a disengaged, objectifying stance of treatment and control, the only two options presented by Strawsonian philosophies of blame and excuse. Instead of reacting with blame, persons who are mistreated might instead come to believe that the obstacles the wrongdoer encountered – circumstantial pressures, strong impulses, personal trauma, social alienation – were understandably, although not justifiably, mishandled. Though it is easiest to accept that it is the victim who is morally permitted to refrain from blaming, others who are involved might also suspend blame. Even grave moral wrongs might be viewed as tragic for everyone involved (Mohamed 2015). This response is compatible with morality.

The position I am elaborating is compatible with maintaining that there are limits to a reasonable range of moral options for responding to wrongdoing. There are cases in which moral blame is misdirected. An agent might be so immature or impaired, or her circumstances so disabling to moral motivation, that either agency ought not be attributed to her, or her actions, while hers, do not reflect her values, dispositions, motives, and characteristics, that is, what she is like. It is plausible to maintain that when a person fails to meet minimal standards of rationality, or is coerced, moral blame is inappropriate. These sorts of cases might be thought to be represented, in a rough way, by the function of nominate excuses in criminal law, such as insanity, immaturity, duress, and necessity. Excuses recognized by criminal law offer grounds for limiting criminal liability by serving as a defense against criminal charges. These criminal defenses represent an "objective" standard through being very strict – imposing a high bar for a defendant seeking to invoke them to avoid punishment.[9] For example, the defense of insanity requires proof that the defendant had, at the time of acting, no knowledge of the difference between right and wrong. When the relevant standard is met, defendants are not guilty of the criminal charges. Excuses as criminal defenses are seldom successful.

Failure to secure a nominate excuse leaves considerable latitude for contemplating mitigating factors that are compatible with criminal wrongdoing and might reasonably trigger compassion or otherwise justifiably quell vindictive and righteous moral sentiments and dispositions. I am arguing that this wider domain of moral assessment depends on an important subjective element – a choice about whether and how to relate to a wrongdoer, above the threshold set by legally recognized excuses or, more specifically, the moral threshold of basic responsibility those excuses represent. The subjective dimension of evaluation means that imposing criminal punishment should not be used as an opportunity for the state to express blame.

Of course, some defendants do not appear to have suffered any hardship. Relatively privileged people who have been treated well, enjoyed opportunities to satisfy their needs and develop their interests, and are psychologically healthy – or at least not very unhealthy – seem like excellent candidates for blame. Suppose such a person commits a crime. In the absence of any evidence of hardship, might we be required to blame him? Naturally, these cases would not include criminal activity that is deranged, cruel, or compulsive. Perhaps psychologically healthy defendants who have acted out of "ordinary" dishonesty, jealousy, greed, egoism, bias, or selfishness deserve moral blame. Whether they deserve retribution is a further question, but a refined retributive thesis that applies only in cases like this would be more palatable and also radically constrained, though it might often attract nagging suspicions that the people it targets suffer more serious problems that are not obvious.

I conclude that, above the lower limit set by nominate excuses, the possibility of blame for criminal behavior is negotiable, at least in a wide range of cases. Available moral responses have subjective conditions, and if the subjective conditions of blame are as I construe them, collective blame is not morally obligatory. We are each morally entitled, within the relationships in which we stand, personal and impersonal, to blame those who have done us wrong. We are similarly entitled to decide, within reasonable limits set by the acknowledgment of wrongdoing, that blaming does not fit our stance or interest within a relationship. This important domain of moral choice enables us in myriad ways either to distance ourselves from or to confront the psychological and interpersonal dynamics of wrongdoing, something about which we can have differing interests and aptitudes without offending morality.

While there are limits to what counts as a reasonable stance – that is, a stance compatible with recognizing that a moral wrong was done and that the wrongdoer met minimal conditions of rationality – within those limits lies the negotiable territory in which moral relationships take shape and evolve over time. The ethical value of a prerogative to blame or to excuse by engaging the wrongdoer's psychic world with compassion and understanding is evidence for the contingency of blame. In many instances of wrongdoing, a range of attitudes, more or less engaged, more or less demanding, more or less angry or righteous or sympathetic or compassionate are morally permissible. The appropriateness of a response depends on whether the respondent chooses to relate to the wrongdoer as righteous judge, empathetic partner, restrained bystander, or from some other morally acceptable position.

The conditional nature of blame – the subjective aspect of a decision about whether and how to position oneself in relation to a person who has done wrong – entails that blame is a poor foundation for criminal punishment. Though the relationship between a person's ill will and her life circumstances sets some limits to how other people may permissibly respond, it is not the state's job to guide or force us in that personal domain of moral choice. If it is acceptable for victims to refrain from engaging in blame, then it is implausible to think it should be morally required for us collectively, through actions by the state, to blame people who are criminally guilty. An individual's sentence should not be a function of a victim's subjective disposition to blame, or of the state's supposing the moral necessity of a blaming response. Blame is not required as a matter of law or justice. And since the retributive theory insists that there is a punitive blaming response required by justice, we should reject the retributive theory.

A blaming stance does not fit well with the general form of criminal law. It fits poorly with the public nature of criminal law: the collective nature of our obligation through law to redress violations of individual rights. In criminal law, redress is formulated in terms of the public's interest and obligation, which is to make it clear that certain types of behavior are forbidden and intolerable, to discourage people from engaging in those types of behavior, and, when available, to take other measures, such as restitution, to address harms to victims. A duty to redress criminal wrongs generalizes across the citizenry, even though the heaviest burdens appropriately fall on people who have been convicted of crimes.[10] In these respects, the criminal law enterprise is driven by the public moral importance of rights and the equal moral status of right-holders. Its basic function is to guide people's actions, generally speaking, in a way that respects and protects rights, not to engage or disengage moralistically with the meaning of wrongdoing for assessing a wrongdoer's personhood.[11] This is to say that criminal law is rightly act-focused, rather than attitude-focused. We can and should reject behavior that violates public moral norms that are legitimately codified in criminal law. It is the responsibility of the criminal justice system to sanction such conduct as a form of intolerable wrongdoing. We are responsible for maintaining a standard of behavior consistent with the basic rights of all individuals and with important shared interests, and our collective obligation to protect the basic rights and liberties of our fellow citizens supports the permissibility of burdening criminal lawbreakers with punishment when doing so is necessary to defend our basic rights. But there is no blaming stance we are required as citizens to take toward criminal wrongdoers. Although we have obligations to control one another's wrongful behavior, we are not obligated to blame.

Deploying the state's power to condemn the personification of "evil" has historically not gone well. From the Salem witch trials, to fabricated rape charges against Black American men perceived as threats to white women and white male sexuality,[12] to extreme sentences for "crack pushers,"[13] to dubious legal provisions in the war on terror – such as the indefinite detention by the US government of "enemy combatants" and abuse of the Material Witness Law to incarcerate suspects indeterminately (Malhotra 2005) – persons in positions of power have too frequently permitted or manipulated our moral commitments and our fears to rationalize abuses. A criminal justice system that remains focused on evidence of wrongdoing could avoid abuses like these.[14] We could insist on evidence of wrongdoing and dangerousness before applying criminal sanctions, and we could calibrate those sanctions to that evidence. People who commit heinous crimes should be brought to justice, yet using the moral language of evil to motivate the point of criminal justice is, morally speaking, a highly risky prospect, especially in a society characterized by racial injustice, serious socio-economic inequality, and a woefully inadequate safety net.

A legitimate democratic state must defend, with fair defensive measures, the equal rights of all citizens. But it does not need to blame people who are found criminally guilty in order to take measures to do so. Furthermore, the moral basis of a state's permission to burden criminal wrongdoers with punishment does not license its morally righteous condemnation of them. It is enough that it criticize, even condemn, their criminal acts as wrongful violations of the public's interest and, specifically, the public's obligation to protect all people's basic rights. Punishment can and should remain focused on this dimension of wrongdoing. It should not involve moral evaluations of an offender's blameworthiness. Doing without blame fits better with the actual basis of criminal liability in criminal law. Forgoing blame would also enable us better to reintegrate people into society after they serve their sentences, and to consider alternatives to prison when incarceration is not necessary to further the legitimate aims of criminal justice. This reorientation would, however, require a significant revision in the public moral discourse surrounding criminal convictions.

Notes

1 I have developed these arguments in Kelly 2018.

2 Strawson writes:

> The preparedness to acquiesce in that infliction of suffering on the offender which is an essential part of punishment is all of a piece with this whole range of attitudes of which I have been speaking. It is not only moral reactive attitudes towards the offender which are in question here. We must mention also the self-reactive attitudes of offenders themselves. Just as the other-reactive attitudes are associated with a readiness to acquiesce in the infliction of suffering on an offender, within the "institution" of punishment, so the self-reactive attitudes are associated with a readiness on the part of the offender to acquiesce in such infliction without developing the reactions (e.g. of resentment) which he would normally develop to the infliction of injury upon him; i.e. with a readiness, as we say, to accept punishment as "his due" or as "just."
>
> *Strawson 2003: section 6*

3 See *McClesky v. Kemp,* 481 U.S. 279 (1987).

4 *Clark v. Arizona,* 548 U.S. 735 (2006).

5 *State v Patterson,* 131 Conn. App. 65 (2011).

6 See *Atkins v. Virginia* 536 U.S. 304 (2002), *Roper v. Simmons,* 543 U.S. 551 (2005), *Miller v. Alabama* 132 S. Ct. 2455 (2012), and *Jackson v. Hobbs* 132 S. Ct. 548 (2011).

7 *Commonwealth of Massachusetts v. Purdue Pharma.* Superior Court C.A. No. 1884-cv-01808 (BLS2). January 15, 2019. https://d279m997dpfwgl.cloudfront.net/wp/2019/01/Mass_AGO_Pre-Hearing_Memo_and_Exhibits.pdf.

8 Some philosophers who write about forgiveness agree that forgiveness cannot be morally required; see Calhoun 1992. Compare Hieronymi 2001. The view that forgiveness should not be demanded of victims has generated criticism of the South African Truth and Reconciliation Commission, which included the aim that victims forgive perpetrators.

9 It would be possible, on the account of the conditions of moral responsibility I am proposing, to argue for a "subjective" interpretation of some legally recognized excuses. I leave this interesting question for another time.

10 Victor Tadros (2011, especially chapter 12) also relies on a notion of redress in developing a nonretributivist account of punishment. However, he conceives of the duty of redress as falling on individual offenders, while I am suggesting that the duty is collective.

11 Arthur Ripstein (1999) takes a similar position. I agree with Ripstein's emphasis on the distinction between punishment and blame (1999: 146). Where I differ is in the idea that a response to criminal wrongdoing

must involve hard treatment. If it does not, Ripstein argues, the public response to the criminal wrong will function as a mere price tag. I doubt that moral condemnation of criminal acts can be expressed only via hard treatment. On the public nature of criminal law and its relation to democratic equality, see also Vincent Chiao (2018).

12 For a powerful historical overview and analysis, see Alison Edwards (1979).

13 In 2010, the Fair Sentencing Act reduced a 100:1 federal sentencing differential for crack versus powder cocaine to an 18:1 disparity.

14 For example, international criminal tribunals have demonstrated a cautious approach. The International Criminal Court rejects the death penalty and it aims for reconciliation. It is moderated by international standards and is less easily confounded with a particular society's mechanisms of social exclusion, hierarchical structure, or systems of oppression. See Whiting 2009; Scharf and Schabas 2002.

References

Alexander, M. (2010) *The New Jim Crow: Mass Incarceration in the Age of Colorblindness*. New York: New Press.

Bureau of Justice Statistics (2004) "Survey of Inmates in State Correctional Facilities." www.bjs.gov/index.cfm?ty=dcdetail&iid=275.

Calhoun, C. (1992) "Changing One's Heart," *Ethics* 103: 76–96.

Chiao, V. (2018) *Criminal Law in the Age of the Administrative State*. New York: Oxford University Press.

Edwards, A. (1979) *Rape, Racism, and the White Women's Movement: An Answer to Susan Brownmiller,* 2nd edition. Chicago: Sojourner Truth Organization.

Edwards, E., Bunting, W. and Garcia, L. (2013) "The War on Marijuana in Black and White." American Civil Liberties Union. www.aclu.org/sites/default/files/field_document/1114413-mj-report-rfs-rel1.pdf.

Hieronymi, P. (2001) "Articulating an Uncompromising Forgiveness," *Philosophy and Phenomenological Research* 62: 529–55.

Indermaur, D. et al. (2012) "A Matter of Judgment: The Effects of Information and Deliberation on Public Attitudes to Punishment," *Punishment and Society* 14: 147–65.

Jacobs, J.B. (2015) *The Eternal Criminal Record*. Cambridge, MA: Harvard University Press.

James, D.J. and Glaze, L.E. (2006) "Mental Health Problems of Prison and Jail Inmates," Bureau of Justice Statistics Special Report, U.S. Department of Justice. www.bjs.gov/content/pub/pdf/mhppji.pdf.

Kelly, E.I. (2018) *The Limits of Blame: Rethinking Punishment and Responsibility*. Cambridge, MA: Harvard University Press.

Malhotra, A. (2005) "Witness to Abuse: Human Rights Abuses under the Material Witness Law since September 11," in Fellner, J. et al. (eds) *Human Rights Watch* 17. www.hrw.org/report/2005/06/26/witness-abuse/human-rights-abuses-under-material-witness-law-september-11.

Mohamed, S. (2015) "Of Monsters and Men: Perpetrator Trauma and Mass Atrocity," *Columbia Law Review* 115: 1157–1216.

Rabuy, B. and Kopf, D. (2015) "Prisons of Poverty: Uncovering the Pre-incarceration Incomes of the Imprisoned," 9 July, Prison Policy Initiative. www.prisonpolicy.org/reports/income.html.

Ripstein, A. (1999) *Equality, Responsibility and the Law*. Cambridge: Cambridge University Press.

Rovner, J. (2017) "Juvenile Life Without Parole: An Overview," *The Sentencing Project*. www.sentencingproject.org/publications/juvenile-life-without-parole/.

Scanlon, T.M. (2010) *Moral Dimensions: Permissibility, Meaning, Blame*. Cambridge, MA: Harvard University Press.

Scanlon, T.M. (2013) "Giving Desert its Due," *Philosophical Explorations* 16: 101–16.

Scharf, M.P. and Schabas, W.A. (2002) *Slobodan Milosevic on Trial: A Companion*. New York: Continuum.

Strawson, P.F. (2003) "Freedom and Resentment." *Proceedings of the British Academy* 48 (1962): 1–25. Reprinted in Gary Watson, ed., *Free Will*, 2nd ed. Oxford: Oxford University Press.

Tadros, V. (2011) *The Ends of Harm: The Moral Foundations of Criminal Law*. Oxford: Oxford University Press.

The Sentencing Project (2018) "Report of The Sentencing Project to the United Nations Special Rapporteur on Contemporary Forms of Racism, Racial Discrimination, Xenophobia, and Related Intolerance: Regarding Racial Disparities in the United States Criminal Justice System," 19 April. www.sentencingproject.org/publications/un-report-on-racial-disparities/.

Whiting, A. (2009) "In International Criminal Prosecutions, Justice Delayed can be Justice Delivered," *Harvard International Law Journal* 50: 323–64.

Widom, C.S. (1989) "Child Abuse, Neglect, and Adult Behavior: Research, Design, and Findings on Criminality, Violence, and Child Abuse," *American Journal of Orthopsychiatry* 59: 355–67.

Widom, C.S. (1992) "The Cycle of Violence," *National Institute of Justice: Research in Brief*. US Department of Justice.

10
THE RIGHT TO PUNISH

Mike C. Materni

Introduction

Criminal law is the branch of law that, perhaps more than any other, *defines* the system of government of which it is the *political expression*. While all law is, at its core, an eminently political enterprise (Fuller 1934; Llewellyn 1931),[1] criminal law holds special political status because, as one jurist observed about a century ago, "[t]he theory of government is reflected particularly in the penal law, because that is the most powerful legal means which the government has at its disposal to achieve its political objectives" (Battaglini 1933: 278).

In modern-day America, beyond being an eminently political enterprise, criminal law and criminal punishment are also a *pervasive* enterprise. The United States, with an incarceration rate of 666 prisoners per 100,000 US residents, holds the dubious honor of ranking highest among OECD countries for per capita incarceration levels.[2] In fact, with a total population of 2.3 million currently detained,[3] the United States has boasted the highest incarceration rate in the world – with the only exception being the Seychelles.[4] At the same time, there are about 4,500[5] federal laws carrying criminal penalties (Smith 2013). As one commentator put it: "[W]e have too much punishment and too many crimes in the United States today. We overpunish and overcriminalize" (Husak 2008: 4). Thus, the long-debated topic of criminal punishment remains as relevant as ever, as a matter of both theory and practice.

Most of the existing scholarship on criminal punishment has focused its attention on the so-called "purposes of punishment"; namely, retribution, deterrence, rehabilitation, and incapacitation – i.e. the end-goals that criminal punishment is meant (or, at the very least, supposed) to achieve. In this chapter, I adopt a different perspective. Rather than looking at the objectives, or goals, of criminal punishment to offer a justification of the practice, I aim to offer a theory of what principles, conditions, and limits ought to justify, and therefore define, the imposition of criminal punishment by the state. Put another way, I will try to offer a justification of the state's right to punish – or, rather, a theory of *when* resort to criminal punishment by the state is *justified*. This is not to say that there is no pre-existing scholarship that addresses this issue – indeed, there is plenty (see e.g. Ashworth 2008; Brown 2010; Duff et al. 2010, 2011, 2013; Feinberg 1984 [1988]; Hart 1968; Husak 2008; Jareborg 2004; Kadish 1987; Luna 2005; Schonsheck 1994; Smith 2013). Two features, however, distinguish the approach proposed in this chapter.

First, I submit that the principles advocated here should not be endorsed because they are ultimately – in the sense of absolutely, or "metaphysically" – correct. Rather, they should be embraced as a matter of *political choice*. In line with the essay's opening premise that criminal law defines the system of government of which it is the political expression, I will advocate for principles that are suitable for a liberal democracy, defined quite simply – and without any aspiration or pretense to any level of sophistication in political science – as a system of government that is seriously committed to the individual liberties of those that it governs (Materni 2015). Second, I will seek to derive support for that political choice from – indeed, to ground that choice on – existing constitutional doctrine.

The chapter is structured as follows: First, I will present the principle of the *extrema ratio*, or "option of the last resort," as the guiding principle that should inform a liberal criminal law – i.e. the type of criminal law that ought to characterize a liberal democracy. Then, I will expound upon the two key principles upon which a criminal law adhering to the notion of the *extrema ratio* must rest – harm and proportionality. The ultimate thesis proposed in the chapter will be that since in a liberal democracy regulation of conduct through the criminal law should represent the *extrema ratio*, a liberal democracy should adopt a *minimalist criminal law* informed by the principles of harm and proportionality, and it should do so *as a matter of political choice*. In a liberal democracy, only if certain conditions are met will the government have a right to impose criminal punishment as the sanction for undesirable conduct.[6]

The Government's Right to Punish: Criminal Law as the *Extrema Ratio*

The conditions that legitimize the exercise of the government's power to impose criminal punishment have been debated from time immemorial.[7] The vast literature on the purposes of criminal punishment tells us *why*, or *for what purpose*, the state punishes offenders – to give them what they are due (retribution); to prevent them from offending (deterrence); to prevent them from re-offending and, ideally, reintegrate them into society (incapacitation; rehabilitation). These purposes of punishment, however, do not tell us *when* the state should punish. More precisely, they do not tell us *under what circumstances* the state's resort to regulating conduct though the criminal law, and therefore through the imposition of criminal punishment, is *justified*.

I suggest here that to find an answer to the latter question, we should take a *pragmatic approach* and start with *necessity*. Necessity is, arguably, the *ultimate* principle behind government action, including *extreme* government action such as criminal punishment. Whatever theory or concept of just punishment or government intervention or limits to governmental authority one may subscribe to, the empirical reality is that, as Oliver Wendell Holmes, Jr., put it, "[n]o society has ever admitted that it could not sacrifice individual welfare to its own existence. If conscripts are necessary for its army, it seizes them, and marches them, with bayonets in their rear, to death." (1881: 30) We will see shortly that relying on an *unfettered* principle of necessity is a knife that cuts both ways – as the old adage goes, necessity knows no law.[8] However, necessity, I submit here, also constitutes an excellent starting point to begin defining the limits of the government's right to resort to criminal punishment. This much at least believed Cesare Beccaria (1764), who, in a revolutionary book that became one of the most influential works in modern penology,[9] *On Crimes and Punishments*, wrote:

> [E]very act of authority of one man over another *that does not derive from absolute necessity* is tyrannical. This is the foundation, therefore, upon which the sovereign's right to punish crimes is based: the necessity to defend the depository of the public welfare from individual usurpations; and the more just the punishments, the more sacred and inviolable the security and the greater the liberty the sovereign preserves for his subjects.
>
> *(Beccaria 1764: 11; emphasis added)*

Subscribing to a contractual theory of the state favored by many Enlightenment thinkers, Beccaria contended that people, having tired of living in the Hobbesian state of nature, decided to come together and form civil society, "sacrific[ing] a portion of their liberty so that they could enjoy the remainder in security and peace" (10).[10] This, of course, meant that "[n]o man ever freely surrendered ... his own liberty" (11). Rather, Beccaria argued,

> [i]t was ... *necessity* that compelled men to give up part of their personal liberty; and so it is that each is willing to place in the public depository *only the least possible portion* ... The aggregate of these smallest possible portions constitutes the right to punish; everything that exceeds it is abuse, not justice; it is a matter of fact, not of right.
>
> *(12; emphasis added)*

The corollary – in fact, the other side of the coin – to Beccaria's claim that men, because of necessity, surrendered to the government only "the least possible portion" of their liberty is that the government's recourse to the most restrictive means of regulating conduct – the means that most deprives individuals of their liberty, i.e. the imposition of criminal punishment[11] – must be the *extrema ratio*, or option of the last resort. Perhaps more importantly, I suggest in this chapter that such a corollary ought to be adopted today, and that doing so finds support in, and in fact can be grounded upon, *existing* constitutional doctrine.[12]

Begin with the basic principle at the core of the American experiment: the *right* to *individual liberty*.[13] The Fifth and Fourteenth amendments to the United States Constitution mandate that no person shall be deprived of liberty without due process of law;[14] however, defining the meaning and content of "liberty" is neither immediately intuitive nor straightforward. The constitutional meaning of the word "liberty" has, in fact, evolved over time, encompassing a variety of concepts. For instance, "liberty" has been held to include the right to teach the German language to children,[15] the right to send one's child to parochial schools,[16] the right for married and unmarried couples to have access to contraceptives as part of their "right to privacy,"[17] the right to engage in homosexual relations,[18] and the right of same-sex couples to get married.[19]

If, in the words of Justice John Marshall Harlan, II, the liberty protected by the Constitution "is a rational continuum which, broadly speaking, includes a freedom from all substantial arbitrary impositions and purposeless restraints,"[20] then it follows necessarily that the liberty protected by the Constitution must also encompass what Justice Clarence Thomas has identified as the core, original meaning of "liberty" – namely, "freedom from physical restraint."[21] Put differently, if the umbrella of liberty protects – as Justice McReynolds wrote in *Meyer* –

> the right of the individual to contract, to engage in any of the common occupations of life, to acquire useful knowledge, to marry, establish a home and bring up children, to worship God according to the dictates of his own conscience, and generally to enjoy those privileges long recognized at common law as essential to the orderly pursuit of happiness by free men,[22]

then *a fortiori* that umbrella must protect an individual's right against arbitrary physical restraint at the hands of the government. Since regulation of conduct through the criminal law almost always comports *at the very least* an infringement of this freedom from physical restraint, then such regulation should be *prima facie* constitutionally suspect.

Note that this is not an argument that the government may not resort to criminal punishment. Rather, as I wrote elsewhere, it is an argument that

> [b]efore the government can regulate conduct by the most restrictive means at its disposal, infringing upon the *core* of liberty itself, there needs to be a compelling interest to achieve which there exist no less restrictive yet equally effective means. Which is to say, resort to governing by means of the criminal law should be subject to strict scrutiny.
>
> *(Materni 2016: 18)*

A strict scrutiny challenge is notoriously one that is quite difficult for the government to overcome (Winkler 2006). I have made the strict scrutiny argument elsewhere (Materni 2015), and insisting on it here would be beside the point. Rather, what matters for the arguments developed in this chapter is to take stock of the fact that settled constitutional doctrine has long recognized that the "liberty" that the criminal law puts "at stake" is an "interest of immense importance"[23] and of "transcending value."[24] This liberty *begins* with an individual's freedom from physical restraint (what we could call the "core" of "liberty"), but *goes far beyond that.* As a consequence of its violation, criminal law provides for an impairment of "the right to make basic decisions about the future; to participate in community affairs; to take advantage of employment opportunities; to cultivate family, business, and social relationships; and to travel from place to place."[25] Criminal punishment causes "a wrenching disruption of everyday life"[26] and

> seriously interfere[s] with the defendant's liberty, whether he is free on bail or not, and … may disrupt his employment, drain his financial resources, curtail his associations, subject him to public obloquy, and create anxiety in him, his family and his friends.[27]

The principle of the *extrema ratio* demands that, before the constitutionally protected liberty interest – as just defined – be infringed, "[t]he whole arsenal of the legal order must be put to use, and criminal law … may only be employed where other means (*e.g.*, private law litigation, administrative solutions, non-criminal sanctions, etc.) fail" (Jareborg 2004: 523). Which is another way of saying that, under the principle of the *extrema ratio*, the government may resort to criminal punishment only when doing so is *absolutely necessary*.

As anticipated earlier, the problem with necessity is that necessity knows no law. Furthermore, necessity tends to be subject to the "vicissitudes of political controversy"[28] and the turmoil of the times, such that what is "necessary" at any given point in time may be dictated by the dangers, real or perceived, relative to specific historical contingencies. As a matter of fact, some of the most severe abuses and infringements of individual rights in American history have not only been justified, but they have also been given an aura of legality, through the invocation of the principle of necessity – which is ironic, given that necessity was invoked precisely as the pretext for breaking the law.

For instance, when Abraham Lincoln, amidst the unfolding of the Civil War, suspended *habeas corpus* (see, e.g., Rehnquist 1998), he did so by invoking necessity as the rationale. Pointing to the urgency of the situation, and stressing the necessity to defend the Union against rebel forces, Lincoln asked:

> Are all the laws but one to go unexecuted, and the Government itself to go to pieces lest that one be violated? Even in such a case, would not the official oath be broken if the Government should be overthrown when it was believed that disregarding the single law would tend to preserve it?[29]

The answer was clear: a minor violation of a single law *would be justified to save the country from being destroyed.* (That, in any event, didn't matter, because, according to Lincoln, no such violation had occurred – he clearly had the power, under the Constitution, to suspend *habeas corpus* in order to preserve public safety).[30]

After the Civil War, the Supreme Court belatedly rebuked Lincoln, appearing to reject necessity as a reason to depart from the law.[31] However, a string of cases from the beginning of the 20th century, when the Supreme Court found itself deciding claims brought under the Espionage Act of 1917 involving the abridgement of the freedom of speech – a liberty interest expressly protected by the First Amendment and, therefore, having the same, or similar, constitutional rank as the liberty interests put at stake by the criminal law – provide a good example to showcase the power of necessity-based arguments at work, as well as their consequences with respect to the criminal law.

In *Schenck v. United States*,[32] the Supreme Court upheld the conviction of defendants Charles Schenck and Elizabeth Bear, who had printed and mailed leaflets urging conscripted draftees to assert their rights and oppose the draft, which the leaflets claimed was a form of slavery prohibited under the Thirteenth Amendment.[33] In rejecting the defendants' claim that their conduct was protected under the First Amendment, Oliver Wendell Holmes, Jr., writing for a unanimous court, argued that while "in ordinary times [the defendants' conduct] would have been within their constitutional rights … the character of every act depends upon the circumstances in which it is done."[34] Holmes analogized: "The most stringent protection of free speech would not protect a man in falsely shouting fire in a theater and causing a panic."[35] Then, Holmes spelled out the test to determine whether the defendants' conduct was entitled to constitutional protection:

> The question in every case is whether the words are used in such circumstances and are of such nature as to create a clear and present danger that they will bring about the substantive evil that Congress has a right to prevent.[36]

According to Holmes, such a question is "a question of proximity and degree"[37]; in times of war, the normal balance of interests shifts so that things that may normally be said in times of peace "are such a hindrance to [the nation's war effort] that their utterance will not be endured."[38] In other words, the *necessity* to prevent what is perceived to be a serious harm – here, the alleged hindrance to the nation's war effort – *trumped* the liberty interest in free speech, and, consequently, the liberty interest in "freedom from physical restraint."[39]

Following the reasoning laid out in *Schenck*, the Supreme Court, in *Frohwerk* v. *United States*,[40] *Debs* v. *United States*,[41] and *Abrams* v. *United States*[42] upheld the convictions of several World War I "dissidents," as well as four-time Socialist Party Presidential candidate Eugene Debs, for engaging in speech that was found to constitute a "clear and present danger" of hindering the war effort of the United States.[43] Once again, in the balancing exercise between the necessity to stave off a perceived danger in perilous times against the protection of constitutionally protected interests, necessity gained the upper hand.

The most egregious example of a violation of individual rights justified by necessity remains perhaps the internment of both aliens and American citizens of Japanese extraction during World War II. Following the Japanese attack on Pearl Harbor on December 7th, 1941, public pressure – bordering on hysteria – began to mount on the Roosevelt administration to deal with the "Japanese threat" (Stone 2005: 283–310). Ignoring the contrary pleas of Attorney General Francis Biddle, as well as a report by FBI Director J. Edgar Hoover indicating that all those believed to be subversive elements of Japanese descent were in FBI custody, on February 19th, 1942, President Franklin D. Roosevelt signed and issued Executive Order n. 9066, authorizing the Secretary of War to designate certain areas as "military zones." The order was then used to exclude all persons of Japanese ancestry, irrespective of citizen status, from most of the West Coast. In practice, this meant that, under the authority of the military, headed by General John DeWitt, over 100,000 individuals of Japanese extraction were forcibly relocated in internment camps outside of the "military zones" (Stone 2005: 283–310).

When Fred Korematsu, an American citizen of Japanese descent, brought suit challenging the constitutionality of the provisions that excluded him from certain areas on the basis of his race (Korematsu had been convicted for violating a military order to leave one such military zone, in a situation where his only alternatives were to either violate the order, or to voluntarily submit himself to indeterminate confinement in an internment camp), the Supreme Court sided with the government and upheld the constitutionality of the deportation and internment of Japanese-Americans. In *Korematsu* v. *United States*,[44] writing for a majority of six justices, Justice Hugo Black not surprisingly played the necessity card: "[A]ll legal restrictions which curtail the civil rights of a single racial group are immediately suspect [but that does not mean that they] are unconstitutional [because] *pressing public necessity* may … justify … such restrictions."[45] In an opinion granting absolute deference to military authorities (Black condescendingly and somewhat tautologically wrote that, while the military measures undoubtedly imposed substantial hardships on certain citizens, "hardships are part of war, and war is an aggregation of hardships"[46]), Justice Black ruled that "when under conditions of modern warfare our shores are threatened by hostile forces, the power to protect must be commensurate with the threatened danger."[47] The measures whose constitutionality was being challenged were directly related to the prevention of espionage and sabotage;[48] the authority to determine what was required by the necessity to protect the homeland in times of war – determinations over the type, level, and immediacy of the threat, and the best measures to respond to that threat – was given by Congress to the military;[49] and the Supreme Court was in no position to reject *ex-post* the findings of the military authorities.[50] In dissent, Justice Frank Murphy cautioned that the government could validly deprive an individual of his constitutional rights on the basis of necessity only when "the deprivation is reasonably related to a public danger that is so immediate, imminent, and impending as not to admit of delay and not to permit the intervention of ordinary constitutional processes to alleviate the danger."[51]

The foregoing are representative (though by no means exhaustive) historical and legal examples of the fact that relying on necessity can lead to breaching of pretty much any right, whether constitutionally protected or not. These examples also tell us something very important – that by building a system resting on necessity as a limiting principle, we run the risk of having a system with no limiting principle at all. But if the interests of "immense importance" and "transcending value" to individual liberty demand that the criminal law only be employed as the *extrema ratio*, and if the *extrema ratio* substantially coincides with necessity (and with all the baggage that necessity, the knife that cuts both ways, carries with it), then the question becomes one of developing further principles, or criteria, to delimit necessity in such a way as to allow the principle of the *extrema ratio* to function as it was intended to by those – Beccaria chief amongst them – who originally developed it: as a limit to government power; as a principle of civility in light of which "no civilized government sacrifices the citizen more than it can help" (Holmes 1881: 30). In the following sections, I will explore the principles of harm and proportionality as means to achieve precisely that goal.

Harm

The first step toward building principled limitations around necessity is to enlist the assistance of the harm principle. At its most basic level, as illustrated by John Stuart Mill (1863) in his essay *On Liberty*, the harm principle – which traces its roots back to at least Thomas Hobbes (1651) and John Locke (1690) – stands for the proposition that "the only purpose for which power can rightfully be exercised over any member of a civilized community, against his will, is *to prevent harm to others*" (Mill 1863: 23; emphasis added). Thus, we could begin by asserting that resort to criminal punishment as a means of regulating conduct is only necessary – and, therefore, it is only warranted – for conduct that will actually cause harm to third parties.

The advantage of this simplistic formulation is that it is very straightforward; its disadvantage is that, without further elaboration, it doesn't mean anything – and it is, therefore, useless. This is because we live in a complex, highly structured, interdependent society; a society where, like it or not, "[n]o man is an island, entire of himself," (Donne 1624) and, therefore, any activity or restraint thereof will likely cause *some degree of harm* to *some* individual or group (see, e.g., Coase 1960; Materni 2016: 12). Which is to say, "there is probably harm in most human activities and, in most cases, on both sides of the equation (Harcourt 1999: 121)."

This observation has led some to the conclusion that the harm principle has "effectively collaps[ed] under the weight of its own success" (*Id.* 139) and that, since "non-trivial harm arguments are being made about practically every moral offense," (*Id.* 114) the harm principle can no longer serve as a limiting principle (Harcourt 1999).

A first comment in that respect would be to note that the harm principle just referred to is a harm principle so broad that Mill would hardly recognize it. A second, related point to make is that not all harms are created equal; therefore, a key suggestion in this chapter is precisely that not all harms may properly be invoked to justify regulation of conduct through the criminal law. Properly framed, the question is how we can go about identifying those harms that can (see, e.g., von Hirsh 1996). For the harm principle to retain any power as a limiting principle, in fact, we need a way to discern harms that can serve as a predicate to criminal regulation from harms that cannot properly do so.

In prior writings, I suggested that a first distinction between harm that is suitable to constitute criminal harm, and harm that is not, could be the distinction between tangible and intangible harm (Materni 2016). I then proceeded to elaborate that

> *[t]angible* harm is a harm that is, in a sense, physical, at least insofar as it can be seen, or measured, including in terms of economic loss. Conversely, *intangible* harm is a harm that may exist but it is difficult to measure, quantify, and qualify, such as, for example, the harm that pornography might cause to "the interest of the public in the quality of life and the total community environment.
>
> *(Id. 14)*

Upon further reflection, however, I have come to believe that – at least for our purposes – the distinction between tangible and intangible harm should be abandoned. To begin with, as I noted when I proposed drawing that distinction, the distinction itself cannot be absolute, because "[t]here are borderline cases (*e.g.* assault), as well as cases that ... contain elements of both tangible and intangible harm (*e.g.* rape) that would seemingly not fit neatly into a bright tangible/intangible harm distinction" (*Id.* 15). What is more, as I acknowledged before (*Id.* 15–16), there may be instances of (purely) intangible harm that are severe enough to warrant being protected against by means of the criminal law.

This observation suggests that perhaps what matters for purposes of justifying resort to criminal regulation is not the *type* of harm (tangible vs. intangible), but, rather, the *degree* of harm. However, focusing only on degree runs the risk of justifying the criminalization of *all* conduct that causes harm *past a certain threshold*. This, in turn, would lead to a potentially endless amount of criminal regulation, which would be at odds with the principles espoused in this chapter.

A better way to identify and limit what harm(s) can properly serve as predicates for invoking criminal regulation of conduct is instead to take a step back and look at the underlying legal interests that we are seeking to protect against harm, which are, ultimately, the reason for having a criminal law in the first place. This requires flipping our epistemological approach – instead of defining what should be criminal in terms of harm, we will aim to define what counts as harm in function of what counts as crime. This perspective – while perhaps counterintuitive – draws support from (and, in fact, rests on) the writings of the Classical School of Criminal Law – the school of thought that must be credited with developing the modern, objective conception of criminal law (Materni 2015: 339–352).

The Classical School of criminal law, which embodied the principles of the classical liberalism of the 19th century, took to heart the message of Beccaria's *On Crimes and Punishments* (*Id.* 342). Reacting to the tremendous abuses that had characterized the exercise of state power via the criminal law throughout the *Ancien Régime*, the Classical School sought to develop a system grounded upon first principles designed to safeguard against government overreach (*Id.* 339–352; Materni 2016: 24–35). As part of that endeavor, the Classical School argued that the foundational justification of the criminal law was to be found in the principle of the legal protection of rights (see, *e.g.* Carrara 1875). The principle of the legal protection stood for the proposition that the criminal law's existence was justified insofar as it protected the rights of individuals against their infringement by others by attaching to that infringement, as a necessitated consequence, the imposition of criminal punishment

(Materni 2015: 344–347). In that spirit, the Classical School proposed a strictly *legal* definition of "crime" as

> the violation of a law of the state that was enacted to protect the security of citizens, violation which is the result of an external harmful act of the agent, positive or negative, and for which the agent is morally reprehensible.
>
> *(Carrara 1870: 197; quoted in Materni 2015: 348)*

Taking this legal definition of what constitutes a "crime" as the starting premise of our inquiry into what harm ought to be criminally relevant allows us to restrict the scope of criminal harm to harm caused to a subset of legally protected interests – those that have been deemed important enough that their protection has been entrusted to the criminal law by means of "a law of the state that was enacted to protect the security of citizens." This proposition has the benefit of clarifying and limiting the scope of the concept of harm that is relevant for the criminal law. However, this proposition is also circular, in that it begs the question of what interests ought to be considered important enough to warrant their protection by means of criminal regulation. Part of the answer in addressing this problem is to note that in a democracy, the selection of what interests are important enough to warrant protection through criminal regulation ought to be made by legislators, in their quality of elected representatives of the people – in other words, that selection ought to be the product of the democratic process. This, in turn, offers no guarantees that the selection will be informed by the restraint that I have been advocating throughout the chapter.

This answer will probably be quite disappointing for those who were hoping for straight, unequivocal answers; however, this is the price we pay for democracy. Nonetheless – and this is the other part of the answer – acknowledging that ultimately it will be democratically elected representatives who select what rights, or interests, ought to be protected by criminal regulation does not mean that this chapter cannot at least present a general framework that, I suggest, should guide those representatives' legislative choices.

If we postulate – with the Classical School – that the *raison d'être* of the criminal law is the legal protection of rights (or interests), then it follows that the right being protected by the criminal law, both in terms of substance and in terms of scope, is both the reason and limit of the criminal law itself (Materni 2015: 345). Since the criminal law puts "at stake" interests of "immense importance" and "transcending value," then perhaps a good corollary to draw from the perspective endorsed by the Classical School is that only interests of immense importance and transcending value should be protected through the criminal law – and, consequently, that only harm to interests of immense importance and transcending value ought to qualify as predicate to criminal regulation. It is this notion, then, that should guide legislators when they have to choose whether to regulate conduct through criminal legislation. This notion is rooted in (some version of) the principle of proportionality, to which we turn next.

Proportionality

In our endeavor to limit necessity through the harm principle, we have encountered another key notion – proportionality. Proportionality is an extensive and intricate doctrinal area (see, *e.g.*, Barak 2012; Stinneford 2011). In the legal context, perhaps the most immediate connection to proportionality is made with respect to what constitutes "proportionate punishment," which Eighth Amendment jurisprudence has come to define as punishment that is predicated upon "the evolving standards of decency that mark the progress of a maturing society."[52] The concept of proportionality that I propose in this chapter, however, is a slightly different and simplified notion. It does relate to the government's reaction to conduct, but at a different stage. Rather than looking at the *quantum* of punishment, the proportionality invoked here looks at *whether* the government should punish at all, versus some other kind of governmental regulatory intervention – i.e., whether resort to criminal punishment constitutes *a proportionate reaction* by the government.

The approach to proportionality discussed here dovetails with the approach to harm espoused in the previous section. If the criminal law puts at stake interests of "immense importance" and "transcending value," then resort to regulation of conduct through the criminal law will only be proportionate when the conduct being regulated threatens harm to interests of immense importance and transcending value. Once again, existing constitutional doctrine can help us ground this approach – specifically, the arguments laid out in two topical decisions in First Amendment and Fourth Amendment jurisprudence, namely *Whitney* v. *California*, 274 U.S. 357 (1927) and *Terry* v. *Ohio*, 392 U.S. 1 (1968) (*see*, Materni 2016: 38–39).

The First Amendment protects, among other things, the freedoms of speech and assembly; the Fourth Amendment protects the right to be free from unreasonable searches and seizures.[53] In a concurring opinion that constitutes a pillar of the modern approach to freedom of speech, Justice Louis Brandeis argued that only "the probability of serious injury to the State"[54] would legitimize abridgment of the right to free speech and assembly – rights that, like the right to liberty, are constitutionally protected. On the other hand, Brandeis claimed, "[p]rohibition of free speech and assembly is a measure so stringent that it would be inappropriate as the means for averting a relatively trivial harm to society."[55] Similarly, in *Terry* v. *Ohio*[56] the Supreme Court held that the test for determining "reasonableness" under the Fourth Amendment was to "balanc[e] the need to search (or seize) against the invasion that the search (or seizure) entails."[57] This meant that "police officers may proceed to a pat-down of a suspect's outer clothing only if they reasonably suspect that doing so will prevent harm to themselves or others" (Materni 2016: 39).

In *Whitney* as in *Terry*, proportionality was invoked to balance the amount of harm to be avoided against the infringement of constitutionally protected interests. Here, I am making the same argument: the harmful conduct that we want to regulate through the criminal law ought to be balanced against the constitutionally protected right to liberty. And, following the sliding scale approach adopted in *Whitney* and *Terry*, I suggest that the further away conduct is from being suitable to cause harm to an interest of "immense importance" and "transcending value," the less the government is entitled to infringe upon the constitutionally protected right to liberty by regulating that conduct through the criminal law. In other words, the regulatory response by the government should be directly proportional to the degree of the interest threatened by the conduct that is to be regulated – only then resort to criminal law may be deemed *necessary*.

This approach to proportionality allows us to short-circuit the circularity embedded in the proposition that only harm to a subset of pre-determined, legally protected interests ought to qualify for protection by means of the criminal law, which, as I noted earlier, begs the question of how to select those interests to be included in the subset. The interests of "immense importance" and "transcending value" that the criminal law puts at stake can all be subsumed under the constitutionally protected interest to "liberty." Following the approach to proportionality illustrated here, then, only conduct that threatens interests whose weight is equivalent or similar to the interest in liberty protected by the Constitution (= to the interest threatened by the imposition of the criminal sanction) ought to be regulated through the criminal law.

This answer is, of course, still imperfect. Reasonable people in good faith can and will disagree on whether a given interest is weighty enough to at least match if not outweigh the liberty interest threatened by the criminal sanctions – but this should be the discussion. Besides, those disagreements are more likely to occur around hard, or extreme, cases, where the relative comparison between interests is not readily intuitive. Those instances will be resolved necessarily, if perhaps imperfectly, through the political process – as indeed they should. On the other hand, I believe it will be far more likely that reasonable people in good faith will agree on instances where the liberty interests threatened by the criminal law far outweigh whatever other interests the criminal law may be trying to protect. For instance, and regardless of personal feelings and political leanings, I believe most reasonable people would be able to agree that whatever legally protected interest is threatened by vagrancy, laws criminalizing being homeless and imprisoning homeless people – which many cities across the United States have enacted and enforced in the decades since the Supreme Court decided *Papachristou* v. *City of Jacksonville* in 1972 – are hardly a proportional response in line with the principles advocated in this chapter (and this without even pointing to the evidence showing that alternatives to imprisonment of the homeless, including providing free housing to homeless individuals, would constitute a substantially economically cheaper option for the government compared to incarceration of those same individuals).[58] Which is to say, the liberty interest threatened by the criminal law far outweighs the interests allegedly threatened by homelessness, such that a different regulatory response by the state is required – one that does not infringe on liberty to the same degree that criminal regulation does. Some may argue that this example is on the extreme end of the spectrum. Insofar as this is true, however, it only proves that the example is instructive, and suited to provide a baseline from which we can start reviewing existing criminal regulations.

Of course, nowhere in the Constitution does it expressly say that the government's response must be proportional in the sense just described, nor does it say that only conduct creating a certain kind and degree of harm to others may legitimately be criminalized. Rather, these arguments have been drawn from and developed on the basis of well-established constitutional precedents. This, however, means that these arguments are, at the very least, plausible. I submit here that the reason why they should be embraced in a liberal democracy is not that they are ultimately, or absolutely (in a metaphysical sense) correct. Rather, these arguments, and the constraints that they suggest, should be embraced as a matter of political choice. The next section will illustrate why this is the case.

Extrema Ratio as Political Choice

Throughout the chapter, I have argued that in a liberal democracy regulation of conduct through the criminal law should be the *extrema ratio*, or option of the last resort. I have then proceeded to show that the principle of the *extrema ratio* coincides, at its core, with the necessity principle and that, therefore, for the *extrema ratio* to work as a limiting principle, necessity must be constrained by the principles of harm and proportionality. One question remains – why should a liberal democracy adopt the model of criminal law founded on harm and proportionality that I propose? The answer that I offer is, in a way, pretty straightforward: it should do so *as a matter of political choice*.

Recall the two opening premises of this chapter: that a liberal democracy is a system of government that is seriously committed to the individual liberties of those that it governs, and that the criminal law defines the system of government of which it is the political expression. We have seen previously how criminal regulation infringes upon interests of immense importance and of transcending value; indeed, how it infringes upon the core of liberty itself. Aside from the fact that the loss of liberty at issue with the criminal law, as we discussed earlier, is not limited to physical restraint, there are also other, practical costs that come with the imposition of a prison sentence. For instance, prisons often resemble "Dante's inner circles of hell"[59], with inmates hoarded in overcrowded facilities where they are often "assaulted by guards and by other inmates" (Husak 2008: 6), where homosexual rape occurs frequently[60] and where they "retain virtually no privacy rights" (Husak 2008: 6). Following release, former convicts continue to experience severe constrictions to their liberty, as they "lose political, economic, and social rights … many … are explicitly denied benefits under welfare and entitlement programs … [and] face difficulties finding employment and housing [and often] emerge from prison with financial debts" (*Id.*).

What is more, the infringement comes at a very high cost not only for those who are subjected to the criminal sanction (what I referred to elsewhere as "the direct costs of punishment" (Materni 2016: 41)); rather, those costs extend beyond defendants – whether awaiting or at trial, or convicted and incarcerated – and "fall … heavily on a criminal's wife and children" (Holmes 1897: 470). In addressing what I referred to as the "indirect costs of punishment" (Materni 2016: 42), I observed that "[f]amilies are torn apart; broken homes in turn may breed (or offer a more fertile ground for) further criminality" (*Id*). I then pointed to the broader impact on communities, including disparately affected ones, and other collateral consequences of imprisonment (*Id.*, 43–44).

The conclusion that I draw from the foregoing observations is that "society at large pays a steep price for the protection it obtains via the criminal law," and that "[a] system of government that is seriously committed to the individual liberties of the members of the social group it governs should not take these costs lightly," and therefore a liberal democracy should employ the criminal law as the option of the last resort (*Id.*, 43).

There are, of course, other values at stake, and other costs will have to be borne if we elect to reduce the use of criminal regulation. For instance, some may no doubt object that deterrence – supposedly achieved through the threat of criminally prosecuting and punishing undesirable conduct – ought to be considered among the core justifications for the criminal law. After all, Beccaria himself wrote that "[t]he purpose of punishment … is none other than to prevent the criminal from doing fresh harm to fellow citizens and to deter others from doing the same" (Beccaria 1764: 26). The answer to that objection is that the conclusion stipulating the deterrent effect of the criminal law, while seemingly logically sound, has never been empirically *proven* – as one scholar noted, "whether punishment deters certain kinds of crimes at all, whether more severe penalties produce greater deterrence, even these basic questions cannot be answered with confidence" (Schulhofer 1974: 1517). Rather, the deterrent effect of the criminal law remains "[nothing] better than a blind guess" (Holmes 1897: 470). I am not claiming that the criminal law has *no* deterrent effect, nor am I claiming that the notion of deterrence should play absolutely no part in the equation. I am claiming, however, that the cost of (allegedly) lost deterrence is easily outweighed by the cost of protecting interests by means of the criminal law, and therefore deterrence should receive a *de minimis* consideration – the burden should be on those arguing that deterrence should be a driving force justifying criminal regulation to prove why that should not be the case. As of today, however, we still don't know whether "the criminal law … does more good than harm" (*Id.*).

On the other hand, we know from history that the criminal law of oppressive, authoritarian, and totalitarian regimes – i.e., the opposite of what a liberal democracy should aim to be – is characterized by overreach and the imperative to protect "the state" at the cost of the rights of individuals (see, e.g., Materni 2015: 325–360)[61]. Since the criminal law defines the system of government of which it is the political expression, a liberal democracy should *choose*, in light of the lessons that we can take from history, to embrace a criminal law founded upon the principle of the *extrema ratio*, interpreted and constrained in light of the principles of harm and proportionality.

Not everyone will embrace the arguments I have developed in this chapter, or the conclusions I have drawn from those arguments; indeed, some will probably embrace neither. The arguments I advance certainly leave room for further development, especially with respect to the identification of harms that may properly serve as a predicate to criminal regulation. After all, disagreement in this regard by reasonable people in good faith is all but inevitable. This is, however, the point: This chapter does not aim to be the last word on the subject, but it hopefully will contribute to shifting the conversation from what has become a somewhat trite discussion of *why* we punish to a more poignant debate as to *when* we should punish. The starting point is understanding that – as Ronald Coase demonstrated long ago in his essay *The Problem of Social Cost* – everything has a cost, and costs should be balanced against one another. The conversation about criminal justice reform should start with considering what rights, or interests, are sufficiently weighty to command protection through the criminal law, and the provocation that there are strong historical, moral, and – perhaps most importantly from a lawyer's perspective – *constitutional* arguments why the burden of justifying regulation of conduct through the criminal law should fall on those who argue in favor of such regulation.

Notes

1 This is one of the core lessons of the American Legal Realist movement. See, for example, Fuller (1934: 429) and Llewellyn (1931: 1222).

2 Data accurate as May 17th, 2017; see www.statista.com/statistics/300986/incarceration-rates-in-oecd-countries/ (Accessed on February 25th, 2018).

3 This number comprises *all* individuals held into custody, whether in federal prison, state prison, juvenile correctional facilities, local jails, Indian Country jails, military prisons, immigration detention facilities, civil commitment centers, and prisons in the US territories. See, for example, Wagner & Sakala (2017).

4 As of June 30, 2016, according to data provided by the national prison administration there were 699 individuals being held in custody in the Seychelles, which, based on an estimated national population of 94,700 at mid-2016 (from Seychelles national statistics bureau figures), gives the Seychelles an incarceration rate of 738 prisoners per 100,000 population. See World Prison Brief, Seychelles (2018).

5 Smith also estimates that as much as 40% of the thousands of federal criminal laws passed since the civil war have been enacted after 1970. Another commentator has observed that "[t]he number of federal statutes and regulations relevant to criminal conduct is unknown, but likely is immense … Some commentators have estimated that there are more than 4,000 statutes and more than 300,000 regulations that define conduct as criminal or otherwise bear on the proper interpretation of laws that do" (Larkin 2014: 749).

6 While the chapter is written from the perspective of an American lawyer, the principles I endorse herein are not limited or unique to the criminal law of the United States and are thus intended to be applicable to liberal democracies *writ large*.

7 In the Western world, the justifications of the State's punitive power have been discussed from the time of the ancient Greeks to the present, see, for example, Pauley (1994). For an overview of the main theories of punishment from ancient Greece to modern times see also Bedau and Kelly (2010). For purposes of this chapter, I assume that there *should be* a government – and that, at any rate, *there is one*, which brings as a corollary the notion that a legitimate government is, and ought to be, entitled to regulate the conduct of those it governs.

8 See *infra*.

9 The influence of *On Crimes and Punishments* on the development of modern criminal law is undisputed, see Catelan (2004). Among those that were inspired by Beccaria we find such names as Jeremy Bentham (see, e.g., D'Entrèves 1964), John Adams and Thomas Jefferson (see, e.g., Flaherty 1990).

10 Beccaria believed that "[l]aws are the terms by which independent and isolated man united to form a society, once they tired of living in a perpetual state of war where the enjoyment of liberty was rendered useless by the uncertainty of its preservation (10)."

11 See *infra*, notes [con law arguments etc.] and accompanying text.

12 American criminal law has been developed in the absence of any foundational constitutional theory, see, for example, (Stuntz, 2011). The constitutional doctrine referred to in this chapter flows from the Supreme Court's interpretation of constitutional principles over time.

13 As I wrote elsewhere, "Liberty" is not by chance one of the three "unalienable rights" that Thomas Jefferson chose to enumerate in the Declaration of Independence, immediately after "life" and before the "pursuit of happiness," of which "liberty" is the logical [and factual] premise" (Materni 2015: 364). It is perhaps one of history's most tragic ironies that the Declaration of Independence, which features the claim that "all men are created equal," was drafted by Jefferson on a table built for him by a slave.

14 The Fifth Amendment provides, in the relevant part, that "No person shall be … deprived of life, liberty, or property without due process of law." Employing the exact same language, the Fourteenth Amendment provides, in the relevant part, that "No State shall … deprive any person of life, liberty, or property without due process of law."

15 *Meyer* v. *Nebraska*, 262 U.S. 390 (1923).

16 *Pierce* v. *Society of Sisters*, 268 U.S. 510 (1925).

17 *Griswold* v. *Connecticut*, 381 U.S. 479 (1965); *Eisenstadt* v. *Baird*, 405 U.S. 438 (1972).

18 *Lawrence* v. *Texas*, 539 U.S. 558 (2003).

19 *Obergefell* v. *Hodges*, 576 U.S. __ (2015).

20 *Poe* v. *Ullman*, 367 U.S. 497, 543 (1961) (opinion of HARLAN, J., dissenting).

21 *Obergefell v. Hodges,* 576 U.S. __ at 6 (2015) (opinion of THOMAS, J., dissenting). Justice Thomas believes that the meaning of liberty envisioned by the framers "[did not] include anything broader than freedom from physical restraint." *Id.* However, Justice Thomas' reading notwithstanding, it is settled and longstanding constitutional law that, whatever the framers might have thought, the constitutionally protected "liberty" encompasses much more than merely "freedom from physical restraint."

22 *Meyer* v. *Nebraska*, *supra* note [__], at 399.

23 *In re Winship*, 397 U.S. 358, 363 (1970).

24 *Speiser* v. *Randall*, 357 U.S. 513, 525 (1958).

25 *Albright* v. *Oliver*, 510 U.S. 266, 294 (1994) (opinion of STEVENS, J., dissenting).
26 *Young* v. *U.S. ex rel Vuitton and Fils S.A.*, 481 U.S. 787, 814 (1987).
27 *U.S.* v. *Marion*, 404 U.S. 307, 320 (1971).
28 *West Virginia State Bd. of Educ.* v. *Barnette*, 319 U.S. 624, 638 (1943).
29 Abraham Lincoln, July 4th Message to Congress (July 4th, 1861) available online at http://millercenter.org/president/speeches/speech-3508.
30 As Lincoln (1861) put it: "It was not believed that any law was violated. The provision of the Constitution that 'the privilege of the writ of *habeas corpus* shall not be suspended unless when, in cases of rebellion or invasion, the public safety may require it' is equivalent to a provision—is a provision—that such privilege may be suspended when, in cases of rebellion or invasion, the public safety does require it. It was decided that we have a case of rebellion and that the public safety does require the qualified suspension of the privilege of the writ which was authorized to be made. Now it is insisted that Congress, and not the Executive, is vested with this power; but the Constitution itself is silent as to which or who is to exercise the power; and as the provision was plainly made for a dangerous emergency, it can not be believed the framers of the instrument intended that in every case the danger should run its course until Congress could be called together, the very assembling of which might be prevented, as was intended in this case, by the rebellion."
31 *Ex Parte Milligan*, 71 U.S. 2 (1866). Rejecting the claim that the executive had the power to suspend general laws in times of war, the Court held that "[n]o doctrine, involving more pernicious consequences, was ever invented by the wit of man than that any of its provisions can be suspended during any of the great exigencies of government. … [T]he theory of necessity on which it is based is false." (*Id.* 121.)
32 *Schenck* v. *United States*, 249 U.S. 47 (1919).
33 *Id.* at 248–249.
34 *Id.* at 249.
35 *Id.*
36 *Id.*
37 *Id.*
38 *Id.*
39 Schenck and Bear were sentenced to ten years in prison for each of the three counts of violating the Espionage Act they had been convicted on.
40 *Frohwerk* v. *United States*, 249 U.S. 204 (1919).
41 *Debs* v. *United States* 249 U.S. 211 (1919).
42 *Abrams* v. *United States*, 250 U.S. 616 (1919).
43 Frohwerk was sentenced to pay a fine and serve ten years in prison; Debs was sentenced to serve ten years in prison and to be disenfranchised for life; the *Abrams* defendants were sentenced to ten and 20 years in prison.
44 *Korematsu* v. *United States*, 323 U.S. 214 (1944).
45 *Id.* at 216 (emphasis added).
46 *Id.* at 219.
47 *Id.* at 220.
48 *Id.* at 218.
49 *Id.* at 223.
50 *Id.* at 223–224. In a concurring opinion, Justice Felix Frankfurter also made the point that times of war are different than times of peace; and an action that would be lawless in times of peace may not be so in times of war. See *Id.* at 224–225.
51 *Id.* at 235. The other two dissenting justices – Owen Roberts and Robert Jackson – argued, respectively, that convicting a citizen based solely on his ancestry was a "clear violation of Constitutional rights," *Id.* at 225–233; and that while there may be certain military exigencies and necessities in times of war, a military order *per se* – whether legal or not – would not last longer than the emergency that gave rise to it, whereas the Supreme Court's ratification of the order will enshrine it into law. *Id.* at 242–248.
52 *Trop* v. *Dulles*, 356 U.S. 88, 101 (1958).
53 In its entirety, the First Amendment reads, "Congress shall make no law respecting an establishment of religion, or prohibiting the free exercise thereof; or abridging the freedom of speech, or of the press; or the right of the people peaceably to assemble, and to petition the Government for a redress of grievances." The Fourth Amendment, in its entirety, reads: "The right of the people to be secure in their persons, houses, papers, and effects, against unreasonable searches and seizures, shall not be violated, and no Warrants shall issue, but upon probable cause, supported by Oath or affirmation, and particularly describing the place to be searched, and the persons or things to be seized."
54 *Whitney* v. *California*, 274 U.S. 357, 378 (1927).
55 *Id.* at 378.
56 *Terry v. Ohio*, 392 U.S. 1 (1968).
57 *Id.* at 27

58 See, for example, *Homes Not Handcuffs: The Criminalization of Homelessness in U.S. Cities*, A Report by The National Law Center on Homelessness & Poverty and The National Coalition for the Homeless, July 2009, available online at www.nationalhomeless.org/publications/crimreport/crimreport_2009.pdf. In *Papachristou*, 450 U.S. 156 (1972), the Court struck down a Jacksonville, Florida, vagrancy ordinance as unconstitutionally vague, since it failed to give a person of ordinary intelligence notice of what conduct was forbidden under the ordinance. The Court also found that the ordinance gave too much power to the police, and criminalized a broad range of innocent activities. The laws promulgated in the decades since have been narrowly tailored and facially neutral, and presented as laws protecting the "quality-of-life." Yet studies have shown that offering permanent housing rather than relying on enforcement of anti-homeless laws results in substantial savings for the government, resulting in programs that not only became cost-neutral after two years, but also generated surplus for the government. See Marina Fisher, Nathaniel Miller, Lindsay Walter & Jeffrey Selbin, *California's New Vagrancy Laws. The Growing Enactment and Enforcement of Anti-Homeless Laws in the Golden State* (February 12th, 2015), available online at http://ssrn.com/abstract=2558944.

59 Kornfeld (1997: 23, *quotations omitted*) quoting what former Governor of Massachusetts William Weld told a meeting of attorney generals American prisons should look like.

60 See, for example, Sigler (2006: 565) observing that "while reliable data about prison rape is hard to come by, even conservative estimates suggest a problem of considerable magnitude." For example, even in the absence of mandatory reporting requirements, "Congress 'conservatively' estimated that thirteen percent of inmates in the United States have been sexually assaulted in prison … that nearly 200,000 inmates now incarcerated have been or will be the victims of rape [and that t]he total number [of inmates] assaulted in the past 20 years likely exceeds [one million]." *Id.* at 570 (citations omitted). Husak (2008: 6) observes how "[p]rison rape … is likely to elicit sarcasm in social circles that express horror at sexual abuse in the outside world."

61 Describing the criminal law of Fascist Italy and Soviet Russia.

References

Ashworth, A. (2008). Conceptions of Overcriminalization. *Ohio State Journal of Criminal Law*, 5(2), pp.407–425.

Battaglini, G. (1933). The Fascist Reform of the Penal Law in Italy. *Journal of Criminal Law and Criminology (1931–1951)*, 24(1), pp. 278–289.

Barak, A. (2012). *Proportionality. Constitutional Rights and their Limitations*. New York: Cambridge University Press.

Beccaria, C. (1764). *On Crimes and Punishments*. Aaron Thomas (ed.), A. Thomas and J. Parzen (trans.). University of Toronto Press, 2008.

Bedau, H.A., & Kelly, E. (2010). Punishment. *The Stanford Encyclopedia of Philosophy.* Edward N. Zalta (ed.). Available at http://plato.stanford.edu/archives/spr2010/entries/punishment/.

Brown, D.K. (2010). Can Criminal Law be Controlled? *Michigan Law Review*, 108, pp. 971–992.

Catelan, N. (2004). *L'Influence de Cesare Beccaria sur la Matière Pénale Moderne*. Marseille: PUAM.

Carrara, F. 1875. *Cardini Della Scuola Penale Italiana*. Lucca.

Carrara, F. 1870. *I Opuscoli di Diritto Criminale*. Lucca.

Coase, R. (1960). The problem of social cost. *The Journal of Law and Economics*, 3, pp. 1–44.

D'Entrèves, A.P. (1964) Introduction. In A. Manzoni (ed.), *The Column of Infamy: Prefaced by Cesare Beccaria's Of Crimes and Punishments.* Translated by Kenelm Foster and Jane Grigson. London: Oxford University Press.

Donne, J. (1624). Meditation XVII in *Devotions upon Emergent Occasions*.

Duff, R.A., Farmer, L., Marshall, S.E., Renzo, M., & Tadros, V. (eds.) (2010). *The Boundaries of the Criminal Law.* New York: Oxford University Press.

Duff, R.A., Farmer, L., Marshall, S.E., Renzo, M., & Tadros, V. (eds.) (2011). *The Structures of the Criminal Law.* New York: Oxford University Press.

Duff, R.A., Farmer, L., Marshall, S.E., Renzo, M., & Tadros, V. (eds.) (2013). *The Constitution of the Criminal Law.* Oxford University Press.

Feinberg, J. (1984–1988). *The Moral Limits of the Criminal Law, Vols. 1–4*. New York: Oxford University Press.

Flaherty, D.H. (1990). The Enlightenment and the Reform of American Criminal Law, in L. Berlinguer and F. Colao (eds.), *Illuminismo e Dottrine Penali*. Milan: Giuffrè.

Fuller, L. (1934). American Legal Realism. *University of Pennsylvania Law Review and American Law Register*, 82(5), pp. 429–461.

Harcourt, B. (1999). The Collapse of the Harm Principle. *The Journal of Criminal Law and Criminology*, 90(1), pp. 109–194.

Hart, H.L.A. (1968). *Punishment and Responsibility*. New York: Oxford University Press.

Hobbes, T. (1651). *Leviathan*. Richard Tuck (ed.), Cambridge: Cambridge University Press, 1996.

Holmes, O.W. (1881). *The Common Law*. Boston: Little, Brown and Company.

Holmes, O.W. (1897). The Path of the Law. *Harvard Law Review*, 10(8), pp. 457–478.

Husak, D.N. (2008). *Overcriminalization: The Limits of the Criminal Law*. New York: Oxford University Press.
Jareborg, N. (2004). Criminalization as Last Resort (Ultima Ratio). *Ohio State Journal of Criminal Law*, 2(2), pp. 521–534.
Kadish, S.H. (1987). *Blame and punishment: Essays in the Criminal Law*. New York: Macmillan.
Kornfeld, P. (1997). Cellblock Visions: Prison Art in America. Princeton: Princeton University Press.
Larkin, P.J. Jr. (2014). Regulation, Prohibition and Overcriminalization: The Proper and Improper Uses of the Criminal Law. *Hofstra Law Review*, 42, pp. 745–758.
Llewellyn, K. (1931). Some Realism about Realism: Responding to Dean Pound. *Harvard Law Review*, 44(8), pp. 1222–1264.
Locke, J. (1690). *Two Treatises of Government*. Peter Laslett (ed.). New York: Cambridge University Press, 1988.
Luna, E. (2005). The Overcriminalization Phenomenon. *American University Law Review*, 54(3), pp. 703–743.
Materni, M.C. (2015). The 100-plus Year Old Case for a Minimalist Criminal Law (Sketch of a General Theory of Substantive Criminal Law). *New Criminal Law Review*, 18, pp. 331–367.
Materni, M.C. (2016). The Value of Harm. *UCD Law Review*, 16, pp. 1–61.
Mill, J.A. (1863). On Liberty. Boston: Ticknor and Fields.
Pauley, M.A. (1994). The Jurisprudence of Crime and Punishment from Plato to Hegel. *The American Journal of Jurisprudence*, 39(1), pp. 97–152.
Rehnquist, W.H. (1998). *All the Laws but One. Civil Liberties in Wartime*. New York: Vintage Books.
Schonsheck, J. (1994). *On criminalization: An Essay in the Philosophy of the Criminal Law*. New York: Springer.
Schulhofer, S. (1974). Harm and Punishment: A Critique of the Emphasis on the Results of Conduct in the Criminal Law. *University of Pennsylvania Law Review*, 122, pp. 1497–1607.
Smith, S.F. (2013). Overcoming Overcriminalization. *Journal of Criminal Law and Criminology*, 102 (3), pp. 537–591.
Sigler, M. (2006). By the Light of Virtue: Prison Rape and the Corruption of Character. *Iowa Law Review*, 91, pp. 561–607.
Stinneford, J.F. (2011). *Rethinking Proportionality under the Cruel and Unusual Punishment Clause. Virginia Law Review*, 97(4), pp. 899–978.
Stone, G.R. (2005). *Perilous Times: Free Speech in Wartime from the Sedition Act of 1798 to the War on Terrorism*. New York: W.W. Norton & Co.
Stuntz, W.J. (2011). *The Collapse of American Criminal Justice*. Harvard University Press.
von Hirsh, A. (1996). Extending the Harm Principle: 'Remote' Harms and Fair Imputation. In A.P. Simester and A.T.H. Smith (eds.), *Harm and Culpability*, pp. 259–276.
Wagner, P. & Sakala, L. (2017). *Mass Incarceration: The Whole Pie*, www.prisonpolicy.org/reports/pie2017.html (Accessed on February 25th, 2018).
Winkler, A. (2006). Fatal in Theory and Strict in Fact: An Empirical Analysis of Strict Scrutiny in the Federal Courts. *Vanderbilt Law Review*, 59, pp. 793–871.
World Prison Brief, Seychelles (2018). Available at www.prisonstudies.org/country/seychelles (last consulted on February 27, 2018).

11

PROBLEM OF PROPORTIONAL PUNISHMENT

Youngjae Lee

Introduction

The idea that punishment should be proportional to crime is familiar and widely accepted but controversial. H.L.A. Hart has characterized the idea that "the punishment should in some way 'match' the crime" to be "perplexing" to many (Hart 1968), and Oliver Wendell Holmes described the idea of "a … bond between wrong and punishment" as "mystic" (Holmes 1881). Some have also complained about the idea's vagueness and its seeming inability to generate determinate amounts of punishments for different crimes. As Leo Katz has remarked, when considering "proportionate punishment" for, say, the crime of bank robbery, "[o]ur sense of just deserts … seems to desert us" (Katz 1999). As Katz's comment implies, the idea of proportional punishment is closely associated with the philosophy of retributivism (or just deserts), and that, too, has attracted criticism, as some object to the idea of proportionate responses to crimes to the extent that it implies that it is good to make people suffer for their wrongdoing (Tadros 2011). This chapter discusses various problems with the idea of proportional punishment and seeks a better understanding of the problems and potential solutions to them.

Is Proportionality a Retributivist Idea?

Before analyzing the idea of proportional punishment as the retributivist notion that a wrongdoer deserves to be punished and should be punished proportionately, we should note that its traditional rival theory, utilitarianism, has its own version of proportionality and consider the alternative, utilitarian interpretation of the idea.

The utilitarian theory of punishment addresses the questions as to whether someone should be punished and by how much in terms of the consequences such punishment would bring to the society. Punishment is a tool used to reduce harm to society arising from criminal activities by deterring future crimes through threat of punishment, incapacitating criminals through incarceration or death, and rehabilitating criminals through education and character reform. The utilitarian theory also considers the costs of punishment, such as the expense the public has to bear for law enforcement, from investigation and apprehension to conviction and administration of penalties, and the disutility inflicted on the criminals, both through punishment and through the loss of benefits they would have gained from criminal activities (Kaplow and Shavell 2002).

In short, the basic idea behind the utilitarian theory of punishment is, as succinctly stated by Jeremy Bentham, "all punishment is mischief: all punishment in itself is evil," and that punishment should be allowed "as far as it promises to exclude some greater evil" (Bentham 1789). From this idea, Bentham draws a number of prescriptions of general applicability. First, the punishment should be severe enough to outweigh the benefits the crime would bring to the criminal. Second, the more harmful the crime is, the more severe the punishment can be because the cost of the punishment we are willing to live with increases in direct proportion to the amount of harm it prevents. Third, when there are two crimes that a criminal might choose from, punishments for the two crimes should be set so that the criminal would be induced to pick a less serious crime, and, for this to happen, the less serious crime should carry the less severe penalty. Fourth, the less certain the punishment is, the more severe the punishment needs to be, in order to sufficiently deter potential criminals. Fifth, the longer the period between the crime and the punishment, the more severe the punishment should be. It is important to note that these are general principles only, and depending on the way the costs and benefits shake out in a given situation, the principles may be violated to obtain the optimal result.

From these principles, one *could* generate a utilitarian theory of proportionality. The utilitarian theory considers punishment to be evil, prescribes that it be used as sparingly as possible, and recommends that a system of punishment should distinguish among crimes by degrees of harm they cause and put corresponding "prices" on them (Rawls 1955). In other words, built into the utilitarian principle of proportionality are various sources of upward and downward pressure on sentences, and such pressures may generate a schedule of punishments that resembles the one designed on the basis of retributivism.

However, as an interpretation of the idea of proportionality in punishment, the utilitarian theory fares poorly as it regularly can yield results that conflict with it. That is, given two crimes of differing seriousness, A and B, there is no requirement within the utilitarian framework that whichever is the more serious crime will be punished more harshly. If A causes the harm of 100 units and B causes the harm of 200 units, the utilitarian theory would favor punishing B more harshly than A sometimes, but not other times; it depends as much on, say, the probability of conviction as on the seriousness of the crimes.

This is seen more clearly when we look at the more modern version of the utilitarian theory of punishment as updated by the economist Gary Becker, whose theory of optimal sanctions is probably the most influential contemporary version of the utilitarian theory of punishment (Becker 1968). Here is Becker's formulation:[1]

$$L = D(O) + C(p, O) + pfO.$$

L is the social loss from crimes; O is the number of offenses; D is the damage to the society from offenses, which in turn is defined as the harm inflicted on the society by the crime minus the benefit the criminal gained from the crime; C is the cost of apprehension and conviction in terms of both executive and judicial law enforcement expenditures; p is the probability of conviction varying between zero and one; and f is the amount of punishment. The equation as stated also tells us that D is a function of O and that C is a function of p and O. L also includes pfO, which is the cost of punishments borne by both the punished and the society that has to finance the regime.

The goal of the punishment regime, then, is to minimize L, the social loss from crimes, and this is done by adjusting the variables p, the probability of conviction, and f, the amount of punishment. Minimizing L is then done with the following factual assumptions in mind: (1) As O, the number of offenses increases, D, the damage to the society, increases.[2] (2) As f, the amount of punishment increases, O, the number of offenses decreases. (3) As p, the probability of conviction increases, O, the number of offenses decreases. (4) Therefore, in order to drive down crime (O) and the damages from it (D), p, the probability of conviction, and f, the amount of punishment, should be set sufficiently high. (5) However, unless we assume perfect deterrence where $L = 0$, increasing p and f will not always lead to the optimal result because increasing p and f also increases the values of C, which is the cost of apprehension and conviction, and pfO, which is the cost of punishments borne by both the punished and the society that has to finance the regime.

In short, the primary concern of the utilitarian theory is to minimize the social loss associated with criminal activities, and attaining the correct relationship between the gravity of crime and the harshness of punishment does not have a special, overriding normative force. As we can see in Becker's equation, there are a number of variables at issue, and if the probability of conviction is low for a variety of reasons such as, for example, the difficulty of detection, then the only way to bring down the social loss from crimes may be by increasing the amount of punishment.

In fact, given the goal of loss minimization, as long as the multivariable calculation works out to the right number, there is no upper limit on the amount of punishment that is tied to the gravity of the crime, and the punishment can be set high or low based on factors that have nothing to do with the seriousness of the crime committed. This is the truth behind the common objections to the utilitarian theory of punishment – that it would permit the state to "punish the innocent" or pick out a "scapegoat" for the greater good of the society (McCloskey 1965). It was, after all, Bentham himself who advised that we increase punishment "beyond that quantity which, on other accounts, would be strictly necessary" in situations "where the punishment proposed is of such a nature as to be particularly well calculated to answer the purpose of a moral lesson" (Bentham 1789). So, even if a particularly high amount of disutility is assigned to, say, an innocent person being punished, as long as the aggregate utility from prevention of harmful activities adds up to the disutility, then there is no reason to think that anything is amiss.

To be fair, what complicates the argument here is that utilitarians modify their theories in various ways to take into account the fact that not everyone in the world sees it the way they do. For instance, some law-and-economics scholars acknowledge the existence of what they call a "taste for fairness" and include it as one of the variables in their analyses (Kaplow and Shavell 2002). Similarly, Bentham lists as a factor the possible unpopularity of a punishment in cases where the people "happen to conceive, that the offence or the offender ought not to be punished at all, or at least ought not to be punished in the way in question" (Bentham 1789). Becker, too, counts the possibility that "judges or juries may be unwilling to convict offenders if punishments are set very high" as one of the factors to consider in his analysis (Becker 1968). Such complications need not detain us, as the question here is whether the idea of proportional punishment should be interpreted as a retributivist principle, and the suggested modifications to the utilitarian theory are ways to make it generate conclusions that resemble those that would be generated by the retributivist theory. Accordingly, the rest of the chapter assumes that the idea of proportional punishment is the kind that comes out of the retributivist tradition.

In What Sense Do Crimes and Punishments "Match"?

One source of the perceived difficulty with the idea of proportional punishment is that crime and punishment are incommensurable; the two scales, the crime scale and the punishment scale, do not seem to have anything to do with each other. The crime scale cannot be translated into the punishment scale, nor vice versa, in the same way, say, a scale of inches can be translated into a scale of centimeters. As a result of this incommensurability, crime and punishment are incomparable, which seems to be a problem for the idea of achieving equivalence between the two (Kaplow and Shavell 2002: 307; Maclagan 1939: 290).

Many attempts have been made throughout history to give the idea a semblance of intelligibility. For instance, consider the traditional, familiar form of the retributivist notion of proportionality: the Biblical maxim of *lex talionis*. One version in the Bible reads, "If any harm follows, then you shall give life for life, eye for eye, tooth for tooth, hand for hand, foot for foot, burn for burn, wound for wound, stripe for stripe" (Exodus 21:23–25). The basic idea is to do to the offender what the offender has done to the victim.

Kant's version of the same principle formulates it as a "principle of equality (in the position of the needle on the scale of justice), to incline no more to one side than to the other." Under this principle, "[i]f you insult him, you insult yourself; if you steal from him, you steal from yourself; if you strike him, you strike yourself; if you kill him, you kill yourself." Kant further claims that *lex talionis* is the only principle that can "specify definitely the quality and the quantity of punishment," as "all other principles are fluctuating and unsuited" (Kant 1797: 105–06).

However, this is true only if "specifying definitely" includes prescribing preposterous or impossible punishments. As Hegel points out, "it is easy … to exhibit the retributive character of punishment as an absurdity" through examples like "theft for theft, robbery for robbery," especially when imagining what "an eye for an eye, a tooth for a tooth" might mean where "the criminal has only one eye or no teeth" (Hegel 1821: § 101). In other words, following *lex talionis* frequently leads to absurd results because it is unclear how the harm is to be reproduced in cases like fraud, perjury, and blackmail, or how the principle could be applied, for instance, to an indigent criminal who destroys property. Moreover, even if the specified punishment is neither conceptually nor practically impossible, it is nevertheless morally repugnant to reproduce the same acts on the criminal in many cases.

To be fair, Kant recognizes these difficulties as well, worrying

> what is to be done in the case of crimes that cannot be punished by a return for them because this would be either impossible or itself a punishable crime against *humanity* as such, for example, rape as well as pederasty or bestiality?

But his answer is to remark rather unhelpfully that the state should do to the criminal "what he has perpetrated on others, if not in terms of its letter at least in terms of its spirit" (Kant 1797: 130).

Hegel, whose retributivist theory of punishment is based on the notion of "annulment" of the crime, attempts to respond to the absurdity problem of *lex talionis*. His theory is very similar to Kant's, as the "annulment," he posits, comes about through "an injury of the injury." Like Kant, Hegel claims that this theory of punishment specifies the right amount of punishment: "since as existent a crime is something determinate in its scope both qualitatively and quantitatively, its negation" – that is, punishment – "is similarly determinate" (Hegel 1821: § 101).

Hegel immediately makes clear, however, that the "identity" of crime and punishment rests not on "an equality between the specific character of the crime and that of its negation" but on an equality "only in respect of their implicit character, i.e. in respect of their 'value.'" By using the term "value," Hegel stresses that the focus should be on the abstract equality between the "value" of crime and the "value" of punishment "in respect of their universal property of being injuries," or "the inner equality of things which in their outward existence are specifically different from one another in every way" (Hegel 1821: § 101).

Of course, putting things this way does not really clarify the matter, nor does Hegel tell us how such a conversion into the common measure of "value" is to occur. Nevertheless, Hegel maintains that seeing the "comparability of crime and punishment in respect of their value" is absolutely crucial because otherwise punishment turns into "only an 'arbitrary' connexion of an evil with an unlawful action" (Hegel 1821: § 101).

Robert Nozick has offered the following contemporary restatement:

Punishment deserved = $r \times H$,

where H is the magnitude of the wrongness or harm, and r is the degree of responsibility. Under this framework, r varies between 0 and 1, with 0 representing no responsibility (such as insanity) and 1 representing full responsibility (intentional crimes), with intermediate values representing other levels of mens rea. Of course, this formulation leaves several difficult issues unresolved, such as how to assign numerical values to the variables, and how we should understand the equal sign in the formula, which Nozick calls "matching" or "equal" (Nozick 1981: 363).

It appears, though, we have not made any progress on the incommensurability question. All accounts surveyed so far do not stray from the idea of matching crimes to punishments to achieve some level of equivalence or equality. How is that to be done when the two items are incommensurable?

Some have suggested, as a way of giving content to the Hegelian "value" and the Nozickian "matching," that retributivism calls for inflicting the same amount of suffering on the criminal as suffered by the victim of the crime (Cottingham 1979). This proposal, however, immediately runs into difficulties in each of the three required steps: measuring one's experience of pain from the crime, measuring another's experience of pain from the punishment, and comparing the two (Kolber 2009).

The answer, rather, lies in taking a step back and focusing on the idea of deserving a punishment. To understand what it means for punishment to be deserved or undeserved by an individual, it is helpful to start with an analysis of the general concept of desert. As Joel Feinberg explained in his seminal discussion, every desert statement has at least three elements. In the statement, "*S* deserves *X* in virtue of *F*," *S* is the deserving person, *X* is what he deserves, and *F* is the desert basis – that is, the basis for *X* (Feinberg 1970a: 61). To understand how it is that a person deserves something, we must understand two relationships: the relationship between the person who is deserving and the desert basis (*S* and *F*), and that between what is deserved and the desert basis (*X* and *F*).

The person who is deserving and the desert basis (*S* and *F*) are related in that the desert basis has to be an attribute of the deserving person. In the relationship between what is deserved and the basis for desert (*X* and *F*), the key concept is "fittingness" or appropriateness. So, a response to criminal wrongdoing is "fitting" or "appropriate" only if it takes a form that symbolizes or expresses the society's condemnatory attitude towards the criminal conduct (Feinberg 1970a: 67–71; Feinberg 1970b: 98). This is why it would be inappropriate to reward criminals, whereas infliction of suffering is often seen as an appropriate response. Second, a corollary to this is that not every form of loss is an acceptable form of punishment in every society, depending on the symbolic significance the particular form of loss has in the society. For instance, the sanction of "community service" may appear inappropriate for certain crimes given the mixed signals – either as a sanction or as evidence of the participant's generosity and public spiritedness – such service gives (Feinberg 1970b: 114).

The concept of proportionality in punishment follows from the idea of fittingness. In short, the harshness of the punishment should reflect our level of condemnation or disapproval of the criminal act. A punishment would be excessive, then, if the degree of condemnation symbolized by the amount of punishment were too high relative to the criminal's blameworthiness. A punishment also would be excessive in situations where it is imposed on a person who has not committed any acts for which the kind of condemnatory expression that accompanies criminal sanction would be appropriate. A corollary to all of this is that the harshness of the punishment should increase as our level of condemnation or disapproval increases, which in turn should increase as the gravity of the crime increases (von Hirsch 1993: 15–17).

Looking at the question of deserved punishment this way, two objections against the idea of proportionality in punishment seem to quickly weaken. First, nothing in this account seems to *require* suffering as a response to criminal wrongdoing. According to this account, the important feature of desert is that of a "fitting" or "appropriate" response. It is true that what is typically considered to be a "fitting" response to criminal wrongdoing is infliction of suffering, but that is not a requirement of the theory of desert.

Second, the incommensurability problem does not seem as serious as it might at first appear. There are still two different scales, the harshness of punishment and the seriousness of crime, but the idea that the level of condemnation that is expressed by the harshness of punishment should match the level of blameworthiness that corresponds to the seriousness of the crime is not so mysterious. And this account gives some content to the idea of getting the proportion right by getting the right "spirit" (Kant's formulation) or "value" (Hegel's formulation). Considered as a specific instantiation of the idea of desert, it turns out the idea of proportionality between crime and punishment is not perplexing or mystic at all. Or it is only as perplexing as the idea of deservingness as a general matter, and unless we are willing to throw the entire practice of making desert judgments into doubt, the principle of proportionality does not suffer from the problem of being *uniquely* obscure or mysterious.

Is the Idea of Proportional Punishment Too Vague?

Of course, this does not mean that the idea of deserving a punishment is without its problems. Even if we can give some sense to the idea of deserving a punishment, the problem of indeterminacy mentioned above remains. How much punishment is deserved for stealing a car? Six months, two years, or five years? Stated this way, the question looks impossible to answer. If the idea of proportionality is good in theory only because of its indeterminacy, then it cannot be of much use in determining what punishments are due or in placing limitations on amounts of punishment.

Here it may be instructive to look at the United States Supreme Court jurisprudence on excessive punishments. In *Solem v. Helm*, the Court outlined a three-step process in reviewing punishments for excessiveness. First, courts should compare "the gravity of the offense and the harshness of the penalty," the gravity of the offense being determined "in light of the harm caused or threatened to the victim or society, and the culpability of the offender." Second, the Court stated that "it may be helpful to compare the sentences imposed on other criminals in the same jurisdiction" and see whether "more serious crimes are subject to the same penalty, or to less serious penalties." Third, the Court suggested that "courts may find it useful to compare the sentences imposed for commission of the same crime in other jurisdictions."

The first step calls for "matching" of crime and punishment that, as discussed above, has the indeterminacy that we are trying to find a way to mitigate. That leaves the second and third steps. The Supreme Court has given us one striking illustration of a use of the kind of analysis called for in the third step – comparing the sentence for a crime to sentences given for the same crime in other jurisdictions – in *Roper v. Simmons* as it declared the juvenile death penalty unconstitutional as a cruel and unusual punishment. When arriving at this decision, the Court noted that "the United States is the only country in the world that continues to give official sanction to the juvenile death penalty." This statement suggests that one way to give some determinacy to proportionality judgments is by comparing the punishment in one jurisdiction to the punishment in other jurisdictions for similar offenders.

What should we make of this suggestion? To evaluate, let's assume that there are ten countries, A through J. To simplify the analysis, let's also assume that there is only form of punishment, imprisonment, and further assume that there is only one theory of punishment, retribution, that all countries employ to determine the appropriate amounts of punishment. Now assume that there is a way to compare punishments that these countries impose for a crime committed in a certain situation by a certain offender, which we will call "crime *x*." If A's punishment for the crime *x*, measured in terms of amount of time spent in prison, is substantially higher than the punishment that countries B through J are willing to impose, what should the fact of A's apparent harshness compared to the rest of the countries tell us about A's desert judgment?

There are several possibilities. First, A simply got the desert judgment wrong and should bring its punishment in line with all the other countries. This is the argument implied in *Roper* about the juvenile death penalty in the United States. Second, A got the desert judgment right and everyone else is wrong. Third, no country is mistaken, but the punishments look different because A has an inflated scale of imprisonment compared to B through J, so that the message sent by the same amount of punishment may be quite different in different countries. That is, perhaps five years in prison is a mild punishment considering A's overall level of harshness in punishment, whereas B through J would take the same amount of punishment very seriously because imprisonment is rare.

The reason all these possibilities exist is that desert is a concept that is indeterminate and highly context-specific in action (why "gold medal" in the Olympics, for instance?). Different jurisdictions that apply the same desert principles to devise their sentencing regimes may end up producing punishments that look very different, and one jurisdiction may have a different understanding of how blameworthy "crime *x*" is from everyone else in a way that does not violate the principle of desert. Because how much punishment is appropriate for a given crime depends on what level of blameworthiness is expressed by different amounts of punishment, different places may attach different significances to the punishment that looks the same on surface.

To apply this general framework to the juvenile death penalty context, perhaps the fact that "the United States is the only country in the world that continues to give official sanction to the juvenile death penalty" means that the United States is willing to impose on juvenile offenders punishments that are undeservedly harsh. But it is also possible that, for whatever reason, the United States is the only country that is willing to impose on some juvenile offenders the punishment that they deserve, and the rest of the international community should learn from the United States. It is also possible that the United States is willing to hold people fully responsible for their acts at a younger age than other countries do, simply because of the legal system's particular understanding of the age at which people should be held responsible for their acts. It is also possible that the United States does not take the death penalty as seriously as some of the other countries that allow the death penalty. That is, some of these other countries may reserve the death penalty only for the most exceptional circumstances, such as acts of terrorism, genocide, and other instances that qualify as acts of evil of historic magnitude, and crimes committed by juvenile offenders rarely rise to that level.

So, the question is what country A's willingness to impose a sentence of imprisonment that lasts longer than countries B through J for the same crime – "crime *x*" – should tell us about the validity of A's desert judgment. The conclusion that A's desert judgment is wrong is certainly a possibility, but, as we saw, it is not the only possibility. Perhaps, then, the strategy of introducing determinacy to proportionality judgments by comparing punishments across jurisdictions does not seem very promising. What about, though, the other kind of comparison the *Solem* Court articulated – comparing sentences for different crimes given in the same jurisdiction?

There is a sound, desert-based rationale for that sort of comparison. Consider, again, the idea of "fittingness" in desert judgments. It turns out fittingness in desert has both comparative and noncomparative aspects (Feinberg 1974). To illustrate, in the punishment context, the noncomparative aspect stands for the view that a person convicted of a given crime should receive a certain amount of punishment, no matter how other people are treated, while the comparative aspect focuses on what the punishment for a given crime is compared to punishments for different crimes of varying degrees of blameworthiness. For example, if a criminal has been sentenced to five years in prison for stealing a car, noncomparative desert asks whether his deed is serious enough to warrant such a response by the state, regardless of how the state is treating other car thieves and criminals of more and less serious crimes. Comparative desert, by contrast, is about whether the car thief is being treated the same way as other car thieves and other comparably serious criminals and how his punishment compares to punishments imposed on those who have committed more or less serious crimes.

Why do both aspects – comparative and noncomparative – matter? Noncomparative desert matters in the following way: when we say that it would be clearly disproportionate to punish parking violation with one year in prison, that statement would be true even if every parking violation were treated the same way and more serious crimes were treated more harshly. In other words, even if a sentencing scheme generates a series of sentences that are in perfect comparative-desert relationship to one another, it is possible for some or all of those sentences to be too harsh.

The comparative aspect matters, too, as what one deserves is sometimes determined in reference to what others deserve. When the state punishes, it condemns the behavior it punishes as wrong, and the degree to which the behavior is condemned is expressed by varying the amount of punishment. Therefore, how one's punishment stands in relation to punishments for other crimes supplies a crucial piece of information as to how wrong the behavior punished is viewed by the society. This means that a punishment imposed on a criminal would be "undeserved" if it is more severe than the punishment imposed on those who have committed more serious crimes or crimes of the same seriousness, because the judgment it expresses about the seriousness of the criminal's behavior would be inappropriate.

To illustrate, as the death penalty carries a social meaning as the ultimate punishment for the most serious crimes, each time the state imposes a death sentence it shows that it considers the crime at issue to be not only one of the most serious offenses committed against the society, but also an offense that is as serious as other crimes that the society considers to be the most serious. Those who commit offenses less serious than the most serious offenses and are still sentenced to death would be receiving harsher sentences than they deserve, because part of what it means for them to receive the punishment they deserve is that they are punished less harshly than the worst criminal.

In this way, comparative desert functions the way an audience at a play responds to various performers at the end of the performance.[3] Assuming that a given production is good enough to merit applause, the audience members vary the length and intensity of their applause to show their relative levels of appreciation for different members of the cast. There may be noncomparative desert at work here, because if the production as a whole is not worthy of applause, no member of the cast may deserve any showing of appreciation. But barring such a situation, what determines how the audience greets each member of the cast is the principle of comparative desert. That is, other things being equal, generally the cast members with bigger and more difficult parts tend to receive the longer, louder, and more intense applause. The reason this has to be so is that there is a limit as to how long, loud, and intense cheering can get, and the audience has to save their longest applause for the cast member they appreciate the most. If they are too quick to unleash their most enthusiastic showing of appreciation and use it on minor characters, they may not be able to express to the ones with the leading parts how much more they appreciate them than those with lesser roles. And if such a situation unfortunately arises, those who deserve more recognition from the audience would not be receiving what they *deserve*, not just what they *comparatively deserve*. It is in this sense that sometimes what one deserves cannot be determined without considering both comparative and noncomparative aspects.

Now we are ready to see why the indeterminacy problem of desert judgments is overstated. The difficulty of giving a determinate answer to the question of how much punishment is deserved for stealing a car seems less serious once we recognize that the amount of the deserved punishment depends not only on the gravity of the crime but also how the state punishes other crimes of varying gravity. Comparative desert, in short, brings some determinacy to the task of judging how much punishment is too much (von Hirsch 1985: 38–46; Miller 1999: 151–55). As an intuitive matter, the task of ranking crimes in the order of seriousness seems doable, and, as has been remarked in the literature, "[t]here is quite an impressive consensus within and even between modern societies on which types of crimes deserve most punishment and which least" (Braithwaite and Pettit 1990: 178). This is not to say that comparative desert judgments are easy; the difficulties are well known (Duff 2001: 132–133). The point merely is that comparative desert tends to offer far more guidance than noncomparative desert in judging what one deserves, and that the perceived level of difficulty of desert judgments depends on how the problem is framed, or which aspect – comparative or noncomparative – is stressed.

Is the Idea of Proportional Punishment Manipulable and Biased?

Various difficulties remain with the idea of proportional punishment, though, especially when it comes to its use as a limiting principle. For instance, in "Desert, Democracy, and Sentencing Reform," Alice Ristroph expresses some skepticism about the idea that the principle that offenders should be punished only to the extent they deserve and not more than that can be used as a way of putting a cap on severe punishments, and she warns against overenthusiasm for desert as a tool to constrain state punishment. Ristroph argues that desert judgments are "elastic" and "opaque," "elastic" because "desert is hard to quantify and easy to stretch" and "opaque" because the language of desert hides ugly biases and emotions such as "[r]acial bias, fear, disgust" that may be shaping people's reactions to acts of crime (Ristroph 2006).

As to the first claim of "elasticity," Ristroph discusses various examples of the society's changing views on the seriousness of various crimes. She points out for instance that "horse thieves ... were adjudged deserving of death" in early America, that violating airport security regulations are taken much more seriously in the United States nowadays than they were before 9/11, and that date rape and drunk driving are considered to be much more serious offenses today than they were a few decades ago. She also argues that changing desert judgments tend to track changing governmental policies. That is, if the government decides to treat certain crimes more harshly, the public tends to adjust its own perceptions of seriousness of those crimes. Drawing from numerous materials, such as sentencing laws and practices of different states, public discourse as reflected in statements of citizens and institutional actors, and constitutional caselaw, she argues that as the government came to treat repeat offenders, mentally disabled offenders, and juvenile offenders more harshly over time for reasons of deterrence and incapacitation, the public's understanding of deservingness of these categories of offenders changed with them (Ristroph 2006).

In support of her claim that desert judgments are "opaque," Ristroph shifts her focus from law, policy, and rhetoric to how sentencing determinations are made on the ground, especially by jurors in death penalty cases. She cites social science studies that found that "the race of the victim was an important determinant of whether a murder defendant would receive the death penalty," that "the state was more likely to seek the death penalty if the murder victim was white," that "decisions to impose death track the defendant's race as well as the victim's," that "black defendants were more likely to be sentenced to death than white defendants," and that "among black defendants who killed white victims, those that appeared more 'stereotypically black,' in terms of skin color and facial features, were more likely to be sentenced to death." Ristroph finds that class biases and xenophobia play similar roles in sentencing and concludes that "desert may serve as a 'placeholder' for prejudice and bias" (Ristroph 2006).

What should we make of these criticisms? Ristroph is of course correct in noting that desert judgments are "elastic" in the sense that specific beliefs about desert can change over time. She mentions examples of date rape and drunk driving, the perceived blameworthiness of which has gone in one direction. To that list we can also add homosexual conduct, adultery, and miscegenation, the perceived blameworthiness of which has gone in the opposite direction. This kind of elasticity, however, is not a problem for desert. Desert judgments need not remain static over time for them to help us think about state punishment. Levels of public condemnation change as social norms change, and there is nothing surprising or troubling about that.

As to her charge that perceptions of seriousness of crimes change simply as government policies change, that also does not strike me as a problem as long as we are clear on exactly how these changes occur. Ristroph does not distinguish between instances where the government changes perceptions of seriousness of offenses through education and consciousness-raising, and instances where the public mindlessly apes governmental policies or is manipulated.

Ristroph is correct, however, to express some worries about the "opacity" of desert judgments. The difficulty is that desert judgments in the punishment context indicate not just disapproval but also an emotive state. Emotions associated with the practice of blaming are, for example, anger, resentment, indignation, and hatred. Such emotions, while important elements of our everyday existence as morally attuned persons, can be excessive and driven by sentiments such as cruelty, sadism, inhumanity, and racial prejudice. Such corrupting influences can seep in unannounced and infect our desert judgments in ways that are difficult to police.

Concluding Thoughts

Where does this all this leave us? Given the concerns raised, should we walk away from the ideal of proportional punishment? It seems to me, rather, that the problematic nature of desert means that we must be suspicious of our retaliatory impulses and constantly test our specific desert judgments against broad principles of desert and political morality. That desert judgments often seem subjective does not mean that such critical scrutiny is impossible. Desert judgments and their accompanying emotions have a cognitive content that can be evaluated as correct or incorrect.

This is of course not a tidy picture, but there is no way around the mess. Punishment – intentional infliction of pain and deprivation of liberty by the government on its citizens, and on behalf of its citizens – is a troublesome practice, and there are bound to be excesses, blind spots, and cruelties. The task is to do the best we can, and the idea of proportional punishment is one important principle to help us do so.

Notes

1 This is a slightly modified version for ease of explication. The original formula is $L = D(O) + C(p, O) + bpfO$, where b is defined as a coefficient that, when multiplied by p, the level of punishment, tells us the social cost of punishment. The coefficient varies depending on the type of punishment. Under Becker's assumption, b is close to zero if the punishment is a fine because, ignoring the cost of collection, it simply results in a transfer of wealth from the criminal to the society. Imprisonment, however, is costly for everyone involved, so b is a larger number.
2 This assumption comes from the assumption that offenders receive diminishing marginal utility and cause increasing marginal harm from additional offenses.
3 I borrow this example from David Miller (Miller 2003).

References

Becker, G. (1968) "Crime and Punishment: An Economic Approach," *Journal of Political Economy* 76, 169–217.
Bentham, J. (1789) *An Introduction to the Principles of Morals and Legislation*.
Braithwaite, J. and Pettit, P. (1990) *Not Just Deserts: A Republican Theory of Criminal Justice*, Oxford: Oxford University Press.
Duff, R.A. (2001) *Punishment, Communication, and Community*, Oxford: Oxford University Press.
Hart, H.L.A. (1968) *Punishment and Responsibility: Essays in the Philosophy of Law*, Oxford: Clarendon Press.
Holmes, O.W. (1881) *The Common Law*, Boston: Little, Brown.
Cottingham, J. (1979) "Varieties of Retribution," *Philosophical Quarterly* 29, 238–46.
Feinberg, J. (1970a) "Justice and Personal Desert," in *Doing and Deserving*, Princeton: Princeton University Press.
Feinberg, J. (1970b) "The Expressive Function of Punishment," in *Doing and Deserving*, Princeton: Princeton University Press.
Feinberg, J. (1974) "Noncomparative Justice," *Philosophical Review* 83, 297–338.
Hegel, G.W.F. (1821) *The Philosophy of Right*, trans. T. Knox, Oxford: Oxford University Press (1942).
Kant, I. (1797) *The Metaphysics of Morals*, in Mary J. Gregor (trans. and ed.) *Immanuel Kant: Practical Philosophy*, Cambridge: Cambridge University Press, 1996.
Kaplow, L. and Shavell, S (2002) *Fairness Versus Welfare*, Cambridge: Harvard University Press.
Katz, L. (1999) "Criminal Law," in D. Patterson (ed.) *A Companion to the Philosophy of Law and Legal Theory*, Oxford: Blackwell.
Kolber, A. (2009) "The Subjective Experience of Punishment," *Columbia Law Review* 109, 182–236.
Maclagan, W. (1939) "Punishment and Retribution," *Philosophy* 14, 281–98.
McCloskey, H. (1965) "A Non-Utilitarian Approach to Punishment." *Inquiry* 8, 249–63.
Miller, D. (1999) *Principles of Social Justice*, Cambridge: Harvard University Press.
Miller, D. (2003) "Comparative and Noncomparative Desert," in Serena Olsaretti (ed.) *Desert and Justice*, Oxford: Oxford University Press.
Nozick, R. (1981) *Philosophical Explanations*, Cambridge: Harvard University Press.
Rawls, J. (1955) "Two Concepts of Rules," *The Philosophical Review* 64, 3–32.
Ristroph, A. (2006) "Desert, Democracy, and Sentencing Reform," *Journal of Criminal Law and Criminology* 96, 1293–1352.
Roper v. Simmons, 543 U.S. 551 (2005)
Solem v. Helm, 463 U.S. 277 (1983)
Tadros, V. (2011) *The Ends of Harm: The Moral Foundations of Criminal Law*, Oxford: Oxford University Press.
von Hirsch, A. (1985) *Past or Future Crimes: Deservedness and Dangerousness in the Sentencing of Criminals*, New Brunswick: Rutgers University Press.
von Hirsch, A. (1993) *Censure and Sanctions*, Oxford: Clarendon Press.

12
THE GAP

Peter A. Alces

The "gap" to which I refer is not Leibniz's Gap, as such, though it is akin to it. Leibniz had in mind a limitation of our understanding, the necessary space between what we can experience and what we can understand or explain about that experience:

> [T]he *perception*, and what depends on it, is *inexplicable in terms of mechanical reasons*, that is, through shapes and motions. If we imagine that there is a machine whose structure makes it think, sense, and have perceptions, we could conceive it enlarged, keeping the same proportions, so that we could enter into it, as one enters into a mill. Assuming that, when inspecting its interior, we will only find parts that push one another, and we will never find anything to explain a perception.
>
> *(Leibniz 1714: 215)*

Now you could, with the "New Mysterians"[1] and those otherwise taken by the "Hard Problem"[2] presented by the stubborn ineffability of such as "qualia,"[3] decide that there just is no making sense of consciousness, conscious experience at least, from the materialistic perspective science, including brain science, provides. That general quandary is not the focus of this inquiry.

I am instead concerned with a related but distinct inquiry, and it is crucial that the distinction be clear. While philosophers of mind confront the challenge of understanding the relationship between brain and mind, perhaps how mind emerges from brain, that is not so much the concern of the law and the law is what I am concerned with in this contribution to the collection. It will be necessary to spend some time making clear the nature of the legal question and how the legal question is not the same as the philosophical question. We may see that the question is no less difficult, no less vexing, but importantly different. The frustrations of philosophers of mind with Leibniz's Gap need not frustrate our efforts to posit a relationship between neuroscience (broadly construed), philosophy (broadly construed), and punishment (construed in non-instrumental as well as instrumental terms).

My effort will proceed in three parts: First, I shall describe the science of punishment, paying particular attention to the connection between the public object and private consequences of punishment. The idea is to formulate a conception of efficacy, and that requires consideration of what it means for punishment to be efficacious. While non-instrumental and instrumental objects are necessarily inconsistent (Moore 1997), the story of our law of punishment is a story of accommodation between the two. There is no reason that, perhaps by serendipity (what else could it be), a particular punishment could not serve both non-instrumental and instrumental objects, but we must be willing to acknowledge that our criminal law assumes that the two can by design – not serendipity – be accommodated in the same punishment. We'll need to proceed from a sense of what science can bring to the punishment calculus. What can the science tell us about what punishment does?

Second, I will turn to the philosophy of punishment, no longer assuming the plausible accommodation of non-instrumental and instrumental objects. This part will approach the "why" question: Why do we punish? What is it that we want to accomplish through punishment? And, building on the first part, how are the objects of punishment related to the science of punishing? Neuroscience can tell us a good deal about how punishment works in fact, and how it fails in fact too. Indeed, we can see that punishment often, very often, undermines the normative object of punishment fixed by philosophy, non-instrumental or instrumental.

Finally, the third part of my argument will explain how the first two parts demonstrate the Leibniz Gap-like nature of the challenge presented by the science and philosophy of punishment. Once we have reviewed the consequences of punishment, from the scientific and normative perspectives, the nature of the gap that remains between our tools and our object becomes more clear. But the gap is importantly not Leibniz's Gap, and that means that it can be bridged well before we solve the "Hard Problem," though philosophers with even a mild case of neurophobia may not understand, or be willing to admit, that there is much we can do now to improve our law of punishment. There is room for scientists, also, to have a bit more confidence in their work than some are yet willing to acknowledge.

Science and Punishment

The science pertinent to punishment would help us better understand the effect as well as efficacy of extant punishment regimes, even now. The low-hanging fruit has already been harvested: psychopaths are incorrigible, but we can probably render them less dangerous (Kiehl 2014; Caldwell and Van Rybroek 2001; Raine et al. 2015: 509); even violent juveniles "age out of" criminal behavior (Snyder 2012; Piquero et al. 2001; Ulmer and Steffensmeier 2014); isolation has the propensity to profoundly impair the mental health of prisoners (Metzner and Fellner 2013 citing Smith 2006[4]); epigenetic insights reveal relationships between environment and criminal behavior (Caspi et al. 2002; DeLisi et al. 2008; Vaughn et al. 2009). There are other examples, some as stark, some less certainly so, but the connections cited demonstrate that science certainly does tell us something about how punishment works, and how it fails to work.

But science, so far, fails us too, and does so at just those points that might be of concern to instrumentalists. From our current vantage point it is difficult to remember a time when we were not so sure that the brain was fundamental to the normativity of human agents. Indeed, for some, the brain is not the sum and substance of human agency: "brains don't kill people; people kill people" (Fox 2010, quoting Stephen Morse). Now the point of those brain skeptics is not, we would hope, that the heart or even spleen for that matter is capable of murder independent of the brain. The point, instead, must be that we cannot understand human agency just by understanding the brain. There is something more than just the physical stuff of the brain – axons, dendrites, synapses, and the like – that is "responsible" for our actions, and for the moral valence of those actions. Part of the defense of that position is the inscrutability of brain function. We cannot localize brain functions to particular areas of the brain; the brain is plastic, and seems to operate more by facilitating neuronal networks than by designating natural kinds (i.e., emotional reactions) to discrete points on the neuronal map. For example, researchers have been able to identify the limbic system (Noback et al. 2005; Ermer et al. 2012; Harenski et al. 2010, Kiehl et al. 2001: 677), specifically the amygdala,[5] as particularly pertinent to psychopathy. The amygdalae of psychopaths are stunted, at least in comparison with those who do not manifest psychopathic qualities. From there some have emphasized the connection between the amygdala and fear and concluded that psychopaths are what they are because they lack the same access to fear as those with better functioning limbic systems (Birbaumer et al. 2005: 799; Jones et al. 2009: 95). Were the relationship between limbic structure and psychopathy certain, if we were able to diagnose psychopathy by measuring or at least surveying an MRI of the amygdala, then we would have a reliable means to diagnose (perhaps, early on) and even ultimately treat psychopathy. In fact, we might be able to predict the onset of psychopathic behavior by scanning the brains of adolescents, even pre-adolescents.[6] And were we able to do that, how would we react: would we euthanize psychopathic children?

At this point it is necessary to respond to that hysterical hypothetical. If we were able to discover that nature and nurture had created a psychopath, and we could confirm that by brain scan, we would, one would hope, no more execute the psychopath than we would the carrier of a contagious and deadly disease. When, on those rare occasions, we diagnose someone with Ebola or the deadliest forms of tuberculosis, we do not execute them. We treat them. Now we isolate them until we can cure them, but we do not attribute to them moral fault on account of their disease (even, presumably, if they negligently or recklessly exposed themselves to the deadly pathogen). It does not take much imagination to acknowledge that human agents might be no more morally responsible for the function of their brains than they are for their brains' composition.

Fortunately, for the sensibilities of those who would consider euthanasia a viable moral option, the coarseness of extant neuroscience does not permit us to certainly discern psychopathy, or any other brain state, for that matter, in a brain scan. While we can, at something of a gross level, connect the integrity of a portion of the brain with some cognitive capacities, all of the science points in a different direction. Rather than a phrenologically attractive map of brain state and function, we are developing a sense of the networked nature of brain and mind. It is far easier to list the areas of the brain that are certainly not involved in some mental event than it is to list exhaustively all of the brain areas that are involved. Further, all we can read from our different scans is neural activity, not the significance of that activity for state of mind.

The current empirical limitations provide fuel for skeptics who would gainsay the contributions of neuroscience to normative questions, and thereby also provide the graspable thin reed to keep non-instrumental normative theory in play. If we cannot even locate, literally in the brain, the situs of bad behavior, what contribution could neuroscience possibly make to the law of punishment? And there are no shortage of examples of "irrational neuro-exuberance" (Morse 2011) that would indicate an unhealthy neuromania. Even if a brain scan reveals a monstrous arachnoid cyst on the frontal (or "executive") lobe, we cannot certainly connect that physical aberration with conduct beyond the control of its human agent-host (see generally Davis 2017: a comprehensive review of the Herbert Weinstein case). And just because we can, with some confidence, draw a connection between a brain lesion and sexual predation (Burns and Swerdlow 2003), we cannot infer from the presence of that lesion the incapacity of the host to overcome criminal urges. It might be harder for the victim of the lesion to do so, but all of us have our crosses to bear and law should not excuse the victim on account of the lesion, at least not until science can draw a more direct line between the lesion and the ability of the host to resist the criminal urges. There is, after all, nothing in the extant brain science that depicts the moral conflict in terms that should provide the basis of excuse, at least in the way we now understand "excuse" in the criminal law (Berman 2003: explaining that in criminal law, "excuse" prevents attachment of criminal liability to committed acts when act is not committed entirely voluntarily, or in other words, actor is not "blameworthy" for morally wrong behavior).

What remains in the gap between what science can reveal and what is normatively significant, are empirical limitations and not a conceptual barrier. Or, more precisely, we have no reason to believe that the gap that remains is conceptual rather than empirical. Indeed, insofar as brain science advances by closing the gap, we have good reason to believe that the challenges are empirical. While it is not inconceivable that *at some point* we might discover the basis of a conceptual limitation, we have not yet. Our sense of consciousness certainly does not establish such a conceptual limitation, because as we continue to learn more and more about consciousness we are able to account for its mystery in quite prosaic terms. Even if you stop short of concluding that all of consciousness is an illusion

(Wegner 2003),[7] what brain science has taught us about consciousness even so far confirms that the mysteries are not so mysterious.[8] Keep in mind, though, that non-instrumental normative theory is literally out of business if it cannot retain at least enough of the mystery to undermine materialism. So non-instrumentalists will emphasize the limitations of the science while instrumentalists will find a glass half full.

For the non-instrumentalist science matters because interests such as retribution can only be served when we have a sense of the agent's experience of punishment (Kolber 2009). If the idea is to redress imbalance (Aristotle 340 BC, Irwin trans. 1985), or to formulate appropriate retributive punishment in terms of an affective experience, such as guilt (Moore 1997: 163–64), then we would need brain science to help us predict and prescribe. If we take retribution seriously, exacting too much or too little punishment may actually undermine the non-instrumental object (Kolber 2009: 198, 201), and it is not immediately clear that close enough is normatively good enough. In fact, an argument against non-instrumental punishment generally is that we cannot "do the math." Science would reveal the relationship between the punishment and the subject, "the math," in terms that would necessarily be considerate of the non-instrumental object, pretty much however you formulate that object.

From an instrumental perspective, science would be crucial too, insofar as it reveals matters pertinent to the consequentialist calculus: how do you know if you're preventing or causing crime unless you know what impact your punishment has on the immediate subject as well as those whom you might want to influence by way of general deterrence? Insofar as specific deterrence is concerned, the empirical data connecting punishment with criminal behavior suggests that our current practices do not work well. Recidivism rates are persistently high (Alper et al. 2018; Durose et al. 2014) and our failure to treat drug addiction as a disease just about guarantees that punishment will not cure what ails the criminal (or the system). At the other end of the spectrum, established sentencing practices assure that we will continue to punish criminals long after their criminal propensities have waned or ended altogether. Older offenders are shown to engage in less misconduct than younger offenders while incarcerated (Office of the Inspector General 2016; US Sentencing Commission 2017). The expense of that practice, in terms of both cost to the criminal and cost to society, are certainly great and likely incalculable. The instrumental case for the extant punishment regimes defies vindication by reference to costs and benefits, the currency of consequentialism.

The situation may be even more problematic with regard to general deterrence. Indeed, extensive recent studies just about confirm the inefficacy of extant punishment practices so far as general deterrence is concerned.[9] The point here is not that general deterrence fails, though in fact it may; the point is that but for a sense that we are dissuaded from criminal behavior by seeing what happens to many of those who engaged in it, the direct connection between punishment practices and crime rate is obscure, at best. It may be the case that science can alert us to non-punishment practices that more effectively reduce crime than does "punishment."[10] Neuroscience tells us more about the human agent, and the efficacy of instrumental punishment depends on the impact of punishment on human agents. We must be prepared to discover that current punishment practices actually *increase* rather than decrease the instances and severity of crime.[11]

It is true, though, that with regard to instrumental punishment there may be more of a case to be made for rough approximation. You would not want to expend more resources increasing the precision of your punishment than you would gain from less precision but, perhaps, more certainty and predictability. Even making that allowance for imprecision would entail our developing a sense of the costs of the imprecision, and neuroscience can inform calculation of that cost.

Philosophy and Punishment

Now we begin to see parallels with Leibniz's Gap. Philosophy (and here the focus is on non-instrumental theory) posits a conception of human agency that may elude the current science. There may be a gap between what science can reveal about the human agent and what philosophy needs to assume in order to make sense of a particular punishment or punishment regime. The philosophical perspective that is most troubled by the invocation of neuroscientific insights demonstrates the existence and significance of the gap by emphasizing that consciousness is a "Hard Problem," one we must solve before we can reach ultimate conclusions about human agency. And, in turn, we need to know, really know what it means to be human before we can reach such ultimate conclusions in terms that could inform the likes of punishment practices.

Take the accessible case of psychopathy. We know that psychopaths engage in acts, sometimes violent, that would be the proper subject of criminal punishment. But what makes a psychopath? Certainly there is something in the brain that is *necessary* to psychopathy, but there is nothing we have identified so far that is *sufficient* to psychopathy. So, the argument goes, there must be something conceptually inaccessible about psychopathy in terms of brain state and brain state is all science can, at best, ever reveal. That is the mantra that must inform philosophy of mind that sees work for philosophy to do after science has discovered whatever science can discover. The reason we can never "know what it is like to be a bat" (Nagel 1974: 445) is the reason science can never answer the bigger normative questions. Within the ineffable there is the lock that the scientific key cannot open. For philosophers captivated by that argument that lock certainly (or, at least, most plausibly) captures the normative substance of what it means to be human.

But there are two parts of that conclusion, and their relationship might go unnoticed, or unappreciated. First, the conclusion posits a conceptual barrier that may only be a temporary empirical impediment. Consciousness remains a mystery. It is just not clear what affords that sense of agency, of uncaused cause, that permeates our being. We may be the sum of cooperating forces rather than a discrete entity acted upon by the forces, but it sure feels like someone is in charge. That someone may not be a homunculus but it is an executive part of me that steps back and decides, or makes a "choice." Somehow the idea that humans "respond to reasons" is supposed to refute any theory of human agency in mechanistic terms. If we construe response to reasons, choice, as conceptually and not just empirically distinct from the mechanical, then, so non-instrumental theory maintains, we have preserved moral responsibility.

Choice, response to reasons, is asserted to be metaphysically different from mechanical force. But how? If I tell you not to go into that room because by doing so you will expose yourself to the Ebola virus I have probably more surely constrained your action than if I stand between you and the door. My spoken words have vibrated airwaves in a way you decipher as conveying the message that you will experience unpleasant consequences if you enter the room. If I am standing in front of the door you can walk "through" me, but at some inconvenience. In either case you may enter the room, but in both cases you are doing so at some cost. Even if it were the case that there were a truly immovable object between you and the door so that you could not "choose" to go through the door, that is just a more certain way to restrict your movement. But it is not even necessarily more certain. The "reason" I give you for not going through the door may more effectively restrict your movement than introducing a physical impediment. So the distinction is *not* based on the efficacy of the obstruction (reason or physical impediment).

The distinction must be based on the *way* that the two obstacles work. Reason relies on a configuration of your neuronal response to the Ebola warning, and that neuronal response is a *physical* response. Reasons can trigger neuronal reactions in a broad range of sentient beings that determine the beings' action or inaction. The interposition of a wall between you and the door is perhaps more obviously physical – we can see the wall – but it is no more physical therefore. To describe response to reason as choice and so distinguishable from a more obviously physical impediment is to beg the question. Both choice and deference to a physical impediment are conceivable in physical, material terms. Relying on the fact that we cannot *see* (at least very clearly, *yet*) the neuronal operations that result in the human agents not going through the door is just to demonstrate (perhaps) a lack of imagination, and (certainly) a lack of understanding. Nothing about mental processes, including consciousness, need compel the conclusion that they are not, at bottom, mechanical. The insight of neuroscience is that there is no difference between the mental and the physical; the dichotomy is false.

Nonetheless, philosophers of mind could recognize that there is something ineffable about consciousness but reason that we know enough about it to capture a sense of human agency sufficient to appraise punishment practices.[12] That is, neuroscience may not (yet) reveal all there is to reveal about consciousness but we do not need to know everything there is to know about consciousness in order to realize social purposes, such as a punishment regime that serves appropriate normative purposes.

Neuroscience, then, can matter so long as it provides an understanding of human agency *sufficient* to answer the particular normative question presented. The question of what punishment is most efficacious – best designed to reduce the cost (broadly construed) of crime – may be answered without our first determining the nature of consciousness. So there might be something non-physical about qualia, about what it is like to be a bat, about choice and reasons. But why would we assume that whatever that something may be is pertinent to determining the efficacy of a punishment regime, or even constitutive of moral responsibility? So far as law is concerned, we need to understand human agency well enough for law to do what law needs to do. Neurophobes, those who fear the introduction of neuroscientific insights to the resolution of legal questions, seem to cling to the hint of a whiff of the inscrutable to resist the application of neuroscience to law. And they do so without offering anything to support the conclusion that the basis of moral responsibility resides in the ineffable.

Neurophobia relies on, in fact clings to, the unelaborated mysteries of "capacities" (Pardo and Patterson 2013: 31–32), qualia, and consciousness to build a rickety scaffold to support non-instrumental theory and, in particular, retributive theory in the criminal law. The real advantage of that device is its accommodation of an indeterminate range of normative considerations unmoored to any physical reality. It provides the perfect armchair. If the basis of the theory is illusory, how can it be falsified? But if it is unfalsifiable it is no more intellectually durable than theology.

The more thoughtful philosophical response to the dualism posited by those who find room for the immaterial to operate is a thoroughgoing materialism. But even those who surrender to materialism do not always appreciate all that that entails. Both the response and its limitations may be appreciated in terms of the gap that is the focus of this essay. Daniel Dennett, a leading philosopher of mind, depicts the enlightened understanding of materialism as well as the stubborn persistence of the immaterial. Dennett is as responsible as any other philosopher, and much more than most, for revealing the nature of consciousness (Dennett 1991: 412–431). He has had no trouble describing the mechanics of consciousness and denying the efficacy, even existence, of the likes of qualia (Dennett 2005: 151–57). Though he too must imaginatively fill in gaps that the science has yet to fill in, Dennett explains consciousness in wholly physical, material terms (Dennett 2005: 41–42).

Paul Churchland's "Eliminative Materialism" leaves no room for the immaterial and so no obvious room for non-instrumentalism (Churchland 1981: 90). In a purely mechanical universe what work is there for the immaterial to do? For Churchland, folk psychology – the stuff of beliefs, desires, and motives – must be discarded along with everything else supernatural that materialism eliminates. Folk psychology is alchemy, if only a bit less ephemeral. Folk psychology does capture categories of mental states but fails because it denies the relationship between those categories and the appurtenant brain states. "Belief" is not supernatural, inaccessible in other than immaterial terms; "belief" is a constellation of cognitive conditions that supports the type of declaration that has semantic currency. The term works when it works because it triggers sufficiently coordinated understanding of a disposition. I know what you mean when you say that you "believe" something. That is all that we need the term to do: communicate, and thereby accommodate linguistic coordination. There is nothing supernatural about "belief" that is inaccessible to understanding in terms of brain state.

Indeed, a recent study has differentiated "knowledge" and "recklessness" in fMRI scans.[13] Stephen Morse, author of the study (Morse 2015: 253),[14] a somewhat renowned neuroscience skeptic,[15] acknowledged that the study provided "proof of principle" (Vilares et al. 2017: 3222, 3226.) that brain science could distinguish mental states that have different legal significance.[16] Once we can distinguish "knowledge" and "recklessness" on a brain scan, why would we assume that we cannot "locate" (not in the literal sense) the likes of belief, desire, and motive? Each term is just a word. And the effort, after all, so far as law is concerned is not to capture in a brain scan the *experience* of knowing or believing; it is to find the brain state indicative of the state of mind described by the term. That is all law needs brain science to do in order for brain science to undermine the non-instrumentalist reliance on the mystery of mind.

It would seem that, as a logical matter, conceptions of free will fail once we understand how materialism eliminates what materialism eliminates. That is, if we can reduce all of folk psychology to cognitive neuroscience, where would we find room for uncaused cause in human agents? Indeed, where would we find human agency in its more familiar forms? We must assume that human agents have free will, to some degree, in order to support the application of non-instrumental normative theory in response to the actions of human agents.

It is true, though, that some can find room for free will even in a wholly mechanical universe, even within a conception of human agency that posits the identity of brain and mind. "Compatibilism" is the Solomonic position that human agents are both determined and have (something at least like) free will. While we are constrained by the material forces of nature and nurture, there remains a sufficient scintilla of choice to support the imposition of moral responsibility. While I find the position incoherent, I recognize that it may (just, barely) represent the majority view of moral philosophers (Bourget and Chalmers 2014: 476).[17] Even those philosophers who seem most favorably impressed with materialism find some room for choice and so embrace compatibilism. I do not know why or how they are able to do that. I find none of the arguments convincing, or even plausible. Once you posit the mechanical nature of human agency, not only is there no work for the immaterial to do, there is nothing immaterial to do it. Raine tried to accomplish an accommodation between free will and determinism:

> I might argue for a middle ground between these two extremes. Free will likely lies on a continuum, with some people having almost complete choice in their actions, while others have relatively less. Rather than viewing intent in black-and-white, all or nothing terms, as the law does, with a few exceptions, I see shades of gray. … There are degrees of free will, and we all differ on that dimension of agency.
>
> *(Raine 2013: 307)*

Your first reaction might be that the accommodation Raine suggests has some plausibility, and appeal. After all, we all covet the conception of ourselves as uncaused causes, as the authors of our own destiny, just as we fashion excuses for our failings in deterministic terms.

If Raine's accommodation is right, then we are all to differing degrees caused or uncaused. Those with presumably more free will are better able to overcome their nature and nurture; those with less free will are more certainly constrained by the circumstances of their nature and nurture. Consider, though, that we would have to determine what accounts for those differences. What makes one of us more immune from circumstance and another less subject to the forces of nature and nurture? It is not enough that we can attribute to one rather than the other more intelligence, more social facility, more "character" (whatever that might mean). We would have to understand what accounts for that greater free will, and, further, we would have to find a way to attribute that enhanced capacity to something absolutely immune from the forces of nature and nurture. But what would that be? And where would we look for it? Somewhere outside of the brain but still within the human agent?

Most all of us have met people who just seem to have a knack for making better decisions, for having greater discipline. The correlation between capacity for deferred gratification and social success has been documented.[18] And we well might find correlations between demonstrated ability to defer gratification and more stable and nurturing environments (as well as parents who also demonstrate such an ability) (Kidd et al. 2013). If you have been raised in a privileged environment by parents who shared with you the genetic material that helped them provide themselves and their offspring with that environment, you are, perhaps, more likely to defer gratification and trust the researcher who tells you that you will receive two additional marshmallows if you wait 15 minutes before you eat the first one. Patience has served you well in the past; why should you not trust an authority figure this time? But if you have been raised in a less secure environment, perhaps because your parents do not have the means to provide you the same security, you might eat the marshmallow now because who knows whether there really will be any payoff for patience? Deferring gratification may not be the best strategy. You, of course, were not in any way responsible for the environment in which you were raised or for the parents who raised you. So you might seem as though you have less free will, in Raine's sense, but it is not clear that we could correctly attribute your apparent "impatience" to your having *less* free will, rather than a different genetic composition and a different environment in which your genes matured. Raine acknowledged the sources of differing degrees of free will: "What determines the extent of free will? Early biological and genetic mechanisms alongside social and environmental factors play substantial roles. For some, free will is significantly constrained early in life by forces far beyond their control" (Raine 2013: 307). Raine is certainly correct here; we only wish he would elaborate on what factors other than nature and nurture impact degrees of free will.

Another problem with conceptions of free will emerges from that scenario. There is danger we might use conceptions of free will to institutionalize inequality. Indeed, positing the reality of free will and then attributing moral responsibility to human agents who are supposed to have it provides the means to justify disparate treatment based on forces not within control of the subject. It is like "blaming" you for not being able to "dunk" a basketball if you are only 60 inches tall. Sure, there may be some person somewhere with extraordinary leg muscles who stands no more than five foot tall and can shoot down at a regulation basketball hoop, but to measure the athletic ability of all such relatively diminutive players by reference to the extraordinary case would be, to say the least, inefficacious, and maybe cruel. In settings more significant than the sports arena, in the context, for example, of criminal punishment, the result might be perpetuation of institutionalized invidious discrimination for generations (Kaye 2008).[19]

We can appreciate the appeal of compatibilism though, particularly for moral philosophers. Without choice, even the merest scintilla of free will, there can be no moral responsibility and so nothing for moral philosophers to moralize about. While it may be difficult to wrap our heads around the possibility that we are all more or less determined creatures, it is another challenge to deny the moral responsibility system altogether. That, of course, is just what Bruce Waller understands and has explained perhaps better than anyone else (see generally Waller 2011; 2014). For the conduct of everyday human affairs that is discomfiting; for our system of laws, premised on moral responsibility, it is cataclysmic. To paraphrase, "if we are wrong about moral responsibility in law that is as wrong as we've ever been about anything" (Fodor 1987).

But can we salvage choice through compatibilism? Is there a gap between the mechanical and the normative within which resides the sum and substance of moral responsibility? The problem here is that as we learn more about cognitive neuroscience and elaborate on our understanding of nature and nurture by reference to epigenetics, there does not seem to be anything that is not constrained, determined, by forces acting upon rather than generated by the human agent. A moment's reflection confirms that that impression must be right. We certainly conduct ourselves as though nature and nurture were everything: Do those who champion free will or compatibilism care less about their child's nourishment and surroundings? Surely the resources devoted to giving every child the best start and the best opportunities her parents can afford confirms that when we vote with our wallets we vote in favor of determinism. Now we may not like what determinism intimates about moral responsibility (the more well-off do not deserve their advantages), but that dissatisfaction says nothing about the plausibility of the free will fiction. Belief in free will becomes a political and moral matter once the status quo is challenged by hard determinism. What if all the privilege you enjoy is the product of forces wholly beyond your control? You do not deserve that privilege, any more than the victim of destitution deserves deprivation.

The contribution of neuroscience to the free will/compatibilism vs. determinism question is in the science's revelation of the causes of human agents' choice. The brain lesion that explains predatory behavior may seem, at least to some, a plausible and efficient cause of the anti-social behavior, particularly when the behavior stops once the lesion is removed. We may appreciate the behavior modification that can be effected by transcranial magnetism (Medeiros et al. 2012; Nitsche and Paulus 2000; Peterchev et al. 2012; Young et al. 2010: 6753) and understand that behavior as caused by direct intervention of neural circuitry. Neuroscience can correlate specific competence (and incompetence) with specific neural aberrations (Bechara et al. 1999). And proponents of free will can acknowledge the connection between such mechanical interventions and apparent intellectual processes. But once they do admit that much, how and where can they draw the line and say with any confidence that *all* intellectual processes are not merely manifestations of physical properties? All that would seem to remain to leave room for moral responsibility would be the *feeling* of control.

We know, though, that many other feelings about human agency are deceptive, that we are not just motivated by emotion and feelings, but may be determined by affective reactions (Damasio 2018). Indeed, if we were alert to a particular affective reaction we would need to know something about context to determine *for ourselves* what that reaction is: fear, sexual arousal, or a mild case of the flu? (Marsh 2018: 88, 94, 134, 190).[20] Not only do we seem to be the sum total of cooperating forces but we are the sum total of forces of which we are not aware.

It is clear that there is much about being we that we do not understand, much that is inaccessible to us. The feeling of control we experience is illusory, which it ultimately must be if there is no essential "us" rather than situses, of complementary causes, forces that could be in control. Once we pull back the curtain on that sense of control, we have exposed as well the incoherence of free will and compatibilism. We have exposed the human agent as no more "in control," as a moral matter, than any other mechanism is in control. Your car, computer, or toaster oven is not a moral agent, and if there is no such thing as free will, choice, neither are you.

That, of course, does not mean that we cannot use moral suasion as a means to motivate human agents to act in ways we deem more desirable, but it does mean that we should not get too carried away with the idea that morality has some essential, real, meaning. Moral talk is a lever, a mechanism. When you discipline your dog for some discourteous behavior, your dog does not understand your "moral argument," and you do not need her to. It is enough that your dog discerns your disappointment and senses that a consequence of that disappointment might be denial of something the dog considers desirable, the security signaled by your approval, the absence of the anxiety caused by a threat to that security (and the food, shelter, and care that provide that security). That is why we perceive dogs as sociable, because their reactions are adaptive insofar as they mimic what we read as affectionate behavior. They are affectionate because we respond well to displays of affection, which, of course, is why you are affectionate toward other humans too.[21]

If that equation makes sense to you (though it probably does not if you are afraid not to believe in free will) then what else do you need to appreciate determinism and the failure of moral responsibility? Once we can account for ostensibly "moral choices" in mechanical terms there is just no work for free will to do. The burden then shifts to those who would find a role for morality. And the case for morality is currently under attack, if not siege (Nadelhoffer 2014: 165). Arguing that morality vindicates "the better result" from some perspective is not an argument for morality, as such; it is an argument for some position that realizes a psychological or other material object. It is ultimately instrumental.

Policing the Gap

There is a gap between what we know about human agency and everything we could know about what it means to be human. But that gap is no reason for paralysis; indeed, every dimension of human affairs confronts the same gap. We need not know everything; it is enough for us to know all we can know and then do no more with what we do know than it is prudent to do. The greater danger is relying on our despair about not knowing everything in order to justify reliance on what we can be certain is insubstantial. Non-instrumental normative theory is insubstantial and leads to results that would be pernicious even according to its own espoused values. If you believe that there is such a thing as morality, then you believe in desert, blame, and similar cognates of moral responsibility. You would also want your legal system to instantiate your moral sense. Most prominently, people should *deserve* what the law does to and for them. But if "choice" is a fiction, if human agents are determined by nature and nurture to behave and even think in certain ways, if they lack god-like autonomy, if the concept of "self" is a fiction, then extant non-instrumental normative theories punish and reward the undeserving because desert is a fiction. Moral responsibility, though, is a convenient fiction, and it is engrained, for reasons that Waller makes clear (Waller 2014: 253–56).

Once we have developed at least a healthy suspicion of moral responsibility, in some of its dimensions if not in all of its manifestations, then we are in the position to engage in the type of reconsideration of human agents' normativity that Greene and Cohen predicted some years ago (Greene and Cohen 2004: 1784). We already see signs of it in evolving notions of desert with regard to substance, particularly opiate, abuse.[22] When we recognize instances of reduced moral responsibility we have taken the step toward abrogation of moral responsibility concepts altogether. And even if that is where we are headed, as science continues to close the gap between what we know about human agency and what we would need to know to abrogate conceptions of moral responsibility altogether, law can be considerate of the emerging insights and evolving normative consequences. In fact, the evidence law is suited to do just that. As Dean Faigman has recognized, evidence law can facilitate introduction of science that is "ready for prime time" and bar introduction of junk science (Faigman 2016). Contrary to fears of the neurophobic, law need not vow fealty to science. The evidence law expressly accommodates such a dialectic: what is inadmissible at T1 is later admissible at T2. Evidence law provides flexible means to deal with the gap.

Perhaps it is the larger punishment institutions that present the greater challenge. If there is no such thing as moral responsibility, then the case for prisons is compromised severely. The case against prisons has been made and, in years past, attained some currency (Gilmore 2007; Meiners 2007; Richie 2012). Reactionary elements, though, have walked back that normative progress by misrepresentation designed to vindicate dubious moral conclusions. There need be no instrumental case for "locking them up and throwing away the key" if it just feels so good, to some, to exact revenge. Revenge, we say, is "sweet"; that feeling of satisfaction is adaptive in a dyadic setting, the paradigmatic context on the savannah. But once the state assumes monopoly power over punishment, feelings that vindicate evolutionarily adaptive results may, indeed, will, undermine better (read "more efficacious") results. Revenge (just another word for "retribution") yields predictable Old Testament results.

Further, a moral responsibility system inconsiderate of the nature of human agency will undermine both non-instrumental and instrumental objects. We know, to a certainty, that youthful criminals "grow out of" their criminality, not all of them in all cases but many of them in a large percentage of cases (Piquero et al. 2001: 68). The moral responsibility system would require the convicted criminal's incarceration long after the criminal is not the same threat, the same person, that he was when he first offended.[23] Parole systems are impotent to correct such mistakes so long as those who sit on them apply conceptions of moral responsibility or serve on such boards at the pleasure of those who have internalized uncritically the extant moral responsibility system.

Neuroscientific insights can reconceptualize our understanding of what it means to be human in ways that are directly opposite to issues of punishment. Once we recognize that humans are collections of neural connections and that those connections are dynamic, subject to certain change, then we will "punish" differently, and probably eschew the term "punishment" altogether. We would take seriously "correction" and fix reduced social cost (broadly construed) as our measure of justice. What sense, we would ask, does it make to incarcerate the loving but tragically distracted parent who leaves her child to die in a car? Should we "punish" the octogenarian who euthanizes his beloved but suffering spouse of 60 years who just could not stand one more day of pain? What should we do about the octogenarian who was a serial murderer in his relative youth, say 50 years earlier? (Robinson 2008: 4). Those are questions we must confront, but instrumentally, not deontologically. Brain science may answer questions that non-instrumental normative theory can only present.

Notes

1 Chalmers 1996; McGinn 2004: 77–61; McGinn: 21–22; but see Flanagan 1991: 313–14, 317 (actually unlikely that consciousness will *not* be found, considering the trillions of neurons, or places to look for consciousness, within a single human brain).

2 Chalmers 1995: 200–02; see also Nagel 1974: 445 ("If we acknowledge that a physical theory of mind must account for the subjective experience, we must admit that no presently available conception gives us a clue how this could be done.").

3 Materialists and non-materialists alike refer to the hypothetical physical qualities of consciousness as "qualia." The term is essentially a gap filler for the elusive physical makeup of consciousness (See Chalmers 1996; Jackson 1982: 291–94.

4 The negative effects of solitary confinement are especially significant for inmates with preexisting mental disorders (Hayes 1995, citing Schimmel et al. 1989: 20, 22; Human Rights Watch 2003; White et al. 2002: 332).

5 The amygdala is a key structure of the limbic system that is involved in processing the emotional and motivational significance of stimuli (Noback 2005: 387, citing LeDoux 2000).

6 The majority of studies have demonstrated reduced function, volume, and connectivity in the amygdala and frontal cortex in both psychopathic adults and adolescents, suggesting that the adult construct for psychopathy may be extended to juveniles (Umbach et al. 2015; see also Finger et al. 2008: fMRI scans of children with psychopathic traits show abnormal responses in ventromedial prefrontal cortex during reversal learning exercises, compared to children with ADHD and healthy children; White et al. 2012: youths with psychopathic traits show significantly reduced amygdala responses when shown fearful faces compared to healthy children). Attaching the "psychopath" label to juvenile offenders in the criminal justice system can impact the type and severity of sentencing and treatment, and even the transfer of youth to adult court, due to the characterization of psychopaths as dangerous and untreatable (Skeem et al. 2011).

7 "The mechanisms underlying the experience of will are themselves a fundamental topic of scientific study. We should be able to examine and understand what creates the experience of will and what makes it go away. This means, though, that conscious will is an illusion. It is an illusion in the sense that *the experience of consciously willing an action is not a direct indication that the conscious thought has caused the action*" (Wegner 2003: 2).

8 For example, phantom limb is a phenomenon in which a person can still "feel" an amputated body part. The mystery has been solved (see Wegner 2003: 40; Ramachandran & Hirstein 1998).

9 For a deterrence effect to exist, potential criminals must perceive a positive risk of apprehension and some form of punishment (Anderson 2002: 296 n.2). A potential criminal must, in some way, have knowledge of the legal rule and the consequences of breaking that rule (Robinson 2008; Kruger and Dunning 1999: 1121).

10 Drug courts combine alcohol and drug treatment services with the criminal justice system's legal authority to reduce substance abuse and related criminal activity (Mitchell et al. 2012: 61; Porter et al. 2011: 26).

11 In the 1960s and 1970s, activists in the United States pushed for prison abolition (Dubler & Lloyd 2018). More recently, the debate about whether prisons should or will become obsolete has revived (Dubler & Lloyd 2018). Over the last 40 years, the prison population has increased by 500% (The Sentencing Project 2018).

12 For example, despite our failure to know the inner workings of the mind, we do know that certain harsh punishments yield undesirable outcomes (The American Civil Liberties Union Human Rights Watch 2012: 23–24, 29–30).

13 The aim of this study was to examine whether different culpable mental states, specifically knowledge and recklessness, could be predicted using fMRI (Vilares et al. 2017: 3223).

14 Stephen Morse contributed to the research design and wrote the paper (Morse 2015).

15 "Until science conclusively demonstrates that human beings are not responsive to and cannot be guided by reasons and that mental states do not play even a partial causal role in explaining behavior, the folk-psychological model of responsibility will endure as fully justified" (Morse 2015: 253). Morse claims that the

use of neurobiological research in criminal law continues to be "haphazard, ad hoc, and often ill conceived" (Morse 2016: 337) and that neuroscience may provide assistance in evaluating responsibility but it cannot inform how much rationality is required for responsibility, and unless it is demonstrated that no one is capable of minimum rationality, the fundamental criteria for responsibility shall persist (Morse 2004).

16 In criminal law, a person is generally not liable for an act if he does not meet the requisite mental state. For example, in a scenario where a person carries drugs over a border, the person's knowledge (or lack thereof) of the drugs in his possession will impact his culpability and his subsequent punishment (Vilares 2017: 3222).

17 They found that 59% of philosophers are compatibilists, but only 39% of those fully accept the doctrine and 24% merely "lean toward" it. It would be helpful to know what percentage of philosophers who are materialists adopt compatibilism (Bourget and Chalmers 2014).

18 The original "Marshmallow Test" longitudinal study found that a child's ability to delay immediate gratification for a bigger reward later correlated with later life success. Children were considered to have better ability to delay gratification if they were able to resist eating the snack placed in front of them for 15 minutes, motivated by the promise of two snacks after the 15 minute period of resisting temptation (Mischel et al. 1989). More recent studies, however, question that premise, and hypothesize that other factors, such as affluence, may play a larger role in both the child's ability to delay gratification and later successes (Calarco 2018; Mischel and Ayduk 2011).

19 Kaye writes, "We might not have sufficiently coherent desires to be considered competent choicemakers, and choice theory fails to sustain responsibility attributions" (Kaye 2008).

20 Marsh 2018: 88, 94, 134, 190 (activation of amygdala responsible for emotional reactions including love, caring, fear, rage and aggression).

21 See Waller (2015) describing ways in which "free will" appears in animals.

22 As of this writing, 16 states have filed actions against Purdue Pharma and other pharmaceutical manufacturers (Association of State and Territorial Health Officials 2018).

23 Between 2007 and 2010, the number of federal and state prisoners in the US aged 65 or older increased by 63%, whereas the overall population of prisoners grew only 0.7% in the same time period (Human Rights Watch 2012; Amos 2018).

References

Alper, M., Durose, M.R. and Markman, J. (2018) *Bureau of Justice Statistics, 2018 Update on Prisoner Recidivism: A 9-Year Follow-Up Period (2005–2014)*. www.bjs.gov/content/pub/pdf/18upr9yfup0514.pdf.

Amos, O. (2018) "The Teenager Sentenced to 241 Years in Prison" www.bbc.com/news/world-us-canada-43461521

Anderson, D. (2002) "The Deterrence Hypothesis and Picking Pockets at the Pickpocket's Hanging," *American Law and Economics Review* 4(2), 295–313.

Aristotle (340 BC/1985) *The Nicomachean Ethics*, Irwin, T. Trans., Indianapolis: Hackett Publishing Company.

Association of State and Territorial Health Officials (2018) "Overview of State Litigation to Combat Opioid Epidemic" www.astho.org/StatePublicHealth/Overview-of-State-Litigation-to-Combat-the-Opioid-Epidemic/02-22-18/

Bechara, A. et al. (1999) "Different Contributions of the Human Amygdala and Ventromedial Prefrontal Cortex to Decision-Making," *Journal of Neuroscience* 19(13), 5473–5481.

Berman, M. (2003) "Justification and excuse, law and morality," *Duke Law Journal* 53, 1–78.

Birbaumer, N. Veit, R., Lotze, M. et al. (2005) "Deficient Fear Conditioning in Psychopathy: A Functional Magnetic Resonance Imaging Study," *Archives of General Psychiatry* 62(7), 799–805.

Bourget, D. and Chalmers, D.J. (2014) "What Do Philosophers Believe?" *Philosophical Studies* 170(3), 465–500.

Burns, J. and Swerdlow, R. (2003) "Right Orbitofrontal Tumor with Pedophilia Symptom and Constructional Apraxia Sign," *Archives of Neurology* 60(3), 437–440.

Calarco, J. (2018) "Why Rich Kids Are So Good at The Marshmallow Test" www.theatlantic.com/family/archive/2018/06/marshmallow-test/561779/

Caldwell, M. and Van Rybroek, G. (2001) "Efficacy of a decompression treatment model in the clinical management of violent juvenile offenders," *International Journal of Offender Therapy and Comparative Criminology*, 45(4), 469–477.

Caspi, A. et al. (2002) "Role of Genotype in the Cycle of Violence in Maltreated Children," *Science* 297(5582), 851–854.

Chalmers, D. (1995) "Facing Up to The Problem of Consciousness," *Journal of Consciousness Studies*, 2(3), 200 -219.

Chalmers, D. (1996) *The Conscious mind*, Oxford: Oxford University Press.

Churchland, P. (1981) "Eliminative Materialism and Propositional Attitudes," *The Journal of Philosophy* 78(2), 67–90.

Damasio, A. (2018) *The Strange Order of Things*, New York: Pantheon Books.

Davis, K. (2017) *The Brain Defense: Murder in Manhattan and the Dawn of Neuroscience in America's Courtrooms*, London: Penguin.

DeLisi, M. et al. (2008). "The Etiology of Criminal Onset: The Enduring Salience of Nature and Nurture," *Journal of Criminal Justice*, 36(3), 217–223.

Dennett, D. (1991) *Consciousness Explained*, London: Penguin.

Dennett, D. (2005) *Sweet Dreams*, Cambridge, MA: Massachusetts Institute of Technology Press.

Dubler, J. and Lloyd, V. (2018) "Think Prison Abolition in America is Impossible? It Once Felt Inevitable" www.theguardian.com/commentisfree/2018/may/19/prison-abolition-america-impossible-inevitable>

Durose, M., Cooper, A.D. and Snyder, H.N. (2014) "Bureau of Justice Statistics, Recidivism of Prisoners Released in 30 States in 2005: Patterns from 2005 to 2010". www.bjs.gov/content/pub/pdf/rprts05p0510.pdf>.

Ermer, E. et al.. (2012) "Aberrant Paralimbic Gray Matter in Criminal Psychopathy," *Journal of Abnormal Psychology* 121, 649–658.

Faigman, D. (2016) "Michael S Pardo and Dennis Patterson, *Minds, Brains, and Law: The Conceptual Foundations of Law and Neuroscience*. Science and Law 101: Bringing Clarity to Pardo and Patterson's Confused Conception of the Conceptual Confusion in Law and Neuroscience," *Jurisprudence* 7(1), 171–180.

Finger, E. et al. (2008) "Abnormal Ventromedial Prefrontal Cortex Function in Children with Psychopathic Traits During Reversal Learning," *Archives of General Psychiatry* 65(5), 586–594.

Flanagan, O. (1991) *The Science of the Mind*, London: Massachusetts Institute of Technology.

Fodor, J. (1987). *Psychosemantics: The Problem of Meaning in the Philosophy of Mind* (Vol. 2), London: Massachusetts Institute of Technology.

Fox, S. (2010) "Laws Might Change as the Science of Violence Is Explained" www.livescience.com/6535-laws-change-science-violence-explained.html

Gilmore, R. (2007) *Golden Gulag: Prisons, Surplus, Crisis, and Opposition in Globalizing California*, Berkeley, CA: University of California Press.

Greene, J. & Cohen, J. (2004) "For the Law, Neuroscience Changes Nothing and Everything," *Philosophical Transactions of the Royal Society of London. Series B: Biological Sciences*, 359 (1451), 1775–1785.

Harenski, C., Harenski, K., Shane, M. and Kiehl, K. (2010) "Aberrant Neural Processing of Moral Violations in Criminal Psychopaths," *Journal of abnormal psychology* 119(4), 863–874.

Hayes, L. (1995) *National Centre on Institutions and Alternatives, Prison Suicide: An Overview and Guide to Prevention* https://permanent.access.gpo.gov/lps18237/012475.pdf

Human Rights Watch (2003) *Ill-Equipped: U.S. Prisons and Offenders with mental Illness* www.hrw.org/reports/2003/usa1003/usa1003.pdf>.

Human Rights Watch (2012) "Old Behind Bars: The Aging Prison Population in the United States" www.hrw.org/sites/default/files/reports/usprisons0112webwcover_0.pdf>

Jackson, F. (1982) "Epiphenomenal Qualia," *Philosophical Quarterly*, 15, 249–61.

Jones, A. et al. (2009) "Amygdala Hypoactivity to Fearful Faces in Boys with Conduct Problems and Callous-Unemotional Traits," *American Journal of Psychiatry* 166(1), 95–102.

Kaye, A. (2008) "Does Situationist Psychology Have Radical Implications For Criminal Responsibility," *Alabama Law Review* 59, 611–679.

Kidd, C., Palmeri, H. and Aslin, R. (2013) "Rational snacking: Young Children's Decision-Making on the Marshmallow Task is Moderated by Beliefs About Environmental Reliability," *Cognition* 126(1),109–114.

Kiehl, K. (2014) *The Psychopath Whisperer*, London: Oneworld Publications.

Kiehl, K., Smith, A., Hare, R., Mendrek, A., Forster, B.B., Brink, J. and Liddle, P.F. (2001) "Limbic Abnormalities in Affective Processing by Criminal Psychopaths as Revealed by Functional Magnetic Resonance Imaging," *Biological Psychiatry* 50(9), 677–684.

Kolber, A. (2009) "The Subjective Experience of Punishment" *Columbia Law Review* 109, 182–236.

Kruger, J. and Dunning, D. (1999) "Unskilled and Unaware of It: How Difficulties in Recognizing One's Own Incompetence Lead to Inflated Self-Assessments," *Journal of Personality and Social Psychology* 77(6), 1121.

LeDoux, J. (2000) "Emotion Circuits in the Brain," *Annual Review of Neuroscience* 23, 155–184.

Leibniz, G. (1714/1989) "The Monadology" in Roger Ariew & Daniel Garber (trans.) *Philosophical Essays*, Indianapolis: Hackett Publishing Company.

Marsh A. (2018) *The Fear Factor*, New York: Basic Books.

McGinn, C. (2004) *Consciousness and its Objects*, Oxford: Oxford University Press.

Medeiros, L., de Souza, I., Vidor, L., de Souza, A., Deitos, A., Volz, M., Fregni, F., Caumo W. and Torres, I. (2012) "Neurobiological Effects of Transcranial Direct Current Stimulation: A Review," *Frontiers in Psychiatry* 3, 1–11.

Meiners, E. (2007) *Right to Be Hostile: Schools, Prisons, and the Making of Public Enemies*, New York: Routledge.

Metzner, J. and Fellner, J. (2013) "Solitary Confinement and Mental Illness in US Prisons: A Challenge for Medical Ethics" in Grodin, M., Tarantola, D., Annas, G. and Gruskin, S. (eds), *Health and Human Rights in a Changing World*, London: Routledge.

Mischel, W., Shoda, Y. and Rodriguez, M. (1989) "Delay of Gratification in Children," *Science*, 244(4907), 933–938.

Mischel, W. and Ayduk, O. (2011). "Willpower in a cognitive affect processing system: The dynamics of delay of gratification" in Vohs, K.D. and Baumeister, R.F. (Eds.), *Handbook of Self-Regulation: Research, Theory, and Applications* (p. 83–105). Guilford Press.

Mitchell, O., Wilson, D.B., Egghers, A. and MacKenzie, D.L. (2012) "Assessing the Effectiveness of Drug Courts on Recidivism: A Meta-Analytic Review of Traditional and Non-Traditional Drug Courts," *Journal of Criminal Justice* 40(1), 60–71.

Moore, M. (1997) *Placing Blame: A Theory of Criminal Law*, Oxford: Oxford University Press.

Morse, S. (2004) "New Neuroscience, Old Problems: Legal Implications of Brain Science," *Cerebrum: The Dana Forum on Brain Science* 6(4), 81–90.

Morse, S. (2011) "Avoiding Irrational Neurolaw Exuberance: A Plea for Neuromodesty," *Law, Innovation and Technology* 3(2), 209–228.

Morse, S. (2015) "Neuroscience, Free Will, and Criminal Responsibility" in W. Glannon (ed.), *Free Will and the Brain: Neuroscientific, Philosophical and Legal Perspectives*, Cambridge: Cambridge University Press.

Morse, S. (2016) "Actions Speak Louder than Images: the Use of Neuroscientific Evidence in Criminal Cases," *Journal of Law and the Biosciences* 3(2), 336–342.

Nadelhoffer, T. (2014) "Dualism, Libertarianism, and Scientific Skepticism about Free Will," in W. Sinnott-Armstrong (ed.) *Moral Psychology: Neuroscience, Free Will, and Responsibility*, Cambridge, MA: Massachusetts Institute of Technology Press.

Nagel, T. (1974) "What Is It Like to Be a Bat?" *The Philosophical Review*, 83(4), 435–450.

Nitsche, M. and Paulus, W. (2000) "Excitability Changes Induced in the Human Motor Cortex by Weak Transcranial Direct Current Stimulation," *The Journal of Physiology* 527(3), 633–639.

Noback, C., Ruggiero, D.A., Demarest, R.J. and Strominger, N.L. (2005) *The Human Nervous System Structure and Function*, 6th ed., Totowa: Humana Press.

Office of the Inspector General (2016) *The Impact of an Aging Inmate Population on the Federal Bureau of Prisons* <https://oig.justice.gov/reports/2015/e1505.pdf>.

Pardo, M. and Patterson, D. (2013) *Minds, Brains and Law: The Conceptual Foundations of Law and Neuroscience*, Oxford: Oxford University Press.

Peterchev, A. Wagner, T., Miranda, P., Nitsche, M., Paulus, W., Lisanby, S., Pascual-Leone, A. and Bikson, M. (2012) "Fundamentals of Transcranial Electric and Magnetic Stimulation Dose: Definition, Selection, and Reporting Practices" *Brain Stimulation* 5(4), 435–453.

Piquero, A., Blumstein, A., Brame, R., Haapanen, R., Mulvey, E., Nagin, D (2001). "Assessing the impact of exposure time and incapacitation on longitudinal trajectories of criminal offending". *Journal of Adolescent Research*, 16(1), 54–74.

Porter, R., Lee, S. and Lutz, M. (2011) "Balancing Punishment and Treatment: Alternatives to Incarceration in New York City," *Federal Sentencing Reporter* 24, 26–29.

Raine, A. (2013) *The Anatomy of Violence*, London: Penguin.

Raine, A., Portnoy, J., Liu, J., Mahoomed, T. and Hibbein, J. (2015). "Reduction in Behavior Problems with Omega-3 Supplementation in Children Aged 8–16 Years: a Randomized, Double-Blind, Placebo-Controlled, Stratified, Parallel-Group Trial", *Journal of Child Psychology and Psychiatry*, 56(5), 509–520.

Ramachandran, V. and Hirstein, W. (1998) "The Perception of Phantom Limbs: The D.O. Hebb Lecture," *Brain: A Journal of Neurology* 121(9), 1603–1630.

Richie, B. (2012) *Arrested Justice: Black Women, Violence, and America's Prison Nation*, New York: New York University Press.

Robinson, P. (2008) *Distributive Principles of Criminal Law: Who Should be Punished, how Much?* Oxford: Oxford University Press.

Schimmel et al. (1989) "Suicide Prevention: Is it working in the Federal Prison System?" *Federal Prison Journal* 20.

Skeem, J., Polaschek, D., Patrick, C. and Lillenfeld, S. (2011) "Psychopathic Personality: Bridging the Gap Between Scientific Evidence and Public Policy," *Psychological Science in the Public Interest* 12(3), 95–162.

Smith, P. (2006) "The Effects of Solitary Confinement on Prison Inmates: A Brief History and Review of the Literature" *Crime and Justice*, 34(1), 441–528.

Snyder, H. (2012), "Bureau of Justice Statistics, Arrests in the United States, 1990–2010" www.bjs.gov/content/pub/pdf/aus9010.pdf>

The American Civil Liberties Union, Human Rights Watch (2012) *Growing Up Locked Down: Youth in Solitary Confinement in Jails and Prisons Across the United States* www.aclu.org/sites/default/files/field_document/us1012webwcover.pdf>.

The Sentencing Project (2018) *Trends in U.S. Corrections* https://sentencingproject.org/wp-content/uploads/2016/01/Trends-in-US-Corrections.pdf

U.S. Sentencing Commission (2017) *The Effects of Aging on Recidivism Among Federal Offenders* www.ussc.gov/sites/default/files/pdf/research-and-publications/research-publications/2017/20171207_Recidivism-Age.pdf>.

Ulmer, J. and Steffensmeier, D. (2014) "The Age and Crime Relationship: Social Variation, Social Explanations" in *The Nurture Versus Biosocial Debate in Criminology: On the Origins of Criminal Behavior and Criminality*, London: Sage Publications.

Umbach, R., Berryessa, C. and Raine, A. (2015) "Brain Imaging Research on Psychopathy: Implications for Punishment, Prediction, and Treatment in Youth and Adults," *Journal of Criminal Justice* 43(4), 295–306.

Vaughn, M., DeLisi, M., Beaver, K., Wright, J. (2009) "DAT1 and 5HTT Are Associated With Pathological Criminal Behavior in a Nationally Representative Sample of Youth," *Criminal Justice and Behavior*, 36(11), 1113–1124.

Vilares, I., Wesley, M., Ahn, W-Y, Bonnie, R., Hoffman, M., Jones, O., Morse, S., Yaffe, G., Lohrenz, T.and Montague, R. (2017) "Predicting the Knowledge–Recklessness Distinction in the Human Brain," *Proceedings of the National Academy of Sciences* 114(12), 3222–3227.

Waller, B. (2011) *Against Moral Responsibility,* Cambridge, MA: Massachusetts Institute of Technology Press.

Waller, B. (2014) *The Stubborn System of Moral Responsibility,* Cambridge, MA: Massachusetts Institute of Technology Press.

Waller, B. (2015) *Restorative Free Will: Back to the Biological Base*, London: Lexington Books.

Wegner, D. (2003) *The Illusion of Conscious Will*, Cambridge, MA: Massachusetts Institute of Technology Press.

White, S. et al. (2012) "Reduced Amygdala Response in Youths with Disruptive Behavior Disorders and Psychopathic Traits: Decreased Emotional Response Versus Increased Top-Down Attention to Nonemotional Features," *American Journal of Psychiatry* 169(7), 750–758.

White, T., Schimmel, D. and Frickey, R. (2002) "A Comprehensive Analysis of Suicide in Federal Prisons: A Fifteen-Year Review" *Journal of Correctional Health Care*, 9(3), 321.

Young, L., Camprodon, J.A., Hauser, M., Pascual-Leone, A. and Saxe, R. (2010) "Disruption of the Right Temporoparietal Junction with Transcranial Magnetic Stimulation Reduces the Role of Beliefs in Moral Judgments," *Proceedings of the National Academy of Sciences* 107(15), 6753–6758.

13

SCIENCE AND THE EVOLUTION OF AMERICAN CRIMINAL PUNISHMENT

Michele Cotton

Introduction

American law has long maintained scientific aspirations. Harvard Law School's first dean, Christopher Langdell, even promoted the idea of a "science of law," supposing that law is, or at least could be, similarly systematic, meticulous, and rigorous (Langdell 1887). It does indeed matter in law that things be done with precision, that they are documented, that there is consistency and predictability, and that accretion of knowledge occurs, much as is also typical of the sciences. And law, like science, is fundamentally concerned with evidence and with proof. Thus, although few see law as the science Langdell envisioned, legal decision-making does have a natural affinity with the scientific approach.

In addition to these similar characteristics, law also shares certain interests with science, particularly with the behavioral and social sciences. Law is likewise concerned with human behavior, including especially its causation and control, leading to interaction between law and these sciences. In addition, the sciences often inform the processes of the American legal system, such that many determinations of civil liability and criminal guilt depend upon scientific experts as witnesses and scientific tests as evidence. To that extent, law and science work hand in hand.

However, it is also true that the American legal system has had a complicated relationship with science, and the law around criminal punishment especially so. While the forensic sciences have long been an integral part of the criminal legal process, the behavioral sciences and social sciences have played a much more constrained role. Behavioral science evidence about individual defendants and social science evidence about the effect of criminal punishment have had comparatively little impact. Indeed, law has generally been unresponsive to and even dismissive of scientific findings relevant to criminal punishment.

That is apparently because law's concept of criminal behavior reflects traditional moral ideas about blameworthiness that do not align well with the scientific perspective. While science identifies psychological, sociological, biochemical, and neurological factors in human behavior, the law views free will choice as its real cause. And while science evaluates interventions according to their results, law considers criminal punishment to be a retributive imperative that does not depend on socially beneficial impacts for its legitimacy. Because of these differences, the law has had difficulty integrating or even accepting as valid behavioral science evidence regarding the causation of criminal behavior and social science evidence regarding the efficacy of criminal punishment.

Nonetheless, criminal law and the behavioral and social sciences will continue to intersect, posing further challenges to the law's unscientific approach to criminal punishment. The nature of the interaction thus far gives a sense of the obstacles to behavioral and social sciences' integration into law.

But that interaction also makes it possible to envision an eventual greater synthesis and how that might occur.

The Purposes of Criminal Punishment

Despite disciplinary similarities, shared interests, and dependence on science, law is, of course, not a science and is not subject to scientific norms. Still, it would be possible for the American criminal justice system to be scientific in its operation. It could, for example, deal with criminals based on the evidence of what reduces and prevents crime. Medicine, as a comparison, is scientific because it attempts to treat and prevent illness by deploying therapies based on their demonstrated effectiveness. But neither the hypothesis that criminal punishment may prevent criminal behavior, nor the idea that the law should be concerned with the effectiveness of punishment as a means of social control, has much to do with the American legal system as presently constituted. Rather, punishment has mainly been understood as something imposed because the criminal "deserves" it.

This fundamental indifference on the part of law to the potential social impact of punishment is embodied in Immanuel Kant's remark that "[e]ven if civil society were to dissolve itself with the consent of all its members …, the last murderer in prison would first have to be executed in order that each should receive his just deserts …" (Kant 1991: 156). In this view, there is something inherent in criminal behavior that calls for punishment, irrespective of whether any benefit to society can be obtained by imposing it. Such retributive punishment is not scientific because it is not "falsifiable," as by definition retributive punishment successfully achieves retribution.

Nonetheless, American criminal law has experimented with empirically testable purposes for criminal punishment, particularly in the 1960s and 1970s, when the Model Penal Code (MPC) was considered and adopted by most of the States. The MPC was an influential modernized, standardized version of the criminal law developed by a group of scholars and practitioners, and it did not even identify retribution as a valid purpose for criminal punishment (Cotton 2000: 1320). Rather, it described punishment as intended to achieve the utilitarian purposes of deterrence, rehabilitation, and isolation of criminals, as a means of reducing and preventing crime. These are scientific purposes, because they can at least in theory be tested for and demonstrated as being achieved or not achieved. It can, for example, be tested whether harsher criminal punishments are deterring crime or preventing recidivism. It can be tested whether rehabilitation programs are preventing re-offense. However, the extent to which this more scientific orientation was a difficult accommodation for the law is suggested by the alacrity with which those jurisdictions that had adopted the MPC's utilitarian purposes subsequently abandoned them and reinstated retribution as the raison d'être for criminal punishment (Cotton 2000).

Such retrenchment may have occurred because most of the scientific research that was done during the MPC era could not demonstrate that utilitarian purposes were actually being accomplished by criminal punishment. It did not appear, for example, that criminals who went into rehabilitation programs re-offended at a reduced rate (Martinson 1977). It also could not be shown that punishment achieved a deterrent effect – no correlation could be shown between punishment and the crime rate or the rate of re-offense (National Academy of Sciences 1978). Given that scientific research on punishment did not offer any well-supported alternative purpose, it is perhaps understandable that the law returned to its traditional retributive mode.

However, if the American legal system had a truly scientific orientation, the result of such unsuccessful experiments would not have been abandonment of empiricism. If chemistry experiments prove unavailing, the scientific answer is more chemistry experiments, not doubling down on alchemy. When research indicated that criminal punishment was not effective at preventing or reducing crime, that ought to, scientifically speaking, have given rise to a reconsideration of the system's methods or means. American criminal law might at least have continued with its traditional retributive focus while leaving open the question of purpose for further exploration, rather than simply repudiating utilitarian objectives (Cotton 2005). But this repudiation may not have happened solely because it could not be demonstrated that utilitarian purposes were actually being achieved. It may have also reflected the fact that utilitarian purposes were to some extent in tension with traditional retributive punishment. Rehabilitation threatened to lessen the retributive nature of punishment by treating the criminal as someone to reform rather than to discipline. Even a focus on deterrence might have undermined retribution, if, for example, it justified less severe punishments than those perceived as sufficiently retributive. If retribution is in fact the most fundamental and valued purpose, the reason the utilitarian purposes were so fully expunged from law was likely to have been because they were viewed not merely as ineffectual but also as hostile to the law's preferred purpose.

In any event, the MPC and its associated moment of empiricism indicate that the American legal system has some amenability to a more scientific attitude towards criminal punishment. But the idea that the criminal law ought to be used to achieve social benefit and evaluated (and reconfigured) accordingly was still at best given only temporary and tentative acceptance. Any future role for scientific evaluation of efficacy will be difficult to integrate into a system focused on retribution.

Just Deserts

Although the American criminal law's focus on retribution is not based on science, the concept of retribution itself can be examined scientifically. If the "just deserts" required by retributive punishment represents a detectable property of human action – and it presumably must, because otherwise no one can know when and how much to punish – then it would seem that this property is capable of scientific confirmation and measurement. For proponents of retribution, the means by which punishment is determined and justified is through consultation of everyone's conscience, moral sense, or intuition, which supposedly reveals what punishment is deserved for particular actions.

It is a complication for such a theory, however, that moral intuitions tend to vary by person, time, place, and situation. For example, what exactly constitutes a killing that is criminally punishable and to what extent it should be punished is not a constant across cultures or even within our own culture. Whatever it is that is experienced as an intuition about criminal behavior and its just deserts, it is not something definite and consistent. Accordingly, the source of the beliefs about punishment that shape the American legal system may not be something objective perceived by the intuition, but rather something collectively created through ordinary efforts, and therefore subject to rational critique.

It is possible, for example, that what is being perceived by our intuitions as the justification for retributive punishment is not a moral truth but an emotional desire. The philosopher Simon Blackburn has pointed out that

> identif[ying] ethical propositions as objectively true or false, different in content from any empirical or other kind of judgement, and known by a special faculty of 'intuition' … [may] explain[] nothing, but may merely function as a disguise for prejudice or passion.
>
> *(Blackburn 1994: 198)*

We may desire to cause pain to the criminal through retributive punishment primarily because he is the source of our own suffering and apprehension. And the belief that he deserves the punishment we mete out – we are not the ones determining it; it is required by the absolute moral laws – may reassure us that we are not gratuitously or cruelly imposing it.

Science assumes that we cannot be sure of the correctness of our conclusions unless we control in some way for our biases. The scientific method, with its double blinds, has the characteristics that it does to prevent desired outcomes from contaminating the assessment of actual outcomes. That we experience gratification from punishing criminals creates the risk that retribution is not so much a true justification for punishment as a deceptive mechanism for protecting and preserving other unacknowledged benefits. Of course, it may still be the case that such gratification is more worth having than whatever reduction in crime might be achieved by a punishment designed around some utilitarian objective. But whatever pleasure we get out of punishing criminals may be greatly reduced if rather than being something dictated by absolute moral laws it is exposed as merely emotionally satisfying.

Its pleasure would also be lessened if it turned out that retributive punishment was actually socially destructive. It should be acknowledged that it is possible for retributive punishment to achieve substantial social benefits, even if those are not its actual aim. The opprobrium made possible by the retributive attitude may have a real deterrent effect or may rehabilitate those who can be inculcated with its ethos. It is, however, similarly possible that social validation of punishment increases overall societal violence by legitimizing the use of force, or that it causes alienation that diminishes the achievement of deterrence. Because the system's focus on retribution patently disclaims concern for consequences, punishment based on desert will achieve any social good by accident and will have no means of correcting for, or even permit the identification of, any social harms it may cause. In other words, retribution may not only be both a rationalization with motivations we ought to suspect, but also one that may have significant costs for society.

None of that is to say that retributive punishment based on just deserts is indefensible – only that it is not scientifically justifiable. Further, it indicates that the retributive focus of American criminal law acts as a constraint upon the integration of scientific findings about criminal behavior into law. As long as the American legal system treats punishment as retribution that need not justify itself by any practical consideration, law will remain divorced from the scientific concern for the consequences of interventions. As such, this retributive focus in the law also may mean that we lose out on the benefits that could be achieved by a system that was scientifically designed around preventing and reducing crime.

Free Will and Criminal Responsibility

The idea in American law that criminals deserve punishment is based in part on the prevailing theory that the criminal is, through his exercise of free will, the true author of the criminal act. That is, the criminal actor could have done other than he did, and therefore his choice to commit the act makes him blameworthy for it. But this view of the causation of human behavior is not scientific. In the scientific view, the causes of behavior are, roughly speaking, genetic and environmental. Free will – in essence, the ability to escape from the impact of genetic and environmental factors – is not established in science as a human capacity. The criminal law's account of behavior could be described as "folk psychology," to the extent that it is impressionistic rather than scientifically supported.

From a scientific perspective, it is not sufficient to take one's impressions as accurate and reliable evidence. Many initial impressions – that the sun revolves around the earth, or that eyewitness identification is highly reliable – turn out to be demonstrably wrong. It is also true, it should be noted, that belief in free will is not universal. Many philosophers and scientists have questioned whether it exists. And some cultures have been more deterministic or fatalistic about human behavior. The criminal law's assumption of free will is thus far from indisputable.

Further, even American criminal law does not assume that every person accused of a crime must have been exercising free will in acting. Rather, the law recognizes exceptions, such as where the actor was affected by insanity, mental retardation, automatism, and the like. (Note that such terms as "insanity" and "mental retardation" are still used in law, though no longer current in scientific discourse.) This idea in the law of free will causation with occasional exceptions raises the question how it will be determined which unlawful acts are willed by the actor and which are not. Making that determination in the law has to varying degrees involved experts from the behavioral sciences, and the resulting interaction has evidenced the law's difficulty in accommodating scientific understanding of human behavior. That tension is particularly well-illustrated in cases involving the insanity defense.

The insanity defense in Anglo-American law was inspired by the 1843 *M'Naghten* case in England, in which it was held that the defendant would be acquitted if he committed his unlawful act while

> laboring under such a defect of reason, from disease of the mind, as not to know the nature and quality of the act he was doing; or, if he did know it, that he did not know he was doing what was wrong.

This conception identified some criminal defendants as lacking the cognitive capacity to understand the significance of their action, either failing to appreciate what they were doing or failing to understand its moral significance. An additional excusing condition was later added in many jurisdictions, where the defendant might have had such cognitive capacity, but still, as the consequence of experiencing an "irresistible impulse" resulting from a mental disorder, could not have controlled his actions. As psychology and psychiatry and other behavioral sciences developed and became more widely accepted, their practitioners began to give their opinions as experts in criminal cases, helping judges and juries make determinations about the impact of mental disorders and impairments for the purposes of applying the *M'Naghten* test and its variants.

However, as the 20th century progressed, the law's formulations of the insanity defense came under increasing criticism from psychologists and psychiatrists, who viewed them as failing to accurately capture the role that mental disorders play in human behavior. Such criticism was a major factor in the substantial revision in the insanity defense test made by the District of Columbia court in 1954 in the *Durham* case.[1] The "*Durham* rule" established that a criminal defendant should not be held responsible for his actions if his behavior was the "product" of a mental disease or defect.[2] The rule represented an effort by the DC court to be more scientific than the *M'Naghten*-type tests; it committed the jurisdiction to a medical definition of insanity and to the possibility of mental disorder as a determinant of human behavior.

The *Durham* rule also led to a substantial increase in the percentage of defendants in DC found not guilty on the grounds of insanity. While still a small number, it nonetheless represented an exponential change in the success rate. It also evidently exceeded the number that was considered tolerable by many in law and among the general public. The *Durham* rule – which never spread farther than the DC jurisdiction – was heavily criticized, increasingly limited, and finally overruled in 1972.[3] The judges who assailed it expressed increasing frustration with the discrepancy between how behavioral scientists viewed criminal behavior and how they (the judges) did. In the view of many judges, the insanity defense needed to have a legal, not medical, definition[4] (which might be compared to psychiatry deciding that there ought to be a medical definition of robbery).

The insanity defense, and the role of the behavioral sciences in American criminal law, came under further and wider attack after 1982 when John Hinckley Jr. was acquitted on the grounds of insanity after his assassination attempt against President Ronald Reagan. This acquittal (after which Hinckley was confined to a mental institution) led to the instigation of various insanity defense "reforms." For instance, some jurisdictions decreased the scope of the defense by removing the "irresistible impulse" prong, and a few even abolished the defense altogether. These changes represented skepticism toward the idea that mental disorders could have the kind of impact on behavior that behavioral scientists described.

In addition, evidentiary rules were revised to reduce the influence of behavioral science evidence. For example, Rule 704 in the Federal Rules of Evidence (and similar State evidentiary rules) had previously permitted expert witnesses to give their opinions on "ultimate issues," which are the particular elements that must be established in order for a defendant to be found guilty. The revised rules continued to allow expert witnesses to opine on ultimate issues, with the exception of mental health experts in criminal cases. Specifically, the revised Rule 704 said: "In a criminal case, an expert witness must not state an opinion about whether the defendant did or did not have a mental state or condition that constitutes an element of the crime charged or of a defense." While a medical examiner remained capable of opining on the witness stand, for example, that a homicide was "intentional," a treating psychiatrist was not allowed to say that a defendant with schizophrenia lacked capacity to understand the significance of his unlawful act and therefore had not acted "deliberately."

The impact of these changes was to reduce the influence of behavioral science on the legal understanding of criminal behavior and to constrict the influence of behavioral scientists on the criminal legal process. It might seem to many behavioral scientists that a person with diagnosed schizophrenia who, for example, killed his mother after seeing her transform into a "gaseous form with tentacles" could not have used free will to escape the impact of his mental disorder. But the law was a realm where belief in that capacity still prevailed and where conviction and punishment of such a defendant was the appropriate legal remedy.[5] The deterministic accounts of behavioral scientists had essentially "spooked" judges and legislators into backing away from the insanity defense. In rejecting the idea that defendants might have been driven by a mental disorder, future Chief Justice Warren Burger remarked that the law "must proceed, until a firm alternative is available, on the scientifically unprovable assumption that human beings make choices in the regulation of their conduct …."[6]

The guardians of American criminal law saw the risk inherent in adopting a scientific understanding of behavior. If some who commit unlawful acts lack free will in doing so, then it is possible that other (and perhaps even all) defendants lack free will and therefore cannot be held criminally responsible as blameworthy for their actions. In particular, addicts might be able to claim that their actions in the throes of their addiction were similarly outside of their own control. It was evident that behavioral science could deeply undermine the most basic assumption of the criminal law. Visions of the slippery slope may have provoked quick retreat from the legal experiment with a more scientific perspective.

Experience with the insanity defense shows that American criminal law has at least been receptive to the most rudimentary scientific concept that human behavior is occasionally affected, even sometimes dispositively, by psychological factors. This crack in the door allowed behavioral science experts to have some influence (and still to have a little influence) on the understanding of criminal behavior and on the disposition of criminal cases. The law's treatment of the insanity defense indicates that the line that separates willed from unwilled acts in the law remains *potentially* relocatable by the findings of science and scientific developments. But as the experience with the insanity defense suggests, law cannot accommodate a substantial role for behavioral sciences as long as the free will assumption remains fundamental to the law's description of criminal behavior.

Behavioral Sciences versus Forensic Sciences

While American criminal law has engaged in extended conflict with the behavioral sciences, it has had a rather different relationship with the forensic sciences. That difference could be considered surprising, because they might be expected to have parallel roles in the law. Forensic sciences, such as those concerned with DNA evidence and fingerprinting, can help establish that the criminal defendant committed the act. Psychiatry and psychology could in theory play a similar role in establishing whether the defendant had the mental state necessary for the offense. But the criminal law has embraced the forensic sciences while keeping the behavioral sciences at arm's length.

That might be because forensic sciences involved in DNA testing or fingerprinting have demonstrated reliability, while the reliability of behavioral sciences in determining the defendant's mental state at the time of the offense is, frankly, unknown. Indeed, forensic sciences and behavioral sciences are, at least on the surface, very different in their demonstrated reliability when it comes to establishing guilt or innocence. To the extent that the criminal law has resisted behavioral science expertise on defendants' mental state, it might itself be a kind of scientific decision to do so.

However, American criminal courts accepted fingerprinting as valid evidence long before it was scientifically demonstrated to be reliable. And the criminal law has accepted and continues to accept other forensic techniques without substantial scientific research support, including hair and fiber analysis, graphology, blood spatter analysis, and some kinds of fire investigation – forensic techniques that have actually proven dubious when subjected to thorough empirical verification. The law's view of science has not been uniformly skeptical, so its resistance to the behavioral sciences probably cannot be described as resulting from a generally high bar that is placed in front of science by the law on the grounds of reliability.

The law's reluctance to accept behavioral science evidence has generally been described as resulting from its status as an "infant science" and "unproven."[7] It is true that many forensic science techniques have advanced to the extent that they can give highly reliable determinations in some situations, while behavioral sciences can seldom give similarly reliable predictions or explanations of criminal behavior. Nonetheless, there is a kind of irony in the law's conclusion that it cannot accept the findings of the behavioral sciences because they are insufficiently justified, while at the same time relying fundamentally for its theory of criminal punishment on concepts of folk psychology that lack any scientific support.

Further, although forensic science can at times be highly reliable, much of it still deals in probabilities, including unknown degrees of probability, and in that sense has something in common with the behavioral sciences. A partial fingerprint, a bit of fiber, or the pattern of a fire are evidence that forensic experts must often interpret with considerable uncertainty. And courts have often admitted such less-than-conclusive forensic expert testimony, as long as it is considered capable of helping the jury in the decision-making about guilt. On the other hand, behavioral scientists are not allowed to give their interpretations of the defendant's mental state, because it is not based on sufficient certainty.

Rather than being about reliability or even sufficiency of scientific development, the law's different treatment of forensic sciences and behavioral sciences may reflect the fact that the forensic sciences do not call into question the fundamental assumptions of the criminal law – in fact, they help implement them – while behavioral sciences tend to call into doubt those assumptions. Accordingly, the law will not necessarily change its perspective as behavioral sciences – with improved neurological and biochemical analysis – become more objectively reliable and better established. Rather, resistance is likely to continue, because the problem will still exist that these kinds of scientific explanations clash with, rather than facilitate, the application of the law's long-standing theories of guilt and punishment.

The Evolution of the Criminal Law

As various examples indicate, American criminal law and its punishment of criminals is not based on scientific study, scientific findings, or even a scientific attitude. It might seem as if making the law more scientific in this regard would be as simple as getting judges and legislators to recognize that the behavioral and social sciences have a more rational and better supported account of criminal behavior than the law's theory of free will and just deserts. But scientific perspectives on human behavior have not thus far motivated any real and lasting changes in the law, suggesting that more than rational comparisons would be needed for any significant effect to occur.

That something more will indeed be needed is also suggested by Thomas Kuhn's theory of how science itself changes its paradigms (Kuhn 1962). He argued that science does not alter its description of nature through a constant process of revision to take into account new information. Rather, it maintains an existing description until the failure of that paradigm to solve important problems becomes unbearable. Kuhn's theory may also apply to American law and its prospects for adopting a more scientific perspective on criminal guilt and punishment.

The guardians of the law may behave much as scientists as do when faced with contrary information. In Kuhn's words, they "devise … *ad hoc* modifications of their theory in order to eliminate any apparent conflict" rather than abandon the underlying theory as defective (Kuhn 1962: 78). When the law confronts the phenomenon of scientific explanation for criminal behavior, as in psychological and psychiatric evidence about defendants who plead insanity, it changes the definition of insanity to cordon off the source of the conflict, rather than revising the law to take into account any discrepancy. When social science research indicates that criminal punishment is not achieving social benefits, the law returns to endorsing a punishment indifferent to social benefit.

These reactions are not really surprising. Those who make and implement the law have received the existing legal paradigm, and its concern for free will and just deserts, over many years of inculcation and have themselves made a substantial investment in it. As Kuhn points out, those who work with an existing paradigm tend to regard any alternative account primarily as something that fails to accord:

> Consider … the men who called Copernicus mad because he proclaimed that the earth moved. They were not either just wrong or quite wrong. Part of what they meant by "earth" was fixed position. Their earth, at least, could not be moved.
>
> *(Kuhn 1962: 149)*

The existing paradigm thus functions as a benchmark for evaluating alternative evidence, rather than that evidence calling into question the existing paradigm.

Further, the cost of making change itself discourages revision. Kuhn remarks, "As in manufacture so in science – retooling is an extravagance to be reserved for the occasion that demands it" (Kuhn 1962: 75). Accordingly, unless the existing paradigm fails to meet some need that can only be addressed by the new paradigm, the status quo is maintained even in the face of significant contradiction. There has to be some "crisis" that makes the existing paradigm woefully insufficient before it is reconsidered (Kuhn 1962: 84–85).

It is interesting in this regard that most of the attention given by the law to the behavioral and social sciences occurred during the 1960s and 70s during a period of rapidly rising crime, as if the law was proving inadequate to an increasing demand for crime control, and alternatives were being examined out of sheer desperation. But it became evident during that period as well that the behavioral and social sciences were unable to establish the effectiveness of empirically based theories of criminal punishment and moreover offered no clear solution to the problem of crime. Further, as crime fell after 1980, so did the law's attention to the perspective of the behavioral and social sciences. The small foothold that they had obtained in the law diminished, perhaps because the demand for an alternative paradigm had become less exigent as the crime rate dropped.

Thus arises the paradox that as the behavioral and social sciences have since grown in their explanatory power and have compiled greater evidence that criminal behavior may be caused by identifiable factors (other than free will), their role has lessened in the law and in the legal understanding of criminal punishment. But if Kuhn's theory of scientific evolution is accurate when applied to the criminal law, then not even the greater explanatory power of the sciences will by itself alter the law's paradigm. Only some important problem that is perceived as incapable of being solved by the existing paradigm, and that is perceived as better addressed by science, will lead to the real incorporation of the scientific account of human behavior into law.

The mechanism by which such a change could occur is likely to be different in law than it would be in science. The sciences – whatever Kuhn might say about their resistance to change – are still mostly under the control of scientists, which means that those who know the most about science are actually in the position to alter its norms. But that is not true of law. Though the law is made and implemented primarily by persons highly trained in law, it is also, and more fundamentally, shaped by the views of the general public, who have little expertise in law as a discipline. As part of government, the law is subject to political forces and popular views that are more grounded in moral beliefs and social attitudes than in scientific findings. If, for example, the American public concludes that the insanity defense allows too many people to "get away with" serious crimes, the American legal system generally adapts to and reflects these popular views, irrespective of whether evidence indicates that their implementation actually prevents crime or otherwise benefits the social order.

Indeed, scientific findings often fail to dictate public attitudes. Scientific evidence of global warming (for example) is not taken seriously by large numbers of the members of the American public, possibly because it is inconvenient to many societal projects. Evolution is derided as a "mere theory" by many Americans as well, presumably because it does not coincide with certain religious views of human origin. Science may be resistant to modification because of the countervailing influence of disciplinary indoctrination. But the law is likely to be even more recalcitrant, because power over change is mostly held by "outsiders" to the discipline – the general public – who have unscientific interests and influences that weigh more heavily upon their views.

With both global warming and evolution, no absolute scientific proof exists of their correctness, but they are nonetheless accepted by the scientific community as well-established and worthy of belief. Behavioral and social sciences arguably have more complicated data to interpret and less sophisticated tools by which to interpret them, but such research does meet scientific standards and has scientific credibility. Accordingly, a scientific account of human behavior may meet the criteria of science sufficiently to be declared the provisional truth in which science deals, without being found to meet the criteria of the public for altering the criminal law's paradigm. And, as with global warming and evolution, scientific accounts of criminal behavior run up against contrary popular motivations that further impede their acceptance.

But if the American public ever grows sufficiently uncomfortable with the high cost of mass incarceration, the disproportionate punishment of minorities, or the "warehousing" of the mentally ill, then the crisis may arise that allows for the revision of the existing legal paradigm. American criminal law may then be pushed to change to a system more concerned with achieving social benefit and more dependent on the behavioral and social sciences for accomplishing that objective, which is likely to represent a substantial alteration of American criminal punishment as we know it.

Conclusion

Despite its affinity with science, the American legal system remains unscientific in important respects. Free will and just deserts are distinctly unscientific concepts that animate its determinations of criminal guilt and punishment. Indeed, these concepts have largely prevented the behavioral sciences and social sciences from affecting the evolution of the law. Even as these sciences have grown and developed to reflect the changing landscape of their research, the law's concept of criminal behavior has remained much the same as it was in 1843, the year that the *M'Naghten* insanity defense test was first enunciated.

As their occasional encounters have demonstrated, it has been difficult for the behavioral and social sciences to make any inroads in the law. But the fact that the law has, in temporary and limited ways, considered scientific amendments to its impressionistic, folk concepts of criminal behavior indicates that it is not immune to the persuasiveness of the alternative scientific account. While the criminal law could easily remain for some time to come an endeavor that resists many aspects of science, at least those that challenge its basic assumptions, it presumably cannot entirely and forever ignore the conflict between those assumptions and scientific findings.

And as sciences advance, the gap in understanding between science and the law will presumably become more conspicuous and perhaps give rise to greater scrutiny and reevaluation, especially if concerns about mass incarceration and prison reform increase. It could turn out that the law's rejection of behavioral and social sciences represents not so much a true repudiation as the stumbling first steps toward a more scientific view of criminal behavior and criminal punishment.

Notes

1 *Durham v. United States*, 214 F.2d 862 (D.C. Cir. 1954).
2 *Id.* at 874–75.
3 *United States v. Brawner*, 471 F.2d 969 (D.C. Cir.1972) (en banc).
4 *Id.* at 978 ("Mental disease means one thing to a physician bent on treatment, but something different, if somewhat overlapping, to a court of law. [In *McDonald v. United States*, 312 F.2d 847, 851 (1962) (en banc),] [w]e provided a legal definition of mental disease or defect ….")
5 *State v. Love*, 909 S.W.2d 930, 940 (Tex. App. 1995).
6 *Blocker v. United States*, 288 F.2d 853, 865 (D.C. Cir 1961) (en banc) (Burger, J., concurring).
7 See *id.* at 860.

References

Blackburn, S. (1994) *The Oxford Dictionary of Philosophy*, Cambridge: Cambridge University Press.

Cotton, M. (2000) "Back with a Vengeance: The Resilience of Retribution as an Articulated Purpose of Criminal Punishment," *American Criminal Law Review* 37(4), 1313–62.

Cotton, M. (2005) "A Foolish Consistency: Keeping Determinism Out of the Criminal Law," *Public Interest Law Journal* 15, 1–48.

Kant, I. (1991) "The Metaphysics of Morals," in *Kant: Political Writings* (Hans Reiss, ed.).

Langdell, C.C. (1887) "Teaching Law as a Science," *American Law Review* 21, 123–25.

Kuhn, T. (1962) *The Structure of Scientific Revolutions* (2nd ed.), Chicago: University of Chicago Press.

Martinson, R. (1977) "What Works? – A Comparative Assessment" in *Crime and Justice, Vol. III The Criminal Under Restraint* (Sir Leon Radzinomowicz and Marvin E. Wolfgang, eds.).

National Academy of Sciences. (1978) *Deterrence and Incapacitation: Estimating the Effects of Criminal Sanctions on Crime Rates* (Alfred Blumstein et al., eds.).

14
WHAT IS WRONG WITH MASS INCARCERATION?

Chad Flanders

Introduction

It seems fair to say that "mass incarceration" as a problem with the American criminal justice system has hit the legal and political mainstream, if not before the publication of Michelle Alexander's *The New Jim Crow*, then certainly after (Alexander 2012). The facts are indisputable: with only China and Russia as clear competitors, the United States stands as the world's leading jailer with 5 percent of the world's population but 25 percent of its prisoners (Pfaff 2017), and even more if we consider those under some sort of criminal justice surveillance or control (e.g., probation or parole). The literature on the phenomena of mass incarceration – detailing it, diagnosing its sources, listing its effects and suggesting remedies – is massive and growing.

But there is a surprising lacuna in the literature, and that is explaining why, at bottom, mass incarceration itself might be wrong. I should be clear about what I mean. There is no shortage of allegations that American criminal justice is racist, or that American criminal laws are poorly drafted and arbitrarily enforced, or that sentences are too long and that prison conditions are too harsh. These, however, are not problems with mass incarceration *per se*: they would be problems even if the United States incarcerated less than half of the people it does now.

It is also the case that, if fewer people were incarcerated, there would be less in the way of the many deleterious social consequences of mass imprisonment. Communities and families who have members in prison would be less devastated by their absence; so too would a smaller number of people suffer in prison and face the resulting challenge of reintegrating into society. But these consequences themselves do not get to the problem I mean to identify. I think that mass incarceration certainly makes these consequences worse, but they do not explain why mass incarceration itself might be bad, that is, why it might be bad in itself for a state to punish and incarcerate a large percentage of its population, even independently of the causes and the symptoms of mass incarceration.

The problem of mass incarceration, as I will be considering it, is simply this: what is wrong with a nation imprisoning a substantial portion of its citizenry?[1] This is a harder question to answer than it first appears. The study of mass incarceration now mostly focuses on the causes and the consequences of mass incarceration, but it leaves open the question of whether just having a large amount of people in prisons and jails might itself be bad. Nor is there anything within the major theories of punishment (deterrence, retribution, and rehabilitation) to explain why jailing a large number of people is *per se* wrong. Indeed, if jailing a large number of people is consistent with the need to deter others, or to give people what they deserve, then these theories would positively *mandate* that we should mass incarcerate.

The answer to this question, I think, needs to come, not from the philosophy of punishment, but from political philosophy. We need to explain why a state that punishes such a large number of its own citizens risks being not just an illegitimate punisher, but an illegitimate state. Telling this story means stepping outside of the usual confines of philosophy of punishment, and even of the criminal law, and explaining what makes states legitimate or illegitimate. It means, as well, telling a story that moves beyond the sociological study of the causes and consequences of mass incarceration.

I tell that story in four parts. In the first part, I try to locate the nature of the problem of mass incarceration. This means separating what is wrong with some things that may cause or be a product of mass incarceration, and what is wrong with mass incarceration itself. I want to focus the inquiry of this paper in a certain way without denying that there are many bad things that are associated with mass incarceration. What I want to focus on, instead, is whether there is one intrinsic thing wrong with mass incarceration, as opposed to a lot of contingent things that may make mass incarceration problematic. In the second part, I show how the major theories of punishment go *none* of the way toward telling us why mass incarceration is wrong, that is to say, intrinsically wrong. The aim of the first two parts is to establish the idea that there is an "intrinsic" problem with mass incarceration.

In the third part, I bring the resources of political philosophy to bear on the problem. I show, first, that John Rawls in his *Theory of Justice* seems to condone the possibility of mass incarceration (Rawls 1971). Rawls does not say that there would be anything intrinsically wrong with a state imprisoning large numbers of people (in fact, in some circumstances, this could be *required* by his theory of justice-as-fairness). I then reinterpret Rawls to show how, on his own terms, a state that incarcerates a large number of its population is presumptively illegitimate.

I should emphasize that I intend only to suggest that there is an additional problem of mass incarceration, an intrinsic problem that exists on top of and in addition to the other and very serious problems of, e.g., overcriminalization and prisoner re-entry. In the end, I hope to open a path to further inquiry, not to dismiss or displace other equally worthy inquiries. Much work still needs to be done, on many and varied fronts. The problem of mass incarceration demands no less than an all-out assault (see Chiao 2017; Stewart 2018).

Is the Intrinsic Problem of Mass Incarceration Sociological or Philosophical?

The dominant way of looking at mass incarceration for the past 20 years has been sociological: a focus on (a) explaining why mass incarceration has happened and (b) detailing the larger social consequences mass incarceration has produced. These studies, as I will put it, focus on the *causes* and the *symptoms* of mass incarceration. They cite the growing punitiveness of American criminal law, for instance, or its racism. They also look at how putting so many people in jail can devastate communities and families.

These are real problems with mass incarceration, and I do not mean to deny them. But for one, they are contingent problems. They may or may not be the case, and we could in principle solve them. We might limit the number of things we criminalize, or we might make it easier for criminals to re-enter society. We could, in other words, potentially mitigate the causes and the symptoms of mass incarceration.

But I want to maintain that even if we did solve them or mitigate them, and *nonetheless* had a large number of people in jail, there would still be a problem with mass incarceration as a matter of state policy. How this could be so will only fully be clear in the next section. In this section, I want only to gesture at that possibility: to show that if we only focus on the contingent causes and effects of mass incarceration, we may miss the possibility that there could be another, intrinsic problem with mass incarceration.

Mass Incarceration: Causes and Symptoms

The focus of the historical and sociological literature about mass incarceration has been on causes and symptoms: why there is mass incarceration (causes) and the social effects of mass incarceration (symptoms). In this section, I explain what broadly speaking a "sociological" study of mass incarceration yields in terms of the causes and symptoms of mass incarceration. In the next section, I explain why this way of studying the problem does not exhaust what I consider to be a central normative problem with mass incarceration.

(1) *Cause: Overcriminalization.* If there are too many things made criminal, there will be too many people convicted of crimes, and if it is common that people convicted of crimes go to jail, there will be too many people in jail (Husak 2010; Reynolds 2013). Thus, one way of looking at mass incarceration is as a problem of mass criminalization: too many people in prisons and jails is a direct result of too many criminal laws. If it is the case that nearly everyone has committed a crime, and prosecutors are relatively free to charge someone of a crime, then the possibility of mass imprisonment comes close to being guaranteed.

Some have challenged overcriminalization as a cause of mass incarceration. There may be too many criminal laws, but not everyone who commits a crime is actually charged with a crime, and of those charged, fewer are convicted and still fewer go to jail. Moreover, those who ascribe mass incarceration to overcriminalization need to say *in what way* there are too many criminal laws. This is no easy task, and the empirical data doesn't necessarily support the intuition that too many people are in prison because of laws that we would think of as necessarily unjust, such as laws against drug possession. Many people are in prison not for violating minor, regulatory laws, but for committing violent crimes (Forman 2012: 47). At most, overcriminalization is an incomplete explanation for mass incarceration.

(2) *Cause: Mandatory minimums.* We come closer, perhaps, to a chief cause of mass incarceration when we focus not merely on the criminal laws in general (which may or may not be enforced, and which may or may not carry with them lengthy prison terms) when we turn to mandatory minimum sentences (Luna & Cassell 2012). If we focus on the fact that many crimes carry with them long sentences which judges have no discretion not to impose, then we have a much tighter causal connection between the cause (mandatory minimums) and the result (mass incarceration). Mandatory minimums extend the time people are in prison, which expands the prison population by not letting people out, rather than by having too many laws that put them in (overcriminalization).

But of course, the two things (overcriminalization and mass incarceration) likely work in tandem and *this* may be the best, or at least a better causal explanation for mass incarceration. First, we have too many criminal laws that possibly overcriminalize more or less harmless behavior. Second, we attach punishments to those laws which require people to stay in prison much longer than is rational. The result is that there are too many people getting into prison (the front-end cause of overcriminalization) and who cannot be released (the back-end cause of mass imprisonment).

(3) *Cause: Racism.* But now we can add a third factor that might also contribute to mass incarceration in its present form. For mass incarceration, as it is commonly discussed, is not merely a problem for people in general, but for a particular subset of people, namely African-Americans, especially poor African-Americans. This is the troubling story that Michelle Alexander tells in *The New Jim Crow*, and the title neatly sums up that story: mass imprisonment is a new means for the very old tradition of brutally subordinating African-Americans. Racism both gives a particular cast to the problem of overcriminalization and mandatory minimums (highlighting the group that suffers the most from these trends) but also shows perhaps the *motivation* for those trends. Mass incarceration is itself a symptom of two features of our criminal justice system

(overcriminalization and mandatory minimums) which in turn may be a symptom of something even deeper, viz., systemic racism.

(4) *Symptom: Overcrowding.* More people in prison means overcrowded prisons. Many (if not most) prisons are operating at near or over their capacity.[2] Prisoners are sleeping in libraries, or in rooms designed to hold many fewer people. Of course, overcrowding is not merely a function of too many people being sent to jail: it is also a function of not enough prisons and jails being built. So in this respect, overcrowding is only a contingent feature of mass incarceration: we could have massive numbers of prisons and jails, but no overcrowding. Nonetheless, in the status quo, absent any real drive to build more prisons (which cost money) or greater efforts at release, mass incarceration means and will continue to mean overcrowded prisons.

(5) *Symptom: Displacement.* But there are also symptoms of mass incarceration outside of the prisons and jails people occupy. When many people are in prison, they are obviously not anywhere else, meaning in particular that they are not participants in their families or in their communities. When many people are in prison, more families and communities are affected, sometimes devastatingly so. Families are without mothers and fathers; businesses are without employees; local governments are without voters or representatives. Of course, each person put in prison has a marginal effect on a family and a community, but there comes a tipping point when whole communities are decimated by imprisonment, so that they barely exist. The structural racism of the criminal justice system means, of course, that black communities are often the ones that are hit the hardest (Roberts 2004).

(6) *Symptom: Re-Entry.* Many people in prison, even for long periods of time, re-enter society. But when they return to society, they find it not only different from when they entered prison, they find themselves ill-equipped to cope. Whatever skills they had before prison, whatever relationships they had, are degraded by the experience of prison. When people are imprisoned and then are not prepared to re-enter their communities, they and their communities suffer: they cannot get jobs and they cannot be responsible members-of-households. Their problems reintegrating are compounded by certain disabilities they have after incarceration (in getting housing, or employment, or in voting), but incarceration itself seems to be the chief cause of their difficulties. When one person has a problem reintegrating, this is of course bad and a tragedy, when it is *many* people, the problem is even worse. As was the case with displacement, whole communities can be obliterated, not because the communities are deprived of people, but because the people who have come back to those communities find themselves unable to cope.[3]

Does Sociology Explain the Intrinsic Wrong of Mass Incarceration?

Does the sociological approach help us get closer to the wrong of mass incarceration? We might first consider the fact that the input and output problems would still be problems if there were no "mass" incarceration. This fact seems especially true with regard to the causes. Overcriminalization, if by that we mean the criminalization of activity that is not truly "criminal" according to some moral theory, is wrong even if one person is wrongly prosecuted for a non-crime. A mandatory minimum sentence would still be morally wrong if it represented an overly harsh or severe punishment for a crime for even one person. Finally, and most obviously, racism in the execution of criminal justice would still be wrong even if it involved one racist cop or one racist prosecutor or one racist judge. Something similar can be said about the symptoms. The problem of displacement is a problem even if it only affects one household. The problem of re-entry is a problem if it is only one person who, upon release, struggles with reintegrating with the larger society. In other words, the problems with the causes and effects of mass incarceration would be problems in themselves even if it were not the case that American imprisoned too many people (see also Levin 2018).

But certainly, the symptoms if not the causes of mass incarceration are worrying precisely because of *mass* incarceration. This is true: displacement and re-entry, for example, become significantly more problematic when we are dealing with large numbers of people rather than small numbers. As I said earlier, this is when mass incarceration threatens the destruction of communities, and this seems a wrong over and above the wrong that one or two or three people might have with re-entry (compare this with the wrongs of overcriminalization, mandatory minimums, and racism, which are wrongs in the same way whether they happen to one person or to many). So it is not incorrect to see the symptoms of mass incarceration as importantly related to what makes mass incarceration so worrisome. At the same time, I do not think that they fully explain the wrong of mass incarceration.

If it were the case that incarceration did not cause displacement or the effects of displacement were mitigated by a strong safety net and strong family ties, or if it were also the case that states instituted prisoner re-entry programs that ameliorated the problems prisoners face when released, we might still have *many people in prison* and we might *still* think that that is wrong. It would not eliminate the wrongness of mass incarceration if the symptoms did not exist, and this particular aspect of the wrongness of mass incarceration is what I want to isolate by speaking of the *intrinsic* wrongness of mass incarceration. We could fix the symptoms or the symptoms might magically disappear, but the intrinsic wrong would remain: the wrong of having a state that massively imprisons people, that has imprisonment as one of its main tools of social control. In part, this point is simply conceptual: there may be empirical contingent problems with mass incarceration, but there may also be an intrinsic problem with it.

This is also true with regard to the causes, which are also contingent. Even if the laws only criminalized those things that ought to be criminalized, and even if sentences were wholly just, there might *still* be a problem with having too many people in prison, that is, a problem of mass incarceration. Mass incarceration would still be a problem even if all the criminal laws and criminal sentences were just; it would be problem that, in a way, we could read off simply from the fact that a lot of people are in prison. That fact itself, and not the causes or the symptoms of it, might be reason enough to say that there is a problem. If this intuition is sound, then we have not merely a contingent set of problems with what causes or effects might be associated with mass incarceration: we would have a problem with mass incarceration itself.

We can see better how this might be so if we turn to what the philosophy of punishment has to say (or rather *not* say) about mass incarceration as a problem. This, again, is both a preliminary and substantive inquiry: it is preliminary because it is aimed at isolating the problem I want to focus on (the intrinsic problem of mass incarceration) and it is substantive because it is meant, in part, to be a criticism of mainstream philosophy of punishment.

Is Mass Incarceration Wrong from the Point of View of Punishment Theory?

The problem with what I called the "sociological" approach to mass incarceration was that, while it identified problems that were related to mass incarceration – either things that caused mass incarceration or were symptoms of mass incarceration – they did not locate the intrinsic wrong of mass incarceration. They showed at most that there were bad things that contributed to mass incarceration (criminalization, mandatory minimums) or things that were made worse by mass incarceration (displacement, re-entry). This was in part a conceptual move; I wanted to focus on what might be wrong with mass incarceration itself, quite apart from its causes and effects. But it was also meant to spur a question: suppose we didn't have these problems (i.e., the causes and symptoms) would we still think that there was a problem with mass incarceration, with the millions of people in prisons and jails in America? If so, we would be dealing with the intrinsic problem of mass incarceration.

I want in this part to show that if the sociological approach at least places us *near* the intrinsic problem of mass incarceration, punishment theory cannot really say why mass incarceration would be intrinsically wrong. I take this to be a failure of punishment theory, at least how it is usually done: it lacks the right perspective on many of the most pressing problems in punishment today. It in fact renders those problems invisible. Consider the three main theories of punishment today: retribution, deterrence, and rehabilitation. *None* of them, I will argue, can get at the intrinsic wrongness of mass incarceration, because they can only say that mass incarceration is contingently wrong – that is, it is wrong if certain other things are true.

The Theories and Their Limits

(1) *Retribution.* The core idea of retribution is that people should be punished because they deserve it, because they have done something wrong (either by doing something wrong in itself, or simply by breaking the law) (Flanders 2014). If nobody deserves to be punished, there will be nobody in prison or in jail. By contrast, if *many* people break the law and commit crimes, then the prisons and jails will be full or over full. Whether or not we have mass incarceration depends on how many people have committed crimes. Nothing in retributivism puts a limit on the number of people who are in jail. Indeed, if a lot of people deserve jail, then we *should* have mass imprisonment (see also Chiao 2017).

We might think that retributivism can say something about mass incarceration, because we can conceive of retribution as not only giving a positive command to punishment, but also a negative command to not punish too much. In short, retributivism can be a limiting principle on the amount of punishment (Flanders 2010). But how does this limit work? There are two problems here, one conceptual and one empirical. The conceptual problem is that it is hard to say how much punishment anyone deserves for any given crime. We do not know, on most retributivist theories, whether a punishment is excessive or not. For example, I do not know of a successful retributivist argument that three strikes laws (laws that provide for life imprisonment after a third offense) are *per se* illegitimate according to retributive theory. At the level of abstract theory, retributivism is simply too indeterminate to give it any critical purchase on harsh punishment.

But there is a further empirical problem with retributivism as it relates to mass incarceration. Even if retributivism could set limits on appropriate punishment with some specificity, we do not know that most people in prison *now deserve* their sentences, or that it is possible that *most people* could deserve their sentences. A retributivist who looks at the number of people incarcerated today cannot say anything is wrong with it until she knows whether many of those incarcerated do not belong there. If there is anything wrong with mass incarceration, it is not due to its massiveness, but to the individuals who are imprisoned unjustly. As a phenomenon that might be wrong in itself, mass incarceration is invisible to retributive theory.

(2) *Deterrence.* Probably a more fundamental justification for punishment is deterrence, both in the sense of deterring particular offenders from offending again (both by incapacitating them, and by threatening them with future punishment) and society at large. Here, the recent debate over imprisonment and the decline in crime has already mirrored the point I wish to make, at least partly. There is significant debate over the question of whether the rise in mass imprisonment has, in fact, resulted in greater deterrence, or whether this is due to other causes, or no specific cause at all (Zimring 2006). Whether those who claim that imprisonment has caused a decline in crime are correct is surprisingly less relevant to my point than the fact that it *could.* The possibility that mass imprisonment could be justified by a deterrence rationale shows that there is nothing in principle wrong with mass incarceration from the standpoint of deterrence. Indeed, if we are interested in deterrence, and the more people locked up the more deterrence there is, then the deterrence rationale, far from discouraging mass incarceration positively *licenses* it.

The deterrence-theorist could reply that there may be some point where the value of deterring crime costs too much, and so it doesn't make sense to keep on punishing people *no matter the cost.* And of course this is true if the deterrence theorist is also a consequentialist. But my point now is that we *don't know* whether this is the case. It could be that we are significantly underdeterring crime; that there is a lot more crime that we could deter were we only to imprison more people. If this were the case and the costs outweighed the benefits, we should keep on imprisoning people, up to and even past the point of mass incarceration. At best, the restriction on mass incarceration is a contingent one, not a necessary one.[4]

(3) *Rehabilitation.* Rehabilitation as a rationale for punishment has sadly fallen out of favor as a matter of theory, due in part to a belief that prisons and jails simply cannot rehabilitate. But this conclusion seems to be empirical, and not normative (Flanders 2015). There seems to be no in principle reason why prisons could *not* be used for rehabilitation; it may take more resources than we are now willing to invest, but this again is a contingent fact about the world and not a truth about the rehabilitative justification for punishment.

If prison and jails are *for* rehabilitation, then again there seems reason to think that many people will need to be rehabilitated, and for a long period of time. Indeed, one of the major worries during the heyday of rehabilitative theory in the mid-20th century was that there was no limit to the "punishments" that rehabilitation could require: so long as the state concluded you were sick and needed further treatment, you could stay locked up for years on end (retributive theory was thought, mistakenly in my view, to put firm limits on how much punishment you could be given for a crime). Again, the incompatibility of rehabilitation and mass incarceration seems to hang on a contingency. If not many people need rehabilitation, then we don't need to imprison them. If, however, many, many people need rehabilitation, there is nothing intrinsically wrong with putting them all in prison.

The Emptiness of Punishment Theory

Why is it that punishment theory can tell us nothing illuminating about mass incarceration, at least as a wrong in itself? On none of the major theories (retributive, deterrent, rehabilitative) does mass incarceration even arise as a problem *in itself.* The question for punishment theory, at least in 20th-century Anglo-American philosophy of law, has been: what gives the state the right to punish *this person* in *this amount*? Is it because he deserves it? To deter him or others? Or is it for his own good? When asked in this individualistic way, the question does not change if we go from one person to many people: it is still the same question, of whether we punish many people because they deserve it, or for other reasons.

The problem of mass incarceration doesn't arise when we ask the question this way because we're asking the problem basically of *each person*, taken one by one, and not about the role of punishment in the state, in relationship to all of its citizens. In short, we've removed philosophy of punishment from political theory, and as a result, certain problems don't even come up, such as whether it becomes a problem when punishment becomes an instrument of state policy against a sizable number of its citizens. Punishment theory, for reasons which are still unclear (see Flanders 2016) has been mostly divorced from larger questions of political theory, and the result is that it cannot address in any straightforward way structural problems with how a state punishes.

An example from another area of political philosophy might be helpful. It could be that, one by one, each economic transaction we make could be justified: both parties have consented to the transaction for instance and have relatively full information in making the transaction. Still, we might still have a problem on another level, if the aggregate of those transactions resulted in vast economic inequality. If we looked solely at the level of each individual transaction, we would never see a problem. But if we went to the level of *society*, the problem of income inequality might emerge as a real problem (see, e.g., Cohen 1995, chapter 1). So too, with the individualistic perspective of punishment theory: it can't see the problem of mass incarceration because the only way it can evaluate punishment is by asking if a particular punishment was just. It cannot take the wider perspective of whether the punishment system as a whole is just if it punishes too many people, even when those punishments might be individually justified. It is this perspective I urge us to take in the last part of this chapter.

How To Look At Mass Incarceration, and Why (Again) Punishment Theory Fails.

If mass incarceration is indeed a structural problem, one that is something more than individual instances of unjust or inefficient or ineffective punishment, then we cannot look at it in isolation from other structural factors – and we can't say why it is bad without looking at how those structural factors make it bad. In her book *The New Jim Crow*, Michelle Alexander defines mass incarceration as

> a set of structural arrangements that locks a racially distinct group into a subordinate political, social, and economic position, effectively creating a second-class citizenship. Those trapped within the system are not merely disadvantaged, in the sense that they are competing on an unequal playing field or face additional hurdles to political or economic success; rather, the system itself is structured to lock them into a subordinate position.
>
> *Alexander 2012: 185*

There is much that needs to be unpacked in this rich and evocative passage. Mass incarceration, Alexander urges, is *structural* arrangement that results in the subordination of a subset of the population, and what makes it wrong is something that is wrong on a system-wide level, not on the individual level, not on the level of "additional hurdles" this or that person may face, but on the level of the *whole thing* – where this is not a matter of individual instances of economic hardship or racial discrimination or of this or that unjust criminal law but a matter of many factors conspiring together.

And when we raise it to this level, we surely cannot ask just about the moral blameworthiness of one individual; nor do we capture the justice or injustice of punishment when we talk about the marginal deterrence value of punishing this or that person. We have to ask about a system that is supported or at least tolerates the fact that a large number of its members are incarcerated, and (importantly for Alexander's purposes) how this came about. Alexander's focus is on the larger, systemic consequences of American racism, of course, but the point can also apply to mass incarceration on the whole.

Punishment theory today not only does not ask these sorts of systemic questions, it blinds us to the fact that these questions need to be asked. Punishment theory leads us back to the individual, and about how to justify *this* punishment for *this* person. But again, this ignores the injustice that may supervene on individual instances of punishments when they are taken as a whole, possibly even if all of the individual instances of punishment can themselves be justified. Punishment theory cannot get at this political problem of mass incarceration, the separate and intrinsic problem, that goes beyond the individual injustices and bad effects of imprisonment on a wide scale.

Toward Mass Incarceration as an Intrinsic Wrong

If the first part of this chapter tried to get clearer on the nature of the wrong of mass incarceration, and the second part pointed to a structural approach to the problem, in this part, I want to try to diagnose how mass incarceration might be intrinsically wrong. In doing so, I take my lead from John Rawls, who offers us the resources to present the intrinsic problem of mass incarceration, or the way in which mass incarceration might be wrong as a matter of state policy.[5] While Rawls's framework is a good one, he does not use it to explain how mass incarceration might be wrong. Indeed, in his theory Rawls treats the problem of mass incarceration in a way that it becomes invisible, much like the theories of punishment do.

My discussion of Rawls has two steps. First, I sketch what Rawls says about the problem of punishment in a just society and how he resolves it. Second, using Rawls's method but disagreeing with Rawls's conclusions, I show how mass incarceration should be considered as something that is intrinsically wrong as a matter of political theory. As I say in my conclusion, I do not think this is the only way we can see mass incarceration as intrinsically wrong, but it at least gets the general approach right.

Rawls on Punishment in the Just Society

Rawls's remarks on punishment are painfully brief, but they are insightful, and even at points a little bit troubling. In explaining the nature of a just society in Part III of *A Theory of Justice*, Rawls writes (to summarize brutally) that the just society for its members should not be a disaster for how their lives go. That is, there should be some "congruence" between a person's happiness and his life in a just society (Freeman 2003: 277). If the two things come apart too much – if people who live justly in a just society are miserable – then something has gone wrong, really wrong. Rawls even suggests that a society in which the rule of just laws makes our lives difficult and unhappy may not merely have a problem with stability (unhappy people will not settle for being unhappy for long) but with legitimacy. Rawls sometimes puts this concept in terms of the "strains of commitment": a society which does not allow its members to achieve their good "strains" their ability to fully commit to the regime (Weithman 2010; Banting & Kymlicka 2017). Importantly, Rawls sees this not merely as a matter of whether the state will be one in which people will be happy. Rather, the fact that some states may strain the commitment of their members goes to the foundational question of whether that state *should* endure over time.

It is in this context that Rawls makes his remarks on punishment, which he admits are not fully fleshed out (Flanders 2016). Some people in a society may not be happy in affirming what Rawls says are the principles of justice. They will have, for whatever reason, a motive for not obeying the principles of justice, and when they fail to heed those principles, we as a society have to decide what to do with them. And here Rawls is unequivocal: we should punish them and enforce the principles of justice. The problem is not in the principles themselves, but in those who for whatever reason do not find their happiness in them. Their nature, Rawls says, is their misfortune (Rawls 1971: 576). In other words, the fault lies not in the laws, but in those unhappy individuals themselves, even if those laws "strain the commitment" of the members who are tempted, and who commit, crimes.

That this is Rawls's conclusion becomes very clear in the paragraph immediately following Rawls's statement about the natures of those who do not find their good in obeying the laws. For in response to the possibility that some will not be happy even in a regime with just rules, Rawls says that it may be that if many are unhappy, "penal devices will play a much larger role in the social system" (Rawls 1971: 576). If happiness and justice are not congruent for many, then many will be made to suffer penal sanctions. Thus does Rawls implicitly concede the possibility of mass incarceration even in a perfectly just regime, a regime that follows the right principles of justice.[6]

Mass Incarceration as a Challenge to Justice

I think we can start with Rawls's point of view about justice and happiness (and also stability) without following him to his conclusion about the possible large role that penal devices may play even in a society with just rules. Rawls's concern with stability and legitimacy is a sound one, but there seems to be something wrong with a "just" society in which it is admitted that penal devices *must* play a large role. The difficulty is that Rawls sees himself as having only two choices: either the problem is with the laws, or with the nature of those who don't find their good in the laws. Because Rawls assumes that the laws are just, the problem must be with the nature of the people themselves who disobey the laws and the solution to that is to use penal sanctions against them.

But there might be a third option. A society may have just laws, but it may be wrong to use penal sanctions against many of members of that society. There may be a further injustice that lies not in the laws but in the use of mass incarceration as an instrument of state policy. If the problem is the congruence between justice and happiness, maybe in some cases justice in the form of punishment or penal sanctions has to go. A just society may have to tolerate some unpunished criminality to preserve its status as a just society: not because its laws are unjust, but because the penal response to that injustice may be inappropriate. There may be a problem, in other words, when penal sanctions get applied as *the means to compliance* for a substantial part of society, even a society with just laws.

Rawls was right to worry about the stability of a just society in the third part of *A Theory of Justice*, but he unhelpfully saw stability as being guaranteed by penal sanctions enforcing just laws. But penal sanctions may be a source of *instability*, and not only in the empirical sense that imprisonment can displace people and make it difficult for them to function in society when they return from prison (although here we can see how the symptoms of mass incarceration may matter not just from an empirical standpoint but also from a legitimacy standpoint). Rather, mass incarceration can show that society will be a bad deal for many people, even if that society has the right rules. A society which puts penal sanctions to heavy use may lose its claim to allegiance from those people who suffer from those sanctions, and perhaps it should.

The reason for this is simple, and somewhat familiar: if a society has not made it possible for some to flourish or be happy outside of committing a crime, then that society may lose its normative ability to punish that crime (see also Matravers 2011). We might have the just rules, but we might have not given citizens the abilities or the means to live up to those rules (in Rawls's terms, we have not given citizens enough of an opportunity to develop a "sense of justice"). The result is not that those rules are unjust (we have been assuming that they are just), but that society's expectations for compliance with the rules are too high: accordingly society may have to tolerate some crimes that ideally it would not. We might have to tolerate a rise in the crime rate (Glazek 2012). Ironically, we may have to tolerate this in part because the alternative (the heavy use of penal sanctions) may threaten societal stability in the long run. Both excessive crime (which Rawls was worried about) and excessive punishment (which Rawls does not consider) can be threats to the ongoing legitimacy of a state.

Of course, if the laws of the state are unjust and this is partly why there is mass incarceration, this makes the threat to legitimacy of a state from punishment even worse (this is how overcriminalization can add to the intrinsic wrong of mass incarceration). But I have been arguing that penal sanctions as a tool of policy represent a threat in themselves, and not just because of the effects of that policy. Mass incarceration reveals a form of society that is unable to continue over time simply by having just rules. That state requires another material incentive (punishment) to be added to this. Used selectively and occasionally, the use of these incentives may not put into question that state's legitimacy, and sometimes those sanctions may be necessary for that society to survive. But used as a default mode of securing compliance, we have to ask: does this society represent a tolerable deal for those living in it? When a large percentage of the population answers this question with a *no* because they are incarcerated, we can doubt that state's legitimacy. A government that is in a perpetual state of war against a large percentage of its people cannot—or perhaps *should not*--remain stable for very long.

Finally, we might connect what Rawls says in *Theory* about stability to what he says in his more recent work on political liberalism. There Rawls develops the idea of "stability for the right reasons." A society is stable "for the right reasons" if it is just and people are able to see their good in following the rules of the society (Rawls 1993: xlii). Rawls contrasts this with a society that is stable primarily through the use of penal sanctions, or coercion. In *Political Liberalism*, Rawls's example of a society that was stable for the wrong reasons had to do with a society that used coercion to enforce one single vision of the good life (or comprehensive doctrine) on everybody. But a more obvious example of stability for the wrong reasons might also be available: a society, even a society with just laws, which had to enforce those laws through a policy of mass incarceration. Such a society also could not endure over time, if it had to rely on extensive coercion or containment in order to maintain compliance with the laws. Such a society would not be "stable for the right reasons." It would not win compliance through winning the voluntary compliance of its citizens, but through coercion.

Conclusion

If we focus on simply the causes and effects of mass incarceration, or if we look at mass incarceration from the standpoint of punishment theory, we are apt to miss the larger picture, or what I have been calling the "intrinsic problem" of mass incarceration. The problem only becomes evident when we look at it normatively, and from the perspective of state policy: how the state relates to its citizens, and whether it offers them a fair deal when it comes to their happiness and the stability of society as whole over time. Whether or not it is a fair deal will not only depend on the nature of people or the nature of society's laws. It will also depend on how those laws are enforced, and on how many people. If prison is a *de facto* inevitability for a large segment of society, we might wonder whether the state that imprisons is offering that segment a fair deal, and whether a society that is moved to imprison a large part of its population can stay stable "for the right reasons." Both of these points raise issues of state legitimacy, which in the end is the intrinsic problem of mass incarceration. That is, there may be a point where the excessive use of the state's coercive power, even in the service of just ends, renders the use of that power unjust. If I have at least pointed to the possibility that there is this intrinsic, political problem of mass incarceration, then this chapter has been a success, even if the ultimate diagnosis of that problem remains elusive.

Acknowledgements

Thanks to Vincent Chiao, Danny Priel, and Zach Hoskins for comments and discussion on a previous draft, and to Hamish Stewart for providing me with a draft of his work on the same subject as my chapter. An audience at a Georgia State University conference on "Overcriminalization" in 2017 provided helpful feedback, especially Doug Husak and Andrew Jason Cohen. Desiree Austin-Holliday provided excellent research and editing assistance.

Notes

1 It may be worthwhile to deal with the question, early on, of what counts as "substantial" because it strikes me that there is no clear answer. But for the purposes of this chapter, I do not need one—or at least the need is less pressing. That's because the concept I am pairing with mass incarceration, "legitimacy," is not an all or nothing concept. It is rather a scalar one. The more people we incarcerate – that is, the more people that are complying with the laws because at the limit they are *coerced* to – the less legitimate our state is.

2 *See, e.g.,* Brown v. Plata, 131 S. Ct. 1910, 1923–26 (2011)

3 "Of the over 2 million people in state and federal prisons and jails, about 630,000 are released annually back into the poor, inner-city communities from which they are drawn. More than one in five of those former prisoners, having fully served their sentences, will receive no formal government help readjusting upon their return." (Miller 2007).

4 More fundamentally, I do not think that the consequentialist can say why mass incarceration is *unjust* rather than inefficient.

5 Rawls may not be the only political philosopher who can help us here (see Flanders 2019).

6 Of course, as a matter of empirical fact, a just society may not have many who commit crimes or who need the threat of penal sanctions in order to obey the law. But the point remains: in theory, justice-as-fairness can condone mass incarceration.

References

Alexander, Michelle (2012) *The New Jim Crow (Revised)*. New Press.

Banting, Keith G., and Kymlicka, Will (2017) *The Strains of Commitment: The Political Sources of Solidarity in Diverse Societies*. Oxford University Press.

Brown v. Plata, 131 S.Ct. 1910 (2011).

Chiao, Vincent (2017) "Mass Incarceration and the Theory of Punishment." *Criminal Law and Philosophy*, 11, 3, pp. 431–452. doi:10.1007/s11572-015-9378-x.

Cohen, G.A. (1995). *Self-Ownership, Freedom, and Equality.* Cambridge University Press.
Flanders, Chad (2010) "Retribution and Reform." *Maryland Law Review*, 70, pp. 87–140.
Flanders, Chad (2014) "Can Retributivism Be Saved?" *Brigham Young University Law Review*, 2014, pp. 309–362.
Flanders, Chad (2015) "The Supreme Court and the Rehabilitative Ideal" *Georgia Law Review*, 48, pp. 383–432.
Flanders, Chad (2016) "Criminals Behind the Veil: Political Philosophy and Punishment." *Brigham Young University Journal of Public Law*, 31, pp. 83–109.
Flanders, Chad (2019) "Political Philosophy and Punishment." in Ferzan, Kim and Larry Alexander, eds. *The Palgrave Handbook on Applied Criminal Justice*, pp. 521–546
Freeman, Samuel (2003) "Congruence and the Good of Justice." *The Cambridge Companion to Rawls*, pp. 277–315. doi:10.1017/ccol0521651670.008.
Forman, Jr., James (2012) "Racial Critiques of Mass Incarceration: Beyond the New Jim Crow." *New York University Law Review,* 83, pp. 101–146.
Glazek, Christopher (2012) "Raise the Crime Rate," *N+1*, Jan. 26, 2012, http://nplusonemag.com/raise-the-crime-rate
Husak, Douglas N. (2010) *Overcriminalization: the Limits of the Criminal Law.* Oxford University Press.
Levin, Benjamin (2018) "The Consensus Myth in Criminal Justice Reform" *Michigan Law Review*, 117, pp. 259–318.
Luna, Erik and Cassell, Paul G. "Mandatory Minimalism." (2012) *SSRN Electronic Journal*, doi:10.2139/ssrn.2181092.
Matravers, Matt (2011) "Political Theory and the Criminal Law" in Duff, R.A., and Stuart P. Green. *Philosophical Foundations of Criminal Law.* Oxford University Press, pp. 67–82.
Miller, Eric J. (2007). "The Therapeutic Effects of Managerial Reentry Courts." *Federal Sentencing Reporter*, 20, pp. 127–135., doi:10.1525/fsr.2007.20.2.127.
Pfaff, John F. (2017) *Locked in: the True Causes of Mass Incarceration--and How to Achieve Real Reform.* Basic Books.
Rawls, John (1993) *Political Liberalism.* Columbia University Press.
Rawls, John (1971) *A Theory of Justice.* Harvard University Press.
Reynolds, Glenn Harlan (2013) "Ham Sandwich Nation: Due Process When Everything Is a Crime." *SSRN Electronic Journal*, doi:10.2139/ssrn.2203713
Roberts, Dorothy E. (2004) "The Social and Moral Cost of Mass Incarceration in African American Communities," *Stanford Law Review*, 56, pp. 1271–1305.
Stewart, Hamish. (2018) "The Wrong of Mass Punishment." *Criminal Law and Philosophy*, 12, 1, pp. 45–57. doi:10.1007/s11572-016-9409-2
Weithman, Paul (2010). *Why Political Liberalism?* Oxford University Press.
Zimring, Franklin E. (2006) "The Size and Character of the Crime Decline." *The Great American Crime Decline*, pp. 3–24., doi:10.1093/acprof:oso/9780195181159.003.0010

PART III

Sciences, Prevention, and Punishment

15
PUNISHMENT, SHAMING, AND VIOLENCE

James Gilligan

When a man is suffering from an infectious disease, he is a danger to the community, and it is necessary to restrict his liberty of movement. But no one associates any idea of guilt with such a situation. On the contrary, he is an object of commiseration to his friends. Such steps as science recommends are taken to cure him of his disease, and he submits as a rule without reluctance to the curtailment of liberty involved meanwhile. The same method in spirit ought to be shown in the treatment of what is called "crime".

(Bertrand Russell, 1918)

Violence is every bit as much a public health issue for me and my successors in this century as smallpox, tuberculosis, and syphilis were for my predecessors in the last two centuries.

(C. Everett Koop, MD, Surgeon General of the United States, 1984)

Punishment as a Form of Violence

If we define violence as the infliction of injury on a person by a person, then it is clear that the injuries forbidden by law, called violent crimes, are not the only behaviors that constitute violence. When the infliction of injury, rather than being forbidden, is explicitly permitted or even commanded by the law, we call it punishment. That is, from a public health standpoint, punishment and crime are simply more or less equivalent forms of violence, whose effects on the victims are more or less the same – death, injury, pain, disability, terror, humiliation, hate, and the loss of autonomy that results from being dominated by someone more powerful (Gilligan 2000a, 2000b). That is especially clear when we speak of physical punishments, such as capital punishment and corporal punishment (whose effects, from a medical standpoint, are the same as murder and aggravated assault, respectively).

But even the infliction of non-physical punishment constitutes social and psychological violence, which can be just as painful and lethal as physical violence and torture (Gilligan 1999a). For example, the subjection of human beings to prolonged solitary confinement, even when it is not accompanied by assaulting their bodies, is regarded by the United Nations and the European Court of Human Rights as a form of (psychological) torture, so that the European Union and virtually every developed nation on earth, with the notable exception of the United States, forbids it (Conley 2013; UN Standard Minimum Rules for the Treatment of Prisoners 1995:72). I have personally examined inmates in US state prisons who have been held in uninterrupted solitary confinement, despite having broken no prison rules during that time (according to the prison's own records), for as long as 30 years. Many survivors of solitary confinement, such as John McCain (Gawande 2009) and

Nelson Mandela (1994: 47), have testified that that form of purely social and psychological torture was more painful than any other aspect of prison life, including beatings and physical torture. And the social isolation and sensory deprivation of solitary confinement are notorious for provoking both psychosis and suicide among those who have been subjected to this form of punishment. For all these reasons, and others that I will document below, it is clear that punishment is just as much a threat to public health as so-called violent crime is, so that it is just as important to learn about the causes, consequences and prevention of punishment as it is of violent crime.

Does Punishment Achieve Justice and Prevent Violence?

Historically, the commonest cause of the form of violence called punishment has been the form of thinking and feeling called morality: that is, moral value systems, judgments and commandments. Central to this is the moral claim that punishing those who are guilty of injuring people is something we are morally obligated to do in order to achieve justice; and that it is by this means, and only by this means, that we can in fact achieve the moral goal called justice. As John Stuart Mill (1861: 246) put it, "We do not call anything wrong, unless we mean to imply that a person ought to be punished in some way or other for doing it…."

But this is often assumed to mean that the purpose of punishment is to achieve justice *for the victim*. However, that assumption becomes untenable once we notice that in our society the government officials and others who pursue justice through punishment spend far more time and money (sometimes millions of dollars over a period of decades) inflicting pain on the guilty than they do in compensating the victims or survivors of violence for their loss, or in helping them to rebuild their lives. So we cannot take seriously the argument that punishing violent criminals is done out of concern for their victims.

Another argument in favor of punishment is the untested assumption that legal violence is an effective means of preventing or deterring illegal violence, simply because preventing violence is supposedly one of its purposes. As Oliver Wendell Holmes (1881: 46) put it, "There can be no case in which the law-maker makes certain conduct criminal without his thereby showing a wish and purpose to prevent that conduct. Prevention would accordingly seem to be the chief and only universal purpose of punishment." In what follows, I will attempt to clarify why punishment, even though its only rational purpose would be to prevent violence, is actually, in addition to being a form of violence itself, among the most powerful stimulants of further violence, including its illegal forms, that we have yet discovered (Gilligan 2000a).

This chapter will attempt to clarify the many ways in which the psychology of punishment is the same as the psychology of crime – both in its causes (motives), its consequences, and its prevention.

What is punishment, psychologically? The etymology of words is one of the royal roads to understanding the collective or cultural unconscious, and the etymology of "punishment" tells us what its underlying meaning is. The word derives from the Greek *poine,* and its Latin derivative, *poena*, which mean revenge. Indeed, *Poine* was the name of the Greek goddess of revenge. *Poine* and *poena* are also the roots of our word "pain," as well as of penalty, penal (system), penitentiary, and penance. Hence, *punishment is the deliberate infliction of pain on a person for the sake of revenge* (no matter what other goals it may also be intended to achieve). And penitentiaries, or prisons, are institutions a central purpose of which is to inflict pain on the prisoners for the sake of revenge (a task at which all but the most enlightened of them are all too successful). But as one of the children whom Piaget (1932) interviewed for his studies of moral development recognized, the trouble with revenge is that it is endless: the moment one person gets revenge, the person on whom revenge was taken is motivated to return the favor, leading to counter-revenge, counter-counter-revenge, and so on, ad infinitum. ("Out of the mouths of babes…") Thus, insofar as punishment is revenge, it does not prevent violence, it stimulates it.

The most popular euphemism for both "punishment" and "revenge" is "justice" – specifically, retributive justice. But "retribution" itself is just another euphemism for revenge.

Do We Want to Revenge Violent Behavior or Prevent It?

The main cognitive handicap that we impose on ourselves by defining violence as a moral and legal problem (the solution to which is justice), is that that point of view is incapable of informing us as to what causes violence and how we could prevent it. The traditional moral and legal way of thinking, as it is actually conducted in criminal trials, contradicts Holmes's description of the only rational purpose of punishment, for in determining guilt the criminal law neither asks questions about the prevention of violence, nor attempts to answer them. The criminal law up to now has restricted itself to asking the moral questions "How evil was this particular person, and how much punishment does he deserve?" And even if it were possible to gain the knowledge that would be necessary in order to know how evil the person is, and how much pain he deserves (which no one yet has demonstrated the ability to do), the answers would not help us in the least to understand either what causes violence or how we could prevent it. Those are not moral or legal questions, they are empirical ones. And they can be answered only by empirical research, not moral or legal reasoning.

The concept of legal guilt is ultimately a moral value judgment, not a finding of fact. For legal guilt does not consist merely of having committed an act that is forbidden by law (an *actus reus*, in the Latin of the law). From a legal standpoint, no one can be found guilty without the additional judgment that he committed his *actus reus* with a *mens rea* – that is, an evil or guilty mind. And that is a moral value judgment, not an empirical datum or finding of fact (Stone 1975; Gilligan 2015, 2018).[1]

But even if it were possible to obtain the knowledge we would need in order to be able to answer those moral questions, the answers would be of no practical help to us if what we really need to know, in order to protect and preserve life, are answers to the practical questions: "What causes violence, and how can we prevent it?" Or in other words: what biological, psychological and social forces and processes interact with each other to destroy life by causing the various forms of violent behavior – from homicide and suicide to war and genocide? And which ones do so in ways that protect, preserve and maintain life, by preventing both behavioral and structural violence, including the deaths caused by poverty? (Gilligan 1996, 1999b, 2001; Hsieh and Pugh 1993).

That is why we need to replace the old moral, legal, and political questions, whether or not we could gain the knowledge we would need in order to answer them, with empirical questions, which can be answered by means of clinical, epidemiological and experimental research: not "How *should* we live?" but "How *can* we live?" That is, what biopsychosocial conditions protect life, and which ones cause death? To ask those questions is to reconceptualize violence as an empirical problem in public health and preventive medicine, rather than as a moral and legal problem (Gilligan 2000b). And just as we recommend evidence-based medicine, isn't it time that we sought to create evidence-based law and politics? If we did that, we would be replacing the irrelevant, futile and ultimately life-destroying presumption that we are capable of knowing how much pain we are morally obligated to inflict on someone because he deserves it, with the kinds of knowledge that are the subject matter of, and can be progressively augmented by, the human sciences: human biology, psychology, and the social sciences. As one of the founders of the discipline of public health and preventive medicine, Rudolph Virchow, put it, "Medicine is a social science, and politics is simply medicine writ large" (Virchow 1958).

We can begin that project by supporting and cooperating with relatively recent developments in the legal system itself, as it evolves beyond its previous restriction to the pursuit of revenge, to such new initiatives as "therapeutic jurisprudence;" replacing "retributive justice" (punishment, or revenge) with "restorative justice;" diverting defendants from criminal courts to drug courts and mental health courts specializing in resolving social and behavioral problems associated with drug addiction and mental illness; and so on. Indeed, I do not think I am proposing an agenda for the law that is substantially different from the one proposed by Oliver Wendell Holmes, as I quoted him above – except that I am adding the caveat that, as the evidence I will review below shows, punishment cannot achieve the prevention of violence, it can only result in the exacerbation of it.

What Causes Violence?

I have used prisons as my social-psychological laboratories for research on the causes and prevention of violence. For example, when I would ask the most violent people our society produces why they had killed or assaulted someone, they would almost always give me the same answer: "Because he disrespected me." In fact, they used that expression so often they abbreviated it into the slang term, "He dis'ed me." And it occurred to me that when people use a word so often that they abbreviate it, that tells you how central it is in their moral and emotional vocabulary. (I speak of both the perpetrators and the victims of lethal violence as "he" because the vast majority of both groups are male.)

From that, and many other types of data, as I have written about elsewhere (Gilligan 1996, 2003), I have concluded that there is a pathogen that is necessary but not sufficient for the causation of violence, in the same sense that the tubercle bacillus is necessary, but not sufficient, to cause tuberculosis; except that in the case of violence, it is not a micro-organism, it is an emotion: the emotion of shame and humiliation (for which there are dozens of synonyms, which in itself tells you how central it is: the feelings of being disrespected, dishonored, disgraced, demeaned, defeated, insulted, slighted, rejected, ridiculed, or treated with contempt, as someone who is inferior, weak, ignorant, poor, worthless, unemployed, unimportant, or experienced any other variety of what psychoanalysts call "narcissistic injuries").

However, there was something else that was equally important in the causation and prevention of violence. My colleagues and I, in the Mental Health Service that I directed in the Massachusetts prison system, used to say that you never meet a guilty man in prison. What we meant by that was not that they would deny that they had committed the act for which they had been imprisoned (only a small minority protested innocence on those grounds – some of whom may indeed have been innocent of the crime of which they had been convicted). Almost everyone with whom we worked simply felt that the violent act that they freely acknowledged having committed was fully justified: "The bitch deserved it" or "The son of a bitch deserved it." Or "I had to do it – what else could I have done? I would have been a punk if I hadn't zapped him." Nor was is it that they necessarily felt that their *physical* lives had been threatened by the victims of their violence. It was that they felt that their *psychological* survival was threatened; that is, that they would be overwhelmingly humiliated or dishonored if they did not stand up for what they felt was their moral "right," or the respect that was morally due to them – in which case they would be vulnerable to experiencing what they have described to me in terms that I have paraphrased as the "death of the self" (Gilligan, 1996), and which others have called "soul murder" (Shengold 1989).

In fact, the more heinous the crime they had committed, the less was their feeling of guilt. And it struck me that that was one reason they had been capable of committing their act of violence in the first place: because they were not inhibited, as any normal person would have been, by the capacity for feelings of guilt and remorse about giving pain to someone else (together with the capacity for feelings of sympathy, care, and some degree of love for other people and responsibility for their welfare).

Freud (1930) commented that no one feels guiltier than the saints. And he was right, as even a cursory examination of their biographies and autobiographies demonstrates. They are forever saying "Mea culpa, mea maxima culpa" – my guilt (or crime, or sin) – and punishing themselves, sometimes with grotesque acts of penance, for their sinfulness. And that is one reason why they are saints – because they feel so guilty about even being tempted to cause pain or harm to anyone, even those who were guilty of the most grievous sins, that they feel too guilty to harm anyone (except themselves). Their goal is to forgive other people, not to punish them for their sins.

But I would add to Freud's insight about saints my own observation of a group with whom he had no experience: that no one feels more innocent than the criminals. That is why they are capable of being criminals: because they lack the capacity for the feelings of guilt and remorse that would inhibit the rest of us from ever committing the crimes that led to their being sentenced to prison.

The Psychology of Shame and Guilt

The moral emotions, shame and guilt (and their opposites, the feelings of pride and innocence, respectively) are as central among the motivations for human behavior as love and hate are – for the simple reason that they are love and hate, except as directed toward the self, not others. That is, pride is self-love, and shame is the absence of self-love. Guilt is self-hate, and innocence is the absence of self-hate. Thus, while we speak of shame as an emotion, it is actually the absence or deficiency of an emotion – namely, the emotion of self-love, or pride (i.e. the feeling of self-esteem, self-worth and self-respect).

Shame and guilt are antagonistic, antithetical emotions, so that whatever increases feelings of shame decreases feelings of guilt, and vice versa. Thus, increases of shame (such as being subjected to the shame of punishment) are accompanied by decreases in the feeling of guilt (which is why punishment disinhibits and facilitates violence toward others). And decreases of shame (increases of pride) are accompanied by increases in the feeling of guilt. Thus, it is not surprising that pride is considered the deadliest of the "Seven Deadly Sins" in the guilt-ethic of Christianity. And it is why the guilt-ridden (i.e., the saints) place the highest value on humility (which to the shame-driven personality is equivalent to self-humiliation) – because it reduces the pain of guilt, which tends to increase when pride does.

Shame and guilt are also central determinants of the degree to which people direct love and hate toward others. Shame motivates directing love toward the self, in the form of narcissism and self-glorification, since it is the pain of having insufficient love for the self – both from oneself, in the form of pride and self-esteem, and from others, in the form of respect, admiration and praise. Shame also motivates directing hate toward others, ultimately in the form of violence, whether it is called crime or punishment, as a means of demonstrating one's power over others, and of achieving an ersatz substitute for respect, namely, fear, when one is not able to elicit actual, positive respect and admiration from others.

Guilt, by contrast, motivates directing love toward others (in the form of altruism, as a "reaction-formation" against the hate that one actually feels toward those whom one also loves, albeit ambivalently), and directing hate against the self (i.e., self-punishment, as a means of avoiding directing one's hate against others, by diverting it onto the self).

One precondition that needs to be present before shame will cause violence is the absence of access to non-violent sources of pride and self-esteem, such as the skills and knowledge that are gained through education; a job, career, or profession that brings self-respect and respect from others; some standing and respect from one's friends, family and community. Those who are most vulnerable to resorting to physical violence when they feel humiliated or slighted are lacking in almost all of the above. They are statistically far more likely to be not only uneducated but even illiterate, unemployed, poor, homeless, and members of relatively less powerful demographic groups that are treated by the wealthier and more powerful members of society as inferior in intelligence, morality, and overall worth (e.g., African-Americans, Latinos, native Americans, and the poor among all races and ethnic groups).

When I was directing the mental health system in the Massachusetts prisons, we came across empirical evidence in support of this last point. We found that of all the self-help programs that were available to the prisoners, the one that was most successful in preventing recidivism, or reoffending, after they were released from prison was gaining a college degree while in prison. Over a 25-year period, not one prisoner, out of the more than 200 who had gained at least a college degree (and in some cases a master's degree) while in prison, returned for a new crime. And we found that the state of Indiana had had the same result, as had Folsom state prison in California. Now of course nothing is 100 per cent everywhere and forever, but many national surveys have confirmed the general finding that education, especially higher education, is the most effective single means of preventing crime and violence (Davis et al. 2014).

Why would education be so effective in preventing violence? Clearly, the acquisition of skills and knowledge through education is one of the most direct and successful means for increasing people's self-esteem, their self-respect, and their respect from others. So if there is any validity to the general theory of the relationship between shame and violence that I am presenting here, we would certainly expect the finding I have just mentioned – namely, that a college education would diminish both shame and violence. The main reason criminals have traditionally been considered untreatable is because our society has not made a serious, prolonged effort to treat them.

Does Punishment Prevent Violence or Cause It?

The first thing I learned about violent prisoners when I first began working with them 50 years ago was that they had already been punished, far beyond anything I realized occurred in our society. For example, one man's body was covered with burn scars, because when he was a child his mother, instead of speaking with him, or even spanking him, threw scalding water on him. Another man, who had raped and murdered a woman whose apartment he had broken into, had scars on his ankles and wrists, because when he was a child, his mother's way of punishing him was to take her pistol and shoot him – not where it would kill him, but where it would teach him a lesson (which, of course, it did). Another man had brain damage, from being locked in an empty refrigerator long enough to suffer deprivation of oxygen. I could give a hundred other examples, confirmed by independent documentation of their life histories. But the point is that if punishment would prevent or inhibit violence, instead of stimulating it, these men would never have become violent in the first place. For they had already been punished as severely as anyone can be without actually being killed (physically, that is; they had in fact become victims of "soul murder"), long before they began assaulting or killing others. Indeed, the most violent among them were the survivors of their own attempted murder (i.e., capital punishment), usually by a parent.

I observed these same patterns of behavior in the prisons on a daily basis: the more severely prisoners were punished, the more violent they became (both toward other inmates, and toward prison officers), and the more violent they became, the more severely they were punished – until finally they became so enraged and humiliated that they became ready to sacrifice the lives of their bodies if that was the only way they could save their souls (or resurrect their dead souls). The most violent among them told me that they had resolved to provoke their own (physical) death in an apocalyptic "blaze of glory" in which they would take down as many other people as they could, until they themselves were finally killed by the officers. Nor were these empty threats: many actually behaved in that way, both in the prisons and on the streets. Their deaths, which occur throughout the United States by the hundreds each year, are classified by vital statisticians as due to "legal intervention." In fact, this behavior is so common that the police have a nickname for it: "suicide by cop."

But one does not have to interview violent prisoners in order to learn this. We now have at least a century's worth of research on child-rearing, focusing on the effects of different parenting and disciplinary practices on the development of moral reasoning, conscience, violence and aggression, other antisocial behavior, capacities for empathy and altruism, and so on. Child-rearing is such an inherently complicated and ambiguous enterprise, and involves so many different variables not all of which are possible to control for, that it is not surprising that there are few findings from this research that are consistently replicated. But there is one finding that has been so consistent that it has earned a substantial consensus among researchers: that the more severely children are punished, the more violent they become – both during childhood itself, and in adulthood. For example, as Roger Brown summarized this research,

> Very few associations have been reliably established between child-rearing practices and child personality. The association between physical punishment and an aggressive child has more evidence behind it than any other. ... the evidence relating punishment and aggression is ... better [than for any other association, such as that between early independence training and a strong achievement motive in the child]. ... Severe punishment went with more aggression.
>
> *(Brown 1965: 387)*[2]

How Can We Transcend the Moral Commandment to Commit Punishment and Violence?

If we consider shame as the thesis, then guilt is its antithesis. What transcending shame and guilt requires is developing the capacity to love both self and others – that is, to become capable of pride without guilt, and innocence without shame – which we can consider the synthesis. Preventing punishment and all the other forms of violence, in other words, will require us to transcend the moral emotions and the moral, legal, and political behaviors and ideologies that they motivate, by developing the capacity for the emotion that makes moral value judgments and commandments unnecessary, redundant, and irrelevant – namely, the ability to love and respect oneself and others. When people love, they do not need moral commandments to order them to treat those they love well. They spontaneously and automatically want to do so. That is what it means to love. That is, an operational definition of love would be: the emotion that motivates us to enhance the lives and welfare of those we love.

We only need morality when, and to the extent that, we do not love. But the problem with morality is that it inhibits love. Shame, and shame-driven ethics, inhibit love toward others; and guilt, and guilt-motivated ethics, inhibit self-love (Gilligan 1975, 1996). As Freud put it, neurosis – and by implication, all psychopathology – consists of the inhibition of the capacity to love. Thus, mental health and maturity require transcending morality, or neurosis (which means transcending shame and guilt, which are the ultimate emotional sources of both morality and neurosis), and developing the capacity to love both self and others.

As Aristotle (2009: VIII.i.4) put it, "if men are friends [*philon*], there is no need of justice [*dikaiosunes*] between them; whereas merely to be just is not enough." In other words, where love (*philia*: "affection" or "friendship") is present, moral commandments and value judgments (such as *dike*: justice) are not needed; and for those who know what love and friendship are, morality or justice alone is a pale substitute. Hume (1751) said much the same thing – that "strong, extensive benevolence" cannot be the original motive of morality (justice), since it would render justice unnecessary – because the person who loves another does not need to be told, by moral or any other commandments, to be "good" to that person, and in fact may want to give even more to the loved person than the laws of justice would command as the minimal obligatory "just" or "fair" amount. As Hume put it, maliciously but entirely accurately, justice is the "cautious, jealous virtue" (Hume 1739: III.ii.2; 1751: III.i.145). Or as St. Augustine (1956: VII, 8) put it, "Love, and do what you will; ... let the root of love be within, of this root can nothing spring but what is good."

The only empirically demonstrated way to diminish the frequency and severity with which violent criminals reoffend is to treat them with respect, not strip them of their human dignity (that has already been accomplished, the result of which has been the violence they have already committed); and to give them access to non-violent sources of self-esteem (such as education), and psychotherapeutic means of healing the traumas they have already experienced, such as the degree of child abuse that I described above. The underlying insight here is that only damaged people damage people. Our job is to identify the injuries and damage, and find ways to facilitate people's ability to heal from the injuries they have suffered, so that they will not inflict other versions of the same wounds on other people or on themselves. As Jesus put it (Mark 2:17), "It is not the healthy who need a doctor, but the sick. I have not come to call the righteous, but sinners." Unless our criminal justice system can take the same attitude, it will only continue to do what it is already doing, namely, set in place a self-reinforcing chain reaction of revenge and counter-revenge which can only increase the eventual number of victims and further endanger everyone.

What Alternatives Are There to Prisons and Punishment?

I am not advocating simply unlocking the doors of our prisons and letting their inmates run free if they have assaulted, murdered or raped people, and are still at high risk of doing so again if they are returned to the community. But I am stressing the distinction between restraint and punishment. We all know what that difference is. When two-year-olds start running in front of traffic and do not respond to verbal commands to stop, we put our arms around them and restrain them. But we don't do that in order to inflict pain or injury on them. We do so in order to prevent them from suffering pain and injury.

I have often been asked if I believe in prison reform. I have had to answer no, because I do not believe prisons can be reformed. I think they can only be abolished, demolished and replaced with something more effective at preventing violence toward everyone. The prisons we have today are almost all designed with the same architecture that used to guide the construction of zoos: concrete cells with bars on the windows. Zoo-keepers learned that when animals were kept in such cages, they died, so they replaced them with zoological parks designed to reproduce the environments in which the animals had evolved to live. Yet we still house human beings in the types of cage in which no zoo-keeper would be allowed to house his or her animals. And then when these human beings behave like animals (or worse), we use that as our excuse: "See, they are animals, and animals belong in cages." It is thus not surprising that the most effective way to turn a non-violent person into a violent one is to send him to prison.

There is, however, an alternative. If we really wanted to prevent violence, we would create locked, safe, secure residential colleges and therapeutic communities, in which the residents would be able to acquire as much education as they were capable of, and as much therapy of all kinds as they needed, for everything from psychiatric disorders and drug and alcohol addictions, to medical and dental care. These communal residences should be as dignified and homelike as possible, since their goal would be to facilitate the residents' ability to gain the sense of personal dignity that is the only effective barrier to violence against others, and to get practice in learning how to live peaceably and cooperatively with others when they return home.

The modern prison system is a fairly recent invention, a failed experiment in social engineering which is a product of the Enlightenment, dating back only to the late 18th century. Its failure became recognized soon after it was first put into effect (Friedman 1993). Yet prisons have been continued, despite their manifest failure to do more than serve as "schools for crime," because (among other reasons) we have not had the ingenuity or generosity to come up with any other model for coping with the violence that is caused, mostly, though not entirely, by our dysfunctional political system, which creates extremes of social and economic inequality that expose those at the bottom of the class and caste hierarchy to extremes of shame and humiliation (Gilligan 2011; Lee, Wexler and Gilligan, 2014). Where that system has been reformed (as it has been, most successfully so far, in the social-democratic "welfare states" of Western Europe, and all of the English-speaking democracies except the United States), murder rates have been reduced to levels that are on average only about one-seventh as high as ours. Not only have they all eliminated capital punishment and solitary confinement, a number of them have replaced prisons with group homes similar to the model I am recommending here. Those are among the reasons I recommend that we phase out the whole notion that prisons should be for punishment rather than for education and therapy, so that people can learn how to live like normal, healthy, non-violent human beings, who will be treated with respect and thereby learn to treat others with respect.

Does Imprisonment Prevent Violence?

The incarceration rate in the United States is roughly ten times higher than it is in the other developed nations of the world, such as in Western Europe. In fact, for several years now we have had the highest imprisonment rate in the entire world: even higher than in those nations that we call "police states." And we are the only Western democracy that still practices capital punishment and prolonged solitary confinement. If imprisonment and capital punishment and solitary confinement prevented violence, you would think that our homicide rates would be at least ten times *lower* than theirs. In fact, however, as I said, our homicide rates are on average seven times *higher* than those of the other Western nations.

Even in the US, the highest murder rates are found in the states with the highest rates of imprisonment, which are also those with the highest rates of capital punishment (Gilligan, 2011; Lee, Wexner and Gilligan, 2014). In other words, the higher the rates of the most extreme forms of punishment, the higher the rates of the most extreme forms of violence. And vice versa – the less the punishment, the fewer the murders.

I believe it will also be essential, in addition to abolishing and demolishing the prisons, to make the job description called "prison officer" or "guard" as obsolete as buggy whips became after the invention of the automobile. For that occupational role has been irreversibly deformed by its association with punishment. The earliest word for prison, in ancient Sumerian, has been translated as "house of darkness." Throughout history, prisons have been represented, and intended – psychologically, socially, and even physically –as the earthly equivalent of hell. That is, their purpose from the time of their first invention at the dawn of civilization has always been to serve the same function during people's life-times as the one that hell was presumed to serve after death and under-ground: a place where people would be punished for their sins. In the Italian Renaissance, paintings of hell based the torments depicted in them on the punishments (really, tortures) to which criminals in the prisons of that day were subjected (Edgerton 1985). Dante's *Inferno* depicts much the same thing, though in poetry rather than visual art. And the demons and devils who were inflicting those torments on the sinners condemned to hell were the role models for the prison guards of that day – a model that still persists, and not only in our cultural unconscious.

For example, a Harvard graduate student with whom I worked became a prison guard in order to do the research for her doctoral dissertation (and book) on "Prison Officers and Their World" (Kauffman 1988). What she found was that the attitudes that most of the prison officers had toward the prisoners were quite humane and understanding. Many of them came from backgrounds similar to those of the inmates, and recognized that the prisoners were very troubled (and often very traumatized) individuals who needed help. But they thought that most of their fellow officers despised the inmates and thought they were animals, who deserved all the punishment they were receiving. But of course that is a mathematical impossibility. That is, if the opinions of each of the officers were humane, then the opinions of each of the other officers could not be inhumane. My point is that this is an example of how prisons possess what has been described, in another context, as a "subculture of violence" (Wolfgang and Ferracuti 1967), which makes it very difficult for even the most humane correction officer to operate independently of the cultural atmosphere – the set of collective norms, assumptions, and expectations – in which he (or she) works. And those assumptions have roots that go so far back into the history of civilization that I cannot see how we could ever change them, except by repudiating the whole notion of prisons and punishments as our responses to violence.

The San Francisco Violence-Prevention Experiment

I say this because I served as the "principal investigator" in a violence prevention experiment in the jails of San Francisco, 1996–2004 (Schwartz, with Boodell 2009). What we discovered there is that when we engaged every man in a 65-bed cell-block, all of whom were in jail for violent crimes, in highly structured educational and therapeutic programs six days a week, 12 hours a day, and moved them out of their cells into an open dormitory, the rate of in-house violence (which had occurred at a rate of three-dozen serious violent incidents a year prior to the beginning of the experiment, and continued at that rate in an otherwise identical "control group" in a conventional jail during the years of the experiment) dropped to zero, for 12 months at a time (Lee and Gilligan 2005). Correction officers who had petitioned to work elsewhere when the program first began, because of their fear that an open dormitory filled entirely with violent inmates would be a recipe for a riot, began petitioning to return to work on this unit, because it had become the safest cell-block in the entire jail system.

The inmates did not perceive their experience in our experimental unit as punishment. On the contrary, one man commented to me that "I should be in this program for four years, not four months, because I'm trying to change the habits of a lifetime." (So much for the notion that prisoners' main goal is to escape.) Because they were learning how their coping strategies, their strategies for living, had been shaped (and mis-shaped) by a whole set of assumptions and beliefs and practices that they had not even realized they had been taught and had internalized, and which were ruining or had ruined their lives and relationships, they expressed gratitude for what we had helped them to learn, and expressed a desire to teach new, incoming inmates what they had learned about themselves. So we trained them, with role-playing and other kinds of supervision, to become group therapists themselves, for new inmates (and after they left the jail, for people in the community), just as members of Alcoholics Anonymous serve as the equivalent of therapists or mentors for others who have struggled with an addiction to alcohol. Except that in this case the addiction was to violence. And of course the teaching and learning went in both directions: for much of what we knew about them we had learned from them.

The rate of violent recidivism following release back into the community was 83 percent lower than it was in a matched control group in an ordinary jail during their first year after release (which is when most recidivism occurs), among those who had participated in it for at least, but not necessarily longer than, four months (Gilligan and Lee 2005). As a result, this program was awarded a national prize from the Kennedy School of Government at Harvard for "innovations in American governance," in a competition among some 800 other legal and governmental programs around the country.

Yes, violence can be prevented. The only question is, do we want to prevent violence, to the greatest degree that is humanly possible, or do we want to retain it? Which do we care more about: saving the potential victims in our communities from being subjected to violence, or preserving our ability to punish those who have already become victims of, and thus serve as scapegoats for, the pathogenic components of our dysfunctional political and economic system?

Conclusion

Punishment inflicts shame on people in many ways, including the fact that the punisher is thereby demonstrating that he is more powerful than the person he is punishing. And also that he has no love for his victim, he hates him, which is the emotional message that inflicting pain without any attempt to mitigate it communicates. But punishment also diminishes the feeling of guilt. That psychological principle has been institutionalized for more than a thousand years by the Catholic Church, whose rituals of confession and penance (self-humiliation and self-punishment) lead to the diminution of guilt and the achievement of innocence (the "absolution of sins"). The administration of punishment by the prison system accomplishes the same thing, as it is intended to do. For the lesson the law is designed to teach is that by suffering the pain the criminal justice system inflicts on him, the prisoner expiates his guilt by "paying his debt" to society, so that it would be irrational for him to continue to feel guilty. Thus, punishment achieves the maximization of shame and the minimization of guilt: the very combination of emotional conditions that are the most powerful psychological precursors of violence toward others.

In other words, if our criminal justice system were deliberately and consciously attempting to create the conditions that would be most effective in maximizing the frequency and severity of violence in our society, and of reoffending among those we have imprisoned, it could hardly have found a more successful formula than the ones called "punishment" and "prisons."

Notes

1 Among the few exceptions to this, among violent crimes, is the status of statutory rape (engaging in sexual activity with an individual regarded as too young to be capable of voluntary consent), which is frequently, though not always, treated as a case of "strict liability" in which the offender may be found guilty simply because he committed an *actus reus*, whether or not he did so with a *mens rea*. See Carpenter, C.L. 2003. See also *Morissette v. United States*, 342 U.S. 246 (1952)

2 For a detailed review of research on this subject, see Gilligan (2000a).

References

Aristotle (2009) *The Nicomachean Ethics*, New York: Oxford University Press

Augustine, Saint (1956) In epistulam Ioannis ad Parthos: Homily 7 on the First Epistle of John, Paragraph 8 (Tractatus VII, 8) in Schaff, P. (ed.) *A Select Library of the Nicene and Post-Nicene Fathers of the Christian Church*, Vol. 7, Grand Rapids, MI: W.R. Eerdmans Pub. Co.

Brown, R. (1965) *Social Psychology*, New York: Free Press.

Carpenter, C.L. (2003) "On Statutory Rape, Strict Liability, and the Public Offense Model," *American University Law Review* 53(2): 313–391.

Conley, A. (2013) "Torture in US Jails and Prisons: An Analysis of Solitary Confinement Under International Law," *Vienna J. on International Constitutional Law* 7(4): 415–453.

Davis, L. M., Steele, J.L., Bozick, M., Williams, V., Turner, S. Miles, J.N.V., Saunders, J. and Steinberg, P.S. (2014) "*How Effective Is Correctional Education and Where Do We Go from Here? The Results of a Comprehensive Evaluation*" (available at www.rand.org/pubs/research_reports/RR564.html)

Edgerton, S.Y. (1985) *Pictures and Punishment: Art and Criminal Prosecution during the Florentine Renaissance*, Ithaca: Cornell Univ. Press.

Freud, S. (1930). Civilization and its Discontents, in J. Strachey (ed.), *The Standard Edition of the Complete Psychological Works of Sigmund Freud*, Vol. 21, pp. 57–146, London: Hogarth Press and the Institute of Psychoanalysis.

Friedman, L.M. (1993) *Crime and Punishment in American History*, New York: Basic Books.

Gawande, A. (2009). "Annals of Human Rights: Hellhole: The United States holds tens of thousands of inmates in long-term solitary confinement. Is this torture?," *New Yorker*, March 30, 2009

Gilligan, J. (1975) "Beyond Morality: Psychoanalytic Reflections on Shame, Guilt and Love," In *Moral Development and Behavior: Theory, Research and Social Issues*, T. Lickona (ed.) New York: Holt, Rinehart and Winston, pp.144–158.

Gilligan, J. (1996) *Violence: Our Deadly Epidemic and Its Causes*, New York: Grosset/Putnam (also published in paperback as *Violence: Reflections on a National Epidemic*, New York: Vintage Books, 1997; as *Violence: Reflections on Our Deadliest Epidemic*, London: Jessica Kingsley Publishers, 2000); and in various translations in other nations.

Gilligan, J. (1999a) "Psychological Violence," in *Violence in America: An Encyclopedia*, Vol. 2, pp. 626–631, R. Gottesman (ed.), New York: Charles Scribners Sons

Gilligan, J. (1999b) "Structural Violence," in *Violence in America: An Encyclopedia*, Vol. 3, pp. 229–233, R, Gottesman (ed.), New York: Charles Scribners Sons

Gilligan, J. (2000a) "Punishment and Violence: Is the Criminal Justice System Based on One Huge Mistake?," *Social Research* 67(3): 745–772.

Gilligan, J. (2000b) "Violence as a Problem in Public Health and Preventive Medicine," *Lancet* 355: 1802–04.

Gilligan, J. (2001) *Preventing Violence: An Agenda for the Coming Century*, London and New York: Thames and Hudson.

Gilligan, J. (2003) "Shame, Guilt and Violence," *Social Research* 70 (4): 1149–1180

Gilligan, J. (2015) "A Modest Proposal to Universalize the Insanity Defense and Replace Prisons and Punishment with Treatment and Education," *Int. J. Applied Psychoanalytic Studies,* 12(2): 134–142.

Gilligan, J. (2018) "Violence," Chapter 17 in *Textbook of Applied Psychoanalysis*, S. Akhtar and S. Twemlow (eds.) London and New York: Karnac Books.

Gilligan, J. and B. Lee (2005) "The Resolve to Stop the Violence Project: Reducing Violence in the Community through a Jail-Based Initiative," *J. Public Health*, 27(2): 143–148.

Gilligan, J. (2011) *Why Some Politicians Are More Dangerous than Others*, Cambridge: Polity Press.

Holmes, O.W. (1881). *The Common Law*. New York: Dover Publications, 1991.

Hume, D. (1739) *A Treatise of Human Nature: Being an Attempt to Introduce the Experimental Method of Reasoning into Moral Subjects*, London: Printed for John Noon

Hume, D. (1751) An Enquiry Concerning the Principles of Morals: A Critical Edition, Beauchamp, T. (ed.), Oxford: Clarendon Press; New York: Oxford University Press, 1998

Kauffman, K. (1988) *Prison Officers and Their World*, Cambridge, MA: Harvard University Press.

Koop, C. Everett (1984) quoted N. Meredith, "The Murder Epidemic," *Science*, 84: 42–48.

Lee, B. and J. Gilligan (2005) "The Resolve to Stop the Violence Project: Transforming an In-House Culture of Violence Through a Jail-Based Programme," *Journal of Public Health*, 27(2): 149–155.

Lee, B. X., B. E. Wexler and J. Gilligan (2014) "Political Correlates of Violent Death Rates in the U.S., 1900–2010: Longitudinal and Cross-Sectional Analyses," *Aggression and Violent Behavior*, 19: 721–728.

Holmes, O.W. (1881) *The Common Law,* New York: Dover Publications (1991).

Hsieh, C.-C. and M. D. Pugh (1993) "Poverty, Income Inequality, and Violent Crime: A Meta-Analysis of Recent Aggregate Data Studies." *Criminal Justice Review*, 18: 182–202.

Mandela, N. (1994) *The Long Walk to Freedom,* London: Abacus. (p. 47)

Mill, J. S. (1861). Utilitarianism, in *The Collected Works of John Stuart Mill*, edited by J.M. Robson, vol. 10 (Toronto: Univ. of Toronto Press, 1965), pp. 203–260.

Piaget, J. (1932). *The Moral Judgment of the Child.* New York: Free Press, 1965.

Russell, B. (1918). *Roads to Freedom: Socialism. Anarchism, and Syndicalism*. New York: Barnes and Noble, 1965.

Schwartz, S. with Boodell, D. (2009) *Dreams from the Monster Factory: A Tale of Prison, Redemption and One Woman's Fight to Restore Justice to All*, with an introduction by J. Gilligan, New York: Scribner.

Shengold, L. (1989) *Soul Murder: The Effects of Childhood Abuse and Deprivation*, New Haven: Yale University Press

Stone, A. (1975). *Mental Health and Law: A System in Transition*. Rockville, MD: Center for Studies of Crime and Delinquency, National Institute of Mental Health.

United Nations Office on Drugs and Crime (UNODC) (1995) *The United Nations Standard Minimum Rules for the Treatment of Prisoners (The Nelson Mandela Rules)*. www.unodc.org/documents/justice-and-prison-reform/GA-RESOLUTION/E_ebook.pdf

Virchow, R. (1958) *Disease, Life and Man*, Stanford: Stanford University Press, p. 6.

Wolfgang, M. E. and F. Ferracuti (1967), *The Subculture of Violence: Towards an Integrated Theory in Criminology,* New York: Routledge.

16

HUMANIZING PRISON THROUGH SOCIAL NEUROSCIENCE

From the Abolition of Solitary Confinement to the Pursuit of Social Rehabilitation

Federica Coppola

16.1 Introduction

Since its inception in the 18th century, prison has been the emblem of criminal punishment (Foucault 1977). Prison was originally conceived of as a "more humane alternative to frequent executions" (Bessler 2016:156) as well as an effective way to reform "the soul of delinquents" through isolation, punitiveness, and control (Foucault 1977). Prison is still viewed as the *par excellence* means of meeting the retribution, deterrence, incapacitation, and rehabilitation needs of criminal justice. Despite differences in correctional facilities and regimes, the basic narrative underlying prison – especially in punitive systems such as that of the United States – is that the pain of detention in exclusionary conditions is a consequence that wrongdoers deserve that will allow them to understand the wrongfulness of their misbehavior (Lippke 2003). As a result, they will refrain from reoffending in the future (Johnson 2013).

Specific methods of detention maximize this narrative of incarceration. In the United States, the most representative method is solitary confinement. Notwithstanding the harsh criticism at both national and international levels regarding the excessive (ab)use of solitary confinement on the part of prison administrations, this practice has found robust support within legislative, administrative, and judiciary bodies on the basis of the alleged efficacy of extreme isolation to meet the discipline, security, and safety needs of prisons (Coppola 2019). In view of these supposed penological functions, solitary confinement remains heavily practiced across states. Even when applied for prolonged periods of time, solitary confinement has hardly been found to constitute cruel and unusual punishment under the Eighth Amendment of the US Constitution (Coppola 2019).

Prisons privilege punitiveness, physical separation, and social and moral exclusion – often in precarious settings – to presumably rationalize the infliction of punishment on a perpetrator. Thereby, they abandon and discount the human dimension of incarcerated people. Abundant psychological evidence demonstrates the negative and long-lasting effects of incarceration (e.g., Haney 2012). Notably, behavioral studies have reported that the act of imprisonment as well as the restrictive and exclusionary conditions of prison life can produce or aggravate a number of affective, cognitive, and behavioral deficits, including cognitive decline and affective disturbances such as decreased affect, lack of self-esteem, increased feelings of rejection and humiliation, chronic anger and rage, and problems with self-regulation (e.g., Gilligan 2000; Umbach et al. 2018; Meijers et al. 2018). A crucial finding is that incarceration can stimulate the same negative emotional feelings and behavioral tendencies that have consistently qualified as risk factors for antisocial conduct and violence in particular (Gilligan 2000).

Psychological perspectives of the deleterious mental effects of incarceration have been supported by the body of social neuroscience research on brain plasticity, social interaction, and environmental stimulation for physiological brain function, mental health, and social behavior. Such foundation has emerged from the specific line of research on the adverse neurobiological effects of negative social environments, social exclusion, and socio-environmental deprivation. Overall, as a complement to behavioral studies, research on the relationship between the brain and the social environment has offered critical insights that further highlight the vital role of enriched environments and positive social relationships for healthy brain development and function. On the other hand, these studies indicate that socially and environmentally poor settings (such as those analogous to prisons) contribute to or intensify problematic neurobiological patterns that negatively correlate with mental well-being and, ultimately, socially functional behavior.

The intention of this chapter is to employ this body of neuroscientific knowledge to propose a drastic rethinking of the prison system. It aims to utilize this neuroscientific perspective to illustrate why common features of the prison system (i.e., punitiveness, social exclusion, isolation and poor environments) may be extremely damaging for the brain and behavior and can consequently pose a serious risk to an individual's progress toward positive change and reintegration into the community as a socially functional individual.

Based on a review of the studies in Sections 16.2 and 16.3, Section 16.4 offers several suggestions for embracing this body of knowledge to reform the prison model at both practical and theoretical levels. Section 16.4.1 argues for transforming the ethos of prisons to embrace the values of belongingness, dialogue, cooperation, and accountability as well as for re-designing the physical layout of correctional facilities to make these settings as dignified and home-like as possible. Section 16.4.2 illustrates the potential of this body of social neuroscience to challenge the constitutionality of solitary confinement and, as a consequence, to support its abolition or at least a radical reform of its regimes. Finally, Section 16.4.3 emphasizes the compatibility of the demonstrated insights from social neuroscience with the tenets of social rehabilitation. Hence, the section argues for the pursuit of social rehabilitation as the most rational and effective goal of the prison system and, ultimately, of criminal justice. The chapter concludes with several remarks about the critical but indirect contribution of social neuroscience to making the criminal justice system more humane.

16.2 The Ineradicable Bond Between the Brain and the Social Environment

In a famous article, Baumeister and Leary (1995) posited that human beings possess a universal need to belong. The authors characterized this need as a drive to form and maintain strong, stable interpersonal relationships. Moreover, they crucially argued that such need is satisfied by frequent human contact and genuine bonds of caring between individuals. Baumeister and Leary's arguments are in line with a robust body of studies from evolutionary and social psychology that have largely demonstrated that humankind exhibits an ineradicable biological need for social bonds and relationships.

The essence of human beings as social animals lies in the nature of the human brain as a social organ (Siegel 2012). The brain enables us to socially interact, perform social thinking, and navigate and communicate with our social environment (Goleman 2006:4). On the other hand, the social environment continuously shapes our brain morphology and activity, modulates our neurological and physiological reactions, and permits the brain to perform its natural functions (Hari et al. 2015; Davidson & McEwen 2012).

The "social brain hypothesis" has been highly accredited within the literature to explain the strict mutual relationship between the brain and the social environment (Dunbar 1998; Lieberman 2013).

According to this account, humans possess larger brains (and especially larger prefrontal cortices) compared to other species precisely because humans are biologically designed to navigate the most complex social environments. In other words, the size of the human brain is directly proportional with the complexity of its expected social environments. The human brain needs to constantly receive stimulation from its social environment in order to work properly and perform its natural functions.

Research on the relationship between the brain and the social environment has intersected with findings about brain plasticity. A key insight from neuroscience concerns the dynamic nature of the brain. While it was once assumed that the adult brain structure was static and mostly unaltered by the environment or behavior, it has been firmly established that the brain is constantly in flux (Power & Bradley 2017). Thereby, it creates and alters neural pathways throughout a person's life to adapt to new experiences, learn information, and create memories, and its structure and function are ceaselessly molded by socio-environmental influences (Hari et al. 2015).

Research has indicated a positive influence of specific socio-environmental factors – so-called dynamic factors of protection – on brain development and function, mental health, and social behavior (e.g., House et al. 1988; Seeman & McEwen 1996; Whittle et al. 2014). Notably, certain social, economic, and environmental factors, including secure attachments, good child rearing, positive social engagement, exposure to positive environments, and social acceptance, appear to be essential to the development and functioning of key brain areas that support cognitive and affective skills that are linked to (pro)social behavior, such as emotion processing, emotion regulation, or empathic responding (e.g., Cozolino 2014; Lieberman 2013).

Consistent with these insights, key research on brain plasticity has revealed that positive social engagement induces positive changes in the neural circuits that underlie cognitive functions, socio-affective skills (e.g., empathy), and social behavior over the entire lifespan (e.g., Kelly et al. 2017; Hari et al. 2015; Valk et al. 2017). These changes have been associated with higher cognitive performance, emotional responsiveness, psychological well-being, and prosocial behavior (Davidson & McEwen 2012).

The relevance of the social environment for brain function and behavior has been famously reported in studies with rodents. Several experiments have indicated that rodents that were reared in "enriched environments" (Slater & Cao 2015) – ample cages with toys and changing stimuli – and surrounded by their peers exhibited functional developmental pathways as well as normal sociable tendencies (e.g., Rosenzweig & Bennett 1972; Neil et al. 2018). In contrast, rodents that were reared in deprived environments and under conditions of social isolation exhibited cognitive deficits, aggressive tendencies, hostility, and an incapacity to live in a social environment (e.g., Wongwitdecha & Marsden 1996; Tanaka et al. 2010). As discussed shortly, such behavioral dysfunctions correlate with a variety of morphological and functional alterations in the brain. These alterations are an immediate outcome of the persistent conditions of socio-environmental deprivation.

The few studies that have been conducted with humans have replicated these results. For instance, research with children raised in orphanages (Sheridan et al. 2012; Gee at al. 2013) has indicated that such children, who had suffered from early maternal deprivation and diminished attachments, exhibited smaller cortical gray matter volume, atypical amygdala-prefrontal cortex connectivity, and increased cortisol levels compared to children who were raised in home-like settings or family environments. In commenting on these studies, Baskin-Sommers and Fonteneau (2016: 428) have highlighted a parallel between this kind of institutionalized setting and correctional facilities, and observed that settings that are characterized by diminished social contact and deprivation contribute to problematic neurobiological patterns.

Collectively, social neuroscience research offers a critical contribution to clarify the mutual influence of the brain and the social environment on mental health, psychological well-being, and socio-behavioral functioning. The key insight that emerges from this body of research regards the development and maintenance of positive and secure social relationships and the surrounding of stimulating environments for physiological brain function. As discussed in the next section, the absence or breakdown of these protective socio-environmental factors – which often occurs within correctional facilities – risks producing a series of deleterious effects at the neurobiological level. In turn, these effects may translate into potentially permanent mental issues and behavioral dysfunctions. Thus, when a (positive) social environment is lacking, the brain – and the person, as a consequence – is likely to undergo profoundly traumatic consequences in the (very) long term.

16.3 The Neurobiological Effects of Negative Social Environments, Social Exclusion, and Socio-Environmental Deprivation

The relevance of social interactions and environmental stimulation for the brain and behavior finds further support within the body of neuroscientific studies that have explored the adverse neurobiological effects of negative social environments and socio-environmental deprivation.

While more data are needed, an increasing amount of studies have emphasized the deleterious influence of specific socio-environmental factors (so-called "positive factors of risk"), which include a lack of secure attachments, social exclusion, history of abuse, or chronic exposure to violence, on one's neurobiology (e.g., McCrory et al. 2010; Hart & Rubia 2012). Specifically, these factors have been found to entail structural and functional alterations across various brain areas that support both cognitive and affective functions, such as empathy or emotion regulation, with adverse implications for (pro)social behavior (Tost et al. 2015).

For instance, several neuroscientific studies have investigated the relationship between cortisol levels (i.e., biological stress response), psychosocial stressors, and violence in adolescence and young adulthood in particular (Ayer et al. 2014). In principle, these studies have suggested that the presence of chronic stressors and inadequate emotional and social support to mitigate the effects of such stressors produces adverse and dysregulating outcomes for an individual's biological stress response, as well as long-term negative effects on the brain, mental health, and social behavior (Ayer et al. 2014). For instance, exposure to violence and contextual stressors has been associated with elevated cortisol levels and hyperresponsivity to threats in the long term. This chronic or long-lasting hyperresponsivity to threats could explain why people (especially youth) who live in violent communities may experience "pathological adaptations" that include a desensitization to violence (Garbarino et al. 2002). Likewise, abuse, trauma, and maltreatment are associated with elevated cortisol levels in both adolescents and adults as well (McCrory et al. 2010). Notably, chronic stress has been evidenced to alter physiological brain function in the long term and especially in brain regions such as the hippocampus, amygdala, and various parts of the prefrontal cortex (PFC) (Brenmer 2006). Dysfunctions in these brain regions have been demonstrated to negatively affect moral reasoning and social functioning and increase the risk of engaging in criminal behaviors that involve aggression and violence (Nee & Vernham 2017: 40).

Other studies have explored the effects of social exclusion on the brain. Of particular relevance is the body of research that has investigated the neurological nature of social pain, which refers to the painful feelings that follow social rejection, social exclusion, or social isolation (Eisenberger 2012a). From a psychological standpoint, social pain has been associated with a variety of psychological symptoms and negative action tendencies that includes anxiety, humiliation, lack of self-esteem, greater rejection sensitivity, and aggression (Eisenberger 2012a). Moreover, several studies have linked the experience of social pain with a stronger predisposition to develop pain disorders (Landa et al. 2012), physical diseases, mental issues, and even a higher risk of mortality (Eisenberger 2012b). Thus, regardless of whether the traumatic effects of social pain are immediately visible, they may manifest and grow over time.

Over the past decade, neuroscientific studies have started to examine the neurological representation of social pain. According to the most influential account in the literature, which is the "shared representation hypothesis," social pain is neurologically akin to physical pain, which is the pain that follows a physical injury. This account holds that, neurologically speaking, social pain shares the same affective component as physical pain. Specifically, it appears to recruit the same neural circuitry, including the dorsal anterior cingulate cortex and the anterior insula (Eisenberger 2012b; Lieberman & Eisenberger 2008).

However, a more recent study (Woo et al. 2014) has suggested that physical pain and social pain involve distinct neural representations within and across brain regions. Thus, the neurological overlap between these two types of pain seems to occur only at a gross anatomical level. Overall, according to this study, social pain and physical pain possibly consist of diverse affective experiences, which entail unique psychological consequences and require different interventions.

Notwithstanding this contrast in the literature, a key insight that has emerged from this body of research is that social pain has a physical reality in the brain, and its experience is no less serious or deleterious than that of physical pain. On the contrary, the consequences of social pain could be more distressful, harmful, and long-lasting for an individual compared to those that follow forms of physical pain.

The study of social pain following social disconnection has integrated with and formed a significant part of the body of social neuroscience research on the neurobiological, psychological, and behavioral effects of socio-environmental deprivation (i.e., extreme isolation) on the brain. Studies on socio-environmental deprivation with animal models have collectively evidenced a variety of brain damages following extreme isolation. Notably, these studies have revealed that extreme isolation may induce a number of structural and functional alterations in both cortical and subcortical regions, including reduced cortical volume, diminished neuronal connections in cortical areas and the hippocampus (Djordjevic et al. 2012), decreased myelin production (Liu et al. 2012), and altered activity in the reward system (Cacioppo et al. 2009) and amygdala (Fowler et al. 2008).

For instance, robust research on the neurobiological impact of chronic stress induced by extreme isolation has found that chronic stress had deleterious effects on brain regions, notably the hippocampus, that support spatial information processing, memory, social information, and emotion regulation (Fone & Porkess 2008; Djordjevic et al. 2012; Cacioppo et al. 2009; Ieraci et al. 2016). These alterations have been reported for certain mental illnesses in humans, including post-traumatic stress disorder, depression, and neurocognitive diseases such as Alzheimer's (Logue et al. 2018; Wang et al. 2014; Ouanes & Popp 2019). Moreover, such alterations have been reported in a series of psychological symptoms and negative action tendencies, such as aggression (Fone & Porkess 2008), which are risk factors for socially dysfunctional behaviors.

Studies on the effects of extreme isolation on the brain and behavior have crucially highlighted that structural and functional alterations in the brain may manifest even within a short period of time (Makinodan et al. 2012). Furthermore, these alterations may persist even after the reintroduction of the subject into a "normal" social environment (Makinodan et al. 2012). Thus, the studies reflect that socio-environmental deprivation may lead to potentially permanent deleterious effects for the individual.

Although more research on human samples is needed, reliable evidence exists demonstrating that increased social isolation and diminished physical contact in environments that are analogous to prisons contribute to and reinforce problematic neurobiological patterns. Hence, the socially scarce conditions of a prison setting are likely to

> generate or exacerbate neurobiological deficits and maladaptive behaviors…[t]his becomes a significant issue, especially for individuals who are chronic offenders, where existing neurobiological vulnerabilities are intensified in settings of confinement and segregation, thereby reinforcing maladaptive patterns of behavior.
>
> *(Baskin-Sommers & Fonteneau 2016: 428)*

16.4 Humanizing Prison

While converging with psychological perspectives, findings from social neuroscience provide additional critical information to challenge the efficiency of the current apparatus of the prison system. Notably, these insights support severe criticism of the punitiveness, social disconnection, and (often) precarious environmental conditions that characterize the lives of incarcerated people. Hence, social neuroscience offers another perspective that may encourage a radical reconsideration of the philosophy and reality of prison that can achieve a greater humanization of not only prison facilities but also their internal policies and underlying goals.

The remainder of this chapter precisely illustrates three main implications of the literature review for the prison context. The first implication concerns the transformation of the prison environment. The second, more specific implication has increasingly attracted attention in the United States and regards the unconstitutionality and, ideally, the abolition or reduction of solitary confinement. The third, theoretical implication refers to the pursuit of social rehabilitation as the ultimate goal of incarceration.

16.4.1 *Prison Environment*

The most essential information to emerge from social neuroscience research concerns the mutually ineradicable tie between the brain and the social environment. As reported above, studies with both animal and human models have indicated the fundamental significance of positive social interactions and stimulating environments for physiological brain function, psychological well-being, and prosocial behavioral tendencies. In combination, these insights highlight the importance of constant positive interactions in stimulating environments for the cultivation of prosocial attitudes precisely because these factors act as positive incentives for brain function and health. Thereby, they stimulate cognitive and socio-emotional competencies that are vital to social and moral life.

This body of empirical knowledge strongly encourages a profound rethinking of the social and physical environment of prisons. In regard to the former, these insights appear to strengthen the position of several authors (Reisel 2015; Gilligan 2000) who have argued for the involvement of positive social engagements and activities as a central feature of prison programs. According to these authors, inclusionary and relationally based approaches are more likely to aid people in eliminating profound feelings of rejection, exclusion, and humiliation, as well as to stimulate them to act in prosocial ways through training, dialogue, and inclusion. Thus, it may be essential for facilities to allow space for human connections in terms of frequent contact with the outside world, education programs, social and recreation activities, and paid labor. These elements can enhance the skills and accomplishments of incarcerated people, which can serve as internalized and reality-based sources of self-respect and self-esteem as well as attract respect and esteem from others and motivate their process of reconstructing their self-identity and a life without crime.

On the other hand, an increasing number of authors (Dhami et al. 2009; Toews 2006; Braswell et al. 2001) have supported the implementation of restorative justice (RJ)-based programs, which aim to allow people in prison to critically take accountability and acknowledge the consequences of their negative behavior through dialogue and confrontations with victims (either actual or surrogate victims, depending on the circumstances), as well as with community members. Notably, empirical evaluations of existing RJ programs in prisons worldwide have reported encouraging results in terms not only of individuals' positive change and healing (e.g., Feasey & Williams 2009) but also crime desistance and lower recidivism rates (Lauwaert & Aertsen 2015).

The second implication of this body of neuroscientific knowledge for the prison environment is the transformation of the physical layout of correctional facilities. The empirical research above has illustrated the fundamental importance of stimulating and enriched environments for physiological brain activity, mental health, and positive sociable tendencies. On the other hand, the research has suggested that environmental deprivation, which is understood as living in scarce or poor environments without significant external stimuli, may have negative repercussions for several brain areas that are linked with a variety of cognitive, affective, and social functions.

Taken together, these insights strongly support the replacement of current detention facilities with locations that are as dignified, humane, and approximated to general living conditions as possible. These settings should allow the people within them to have as much internal freedom as possible considering their temporary deprivation of liberty and separation from the community. In this regard, several scholars and national associations have recommended the transformation of jails and prisons from exclusionary and often precarious facilities into secure yet humane settings, such as residential centers or therapeutic communities (e.g., Gilligan 2000). For instance, the VERA Institute of Justice, a US non-profit organization for criminal justice, has partnered with a team of architects from MASS Design Group to launch an experimental project that targets the development of future correctional facilities (VERA Institute of Justice 2019). By recalling the "Norwegian prison model," the project reimagines the physical layout of prison facilities to achieve a design that conveys respect for human dignity and promotes inclusivity, dialogue, and effective rehabilitation. This project would transform "prisons" into open yet secure spaces wherein the people who reside there can heal and feel empowered to change their own lives. This design for prisons would facilitate personal growth and change, and, ultimately, restore communities.

Such an ideal prison model admittedly promotes the implementation of the previously reported dynamic socio-environmental factors of protection for mental health, psychological well-being and prosocial attitudes. Thus, while encouraging individual change, a humanized detention environment that favors inclusion, social relationships, dialogue, and dignity could also be instrumental in resolving the excessive violence in institutionalized settings and eventually decreasing recidivism rates. Altogether, the transformation of correctional facilities into the described centers could be a vital change not only to improve the lives of the people they house but also more fully satisfy public demands for safety and security to ameliorate the workings and outcomes of criminal justice as a whole.

16.4.2 *Solitary Confinement*

The implications of the above insights from social neuroscience are even more glaring when applied to solitary confinement. In the United States, solitary confinement is a correctional measure that prison officials use to meet disciplinary, protection, or security needs of prisons (Labrecque 2016: 51–53). People who are forced into solitary confinement live in conditions of extreme isolation, which entail tiny cells, an absence of meaningful social contacts, subjection to absolute control by prison guards, and potentially indefinite periods of time. Although the harshness of solitary confinement regimes in the United States has received heavy criticism at both the national and international levels, this correctional measure is still legitimate and has not been found to constitute cruel and unusual punishment under the Eighth Amendment of the US Constitution. In brief, solitary confinement per se is completely constitutional.

The standard set of the Supreme Court for assessing whether solitary confinement "becomes" cruel and unusual punishment requires that one or more *accompanying material conditions* of solitary confinement result in "a wanton and unnecessary infliction of pain" (*Gregg v. Georgia* 1976) upon the individual who was forced into extreme isolation. This requirement is met when such conditions involve a "deprivation of basic identifiable human needs" (*Rhodes v. Chapman* 1981) to an extent that they "inflict harm or create a risk of objectively serious harm," (*Farmer v. Brennan* 1994), and they are enacted with "deliberate indifference" (*Wilson v. Seiter* 1991) by prison personnel. With limited exceptions (e.g., *Wilkerson v. Stalder* 2007*),* the Supreme Court and lower federal courts have perpetuated a narrow application of these standards. Specifically, courts have tended to interpret the objective prong of the standard by narrowing it down to identifiable physical human needs, including nutrition or shelter (e.g., *Wilson v. Seiter* 1991: 304–05), the lack of which may lead to the infliction of physical harm, such as physical disease or death (see e.g., Matter, 2010: 296). Thus, courts have often discounted the generalized mental pain that is caused by extreme isolation as a sufficient ground to qualify solitary confinement as a form of torture (*see* Lobel 2008).

In a famous federal class action lawsuit before the District Court for the Northern District of California (*Ashker v. Governor of California* 2014), social neuroscience-based evidence was successfully introduced to challenge such dominant interpretation of the conditions of confinement standards and, consequently, to support Eighth Amendment challenges to prolonged solitary confinement (Lobel & Akil 2018). The case concerned the horrors that were suffered by more than 1,000 prisoners who were forced into extreme isolation for prolonged periods of time at California's Pelican Bay State Prison. The plaintiffs introduced expert neuroscience testimony to support their Eighth Amendment claims.

The core arguments of the expert testimony were that social interaction is fundamental to physiological brain function and health, and the psychological deteriorations (mental harm) that follow social and environmental deprivation are linked to alterations that occur in the brain (Lobel & Akil 2018). Such brain alterations can lead to a wide range of adverse psychological effects, many of which may be long-lasting or even permanent. Based on this evidence, the plaintiffs successfully[1] argued that the harsh conditions of solitary confinement into which the Pelican Bay prisoners were forced could cause or create a substantial risk of causing serious *physical* damage "to a degree prohibited by the Constitution" (Lobel & Akil 2018: 67).

The Ashker case has prompted subsequent (ongoing) legal research into the potential of social neuroscience to support challenges to prolonged solitary confinement. Within such research, some authors (e.g., Bennion 2015; Coppola 2019) have more radically maintained that this body of scientific knowledge may be used to validate the claim that *solitary confinement should be viewed as per se unconstitutional.*

Overall, arguments for the per se unconstitutionality of solitary confinement in view of neuroscience-based evidence include three main claims. The first is that social interaction and environmental stimulation *are* basic human physical needs that are essential to physiological brain function and mental health. Thus, regardless of its duration or accompanying material conditions, extreme isolation is sufficient per se to deprive a person of his or her fundamental biological needs. Thus, the aspects of duration and material conditions should be viewed as *pejorative* circumstances that may aggravate the underlying condition of extreme isolation that already qualifies as a severe deprivation of a minimal life necessity (Coppola 2019).

The second and consequential claim concerns the "objectively serious risk of [physical] harm" (i.e., brain damage) due to extreme isolation alone. As Bennion has noted (2015: 776), even if a physical (brain) damage following a period in solitary confinement never materializes, "[this] is not dispositive for…the test." Indeed, all that matters for the purposes of the test is that the risk of undergoing serious brain deterioration following solitary confinement is objective – that is, it is universal. Neuroscientific findings suggest that *any* person who lives in extreme isolation – even for a short period – is vulnerable to such risk. Moreover, the harm that solitary confinement risks imposing on the brain underpins a number of long-lasting and potentially permanent mental, physical, and physiological conditions. Therefore, the possible harms of solitary confinement are not only disfiguring but may also be permanent (Coppola, 2019).

The third and final argument concerns the "deliberate indifference" requirement. With acknowledging that the core condition of solitary confinement, namely extreme isolation, amounts per se to a wanton and unnecessary infliction of pain and hence constitutes cruel and unusual punishment, "the subjective prong of the test loses its *raison d'être* and becomes superfluous" (Coppola 2019). Given the growing general awareness of the risks that have been linked to life in extreme isolation, proof that a prison official acted with "deliberate indifference" should be inferred from the very act of isolating someone. Imposing extreme isolation on a prisoner entails an objectively serious and well-known risk of harm; any further subjective inquiry is simply unnecessary.

A serious acknowledgment that extreme isolation alone is constitutionally problematic under current standards may support the abolition – or at least a drastic reform – of solitary confinement regimes. Specifically, it may facilitate the replacement of isolation with alternative measures to meet the security and safety needs of prisons, thereby relegating the separation of a person from the rest of the prison population to a last-resort intervention that is applicable only once all other measures have been exhausted without success. However, even if the latter extreme case should occur, strict time limits as well as sociability and environmental standards should apply.

In regard to time limits, more empirical research is needed to assess the exact maximum time limit for depriving an individual of constant social contact without causing damages. Nevertheless, given the current paucity of jurisprudence on duration limits for solitary confinement, all jurisdictions should ideally abide by international guidelines that mandate a maximum of 15 days of separation of a person from the rest of the prison population (*see* also Haney 2018: 302). With respect to sociability conditions, temporarily separated people should still be able to access as much social engagement as possible, including through education and job programs, rehabilitation and recreation activities, and time with visitors (*see* also Kupers 2017: 171–209). Finally, the design of "separation" settings should follow strict environmental standards. In line with the aforementioned suggestions for rethinking general prison settings, separation settings should also be re-designed as spaces that are as secure yet home-like as possible to allow the people who live in them to experience their incarceration in the most dignified and humanized conditions.

16.4.3 *Social Rehabilitation*

From a more theoretical perspective, the above research from social neuroscience offers support to social rehabilitation (also known as "re-socialization"). As a typical penological goal of most continental European systems, social rehabilitation is a rehabilitative approach to crime that aims to reintegrate convicted persons into society upon their release to allow them to lead law-abiding and self-supporting lives (Ashworth et al. 2009). Thus, social rehabilitation seeks to re-establish positive relationships between perpetrators and the rest of society by facilitating (self-)reform and change on the basis of relational processes.

Social rehabilitation, which is akin to restorative justice in many respects, is grounded in a view of the individual that is *morally dynamic* and *holistic*. Like restorative justice, social rehabilitation endorses the view that people who are involved in the criminal justice system are not "irredeemable" individuals (Maruna 2016). Furthermore, their moral character should not be determined by their wrongdoings. Rather, social rehabilitation maintains a strict separation between a person and his or her actions, and it values the multiple aspects of a person's social identity, especially his or her capacity for positive change. Thus, social rehabilitation recognizes the powers of self-determination and self-efficacy of perpetrators in their process of (self)change. Hence, it attributes an active role to perpetrators within the reconstruction of their individual and social lives.

Beyond valuing a person's capacity for change, social rehabilitation acknowledges the holistic (i.e., social) dimension of the individual. Social rehabilitation recognizes that individual change can hardly occur on its own or without the necessary motivation and support. Thus, social rehabilitation highlights the importance for people in prison to maintain or develop positive social bonds and relationships that may encourage feelings of belongingness and consequently motivate them to act in prosocial ways.

Altogether, the aim of the socio-rehabilitative approach is to reintegrate the perpetrator "by tackling not only individual behavior but also social and structural advantages relevant to him or her, which include social bonds, employment, education, and other benefits" (Ashworth et al. 2009: 4). To this end, social rehabilitation values and hinges on the power of human connections to motivate individuals to change and live socially as law-abiding citizens.

When applying the lens of social rehabilitation, prison becomes a venue of dialogue, support, cooperation, and accountability wherein an individual can feel prompted to assume actual responsibility for his or her misbehavior and find constructive ways to enact and be motivated to achieve positive change. A prison that adheres to this ideal can give its residents the chance to value the positive aspects of their social identities with the necessary social and emotional support in a humane context. Overall, a prison that pursues the goals of social rehabilitation provides perpetrators with the appropriate conditions to feel motivated to change and live as law-abiding citizens.

Nevertheless, adapting the philosophy and dynamics of prison life implies neither a denial of people's criminal responsibility nor a reduction of the legal and social gravity of certain behaviors. As Pickard has rightly claimed, "we can aim to hold people responsible and to account in a way which supports people to change and so promotes crime reduction as well as actual rehabilitation and reform" (Pickard 2018: 8). Hence, the proposed model of prison would still represent the imposition of consequences that are appropriate for the behavior in response to blameworthy conduct. However, it would not subject perpetrators to harsh treatment, stigma, or censure and exclusion from the community. On the contrary, such a model is founded on a person's potential capacity as a responsible agent not only in regard to his or her past but also with respect to his or her present and future. It encourages offenders to acknowledge the wrongness of their conduct and endeavor to improve.

In view of the empirical evidence that has been canvassed in this chapter, such an approach is likely to be instrumental for successfully addressing people who are affected by the criminal justice system and, ultimately, for prompting and encouraging them to choose and pursue a life without crime. Claims to the contrary, which assert that prisons must punish individuals for their misdeeds in exclusionary conditions in order to be effective, are grounded in outdated intuitions. These intuitions, beyond having been proven inhumane, heavily ignore the (neuro)biology of people as dynamic social beings.

16.5 Conclusion

Prison, in its current conception, is dehumanizing. It determines the social death of a person and does not contribute to his or her social functioning. On the contrary, it seriously risks compromising such functioning and, consequently, the individual's reintegration into wider society. A prison that excludes, stigmatizes, or isolates poses inevitable risks for individuals in terms of erasing their social identity, damaging their neurobiology, devastating their psychological well-being, and increasing the difficulty of their life in the community.

A prison system that considers the social needs of the people within it and acknowledges and stimulates their capacity for positive change may be vital to adequately addressing crime, and key to a truly efficient criminal justice system. Therefore, a radical reform of prisons into a system that empowers individuals to become active decision-makers in their change process while guaranteeing social relationships is warranted for the sake of individuals' social functioning and public safety.

After all, to "humanize" is to attribute universal human capacities to others (Haslam 2006), including the capacities to critically think about one's own behavior, admit one's own mistakes, experience the usual social emotions due to hurting someone else, and choose to take action to repair the negative consequences of his or her behavior and improve in the future. Essentially, "humanizing" refers to valuing the human dimension of the other, including his or her fallibility, and, simultaneously, his or her capacity to change.

Hence, a "humanized prison" is a place wherein a person can be motivated, encouraged, and supported to achieve positive change, value his or her social identity, and have a voice within his or her change process. Hence, it is a site that replaces the narrative and logic of exclusion, suffering, and isolation with the values of dialogue, respect, re-engagement, support, and personal responsibility. The aim is to help individuals prepare for their re-entry into society as functional members.

I believe that "humanization" is the actual potential of social neuroscience for not only incarceration but also, and more broadly, criminal justice. Admittedly, social neuroscience alone cannot certainly dismantle centuries of theories of punishment. Moreover, neither social neuroscience nor any other empirical science can define the ultimate goal of punishment. Nevertheless, I argue that social neuroscience can significantly, though indirectly, contribute to making criminal justice more humane by educating the law and public about the importance of social relationships and positive environments for fostering positive behavioral change. To this end, it can provide a different narrative of wrongdoing and responses to it that values social and emotional support as well as the empowerment of the individual. This approach would encourage alternative ways of addressing crime that reject isolation, stigma, and social exclusion.

Critics may object that prison is intended to respond to "certainty-of-punishment" needs and lay people's demands or it is not designed for comfort given the reasons for incarceration. Yet, I find it bizarre that despite so much progress in understanding human behavior and social relationships over the centuries, humankind has not been able to imagine any approach beyond the use of cages, cells, and bars to lock other humans up and treat them as if they are ferocious creatures that should be feared. The time is ripe for criminal justice to embrace the progress of the empirical sciences in clarifying the dynamics of social behavior and take action to reduce the gap between "us" and "them" (Garland 2001: 135) by implementing alternative modes of addressing crime. Maintaining this gap only fuels (too often) ill-founded fears without offering any resolution for them.

Note

1 The lawsuit was settled on September 1, 2015. Soon after, the people who had been in solitary confinement for as long as three decades were released into general prison population or into transitional "step-down" programs.

References

Ashker v. Governor of the State of California, 4:09-cv-05796-cw (N.D. Cal., 2014).

Ashworth, A., von Hirsh, A. & Roberts, J. (eds.) (2009) *Principled Sentencing: Readings on Theory and Policy, 3rd edn.* Portland: Hart Publishing.

Ayer S.M., Heinze, J., Miller, A., Stoddard, S. & Zimmerman, M. (2014) "Exposure to Violence Predicting Cortisol Response During Adolescence and Early Adulthood: Understanding Moderating Factors," *Journal of Youth Adolescence* 43(7): 1066–79.

Baskin-Sommers, A. & Fonteneau, K. (2016) "Correctional Change Through Neuroscience," *Fordham Law Review* 85(2): 423–36.

Baumeister, R. & Leary, M. (1995) "The Need to Belong: Desire for Interpersonal Attachments as a Fundamental Human Motivation," *Psychological Bulletin* 117(3): 497–529.

Bennion, E. (2015) "Banning the Bing: Why Extreme Solitary Confinement is Cruel and Far Too Usual," *Indiana Law Journal* 90: 741–86.

Bessler, J. (2016) "The Italian Enlightenment and the American Revolution: Cesare Beccaria's Forgotten Influence on American Law," *Mitchell Hamline Law Journal of Public Policy and Practice* 37(1): 1–184.

Braswell, M. et al. (2001) *Corrections, Peacemaking and Restorative Justice: Transforming Individuals and Institutions*, New York: Routledge.

Brenmer, J.D. (2006) "Traumatic Stress: Effects on the Brain," *Dialogues in Clinical Neuroscience* 8(4): 445–61.

Cacioppo, J.T., Norris, C., Decety, J., Monteleone, G. & Nusbaum, H. (2009), "In the Eye ofThe Beholder: Individual Differences in Perceived Social Isolation Predict Regional Brain Activation to Social Stimuli," *Journal of Cognitive Neuroscience* 21(1): 83–92.

Coppola, F. (2019) "The Brain in Solitude: An(other) Eighth Amendment Challenge to Solitary Confinement," *Journal of Law and the Biosciences.* DOI:10.1093/jlb/lsz014

Cozolino, L. (2014) *Neuroscience of Human Relationships: Attachment and the Developing Social Brain, 2nd edn.*, New York: W.W. Norton & Company.

Davidson, R. & McEwen, B. (2012) "Social Influences on Neuroplasticity: Stress and Interventions to Promote Well-being," *Nature Neuroscience* 15(5): 689–95.

Dhami, N., Mantle, G. & Fox, D. (2009) "Restorative Justice in Prisons," *Contemporary Justice Review: Issues in Criminal, Social, and Restorative Justice* 12(1): 433–38.

Djordjevic, J., Djordjevic, A., Adzic, M. & Radojcic, M. (2012) "Effects of Chronic Social Isolation on Wistar Rat Behavior and Brain Plasticity Markers," *Neuropsychobiology* 66(2):112–19.

Dunbar, R. (1998) "The Social Brain Hypothesis," *Evolutionary Anthropology* 6(5): 178–90.

Eisenberger, N. (2012a) "The Neural Bases of Social Pain: Evidence for Shared Representations with Physical Pain," *Psychosomatic Medicine* 74(2): 126–35.

Eisenberger, N. (2012b) "The Pain of Social Disconnection: Examining the Shared Neural Underpinnings of Physical and Social Pain," *Nature Reviews of Neuroscience* 13: 421–34.

Farmer v. Brennan, 511 U.S. 825 (1994).

Fone, K. & Porkess, M.V. (2008) "Behavioural and Neurochemical Effects of Post-weaning Social Isolation in Rodents – Relevance to Developmental Neuropsychiatric Disorders," *Neuroscience & Biobehavioral Review* 32(6): 1087–102.

Foucault, M. (1977) *Discipline and Punish: The Birth of the Prison,* New York: Vintage Books.

Fowler, C., Liu, Y. & Wang, Z. (2008) "Estrogen Adult Neurogenesis in the Amygdala and Hypothalamus," *Brain Research Review* 57(2): 342–51.

Feasey, S. & Williams, P. (2009) "An Evaluation of the Sycamore Tree Programme: Based on an Analysis of Crime Pics II Data," at http://shura.shu.ac.uk/1000/1/fulltext.pdf.

Garbarino, J., Bradshaw, C. & Vorrasi, J. (2002) "Mitigating the Effects of Gun Violence on Children and Youth," *Future of Children* 12(2): 73–85.

Garland, D. (2001) *The Culture of Control: Crime and Social Order in Contemporary Society*, New York: Oxford University Press.

Gee D.G., Gabard-Durnam, L., Flannery, J., Goff, B., Humphreys, K. Telzer, E., Hare, T., Bookheimer, S. & Tottehnam, N. (2013) "Early Developmental Emergence of Human Amygdala-Prefrontal Connectivity After Maternal Deprivation," *PNAS* 110(39): 15638–43.

Gilligan, J. (2000) "Punishment and Violence: Is Criminal Law Based on a Huge Mistake?," *Social Research* 67(3): 745–72.

Goleman, D. (2006) *Social Intelligence: The New Science of Human Relationships*, New York: Arrow Books.

Gregg v. Georgia, 428 U.S. 153 (1976).

Johnson, C. (2013) "The Effects of Imprisonment," in F. Cullen and P. Wilcox (eds.) *The Oxford Handbook of Criminological Theory and Criminal Justice*, New York: Oxford University Press.

Haney, C. (2012) "Psychological Effects of Imprisonment," in J. Petersilia and K. Reitz (eds.), *The Oxford Handbook of Sentencing and Corrections*, New York: Oxford University Press.

Haney, C. (2018) "Restricting the Use of Solitary Confinement," *Annual Review of Criminology* 1: 285–310.

Hari, R., Henriksson, L., Malinen, S. & Parkonnen, L. (2015) "Centrality of Social Interaction for Adult Brain Function," *Neuron* 88(1): 181–93.

Hart, H. & Rubia, K. (2012) "Neuroimaging of Child Abuse: A Critical Review," *Frontiers in Human Neuroscience* 6: 1–24.

Haslam, N. (2006) "Dehumanization: An Integrative Review," *Personality and Social Psychology Review* 10(3): 252–64.

House, J.S., Landis, K. & Umberson, D. (1988) "Social Relationships and Health," *Science* 241(4865): 540–45.

Ieraci, A., Mallei, A. & Popoli, M. (2016) "Social Isolation Stress Induces Anxious-Depressive-Like Behavior and Alterations of Neuroplasticity-Related Genes in Adult Male Mice," *Neural Plasticity.* DOI: 10.1155/2016/6212983

Kelly, M., Duff, H., Kelly, S., McHugh Power, J., Brennan, S., Lawlor, B. & Loughrey, D. (2017) "The Impact of Social Activities, Social Networks, Social Support and Social Relationships on the Cognitive Functioning of Healthy Older Adults: A Systematic Review," *Systematic Reviews.* DOI: 10.1186/s13643-017-0632-2

Kupers, T. (2017) *Solitary: The Inside Story of Supermax Isolation and How We Can Abolish It*, Oakland, CA: University of California Press.

Labrecque, R. (2016) "The Use of Administrative Segregation and Its Function in the Institutional Setting," in *National Institute of Justice 2503157, Restrictive Housing in the U.S.: Issues Challenges and Future Directions*, Washington, DC: U.S. Department of Justice.

Landa, A., Peterson, B. & Fallon, B. (2012) "Somatoform Pain: A Developmental Theory and Translational Research Review," *Psychosomatic Medicine* 74(7): 717–27.

Lauwaert, K., Aertsen, I. (eds.) (2015) "Desistance and Restorative Justice: Mechanisms for Desisting from Crime within Restorative Justice Practices," *European Justice Forum*.

Lieberman, M. (2013) *Social: Why Our Brains Are Wired to Connect*, New York: Crown.

Lieberman, M. & Eisenberger, N. (2008), "The Pains and Pleasures of Social Life: A Social Neuroscience Approach," Neuroleadership Journal, at www.scn.ucla.edu/pdf/Pains&Pleasures(2008).pdf

Lippke, R. (2003) "Retribution and Incarceration," *Public Affairs Quarterly* 17(1): 29–48.

Liu, J. et al. (2012) "Impaired Adult Myelination in the Prefrontal Cortex of Socially Isolated Mice," *Nature Neuroscience* 15(2): 1621–23.

Lobel, J. (2008) "Prolonged Solitary Confinement and the Constitution," *University of Pennsylvania Journal of Constitutional Law* 11: 115–38.

Lobel, J. & Akil, H. (2018) "Law & Neuroscience: The Case of Solitary Confinement," *Daedalus* 147(4): 61–75.

Logue, M.W. et al. (2018) "Smaller HippocampalVolume in Posttraumatic Stress Disorder: A Multisite ENIGMA-PGC Study: SubcorticalVolumetry Results from Posttraumatic Stress Disorder Consortia," *Biological Psychiatry* 1(83): 244–53.

Makinodan, M., Rosen, K., Ito, S. & Corfas, G. (2012) "A Critical Period for Social Experience-dependent Oligodendrocyte Maturation and Myelination," *Science* 337(6100): 1357–60.

Maruna, S. (2016) "Desistance and Restorative Justice: It's Now or Never," *Restorative Justice: An International Journal* 4(3): 289–301.

Matter, L. (2010–2011) "'Hey, I Think We're Unconstitutionally Alone Now': The Eighth Amendment Protects Social Interaction as a Basic Human Need," *Journal of Gender, Race & Justice* 14: 265–99.

McCrory, E., De Brito, S. & Viding, E. (2010) "The Neurobiology and Genetics of Maltreatment and Adversity," *Journal of Child Psychology and Psychiatry* 51(10): 1079–95.

Meijers, J., Harte, J., Meynen, G., Cuijpers, P. & Schreder, E. (2018) "Reduced Self-Control After 3 Months of Imprisonment: A Pilot Study," *Frontiers in Psychology.* DOI: 10.3389/fpsyg.2018.00069

Nee C. & Vernham, Z. (2017), "Expertise and Its Contribution to the Notion of Protective Factors in Offender Rehabilitation and Desistance," *Aggression and Violent Behavior* 32: 37–44.

Neil, S., Kent, M., Bardi, M. & Lambert, K. (2018) "Enriched Environment Exposure Enhances Social Interactions and Oxytocin Responsiveness in Male Long-Evans Rats," Frontiers in Behavioral Neuroscience. DOI:10.3389/fnbeh.2018.00198

Ouanes, S., Popp, J. (2019) "High Cortisol and the Risk of Dementia and Alzheimer's Disease: A Review of the Literature," *Frontiers in Aging Neuroscience.* DOI:10.3389/fnagi.2019.00043

Pickard, H. (2018) "Rethinking Justice: The Clinical Model of Responsibility Without Blame," *Howard League for Penal Reform – Early Academics Network Bulletin* 4–10.

Power, J., Bradley, L. (2017) "Neural plasticity across the lifespan," *Wiley Interdisciplinary Review of Developmental Biology.* DOI:10.1002/wdev.216

Reisel, D. (2015) "Towards a Neuroscience of Morality," in T. Gavrielides (ed.) *The Psychology of Restorative Justice: Managing the Power* from Within, New York: Ashgate Publishing.

Rhodes v. Chapman 452 U.S. 337 (1981).

Rosenzweig, M.R. & Bennett, E. L. (1972) "Cerebral Changes in Rats Exposed Individually to an Enriched Environment," *Journal of Comparative and Physiological Psychology* 80(2): 304–13.

Seeman, T.E. & McEwen, B.S. (1996) "Impact of social environment characteristics on neuroendocrine regulation," *Psychosomatic Medicine* 58: 459–71.

Sheridan M.A., Fox, N., Zaehnan, C., McLaughlin, K. & Nelson, C. et al. (2012) "Variation in Neural Development as a Result of Exposure to Institutionalization Early in Childhood," *PNAS* 109(32): 12927–32.

Siegel D. (2012) *The Developing Mind: How Relationships and the Brain Interact to Shape Who We Are,* New York: Guildford Press.

Slater, A. & Cao, L. (2015) "A Protocol for Housing Mice in Enriched Environments," *Journal of Visualized Experiments.* DOI:10.3791/52874

Tanaka, K., Osako, Y. & Yuri, K. (2010) "Juvenile social experience regulates central neuropeptides relevant to emotional and social behaviors," *Neuroscience* 166 (4):1036–42.

Toews, B. (2006) *The Little Book of Restorative Justice for People in Prison: Rebuilding the Web of Relationships,* Good Books.

Tost H., Champagne, F., Meyer-Lindenberg, A.(2015) "Environmental Influence in the Brain, Human Welfare and Mental Health," *Nature Neuroscience* 18(10): 4121–31.

Umbach, R., Raine, A. & Leonard, N. (2018) "Cognitive Decline as a Result of Incarceration and the Effects of a CBT/MT Intervention: A Cluster Randomized Controlled Trial," *Criminal Justice and Behavior* 45(1): 31–55.

Valk, S. L., Bernhardth, B., Trautwein, F.M., Böckler, A., Kanske, P., Guizard, N., Louis Collins, D. & Singer, T. (2017) "Structural Plasticity of The Social Brain: Differential Change After Socio-Affective and Cognitive Mental Training," *Science Advances.* DOI:10.1126/sciadv.1700489

Vera Institute of Justice (2019) "Human Dignity and Prison Design", at www.vera.org/research/human-dignity-and-prison-design

Wang, X., Cai, L., Qian, J. & Peng, J. (2014) "Social Support Moderates Stress Effects on Depression," *International Journal of Mental Health Systems.* DOI:10.1186/1752-4458-8-41

Whittle, S., Simmons, J., Dennison, M., Viyajakumar, N., Schwartz, O., Yap, M., Sheeber, L. & Allen, N. (2014) "Positive parenting predicts the development of adolescent brain structure: A longitudinal study," *Developmental Cognitive Neuroscience* 8: 7–17.

Wilkerson v. Stalder, 639 F. Supp. 2d 654 (M.D. La. 2007).

Wilson v. Seiter 501 U.S. 294 (1991).

Wongwitdecha, N. & Marsden, C.A. (1996) "Social Isolation Increases Aggressive Behaviour and Alters the Effects of Diazepam in the Rat Social Interaction Test," *Behavioral Brain Research* 75(1–2): 27–32.

Woo C., Kobam, L., Kross, E., Lindsquit, M., Banich, M., Ruzik, L., Andrews-Hanna, J. & Wager, T. (2014) "Separate Neural Representations for Physical Pain and Social Rejection," *Nature Communications.* DOI: 10.1038/ncomms6380

17

EFFECTS OF PRISON CROWDING ON PRISON MISCONDUCT AND BULLYING

Ivana Sekol, David P. Farrington, and Izabela Zych

As prison populations rise rapidly in many countries worldwide (Walmsley 2015), the effect of incarceration on prisoners' well-being has become an urgent social concern (Murray, Farrington & Sekol 2012). Prison misconduct and violence, including bullying and violence amongst prisoners, are one of the greatest threats to prisoners' mental health and behavior, decreasing prisoners' chances of successful rehabilitation and reintegration back into the community. Since more than 90% of all prisoners will be released back to their communities eventually (Levan 2012), getting "smart on crime" requires minimizing the negative effects of imprisonment and providing opportunities for prisoner rehabilitation (Woolf 1991).

It is hard to imagine, however, how effective rehabilitation can take place in an environment where violence seems to be the norm rather than the exception. In the UK, the prevalence of bullying occurring on a monthly basis is as high as 74% in some studies, while the prevalence of victimization is around 80% (e.g. Ireland & Ireland 2008; Turner & Ireland 2010). In Canada, the prevalence of weekly victimization is 73%, while the prevalence of bullying is 58% (Ireland & Power 2012). In Croatia, the weekly prevalence of victimization and bullying is 55% and 40% respectively (Sekol, Vidranski & Jolliffe 2020).[1]

The importance placed on establishing and maintaining prison order and safety has generated numerous studies of the causes and correlates of prison misconduct (Steiner, Butler & Ellison 2014). Following the above-mentioned rapid increases in incarceration rates in many countries, one of the most often examined environmental predictors of either violent or non-violent prison misconduct over the past four decades has been prison crowding. However, although the intuitive hypothesis would be that crowding and prison misconduct are positively related, the results of primary studies examining these relationships have been conflicting.

The main aims of this chapter are to: (1) summarize the evidence about the relationship between prison crowding and prison misconduct, including bullying among prisoners; (2) discuss different methods of measuring prison crowding, misconduct and bullying as well as whether taking account of differing methodology allows for more robust summaries of the results of the existing studies; (3) identify the gaps in knowledge and propose guidance for future research. Section 1 provides an overview of the causes and context of rapid increases in prison populations in many countries. Section 2 defines prison crowding and discusses its prevalence and methods for collecting the data about it. Section 3 does the same for prison misconduct and bullying. Section 4 gives a brief overview of theoretical models that are used to explain prison misconduct, including bullying. Section 5 summarizes evidence about the effects of prison crowding on prison misconduct and bullying, while

Section 6 identifies the gaps in knowledge and proposes guidance for future research. Because of space limitations, we do not attempt to review the effect of prison crowding on recidivism (see e.g. Farrington & Nuttall 1980).[2]

1. Increase in Prison Populations

Following Martinson's (1974) conclusion that "nothing works" in the 1970s, prison populations have been growing in many countries ever since. The increase has particularly been noticeable in the United States, which currently has an incarceration rate of 655 inmates per 100,000 residents, compared with the average rate of 127 among other nations in the Organisation for Economic Co-operation and Development (Walmsley 2015). Currently, around 2.12 million people are incarcerated in American federal or state prisons and jails, compared to around half a million people who used to be incarcerated on a daily basis in the USA in the 1980s (Walmsley 2015). Although not as dramatically as in the United States, many other high-income countries (e.g. the United Kingdom and Belgium) and middle-income countries (e.g. Croatia and Brazil) have also experienced rather large increases in their prison populations (Aebi, Tiago & Burkhardt 2016; Walmsley 2015). Since the United States has the highest total number of prisoners in the world, as well as the highest prison population rate, this chapter will mainly focus on the United States.

There are three broad reasons for increases in prison populations. First, following the "Nothing Works" paradigm and an increase in crime in the 1970s, there was a shift in focus from offender-orientated rehabilitative policies to punitive offense-based prison policies (Besemer & Murray 2014; Tonry 2009). In the early 1980s, tougher crime policies started being employed not only within the prison walls but also in the community, resulting in harsher sentences for less serious offenses. Specifically, it was the "War on Drugs" that led to the unprecedented growth in prison populations from the 1980s onwards. For instance, in 1979 drug offenders accounted for approximately 6% of the US prison population. By 2012 drug offenders accounted for 52% of the US federal prison population (Taxy, Samuels & Adams 2015). Although by November 2018 the number of drug offenders in prisons had declined to 46%, they still constituted a considerable proportion of the US federal prison population (Federal Bureau of Prisons 2018). The tough-on-crime measures culminated in the 1990s with the introduction of the "Three Strikes and You are Out" legislation, which was implemented in over half of all states in the USA and which further increased the nation's prison population and the length of prison sentences (Vitiello 2017).

Second, the security and terrorism agenda following the 9/11 attacks in the USA and terrorist attacks in the EU, as well as the broader processes of migration and globalization in the new millennium, have resulted in additional rises in prison populations, especially in terms of increasing numbers of foreigners in many prison systems (Scharff-Smith 2016). Finally, a concept of penal populism, in which politicians and the media fed into the idea that both crime and terrorism were spiraling out of control and that more people needed to be sent to prisons for longer (Besemer & Murray 2014), further contributed to illegitimately justifying the above described tough-on-crime measures.

While advocates of severe incarceration policies claim that punitive penal policies have reduced crimes rates, the opponents of such measures argue that conclusions about the effectiveness of the "War on Drugs" and "Three Strikes" laws have predominantly been based on biased methodology that lacked appropriate research rigor. More sophisticated analyses of the effectiveness of tough-on-crime measures suggest that the "toughest" sentencing policies might not necessarily be the most effective ones (Chen 2008). Mass incarceration has resulted in prison crowding, a problem that many US states are still facing, regardless of the growing private prison industry and newly built prisons over the past few decades. As of December 31 2016, at least 20 US states had prison systems operating above their design capacity (Carson 2018).[3]

There is evidence that prison crowding is related to numerous problems within the prison walls, including deterioration of the physical and psychological health of prisoners (Cox, Paulus & McCain 1984), prison suicides (Cox et al. 1984; Huey & Mcnulty 2005), deterioration of the physical, operational, and social conditions of the prison (Leone & Kinkade 1994), and staff burnout and turnover (Martin et al. 2012). The incarceration explosion has also had a marked negative impact on the rest of the criminal justice system and society in general, causing strain on local law enforcement operations and courts (Austin et al. 1999), placing a significant burden on state budgets and taxpayers (Vaughn 1993) and having long-lasting adverse effects on prisoners' children and families (Murray, Farrington & Sekol, 2012).

2. Prison Crowding

Prison crowding can be conceptualized in different ways. Some authors have defined prison crowding as the percentage of inmates who shared cells with other inmates or were housed in dormitories relative to the percentage of inmates housed in single cells (e.g Tartaro 2002). Others have assumed that a good indicator of prison crowding is whether prisons are under a court order for crowding (e.g. McCorkle et al. 1995) or that crowding can be operationalized by changes in the prison environment, such as those related to conditions before and after double bunking was introduced in a prison (Pelissier 1991). Defining crowding as the degree to which prisoners perceive their environment to be crowded has also been documented (e.g. Paulus & Dzindolet 1993). There have also been attempts to treat total population counts as proxy measures of crowding (Steiner & Wooldredge 2009).

Most frequently, however, prison crowding has been operationalized as the ratio of a facility's total population to the maximum design or rated capacity, and this is known as the "crowding index" (Camp et al. 2003; Farrington & Nuttall 1980; Ruback & Carr, 1993; Steiner & Wooldredge, 2009).[4] "Design capacity" refers to the number of inmates that planners or architects intended for a prison. According to this definition, a prison is considered crowded if the number of prisoners exceeds its original planned capacity. The "rated capacity" is determined by corrections officials or a national corrections organization. There is also "operational capacity," which is the number of inmates a prison can hold while being managed properly, and it is based on a number of staff, existing programs, and services (Carson 2018; Tartaro 2002). The data on any of the three types of capacity-related measures of crowding, which are sometimes also referred to as "spatial density,"[5] can be collected either at one point in time or longitudinally, focusing on monthly values. Using an average value for a fiscal year is also relatively common (Steiner & Wooldredge, 2009).

Prison crowding measures standardized by capacity are often considered to be better suited for measuring crowding than, for instance, measures of the way in which prisoners perceive crowding or measures of prison size or population counts. The advocates of capacity-related crowding measures center their assumptions around three main points. First, prisoners' perceptions of crowding are individual-level subjective measures, as prisoners' views of the same environment can easily change over a short time period, thus having little policy relevance (Gaes 1985; Steiner & Wooldredge 2009). Second, given large differences in prison capacities across prisons, total population counts are difficult to interpret without taking capacity into account. For instance, a prison with a large population might not be crowded if its capacity is large enough. Standardizing measures of crowding by capacity, therefore, allows comparisons across different prisons. Finally, the aggregate (prison-level) nature of the capacity related-crowding measures also has stronger policy implications because the admission rates and available bed space are more easily controlled than, for instance, prisoners' perceptions of their environment (Steiner & Wooldredge 2009).

Of measures of crowding standardized for capacity, design capacity is usually treated as superior to rated capacity and operational capacity. The reason for this is twofold. First, it is believed that rated and operational capacities can be manipulated by prison officials to give socially desirable answers and the impression that prisons can accommodate more inmates than they were designed to house. Second, the more objective nature of design capacity makes the data on prison crowding more available for both longitudinal and cross-sectional research because a crowding index (the ratio of a prison's total population to the maximum design capacity) could be calculated for virtually any point in time (Steiner & Wooldredge 2009).

Although measures of spatial density, especially the measure of design capacity, seem to be generally preferred among prison crowding researchers, some scholars have argued that spatial density measures are rather crude and that crowding might be assessed more accurately by measuring inmates' feelings and perceptions of being crowded, especially if those feelings are construed as stressful (Gendreau, Low & Goggin 1997). For instance, some authors argue that individuals in a densely populated setting may not necessarily feel crowded or find their circumstances stressful and that crowding research should focus on conditions other than spatial density (Bleich 1989; Paulus 1988). A more objective measure of crowding might focus on the number of square feet per prisoner. In England and Wales, a measure of crowding could be based on the frequency of two or three inmates being housed in a cell designed for one inmate.

3. Prison Misconduct and Bullying Among Prisoners

The dramatic increase in US prison and jail populations over the past four decades has renewed scholarly interest in prisoners' experiences and the challenges that prisons face in maintaining order and safety (Toman 2017). According to the U.S. Bureau of Prisons (2012, hereafter BOP) the growth in the federal inmate population has negatively affected inmates, staff, and infrastructure, resulting in waiting lists for education and drug treatment programs, limited meaningful work opportunities, increased use of double and triple bunking, and increased inmate-to-staff ratios. All these factors, as BOP further argues, contribute to increased inmate misconduct. Prison systems usually define prison misconduct as deviations from the formal prison rules that regulate a prisoner's behavior in a prison (Steiner, Butler & Ellison, 2014). Prison misconduct includes behaviors that have been prohibited because of the aim of maintaining order and security within a prison (e.g. disrespecting staff or other inmates), as well as behaviors that would be considered criminal offenses if they were committed outside the prison, such as assaults (Steiner 2018).

Given that prison misconduct negatively affects the safety and security of inmates and staff (BOP 2012), from a policy standpoint, understanding the causes and correlates of prison misconduct is of great importance. In this context, several points need to be taken into account. First, there is evidence that inmates who are involved in prison misconduct are more likely to continue offending upon release (Trulson, DeLisi & Marquart 2011). It is, therefore, particularly important to try to establish whether imprisonment, or prison-based interventions, are effective in encouraging desistance from offending upon release (Steiner et al. 2014). If not, it is essential to identify prison-based risk factors for misconduct as possible mediators of later re-offending, and develop programs to eradicate them. Relatedly, as already mentioned, it is unlikely that effective rehabilitation can take place in an environment where prisoners constantly fear for their safety. On the contrary, it is more likely that an atmosphere of fear would result in adverse outcomes both within and outside the prison walls, even among the prisoners who obey prison rules.

Also, there is evidence that, in the general population, there is continuity in bullying behavior across time and settings, implying that bullying is only one element of aggression and aggression is only one element of a larger syndrome of antisocial behavior (Farrington 1993; Zych et al. 2019). Bullying also appears to be stable across time and settings among young people in children's and correctional homes (Sekol & Farrington 2016). Similarly, in a prison setting, there is a large overlap between bullies and victims, meaning that a large proportion of prisoners who bully others are also victims of bullying (Ireland 1999a, 1999b, 1999c; 2002a; 2005a; Ireland & Monaghan 2006; Sekol & Vidranski 2020) and that prison policies should systematically target prison bullying as a special type of misconduct. Finally, living in an atmosphere of fear violates basic prisoners' rights set forth by the

UN Human Rights Committee (1992), according to which prisoners may not be subjected to any hardship other than that resulting from the deprivation of liberty (General comment No. 21: Article 10 - Humane treatment of persons deprived of their liberty) and that no-one in a prison should fear for his or her physical safety (UN, 2005).

Given that prison misconduct includes a wide variety of behaviors, it is important to note that not all misconduct is necessarily violent. For instance, alcohol or drugs related offenses might not include violence at all. Similarly, not all violent misconduct (e.g. verbal attacks) includes physical violence. Further, while all types of bullying include direct or indirect aggression, not all prisoner-to-prisoner violence involves bullying. Just as in other settings, bullying in prisons requires an element of repetition. The most widely used definition of prison bullying was proposed by Ireland (2002b) and assumes that prisoners are being bullied when they are victims of indirect or direct aggression happening on a weekly basis, by the same or different perpetrator(s). However, given the special nature of the closed social prison environment, the definition of prison bullying is somewhat wider than the definition of bullying in a school setting. School-based definitions of bullying require not only the element of repetition, but also assume the intent of bullies to harm their victims and the imbalance of power between the bully and his/her victim(s). In a prison setting in which victims are permanently "trapped", an aggressive act can be considered bullying if the victim believes that s(he) had been aggressed against, regardless of the intention of the bully to cause harm. For instance, in a prison setting bullying behavior might be so normalized that prisoners might unconsciously bully others, thinking that they are just "playing a joke."

Similarly, bullying in prison can also exist when the imbalance of power between the bully and his/her victim is not immediately evident. This is the case in situations such as "baroning" in which goods are given to one prisoner by another prisoner (a "baron") who later demands a high repayment. Since the victim enters this relationship voluntarily, the relationship is not initially based on an imbalance of power (for a more detailed discussion of definitions of bullying in prisons, see Ireland, 2002b: 25–27). Although Ireland (2002b) has argued that, in a prison setting, single incidents of aggression might be considered bullying if the victim fears future victimization after the incident, in line with school-based bullying research, single incidents of inmate-to-inmate aggression are defined as peer violence, not bullying.

Most frequently, bullying in prisons is measured by the widely used self-report Direct and Indirect Prisoner Behaviour Checklist-Revised (DIPC-R ©Ireland 2002c, for details see Ireland & Ireland 2008), in which prisoners are asked to indicate whether they have been subjected to or whether they have engaged in a wide range of direct (e.g. name calling or hitting someone) or indirect (e.g. gossiping or socially excluding someone) aggressive behaviors in the past week. Using this scale, prisoners are classified as bullies or victims if they reported at least one behavior indicative of bullying others or being bullied in the past week. Interestingly, despite the fact that most other types of prison research have been conducted in the US, research on prison bullying has mainly been conducted in the UK, where the prevalence of bullying occurring on a monthly basis is as high as 74% in some studies, while the prevalence of victimization is around 80% (e.g. Ireland & Ireland, 2008; Turner & Ireland, 2010). More recently, prison bullying has also been studied in other countries (for details see Ireland & Power, 2012, and Sekol & Vidranski 2020).

Unlike prison bullying, which is mainly measured by means of self-report, the data on prison misconduct is usually collected through official reports. Official reports include official counts of reported total rule infractions (regardless of the type of misconduct) or official counts of certain types of misconduct (e.g. the number of assaults on other inmates or staff, the number of drug offenses, the number of property offenses). Sometimes official reports include only officially sanctioned or "convicted" rule infractions. On other occasions, official reports comprise dichotomized measures of whether inmates engaged in any or type-specific rule infractions. Aggregate measures of the dichotomous data, which reflect the proportion of inmates who engaged in rule infractions, have also been documented (for a summary of major studies conducted before 2009 which used different types of official misconduct measures see Steiner & Wooldredge 2009: 210–214). Although the majority of studies on prison misconduct have employed official measures, some researchers have examined both self-reported and officially reported prison misconduct (e.g. Steiner & Wooldredge 2014).

Both official reports and self-reports have advantages and disadvantages. Official measures of misconduct often underestimate the prevalence of prison misconduct because a lot of offences go undetected by staff. Official measures also depend on the discretion of the prison officials, meaning that even some incidents of misconduct that are known to prison officials fail to be officially reported and processed. Also, official data increase the likelihood of finding spurious effects if the probability of incidents remaining unreported is associated with certain inmate or prison characteristics. One problem of self-reports is that prisoners might underreport their misconduct or bullying because of the fear of reprisal in case their identity is revealed (Steiner & Wooldredge 2009). Prisoners might also underreport being victims of bullying or peer violence for fear of being labelled as "grassers" by other prisoners, even when anonymous questionnaires are employed, especially if the questionnaires are being completed in groups (Connell & Farrington, 1996; Ireland, 1999a).

On the other hand, it has been demonstrated that anonymous self-reports of bullying and victimization are more valid and reliable than staff reports and peer reports in children's homes and juvenile correctional homes (Sekol & Farrington, 2013) as well as in young offender institutions (Connell & Farrington 1997). The main advantage of self-report measures of bullying is that they can measure less visible forms of indirect bullying, about which other informants (i.e. staff) often do not have enough information (Farrington 1993; Tattum 1997) and which official records often do not include (Ireland 2005b). Self-reports of prison bullying have proved to be particularly useful when using behavior checklists (such as the above-described DIPC-R) because they avoid the term "bullying", which is an emotive and stigmatizing term that has negative connotations for both perpetrators and victims (Ireland 2002a). The use of "bullying" can encourage dishonest answers because participants might feel pressured to provide socially desirable responses (Theriot et al. 2005). Similarly, prisoners may have different interpretations of the term (Connell & Farrington 1996) and may not perceive their behavior as bullying and therefore not report it when asked directly (Ireland 2002a). Finally, there is evidence that victimization must be severe and frequent before participants identify it as bullying (Connell & Farrington, 1996; Theriot et al. 2005).

While the validity and reliability of self-report, staff-report and peer-report bullying measures in secure settings have been empirically examined, this has not been the case for measures of other types of prison misconduct. Until more research on the reliability and validity of prison self-report, staff-report or peer-report misconduct is conducted, it might be useful to use official data when studying prison misconduct (especially violent misconduct) and self-report data when examining prison bullying.

4. Theories of Prison Misconduct and Bullying

In order to examine correlates and possible causes of prison misconduct, researchers have built upon classic prison theories, namely those referring to deprivation and importation models. These opposing models attempt to explain prison misconduct as a product of the special nature of the closed prison environment and specific experiences within this environment (the deprivation model) or as a result of characteristics that inmates bring with them into the prison from the outside world (the importation model).

The deprivation model is based on the classic texts of prison sociology, namely those of Clemmer (1940), Sykes (2007/1958), and Goffman (1961), and assumes that it is the characteristics of the physical and social prison environment that contribute to misconduct in prisons. According to Sykes (2007/1958) these characteristics contain five main deprivations typical of prison life, also known as "pains of imprisonment", and there are three main ways in which prisoners can adapt or respond to these pains of imprisonment. The five main deprivations include deprivation of liberty, deprivation of goods and services, deprivation of heterosexual relationships, deprivation of autonomy, and deprivation of security. The three possible ways in which prisoners may respond to the pains of imprisonment include the development of inmate solidarity (but hostility towards staff), withdrawal (e.g. prisoners give up attempts to achieve their goals or meet their needs), and misbehavior (including misconduct and bullying). Any of the five deprivations may lead to any of the three responses. In their totality, the pains of imprisonment and the ways in which prisoners adapt to them create a specific prisoner subculture organized around the inmate value system or "inmate code" that then further directs prisoners' behavior.

Sykes described the second pain, deprivation of goods and services, as a factor that creates "a harshly Spartan environment which [a prisoner] finds painfully depriving" (2007/1958: 68). Such an environment fails to adequately meet prisoners' basic human needs, such as those related to access to varied foods, proper health care, exercise, clothing, certain material possessions (e.g. cigarettes), privacy, and appropriate living arrangements. Although contemporary prisons are not as depriving of material goods and services as they might have been in the 1950s, more recent prison ethnographies still find the concept of pains of imprisonment relevant. In the era of mass incarceration, crowding is a likely contributing factor to the modern pains of imprisonment. As such, of all predictors of prison misconduct included in the deprivation model, crowding has been one of the most frequently examined predictors in quantitative prison research.

The deprivation model was first challenged by Irwin and Cressey (1962), who argued that prisoners' behavior within the prison is determined by prisoners' personal characteristics and cultures that they "import" with them into the prison, rather than by specific features of the prison environment. According to the importation model, prisoners' misconduct is just a continuation of their previous criminal careers, meaning that the correlates of prison misconduct are fundamentally the same as those of criminal behavior in general (Innes 1997). The importation model therefore examines the demographic (e.g. age, gender, previous history of violence or convictions), social (e.g. family relationships, peer support, adverse childhood experiences), and psychological (e.g. empathy, self-esteem, impulsivity, personality traits) characteristics of inmates that influence prison misconduct.

Based on the results of her extensive research on prison bullying over the past two decades, Ireland (2012) has proposed a Multifactor Model of Bullying in Secure Settings (MMBSS). Incorporating the elements of both the deprivation and importation models, the MMBSS argues that bullying amongst prisoners is determined by an interaction between the individual characteristics of prisoners and the prison environment. It describes two main pathways that lead to bullying in prisons, both driven by the prison environment. The first, "desensitization pathway", assumes that violence in prisons is normalized, which makes prisoners become desensitized to aggression. This in turn amplifies prisoners' *stable dynamic individual characteristics*, which further promote prisoners' existing beliefs and attitudes supportive of aggression, as well as their emotions of fear, anger and hostility (*acute dynamic individual factors*). Once bullying behavior occurs, it is likely to be reinforced by the social prison environment that is accepting of aggression.

The second, "environment and prior characteristic" pathway argues that the physical and social aspects of the prison environment both reinforce preexisting individual traits of prisoners who are prone to bullying. In line with the deprivation model, this model describes the physical prison environment as a setting marked by limited access to material goods, large numbers of prisoners detained together in a small space (as a proxy measure of crowding), low supervision because of a high prisoner to staff ratio, and insufficient environmental stimulation. The social prison environment includes authoritarian relationships between staff and prisoners, prisoner subcultures based on values that promote dominance relations and peer hierarchies, negative attitudes towards victims, and low attachment relationships (for more details, see Ireland 2012).

5. Empirical Support for the Relationship Between Prison Crowding and Misconduct and Bullying

Numerous studies of the causes and correlates of prison misconduct have been conducted, mainly examining the socio-demographic and psychological inmate variables that are included in the importation model. Deprivation theory has been quantitatively tested less frequently, with prison crowding being its most often examined element.

The results of primary studies examining the relationship between prison crowding and inmate misconduct (excluding bullying *per se*) have been conflicting. Thus far, our recent extensive literature search identified 13 studies that found a significant positive relationship between crowding and either violent or non-violent prison misconduct (Cabanillas 2012; Cox, Paulus & McCain 1984; Gaes & McGuire 1985; Glazener 2016; Harer & Steffensmeier 1996; Jan 1980; Kurzfeld 2017; Lahm 2008; Megargee 1977, Nacci, Teitelbaum & Prather 1977; Porporino 1986; Ruback & Carr 1993; and Steiner & Wooldredge 2014). However, we also identified 12 studies that found no such relationship (Atlas 1982; Dâmboeanu & Nieuwbeerta 2016; Dietz 1999; Bonta & Kiem, 1978; Camp, Gaes, Langan & Saylor, 2003; Bonta & Nanckivell, 1980; Clayton & Carr 1984; Ekland-Olson, Barrick & Cohen 1983; McCorkle et al. 1995; Porporino & Dudley 1984; Steiner 2009; Useem & Reisig 1999). One project based on the analyses of 646 jails in the United States (Tartaro 2002) found a significant negative relationship between crowding and inmate-to-inmate assaults.[6]

Of the above studies which reported a significant positive relationship between prison crowding and misconduct, only two studies (i.e. Ruback & Carr 1993; Steiner & Wooldredge 2014) found that this relationship held after controlling for other factors examined. For instance, Ruback and Carr (1993) reported that crowding was a significant predictor of both violent and non-violent misconduct even after controlling for factors such as age, race, number of violent convictions, annual prison budget, number of inmates backlogged in jails, number of individuals on probation, custody level, number of employees, and prison size.

The problem with counting significant versus non-significant results (the "vote-counting" method) of prior primary studies is that statistical significance depends partly on sample size and partly on effect size. Some of the non-significant results might actually reflect a large effect in a small sample. The best way to estimate effect sizes is to conduct a meta-analysis. Although some authors have argued that the differing methods and levels of analyses that are employed in primary studies on the relationship between crowding and prison misconduct do not allow for a quantitative synthesis (e.g. Gaes 1994), there have been attempts to summarize the conflicting findings of the primary studies in systematic reviews. Systematic reviews use rigorous methods for locating, appraising, and synthesizing all relevant evidence from prior primary studies. They have Methods and Results sections, explicit criteria for including or excluding studies, a structured report, and are marked by the same level of rigor that characterizes high quality original research (Farrington & Petrosino 2000). They may or may not include a meta-analysis. Because they synthesize various types of prior research and policy evidence, systematic reviews are particularly useful for evidence-based research and practice, especially in cases where meta-analysis can be conducted.

To date, only one systematic review has explicitly attempted to rigorously synthesize the findings from the above primary studies (Franklin, Franklin & Pratt, 2006). An additional three systematic reviews and meta-analyses have been conducted (Bonta & Gendreau, 1990; Gendreau, Low & Goggin 1997; Gonçalves et al. 2014), but their aims were to examine various prison and personal predictors of numerous outcomes, including prison misconduct. Each of these reviews and/or their research designs employed are, however, either dated or limited in scope, which makes it challenging to uniformly interpret their differing findings. For instance, while Bonta and Gendreau (1990), Gendreau et al. (1997), and Franklin et al. (2006) discovered that crowding was significantly (but weakly) related to prison misconduct, Gonçalves et al. (2014) found no such relationship. Franklin et al. (2006), however, concluded that the effect of crowding on prison misconduct was much larger for young offenders, and Bonta and Gendreau (1990) also suggested that prisoners' age might be an important moderator of the relationship between crowding and misconduct.

In terms of the limited scope and/or methodology of the existing reviews, Bonta and Gendreau (1990), Franklin et al. (2006); and Gendreau et al. (1997) all based their conclusions on a synthesis of data collected predominantly on an aggregate/prison level. The problem with the aggregate level of analysis, however, is that other individual factors, such as prisoners' age or the length of the sentence, may moderate the relationship between crowding and prison misconduct (Bonta & Gendreau, 1990). Similarly, only Gonçalves et al. (2014) synthesized the primary studies based on both self-reports and official reports of misconduct. As already discussed, the problem with official records is that a large portion of prisoner misconduct remains undetected by staff and is consequently often missing from official records. Therefore, as empirically confirmed by Steiner and Wooldredge (2014) officially recorded misconduct underestimates the total volume of inmate infractions.

Further, in the majority of the above-mentioned reviews, it remains unclear what criteria of methodological quality were used for including primary studies. Only Bonta and Gendreau (1990) stated that they had included correlational or quasi-experimental primary studies. It is, however, important that only primary studies with high internal validity are included in systematic reviews. When it comes to systematic reviews of evaluation studies, reviewers normally aim to include at least quasi-experimental evaluations (Farrington, Weisburd & Gill, 2011). In the case of systematic reviews synthesizing evidence on risk factors, reviewers should ideally aim to include only longitudinal studies in order to determine causal order, although cross-sectional and quasi-experimental studies may also be included.

The search strategies of the existing reviews were often either vaguely described or limited in scope. For instance, Franklin et al. (2006) only included studies published in peer reviewed journals and did not specify the time period over which they had conducted their searches or whether they had considered studies published in languages other than English. Also, they only searched three electronic databases and conducted no hand-searches of the literature. Gonçalves et al. (2014) only included primary studies conducted between 1996 and October 2012 and only those that were conducted with adult male prisoners, relying only on electronic database searches. Furthermore, although some of the above reviews (i.e. Franklin et al. 2006) did look at inmate-to-inmate assaults as an outcome, none of them examined the relationship between crowding and bullying *per se*. Given that, unlike single incidents of violence between prisoners, the repetitive nature of bullying might have more severe psychological consequences for victims, systematic reviews should distinguish between bullying and other types of inmate-to-inmate violence. The growing body of recent research on prison bullying should allow for this.

Finally, apart from Franklin et al. (2006), who found that the effect of crowding on prison misconduct was much larger for young offenders, no other reviews examined whether crowding might be related to prison misconduct and bullying through one or more intervening influences. Apart from prisoners' age, it is possible that crowding effects are moderated by prison population compositions (e.g. male vs. female prisons), security levels, inmate turnover, management style, levels of inmate program involvement and the like (Gendreau et al. 1997; Klofas, Stojkovic & Kalinich 1992; Steiner & Wooldredge 2009).

6. Conclusions

This chapter provided an overview of theories, methods and empirical evidence on the relationship between prison crowding and misconduct, including bullying among prisoners. It demonstrated that there are numerous methodological and conceptual options from which researchers can choose when deciding how to collect, measure and analyze the data on both prison crowding and misconduct. Presumably because of different operational definitions, methods and levels of analyses employed in different studies, empirical evidence about the effects of crowding on prison misconduct is mixed. For the time being our literature review suggests that there appears to be slightly more evidence about prison crowding being a risk factor for both violent and non-violent misconduct. However, more primary research comparing crowded (experimental group) and non-crowded (control group) prisons is needed if we are to draw stronger conclusions. Similarly, more primary studies that would allow for examining whether crowding is an independent predictor of prison misconduct, after taking into account other relevant individual or prison variables, are needed. However, this is not to say that a non-significant direct effect of crowding on misconduct is irrelevant. A non-significant effect (e.g. in a regression analysis) together with a significant zero-order correlation could suggest that crowding is linked to misconduct via one or more intervening variables (Steiner & Wooldredge 2009). In terms of policy and practice, identifying and targeting possible intervening influences in the relationship between crowding and misconduct is as important as identifying possible direct effects of crowding on infractions.

7. Recommendations for Future Meta-Analytic Research

While acknowledging that quantitative synthesis of the existing results is indeed a challenging task because of the different methodologies and levels of analysis employed in primary studies, we believe that a high quality systematic review examining the relationship between prison crowding and misconduct is not only warranted, but also possible. In fact, we are currently in the process of finalizing our systematic review in which we screened over 23,000 references extracted from over 25 electronic databases and a number of hard copy journals. Our review aims to answer the following questions: (1) To what extent is prison crowding associated with prison misconduct, including bullying?; (2) Are any of these relationships **moderated** by the prison's population composition (e.g. male vs. female prisons; juvenile vs. adult prisons), the prison security level, inmate turnover, management style, and levels of inmate program involvement?; (3) Do the results vary according to **study methodological characteristics** (e.g., type of study design, level at which the data were collected, and publication type)?

To be included in our review each study needed to meet all of the following five criteria: (1) The study included (prisoners from) crowded prisons and a comparison group of (prisoners from) non-crowded prisons. Methodologically sound correlational studies are acceptable; (2) The study included self-reported or officially reported data on bullying amongst prisoners or violent or non-violent misconduct as outcome measures; (3) Bullying and misconduct were measured during the exposure (or not) to crowding; (4) The study used the same outcome measures for prisoners from crowded and non-crowded prisons (or more crowded vs. less crowded prisons); (5) At least one effect size was reported, or there was enough information to calculate an effect size.

We are currently coding the possibly eligible studies and converting their effect sizes into common metrics. By statistically synthesizing data, we believe that this will be the first systematic review that will be able to pool all relevant and methodologically sound evidence arising from both individual-level and aggregate studies. We hope that the results of our meta-analysis will help scholars to draw evidence-based conclusions about prison crowding as a possible cause of prison misconduct and bullying. Similarly, we hope that our results would be a useful practical guide for practitioners and policy makers. In the case that there is a relationship (either direct or indirect) between crowding and prison misconduct and bullying, our review should help policy makers to develop and implement policy solutions targeting crowding or other factors that intervene in its relationship with misconduct.

While our systematic review is expected to contribute to the body of knowledge concerning prison research, it is important to note that crowding is only one risk factor or possible cause of prison misconduct and bullying. To develop effective comprehensive prison policies, more systematic reviews examining the same set of outcomes (misconduct and bullying), and other risk factors (both individual and prison-related), are needed.

Notes

1 Generally, it is important to distinguish between bullying and violence between prisoners. While all bullying includes either direct or indirect violence, not all violence is bullying. To be considered bullying, a violent act needs to be repeated (for details of the definition of bullying see page 205 of this chapter). All studies reported in this paragraph measured bullying and victimization using different versions of the self-report Direct and Indirect Prisoner Behaviour Checklist (Ireland & Ireland 2008), which we describe in more detail on page 205 of this chapter. Using this scale, the studies reported in this chapter defined the prevalence of bullying as the percentage of prisoners who reported engaging in at least one behavior indicative of bullying other prisoners (e.g. deliberately intimidating another prisoner), either during the previous month or during the previous week. Similarly, the prevalence of victimization was measured as the percentage of prisoners who reported being the victim of at least one behavior indicative of being a victim of bullying (e.g. having been hit by another prisoner), either during the previous month or during the previous week.

2 Farrington and Nuttall (1980) found that, after controlling for types of inmates incarcerated in each prison, there was a high positive relationship between crowding and recidivism over prisons. The authors concluded that it was unlikely that such a high negative relationship between crowding and prison effectiveness could have been explained by some other set of variables.

3 Given that the design capacity was unknown for 20 states in Carson's (2018) report, it was not possible to classify those states as having prison systems operating below or above their capacity. Some of those states might have had the number of prisoners exceeding their designed capacity.

4 The terms "crowding" and "overcrowding" are often used interchangeably. However, the term "overcrowding" is redundant, since crowding already assumes more prisoners than a prison is designed to hold (Bleich, 1989). For this reason, we use the term "crowding" in this chapter.

5 A closely related concept to spatial density is social density. The main difference is that spatial density assumes the reduction of available space without changes in the number of individuals, while social density assumes increases of the number of individuals in the same given space (Loo, 1973).

6 The numbers of studies reported in this paragraph were identified in the first stage of the screening process of our ongoing systematic review. Since we still have not coded all the studies, these numbers are likely to change in our final review.

References

Aebi, M.F., Tiago, M.M. and Burkhardt, C. (2016) SPACE I – Council of Europe Annual Penal Statistics: Prison populations. Survey 2015, Strasbourg: Council of Europe.

Atlas, R. (1982) "Violence in Prison: Architectural Determinism," Ph.D. thesis, Department of Criminology, University of Florida.

Austin, J., Clark, J., Hardyman, P., and Henry, D.A. (1999). "The Impact of 'Three Strikes and You're Out'," *Punishment and Society* 1: 131–162.

Besemer, S., and Murray, J. (2014) "Prison as an Environmental Pathogen", in M. DeLisi and M.G. Vaughn (eds) *The Routledge International Handbook of Biosocial Criminology*, London: Routledge.

Bleich, J. (1989) "Politics of Prison Crowding," *California Law Review* 77: 1125–1180.

Bonta, J.L, and Gendreau, P. (1990) "Reexamining the Cruel and Unusual Punishment of Prison Life," *Law and Human Behavior* 14: 347–372.

Bonta, J.L., and Kiem, T. (1978) "Institutional Misconducts in a Jail Setting: Preliminary Findings and a Note of Caution," *Crime and/et Justice* 6: 175–178.

Bonta, J. L., and G. Nanckivell (1980) "Institutional Misconducts and Anxiety Levels Among Jailed Inmates," *Criminal Justice and Behavior* 7: 203–213.

BOP (U.S. Bureau of Prisons) (2012) *Growing Inmate Crowding Negatively Affects Inmates, Staff, and Infrastructure*, Washington, DC: United States Government Accountability Office/CreateSpace Publishing.

Camp, S.D., Gaes, G.G., Langan, N.P., and Saylor, W.G. (2003) "Influence of Prisons on Inmate Misconduct: A Multilevel Investigation," *Justice Quarterly* 20: 501–533.

Cabanillas, O.B. (2012) "Conductas violentas y hacinamiento carcelario," *Revista Desarrollo y Sociedad* 69: 33–71.

Carson, E.A. (2018) *Prisoners in 2016*, Bureau of Justice Statistics, at www.bjs.gov/index.cfm?ty=pbdetail&iid=6187

Chen, E.Y. (2008) "Impacts of 'Three Strikes and You're Out' on Crime Trends in California and throughout the United States," *Journal of Contemporary Criminal Justice* 24: 345–370.

Clayton, O., and Carr, T. (1984) "The Effects of Prison Crowding upon Infraction Rates," *Criminal Justice Review* 9: 69–77.

Clemmer, D. (1940) *The Prison Community*, Boston: Christopher.

Connell, A., and Farrington, D. P. (1996) "Bullying among Incarcerated Young Offenders: Developing an Interview Schedule and some Preliminary Results," *Journal of Adolescence,* 19: 75–93.

Connell, A., & Farrington, D.P. (1997) "The Reliability and Validity of Resident, Staff and Peer Reports of Bullying in Young Offender Institutions," *Psychology, Crime and Law.,* 3(4), 287–300.

Cox, V.C., Paulus, P., and McCain, G. (1984) "Prison Crowding Research: The Relevance for Prison Housing Standards and a General Approach Regarding Crowding Phenomena," *American Psychologist* 39: 1148–1160.

Dâmboeanu, C. and P. Nieuwbeerta (2016) "Importation and Deprivation Correlates of Misconduct among Romanian Inmates," *European Journal of Criminology* 13: 332–351.

Dietz, E.F. (1999) "Institutional Violence and Overcrowding: An Examination of the Effects of Increased Social Density and Situational Variables on Increased Rates of Assaults in American Prisons," MA Thesis, Ann Arbor, University of Massachusetts Lowell.

Ekland-Olson, S., Barrick, D.M., and Cohen, L.E. (1983) "Prison Overcrowding and Disciplinary Problems: An Analysis of the Texas Prison System," *Journal of Applied Behavioral Science* **19**: 163–176.

Farrington, D.P. (1993) "Understanding and Preventing Bullying," in M. Tonry (ed) *Crime and Justice: A review of research, Vol 17*, Chicago, IL: University of Chicago Press.

Farrington, D.P., and Nuttall, C.P. (1980) "Prison Size, Overcrowding, Prison violence, and Recidivism," *Journal of Criminal Justice* 8: 221–231.

Farrington, D.P., and Petrosino, A. (2000) "Systematic Reviews of Criminological Interventions: The Campbell Collaboration Crime and Justice Group," *International Annals of Criminology* 38: 49–66.

Farrington, D.P., Weisburd, D. and Gill. C.E. (2011) "The Campbell Collaboration Crime and Justice Group: A Decade of Progress", in C. J. Smith, S. X. Zhang, and R. Barberet (eds) *Routledge Handbook of International Criminology*. New York: Routledge.

Franklin, T.W., Franklin, C.A., and Pratt, T.C. (2006) "Examining the Empirical Relationship between Prison Crowding and Inmate Misconduct: A Meta-analysis of Conflicting Research Results," *Journal of Criminal Justice* 34: 401–412.

Federal Bureau of Prisons (2018) *Statistics*, retrieved from: www.bop.gov/about/statistics/statistics_inmate_offenses.jsp

Gaes, G.G. (1985) "The Effects of Overcrowding in Prison," *Crime and Justice* 6: 95–146.

Gaes, G.G. (1994). "Prison Crowding Research Reexamined," *Prison Journal* 74: 329–363.

Gaes, G.G. and McGuire, W.J. (1985). "Prison Violence – The Contribution of Crowding Versus Other Determinants of Prison Assault Rates," *Journal of Research in Crime and Delinquency 22*: 41–65.

Gendreau, P., Low, M.A., and Goggin, C., (1997). "Predicting Prison Misconducts," *Criminal Justice and Behavior* 24: 414–431.

Glazener, E. (2016) "Exploring the Link between Prison Crowding and Inmate Misconduct: A Panel Data Analysis," MA Thesis. Ann Arbor, University of Maryland, College Park.

Goffman, E. (1961) *Asylums: Essays on the Social Situation of Mental Patients and Other Inmates,* Garden City, NJ: Anchor.

Gonçalves, L.C., Gonçalves, R.A., Martins, C. and Dirkzwager, A.J.E. (2014) "Predicting Infractions and Health Care Utilization in Prison: A Meta-Analysis," *Criminal Justice and Behavior* 8: 921–942

Harer, M., and Steffensmeier, D. (1996) "Race and Prison Violence," *Criminology* 34, 323–355.

Huey, M.P., and Mcnulty, T.L. (2005) "Institutional Conditions and Prison Suicide: Conditional Effects of Deprivation and Overcrowding," *The Prison Journal* 85:4c 90–514.

Jan, L.-J. (1980). "Overcrowding and Inmate Behavior: Some Preliminary Findings," *Criminal Justice and Behavior* 7: 293–301.

Klofas, J. Stojkovic, S., and Kalinich, D.A. (1992) "The Meaning of Correctional Crowding: Steps Toward an Index of Severity," *Crime & Delinquency* 38: 171–188.

Kurzfeld, J. (2017) Prison Crowding and Violent Misconduct (November 15, 2017). Available at SSRN: https://ssrn.com/abstract=2994546 or http://dx.doi.org/10.2139/ssrn.2994546

Lahm, K.F. (2008) "Inmate-On-Inmate Assault," *Criminal Justice & Behavior* 35: 120–137.

Innes, C.A. (1997) "Patterns of Misconduct in the Federal Prison System," *Criminal Justice Review* 22: 157–174.

Ireland, J.L. (1999a) "Bullying Behaviors among Male and Female Prisoners: A study of Adult and Young Offenders," *Aggressive Behavior* 25: 161−178.

Ireland, J.L. (1999b) "Provictim Attitudes and Empathy in Relation to Bullying Behavior among Prisoners," Legal and Criminological Psychology, 4(1), 51−66.

Ireland, J.L. (1999c) "A Recent Bullying Survey: Results and Recommendations for Intervention," *Prison Service Journal* 123: 27−30.

Ireland, J.L. (2002a) "Do Juveniles Bully more than Young Offenders?," *Journal of Adolescence* 25:155−168.

Ireland, J.L. (2002b) *Bullying among Prisoners: Evidence, Research and Intervention Strategies,* Hove: Brunner-Routledge.

Ireland, J. L. (2002c). *Direct and Indirect Prisoner Behaviour Checklist-Revised (DIPC-R)*. Preston. University of Central Lancashire.

Ireland, J.L. (2005a) "Psychological Health and Bullying Behavior among Adolescent Prisoners: A study ofYoung and Juvenile Offenders," *Journal of Adolescent Health* 36: 236−243.

Ireland, J.L. (2005b) "Bullying among Prisoners: The Need for Innovation", in J.L. Ireland (Ed), *Bullying amongst Prisoners: Innovations for Theory and Research*, Cullompton, Devon: Willan.

Ireland, J.L. (2012) "Understanding Bullying among Younger Prisoners: Recent Research and Introducing the Multifactor Model of Bullying in Secure Settings," *International Journal of Adolescent Medicine and Health* 24(1): 63–68.

Ireland, J.L., and Ireland, C.A. (2008) "Intra-group Aggression among Prisoners: Bullying Intensity and Exploration ofVictim-perpetrator Mutuality," *Aggressive Behavior* 34: 76–87.

Ireland, J.L., and Monaghan, R. (2006) "Behaviours Indicative of Bullying among Young and Juvenile Male Offenders: A Study of Perpetrator and Victim Characteristics", *Aggressive Behavior* 32(2): 172–180.

Ireland, J.L., and Power, C.L. (2012) "Propensity to Support Prison Gangs: Its Relationship to Gang Membership, Victimization, Aggression and Other Disruptive Behaviors," *Psychology, Crime and Law* 19: 801–816.

Irwin, J. and Cressey, D. (1962) "Thieves, Convicts and the Inmate Culture," *Social Problems* 10: 145–55.

Leone, M.C., and Kinkade, P. (1994) "New Designs, New Ideas, and New Problems: An Analysis of the Effects of Non-smoking Policies on a 'New Generation' Jail," 8: *Justice Professional* 1–21.

Levan, K. (2012) *Prison violence: Causes, consequences and solutions*, Burlington, VT: Ashgate.

Loo, C. (1973) "Important Issues in Researching the Effects of Crowding in Humans," *Representative Research in Psychology* 4: 219–226.

Martinson, R. (1974). "What Works? – 'Questions and Answers about Prison Reform'," *The Public Interest* 35: 22–54.

Martin, J.L., Lichtenstein, B., Jenkot, R.B., and Forde, D.R. (2012) "They Can Take Us Over Any Time They Want": Correctional Officers' Responses to Prison Crowding," *The Prison Journal* 92: 88–105.

McCorkle, R.C., Miethe, T.D. & Drass, K.A (1995) "The roots of prison violence: A test of the deprivation, management, and "not-so-total" institution models," *Crime & Delinquency* 41: 317–331.

Megargee, E.I. (1977) "The Association of Population Density, Reduced Space, and Uncomfortable Temperatures with Misconduct in a Prison Community," *American Journal of Community Psychology* 5: 289–298.

Murray, J., Farrington, D.P., and Sekol, I. (2012) "Children's antisocial behavior, mental health, drug use, and educational performance after parental incarceration: A systematic review and meta-analysis," *Psychological Bulletin* 138(2): 175–210.

Nacci, P.L., Teitelbaum, H.E., and Prather, J. (1977) "Population Density and Inmate Misconduct Rates in The Federal Prison System," *Federal Probation* 41: 26–31.

Paulus, P.B. (1988) *Prison Crowding: A Psychological Perspective*, New York, NY: Springer-Verlag.

Paulus, P.B., and Dzindolet, M.T. (1993) "Reactions of Male and Female Inmates to Prison Confinement: Further Evidence for a Two Component Model," *Criminal Justice and Behavior* 20: 149–166.

Pelissier, B. (1991) "The Effects of a Rapid Increase in a Prison Population: A Pre-and Posttest Study," *Criminal Justice and Behavior* 18: 427–447.

Porporino, F. (1986) "Managing Violent Individuals in Correctional Settings," *Journal of Interpersonal Violence* 1: 213–237.

Porporino, F. and Dudley, K. (1984) *An Analysis of the Effects of Overcrowding in Canadian Penitentiaries*, Ottawa, Ontario: Research Division, Programs Branch, Solicitor General of Canada.

Ruback, R.B., and Carr, T.S. (1993) "Prison Crowding Over Time: The Relationship of Density and Changes in Density to Infraction Rates," *Criminal Justice & Behavior* 20: 130–148.

Scharff-Smith, P. (2016) "Prisons and Human Rights - Past, Present and Future Challenges", in L. Weber, E. Fishwick and M. Marmo (eds.) *The Routledge International Handbook of Criminology and Human Rights*, New York: Routledge.

Sekol, I. and Farrington, D.P. (2013) "The Reliability and Validity of Self, Peer and Staff Reports of Bullying and Victimisation in Correctional and Care Institutions," *Psychology, Crime & Law* 19: 329–344.

Sekol, I., and Farrington, D.P. (2016) "Psychological and Background Correlates of Bullying in Adolescent Residential Care," *Journal of Social Work* 16: 429–452.

Sekol, I., Vidranski, T., and Jolliffe, D. (2020) "The Relationship between Empathy and Prison Bullying in a Sample of Croatian Prisoners", in D. Jolliffe and D.P. Farrington (eds) *Empathy versus offending, aggression and bullying: Advancing knowledge using the Basic Empathy Scale.* Abingdon, UK: Routlege, in press.

Steiner, B. (2009) "Assessing Static and Dynamic Influences on Inmate Violence Levels," *Crime & Delinquency* 55: 134–161

Steiner, B. (2018) "Measuring and Explaining Prison Misconduct," in J.D. Wooldredge and P. Smith (eds), The *Oxford Handbook of Prison and Imprisonment*, New York: Oxford University Press, p. 235–244

Steiner, B., Butler, H.D., and Ellison, J.M. (2014) "Causes and Correlates of Prison Inmate Misconduct: A Systematic Review of the Evidence," *Journal of Criminal Justice* 42: 462–470.

Steiner, B. and Wooldredge, J. (2009) "Rethinking the Link Between Institutional Crowding and Inmate Misconduct," *The Prison Journal* 89: 205–233

Steiner, B. and Wooldredge, J. (2014) "Comparing Self-Report to Official Measures of Inmate Misconduct," *Justice Quarterly* 31: 1074–1101.

Sykes, G. (2007/1958) *The Society of Captives: A Study of a Maximum Security Prison*. Princeton, NJ: Princeton University Press.

Tartaro, C. (2002) "The Impact of Density on Jail Violence," *Journal of Criminal Justice* 30: 499–510.

Taxy, S., Samuels, J., and Adams, W. (2015) *Drug Offenders in Federal Prison: Estimates of Characteristics Based on Linked Data: Special Report,* Washington, DC: United States Bureau of Justice.

Tattum, D. (1997) "Home and school: Introduction," in D. Tattum and G. Herbert (eds), *Bullying: Home, School and Community*, London: David Fulton.

Theriot, M.T., Dulmus, C.N., Sowers, K.M., and Johnson, J.A. (2005) "Factors Relating to Self-identification among Bullying Victims," *Children and Youth Services Review* 27: 979–994.

Toman, E.L. (2017) "Female Incarceration and Prison Social Order: An Examination of Gender Differences in Prison Misconduct and In-Prison Punishments," PhD Thesis, College of Community and Behavioral Sciences, University of South Florida.

Tonry, M. (2009) "Explanations of American Punishment Policies: A National History," *Punishment & Society* 11: 377–394.

Trulson, C.R., DeLisi, M., and Marquart, J.W. (2011) "Institutional Misconduct, Delinquent Background, and Re-Arrest Frequency among Serious and Violent Delinquent Offenders," *Crime and Delinquency* 57: 709–731.

Turner, P., and Ireland, J.L. (2010) "Do personality characteristics and beliefs predict intra-group bullying between prisoners?" *Aggressive Behavior* 36: 261–270.

UN (United Nations) (2005) *Human Rights and Prisons: Manual on Human Rights Training for Prison Officials*, New York and Geneva: United Nations Publications.

UN Human Rights Committee (HRC) (1992) *CCPR General Comment No. 21: Article 10 (Humane Treatment of Persons Deprived of Their Liberty)*, 10 April 1992, available at: www.refworld.org/docid/453883fb11.html (accessed 14 June 2020)

Useem, B. and Reisig, M.D. (1999) "Collective Action in Prisons: Protests, Disturbances, and Riots," *Criminology* 37: 735–760.

Vaughn, M.S. (1993) "Listening to the Experts: A National Study of Correctional Administrators' Responses to Prison Overcrowding," *Criminal Justice Review* 18: 12–25.

Vitiello, M. (2017) Three Strikes Laws: A Real or Imagined Deterrent to Crime?, American Bar Association, retrieved from: www.americanbar.org/groups/crsj/publications/human_rights_magazine_home/human_rights_vol29_2002/spring2002/hr_spring02_vitiello/

Zych, I., Ttofi, M.M., Llorent, V.J., Farrington, D.P., Ribeaud, D., and Eisner, M.P. (2020) "A Longitudinal Study on Stability and Transitions Among Bullying Roles," *Child Development* 91: 527–545

Walmsley, R. (2015) *World Prison Population List*, 11th edition, London: International Centre for Prison Studies.

Woolf, L.J. (1991) *The Woolf Report: A summary of the Main Findings and Recommendations of the Enquiry into Prison Disturbances*, London: Prison Reform Trust.

18

BIOSOCIAL RISK FACTORS FOR OFFENDING

Olivia Choy

In addition to the contribution of social environmental factors, a growing body of literature has documented the role of biological influences on the development of offending. In light of these scientific findings, over the last two decades, there has been increasing attention on how the neurobiological factors underlying offending may be relevant to the criminal justice system. The consideration of neuroscientific evidence in criminal proceedings has been documented in various countries. Such evidence spans a range of research areas, including genetics, early health, brain imaging, and neuropsychology (Chandler 2016; De Kogel and Westgeest 2016; Denno 2011; McSwiggan et al. 2017).

This chapter aims to highlight salient scientific findings on biological factors related to offending. A broad perspective is taken, whereby offending is referred to as not only the violation of legal codes, but also the larger spectrum of antisocial behavior which encompasses a variety of actions that violate societal norms and the personal or property rights of others. This includes behavioral problems such as violent, psychopathic, and delinquent behavior. Although there may be subtle differences in their etiological origins, this chapter seeks to provide a comprehensive overview of the biological findings in relation to such behaviors. The empirical findings presented cover the fields of genetics, brain imaging, neuropsychology, psychophysiology, and health. Importantly, the interaction of social environmental factors with biological processes to predispose to antisocial behavior is also considered. The link between punishment and biosocial risk factors for offending is considered in a review of research on the impact of incarceration on biology. The chapter concludes with a discussion of how biosocial research on offending may inform alternatives to traditional punitive practices and a discussion of the potential implications of this research for crime prevention.

Genetics

There is compelling evidence from behavioral genetic research, which broadly includes twin, adoption, and family studies, documenting that heritable influences contribute to offending. Results from 51 twin and adoption studies on children, adolescents, and adults suggest that genetic factors explained 41% of the variance in antisocial behavior (Rhee and Waldman 2002). Furthermore, within the broader construct of antisocial behavior, an effort has been made to understand etiological distinctions between physically aggressive and non-aggressive, rule-breaking behaviors. Research on the influence of genetic factors across ages has found that aggressive behavior is primarily influenced by genetic factors, while delinquent and rule-breaking behavior is influenced by both genetic and shared environmental factors (Burt 2009).[1] It has also been documented that variation in the etiology of antisocial behavior may be present across development. Findings suggest that genetic influences may contribute more strongly to early-onset, rather than late-onset antisocial behavior (Taylor et al. 2000). Taken together, findings exhibit substantial support for the influence of genetic factors on offending.

In light of these findings on the heritability of offending, molecular genetic research has investigated candidate genes that may underlie such behavior. One well-studied polymorphism in relation to antisocial behavior is the monoamine oxidase A (MAOA) gene. In a longitudinal study on a birth cohort in New Zealand, childhood maltreatment was found to confer significant risk for violence in adulthood among males with low levels of MAOA expression, but not for males with high MAOA activity (Caspi et al. 2002). These findings have subsequently been corroborated in other gene-environment interaction studies. In recent reviews conducted by Byrd and Manuck (2014) and Buades-Rotger and Gallardo-Pujol (2014) on 20 and 37 studies respectively, additional support was provided for the notion that individuals with the low activity variant of the MAOA gene are predisposed to offending when exposed to adverse environments. Thus, these findings suggest that genetic markers may increase sensitivity to social risk factors for crime.

Although the interaction between the low activity MAOA genotype and childhood maltreatment in predisposing to antisocial behavior is well-replicated, evidence of the main effect of the MAOA gene on offending has been less conclusive. A meta-analysis that included data from 31 studies on children, adolescents, and adults reported a modest association between the low activity allele of the MAOA gene and antisocial behavior (Ficks and Waldman 2014). However, in another comprehensive meta-analysis of 185 studies conducted on over 60,000 individuals investigating genetic associations with aggression and violence, Vassos et al. (2014) found a lack of evidence for significant associations between any candidate genes and antisocial behavior, further underscoring the importance of considering the interaction effects of genes with the environment.

Brain Imaging

There is also a substantial body of literature involving the use of structural and functional brain imaging techniques to investigate the neural basis of antisocial behavior. It has been suggested, from neuroimaging research, that antisocial and violent behavior is associated with structural and functional brain abnormalities in processes subserving moral decision-making (Raine 2018) and emotion processing and regulation (Raschle et al. 2015). In one of the first structural brain imaging studies of antisocial adults, Raine et al. (2000) documented an 11% and 14.7% reduction in gray matter volume in the prefrontal cortex of men with antisocial personality disorder compared to normal controls and a psychiatric control group respectively. Subsequent studies have provided support for the association between reduced prefrontal volumes and increased offending. For example, reduced gray matter volume and thickness in the middle frontal and orbitofrontal cortex, as well as reduced volume and surface deformations in the amygdala have been found in psychopaths with prior convictions compared to psychopaths without convictions and non-psychopathic controls (Yang et al. 2010). Recently, these findings have also extended to sexual offending. Using diffusion tensor imaging, Chen et al. (2016) found that male sex offenders who had committed rape against adult female strangers exhibited decreased fractional anisotropy (connectivity) in white matter near the medial frontal pole compared to matched controls. Their study demonstrated, for the first time, abnormalities in the structural integrity of white matter in the brains of sexual offenders.

Recent studies examining the structural abnormalities associated with offending have begun to examine the striatum, a region critically involved in the cognitive processing of reward-related information. However, findings for the striatum have been mixed as some studies have documented enlarged putamen, nucleus accumbens, and caudate in offenders (Schiffer et al. 2011), while others report findings of smaller nucleus accumbens volumes (Boccardi et al. 2013).

Functional imaging studies provide support for the results obtained from structural imaging studies on the brain differences between offenders and non-offenders. For instance, a meta-analysis of 43 studies revealed that increased antisocial behavior was associated with reduced prefrontal structure and function, particularly in the right orbitofrontal, left dorsolateral prefrontal, and right anterior cingulate cortex (Yang and Raine 2009). Consistent with structural imaging findings, an association between amygdala dysfunction and antisocial behavior has also been documented (Blair 2008). Thus, there is converging evidence from studies investigating brain morphology and brain activity.

The brain abnormalities related to offending have also been observed in younger populations and may predict later offending. An analysis of 13 structural neuroimaging studies on youths with conduct problems revealed that youths characterized by aggressive, antisocial, and oppositional or defiant behaviors during childhood and adolescence showed decreased gray matter volume in the left amygdala, right insula, left medial superior frontal gyrus, and left fusiform gyrus compared to typically developing youths (Rogers and De Brito 2016). Reduced gray matter volume has also been identified particularly in the orbitofrontal and dorsomedial prefrontal cortices in youths with aggressive behavior (Raschle et al. 2015). Evidence to suggest that brain deficits can predict later offending have stemmed from longitudinal studies. It has been documented that males with lower amygdala volumes measured at age 26 years exhibited increased risk for committing violence 3 years later (Pardini et al. 2014). In another study on adult male offenders, lower anterior cingulate activity was found to be associated with a greater likelihood of rearrest (Aharoni et al. 2013).

Few brain imaging studies to date have addressed the role of psychosocial risk factors for offending. Two studies have demonstrated a moderating effect of home background on the relationship between the brain and offending, but in opposing directions. In one study, murderers from non-deprived home backgrounds showed a 14.2% reduction in functioning of the right orbitofrontal cortex relative to murderers from deprived home backgrounds characterized by abuse, neglect, and marital violence (Raine et al. 1998). It was argued that neurobiological deficits are more pronounced among violent individuals who lack the psychosocial deprivation that normally provides a "social push" toward violence. In contrast, a second functional magnetic resonance imaging study showed that violent offenders who had been severely abused as children were more likely to show poor temporal lobe functioning compared to violent offenders lacking abuse (Raine et al. 2001). Despite the limited and mixed findings on biosocial interactions involving brain imaging findings, overall, there is convincing evidence to suggest that there are brain differences that are present between offenders and non-offenders.

Neuropsychology

Neuropsychological studies, which involve indirect, behavior-based assessments of brain dysfunction, have also revealed deficits in specific domains of cognitive functioning in relation to offending. To date, the best-replicated cognitive correlate of antisocial, violent, and criminal behavior among non-mentally ill individuals is general intelligence (e.g. IQ or Full Scale IQ) deficits (Herrnstein and Wilson 1985). Moreover, meta-analytic evidence from 166 independent samples has shown lower verbal relative to spatial/performance in antisocial individuals (Isen 2010). This discrepancy in verbal and non-verbal IQ scores has been found to be characteristic of antisocial females as well as males, and is observed among adolescents and adults. Reduced verbal intelligence has also been documented to predict later offending. For example, Moffitt et al. (1994) found that verbal deficits in early adolescence predicted delinquency in later adolescence for persistent, high-level offenders. It has been suggested that verbal deficiencies relate to increased offending as they serve as a precursor to failure in the socialization process and are associated with difficulty manipulating abstract concepts, which may result in an inability to understand the consequences of one's actions and others' feelings. Verbal abilities are also known to be crucial for educational achievement and for the self-control of emotions, factors which are associated with offending (Isen 2010; Kokko and Pulkkinen 2000).

Nevertheless, spatial deficits remain of etiological significance to offending. This has been documented in longitudinal studies of community-based samples. In a Pittsburgh youth sample including childhood-limited, adolescent-limited, and life-course persistent offenders, both spatial and verbal impairments were found (Raine et al. 2005). Data from Mauritius show that early spatial but not verbal deficits at age 3 years, and later spatial and verbal deficits at age 11 years were exhibited in persistently antisocial individuals (Raine et al. 2002). These results suggest that while early spatial deficits contribute to persistent antisocial behavior, verbal deficits may be developmentally acquired. It has been suggested that early deficits in visuospatial functioning may interfere with mother-infant bonding, possibly reflecting right hemispheric dysfunction that disrupts emotional processing and regulation, to in turn contribute to persistent offending.

Poor executive function is also a well-documented risk factor for offending. Executive functioning deficits are thought to represent impairment in frontal lobe functioning and are indicated by performance errors on neuropsychological tests of strategy formation, cognitive flexibility, or impulsivity (i.e. category, maze-tracing, Stroop interference, card sorting, verbal fluency and tower tests; and go/no-go and gambling tasks). Morgan and Lilienfeld's (2000) classic quantitative review of 39 studies reported that overall executive functioning deficits were observed in antisocial individuals compared to controls. The relationship between deficits in executive function and offending has been observed for different types of offenders. Executive dysfunction has been linked to aggressive, violent, and antisocial personality-disordered populations (Dolan 2012; Hancock et al. 2010; Stanford et al. 2007), property crime offenders (Barker et al. 2007), child molesters (Schiffer and Vonlaufen 2011), murderers with schizophrenia compared to non-violent men with schizophrenia (Hanlon et al. 2012), and offenders characterized by reactive as opposed to instrumental violence (Broomhall 2005). Overall, strongest effects of the executive function-antisocial behavior relationship were found for the Porteus Mazes test and for indices of criminality rather than psychopathy or the clinical syndromes of conduct disorder and antisocial personality disorder (Morgan and Lilienfeld 2000). A subsequent meta-analysis of 126 studies including more than 14,000 participants replicated these findings, documenting that antisocial individuals exhibited poorer executive function and this relationship was strongest when antisocial behavior was defined as the violation of legal norms (Ogilvie et al. 2011).

Nevertheless, some mixed findings have also been found. Findings on children and adolescents have been less consistent. Several studies have found executive functioning deficits to characterize some antisocial youths (e.g., Cauffman et al. 2005), but not others (Moffitt et al. 1994; Nigg et al. 2004). The development of executive functions along with the ongoing myelination of the frontal cortex into and beyond adolescence may explain differential patterns of executive functioning deficits among children and adults. Findings of executive functioning impairments in older maximum security hospital patients (Nestor 1992) and more pronounced impairments on an orbitofrontal neuropsychological task in psychopathic adults than psychopathic children (Blair 2006) provide support for this notion. Additionally, differences have been found between successful psychopaths, who exhibit high levels of psychopathic traits but avoid conviction of any crime, and unsuccessful psychopaths who score similarly highly on psychopathic traits, but have a criminal conviction. Successful, uncaught psychopaths have been found to exhibit significantly *better* dorsolateral prefrontal task performance relative to unsuccessful psychopaths and controls (Ishikawa et al. 2001). In a similar vein, increased executive functioning has been observed among white collar criminals compared to offender controls who had not engaged in white collar crime (Raine et al. 2012).

Biosocial interactions in relation to neuropsychological risk factors for offending have been investigated. In a study of 370 Australian adolescents, Brennan et al. (2003) found that an interaction of biological risk factors including neuropsychological deficits and social risk factors predicted life-course persistent aggression in boys and girls. Other research examining neuropsychological deficits and psychosocial factors in relation to antisocial behavior has documented that neurocognitive deficits indicated by more risky decision-making in the Iowa Gambling Task were associated with psychopathic tendencies only in children with higher socioeconomic status (Gao et al. 2009a).

Psychophysiology

One of the best-replicated findings in the literature on biological risk factors and crime is the association between a psychophysiological measure, low heart rate, and antisocial behavior. Heart rate is influenced by the sympathetic and parasympathetic branches of the autonomic nervous system. In the most recent meta-analysis on heart rate and antisocial behavior, the relationship between low heart rate at rest and higher levels of antisocial behavior was found to be highly replicable, with an effect size of $d = -.20$ (Portnoy and Farrington 2015). This relationship has been documented in both children and adults, for males and females, and for multiple types of antisocial behavior, including violent and non-violent criminality (Latvala et al. 2015; Murray et al. 2016; Portnoy and Farrington 2015).

Moreover, low resting heart rate has been found to predict future levels of antisocial behavior in prospective longitudinal research. For instance, in one study conducted in Mauritius, low resting heart rate as young as age 3 years predicted aggression at age 11 years (Raine, Venables, and Mednick 1997). In the same sample, a low resting heart rate at age 11 years was associated with later criminal offending at age 23 years (Choy et al. 2017). This relationship was observed for violent crimes as well as drug offenses. Consistent with these findings, results from a longitudinal study on London males showed that low resting heart rate at age 18 years predicted offending up to age 50 years independent of numerous covariates, including smoking, sports participation, impulsivity, binge drinking, body mass index, as well as early childhood individual and environmental risk factors, demonstrating that the predictive utility of low resting heart rate can extend into late adulthood (Jennings et al. 2013).

Two major explanations have been proposed for the association between low heart rate and higher levels of offending. According to the fearlessness theory, a low resting heart rate may index a lower level of fear in individuals, who are then more likely to engage in antisocial acts that require a degree of fearlessness to complete (Venables 1987). On the other hand, the stimulation seeking theory posits that low autonomic nervous system arousal is an unpleasant physiological state, leading those with low resting heart rates to seek stimulating behaviors, including antisocial behaviors, in order to increase their level of physiological arousal to a more optimal level (Quay 1965). Recently, two studies have documented that sensation-seeking, but not fearlessness, mediated the relationship between heart rate and antisocial behavior, providing greater empirical support for the stimulation-seeking theory (Portnoy et al. 2014; Sijtsema et al. 2010).

In addition to cardiovascular functioning, skin conductance serves as a popular measure of physiological response in relation to offending. Skin conductance is an index of sympathetic nervous system activity that can be measured at rest or during laboratory tasks. Unlike heart rate, electrodermal activity is regulated exclusively by the sympathetic nervous system. Empirical studies have documented a relationship between lower skin conductance and higher levels of criminal behavior and delinquency (Ellis et al. 2009). As with heart rate, reduced skin conductance has been found to predict future levels of antisocial behavior. Reduced skin conductance fear conditioning as early as age 3 has been found to predict offending at age 23 years (Gao et al. 2009b). In line with these findings, it has been documented that reduced skin conductance arousal in adolescence, at age 15 years, predicted criminal behavior at age 24 years (Raine et al. 1990). Findings from these studies suggest that childhood and adolescent skin conductance may help to explain future levels of criminal behavior.

Research investigating biosocial interactions involving psychophysiology has revealed that low resting heart rate combined with high social risk can increase the likelihood of antisocial behavior (Raine et al. 2014). Similarly, skin conductance has been found to interact with social adversity to predict antisocial behavior, though patterns of interaction are not always consistent, with high skin conductance serving as a risk factor for antisocial behavior amongst children at high social risk in several studies (e.g., Cummings et al. 2007). Taken together, psychophysiological studies suggest a reduced pattern of autonomic arousal in antisocial individuals. Importantly, however, the results may be partly dependent on the individual's social context.

Early Health Factors

Empirical evidence suggests that risk factors experienced early in life such as during the prenatal and perinatal periods of development are associated with longitudinal patterns of offending (Day et al. 2014). Several prenatal and perinatal factors that have been most closely linked to antisocial behavior include prenatal nicotine, alcohol, and lead exposure, minor physical anomalies, and birth complications.

A meta-analysis of 18 empirical studies representing more than 12,000 cases has revealed that maternal cigarette smoking during pregnancy is a moderately important risk factor for criminal and deviant behavior in offspring (Pratt et al. 2006). Prenatal nicotine exposure has been linked to an elevated risk of antisocial behaviors such as juvenile offending, delinquency, conduct disorder, and violent offending (Brennan et al. 1999; Rantakallio et al. 1992; Wakschlag et al. 1997). The effect sizes are most robust within child and adolescent samples, and are stronger in clinical compared to population cohort samples. In particular, a dose-response relationship has been observed between the degree of prenatal maternal smoking and the extent of offspring's non-violent and violent offending assessed at age 34 years (Brennan et al. 1999). However, a debate remains regarding whether the nicotine exposure-offending association involves a genetic confound (Glenn and Raine 2014).

Prenatal exposure to alcohol results in cognitive, behavioral, social, and physical deficits, and can lead to a diagnosis of Fetal Alcohol Syndrome (FAS). In studies on children, adolescents, and adults, fetal alcohol exposure has been documented as a risk factor for antisocial outcomes (Fast et al. 1999; Olson et al. 1997). Even without FAS, high rates of delinquency have been found in children and adolescents with heavy fetal alcohol exposure (Mattson and Riley 2000). It has been reported that there is a high prevalence of individuals with fetal alcohol spectrum disorder in correctional systems, with estimates showing that youths with fetal alcohol spectrum disorder are 19 times more likely to be incarcerated in a given year compared to youths without fetal alcohol spectrum disorder (Popova et al. 2011).

Besides nicotine and alcohol exposure, prospective studies have documented a link between prenatal lead exposure and later offending. In a longitudinal study on 195 adolescents, lead levels from the prenatal period to 6.5 years of age were associated with delinquent and antisocial behavior in middle adolescence (Dietrich et al. 2001). This pattern of findings has also been observed for antisocial behavior in adulthood. In a study on 250 individuals, Wright et al. (2008) found prenatal maternal blood lead concentrations during the first and second trimesters of pregnancy to be associated with higher rates of criminal arrests assessed at ages 19 to 24 years. Although few longitudinal studies in this area exist, these studies provide some empirical evidence that prenatal lead exposure is associated with the development of offending.

Minor physical anomalies (MPAs) have also been linked to offending. MPAs such as low seated ears, a single palmar crease, and a furrowed tongue are considered indicators of fetal neural maldevelopment near the end of the first trimester or the beginning of the second trimester of pregnancy. Studies have found that an increase in MPAs is associated with greater antisocial behavior in children, adolescents, and adults (Glenn and Raine 2014). This has been particularly observed for violent as opposed to non-violent offending. For example, MPAs measured at age 14 years were found to predict violent, rather than non-violent delinquency in 170 males at age 17 years, independent of childhood physical aggression or family adversity (Arseneault et al. 2000). A larger number of MPAs has also been documented to be associated with recidivistic violent criminal behavior. In a study by Kandel et al. (1989), recidivistic violent offenders assessed between ages 20 and 22 years were found to have had more MPAs between ages 11 and 13 years compared to individuals with one or fewer violent offenses.

Birth complications, such as preeclampsia, preterm birth, and breech fetal positioning, constitute another risk factor for offending later in life (e.g., Liu et al. 2009). Findings from a Danish birth cohort have shown that high delivery complications were related to violent offending when individuals were assessed between ages 20 and 22 years (Kandel and Mednick 1991). In another longitudinal study, the Fragile Families and Child Well-being Study, low birth weight was shown to be associated with serious aggression and destructive behavior at an earlier age of age 5 years (Vaske et al. 2013). Furthermore, some empirical evidence suggests that the low birth weight-antisocial behavior relationship is mediated by verbal skills.

It has also been documented that these prenatal and perinatal factors interact with social factors to predispose to later offending. For example, prenatal nicotine exposure was found to lead to an 11.9-fold and 14.2-fold increase in recidivistic violent offending in adulthood when combined with the individual social risk factor of being raised in a single-parent family and with a group of psychosocial risk factors respectively (Räsänen et al. 1999). Increased risk has particularly been observed for persistent violent offending (Brennan et al. 1999; 2002; Gibson and Tibbetts 2000). Moreover, Mednick and Kandel (1988) found that MPAs in boys at age 12 years were related to violent, but not non-violent property offending at age 21 years, but only for individuals reared in unstable homes. Similarly, Brennan et al. (1997) and Pine et al. (1997) found higher rates of adult violent crime in males and greater risk for disruptive behavior and conduct disorder at age 17 years among individuals with both MPAs and social risk factors. Birth complications combined with early maternal rejection measured at age 1 year increased the likelihood of violent offending at ages 18 and 34 years (Raine et al. 1994; Raine et al. 1997). Birth complications have also been found to interact with other psychosocial factors such as poor parenting (Hodgins et al. 2001), family adversity (Arseneault et al. 2002), and being an only child (Kemppainen et al. 2001) to lead to increased adult violent offending.

The Impact of Incarceration on Biological Risk Factors for Offending

Biological processes associated with offending are relevant to consider in discussions of punishment. It has long been speculated that punishment in the form of incarceration can have negative effects on cognition and psychological well-being (Goodstein et al. 1984; Haney 2012). However, only recently have empirical investigations been conducted to test whether imprisonment has an impact on the brain. These studies have used neuropsychological assessments. One study examined 201 male adolescents incarcerated in a high-security correctional facility in the United States. Performance on an attention task worsened when the adolescents were assessed at a four-month follow-up compared to baseline (Leonard et al. 2013). Another study on 197 adolescent offenders from the same sample assessed three other executive functions using an emotional go/no-go task that has been documented to engage the prefrontal cortex and the amygdala (Hare et al. 2008; Umbach et al. 2018). The incarcerated male offenders exhibited deficits in executive functioning, in the form of poorer cognitive control, response inhibition, and emotion regulation four months later. Similar findings were documented in a study of 37 male inmates in the Netherlands. An increase in risk taking and a decline in attention were observed when the incarcerated individuals were retested on neuropsychological measures after three months of imprisonment (Meijers et al. 2018). In contrast to these findings, an improvement in the offenders' planning was noted at the three-month follow-up, which may have been attributable to practice effects.

Despite the limited body of research, there is some empirical evidence that incarceration can worsen a biological risk factor, executive function impairment, that is associated with increased offending. Notably, the decline can be observed after only a few months of incarceration. These findings are in line with the extant literature on the influence of adverse environments and stress on the brain. It has been documented that the most consistent neurobiological findings in children with adverse psychosocial experiences involve impaired prefrontal cortical functioning (Danese and McEwen 2012). Deficits in other regions of the brain such as the amygdala are also linked to greater life stress (Hanson et al. 2015). These findings on the relationship between incarceration and the brain provide support for considering alternative approaches to traditional punitive practices.

Implications of Biosocial Research on Offending for Rehabilitation

There is evidence of support for alternative forms of punishment. In a recent national survey evaluating the views of victims on safety and justice, victims of violent and non-violent crime were found to show preference for the criminal justice system to focus more on rehabilitation compared to punishment (Alliance for Safety and Justice 2016). Scientific evidence on the biosocial underpinnings of offending may assist in informing rehabilitative efforts through the development of novel treatment strategies.

Biological risk factors for offending may be targets for behavioral change. Interventions that target biological functioning can protect against the cognitive decline that has been observed from incarceration. In Leonard et al.'s (2013) and Umbach et al.'s (2018) studies on incarcerated adolescents, offenders who were randomly assigned to a multi-session, group-based cognitive behavioral therapy and mindfulness intervention did not show the same decrease in attention, response inhibition, and emotion regulation over time that was observed in an active control group that did not undergo this treatment. Furthermore, individuals who practiced mindfulness outside of the intervention sessions exhibited better executive functioning compared to those who did not practice or did not receive the cognitive behavioral therapy and mindfulness intervention (Leonard et al. 2013). Their performance on the attention task remained stable over time. Thus, there is some evidence that interventions can alter neuropsychological factors that are associated with offending.

Although there is a limited number of studies on biological treatments for offending, one benign biological intervention that has been tested is nutritional supplementation. In particular, omega-3 has been proposed as a treatment for antisocial and aggressive behavior as it has been known to improve brain structure and function (Yehuda et al. 2005). Fatty acids such as omega-3 regulate the activity of membrane enzymes, protect neurons from cell death, increase the size of the cell, stimulate neurite outgrowth, and enhance synaptic functioning and dendritic branching. Randomized controlled trials involving omega-3 supplementation have been found to enhance dorsolateral prefrontal functioning in children (McNamara and Carlson 2006), a brain region in which deficits have been observed in antisocial individuals (Yang and Raine 2009). Experimentally, randomized controlled trials have found promising support for the efficacy of omega-3 supplementation in reducing offending. For example, one trial on 231 young adult English prisoners documented that an intervention comprised of omega-3 and multivitamin supplementation for 142 days was associated with a significant 26.3% reduction in antisocial and aggressive behavior (Gesch et al. 2002). These findings were replicated in a randomized controlled trial of institutionalized young offenders in the Netherlands (Zaalberg et al. 2010). In non-incarcerated samples, similar findings of reduced antisocial behavior following omega-3 supplementation have been observed in the United States (Zanarini and Frankenburg 2003), Thailand (Hamazaki et al. 2002), and Wales (Long and Benton 2013). All in all, these cross-cultural findings provide initial empirical support that omega-3 supplementation can reduce antisocial behavior in adults.

Recently, another tool that has been tested in experimental study designs to target the prefrontal brain impairment that predisposes to offending is non-invasive brain stimulation. One form of non-invasive brain stimulation is transcranial direct current stimulation (tDCS), which is a neuromodulatory technique that allows for either the facilitation or inhibition of spontaneous neuronal activity by delivering a direct, continuous, low-intensity electrical current transcranially to cortical areas between anodal and cathodal electrodes (Brunoni et al. 2012). Its safety in human trials has been documented (Bikson et al. 2016). Anodal direct current stimulation generally increases cortical excitability, while cathodal stimulation decreases it. Thus, studies that have applied tDCS to the study of antisocial behavior have examined whether upregulating the prefrontal cortex using anodal stimulation can reduce such behaviors.

Seven randomized controlled trials examining the effect of stimulation over the prefrontal cortex on aggression have been conducted on adult samples. In an incarcerated sample of 41 male violent offenders, three consecutive sessions of tDCS applied to enhance cortical excitability in the dorsolateral prefrontal region resulted in decreases in self-reported aggressiveness (Molero-Chamizo et al. 2019). This reduction was observed among murderers and non-murderers. Other studies have assessed non-incarcerated individuals. Using the Taylor Aggression Paradigm, one study on 32 healthy university students documented that compared to a sham (placebo) condition, upregulating the right dorsolateral prefrontal cortex significantly reduced proactive aggression (Dambacher et al. 2015b). However, this effect was only observed in males. It has been suggested that this may be attributable to the low levels of aggression observed among females. Stimulation over another prefrontal region, the right ventrolateral prefrontal cortex, has been found to reduce aggression following social exclusion and exposure to violent video games in healthy university students (Riva et al. 2015; Riva et al. 2017). Although preliminary, there is also experimental evidence that anodal stimulation over the prefrontal cortex can reduce intentions to commit aggression (Choy, Raine, and Hamilton 2018). However, some mixed findings have also been observed. In a study on 60 undergraduates, individuals who received tDCS to increase activity in the left dorsolateral prefrontal cortex exhibited more aggressive behavior when they were angry (Hortensius et al. 2011). This effect, however, was not observed among individuals who received stimulation to increase right dorsolateral prefrontal cortical activity. In a similar vein, anodal stimulation over the right or left inferior frontal cortex did not result in any significant reductions in aggressive behavior (Dambacher et al. 2015a).

It is apt to note that research on relatively benign interventions, such as nutrition and non-invasive brain stimulation, that aim to target biological risk factors for offending is nascent.

Several challenges remain. Ethical concerns, such as the safety of interventions, informed consent, the ability to intervene in personal identity, and mandated versus offered biological treatment require careful consideration (Choy, Focquaert, and Raine 2018; Focquaert and Schermer 2015; Greely 2007). The finding of evidence for efficacy in some randomized controlled trials and not in others highlights the need for replication and extension of these findings in methodologically strong studies. Appropriate caution is emphasized as research on the effectiveness of treatments can provide a mixed picture, with a risk of interventions producing counterproductive effects (e.g., Dambacher et al., 2015a; Hortensius et al., 2011; Mews et al. 2017). From a methodological perspective, longitudinal studies are required to test for change in offending in longer-term follow-ups. Furthermore, conducting dose-ranging studies to determine the adequate dosage required for behavioral change and research to investigate the mechanisms of action underlying any treatment-outcome relationship would help to elucidate the benefits of adopting such interventions. These studies on relatively benign interventions provide some initial evidence to support the notion that treatment programs for offending may be improved by taking into account the biological mechanisms that underlie antisocial behavior. However, any potential benefits must be weighed against possible risks.

It has also been suggested that knowledge about the biological underpinnings of antisocial behavior may be beneficial in improving the efficacy of intervention programs by leading to more tailored treatment options for offenders (Sabatello and Appelbaum 2017). This has stemmed from the accumulating empirical evidence that the effects of interventions for offending may vary as a function of an individual's biological make-up. For example, a review of 10 studies by Cornet et al. (2014) revealed that certain neurobiological variables, such as psychophysiological and neuropsychological factors at baseline were predictive of treatment outcome among individuals with antisocial behavior. Several recent studies have also provided empirical evidence that genetic factors may influence response to interventions (e.g. Bakermans-Kranenburg et al. 2008; Brett et al. 2015). Despite the limited number of extant studies, they shed light on biological sources of treatment outcome variability among offenders and show, to some extent, that knowledge of biological risk factors for crime may play a role in determining treatment efficacy.

Implications of Biosocial Research on Offending for Prevention

With the growing body of literature documenting the association between biological factors and offending, a stronger focus on crime prevention has emerged to address biological risk factors early in life (Rocque et al. 2012). Importantly, these efforts have been conducted in a sociologically-sensitive manner that does not negate social environmental influences on offending. For example, research on early health factors and offending has resulted in calls for improvements in prenatal and maternal care. One such evidence-based preventive intervention is the Nurse-Family Partnership. In a randomized controlled trial conducted in the United States, 400 first-time mothers were assigned to either receive home visits from nurses during pregnancy, to receive visits during pregnancy up to the first two years of life, or to a control group without visits (Olds et al. 1998). The home visits promoted aspects of maternal functioning including positive health-related behaviors such as avoiding smoking and drinking during pregnancy, competent prenatal and postnatal care of the child, and maternal personal development. Follow-up assessments revealed that at age 15 years, adolescents born to women who had received nurse visits during pregnancy and postnatally, and whose mothers were unmarried and from low socioeconomic status families, had fewer arrests, convictions, and violations of probation compared to individuals in the control group. There is also empirical evidence to suggest that adolescents born to nurse-visited women from pregnancy to the first two years of life and who were at high social risk exhibited fewer behavioral problems related to the use of alcohol and other drugs (Olds et al. 1998). The findings demonstrate that programs that address prenatal and perinatal risk factors for crime may contribute to reduced antisocial behavior later in life.

Other programs have aimed to target another biological factor associated with offending, neurocognitive functioning. For instance, the Perry Preschool Project and the Carolina Abercedarian Project represent intellectual enrichment programs provided to children at age 3 years. Data from studies examining the long-term effect of these programs on antisocial outcomes have provided evidence for trends that the experimental groups exhibit lower levels of offending in adulthood compared to the control groups who were not assigned to the programs (Campbell et al. 2002; Schweinhart et al. 1993). These studies suggest that biosocial science regarding offending has the potential to inform evidence-based prevention. It may be particularly advantageous to keep individuals away from detainment environments, which have shown to have negative impacts on biology, which may in turn lead to later antisocial outcomes that carry significant costs to society.

From an ethical perspective, there remain concerns about the false-positive rate in identifying children at risk for later offending. Additionally, it has been proposed that intervening early in life may serve to label and stigmatize individuals to result in a self-fulfilling prophecy of future violence (McAra and McVie 2010). Some researchers have proposed that ensuring that benefits outweigh any potential risks, framing interventions such that they emphasize the provision of support mechanisms, and targeting all of the children and families in particular at-risk neighborhoods may help address these concerns.

Conclusion

A substantial body of research shows that antisocial behavior is a construct of both biological and social influences. This chapter highlights a range of biological factors that have been documented in the extant literature to be associated with higher levels of offending, such as the low activity variant of the MAOA gene, structural and functional brain abnormalities, deficits in cognitive functioning, low psychophysiological arousal, and early health factors including prenatal nicotine, alcohol, and lead exposure, minor physical anomalies, and birth complications. Some of these biological risk factors may be exacerbated by incarceration. Scientific evidence on the biosocial basis of offending can have implications for rehabilitation and crime prevention. Programs targeting prenatal and perinatal risk factors associated with crime have been associated with reduced offending in later in life. In addition, research suggests that potential rehabilitative efforts can be made to take into account not only social environmental risk, but also the biological risk factors associated with offending.

Note

1 Burt's (2009) meta-analysis distinguished between physically aggressive and non-aggressive rule-breaking behavior by including twin and adoption studies that (a) explicitly referenced symptoms of aggression or rule-breaking in the Diagnostic and Statistical Manual of Mental Disorders, (b) provided evidence that the measure used successfully discriminated clinical and normative samples on aggression or rule-breaking behavior, such as on the Achenbach Child Behavior Checklist or Teacher Report Form (Achenbach and Rescorla 2001), or (c) had a measure that was significantly associated with a validated measure of either aggression or rule-breaking.

References

Achenbach, T. M. and Rescorla, L. A. (2001) *Manual for ASEBA School-age Forms & Profiles*. Burlington, VT: University of Vermont, Research Center for Children, Youth, & Families.

Aharoni, E., Vincent, G. M., Harenski, C. L., Calhoun, V. D., Sinnott-Armstrong, W., Gazzaniga, M. S. and Kiehl, K. A. (2013) "Neuroprediction of Future Rearrest," *Proceedings of the National Academy of Sciences* 110 6223–8.

Alliance for Safety and Justice (2016) *Crime Survivors Speak: The First-Ever National Survey of Victims' Views on Safety and Justice*. Retrieved from: https://allianceforsafetyandjustice.org/crimesurvivorsspeak/

Arseneault, L., Tremblay, R. E., Boulerice, B. and Saucier, J. F. (2002) "Obstetrical Complications and Violent Delinquency: Testing Two Developmental Pathways," *Child Development* 73 496–508.

Arseneault, L., Tremblay, R. E., Boulerice, B., Seguin, J. R. and Saucier, J. F. (2000) "Minor Physical Anomalies and Family Adversity as Risk Factors for Violent Delinquency in Adolescence," *American Journal of Psychiatry* 157 917–23.

Bakermans-Kranenburg, M. J., Van IJzendoorn, M. H., Mesman, J., Alink, L. R. and Juffer, F. (2008) "Effects of an Attachment-Based Intervention on Daily Cortisol Moderated by Dopamine Receptor D4: A Randomized Control Trial on 1-to 3-Year-Olds Screened for Externalizing Behavior," *Development and Psychopathology* 20 805–20.

Barker, E. D., Séguin, J. R., White, H. R., Bates, M. E., Lacourse, E., Carbonneau, R. and Tremblay, R. E. (2007) "Developmental Trajectories of Male Physical Violence and Theft: Relations to Neurocognitive Performance," *Archives of General Psychiatry* 64 592–9.

Bikson, M., Grossman, P., Thomas, C., Zannou, A. L., Jiang, J., Adnan, T., Mourdoukoutas, A. P., Kronberg, G., Truong, D. and Boggio, P. (2016) "Safety of Transcranial Direct Current Stimulation: Evidence Based Update 2016," *Brain Stimulation* 9 641–61.

Blair, R. (2006) "The Emergence of Psychopathy: Implications for the Neuropsychological Approach to Developmental Disorders," *Cognition* 101 414–42.

Blair, R. (2008) "The Amygdala and Ventromedial Prefrontal Cortex: Functional Contributions and Dysfunction in Psychopathy," *Philosophical Transactions of the Royal Society B: Biological Sciences* 363 2557–65.

Boccardi, M., Bocchetta, M., Aronen, H. J., Repo-Tiihonen, E., Vaurio, O., Thompson, P. M., Tiihonen, J. and Frisoni, G. B. (2013) "Atypical Nucleus Accumbens Morphology in Psychopathy: Another Limbic Piece in the Puzzle," *International Journal of Law and Psychiatry* 36 157–67.

Brennan, P. A., Grekin, E. R. and Mednick, S. A. (1999) "Maternal Smoking During Pregnancy and Adult Male Criminal Outcomes," *Archives of General Psychiatry* 56 215–9.

Brennan, P. A., Grekin, E. R., Mortensen, E. L. and Mednick, S. A. (2002) "Relationship of Maternal Smoking During Pregnancy with Criminal Arrest and Hospitalization for Substance Abuse in Male and Female Adult Offspring," *American Journal of Psychiatry* 159 48–54.

Brennan, P. A., Hall, J., Bor, W., Najman, J. M. and Williams, G. (2003) "Integrating Biological and Social Processes in Relation to Early-Onset Persistent Aggression in Boys and Girls," *Developmental Psychology* 39 309–23.

Brennan, P. A., Mednick, S. A. and Raine, A. (1997) "Biosocial Interactions and Violence: A Focus on Perinatal Factors" in A. Raine, P. A. Brennan, D. P. Farrington, and Sarnoff A. Mednick (eds) *Biosocial Bases of Violence*, New York: Plenum.

Brett, Z. H., Humphreys, K. L., Smyke, A. T., Gleason, M. M., Nelson, C. A., Zeanah, C. H., Fox, N. A. and Drury, S. S. (2015) "Serotonin Transporter Linked Polymorphic Region (5-Httlpr) Genotype Moderates the Longitudinal Impact of Early Caregiving on Externalizing Behavior," *Development and Psychopathology* 27 7–18.

Broomhall, L. (2005) "Acquired Sociopathy: A Neuropsychological Study of Executive Dysfunction in Violent Offenders," *Psychiatry, Psychology and Law* 12 367–87.

Brunoni, A. R., Nitsche, M. A., Bolognini, N., Bikson, M., Wagner, T., Merabet, L., Edwards, D. J., Valero-Cabre, A., Rotenberg, A. and Pascual-Leone, A. (2012) "Clinical Research with Transcranial Direct Current Stimulation (tDCS): Challenges and Future Directions," *Brain Stimulation* 5 175–95.

Buades-Rotger, M. and Gallardo-Pujol, D. (2014) "The Role of the Monoamine Oxidase a Gene in Moderating the Response to Adversity and Associated Antisocial Behavior: A Review," *Psychology Research and Behavior Management* 7 185–200.

Burt, S. A. (2009) "Are There Meaningful Etiological Differences within Antisocial Behavior? Results of a Meta-Analysis," *Clinical Psychology Review* 29 163–78.

Byrd, A. L. and Manuck, S. B. (2014) MAOA, Childhood Maltreatment, and Antisocial Behavior: Meta-Analysis of a Gene-Environment Interaction," *Biological Psychiatry* 75 9–17.

Campbell, F. A., Ramey, C. T., Pungello, E., Sparling, J. and Miller-Johnson, S. (2002) "Early Childhood Education: Young Adult Outcomes from the Abecedarian Project," *Applied Developmental Science* 6 42–57.

Caspi, A., McClay, J., Moffitt, T. E., Mill, J., Martin, J., Craig, I. W., Taylor, A. and Poulton, R. (2002) "Role of Genotype in the Cycle ofViolence in Maltreated Children," *Science* 297 851–4.

Cauffman, E., Steinberg, L. and Piquero, A. R. (2005) "Psychological, Neuropsychological and Physiological Correlates of Serious Antisocial Behavior in Adolescence: The Role of Self-Control," *Criminology* 43 133–76.

Chandler, J. A. (2016) "The Use of Neuroscientific Evidence in Canadian Criminal Proceedings," *Journal of Law and the Biosciences* 2 550–79.

Chen, C.-Y., Raine, A., Chou, K.-H., Chen, I.-Y., Hung, D. and Lin, C.-P. (2016) "Abnormal White Matter Integrity in Rapists as Indicated by Diffusion Tensor Imaging," *BMC Neuroscience* 17 45–52.

Choy, O., Focquaert, F. and Raine, A. (2018) "Benign Biological Interventions to Reduce Offending," *Neuroethics* 1–13.

Choy, O., Raine, A. and Hamilton, R. H. (2018) "Stimulation of the Prefrontal Cortex Reduces Intentions to Commit Aggression: A Randomized, Double-Blind, Placebo-Controlled, Stratified, Parallel-group Trial," *Journal Of Neuroscience* 38 6505–12.

Choy, O., Raine, A., Venables, P. H. and Farrington, D. P. (2017) "Explaining the Gender Gap in Crime: The Role of Heart Rate," *Criminology* 55 465–87.

Cornet, L. J., de Kogel, C. H., Nijman, H. L., Raine, A. and van der Laan, P. H. (2014) "Neurobiological Factors as Predictors of Cognitive–Behavioral Therapy Outcome in Individuals with Antisocial Behavior: A Review of the Literature," *International journal of Offender Therapy and Comparative Criminology* 58 1279–96.

Cummings, E. M., El-Sheikh, M., Kouros, C. D. and Keller, P. S. (2007) "Children's Skin Conductance Reactivity as a Mechanism of Risk in the Context of Parental Depressive Symptoms," *Journal of Child Psychology and Psychiatry* 48 436–45.

Dambacher, F., Schuhmann, T., Lobbestael, J., Arntz, A., Brugman, S. and Sack, A. T. (2015a) "No Effects of Bilateral Tdcs over Inferior Frontal Gyrus on Response Inhibition and Aggression," *PloS One* 10 e0132170.

Dambacher, F., Schuhmann, T., Lobbestael, J., Arntz, A., Brugman, S. and Sack, A. T. (2015b) "Reducing Proactive Aggression through Non-Invasive Brain Stimulation," *Social Cognitive and Affective Neuroscience* 10 1303–9.

Danese, A. and McEwen, B.S. (2012) "Adverse Childhood Experiences, Allostasis, Allostatic Load, and Age-related Disease," *Physiology & Behavior* 106 29–39.

Day, D. M., Wanklyn, S. G. & Yessine, A. K. (2014) "Review of Terminological, Conceptual, and Methodological Issues in the Developmental Risk Factor Literature for Antisocial and Delinquent Behavior," *Child & Youth Care Forum* 43 97–112.

De Kogel, C. and Westgeest, E. (2016) "Neuroscientific and Behavioral Genetic Information in Criminal Cases in the Netherlands," *Journal of Law and the Biosciences* 2 580–605.

Denno, D. W. (2011). "Courts' Increasing Consideration of Behavioral Genetics Evidence in Criminal Cases: Results of a Longitudinal Study," Michigan State Law Review 967–1047.

Dietrich, K. N., Douglas, R. M., Succop, P. A., Berger, O. G. and Bornschein, R. L. (2001) "Early Exposure to Lead and Juvenile Delinquency," *Neurotoxicology and Teratology* 23 511–8.

Dolan, M. (2012) "The Neuropsychology of Prefrontal Function in Antisocial Personality Disordered Offenders with Varying Degrees of Psychopathy," *Psychological Medicine* 42 1715–25.

Ellis, L., Beaver, K. M. and Wright, J. (2009) *Handbook of Crime Correlates*, Oxford: Academic Press.

Fast, D. K., Conry, J. and Loock, C. A. (1999) "Identifying Fetal Alcohol Syndrome among Youth in the Criminal Justice System," *Journal of Developmental and Behavioral Pediatrics* 20 370–2.

Ficks, C. A. and Waldman, I. D. (2014) "Candidate Genes for Aggression and Antisocial Behavior: A Meta-Analysis of Association Studies of the 5HTTLPR and MAOA-uVNTR," *Behavior Genetics* 44 427–44.

Focquaert, F. and Schermer, M. (2015) "Moral Enhancement: Do Means Matter Morally?" *Neuroethics* 8 139–51.

Gao, Y., Baker, L. A., Raine, A., Wu, H. and Bezdjian, S. (2009a) "Brief Report: Interaction between Social Class and Risky Decision-Making in Children with Psychopathic Tendencies," *Journal of Adolescence* 32 409–14.

Gao, Y., Raine, A., Venables, P. H., Dawson, M. E. and Mednick, S. A. (2009b) "Association of Poor Childhood Fear Conditioning and Adult Crime," *American Journal of Psychiatry* 167 56–60.

Gesch, C. B., Hammond, S. M., Hampson, S. E., Eves, A. and Crowder, M. J. (2002) "Influence of Supplementary Vitamins, Minerals and Essential Fatty Acids on the Antisocial Behaviour of Young Adult Prisoners," *The British Journal of Psychiatry* 181 22–8.

Gibson, C. L. and Tibbetts, S. G. (2000) "A Biosocial Interaction in Predicting Early Onset of Offending," *Psychological Reports* 86 509–18.

Glenn, A. L. and Raine, A. (2014) "Neurocriminology: Implications for the Punishment, Prediction and Prevention of Criminal Behaviour," *Nature Reviews Neuroscience* 15 54–63.

Goodstein, L., MacKenzie, D.L. and Shotland, R.L. (1984) "Personal Control and Inmate Adjustment to Prison," *Criminology* 22 343–69.

Greely, H. T. (2007) "Neuroscience and Criminal Justice: Not Responsibility but Treatment," *University of Kansas Law Review* 56 1103–38.

Hamazaki, T., Thienprasert, A., Kheovichai, K., Samuhaseneetoo, S., Nagasawa, T. and Watanabe, S. (2002) "The Effect of Docosahexaenoic Acid on Aggression in Elderly Thai Subjects—A Placebo-Controlled Double-Blind Study," *Nutritional Neuroscience* 5 37–41.

Hancock, M., Tapscott, J. L. and Hoaken, P. N. (2010). "Role of Executive Dysfunction in Predicting Frequency and Severity of Violence," *Aggressive Behavior* 36 338–49.

Haney, C. (2012). "Prison Effects in the Era of Mass Incarceration," *The Prison Journal* 92 1–24.

Hanlon, R. E., Coda, J. J., Cobia, D. and Rubin, L. H. (2012) "Psychotic Domestic Murder: Neuropsychological Differences between Homicidal and Nonhomicidal Schizophrenic Men," *Journal of Family Violence* 27 105–13.

Hanson, J. L., Nacewicz, B. M., Sutterer, M. J., Cayo, A. A., Schaefer, S. M., Rudolph, K. D., Shirtcliff, E. A., Pollak, S. D. and Davidson, R. J. (2015) "Behavioral Problems after Early Life Stress: Contributions of the Hippocampus and Amygdala," *Biological Psychiatry* 77 314–23.

Hare, T. A., Tottenham, N., Galvan, A., Voss, H. U., Glover, G. H. and Casey, B. J. (2008) "Biological Substrates of Emotional Reactivity and Regulation in Adolescence During an Emotional Go-nogo Task," *Biological Psychiatry* 63 927–34.

Herrnstein, R. and Wilson, J. Q. (1985) *Crime and Human Nature*, New York: Simon and Schuster.

Hodgins, S., Kratzer, L. and McNeil, T. F. (2001) "Obstetric Complications, Parenting, and Risk of Criminal Behavior," *Archives of General Psychiatry* 58 746–52.

Hortensius, R., Schutter, D. J. and Harmon-Jones, E. (2011) "When Anger Leads to Aggression: Induction of Relative Left Frontal Cortical Activity with Transcranial Direct Current Stimulation Increases the Anger–Aggression Relationship," *Social Cognitive and Affective Neuroscience* 7 342–7.

Isen, J. (2010) "A Meta-Analytic Assessment of Wechsler's P>V Sign in Antisocial Populations," *Clinical Psychology Review* 30 423–35.

Ishikawa, S. S., Raine, A., Lencz, T., Bihrle, S. and Lacasse, L. (2001) "Autonomic Stress Reactivity and Executive Functions in Successful and Unsuccessful Criminal Psychopaths from the Community," *Journal of Abnormal Psychology* 110 423–32.

Jennings, W. G., Piquero, A. R. and Farrington, D. P. (2013) "Does Resting Heart Rate at Age 18 Distinguish General and Violent Offending up to Age 50? Findings from the Cambridge Study in Delinquent Development," *Journal of Criminal Justice* 41 213–9.

Kandel, E., Brennan, P. A., Mednick, S. A. and Michelson, N. M. (1989) "Minor Physical Anomalies and Recidivistic Adult Violent Criminal Behavior," *Acta Psychiatrica Scandinavica* 79 103–7.

Kandel, E. and Mednick, S. A. (1991) "Perinatal Complications Predict Violent Offending," *Criminology* 29 519–29.

Kemppainen, L., Jokelainen, J., Järvelin, M.-R., Isohanni, M. and Räsänen, P. (2001) "The One-Child Family and Violent Criminality: A 31-Year Follow-up Study of the Northern Finland 1966 Birth Cohort," *American Journal of Psychiatry* 158 960–2.

Kokko, K. and Pulkkinen, L. (2000) "Aggression in Childhood and Long-term Unemployment in Adulthood: A Cycle of Maladaptation and Some Protective Factors," *Developmental Psychology* 36 463–72.

Latvala, A., Kuja-Halkola, R., Almqvist, C., Larsson, H. and Lichtenstein, P. (2015) "A Longitudinal Study of Resting Heart Rate and Violent Criminality in More Than 700,000 Men," *JAMA Psychiatry* 72 971–8.

Leonard, N. R., Jha, A. P., Casarjian, B., Goolsarran, M., Garcia, C., Cleland, C. M., Gwadz, M.V. and Massey, Z. (2013) "Mindfulness Training Improves Attentional Task Performance in Incarcerated Youth: A Group Randomized Controlled Intervention Trial," *Frontiers In Psychology* 4 792.

Liu, J., Raine, A., Wuerker, A., Venables, P. H. and Mednick, S. (2009) "The Association of Birth Complications and Externalizing Behavior in Early Adolescents: Direct and Mediating Effects," *Journal of Research on Adolescence* 19 93–111.

Long, S. J. and Benton, D. (2013) "A Double-Blind Trial of the Effect of Docosahexaenoic Acid and Vitamin and Mineral Supplementation on Aggression, Impulsivity, and Stress," *Human Psychopharmacology: Clinical and Experimental* 28 238–47.

Mattson, S. N. and Riley, E. P. (2000) "Parent Ratings of Behavior in Children with Heavy Prenatal Alcohol Exposure and IQ-Matched Controls," *Alcoholism: Clinical and Experimental Research* 24 226–31.

McAra, L. and McVie, S. (2010) "Youth Crime and Justice: Key messages from the Edinburgh Study of Youth Transitions and Crime," *Criminology & Criminal Justice* 10 179–209.

McNamara, R. K. and Carlson, S. E. (2006) "Role of Omega-3 Fatty Acids in Brain Development and Function: Potential Implications for the Pathogenesis and Prevention of Psychopathology," *Prostaglandins, Leukotrienes and Essential Fatty Acids* 75 329–49.

McSwiggan, S., Elger, B. and Appelbaum, P. S. (2017) "The Forensic Use of Behavioral Genetics in Criminal Proceedings: Case of the MAOA-L Genotype," *International Journal of Law and Psychiatry* 50 17–23.

Mednick, S. A. and Kandel, E. S. (1988) "Congenital Determinants of Violence," *Bulletin of the American Academy of Psychiatry and the Law* 16 101–9.

Meijers, J., Harte, J. M., Meynen, G., Cuijpers, P. and Scherder, E. J. (2018) "Reduced Self-Control after 3 Months of Imprisonment; A Pilot Study," *Frontiers in Psychology* 9 1–7.

Mews, A., Di Bella, L. and Purver, M. (2017) *Impact Evaluation of the Prison-based Core Sex Offender Treatment Programme.* London: Ministry of Justice.

Moffitt, T. E., Lynam, D. R. and Silva, P. A. (1994) "Neuropsychological Tests Predicting Persistent Male Delinquency," *Criminology* 32 277–300.

Molero-Chamizo, A., Riquel, R. M., Moriana, J. A., Nitsche, M. A. and Rivera-Urbina, G. N. (2019) "Bilateral Prefrontal Cortex Anodal tDCS Effects on Self-Reported Aggressiveness in Imprisoned Violent Offenders," *Neuroscience* 397 31–40.

Morgan, A. B. and Lilienfeld, S. O. (2000) "A Meta-Analytic Review of the Relation between Antisocial Behavior and Neuropsychological Measures of Executive Function," *Clinical Psychology Review* 20 113–36.

Murray, J., Hallal, P. C., Mielke, G. I., Raine, A., Wehrmeister, F. C., Anselmi, L. and Barros, F. C. (2016) "Low Resting Heart Rate Is Associated with Violence in Late Adolescence: A Prospective Birth Cohort Study in Brazil," *International Journal of Epidemiology* 45 491–500.

Nestor, P. G. (1992) "Neuropsychological and Clinical Correlates of Murder and Other Forms of Extreme Violence in a Forensic Psychiatric Population," *Journal of Nervous and Mental Disease* 180 418–23.

Nigg, J. T., Glass, J. M., Wong, M. M., Poon, E., Jester, J. M., Fitzgerald, H. E., Puttler, L. I., Adams, K. M. and Zucker, R. A. (2004) "Neuropsychological Executive Functioning in Children at Elevated Risk for Alcoholism: Findings in Early Adolescence," *Journal of Abnormal Psychology* 113 302–14.

Ogilvie, J. M., Stewart, A. L., Chan, R. C. and Shum, D. H. (2011) "Neuropsychological Measures of Executive Function and Antisocial Behavior: A Meta-analysis," *Criminology* 49 1063–107.

Olds, D., Henderson Jr, C. R., Cole, R., Eckenrode, J., Kitzman, H., Luckey, D., Pettitt, L., Sidora, K., Morris, P. and Powers, J. (1998) "Long-Term Effects of Nurse Home Visitation on Children's Criminal and Antisocial Behavior: 15-Year Follow-up of a Randomized Controlled Trial," *JAMA* 280 1238–44.

Olson, H. C., Streissguth, A. P., Sampson, P. D., Barr, H. M., Bookstein, F. L. and Thiede, K. (1997) "Association of Prenatal Alcohol Exposure with Behavioral and Learning Problems in Early Adolescence," *Journal of the American Academy of Child & Adolescent Psychiatry* 36 1187–94.

Pardini, D. A., Raine, A., Erickson, K. and Loeber, R. (2014) "Lower Amygdala Volume in Men Is Associated with Childhood Aggression, Early Psychopathic Traits, and Future Violence," *Biological Psychiatry* 75 73–80.

Pine, D. S., Shaffer, D., Schonfeld, I. S. and Davies, M. (1997) "Minor Physical Anomalies: Modifiers of Environmental Risks for Psychiatric Impairment?" *Journal of the American Academy of Child & Adolescent Psychiatry* 36 395–403.

Popova, S., Lange, S., Bekmuradov, D., Mihic, A. and Rehm, J. (2011) "Fetal Alcohol Spectrum Disorder Prevalence Estimates in Correctional Systems: A Systematic Literature Review," *Canadian Journal of Public Health* 102 336–40.

Portnoy, J. and Farrington, D. P. (2015) "Resting Heart Rate and Antisocial Behavior: An Updated Systematic Review and Meta-Analysis," *Aggression and Violent Behavior* 22 33–45.

Portnoy, J., Raine, A., Chen, F. R., Pardini, D., Loeber, R. and Jennings, J. R. (2014) "Heart Rate and Antisocial Behavior: The Mediating Role of Impulsive Sensation Seeking," *Criminology* 52 292–311.

Pratt, T. C., McGloin, J. M. and Fearn, N. E. (2006) "Maternal Cigarette Smoking During Pregnancy and Criminal/Deviant Behavior: A Meta-analysis," *International Journal of Offender Therapy and Comparative Criminology* 50 672–90.

Quay, H. C. (1965) "Psychopathic Personality as Pathological Stimulation-Seeking," *American Journal of Psychiatry* 122 180–3.

Raine, A. (2018) "The Neuromoral Theory of Antisocial, Violent, and Psychopathic Behavior," *Psychiatry Research* 277 64–9.

Raine, A., Brennan, P. and Mednick, S. A. (1994) "Birth Complications Combined with Early Maternal Rejection at Age 1 Year Predispose to Violent Crime at Age 18 Years," *Archives of General Psychiatry* 51 984–8.

Raine, A., Brennan, P. and Mednick, S. A. (1997) "Interaction between Birth Complications and Early Maternal Rejection in Predisposing Individuals to Adult Violence: Specificity to Serious, Early-Onset Violence," *American Journal of Psychiatry* 154 1265–71.

Raine, A., Fung, A. L. C., Portnoy, J., Choy, O. and Spring, V. L. (2014) "Low Heart Rate as a Risk Factor for Child and Adolescent Proactive Aggressive and Impulsive Psychopathic Behavior," *Aggressive Behavior* 40 290–29.

Raine, A., Laufer, W. S., Yang, Y., Narr, K. L., Thompson, P. and Toga, A. W. (2012) "Increased Executive Functioning, Attention, and Cortical Thickness in White-Collar Criminals," *Human Brain Mapping* 33 2932–40.

Raine, A., Lencz, T., Bihrle, S., LaCasse, L. and Colletti, P. (2000) "Reduced Prefrontal Gray Matter Volume and Reduced Autonomic Activity in Antisocial Personality Disorder," *Archives of General Psychiatry* 57 119–27.

Raine, A., Moffitt, T. E., Caspi, A., Loeber, R., Stouthamer-Loeber, M. and Lynam, D. (2005) "Neurocognitive Impairments in Boys on the Life-Course Persistent Antisocial Path," *Journal of Abnormal Psychology* 114 38–49.

Raine, A., Park, S., Lencz, T., Bihrle, S., LaCasse, L., Widom, C. S., Al-dayeh, L. and Singh, M. (2001) "Reduced Right Hemisphere Activation in Severely Abused Violent Offenders During a Working Memory Task: An fMRI Study," *Aggressive Behavior* 27 111–29.

Raine, A., Phil, D., Stoddard, J., Bihrle, S. and Buchsbaum, M. (1998) "Prefrontal Glucose Deficits in Murderers Lacking Psychosocial Deprivation," *Neuropsychiatry Neuropsychology, and Behavioral Neurology* 11 1–7.

Raine, A., Venables, P. H. and Mednick, S. A. (1997) "Low Resting Heart Rate at Age 3 Years Predisposes to Aggression at Age 11 Years: Evidence from the Mauritius Child Health Project," *Journal of the American Academy of Child & Adolescent Psychiatry* 36 1457–64.

Raine, A., Venables, P. H. and Williams, M. (1990) "Relationships between Central and Autonomic Measures of Arousal at Age 15 Years and Criminality at Age 24 Years," *Archives of General Psychiatry* 47 1003–7.

Raine, A., Yaralian, P. S., Reynolds, C., Venables, P. H. and Mednick, S. A. (2002) "Spatial but Not Verbal Cognitive Deficits at Age 3 Years in Persistently Antisocial Individuals," *Development and Psychopathology* 14 25–44.

Rantakallio, P., Läärä, E., Isohanni, M. and Moilanen, I. (1992) "Maternal Smoking During Pregnancy and Delinquency of the Offspring: An Association without Causation?" *International Journal of Epidemiology* 21 1106–13.

Räsänen, P., Hakko, H., Isohanni, M., Hodgins, S., Järvelin, M.-R. and Tiihonen, J. (1999) "Maternal Smoking During Pregnancy and Risk of Criminal Behavior among Adult Male Offspring in the Northern Finland 1966 Birth Cohort," *American Journal of Psychiatry* 156 857–62.

Raschle, N. M., Menks, W. M., Fehlbaum, L. V., Tshomba, E. and Stadler, C. (2015) "Structural and Functional Alterations in Right Dorsomedial Prefrontal and Left Insular Cortex Co-Localize in Adolescents with Aggressive Behaviour: An Ale Meta-Analysis," *PLoS One,* 10(9): e0136553.

Rhee, S. H. and Waldman, I. D. (2002) "Genetic and Environmental Influences on Antisocial Behavior: A Meta-Analysis of Twin and Adoption Studies," *Psychological Bulletin* 128 490–529.

Riva, P., Gabbiadini, A., Romero Lauro, L. J., Andrighetto, L., Volpato, C. and Bushman, B. J. (2017) "Neuromodulation Can Reduce Aggressive Behavior Elicited by Violent Video Games," *Cognitive, Affective, & Behavioral Neuroscience* 17 452–9.

Riva, P., Romero Lauro, L. J., DeWall, C. N., Chester, D. S. and Bushman, B. J. (2015) "Reducing Aggressive Responses to Social Exclusion Using Transcranial Direct Current Stimulation," *Social Cognitive and Affective Neuroscience* 10 352–6.

Rocque, M., Welsh, B. C. and Raine, A. (2012) "Biosocial Criminology and Modern Crime Prevention," *Journal of Criminal Justice* 40 306–12.

Rogers, J. C. and De Brito, S. A. (2016) "Cortical and Subcortical Gray Matter Volume in Youths with Conduct Problems: A Meta-Analysis," *JAMA Psychiatry* 73 64–72.

Sabatello, M. and Appelbaum, P. S. (2017) "Behavioral Genetics in Criminal and Civil Courts," *Harvard Review of Psychiatry* 25 289–301.

Schiffer, B., Muller, B. W., Scherbaum, N., Hodgins, S., Forsting, M., Wiltfang, J., Gizewski, E. R. and Leygraf, N. (2011) "Disentangling Structural Brain Alterations Associated with Violent Behavior from Those Associated with Substance Use Disorders," *Archives of General Psychiatry* 68 1039–49.

Schiffer, B. and Vonlaufen, C. (2011) "Executive Dysfunctions in Pedophilic and Nonpedophilic Child Molesters," *The Journal of Sexual Medicine* 8 1975–84.

Schweinhart, L. J., Barnes, H. V. and Weikhart, D. P. (1993) *Significant Benefits: The High/Scope Perry Preschool Study through Age 27*, Ypsilanti, MI: High/Scope.

Sijtsema, J. J., Veenstra, R., Lindenberg, S., van Roon, A. M., Verhulst, F. C., Ormel, J. and Riese, H. (2010) "Mediation of Sensation Seeking and Behavioral Inhibition on the Relationship between Heart Rate and Antisocial Behavior: The TRAILS Study," *Journal of the American Academy of Child and Adolescent Psychiatry* 49 493–502.

Stanford, M. S., Conklin, S. M., Helfritz, L. E. and Kockler, T. R. (2007) "P3 Amplitude Reduction and Executive Function Deficits in Men Convicted of Spousal/Partner Abuse," *Personality and Individual Differences* 43 365–75.

Taylor, J., Iacono, W. G. and McGue, M. (2000) "Evidence for a Genetic Etiology of Early-Onset Delinquency," *Journal of Abnormal Psychology* 109 634–43.

Umbach, R., Raine, A. and Leonard, N. R. (2018) "Cognitive Decline as a Result of Incarceration and the Effects of a CBT/MT Intervention: A Cluster-Randomized Controlled Trial," *Criminal Justice and Behavior* 45 31–55.

Vaske, J., Newsome, J. and Boisvert, D. (2013) "The Mediating Effects of Verbal Skills in the Relationship between Low Birth Weight and Childhood Aggressive Behaviour," *Infant and Child Development* 22 235–49.

Vassos, E., Collier, D. and Fazel, S. (2014) "Systematic Meta-Analyses and Field Synopsis of Genetic Association Studies of Violence and Aggression," *Molecular Psychiatry*, 19, 471–7.

Venables, P. H. (1987) "Autonomic Nervous System Factors in Criminal Behavior," in S. A. Mednick, T. E. Moffitt, and S. A. Stack (eds) *The Causes of Crime: New Biological Approaches*, New York: Cambridge University Press.

Wakschlag, L. S., Lahey, B. B., Loeber, R., Green, S. M., Gordon, R. A. and Leventhal, B. L. (1997) "Maternal Smoking During Pregnancy and the Risk of Conduct Disorder in Boys," *Archives of General Psychiatry* 54 670–6.

Wright, J. P., Dietrich, K. N., Ris, M. D., Hornung, R. W., Wessel, S. D., Lanphear, B. P., Ho, M. and Rae, M. N. (2008) "Association of Prenatal and Childhood Blood Lead Concentrations with Criminal Arrests in Early Adulthood," *PLoS Medicine*, 5, e101.

Yang, Y. and Raine, A. (2009) "Prefrontal Structural and Functional Brain Imaging Findings in Antisocial, Violent, and Psychopathic Individuals: A Meta-Analysis," *Psychiatry Research: Neuroimaging* 174 81–8.

Yang, Y., Raine, A., Colletti, P., Toga, A. W. and Narr, K. L. (2010) "Morphological Alterations in the Prefrontal Cortex and the Amygdala in Unsuccessful Psychopaths," *Journal of Abnormal Psychology* 119 546–54.

Yehuda, S., Rabinovitz, S. and Mostofsky, D. (2005) "Essential Fatty Acids and the Brain: From Infancy to Aging," *Neurobiology of Aging* 26 98–102.

Zaalberg, A., Nijman, H., Bulten, E., Stroosma, L. and Van Der Staak, C. (2010) "Effects of Nutritional Supplements on Aggression, Rule-Breaking, and Psychopathology among Young Adult Prisoners," *Aggressive Behavior* 36 117–26.

Zanarini, M. C. and Frankenburg, F. R. (2003) "Omega-3 Fatty Acid Treatment of Women with Borderline Personality Disorder: A Double-Blind, Placebo-Controlled Pilot Study," *American Journal of Psychiatry* 160 167–9.

19

BRAIN ABNORMALITIES ASSOCIATED WITH PEDOPHILIA

Implications for Retribution and Rehabilitation

Colleen M. Berryessa

Introduction

Historically, sexual crimes against children have been singled out by society as some of the most heinous and monstrous acts possible (Simon 1998). Heightened media coverage of these crimes over the last several decades, including high-profile sexual abuse scandals, have created further panic within the general public about the dangers that sexual predators pose to children and their likelihood of victimization (Lynch 2002). Pedophilia, a clinically diagnosable psychiatric disorder marked by sexual attraction to and arousal by prepubescent children, has been particularly at the forefront of this concern of the general public; a substantial amount of societal resources have thus been dedicated to understanding and preventing offending by pedophilic sex offenders in recent years (Hall & Hall 2007). Unfortunately, research has established that existing legislation crafted to combat and prevent pedophilic sexual offending, such as sex offender registration and community notification, are most often ineffective deterrents to reduce sexual offending against children (Tewksbury & Lees 2007).

In parallel, increased societal interest and concerns surrounding pedophilia have led to a growth of neurobiological, genetic and other biological research on the potential causes and contributions to the development of pedophilia (Hall & Hall 2007). A great deal of this literature has focused on understanding the pathology of the disorder as a psychiatric and medical condition, its etiology, and biological characteristics or abnormalities specific to the development of pedophilia. Correspondingly, there have also been many recent studies attempting to develop effective, noninvasive treatments to hinder or regulate pedophilic ruminations and actions that target certain brain regions or biological abnormalities associated with pedophilia (Bradford 2001). As some estimates report that 20% of all individuals that sexually offend meet the diagnostic criteria for pedophilia (Van Gijseghem 2011), this research is exceedingly important to better understanding the true nature and origins of pedophilic sexual offending and, ultimately, should be able to aid in providing more effective mechanisms to prevent it from occurring in the future.

As literature on the biological influences on pedophilia has increased, so has academic dialogue concerning how knowledge of biological contributions to antisocial behavior and mental disorders, as they relate to offending, may influence perceptions of legal responsibility, objectives of punishment, and ultimately rendered justice in the courtroom (Aharoni et al. 2008; Berryessa 2014; Garland & Frankel 2006; Goodenough & Tucker 2010). Existing literature has also voiced optimism that neurobiological research may ultimately support the development of more effective treatment options for offenders in order to better prevent reoffending (Greely 2007). In addition to better understanding the development of the disorder, it is likely that growing areas of biological research on the development and manifestation of pedophilia may also produce distinct implications for the prosecution, punishment, and treatment of pedophilic sex offenders within the criminal justice system (Berryessa 2014). Yet, to date, there has been little literature on these issues.

Thus, in an attempt to fill this gap in the literature, this chapter examines potential ways in which neurobiological research on pedophilia may influence perceptions of retribution and rehabilitation in the criminal justice system, particularly focusing on reported neurobiological, rather than physiological, genetic, or other biological, aspects of pedophilia. After defining the prevalence, as well as diagnostic and clinical characteristics, of pedophilia, this chapter will provide a brief overview of the existing research on neural abnormalities and deficits associated with pedophilia, focusing on structural and functional neuroimaging literature. Thereafter, the remainder of this chapter will discuss how this research may affect two of the core objectives of punishment in our legal system: retribution and rehabilitation. Research on the neural abnormalities associated with pedophilia may also not only influence the conventional prosecution and rendered punishments of pedophilic sex offenders within the legal system, which historically have been heavily retributive in nature, but also extremely punitive perceptions and stigma surrounding pedophilia, commonly held by juries and judges, that may affect their legal decisions. Correspondingly, knowledge on the neural abnormalities associated with pedophilia, paired with the growing amount of research on potentially effective biological treatments to regulate or deter pedophilic behaviors, may influence existing perceptions of the purposes and appropriateness of punishments for pedophilic sex offenders, which could lead to more open attitudes toward sentences aimed at rehabilitation. Finally, this chapter will discuss literature on three promising treatments that target the neural abnormalities observed in pedophilia. These treatments could possibly one day be utilized as rehabilitative sentencing alternatives, instead of or in addition to retributive punishments (Gilbert & Focquaert 2015). This chapter adopts a similar structure to Berryessa (2014), which reviews genetic research on pedophilia and how it may affect objectives of punishment.

Pedophilia: Diagnosis and Definition

The fifth edition of the Diagnostic and Statistical Manual of Mental Disorders (DSM-5) defines pedophilic disorder as a disorder in which "adults or adolescents 16 years of age or older have intense and recurrent sexual urges toward and fantasies about prepubescent children that they have either acted on or which cause them distress or interpersonal difficulty" (American Psychiatric Association 2013). Prepubescent is considered 13 years of age or younger (Williams & Currie 2000). Since the DSM-5, pedophilic disorder has been distinguished from pedophilia, which is defined as sexual arousal or response to prepubescent subjects, but without recurrent sexual urges, interpersonal difficulty, or actions based upon those urges (American Psychiatric Association 2013). Pedophilia is often included as a psychiatric symptom of several DSM-5 diagnosable paraphilic disorders, but is not a separate disorder.

The psychiatric community ultimately chose to differentiate pedophilia from pedophilic disorder in the DSM-5 because the sexual preference for children in pedophilia, without urges or actions associated with it, has been "depathologized" (Mohnke et al. 2014). The sexual preference alone, without urges or actions, does not create harm to either the individual with symptoms of pedophilia or to children, and therefore it does not require treatment. As pedophilic sex offenders are those who have attempted to or indeed acted upon their sexual urges toward children, the current discussion concerns what is now clinically diagnosed as pedophilic disorder. However, the term "pedophilia" will instead be used in this chapter, as "pedophilia" has historically been the terminology used in the neuroscience and criminal justice literature predating the DSM-5 when discussing what is now diagnosed as "pedophilic disorder."

There is also an important distinction between pedophilia and child sexual offending. In the media and amongst the general public, the terms are often used synonymously, but a large portion of child sex offenders do not have a sexual preference for children (Seto 2008). In fact, only 40% to 50% of individuals who sexually offend against children are thought to meet the clinical diagnosis for pedophilia (Maletzky & Steinhauser 2002; Seto 2008). Further, meeting the clinical diagnosis for pedophilia, including exhibiting sexual urges toward children as well as interpersonal difficulties controlling those urges, does not always result in an individual acting upon those urges (Ames & Houston 1990). Meeting the diagnostic criteria for the disorder solely means that sexual urges, sexual ruminations, and difficulty controlling thoughts toward children are present. The epidemiological research on pedophilia is poor, but the prevalence of the disorder has been reported as between 3% to 5% of the population and is significantly more common amongst males (Seto 2009). Seto, Cantor, and Blanchard (2006) report that only 43% of individuals who meet the clinical diagnosis for pedophilia ultimately act upon their urges. Unfortunately, little is known about diagnosed individuals who experience intrapersonal struggles due their sexual urges toward children, but do not act upon them. This chapter is concerned with pedophilic sex offenders, meaning the 40% to 50% of individuals who meet the diagnostic criteria for pedophilia and sexually offend against children.

Finally, there must also be a distinction drawn between non-acquired pedophilia and acquired pedophilia. Acquired pedophilia occurs when an individual with a normal history of sexual behavior and sexual preference, in addition to no prior history of pedophilia, experiences pedophilic urges, commits pedophilic actions, and meets the clinical diagnosis for pedophilia with no warning (Mendez & Shapira 2011). The explanation for this behavior is most often the onset of a degenerative brain disorder, such as Parkinson's disease, certain forms of dementia, or the presence of a tumor, which causes extreme changes in behavior by affecting brain areas involved in regulating sexual behavior, moral decision-making, and impulse control (Burns & Swerdlow 2003; Mendez & Shapira 2011). Most often these individuals are middle-aged, and, in the large majority of known cases, pedophilic actions have occurred during episodes of general hypersexuality caused by the individual's brain disorder, rather than the brain disorder causing pedophilia specifically (Mohnke et al. 2014). Individuals with acquired pedophilia can often be treated or regulated by either medication to control the behavioral symptoms of their brain disorder or by removing the tumor (Mendez & Shapira 2011).

Conversely, non-acquired pedophilia is a life-long individual trait and stable sexual preference (Seto 2012). The clinical diagnosis of pedophilia does not change over the lifetime, and the sexual preference is thought to be a predisposition (Seto 2008, 2012). Research has reported that with treatment, individuals with non-acquired pedophilia can learn to control or refrain from their sexual urges and actions, but the underlying sexual preference cannot be altered (Seto 2012). Accordingly, this chapter is concerned with sex offenders with non-acquired pedophilia.

Neurobiological Research on Pedophilia

To date, neurobiological and brain research on pedophilia has included a limited amount of both structural and functional neuroimaging studies. The following two sections briefly review existing structural and functional neuroimaging research on pedophilia. A more substantive review of the existing literature can be found in papers by Tenbergen et al. (2015) and Mohnke et al. (2014).

Early structural neuroimaging research on pedophilia began in the 1980s and utilized computerized tomography (CT). Some of these first studies observed reduced brain density in pedophilic men (Graber et al. 1982; Hendricks et al. 1988) and found enlargement of the left temporal and anterior horns (Hucker et al. 1986) compared to controls. Wright, Nobrega, Langevin, & Wortzman (1990) reported more brain asymmetry in pedophilic individuals, which was ascribed to temporal lobe abnormalities, compared to controls. Yet, many of these temporal lobe abnormalities were not only observed in pedophilic men, but also observed in non-pedophilic sexually deviant males. The authors argued that observed temporal abnormalities might be involved in a range of sexually impulsive and deviant behaviors, and not solely pedophilia (Wright et al. 1990).

The first magnetic resonance imaging (MRI) study on pedophilic sex offenders was conducted in 2000 and examined a group of 38 imprisoned pedophilic sex offenders (Eher et al. 2000). Structural abnormalities were observed in 17 offenders, including cortical atrophy and white matter lesions. The authors considered that the observed abnormalities may have led to sexual offending by hindering social information processing, but the reported results were largely unspecific to pedophilia (Eher et al. 2000). Beginning in 2007, several other structural studies, including MRI and Diffusion Tensor Imaging, have been since conducted and published in the last 10 years (e.g. Cantor & Blanchard 2012; Cantor et al. 2008, 2015; Lett et al. 2018; Poeppl et al. 2013, 2015; Schiffer et al. 2007, 2017; Schiltz et al. 2007).

For example, a study by Schiltz et al. (2007) evaluated MRI data of 15 pedophilic sex offenders, of which nine individuals had exclusive pedophilic preferences (meaning their victims were of only one sex) and six individuals had non-exclusive pedophilic preferences, and 15 control subjects that were normally sexually attracted to adults. Analysis focused on neural regions generally associated with sexual function, including the amygdala, septal nuclei, stria terminalis, hypothalamus, and substantia innominata. Results showed reduced volume of the right, and possibly the left, amygdala, as well as enlarged right temporal horns, in pedophilic sex offenders compared to control. The authors suggested that these abnormalities might be the result of neurodevelopmental issues, altering normal sexual maturation. There were no significant neural differences between exclusive and non-exclusive pedophilic individuals (Schiltz et al. 2007).

An MRI study by Schiffer et al. (2007) compared 18 pedophilic individuals with 24 community controls, controlling for age, handedness, gender, and other demographic characteristics. Half of both the pedophilic and control groups were attracted exclusively to males, and the other half was exclusively attracted to females. MRI data identified reduced grey matter volume of 11 brain areas, such as the bilateral orbitofrontal cortex, insula, ventral striatum, hippocampus, bilateral amygdala, and cerebellum, in pedophilic individuals compared to controls. These brain areas have been previously associated with impulse and compulsive disorders, and the authors concluded that the results provided evidence for a relationship between obsessive-compulsive disorder and pedophilia (Schiffer et al. 2007).

Cantor et al. (2008) compared 44 pedophilic sex offenders with 53 non-pedophilic non-sexual criminal offenders, controlling for age, education, handedness, and IQ. No differences were observed in grey matter volume between groups, but pedophilic sex offenders showed reduced white matter in temporal and parietal regions compared to the non-pedophilic non-sexual criminal offender group. Cantor and Blanchard (2012) reanalyzed the original 2008 data by separating pedophilic and hebephilic sex offenders; hebephilia involves sexual attraction to pubescent children aged 11 to 14. White matter reductions to bilateral temporal and parietal regions were present in both pedophilic and hebephilic sex offenders. Ultimately, Cantor and Blanchard (2012) proposed that white matter reductions in the temporal and parietal regions of pedophilic individuals may suggest that connectivity between neural areas crucial to normal sexual arousal and processing is significantly impaired. The authors further suggested that diffusion tensor imaging, which observes white matter connectivity by measuring the diffusion of water molecules, might be useful to test this hypothesis in the future (Cantor & Blanchard 2012).

A German MRI study by Poeppl et al. (2013) analyzed eight pedophilic sex offenders compared to 11 criminal offenders who were normally sexually attracted to adults and had no history of sex crimes. The only brain area showing a significant difference between pedophilic individuals and controls was grey matter reductions of the right amygdala. The authors speculated that reduced amygdala volume may be characteristic of neurodevelopmental impairments to normal sexual maturation, resulting in pedophilia (Poeppl et al. 2013). Although the number of MRI studies on pedophilia to date is limited, multiple studies have observed reduced amygdala volume, which may suggest impairments to emotional processing of sexual arousal in pedophilic individuals (e.g. Poeppl et al. 2013; Schiffer et al. 2007; Schiltz et al. 2007) and reduced grey and white matter in total brain volume, particularly in frontal areas related to executive function (e.g. Cantor & Blanchard 2012, Cantor et al. 2008, 2015; Lett et al. 2018; Poeppl et al. 2015; Schiffer et al. 2007, 2015)

There have been several case reports (e.g. Dressing et al. 2001; Habermeyer et al. 2012; Moulier et al. 2012; Schiffer et al. 2009) and numerous studies that have used functional magnetic resonance imaging (fMRI) or positron emission tomography (PET) to examine sexual arousal in pedophilia in the last decade (e.g. Cantor et al. 2016; Cazala et al. 2018; Cohen et al. 2002; Habermeyer et al. 2013a, 2013b; Kärgel et al. 2015; Poeppl et al. 2011; Ponseti et al. 2012; Sartorius et al. 2008; Schiffer et al. 2008a, 2008b; Walter et al. 2007). All of the larger fMRI and PET studies have used similar methods (Mohnke et al. 2014). Sexually arousing pictures, among control images, were presented to both non-pedophilic male controls, who exhibited normal sexual attraction to adults, and pedophilic males. Sexual pictures included both nude or partially clothed children and adults, and control images included neutral pictures and pictures of fully clothed individuals. Between experimental and control groups, studies seek to identify and compare potential differences between the neural activity of pedophilic individuals and controls when processing both the control images and the sexually arousing images that correspond to their sexual preferences (children for pedophilic individuals and adults for controls) (Mohnke et al. 2014).

Overall, there are two main brain areas where functional differences between groups have been observed. First, abnormal and reduced activation in frontal areas of pedophilic individuals was reported in the majority of functional imaging studies when viewing both sexually arousing and control images (e.g. Cantor et al. 2015; Cohen et al. 2002; Dressing et al. 2001; Habermeyer et al. 2013a; 2013b; Kärgel et al. 2015; Poeppl et al. 2011; Schiffer et al. 2008b, 2009; Walter et al. 2007). Significant abnormal activation of the orbitofrontal cortex (OFC), an area associated with the cognitive component of sexual processing, during sexual arousal was observed in at least four of the larger functional studies (e.g. Cohen et al. 2002; Habermeyer et al. 2013a, 2013b; Kärgel et al. 2015; Poeppl et al. 2011; Walter et al. 2007) and one fMRI case report (Dressing et al. 2001). Damage to the OFC has been known to affect the disinhibition of normal sexual behavior and cause problems with emotional processing (Redouté et al. 2000). For example, an fMRI study by Walter et al. (2007) found neural abnormalities in the dorsolateral prefrontal cortex during visual processing of sexually arousing images of children for pedophilic individuals. A PET study by Cohen et al. (2002) found reduced glucose metabolism in frontal regions of pedophilic subjects, which indicated impairment to neural function in these brain areas, during the processing of both sexually arousing images of children and control images. These studies suggest that frontal abnormalities may help to explain the diminished behavioral and impulse control that is characteristic of pedophilia.

Second, several functional imaging studies have reported abnormal activation of the amygdalae in pedophilic individuals (e.g. Dressing et al. 2001; Poeppl et al. 2011; Kärgel et al. 2015; Sartorius et al. 2008; Schiffer et al. 2008a, 2008b). These studies further support the structural imaging evidence for amygdala abnormalities in pedophilic individuals. For example, a 2008 fMRI study found that amygdala activity was higher during the viewing of sexually arousing pictures of children for pedophilic individuals, while the control group showed the reverse pattern of amygdala activation (Sartorius et al. 2008). Dressing et al. (2001) also demonstrated abnormal activation patterns in the amygdala during the viewing of both sexually arousing images of children and control images in a pedophilic patient. The authors suggested the results might be evidence of compromised emotional evaluation and processing in pedophilic individuals (Dressing et al. 2001).

In addition to the frontal regions and amygdala, other brain areas of pedophilic individuals showing abnormal activation compared to controls during the viewing of sexually arousing images of children in functional imaging studies included the temporal areas, anterior cingulate cortex, fusiform gyrus, cerebellum, substantia nigra, and hypothalamus (e.g. Cantor et al. 2016; Cazala et al. 2018; Cohen et al. 2002; Dressing et al. 2001; Habermeyer et al. 2012; Habermeyer et al. 2013a; 2013b; Kärgel et al. 2015; Moulier et al. 2012; Poeppl et al. 2011; Ponseti et al. 2012; Sartorius et al. 2008; Schiffer et al. 2008a, 2008b; Schiffer, Gizewski, and Kruger, 2009; Walter et al. 2007). For example, Walter et al. (2007) reported that compared to controls, pedophilic individuals have reduced activation of the hypothalamus, which regulates physiologic arousal and release of hormones, when shown sexually arousing pictures of adults.

Overall, structural and functional imaging research into pedophilia has indicated abnormalities to several brain regions. Abnormal activation and reduced volume of the amygdala, as well as structural deficits and reduced activation in the frontal areas, have been the most replicated findings across CT, MRI, PET, fMRI, and other imaging studies. Researchers have suggested that pedophilic individuals may have impairments to emotional processing, underlain by abnormal structure and functioning of the amygdala, compared to normally sexually aroused adults. Further, deficits associated with the processing, decision-making, and behavioral control concerning sexually arousing stimuli, underlain by structural and functional frontal area abnormalities, may contribute to pedophilic behavior (Mohnke et al. 2014; Tenbergen et al. 2015). Thus, based on these replicated findings, these brain regions are potentially those to target for future treatment approaches.

Potential Effects on Perceptions of Retribution

Research on the neural abnormalities associated with pedophilia may potentially influence legal perspectives on retributive and rehabilitative punishments. Retribution, which has been commonly considered the main objective of the criminal justice system, is based upon "eye for an eye" justice. Retributive sentences are rendered proportionate to the perceived moral blameworthiness of the offender for the crime. For example, although it is illegal, speeding is not considered to be at the same level of immorality or depravity as murder; as such, speeding only elicits a small fine and murder may result in the death penalty. Retribution is often paired with incapacitation, which seeks to protect society by confining offenders away from the general public in order to prevent future offending (Smith 2005).

Pedophilic sex offenders have historically been subjected to some of the harshest and most retributive punishments rendered by judges and, in select jurisdictions and in capital cases, by juries; these punishments have been chiefly focused on lengthy incapacitating sentences and "shaming" strategies upon release, such as community notification, with virtually no focus on rehabilitation or treatment (Quinn, Forsyth, & Mullen-Quinn, 2004). Judges have called pedophilic sex offenders "the worst of the worst" and the most immoral category of offender (Nhan, Polzer, & Ferguson, 2012). Judges have been known to sentence pedophilic sex offenders in accordance with these beliefs and greatly support retributive and harsh punishments for sex offenders (Bumby & Maddox 1999). Often the members of the general public serving on juries share similar sentiments. A large majority of the population believes pedophilic individuals cannot be rehabilitated and no current punishment can stop pedophilic sex offenders because of their dangerousness (Lave 2011). Overall, criminal sentences for pedophilic sex offenders have appeared to be largely based on perceived stigmas (Bumby & Maddox 1999). However, it is possible that research on neural abnormalities associated with pedophilia may help to counteract some of these stigmas historically associated with pedophilic sex offenders and, at least to a degree, work to reduce the overwhelming retributive attitudes toward pedophilic sex offenders. As such, judges and juries making legal decisions concerning pedophilic sex offenders may be more open to rehabilitative sentences, rather than solely harsh punishments.

In recent decades, neurobiological research, specifically neuroimaging research, has been increasingly presented in court, most often by the defense, in order to provide evidence that an offender's brain is structurally or functionally abnormal (Jones et al. 2013). The argument most often attempted is that the offender's neural abnormalities contributed to or caused the offender's criminal behavior, and, therefore, control over their behavior and responsibility may be compromised; as such, moral blameworthiness is argued to be reduced, and punishment should be mitigated (Batts 2009). Although almost all of the defenses built upon this rationale have been unsuccessful in reducing punishment, certain cases have been successful in recent years, specifically in capital cases (Presidential Commission for the Study of Bioethical Issues 2015). In general, neuroscience evidence has often been described as a "double-edged sword:" evidence could be either be viewed by judges or juries as a mitigator to punishment, based on the view that the offender is less responsible for their crimes because their "brain made them do it," or as an aggravator to punishment, based on the view that an offender is more dangerous and likely to reoffend because their brain is permanently "broken" (Jones & Shen 2012). Accordingly, a judge or jury could potentially choose to either reduce or extend the sentence of an offender based on their perceptions of presented evidence on the offender's biological abnormalities (Aspinwall, Brown, & Tabery, 2012; Barth 2007).

As previously discussed, current attitudes toward pedophilic sexual offenders are almost universally negative, harsh, and result in punitive and incapacitating punishments (Quinn et al. 2004). Thus, it is conceivable that evidence on neural abnormalities associated with pedophilia could further aggravate these attitudes toward pedophilic sex offenders and be used to provide additional evidence of dangerousness and the unlikelihood of rehabilitation. For example, structural and functional abnormalities to the brain's frontal areas, associated with potential impairments to processing, decision-making, and behavioral control surrounding sexual arousal, may be viewed as evidence that pedophilic sex offenders are unable to control their sexual behavior and therefore would be an inherent danger to society's children if released back into the public. This is similar to research suggesting the heritability of pedophilia which might be seen as evidence of future dangerousness and a high likelihood to reoffend (Berryessa 2014). Evidence surrounding a family history of criminality has been previously used in court by the prosecution in an attempt to portray an offender as a likely dangerous recidivist (*Johnston v. Love* 1996). Attitudes such as these could result in continued or added support for retributive punishments for pedophilic sex offenders.

Yet, it is also possible that neurobiological research on pedophilia could be viewed as evidence that pedophilic sex offenders act, at least in part, due to their neural differences and abnormalities; this could lead judges or juries to believe that pedophilic sex offenders, although legally responsible for their crimes, are victims of "broken brains" and are less morally blameworthy (Monterosso, Royzman, & Schwartz, 2005). In the selected cases that have successfully used neuroscientific evidence to reduce punishment, these successes have been largely due to the receptiveness of the judge or jury to the presented evidence; although courts overall have been uncertain of neuroscientific evidence and if it should affect sentencing, past research indicates that at least some judges and juries are potentially open and responsive to defenses based upon neuroscientific evidence as a mitigator to punishment (Moriarty 2008). Further, judges and jurors have been shown to often put a significant amount of weight on scientific expert evidence when making legal decisions (Ivković & Hans 2003). Thus, depending on the openness of a judge or jury to considering evidence on neural abnormalities associated with pedophilia, as well as how much weight is placed on it during sentencing, a judge or jury may perceive a pedophilic sex offender as less morally responsible because of the offender's biological deficits.

These perceptions could also lessen currently held negative attitudes toward pedophilic sex offenders and correspondingly may reduce the punishment given. Specifically, judges and juries may view pedophilic sex offenders, even though they are still legally accountable for their crimes, as pathologically and biologically disordered because of their neural abnormalities. This may influence opinions about the appropriateness of certain punishments. For example, a judge or jury could believe a pedophilic sex offender would be unable to control their sexual behavior, as well as unable to emotionally or morally evaluate their actions, because their neural deficits rendered it impossible for him to do so. Therefore, courts may be more open to delivering sentences to pedophilic sex offenders that are not exclusively retributive and, instead, also include a rehabilitative component. This could potentially provide treatment to the disordered offender that affects their frontal and subcortical deficits, and, therefore, affects and hinders their pedophilic ruminations, actions, and offending behaviors.

Effects on Perceptions of Rehabilitation

Rehabilitative sentences, contrary to retributive sentences, strive to treat the underlying reasons for an offender's criminal behaviors in order to prevent reoffending (Smith 2005). It is perhaps unlikely that retributive sentences would ever be completely eradicated for pedophilic sex offenders given long established sentiments, but neuroscientific research on pedophilia may help to foster support for rehabilitative punishments. If a pedophilic sex offender is thought to be "neurobiologically disordered," rehabilitative treatments that target the biological abnormalities could be the most effective and successful methods to prevent future offending, especially since existing policies created to combat and prevent pedophilic sexual offending have been shown to be almost wholly ineffective (Tewksbury & Lees 2007).

Even though research has indicated that the underlying sexual preference of pedophilia cannot be "cured," in the same way that a homosexual or heterosexual cannot change their sexual preferences (Seto 2009), treatments that target the biological abnormalities associated with pedophilia could ultimately allow pedophilic individuals to have better behavioral and emotional control over their sexual arousal and attain self-management skills in order to regulate their sexual urges. Although still currently used in certain jurisdictions in order to reduce sexual response and deter the offending of repeat pedophilic sex offenders, forms of castration have raised many legal and ethical concerns among academic communities and the general public about their invasiveness, their use as mandatory treatments, potential for non-coerced informed consent, and the constitutional and civil liberties issues that may arise with their use (Hicks 1993; Seto 2009; Thibaut et al. 2016). Less invasive treatments that also biologically target the regulation and reduction of sexual arousal of pedophilic individuals would likely create much less ethical and legal uproar and may be far more widely considered, accepted, and used for treatment.

If the justice system was open to rehabilitative sentencing options to treat and target the neural abnormalities associated with pedophilia moving forward, it is important to review the existing literature on nascent treatments for pedophilia that specifically affect the areas shown by structural and functional neuroimaging research to be abnormal in pedophilic individuals. Recent research has discussed three potential treatment options for pedophilia: (1) a real-time functional magnetic imaging brain computer interface neurofeedback system; (2) pharmacological therapy including the use of selective serotonin reuptake inhibitors and other medications that act on 5-HT receptors; and (3) Berlin Dissexuality Therapy. In the future, these promising treatments could possibly be utilized as rehabilitative sentencing alternatives instead of or in addition to retributive punishments.

First, research on the neural abnormalities associated with pedophilia has led to the formulation of a new, innovative therapy for pedophilia using a real-time functional magnetic imaging (rt-fMRI) brain computer interface (BCI) neurofeedback system (Renaud et al. 2011). Neurofeedback has been previously used for the treatment of several mental disorders, including obsessive-compulsive disorder (Hammond 2004) and attention deficit hyperactivity disorder (Arns et al. 2009). Renaud et al. (2011) argue that the use of this rt-fMRI BCI application would seek to assist pedophilic individuals, by targeting affected frontal and subcortical brain areas, to help individuals develop control control over their sexual arousal and the "cognitive and motor intentionality" that leads to the commission of pedophilic acts. The neural region thought to be best treated and specifically targeted with this system is the anterior cingulate cortex (ACC). The ACC has been shown to be functionally abnormal in pedophilic individuals, but is also associated with obsessive-compulsive behaviors and is active during sexual arousal in both normal adults and pedophilic individuals (Arnow et al. 2002; Schiffer et al. 2008a, 2008b).

Renaud et al. (2011) write that rt-fMRI BCI neurofeedback may be able to train pedophilic individuals to reduce the activation of the ACC, and correspondingly reduce sexual arousal, when presented with erotic or sexually arousing visual or behavioral stimuli involving prepubescent children.

In an rt-fMRI BCI neurofeedback system to treat pedophilic individuals, 3D life-like computer-simulated sexually arousing images of nude or partially nude prepubescent children are presented to pedophilic individuals, and sexual arousal is gauged by tracking eye movements, penile tumescence, and measuring activation in the ACC. Then, a neurofeedback "loop" is used to target and diminish activation in the ACC, paired with the use of a behavioral therapy termed "covert mental rehearsal" to also reduce ACC activation (Johnston et al. 2010; Renaud et al. 2011).

Covert mental rehearsal is a type of covert sensitization in cognitive behavioral therapy (CBT) where an undesirable behavior is paired with an undesirable thought or stimulus, repeatedly rehearsed, and the undesirable behavior is modified. For example, similar aversion therapies using CBT methodology have been used to eradicate undesirable compulsive behaviors, such as pulling out one's hair or scratching, in obsessive-compulsive disorder patients (Foa 2010). Through covert mental rehearsal, the frontal cortex and the subcortical regions, including the ACC and amygdala, are reportedly affected by establishing top-down control of behaviors (Cisek & Kalaska 2004). As discussed above, these are brain areas abnormal in pedophilic individuals and are thought to underlie the impulsivity, regulation of sexual behavior, and decision-making affected in pedophilic individuals (Mohnke et al. 2014). Although this treatment is still in its early stages, it is a promising method to help pedophilic individuals regulate their sexual arousal and behaviors that result from said arousal.

Second, existing literature on neural abnormalities associated with pedophilia has led to recent research on the possibility of using selective serotonin reuptake inhibitors (SSRIs) or other medications that act on 5-HT receptors as a pharmacological therapy to hinder and regulate the sexual urges and behaviors associated with pedophilia. SSRIs target serotonin dysfunction by blocking serotonin reuptake, allowing for increased levels of serotonin to be present in the synaptic gap for longer periods of time, and making it more likely that serotonin will bind to 5-HT receptors on postsynaptic neurons (Frazer 1997). Genetic literature on research on pedophilia has reported abnormalities associated with serotonin and dopamine production and function, particularly contributing to the functional neural deficits observed in the frontal regions of pedophilic patients (Comings 1994; Tost et al. 2004). Abnormal serotonin and dopamine function has been connected to the compulsive thoughts and behaviors associated with pedophilia, leading some to argue that this is evidence for a relationship between pedophilia and obsessive-compulsive disorders (Tost et al. 2004). Functional imaging research has also supported the argument for this relationship (Schiffer et al. 2007), and SSRIs have been often used to treat obsessive-compulsive disorders (Stein 2000).

In recent decades, there have been several preliminary studies to examine whether SSRIs may help pedophilic individuals regulate their sexual urges. Unfortunately, there have been no randomized control trials, and only a limited number of case studies and open-label studies have been reported (e.g. Bradford 2001; Kafka 1994; Kafka & Hennen 2000; Stein et al. 1992). Yet results from these early studies suggest SSRIs have been shown to effectively control the compulsive sexual urges and thoughts in pedophilic patients by diminishing sexual ruminations, improving regulation over impulse control, and dampening sex drive. Reduced sexual libido is actually a noted side effect by individuals taking SSRIs for other psychiatric disorders, and it is usually thought of as a detrimental consequence of the medication; yet, for pedophilic patients who are attempting to control their sexual desires, it may be thought of as a benefit (Bradford 2001). Although much more substantial research must be conducted, including randomized control trials, the preliminary results of selected studies on the efficacy of treating pedophilic urges with SSRIs suggest that its use as a pharmacological therapy to inhibit sexual compulsions and regulate sexual impulses of pedophilic sex offenders may be used as an effective rehabilitative therapy in the future (Gilbert & Outram 2009).

Finally, a recent longitudinal pilot treatment program called the Berlin Dissexuality Therapy (BEDIT) has provided some evidence that cognitive behavioral therapy (CBT) methodology may be effective in enhancing sexual impulse control, reducing cognitive and emotional impairments, and ultimately reducing risk factors for offending in pedophilic individuals (Beier et al. 2015). CBT reportedly increases serotonin receptor functioning (Karlsson, 2011) and increases functionality of prefrontal regions that are integral in cognitive control (DeRubeis, Siegle, & Hollon, 2008). Many argue that CBT fosters top-down regulation of emotions and behaviors, by increasing the control of prefrontal networks over subcortical, limbic structures, specifically the amygdala (Karlsson 2011). CBT aims to regulate and increase frontal activation that normalizes the activation of the amygdala and other limbic structures, thereby establishing better cognitive control and regulation over one's emotions, negative thinking, and behaviors (Karlsson 2011). As research on neural abnormalities associated with pedophilia has observed functional deficits in the prefrontal cortex and the amygdala, CBT may provide pedophilic individuals an effective way to modify and manage their sexual urges and behaviors.

BEDIT utilizes a method of group CBT, including several behavioral, psychological, and sexological intervention strategies to prevent pedophilic sexual offending (Beier et al. 2015). This mode of CBT for pedophilic individuals specifically targets a pedophilic sex offender's motivation to change their behavior, self-esteem, ability to self-monitor and manage their thoughts and behaviors, their ability to regulate their emotions and sexual urges, attitudes that support offending behavior, their ability to experience empathy for child victims of pedophilic acts, and strategies to prevent recidivism (Beier et al. 2015). The BEDIT pilot study followed a group of pedophilic individuals being treated with BEDIT and who had previously acted upon their urges over a three-year period by sexually offending against a child, including a year after the completion of the treatment, and compared them to a group of pedophilic individuals who had offended against a child as well, but received no treatment. Scales measuring offense supportive cognitions, emotional deficits, sexual self-regulation deficits, and child abusive behaviors were administered to pedophilic individuals before, during, and after the completion of BEDIT (Beier et al. 2015). A group of diagnosed pedophilic individuals that had offended by using child pornography, but not by sexually offending against a child, were also studied; their results will not be discussed here.

Beier et al. (2015) reported that treated pedophilic individuals showed a significant reduction in feelings of emotional loneliness, attitudes that support offending behavior, and preoccupations with sexual arousal, thoughts, and behaviors. Pedophilic individuals who had completed BEDIT also significantly increased their abilities to practice empathy toward victims, practice sexual self-regulation, and manage thoughts and behaviors. Interestingly, offenders with a "lifetime" history of pedophilic actions, both demonstrated by their criminal records and by their self-reported past actions, were observed to benefit most from the program (Beier et al. 2015).

Although 20% of treated individuals reported still having problems with sexual arousal or self-admitted committing some type of sexual behavior toward children after treatment, the severity of committed actions by these recidivists was shown to be reduced after treatment compared to their previous actions. The official recidivism rate for treated pedophilic individuals was 0% (Beier et al. 2015). Thus, the BEDIT methodology appears to decrease the risk factors and behaviors associated with offending in pedophilic individuals, as well as appearing to increase behavioral and sexual self-regulation and empathy toward victims that may additionally reduce offending. Further research is necessary into the BEDIT methodology to see if results can be replicated on a larger scale, but BEDIT represents an additional promising rehabilitative treatment option that could potentially combat offending.

Conclusion

In conclusion, societal concerns surrounding the protection of children from pedophilic sexual offending have led to the growth in the amount of neurobiological and other biological research into the development and manifestation of pedophilia and pedophilic behavior. Neuroimaging research on the disorder has reported frontal and temporal region abnormalities, as well as structural and functional deficits in subcortical structures, especially the amygdala, in pedophilic individuals. The literature has reported that observed deficits in these brain regions may contribute to problems with impulse control, behavioral regulation, impairments to sexual and emotional processing, evaluation, and decision-making, and disinhibition of sexual behaviors and compulsions that are characteristic of pedophilia. This existing research on neural abnormalities associated with the disorder has correspondingly led to studies seeking to target these neural deficits to help create better treatments to regulate and deter pedophilic behaviors.

This chapter examines ways in which neurobiological research on pedophilia may affect traditional legal perspectives on retribution and rehabilitation surrounding pedophilic sexual offending. Research on neural abnormalities associated with pedophilia could possibly further aggravate the extremely punitive and retributive sentiments that historically have been held toward pedophilic sex offenders as both very dangerous and untreatable, contributing to the heavily retributive sentences traditionally conferred upon pedophilic sex offenders. Yet, this research could also serve to potentially mitigate retributive sentiments toward pedophilic sex offenders. Depending on how open and receptive a court is to neuroscientific evidence, pedophilic sex offenders could be viewed as individuals with "broken brains" and therefore less morally blameworthy. Consequently, this could not only lead to the mitigation of retributive punishments, but it may influence judges' and juries' perceptions of the likelihood of rehabilitation and the appropriateness of treatments as a more effective means to prevent reoffending of pedophilic sex offenders.

Although research on treatments that target the regulation and deterrence of pedophilic sexual offending is still in its formative stages, the literature on rt-fMRI BCI neurofeedback, SSRI therapy to regulate pedophilia, and BEDIT reports that targeting neural abnormalities observed in pedophilic individuals has favorable effects on influencing and hindering pedophilic behaviors and ruminations. Although these noninvasive rehabilitative treatments are not yet ready to be used in the criminal justice system instead of or in addition to traditional punishments, they represent promising methods that could be used to regulate and treat, rather than solely punish, the behaviors of pedophilic sex offenders in the future.

Future neurobiological research on pedophilia may not only further inform and advance the potential therapies reviewed in this chapter, but also may help to develop other innovative treatment interventions or programs for pedophilic sex offenders that target affected brain areas observed in pedophilic individuals. For example, the use of transcranial direct current stimulation could be a potential option to normalize frontal lobe functioning in pedophilic individuals. This research could also be significant in the future formulation of strategies to preventatively regulate pedophilic urges before an individual sexually offends against a child. Research on these preventative strategies could save children from victimization and at the same time reduce the societal resources devoted to combating sexual offending. Ultimately, as current policies aimed at reducing pedophilic sexual offending are largely ineffective, understanding and treating pedophilia as a disorder with biological contributions and associated abnormalities will likely lead to superior insights into the true nature of pedophilic sexual offending and may also be able to provide the legal system with more effective tools to respond to and prevent pedophilic sexual offending in the future.

References

Aharoni, E., Funk, C., Sinnott-Armstrong, W. and Gazzaniga, M. (2008) "Can neurological evidence help courts assess criminal responsibility? Lessons from law and neuroscience," *Annals of the New York Academy of Sciences* 1124 145–160.

American Psychiatric Association (2013) *Diagnostic and Statistical manual of mental disorders: DSM-5 (5th edn.)*, Washington, DC: APA.

Ames, M.A. and Houston, D.A. (1990) "Legal, social, and biological definitions of pedophilia," *Archives of Sexual Behavior* 19 333–342.

Arnow, B.A., Desmond, J.E., Banner, L.L., Glover, G.H., Solomon, A., Polan, M.L., Lue, T.F. and Atlas, S.W. (2002) "Brain activation and sexual arousal in healthy, heterosexual males," *Brain* 125 1014–1023.

Arns, M., De Ridder, S., Strehl, U., Breteler, M. and Coenen, A. (2009) "Efficacy of neurofeedback treatment in ADHD: the effects on inattention, impulsivity and hyperactivity: a meta-analysis," *Clinical EEG and Neuroscience* 40 180–189.

Aspinwall, L.G., Brown, T.R. and Tabery, J. (2012). "The double-edged sword: Does biomechanism increase or decrease judges' sentencing of psychopaths?," *Science* 337 846–849.

Barth, A.S. (2007) "A double-edged sword: the role of neuroimaging in federal capital sentencing." *American Journal of Law & Medicine* 33 501–522.

Batts, S. (2009) "Brain lesions and their implications in criminal responsibility," Behavioral sciences & the law 27 261–272.

Beier, K.M., Grundmann, D., Kuhle, L.F., Scherner, G., Konrad, A. and Amelung, T. (2015) "The German Dunkelfeld Project: A pilot study to prevent child sexual abuse and the use of child abusive images," *The Journal of Sexual Medicine* 12 529–542.

Berryessa, C.M. (2014) "Potential implications of research on genetic or heritable contributions to pedophilia for the objectives of criminal law," *Recent Advances in DNA & Gene Sequences* 8 65–77.

Bradford, J.M. (2001) "The neurobiology, neuropharmacology, and pharmacological treatment of the paraphilias and compulsive sexual behaviour" *The Canadian Journal of Psychiatry* 46 26–34.

Bumby, K.M. and Maddox, M.C. (1999) "Judges' knowledge about sexual offenders, difficulties presiding over sexual offense cases, and opinions on sentencing, treatment, and legislation," Sexual Abuse 11 305–315.

Burns, J.M. and Swerdlow, R.H. (2003) "Right orbitofrontal tumor with pedophilia symptom and constructional apraxia sign," *Archives of Neurology* 60 437–440.

Cantor, J.M. and Blanchard, R. (2012) "White matter volumes in pedophiles, hebephiles, and teleiophiles," *Archives of Sexual Behavior* 41 749–752.

——, Kabani, N., Christensen, B.K., Zipursky, R.B., Barbaree, H.E., Dickey, R., Klassen, P.E., Mikulis, D.J., Kuban, M.E., Blak, T. and Richards, B.A. (2008) "Cerebral white matter deficiencies in pedophilic men," *Journal of Psychiatric Research* 42 167–183.

——, Lafaille, S.J., Hannah, J., Kucyi, A., Soh, D.W., Girard, T.A. and Mikulis, D.J. (2016) "Independent component analysis of resting-state functional magnetic resonance imaging in pedophiles," *The Journal of Sexual Medicine* 13 1546–1554.

——, Lafaille, S., Soh, D.W., Moayedi, M., Mikulis, D.J. and Girard, T.A. (2015) "Diffusion tensor imaging of pedophilia," *Archives of Sexual Behavior* 44 2161–2172.

Cazala, F., Fonteille, V., Moulier, V., Pélégrini-Issac, M., De Beaurepaire, C., Abondo, M., Bodon-Bruzel, M., Cano, J., Cochez, F., Fouli, T. and Thevenon, C. (2018) "Brain responses to pictures of children in men with pedophilic disorder: a functional magnetic resonance imaging study," *European Archives of Psychiatry and Clinical Neuroscience* 1–17.

Cisek, P. and Kalaska, J.F. (2004) "Neural correlates of mental rehearsal in dorsal premotor cortex" *Nature* 431 993–996.

Cohen, L.J., Nikiforov, K., Gans, S., Poznansky, O., McGeoch, P., Weaver, C., King, E.G., Cullen, K. and Galynker, I. (2002) "Heterosexual male perpetrators of childhood sexual abuse: a preliminary neuropsychiatric model" *Psychiatric Quarterly* 73 313–336.

Comings, D.E. (1994) "Role of genetic factors in human sexual behavior based on studies of Tourette syndrome and ADHD probands and their relatives," *American Journal of Medical Genetics* 54 227–241.

DeRubeis, R.J., Siegle, G.J. and Hollon, S.D. (2008) "Cognitive therapy versus medication for depression: treatment outcomes and neural mechanisms" *Nature Reviews Neuroscience* 9 788.

Dressing, H., Obergriesser, T., Tost, H., Kaumeier, S., Ruf, M. and Braus, D.F. (2001) "Homosexual pedophilia and functional networks-an fMRI case report and literature review" *Fortschritte der Neurologie-Psychiatrie* 69 539–544.

Eher, R., Aigner, M., Fruehwald, S., Frottier, P. and Gruenhut, C. (2000) "Social information processed self-perceived aggression in relation to brain abnormalities in a sample of incarcerated sexual offenders" *Journal of Psychology & Human Sexuality* 11 37–47.

Foa, E.B. (2010) "Cognitive behavioral therapy of obsessive-compulsive disorder," *Dialogues Clin Neurosci* 12 199–207.

Frazer, A. (1997) "Pharmacology of antidepressants," *Journal of Clinical Psychopharmacology* 172 S-18S.

Garland, B. and Frankel, M.S. (2006) "Considering convergence: a policy dialogue about behavioral genetics, neuroscience, and law," *Law and Contemporary Problems* 69 101–113.

Gilbert, F. and Focquaert, F. (2015) "Rethinking responsibility in offenders with acquired paedophilia: Punishment or treatment?" *International Journal of law and Psychiatry* 38 51–60.

Gilbert, F. and Outram, S. (2009) "Chemical interventions and ethical side effects," *Canadian Chemical News* September 20–21.

Goodenough, O.R. and Tucker, M. (2010) "Law and Cognitive Neuroscience," *Annual Review of Law and Social Science* 6 61–92.

Graber, B., Hartmann, K., Coffman, J.A., Huey, C.J. and Golden, C.J. (1982) "Brain damage among mentally disordered sex offenders," *Journal of Forensic Science* 27 125–134.

Greely, H.T. (2007) "Neuroscience and criminal justice: Not responsibility but treatment," *U. Kan. L. Rev.* 56 1103–1159.

Habermeyer, B., Esposito, F., Händel, N., Lemoine, P., Klarhöfer, M., Mager, R., Dittmann, V., Seifritz, E. and Graf, M. (2013a) "Immediate processing of erotic stimuli in paedophilia and controls: a case control study," *Bmc Psychiatry* 13 88.

——, Esposito, F., Händel, N., Lemoine, P., Kuhl, H.C., Klarhöfer, M., Mager, R., Mokros, A., Dittmann, V., Seifritz, E. and Graf, M. (2013b) "Response inhibition in pedophilia: An fMRI pilot study," *Neuropsychobiology* 68 228–237.

Habermeyer, B., Händel, N., Lemoine, P., Klarhöfer, M., Seifritz, E., Dittmann, V. and Graf, M. (2012) "LH-RH agonists modulate amygdala response to visual sexual stimulation: A single case fMRI study in pedophilia," *Neurocase* 18 489–495.

Hall, R.C. and Hall, R.C. (2007) "A profile of pedophilia: definition, characteristics of offenders, recidivism, treatment outcomes, and forensic issues," *Mayo Clinic Proceedings* 82 457–471.

Hammond, D. C. (2004) "Treatment of the obsessional subtype of obsessive–compulsive disorder with neurofeedback," *Biofeedback* 32 9–12.

Hendricks, S.E., Fitzpatrick, D.F., Hartmann, K., Quaife, M.A., Stratbucker, R.A. and Graber, B. (1988), "Brain structure and function in sexual molesters of children and adolescents," *The Journal of Clinical Psychiatry* 49 108–112.

Hicks, P.K. (1993) "Castration of sexual offenders. Legal and ethical issues," *Journal of Legal Medicine* 14 641–667.

Hucker, S., Langevin, R., Wortzman, G., Bain, J., Handy, L., Chambers, J. and Wright, S. (1986) "Neuropsychological impairment in pedophiles," *Canadian Journal of Behavioural Science* 18 440–448.

Ivković, S.K. and Hans, V.P. (2003) "Jurors' evaluations of expert testimony: Judging the messenger and the message," *Law & Social Inquiry* 28 441–482.

Johnston v. Love, 940 F. Supp. 738 (Pennsylvania Eastern District Court, July 22, 1996).

Johnston, S.J., Boehm, S.G., Healy, D., Goebel, R. and Linden, D.E. (2010) "Neurofeedback: A promising tool for the self-regulation of emotion networks," *Neuroimage* 49 1066–1072.

Jones, O.D. and Shen, F.X. (2012) "Law and Neuroscience in the United States," In International Neurolaw, Heidelberg: Springer.

——, Wagner, A.D., Faigman, D.L. and Raichle, M.E. (2013) "Neuroscientists in court," *Nature Reviews Neuroscience* 14 730–736.

Kafka, M.P. (1994) "Sertraline pharmacotherapy for paraphilias and paraphilia-related disorders: an open trial," *Annals of Clinical Psychiatry* 6 189–195.

—— and Hennen, J. (2000) "Psychostimulant augmentation during treatment with selective serotonin reuptake inhibitors in men with paraphilias and paraphilia-related disorders: a case series," *The Journal of Clinical Psychiatry* 61 664–670.

Karlsson, H. (2011) "How psychotherapy changes the brain," *Psychiatric Times* 28 21–23.

Kärgel, C., Massau, C., Weiß, S., Walter, M., Kruger, T.H. and Schiffer, B. (2015) "Diminished functional connectivity on the road to child sexual abuse in pedophilia," *The Journal of Sexual Medicine* 12 783–795.

Lave, T.R. (2011) "Inevitable recidivism—The origin and centrality of an urban legend," *International Journal of Law and Psychiatry* 34 186–194.

Lett, T.A., Mohnke, S., Amelung, T., Brandl, E.J., Schiltz, K., Pohl, A., Gerwinn, H., Kärgel, C., Massau, C., Tenbergen, G. and Wittfoth, M. (2018) "Multimodal neuroimaging measures and intelligence influence pedophile child sexual offense behavior," *European Neuropsychopharmacology* 28 818–827.

Lynch, M. (2002) "Pedophiles and cyber-predators as contaminating forces: The language of disgust, pollution, and boundary invasions in federal debates on sex offender legislation," *Law & Social Inquiry* 27 529–557.

Maletzky, B.M. and Steinhauser, C. (2002) "A 25-year follow-up of cognitive/behavioral therapy with 7,275 sexual offenders," *Behavior Modification* 26 123–147.

Mendez, M. and Shapira, J.S. (2011) "Pedophilic behavior from brain disease," *The Journal of sexual medicine* 1092–1100.

Mohnke, S., Mueller, S., Amelung, T., Krüger, T.H., Ponseti, J., Schiffer, B., Walter, M., Beier, K.M. and Walter, H. (2014) "Brain alterations in paedophilia: a critical review," *Progress in Neurobiology* 122 1–23.

Monterosso, J., Royzman, E.B. and Schwartz, B. (2005) "Explaining away responsibility: Effects of scientific explanation on perceived culpability," *Ethics & Behavior* 15 139–158.

Moriarty, J.C. (2008) "Flickering admissibility: neuroimaging evidence in the US courts," Behavioral Sciences & the Law 26 29–49.

Moulier, V., Fonteille, V., Pélégrini-Issac, M., Cordier, B., Baron-Laforêt, S., Boriasse, E., Durand, E. and Stoléru, S. (2012) "A pilot study of the effects of gonadotropin-releasing hormone agonist therapy on brain activation pattern in a man with pedophilia," *International Journal of Offender Therapy and Comparative Criminology* 56 50–60.

Nhan, J., Polzer, K. and Ferguson, J. (2012) "More dangerous than hitmen": Judicial perceptions of sexual offenders," *International Journal of Criminology and Sociological Theory* 5.

Poeppl, T.B., Eickhoff, S.B., Fox, P.T., Laird, A.R., Rupprecht, R., Langguth, B. and Bzdok, D. (2015) "Connectivity and functional profiling of abnormal brain structures in pedophilia," *Human Brain Mapping* 36 2374–2386.

——, Nitschke, J., Dombert, B., Santtila, P., Greenlee, M.W., Osterheider, M. and Mokros, A. (2011) "Functional cortical and subcortical abnormalities in pedophilia: a combined study using a choice reaction time task and fMRI," *The Journal of Sexual Medicine* 8 1660–1674.

——, Nitschke, J., Santtila, P., Schecklmann, M., Langguth, B., Greenlee, M.W., Osterheider, M. and Mokros, A. (2013) "Association between brain structure and phenotypic characteristics in pedophilia," *Journal of Psychiatric Research* 47 678–685.

Ponseti, J., Granert, O., Jansen, O., Wolff, S., Beier, K., Neutze, J., Deuschl, G., Mehdorn, H., Siebner, H. and Bosinski, H. (2012) "Assessment of pedophilia using hemodynamic brain response to sexual stimuli," *Archives of General Psychiatry* 69 187–194.

Presidential Commission for the Study of Bioethical Issues (2015) *Gray matters: Integrative Approaches at the Intersection of Neuroscience, Ethics, and Society* (Vol. 2), Washington, DC: Presidential Commission for the Study of Bioethical Issues.

Quinn, J.F., Forsyth, C.J. and Mullen-Quinn, C. (2004), "Societal reaction to sex offenders: A review of the origins and results of the myths surrounding their crimes and treatment amenability," *Deviant Behavior* 25 215–232.

Redouté, J., Stoléru, S., Grégoire, M.C., Costes, N., Cinotti, L., Lavenne, F., Le Bars, D., Forest, M.G. and Pujol, J.F. (2000) "Brain processing of visual sexual stimuli in human males," *Human Brain Mapping* 11 162–177.

Renaud, P., Joyal, C., Stoleru, S., Goyette, M., Weiskopf, N. and Birbaumer, N. (2011) "Real-time functional magnetic imaging—brain–computer interface and virtual reality: promising tools for the treatment of pedophilia," In *Progress in Brain Research.*

Sartorius, A., Ruf, M., Kief, C., Demirakca, T., Bailer, J., Ende, G., Henn, F.A., Meyer-Lindenberg, A. and Dressing, H. (2008) "Abnormal amygdala activation profile in pedophilia," *European Archives of Psychiatry and Clinical Neuroscience* 258 271–277.

Schiffer, B., Amelung, T., Pohl, A., Kaergel, C., Tenbergen, G., Gerwinn, H., Mohnke, S., Massau, C., Matthias, W., Weiß, S. and Marr, V. (2017) "Gray matter anomalies in pedophiles with and without a history of child sexual offending," *Translational psychiatry* 7 e1129.

——, Gizewski, E. and Kruger, T. (2009) "Reduced neuronal responsiveness to visual sexual stimuli in a pedophile treated with a long-acting LH-RH agonist," *The Journal of Sexual Medicine* 6 892–894.

——, Krueger, T., Paul, T., de Greiff, A., Forsting, M., Leygraf, N., Schedlowski, M. and Gizewski, E. (2008a) "Brain response to visual sexual stimuli in homosexual pedophiles," *Journal of Psychiatry & Neuroscience* 33 (1) 23–33.

——, Paul, T., Gizewski, E., Forsting, M., Leygraf, N., Schedlowski, M. and Kruger, T.H. (2008b) "Functional brain correlates of heterosexual paedophilia," *Neuroimage* 41 80–91.

——, Peschel, T., Paul, T., Gizewski, E., Forsting, M., Leygraf, N., Schedlowski, M. and Krueger, T.H. (2007) "Structural brain abnormalities in the frontostriatal system and cerebellum in pedophilia," *Journal of Psychiatric Research* 41 753–762.

Schiltz, K., Witzel, J., Northoff, G., Zierhut, K., Gubka, U., Fellmann, H., Kaufmann, J., Tempelmann, C., Wiebking, C. and Bogerts, B. (2007) "Brain pathology in pedophilic offenders: evidence of volume reduction in the right amygdala and related diencephalic structures," *Archives of General Psychiatry* 64 737–746.

Seto, M.C. (2008) *Pedophilia and Sexual Offending Against Children: Theory, Assessment, and Intervention*, Washington, DC: American Psychological Association.

——(2009) "Pedophilia," *Annual Review of Clinical Psychology* 5 391–407.

—— (2012) "Is pedophilia a sexual orientation?," *Archives of Sexual Behavior* 41 231–236.

——, Cantor, J.M. and Blanchard, R. (2006) "Child pornography offenses are a valid diagnostic indicator of pedophilia," *Journal of Abnormal Psychology* 115 610–615

Simon, J. (1998) "Managing the monstrous: Sex offenders and the new penology," *Psychology, Public Policy, and Law* 4 452.

Smith, N. (2005) "Punishment," In P. Gerstenfeld (Ed.), *Criminal Justice Encyclopedia,* Pasadena, CA: Salem Press.

Stein, D.J. (2000) "Neurobiology of the obsessive–compulsive spectrum disorders," *Biological Psychiatry* 47 296–304.

Stein, D.J., Hollander, E., Anthony, D.T., Schneier, F.R., Fallon, B.A., Liebowitz, M.R. and Klein, D.F. (1992), "Serotonergic medications for sexual obsessions, sexual addictions, and paraphilias," *The Journal of Clinical Psychiatry.*

Tenbergen, G., Wittfoth, M., Frieling, H., Ponseti, J., Walter, M., Walter, H., Beier, K.M., Schiffer, B. and Kruger, T.H. (2015) "The neurobiology and psychology of pedophilia: recent advances and challenges," *Frontiers in Human Neuroscience* 9 1–20.

Tewksbury, R. and Lees, M.B. (2007) "Perceptions of punishment: How registered sex offenders view registries," *Crime & Delinquency* 53 380–407.

Tost, H., Vollmert, C., Brassen, S., Schmitt, A., Dressing, H. and Braus, D.F. (2004) "Pedophilia: neuropsychological evidence encouraging a brain network perspective," *Medical Hypotheses* 63 528–531.

Van Gijseghem, H. (2011) Proceedings of standing committee on justice and human rights on bill c-54, an act to amend the criminal code (sexual offences against children), *Ottawa, Ontario, Canada.* Retrieved from www.parl.gc.ca/HousePublications/ Publication.aspx?Language=E&Mode=1&DocId=4959361&File=0

Walter, M., Witzel, J., Wiebking, C., Gubka, U., Rotte, M., Schiltz, K., Bermpohl, F., Tempelmann, C., Bogerts, B., Heinze, H.J. and Northoff, G. (2007) "Pedophilia is linked to reduced activation in hypothalamus and lateral prefrontal cortex during visual erotic stimulation," *Biological Psychiatry* 62 698–701.

Thibaut, F., Bradford, J.M., Briken, P., De La Barra, F., Haessler, F., Cosyns, P. and WFSBP Task Force on Sexual Disorders (2016) "The World Federation of Societies of Biological Psychiatry (WFSBP) guidelines for the treatment of adolescent sexual offenders with paraphilic disorders," *World Journal of Biological Psychiatry* 17 (1) 2–38.

Williams, J.M. and Currie, C. (2000) "Self-esteem and physical development in early adolescence: Pubertal timing and body image," *The Journal of Early Adolescence* 20 129–149.

Wright, P., Nobrega, J., Langevin, R. and Wortzman, G. (1990) "Brain density and symmetry in pedophilic and sexually aggressive offenders," *Annals of Sex Research* 3 319–328.

Further Reading

Berryessa, C.M. (2014) "Potential implications of research on genetic or heritable contributions to pedophilia for the objectives of criminal law," *Recent Advances in DNA & Gene Sequences* 8 65–77. (A discussion of how genetic research may affect perceptions on the objectives of punishment.)

Hall, R.C. and Hall, R.C. (2007) "A profile of pedophilia: definition, characteristics of offenders, recidivism, treatment outcomes, and forensic issues," *Mayo Clinic Proceedings* 82 457–471. (A thorough review of pedophilia as a clinical disorder.)

Mohnke, S., Mueller, S., Amelung, T., Krüger, T.H., Ponseti, J., Schiffer, B., Walter, M., Beier, K.M. and Walter, H. (2014) "Brain alterations in paedophilia: a critical review," *Progress in Neurobiology* 12 21–23. (A thorough review of neurobiological research on pedophilia.)

Tenbergen, G., Wittfoth, M., Frieling, H., Ponseti, J., Walter, M., Walter, H., Beier, K.M., Schiffer, B. and Kruger, T.H. (2015) "The neurobiology and psychology of pedophilia: recent advances and challenges," *Frontiers in Human Neuroscience* 91–20. (A thorough review of neurobiological research on pedophilia.)

Quinn, J.F., Forsyth, C.J. and Mullen-Quinn, C. (2004) "Societal reaction to sex offenders: A review of the origins and results of the myths surrounding their crimes and treatment amenability," *Deviant Behavior* 25 215–232. (A discussion about societal reactions to and perceptions of sex offenders.)

20
CURRENT TRENDS IN COGNITIVE NEUROSCIENCE AND CRIMINAL PUNISHMENT

Corey H. Allen and Eyal Aharoni[1]

Introduction

Recently, while attending a seminar on neuroscience, philosophy, and the law, one of us received an unexpected phone call: a childhood friend had shot and killed his own parents in their sleep before turning the gun on himself. When tragic events like this occur, a barrage of questions rapidly comes to mind: Was he a victim of abuse? Was he suffering from mental illness? Had he been showing signs of distress? Was he under the influence? Did he keep a diary? What the hell was he *thinking*? In such situations, we consistently ruminate on roughly the same short list of questions, as if to apprehend the contents of the perpetrator's mental state – a desperate instinct, perhaps, to form an attitude about his internal moral culpability.

The criminal law works in much the same way, but with far-reaching consequences. Beneath a complex lattice of policies and procedures is a system attempting to deliver punishment to all those – and only those – who deserve it. And to make that determination satisfactorily, the system tasks itself to somehow assess and build a representation of the defendant's mental environment. In this way, criminal law is fundamentally psychological.

To inform the question of the defendant's mental states, trial courts have traditionally relied on subjective and qualitative judgments. Today, lawyers are increasingly querying evidence from the brain sciences (Farahany 2015). Since the mind, after all, is a product of the brain, it is reasonable to ask whether the brain contains clues about the offender's mental health, mental capacities, and perhaps even his past intentions or future risk of reoffending. But to date, judicial opinions have not always been favorable to neuroscience evidence, which has often failed to demonstrate a legally compelling link between brain, mind, and crime (Farahany 2015). According to its critics, the physicalist perspective taken by neuroscience is unlikely to tell us anything that couldn't already be discerned using a traditional, folk psychological observation of the offender's behavior (Morse 2016).

The legal and ethical standards for evaluating neuroscientific evidence and why this evidence has often fallen short have been examined elsewhere (Brown & Murphy 2010; Buckholtz & Faigman 2014; Glannon 2011 Pardo & Patterson 2010). Much of this scholarship has focused on questions bearing on the defendant's mental health in the guilt phase of a trial, such as evaluations of legal insanity and competency to stand trial (Aharoni et al. 2008; Edersheim, Brendel & Price 2012; Meixner 2016). Less attention has been paid to questions arising at the sentencing phase, such as questions of the defendant's dangerousness. Even less attention has been paid to insights to be gleaned, not just from the defendant's brain, but from those of other players in criminal procedures, such as jurors and judges who evaluate facts and make punishment recommendations or rulings. Yet, as the brain sciences mature, it is important to anticipate the potential uses and misuses of the neuroscience evidence for such purposes.

The relevance of the brain sciences to punishment decisions can be examined from various perspectives including scientific, ethical, and legal ones. The ethical perspective asks questions like: when, if ever, is it justified to use information about a defendant's brain in sentencing decisions? What constitutes a responsible use of neurotechnology in the court? The legal perspective raises questions about whether neurobiological evidence meets standards of evidence and admissibility, and whether we need to change these standards in light of this advancing technology. The scientific perspective includes questions like: can an understanding of the *defendant's* brain function inform questions of his dangerousness? Can sentencing decisions in any way be informed by the *punisher's* brain? And when making judgments about a defendant's responsibility, what role is played by *lay* perceptions of brain evidence? Since the ethical and legal questions surrounding brain evidence in the court depend heavily on the state of the science, the focus of this chapter will be the scientific questions.

In this chapter, we review current research trends in neuroscience research bearing on defendant dangerousness as well as how punishment judgments are made. We consider their methodological strengths and limitations, and we touch upon several ways in which these research developments may, and in some cases, may not, be relevant to criminal sentencing decisions. We conclude that while the results of current neuroscience research and application are still very inferentially limited, their potential is growing rapidly, and so efforts aiming to characterize the neural mechanisms underlying antisocial actions and punitive judgments should be taken seriously as potentially relevant contributors to our understanding of human behavior, both virtuous and vicious. Ultimately, a deeper understanding of the relationship between mind, brain, and behavior will be essential for the development of legal procedures that effectively balance the public's safety against defendants' civil liberties.

Can an Understanding of the Defendant's Brain Function Inform Questions of Future Dangerousness?

Is there any structure or operation of the brain whose measurement can reveal something useful about the probability that a criminal defendant will cause harm in the future? An answer to this question could be useful not just for traditional sentencing decisions but also for indictment, plea bargaining, diversion, and rehabilitation decisions. Unfortunately, the question is fundamentally flawed. It's flawed because dangerousness is a broad, normative attribution that people make based on a complex relationship between a variety of different causal factors, many of which operate in social environments outside the mind, few if any of which are necessary or sufficient for evoking the dangerous outcome. In short, there is no "danger" part of the brain (Specker et al. 2018).

To break down this question into more useful components, at minimum, it would be necessary to operationally define some specific types of dangerousness, for instance, the probability that a domestic abuser will commit a new act of domestic violence within some specific period of time, holding constant various situational/contextual factors. But a narrow definition of dangerousness is not enough. It is also prudent to have a theory about which known properties of human cognition are likely to place that abuser at elevated risk of a new offense. Alas, the field of cognitive neuroscience does not have a comprehensive theory of all the cognitive mechanisms likely to play a role in every type of reoffense. Nonetheless, we can look to the existing literature to see how scholars have approached the question, and then consider some of their strengths and limitations. We can group their approaches into several methodological categories: correlation, quasi-experimentation, retrodiction, prediction, and stimulation approaches. We discuss examples of each approach and how it might contribute to discourse on dangerousness.

Neuroimaging Approaches to Questions of Dangerousness: Correlational Methods

Correlational methods are widely used for getting a lay of the neurological land. In a typical correlational approach, neurotechnologies such as magnetic resonance imaging (MRI) and electroencephalography (EEG) serve as passive recording devices that help scientists measure associations between brain states and behaviors. Importantly, these technologies do not actively manipulate those brain states, so they cannot independently demonstrate that such states cause a particular behavior. Even so, when collected during an experimental task, such techniques are valuable for the development of hypotheses about neural mechanisms of a particular behavior, in large part, because they help to reduce the number of candidate causal factors to a manageable list.

Many of the correlational neuroimaging studies to date have focused on populations with elevated risk such as incarcerated offenders and those with psychopathic personality traits. The psychopathic personality is a research classification that includes a cluster of traits, such as impulsivity, manipulativeness, and lack of empathy, which together predict antisocial outcomes such as reoffending (Tengström et al. 2000). Forensic and psychopathic populations can be particularly informative for the study of the brain's contribution to dangerous behavior.

In one study, researchers examined the neural circuitry underlying reward-related decision making in a sample of 49 incarcerated offenders who varied in psychopathic personality traits (Hosking et al. 2017). In theory, some criminal offenses (i.e., impulse crimes) could result from a tendency to overvalue immediate rewards relative to delayed rewards, without regard for future consequences (e.g., the probability of arrest). The researchers found that when making such valuation trade-offs, participants higher in psychopathic personality traits exhibited greater activity in the nucleus accumbens (NAcc), an area known to underlie the processing of reward. The NAcc in these participants also showed less functional connectivity to the ventromedial prefrontal cortex (vmPFC), a region involved in regulation of the NAcc, representation of delayed value outcomes, and moral decision making (Economides et al. 2015; Raine & Yang 2006). Interestingly, NAcc-vmPFC functional connectivity was negatively correlated with criminal convictions. These findings suggest that dysregulation of the neural circuitry underlying cost/benefit valuation may play an important role in the proclivity to favor short-term over long-term rewards, which in turn may contribute to impulsive and perhaps, criminal decision making.

Another potential contributor to criminal behavior is the failure to recognize moral concepts or violations. In one test of this theory, Fede and colleagues (2016) employed functional MRI to examine the neural activity underlying the classification of words or phrases with moral content related to being wrong (e.g., murder, lying, stealing), not wrong (e.g., charity, kindness, saving lives), or ambiguous (e.g., animal testing, gun, control, prostitution) in nearly 250 criminal offenders who varied in psychopathic personality traits. Individuals high in psychopathy (incorrectly) rated a larger portion of the moral stimuli as being "not wrong". Furthermore, during presentation of morally "wrong" stimuli, these higher psychopathy individuals showed less activity than their low-psychopathy counterparts in the anterior cingulate cortex (ACC), a region found to be involved in the detection of norm-violations (Güroğlu et al. 2010). While processing morally ambiguous stimuli, those high in psychopathy also showed less activity than those low in psychopathy in the temporal-parietal junction (TPJ), a region previously implicated in the processing of ambiguous moral stimuli in healthy populations (Schaich Borg et al. 2011), and the dorsolateral prefrontal cortex (dlPFC), a region engaged when exerting cognitive control over emotions (Tassy et al. 2009).

Some evidence suggests that brain differences associated with psychopathy may even be observable at the structural level. Using a structural, correlational technique known as voxel-based morphometry, one study examined gray matter differences in nearly 300 incarcerated men (Ermer et al. 2012). The researchers reported that participants higher in psychopathy exhibited decreased gray matter in limbic, paralimbic, and orbitofrontal areas. These differences accounted for 20% of the variance in psychopathy scores and converge with previous research (e.g., Kiehl 2006, Kiehl et al. 2001; Walton, Devlin & Rushworth 2004).

Studies of neurobiological differences among former offenders have revealed distinct patterns underlying the processing of reward and moral norms. And these findings cohere with existing models about the cognitive functions typically associated with these networks. As noted, however, because of their correlational design, they cannot, by themselves, demonstrate that the observed brain abnormalities cause people to behave in risky ways. Instead, these effects could represent indicators of some other causal process or could even be an effect of the high-risk behavior itself. In the next subsections, we review studies that attempt to draw causal links between brain function and potentially dangerous behavior.

Neuroimaging Approaches to Questions of Dangerousness: Quasi-Experimental and Retrodictive methods

One method of uncovering causal links between brain and behavior is quasi-experimental design. Quasi-experimental designs permit researchers to rely on pre-defined groups when experimental manipulation is not feasible, such as the examination of the adverse consequences of pre-existing brain lesions.

Schofield and colleagues (2015) used this method to determine whether there was an association between criminal convictions and pre-existing brain lesions. The researchers retrospectively analyzed criminal and medical records spanning over 30 years on nearly 8,000 individuals with brain lesions, and compared these records to sibling and general population matched control data. The investigators reported that the presence of a brain lesion was associated with increased conviction rates (for any crime as well as violent crimes specifically) in both men and women relative to the general population, and that these relationships largely held even when limiting the analysis to those with sibling controls ($n \approx 2{,}400$). The researchers interpreted these findings as evidence that brain lesions (of any sort) may increase behavioral dysregulation, aggression, or impulsivity, which may, in turn, increase the risk of criminal offending. One known limitation of quasi-experimental methods is that the pre-defined groups may vary in a variety of unknown ways, and Schofield and colleagues acknowledged this inability to rule out the influence of a third variable: a particular phenotype, perhaps, that could place some individuals at risk of both criminality and impulsive, aggressive behavior.

Another method of uncovering causal links between brain and behavior is retrospective prediction, or "retrodiction". Retrodiction refers to the retrospective assessment of a pre-existing explanatory factor given a known outcome. In a similar fashion, Darby and colleagues (2018) evaluated brain scans of convicted offenders with pre-existing lesions in order to understand how these lesions might precipitate changes in the functional connectivity (an analysis known as lesion network mapping) between regions commonly engaged in moral decision-making tasks. The researchers reported two main findings: First, lesions that were temporally associated with criminal activity were confined to a single brain network (consisting primarily of the inferior orbitofrontal cortex, anterior temporal lobes, vmPFC, NAcc, intraparietal sulcus, and dlPFC), which was distinct and separate from networks affected by lesions that were not temporally connected to criminal activity. Second, the locations of these lesions were functionally connected to areas engaged in moral decision making, value-based decision making, and theory of mind tasks, domains that are potentially relevant to decisions to commit a crime. These results raise the possibility that this unique pattern of brain connectivity can help to explain why some individuals with lesions are likely to commit crimes whereas others are not, while at the same time potentially demarcating candidate causal factors shaping criminal activity.

These studies suggest potential candidates for causal mechanisms in the development of antisocial behavior. However, we caution against over-interpretation because quasi-experimental and retrodictive methods carry risks of misattributing the source or overestimating the strength of their effects, largely due to an inability to remove and control for confounding variables during the sampling process. One way to reduce these risks is using prospective methods.

Neuroimaging Approaches to Questions of Dangerousness: Prospective Prediction

Prospective prediction is achieved by tracking changes in the outcome variable over time and employing an a priori hypothesis to test whether information at Time 1 predicts outcomes at Time 2. It asks: of a sample of people with a varying attribute, what proportion will later exhibit a particular outcome? Evidence of a time-dependent relationship between a potentially explanatory factor and outcome increase confidence that the relationship is a causal one. Prospective prediction has been validated in the context of violence risk assessment using structured, actuarial instruments that measure a variety of person-level characteristics, including behavioral ones (e.g., Monahan 2008; Nicholls, Ogloff & Douglas 2004). These instruments rely on normative samples – large groups of former offenders that have been observed over time – to serve as a basis to estimate a new individual's prospects by comparing the two along predefined dimensions. The accuracy with which these classification tools predict individual violent reoffending has been shown to significantly exceed that of traditional unstructured risk assessment methods (Grove & Meehl 1996; Monahan 1981).

The notion that structured risk assessment could be further improved by functional brain metrics seems ambitious. But a growing line of research in "neuroprediction" lends credence to this possibility. Indeed, there are strong empirical reasons to expect the existence of substantial causal links between brain function and violent behavior (see Liu 2011). For example, prospective studies have demonstrated that early lead exposure can increase risk of violence by affecting critical brain networks. In one longitudinal study, Wright and colleagues (2008) measured blood lead levels in pregnant women and their children throughout the first six years of life. Years later, the investigators tracked the children's violent behavior using criminal arrest records and found a predictive relationship between early lead concentrations and arrests for violent crimes, even after controlling for other contributing factors. In a separate longitudinal study, investigators found a significant association between early childhood lead exposure and brain volume (Cecil et al. 2008), specifically gray matter loss in the ACC, a region formerly associated with the ability to control aggressive impulses (Devinsky, Morrell & Vogt 1995). The evidence for the damaging effects of lead exposure is strong enough that it has been used to argue that it should qualify as a potentially mitigating factor in criminal sentencing decisions (Kittilstad 2018).

In another longitudinal study, Pardini and colleagues administered a battery of psychological assessments to young boys, and then assessed their brain volumes, violence and delinquency approximately 20 and 23 years later (Pardini et al. 2014). Using this design, the researchers were able to correlate brain volume with violence and aggression both retrospectively and prospectively. Retrospectively, they found that lower amygdala volumes were associated with more aggression and psychopathic tendencies in childhood and early adulthood. Prospectively, lower amygdala volumes were associated with increased risk for aggression, violence, and psychopathic traits. Their findings are consistent with previous research (Bobes et al. 2013), including evidence that the amygdala plays a crucial role in emotional processing and the development of antisocial traits (Phelps & LeDoux 2005).

A growing number of prospective prediction studies have demonstrated the utility of neurocognitive models in the prediction of antisocial outcomes including substance abuse relapse (Janes et al. 2010; Paulus, Tapert & Schuckit 2005), treatment completion (Fink et al. 2016; Steele et al. 2014; Steele et al. 2018), and rearrest (Aharoni et al. 2013; Aharoni et al. 2014; Delfin et al. 2019; Kiehl 2018; Steele et al. 2015). Importantly, evidence of prospective statistical relationships between brain and behavior do not necessarily imply that the relationship is strong enough to be used as biomarkers for diagnostic uses in individual cases. High diagnostic specificity would be useful for the provision of tailored treatment to individuals at risk, and arguably for legal decisions such as involuntary civil commitment, but it requires that these models achieve classification accuracy levels determined by some pre-existing normative standard. In legal contexts, this standard is often likely to be prohibitively high given the highly multivariate nature of criminal behavior. At least one group of prospective neuroimaging studies, however, has evaluated the classification accuracy of a neurocognitive model in predicting antisocial outcomes. In a sample of 96 offenders, the investigators found that activity within the ACC prospectively predicted rearrest up to three years following release. Furthermore, this neurocognitive model correctly classified rearrest at levels that rival validated actuarial risk tools (Aharoni et al. 2013; Aharoni et al. 2014; Steele et al. 2015).

Although these results provide a proof of concept about the potential of neuroprediction models, much work remains to be done to demonstrate whether such effects are reliable and specific enough for legal and treatment applications. For example, as others have noted (e.g., Poldrack et al. 2018), the gold standard for estimating the predictive utility of a model is to test it on a second, independent sample – a technique known as out-of-sample validation. Prospective imaging studies have only recently risen to this challenge. For instance, a recent study by Kiehl and colleagues (2018) successfully used a structural model of brain age to predict rearrest in an independent sample. Their model implicated many of the same regions reported in previous studies, including the ACC and amygdala.

The growing body of research on neuroprediction suggests that the function and structure of the brain plays an instrumental role in the expression of many harmful behaviors. So, while predictive modeling is unlikely to become accurate enough for use in criminal sanctioning decisions, efforts to prospectively predict risk outcomes in lower stakes domains, such as the provision of treatment resources to those most likely to benefit from it, may be scientifically meaningful and empirically tractable (see also Faigman et al. 2013; Heilbrun 2009).

Neuroimaging Approaches to Questions of Dangerousness: Brain Stimulation

Another promising method of building causal, potentially predictive, models of antisocial behavior is the use of brain stimulation. Depending on the stimulation technique used, researchers can increase or decrease the excitability of areas in the brain, through the targeted application of positively or negatively charged ions. This approach has been used to elucidate neural contributors to antisocial behavior as well as ways to regulate such behavior.

For example, Gilam and colleagues (2018) employed concurrent transcranial direct current stimulation (tDCS) and fMRI to test whether facilitation of vmPFC activity aids in anger regulation – as measured by the acceptance of unfair offers in an economic game – and aggressive behavior in subsequent reactive aggression tasks. As expected, active stimulation to the vmPFC during the economic task led to a larger acceptance rate of unfair offers and a decrease in self-reported anger following the task, yet there were no differences between active and sham stimulation in reactive aggression. Similarly, there was increased vmPFC activity during the processing of unfair offers for those undergoing active stimulation. These results obtained by combining correlational and causational methodologies suggest a causal role for vmPFC functionality in the expression and regulation of anger.

Similarly, Choy and colleagues (2018) utilized tDCS to test whether a brain area known as the dlPFC plays a causal role in the ability to inhibit aggressive behavior (Anderson et al. 1999). After receiving active or sham stimulation, the participants (members of the general public) read hypothetical vignettes involving a physical and sexual assault and rated how likely they were to behave as the criminal protagonist in the scenario had behaved and how morally wrong that behavior was. A secondary task was also administered to measure implicit aggression behaviorally. On a computer workstation, participants were given an opportunity to stick virtual needles into an image of a doll that represented someone for whom the participant harbored ill will (as validated by Dewall et al. 2013). Consistent with their hypotheses, the researchers found that the active stimulation group reported significantly lower likelihood of committing physical and sexual assault compared to the mock stimulation group, and found sexual assault to be more morally wrong than the mock stimulation group,

However, stimulation of the dlPFC did not change the rate of aggression as measured in the behavioral task. These findings support the hypothesis that the dlPFC functions to modulate wrongfulness judgments and the self-reported likelihood of committing such acts, though is not necessarily sufficient to control aggressive behavior.

A study by Dambacher and colleagues (2015) provides converging evidence for the dlPFC as an inhibitor of aggression. After receiving either active or sham tDCS stimulation, 32 male and female participants completed questionnaires and behavioral tasks designed to assess transient states of reactive and proactive aggression. The researchers found that active stimulation of the dlPFC selectively decreased proactive aggression in men, but had no effect on reactive aggression. These results suggest a potential gender difference in receptivity to clinical interventions and also suggest a neural dissociation between different types of aggression.

In another stimulation study (Riva et al. 2015), researchers sought to test the function of the right ventrolateral prefrontal cortex (rvlPFC), a region believed to be involved in the regulation of aggressive impulses (Aron & Poldrack 2005). In their experiment, 79 participants played a violent or non-violent video game while receiving active or sham stimulation over the rvlPFC. They then completed a task designed to assess both provoked and unprovoked aggression. The task pits participants against each other in a competitive reaction-time game, one that they are able to deliver provoked and unprovoked aversive noises to the opponent. For participants receiving sham stimulation, the experimenters found that unprovoked aggression was higher in those assigned to play violent (as opposed to nonviolent) games, as might be expected. Importantly, active stimulation reduced unprovoked aggression such that there were no group differences according to game type. These results suggest an important role for the rvlPFC in mediating psychologically aggravated levels of unprovoked aggression.

One common characteristic of these studies is the tendency to sample from the general public, whose base rate of dangerous, criminal behavior is fairly low. This limits the ability to generalize to those with elevated risk of criminal behavior. A further limitation is the ecological validity of laboratory aggression measures. Since experimental manipulation of criminal risk is ethically problematic, this increases experimenters' reliance on more distal proxies for real-world aggression. This heavy reliance on distal proxies for aggressive behavior may help to explain the apparent disconnect in the evidence identifying neural contributors to outward aggressive behavior versus mental states theorized to motivate that behavior (such as anger). Though both types of evidence have been demonstrated, just how these mental states give rise to aggressive and criminal behavior remains relatively unknown.

Despite these limitations, these early advancements will help future investigators develop more refined hypotheses that enable them to selectively target the neural circuitry that most facilitates aggressive behavior. Such efforts would not necessarily have direct implications for legal procedure, but could potentially yield therapeutic insights, which in turn, may become relevant during legal processes such as forensic evaluation, adjudication, and sentencing.

How Can Sentencing Decisions Be Informed by the Punisher's Brain Function?

The intersection of law and neuroscience has focused primarily on the brains of criminal offenders. Much less attention has been paid to the role of those called upon to assign blame and to make punishment judgments or recommendations, such as judges and jurors. Although specific legal applications of this research are still ill-defined, investigating the punisher's brain could help to uncover some of the proximate mechanisms shaping typical punishment decisions. A small set of experiments provide converging evidence that typical punishment decisions might be subserved by a host of dynamic brain networks. We discuss what these studies suggest about typical punishment decision making in the brain including the effects of both endogenous factors (e.g., attributions of the defendant's mental state at the time of the crime) and exogenous factors (e.g., contextual cues) in this process.

In an early attempt to elucidate the neural mechanisms of third-party punishment, Buckholtz and colleagues (2008) conducted an event-related fMRI experiment investigating brain areas that are selectively associated with ascriptions of criminal responsibility and punishment. In the experiment, participants made punishment judgments after reading about different protagonists performing criminal and non-criminal actions with varying degrees of mitigating circumstances (such as a lack of requisite knowledge of the risk of harm). For the crimes with mitigating circumstances, participants recommended smaller punishments, as to be expected. During these trials, the rTPJ was engaged, an area commonly attributed to the process of mentalizing others.[2] During trials lacking mitigating circumstances, and trials in which participants chose to punish, the rdlPFC, an area found to play an integral role in norm enforcement, was uniquely engaged (Sanfey et al. 2003). The investigators attributed the activation of the rTPJ to the period when participants made judgments about the offender's level of responsibility for the act, and the rdlPFC, in contrast, was attributed to the actual decision to punish.

Buckholtz and colleagues (2008) also observed engagement of the right amygdala during trials lacking mitigating circumstances, an area credited as a hub for social and affective processing generally (Murray, Brosch & Sander 2014). This engagement persisted even when the investigators controlled for the emotional arousal inherent to the scenarios. This signal was positively correlated with the magnitude of punishment recommended, suggesting that the amygdala might play a distinct role in the formation of punishment judgments beyond the processing of emotional arousal, such as the processing of harm, as proposed by two of the authors in a later commentary on this experiment (Buckholtz & Marois 2012).

Similarly, Yamada and colleagues (2012) varied whether crime vignettes included mitigating circumstances intended to evoke sympathy (e.g., the offender felt pity for his terminally sick wife and thus killed her) or lacked mitigating circumstances. The investigators then solicited sympathy ratings and punishment recommendations in an fMRI setting. As expected, participants reported more sympathy and less punishment toward the offender for crimes committed with mitigating circumstances. The investigators found three brain regions that were associated with sympathy ratings and the mitigation of punishment: the TPJ, precuneus, and dorsomedial prefrontal cortex (dmPFC) – all regions previously identified to be involved in mentalizing and moral conflict (Yamada et al. 2012).

Ginther and colleagues (2016) sought to characterize the neural processes underlying evaluations of harm and criminal intent. They systematically varied these constructs and solicited punishment recommendations in an fMRI setting. They also measured self-reported difficulty of the decision. Attributions of harm were negatively associated with activity in the right lateral prefrontal cortex (rlPFC), and difficulty attributing harm was associated with the orbitofrontal cortex (OFC). These results align with previous literature suggesting that the rlPFC is commonly involved in the processing of other's pain, and the OFC in cost benefit analysis (Janowski, Camerer & Rangel 2013; Lamm, Decety & Singer 2011). Attributions of intent were positively associated with activation of the posterior cingulate cortex (PCC), which the authors suggest is indicative of the negative valence associated with increasing culpability (Maddock, Garrett & Buonocore 2003). Increasing difficulty of attributing intent was associated with activity within the TPJ, dmPFC, and superior temporal sulcus, a network active during mentalization (Ginther et al. 2016). This pattern of results suggests separable mechanisms for assessing the magnitude of these concepts, and the difficulty with which they are conceived.

The researchers were also interested in how information about the crime (such as the level of harm and intent) interact to produce a punishment judgment. Following participants' initial appraisal of harm and intent, they observed sequential activation of the bilateral amygdalae and right dlPFC which anticipated the judgment, similar to previous research by Buckholtz and colleagues (2008).

In a similar study, researchers sought to understand how participants respond to conflicting instances of sentencing decisions: instances where acts committed were deemed morally right but legally wrong (Yang et al. 2019). Perhaps unsurprisingly, moral acceptability was correlated with punishment decisions, and crimes of good intention were punished less so than those of bad intention. Consistent with previous research, activation of the rTPJ was found to be higher in the evaluation of well-intentioned acts compared to those of bad intentions. Furthermore, crimes of good intent elicited greater activation in the dlPFC, and correspondingly, a greater connectivity from the dlPFC to the mPFC. In both previous experiments, the researchers interpret this pattern as evidence that these brain regions work in concert to integrate relevant information, such as the level of harm and intent, and then select a level of punishment scaled to that integrated information.

Other studies have focused on contextual factors likely to influence attributions of responsibility and punishment. Capestany and Harris (2014), for example, examined punitive responses to emotionally evocative language and the evidence presented about the defendant's character. Using hypothetical crime scenarios, the researchers systematically varied disgust evoking language of the crime (low vs. high disgust) and the method by which the defendant's personality was clinically assessed (behavioral vs. neurobiological). As expected, behavioral explanations of personality yielded greater ascriptions of responsibility than neurobiological explanations. Furthermore, disgust language and behavioral explanations of personality yielded more severe punishments than descriptions lacking disgust language and neurobiological personality assessments. During responsibility judgments, the investigators observed increased activation in the lingual gyrus and PCC when the defendant's personality was assessed behaviorally. These regions have been shown to be involved in logical deduction and emotional salience, respectively (Barack, Chang & Platt 2017; Goel et al. 2004). During the actual decision to punish, the superior frontal gyrus and the superior parietal lobule were increasingly engaged in the presence of disgust language. These regions have been shown to be involved in executive function and the manipulation of working memory (Boisgueheneuc et al. 2006; Koenigs et al. 2009). Engagement of the amygdala, inferior parietal lobule, middle frontal gyrus, and insula were associated with the magnitude of punishment recommended – all regions associated with affective processing (Capestany & Harris 2014).

Using a similar approach, Treadway and colleagues (2014) examined the neural mechanisms underlying attributions of criminal intent and harm with and without the use of graphic language to describe the crime, as well as those underlying the decision to punish or not. Similar to the findings of Buckholtz and colleagues (2008), when scenarios lacked mitigating circumstances and when participants chose to punish, the researchers found that the dlPFC was more engaged when the crime was intentional compared to unintentional, as well as when participants chose to punish the offender compared to when they chose not to do so. For intentional crimes, the left amygdala was more engaged when the crime was described using graphic language rather than plain language, and, correspondingly, participants selected harsher punishments in this condition, suggesting that the amygdala's role in emotional arousal may also operation in punitive decision making. A similar pattern emerged for level of harm: the amygdala was engaged increasingly with level of harm, yet only when the crime was intentional.

Despite their strengths, traditional fMRI study designs do not permit the inference that a particular cognitive function is directly caused by a given neural pattern. In attempt to overcome this limitation, Treadway and colleagues (2014) also utilized the post hoc statistical technique of Granger Causality Modeling (GCM). GCM is designed to determine whether certain fMRI signals from particular brain regions explain variance in others, allowing the researchers to create a temporally defined map of which signals give rise to others in the brain. They found that the functional connectivity between the amygdala and dlPFC was strengthened in the presence of graphic language, but *only* when the crime was intentional. In cases where the offender committed a crime unintentionally, there was greater functional connectivity from the lTPJ to the dorsal ACC (dACC), which has been previously implicated in the detection of norm violations (Güroğlu et al. 2010), as well as from the dACC to the amygdala. Together, these results suggest that in cases of intentional crimes, graphic language can serve to aggravate punishment recommendations via the functional connectivity from the left amygdala to the dlPFC, yet this aggravating effect can be down-regulated by a top-down connection from the lTPJ-dACC pathway to the amygdala, consistent with motivations to withhold punishment from less-blameworthy offenders.

Another attempt to elucidate the causal mechanisms of punishment decisions was made by Bellucci and colleagues (2017). While participants were deciding how much to punish a defendant for a hypothetical crime (compared to a control task of estimating the number of syllables in each vignette), several regions were found to be engaged within what they describe as the mentalizing network – including the vmPFC, dmPFC, PCC, left temporal pole, and the lTPJ – and the central executive network, particularly, the left dlPFC. In a GCM analysis, the investigators identified two regions (the left dmPFC and left temporal pole) that sent output to every other region reportedly involved in their punishment task. Further, the dmPFC was found to receive input only from the temporal pole, suggesting that it may serve as a communication hub in the mentalizing network. The investigators interpreted this pattern as evidence that the dmPFC plays an important causal role in the integration of all relevant signals in third-party punishment decisions. More generally, these results suggest a broad and complex network of brain regions underlying third party punishment.

Across studies on the punisher's brain, we find some consistency among brain regions during punishment judgments, including activation of the TPJ, dmPFC, PCC, amygdala, temporal pole, and dlPFC. These regions have been formerly implicated in cognitive functions including theory of mind, affective processes, and higher order cognitive functions in this process (Bellucci et al. 2016; Buckholtz et al. 2008; Capestany & Harris 2014; Ginther et al. 2016; Treadway et al. 2014; Yamada et al. 2012; Yang et al. 2019; Young et al. 2010), and it would not be surprising if such cognitive functions are recruited in the formation of typical punishment judgments. Future research would benefit from going beyond study designs optimized to localize cognitive functions in the brain and directly test how these functions unfold in terms of stages of processing. Understanding the stages of cognitive processing could potentially reveal, not just where, but how punishment judgments are likely to be made and when they are likely to conform to or depart from normative preferences or expectations. Until the research can move from questions of "where" to how and when, the direct relevance of this research to legal decision making seems limited, at best. However, research on the punisher's brain may at least retain indirect relevance as part of a broader, basic research question about the contributors to punishment decisions.

How Can Sentencing Decisions Be Informed by the Punisher's *Perceptions* Of Brain Function?

Another way that neuroscience might influence sentencing decisions is in the way neuroscientific evidence is interpreted by non-experts, such as judges and jurors. A growing body of research suggests that laypeople may place undue confidence in neuroscientific evidence, and this can affect their ascriptions of responsibility and punishment.

In two studies, Weisberg and colleagues (2008, 2015) found that when scientific explanations were offered for a behavior, laypeople's ability to distinguish between good and bad quality explanations was hindered when irrelevant neuroscientific information was included. More specifically, explanations that included irrelevant neuroscientific information were judged as stronger and more satisfying than those without it. Further research has suggested that particular aspects of neuroscientific arguments, such as brain images in particular, are especially persuasive when it comes to credibility judgements (McCabe & Castel 2008; but see Farah & Hook 2013; Michael et al. 2013).

Is this "seductive allure" of neuroscientific information likely to impact legal decisions? In a vignette study with US trial court judges, Aspinwall, Brown, and Tabery (2012) found that including a neurobiological description of a defendant's mental illness reduced ratings of responsibility and punishment. Similarly, in a study of mock jurors, Greene & Cahill (2012) found that neuroscientific evidence of the defendant's psychosis reduced death sentence recommendations compared to a diagnosis of psychosis sans neuroscientific evidence. One explanation for these mitigating effects is the perception that the presence of biological causes implies that the defendant had less control over his actions.

Although biological evidence of behavior seems to reduce judgments of a defendant's responsibility, some research has suggested that this perception can be double-edged if that evidence increases perceptions of future dangerousness (Aspinwall et al. 2012; Berryessa 2017; Chandler 2015; Fuss 2016; Hardcastle & Lamb 2018). In support of this prediction, McCabe and colleagues (2011) found that inculpatory evidence (that is, evidence suggesting guilt) from ostensible lie detection technologies produced more guilt recommendations when the technology was described as fMRI as opposed to a traditional polygraph, thermal facial imaging, or no evidence at all. Similarly, Saks and colleagues (2014) found that when the prosecutorial side presented arguments that included neuroimaging evidence, there was an increase in death sentence recommendations.

These studies suggest that perceptions of neurobiological evidence might be consequential for legal proceedings. Yet, the effects across studies have been somewhat inconsistent. And despite the observation of both mitigating and aggravating effects of neuroscientific evidence on sentencing decisions, no single study has observed both patterns side by side, and several studies have reported null results (Blakey & Kremsmayer 2018; LaDuke, Locklair & Heilbrun 2018; Remmel, Glenn & Cox 2018; Schweitzer et al. 2011). These inconsistencies raise questions about the robustness of the effects across different methods. One commonality of these studies is the use of fairly simple punishment measures such as a single prison sentencing scale. Such scales, though, are not equipped to distinguish between distinct motives for punishment such as retribution, rehabilitation, or deterrence. This fact may be important because the theories about aggravation and mitigation imply the interaction of distinct punitive motives.

In support of this interpretation, recent research by Allen and colleagues (2019) conducted the first quantitative demonstration of the theorized double-edge effect by including multiple measures designed to separately elicit distinct motives for punishment. In their mock trial study, the researchers found that while neurobiological evidence of an impulse control disorder mitigated prison sentence recommendations, it also aggravated involuntary hospitalization recommendations compared to equivalent psychological evidence. The implication is that fact-finders may be unduly influenced by neurobiological framing of the evidence, and that this framing can cut both ways depending on the type of decision at hand.

Further validation of these effects are needed before gleaning confidence in exactly how and under what conditions they are likely to play out in real criminal punishment decisions. Even so, it raises questions regarding how policy makers can manage these effects (see de Kogel & Westgeest 2016, and Meynen 2013 for further discussion). For example, should judges and juries be trained on the interpretation of neurobiological evidence? Should the presentation of neurobiological evidence be accompanied by a statement about its potentially biasing effects? When is neurobiological evidence adequate to stand alone, and when must it be accompanied by behavioral evidence? Further scholarship is needed to explore the answers to such questions, but, as a whole, the growing body of research on how people perceive neuroscience evidence does suggest that such perceptions will be consequential for criminal law practice.

Conclusion

In this chapter, we sought to examine current developments in the brain sciences that pertain to risk of reoffense and to punitive decision making. While comprehensive neurobiological models of criminal behavior and punitive decision making remain a distant goal, the existing literature on these subjects suggests important progress. Across studies, several brain regions make repeat appearances. The ACC and amygdala, for example, appear to play consistent roles in the impulsivity and development of criminal behavior (Aharoni et al. 2013; Aharoni et al. 2014; Kiehl 2018; Steele et al. 2015).

Likewise, the TPJ, dmPFC, PCC, amygdala, temporal pole, and dlPFC show some consistency in punishment judgments, suggesting a possible role of theory of mind, affective processes, and higher order cognitive functions in this process (Bellucci et al. 2016; Buckholtz et al. 2008; Capestany & Harris 2014; Ginther et al. 2016; Treadway et al. 2014; Yamada et al. 2012; Yang et al. 2019; Young et al. 2010).

Across these subject matter domains, we identified several priorities for future research. First, this research should aspire to move beyond traditional correlational study designs toward methods that permit stronger causal inference between brain functions and particular behavioral outcomes. A key metric for validating these models is the extent to which they make accurate predictions. Accurate predictive models might, in turn, be valuable for the development of tailored treatments for high risk offenders. Second, this research should further examine how disparate cognitive functions are integrated neurobiologically into a final punishment judgment (e.g., Bellucci et al. 2016; Ginther et al. 2016). To achieve this objective, however, it may be necessary to specify more precise, conceptual cognitive models of crime and punishment. Part of this effort should entail probing the relevant stages of cognitive processing that culminate in a punishment judgment, such as the sequence in which we appraise information about an actor's intentions, or the harmfulness of the act, and the integration of such information in service of the judgment. Third, further research is needed to address how fact-finders interpret neuroscientific evidence. This effort should show consideration for the plurality of motivations that drive fact-finders punishment recommendations.

As we consider future directions, it is important to acknowledge the narrowness of this chapter's scope. For example, we did not discuss the neurocognitive effects of incarceration on inmates. We also ignored a large literature on cognitive heuristics and biases, as well as gender and racial biases (see Peer & Gamliel 2013 for a review of cognitive heuristics and biases relevant to criminal sentencing, and Ward, Hartley & Tillyer 2016 for an in depth analysis of potential drivers in gender and racial biases in drug sentencing decisions). Likewise, we were silent on the many contextual and structural factors that undoubtedly shape criminal behavior, sentencing, and associated neurobiological function. Although such topics were beyond this scope of this chapter, their growing contribution to the field of neuroscience and law will bring theoretical clarity and nuance to neurobiological models of criminal and legal decision making and cannot be overstated.

Just how this laboratory evidence may or may not bear on real legal punishment decisions remains an open question. As this research develops, some people may be tempted to stretch the findings for questionable uses, such as to justify a sentencing increase, diagnose judicial bias, or predict the outcome of a particular trial. But, in order to be of any use to trial procedures, neuroscience evidence – like any scientific evidence – must first demonstrate that it will be relevant to the legal question. For many legal questions, neuroscientific explanations do not meet this basic standard (Morse 2011). Even if they are deemed relevant, they would have to meet levels of specificity and reliability that are not observed in the current scientific literature. Amidst these legal challenges are a variety of unresolved ethical questions that must be addressed in stride with the scientific advances.

Despite the current limitations of the brain sciences in informing specific legal practices, these sciences nonetheless hold promise in addressing humbler goals. Neuroscience methods carry the potential to validate behavioral findings about antisocial behavior and punishment behavior, generate new hypotheses about cognitive mechanisms, and lend incremental utility to models attempting to explain and predict that behavior for clinical rather than punitive purposes (see also Coppola 2018). Whether or not the contribution of neuroscience will be probative, let alone pragmatic, are open questions. Until then, studying the factors that drive crime and punishment decisions remains an important objective of basic and clinical research.

Acknowledgements

We thank Nathaniel Anderson, Morris Hoffman, Eddy Nahmias, Saskia Verkiel, and the Cooperation, Conflict, and Cognition Lab for helpful comments.

Notes

1 Authorship is equal.

2 Though this result is correlational in nature, Young and colleagues (2010) has noted the same role for the rTPJ in belief and intent attribution. By utilizing transcranial magnetic stimulation (TMS) the researchers were able to "lesion" the area in order to observe its effects on behavior, and confirm its role with a more causal approach.

References

Aharoni, E., Funk, C., Sinnott-Armstrong, W. and Gazzaniga, M. (2008) "Can neurological evidence help courts assess criminal responsibility? Lessons from law and neuroscience," *Annals of the New York Academy of Sciences*, 1124, pp.145–160.

Aharoni, E., Vincent, G.M., Harenski, C.L., Calhoun, V.D., Sinnott-Armstrong, W., Gazzaniga, M.S. and Kiehl, K.A. (2013) "Neuroprediction of future rearrest,` Proceedings of the National Academy of Sciences of the United States of America, 110(15), pp.6223–6228.

—— et al. (2014) "Predictive accuracy in the neuroprediction of rearrest," *Social Neuroscience*, 9(4), pp.332–336.

Allen, C.H., Vold, K., Felsen, G., Blumenthal-Barby, J.S. and Aharoni, E. (2019) "Reconciling the opposing effects of neurobiological evidence on criminal sentencing judgments," *PLoS One*, 14(1), p.e0210584.

Anderson, S.W., Bechara, A., Damasio, H., Tranel, D. and Damasio, A.R. (1999) "Impairment of social and moral behavior related to Damasio early damage in human prefrontal cortex," *Nature Neuroscience*, 2(11), pp.1032–1037.

Aron, A.R. and Poldrack, R.A. (2005) "The cognitive neuroscience of response inhibition: relevance for genetic research in attention-deficit/hyperactivity disorder," *Biological Psychiatry*, 57(11), pp.1285–1292.

Aspinwall, L.G., Brown, T.R. and Tabery, J. (2012) "The double-edged sword: does biomechanism increase or decrease judges' sentencing of psychopaths?" *Science*, 337(6096), pp.846–849.

Barack, D.L., Chang, S.W.C. and Platt, M.L. (2017) "Posterior cingulate neurons dynamically signal decisions to disengage during foraging," *Neuron*, 96(2), pp.339–347.e5.

Bellucci, G., Chernyak, S., Hoffman, M., Deshpande, G., Dal Monte, O., Knutson, K.M., Grafman, J. and Krueger, F. (2016) "Effective connectivity of brain regions underlying third-party punishment: functional MRI and Granger causality evidence," *Social Neuroscience*, 12(2), pp.124–134.

Berryessa, C.M. (2017) "Jury-eligible public attitudes toward biological risk factors for the development of criminal behavior and implications for capital sentencing," *Criminal Justice and Behavior*, 44(8), pp.1073–1100.

Blakey, R. and Kremsmayer, T.P. (2018) "Unable or unwilling to exercise self-control? The impact of neuroscience on perceptions of impulsive offenders," *Frontiers in Psychology*, 8. [online]. Available from: www.frontiersin.org/articles/10.3389/fpsyg.2017.02189/full [Accessed October 10, 2018].

Bobes, M.A., Ostrosky, F., Diaz, K., Romero, C., Borja, K., Santos, Y. and Valdés-Sosa, M. (2013) "Linkage of functional and structural anomalies in the left amygdala of reactive-aggressive men," *Social Cognitive and Affective Neuroscience*, 8(8), pp.928–936.

Boisgueheneuc, F.D., Levy, R., Volle, E., Seassau, M., Duffau, H., Kinkingnehun, S., Zhang, S. and Dubois, B. (2006). "Functions of the left superior frontal gyrus in humans: a lesion study." *Brain: A Journal of Neurology*, 129(Pt 12), pp.3315–3328.

Brown, T. and Murphy, E. (2010) "Through a scanner darkly: functional neuroimaging as evidence of a criminal defendant's past mental states," *Stanford Law Review*, 62(4), pp.1119–1208.

Buckholtz, J.W., Asplund, C.L., Dux, P.E., Zald, D.H., Gore, J.C., Jones, O.D. and Marois, R. (2008) "The neural correlates of third-party punishment," *Neuron*, 60(5), pp.930–940.

Buckholtz, J.W. and Faigman, D.L.(2014) "Promises, promises for neuroscience and law," *Current Biology*, 24(18), pp.R861–R867.

Buckholtz, J.W. and Marois, R. (2012) "The roots of modern justice: cognitive and neural foundations of social norms and their enforcement," *Nature Neuroscience*, 15(5), pp.655–661.

Capestany, B.H. and Harris, L.T. (2014) "Disgust and biological descriptions bias logical reasoning during legal decision-making," *Social Neuroscience*, 9(3), pp.265–277.

Cecil, K.M., Brubaker, C.J., Adler, C.M., Dietrich, K.N., Altaye, M., Egelhoff, J.C., Wessel, S. and Lanphear, B.P. (2008) "Decreased brain volume in adults with childhood lead exposure," *PLoS medicine*, 5(5), p.e112.

Chandler, J.A. (2015) "The use of neuroscientific evidence in Canadian criminal proceedings," *Journal of Law and the Biosciences*, 2(3), pp.550–579.

Choy, O., Raine, A. and Hamilton, R.H. (2018) "Stimulation of the prefrontal cortex reduces intentions to commit aggression: a randomized, double-blind, placebo-controlled, stratified, parallel-group trial," *Journal of Neuroscience*, pp.3317–17.

Coppola, F. (2018) "Mapping the brain to predict antisocial behaviour: new frontiers in neurocriminology,'new' challenges for criminal justice," *UCL Journal of Law and Jurisprudence – Special Issue*, 1, pp.103–126.

Dambacher, F., Schuhmann, T., Lobbestael, J., Arntz, A., Brugman, S. and Sack, A.T. (2015) "Reducing pro-active aggression through non-invasive brain stimulation," *Social Cognitive and Affective Neuroscience*, 10(10), pp.1303–1309.

Darby, R.R., Horn, A., Cushman, F. and Fox, M.D. (2018) "Lesion network localization of criminal behavior," *Proceedings of the National Academy of Sciences*, 115(3), pp.601–606.

de Kogel, C.H. and Westgeest, E.J.M.C. (2016) "Neuroscientific and behavioral genetic information in criminal cases in the Netherlands," *Journal of Law and the Biosciences*, 2(3), pp.580–605.

Delfin, C., Krona, H., Andiné, P., Ryding, E., Wallinius, M. and Hofvander, B., (2019) "Prediction of recidivism in a long-term follow-up of forensic psychiatric patients: Incremental effects of neuroimaging data," *PLoS One*, *14*(5), p.e0217127.

Devinsky, O., Morrell, M.J. and Vogt, B.A. (1995) "Contributions of anterior cingulate cortex to behavior," *Brain: A Journal of Neurology*, 118 (Pt 1), pp.279–306.

DeWall, C.N., Finkel, E.J., Lambert, N.M., Slotter, E.B., Bodenhausen, G.V., Pond Jr, R.S., Renzetti, C.M. and Fincham, F.D. (2013) "The voodoo doll task: Introducing and validating a novel method for studying aggressive inclinations," *Aggressive Behavior*, 39(6), pp.419–439.

Economides, M., Guitart-Masip, M., Kurth-Nelson, Z. and Dolan, R.J. (2015) "Arbitration between controlled and impulsive choices," *Neuroimage*, 109, pp.206–216.

Edersheim, J.G., Brendel, R.W. and Price, B.H. (2012) "Neuroimaging, Diminished Capacity and Mitigation," In *Neuroimaging in Forensic Psychiatry*. Wiley-Blackwell, pp. 163–193. [online]. Available from: https://onlinelibrary.wiley.com/doi/abs/10.1002/9781119968900.ch10 [Accessed November 5, 2018].

Ermer, E., Cope, L.M., Nyalakanti, P.K., Calhoun, V.D. and Kiehl, K.A. (2012) "Aberrant paralimbic gray matter in criminal psychopathy," *Journal of Abnormal Psychology,* 121(3), pp.649–658.

Faigman, D.L., Jones, O.D., Wagner, A.D. and Raichle, M.E. (2013) "Neuroscientists in Court," *Nature Reviews Neuroscience*, p.730.

Farah, M.J. and Hook, C.J. (2013). "The seductive allure of 'seductive allure'," *Perspectives on Psychological Science*, 8(1), pp.88–90.

Farahany, N.A. (2015) "Neuroscience and behavioral genetics in US criminal law: an empirical analysis," *Journal of Law and the Biosciences*, 2(3), pp.485–509.

Fede, S.J., Borg, J.S., Nyalakanti, P.K., Harenski, C.L., Cope, L.M., Sinnott-Armstrong, W., Koenigs, M., Calhoun, V.D. and Kiehl, K.A. (2016) "Distinct neuronal patterns of positive and negative moral processing in psychopathy," *Cognitive, Affective & Behavioral Neuroscience*, 16(6), pp.1074–1085.

Fink, B.C., Steele, V.R., Maurer, M.J., Fede, S.J., Calhoun, V.D. and Kiehl, K.A. (2016) "Brain potentials predict substance abuse treatment completion in a prison sample," *Brain and Behavior*, 6(8), p.e00501.

Fuss, J. (2016) "Legal responses to neuroscience," *Journal of Psychiatry & Neuroscience*, 41(6), pp.363–365.

Gilam, G., Abend, R., Gurevitch, G., Erdman, A., Baker, H., Ben-Zion, Z. and Hendler, T. (2018) "Attenuating anger and aggression with neuromodulation of the vmPFC: A simultaneous tDCS-fMRI study," *Cortex*, 109, pp.156–170.

Ginther, M.R., Bonnie, R.J., Hoffman, M. B., Shen, F.X., Simons, K.W., Jones, O.D. and Marois, R. (2016) "Parsing the behavioral and brain mechanisms of third-party punishment," *The Journal of Neuroscience: The Official Journal of the Society for Neuroscience*, 36(36), pp.9420–9434.

Glannon, W. (2011) *What Neuroscience Can (and Cannot) Tell Us about Criminal Responsibility*. Oxford University Press. [online]. Available from: www.oxfordscholarship.com/view/10.1093/acprof:oso/9780199599844.001.0001/acprof-9780199599844-chapter-2 [Accessed November 1, 2018].

Goel, V., Shuren, J., Sheesley, L. and Grafman, J. (2004) "Asymmetrical involvement of frontal lobes in social reasoning," *Brain: A Journal of Neurology*, 127(Pt 4), pp.783–790.

Greene, E. and Cahill, B.S. (2012) "Effects of neuroimaging evidence on mock juror decision making," *Behavioral Sciences & the Law*, 30(3), pp.280–296.

Grove, W.M. and Meehl, P.E. (1996) "Comparative efficiency of informal (subjective, impressionistic) and formal (mechanical, algorithmic) prediction procedures: The clinical–statistical controversy," *Psychology, Public Policy, and Law*, 2(2), pp.293–323.

Güroğlu, B., van den Bos, W., Rombouts, S.A. and Crone, E.A. (2010) "Unfair? It depends: Neural correlates of fairness in social context," *Social Cognitive and Affective Neuroscience*, 5(4), pp.414–423.

Hardcastle, V.G. and Lamb, E. (2018) "What difference do brain images make in US criminal trials?" *Journal of Evaluation in Clinical Practice*, 24(4), pp.909–915.

Heilbrun, K. (2009) *Evaluation for Risk of Violence in Adults. 1st edition*. New York: Oxford University Press.

Hosking, J.G., Kastman, E.K., Dorfman, H.M., Samanez-Larkin, G.R., Baskin-Sommers, A., Kiehl, K.A., Newman, J.P. and Buckholtz, J.W. (2017) "Disrupted Prefrontal Regulation of Striatal Subjective Value Signals in Psychopathy," *Neuron*, 95(1), pp.221–231.e4.

Janes, A.C., Pizzagalli, D.A., Richardt, S., Frederick, B.D., Chuzi, S., Pachas, G., Culhane, M.A., Holmes, A.J., Fava, M., Evins, A.E. and Kaufman, M.J., (2010) "Brain reactivity to smoking cues prior to smoking cessation predicts ability to maintain tobacco abstinence," *Biological Psychiatry*, 67(8), pp.722–729.

Janowski, V., Camerer, C. and Rangel, A. (2013) "Empathic choice involves vmPFC value signals that are modulated by social processing implemented in IPL," *Social Cognitive and Affective Neuroscience*, 8(2), pp.201–208.

Kiehl, K. A. (2006) "A cognitive neuroscience perspective on psychopathy: evidence for paralimbic system dysfunction," *Psychiatry Research*, 142(2–3), pp.107–128.

Kiehl, K.A., Anderson, N.E., Aharoni, E., Maurer, J.M., Harenski, K.A., Rao, V., Claus, E.D., Harenski, C., Koenigs, M., Decety, J. and Kosson, D. (2018) "Age of gray matters: Neuroprediction of recidivism," *NeuroImage. Clinical*, 19, pp.813–823.

Kiehl, K.A., Smith, A.M., Hare, R.D., Mendrek, A., Forster, B.B., Brink, J. and Liddle, P.F. (2001) "Limbic abnormalities in affective processing by criminal psychopaths as revealed by functional magnetic resonance imaging," *Biological Psychiatry*, 50(9), pp.677–684.

Kittilstad, E. (2018) "Reduced Culpability Without Reduced Punishment: A Case for Why Lead Poisoning Should be Considered a Mitigating Factor in Criminal Sentencing," *Journal of Criminal Law and Criminology*, 108, p.29.

Koenigs, M., Barbey, A.K., Postle, B.R. and Grafman, J. (2009) "Superior Parietal Cortex Is Critical for the Manipulation of Information in Working Memory," *Journal of Neuroscience*, 29(47), pp.14980–14986.

Kraft, C.J. and Giordano, J. (2017) "Integrating Brain Science and Law: Neuroscientific Evidence and Legal Perspectives on Protecting Individual Liberties," Frontiers in Neuroscience, 11, pp.621–621.

LaDuke, C., Locklair, B. and Heilbrun, K. (2018) "Neuroscientific, Neuropsychological, and Psychological Evidence Comparably Impact Legal Decision Making: Implications for Experts and Legal Practitioners," *Journal of Forensic Psychology Research and Practice*, 18(2), pp.114–142.

Lamm, C., Decety, J. and Singer, T. (2011) "Meta-analytic evidence for common and distinct neural networks associated with directly experienced pain and empathy for pain," *NeuroImage*, 54(3), pp.2492–2502.

Liu, J. (2011) "Early Health Risk Factors for Violence: Conceptualization, Review of the Evidence, and Implications," *Aggression and Violent Behavior*, 16(1), pp.63–73.

Maddock, R.J., Garrett, A.S. and Buonocore, M.H. (2003) "Posterior cingulate cortex activation by emotional words: fMRI evidence from a valence decision task," *Human Brain Mapping*, 18(1), pp.30–41.

McCabe, D.P. and Castel, A.D. (2008) "Seeing is believing: the effect of brain images on judgments of scientific reasoning," *Cognition*, 107(1), pp.343–352.

McCabe, D.P., Castel, A.D. and Rhodes, M.G. (2011) "The influence of FMRI lie detection evidence on juror decision-making," *Behavioral Sciences & the Law*, 29(4), pp.566–577.

Meixner, J.B. (2016) "The use of neuroscience evidence in criminal proceedings," *Journal of Law and the Biosciences*, 3(2), pp.330–335.

Meynen, G., (2013) "A neurolaw perspective on psychiatric assessments of criminal responsibility: Decision-making, mental disorder, and the brain," *International Journal of Law and Psychiatry*, 36(2), pp.93–99.

Michael, R.B., Newman, E.J., Vuorre, M., Cumming, G., and Garry, M. (2013). "On the (non) persuasive power of a brain image," *Psychonomic Bulletin & Review*, 20(4), pp.720–725.

Monahan, J. (1981) "Predicting violent behavior: An assessment of clinical techniques," Sage Publications.

Monahan, J. (2008) "Structured risk assessment of violence," *Textbook of Violence Assessment and Management*, 2, pp.17–33.

Morse, S. (2011) *Lost in Translation? An Essay on Law and Neuroscience.* Rochester, NY: Social Science Research Network. [online]. Available from: https://papers.ssrn.com/abstract=1904488 [Accessed October 10, 2018].

—— (2016) *Neuroethics: Neurolaw.* Rochester, NY: Social Science Research Network. [online]. Available from: https://papers.ssrn.com/abstract=2919011 [Accessed October 10, 2018].

Murray, R.J., Brosch, T. and Sander, D. (2014) "The functional profile of the human amygdala in affective processing: Insights from intracranial recordings," *Cortex*, 60, pp.10–33.

Nicholls, T.L., Ogloff, J.R.P. and Douglas, K.S. (2004) "Assessing risk for violence among male and female civil psychiatric patients: the HCR-20, PCL:SV, and VSC," *Behavioral Sciences & the Law*, 22(1), pp.127–158.

Pardini, D.A., Raine, A., Erickson, K. and Loeber, R. (2014) "Lower amygdala volume in men is associated with childhood aggression, early psychopathic traits, and future violence," *Biological Psychiatry*, 75(1), pp.73–80.

Pardo, M.S. and Patterson, D. (2010) "Philosophical foundations of law and neuroscience," *University of Illinois Law Review*, 2010(4), p.40.

Paulus, M.P., Tapert, S.F. and Schuckit, M.A. (2005) "Neural activation patterns of methamphetamine-dependent subjects during decision making predict relapse," *Archives of General Psychiatry*, 62(7), pp.761–768.

Peer, E. and Gamliel, E. (2013) "Heuristics and Biases in Judicial Decisions," *Court Review*, 49, p.114.

Phelps, E.A. and LeDoux, J.E. (2005) "Contributions of the amygdala to emotion processing: from animal models to human behavior," *Neuron*, 48(2), pp.175–187.

Poldrack, R.A., Monahan, J., Imrey, P.B., Reyna, V., Raichle, M.E., Faigman, D. and Buckholtz, J.W. (2018) "Predicting violent behavior: what can neuroscience add?" *Trends in Cognitive Sciences*, 22(2), pp.111–123.

Raine, A. and Yang, Y., (2006) "Neural foundations to moral reasoning and antisocial behavior," *Social Cognitive and Affective Neuroscience*, 1(3), pp.203–213.

Remmel, R.J., Glenn, A.L. and Cox, J. (2018) "Biological evidence regarding psychopathy does not affect mock jury sentencing," *Journal of Personality Disorders*, pp.1–21.

Riva, P., Romero Lauro, L.J., Vergallito, A., DeWall, C.N. and Bushman, B.J. (2015) "Electrified emotions: Modulatory effects of transcranial direct stimulation on negative emotional reactions to social exclusion," *Social Neuroscience*, 10(1), pp.46–54.

Saks, M.J., Schweitzer, N.J., Aharoni, E. and Kiehl, K.A. (2014) "The impact of neuroimages in the sentencing phase of capital trials," *Journal of Empirical Legal Studies*, 11(1), pp.105–131.

Sanfey, A.G., Rilling, J.K., Aronson, J.A., Nystrom, L.E. and Cohen, J.D. (2003) "The neural basis of economic decision-making in the Ultimatum Game," *Science*, 300(5626), pp.1755–1758.

Schaich Borg, J., Sinnott-Armstrong, W., Calhoun, V.D. and Kiehl, K.A. (2011) "Neural basis of moral verdict and moral deliberation," *Social Neuroscience*, 6(4), pp.398–413.

Schofield, P.W., Malacova, E., Preen, D.B., D'Este, C., Tate, R., Reekie, J., Wand H. and Butler, T. (2015) "Does Traumatic brain injury lead to criminality? A whole-population retrospective cohort study using linked data," *PLoS One*, 10(7), p.e0132558.

Schweitzer, N.J., Saks, M.J., Murphy, E.R., Roskies, A.L., Sinnott-Armstrong, W. and Gaudet, L.M. (2011) "Neuroimages as evidence in a mens rea defense: No impact," *Psychology, Public Policy, and Law*, 17(3), pp.357–393.

Specker, J., Focquaert, F., Sterckx, S. and Schermer, M.H. (2018) "Forensic practitioners' expectations and moral views regarding neurobiological interventions in offenders with mental disorders," *BioSocieties*, 13(1), pp.304–321.

Steele, V.R., Fink, B.C., Maurer, J.M., Arbabshirani, M.R., Wilber, C.H., Jaffe, A.J., Sidz, A., Pearlson, G.D., Calhoun, V.D., Clark, V.P. and Kiehl, K.A. (2014) "Brain potentials measured during a Go/NoGo task predict completion of substance abuse treatment," *Biological Psychiatry*, 76(1), pp.75–83.

Steele, V.R., Maurer, J.M., Arbabshirani, M.R., Claus, E.D., Fink, B.C., Rao, V., Calhoun, V.D. and Kiehl, K.A. (2018) "Machine Learning of functional magnetic resonance imaging network connectivity predicts substance abuse treatment completion," *Biological Psychiatry. Cognitive Neuroscience and Neuroimaging*, 3(2), pp.141–149.

Steele, V.R., Claus, E.D., Aharoni, E., Vincent, G.M., Calhoun, V.D. and Kiehl, K.A. (2015) "Multimodal imaging measures predict rearrest," *Frontiers in Human Neuroscience*, 9. [online]. Available from: www.frontiersin.org/articles/10.3389/fnhum.2015.00425/full [Accessed October 10, 2018].

Tassy, S., Oullier, O., Cermolacce, M. and Wicker, B. (2009) "Do psychopathic patients use their DLPFC when making decisions in moral dilemmas?" *Molecular Psychiatry*, 14(10), pp.908–909.

Tengström, A., Grann, M., Långström, N. and Kullgren, G. (2000) "Psychopathy (PCL-R) as a predictor of violent recidivism among criminal offenders with schizophrenia," *Law and Human Behavior*, 24(1), pp.45–58.

Treadway, M.T., Buckholtz, J.W., Martin, J.W., Jan, K., Asplund, C.L., Ginther, M.R., Jones, O.D. and Marois, R. (2014) "Corticolimbic gating of emotion-driven punishment," *Nature Neuroscience*, 17(9), pp.1270–1275.

Walton, M.E., Devlin, J.T. and Rushworth, M.F.S. (2004) "Interactions between decision making and performance monitoring within prefrontal cortex," *Nature Neuroscience*, 7(11), pp.1259–1265.

Ward, J.T., Hartley, R.D. and Tillyer, R. (2016) "Unpacking gender and racial/ethnic biases in the federal sentencing of drug offenders: A causal mediation approach," *Journal of Criminal Justice*, 46, pp.196–206.

Weisberg, D.S., Keil, F.C., Goodstein, J., Rawson, E. and Gray, J.R. (2008) "The Seductive Allure of Neuroscience Explanations," *Journal of Cognitive Neuroscience*, 20(3), pp.470–477.

Weisberg, D.S., Taylor, J.C. and Hopkins, E.J. (2015) "Deconstructing the seductive allure of neuroscience explanations," *Judgment and Decision Making*, 10(5), p.13.

Wright, J.P., Dietrich, K.N., Ris, M.D., Hornung, R.W., Wessel, S.D., Lanphear, B.P., Ho, M. and Rae, M.N. (2008) "Association of Prenatal and Childhood Blood Lead Concentrations with Criminal Arrests in Early Adulthood," in J. Balmes, ed. *PLoS Medicine*, 5(5), p.e101.

Yamada, M., Camerer, C.F., Fujie, S., Kato, M., Matsuda, T., Takano, H., Ito, H., Suhara, T. and Takahashi, H. (2012) "Neural circuits in the brain that are activated when mitigating criminal sentences," *Nature Communications*, 3, p.759.

Yang, Q., Shao, R., Zhang, Q., Li, C., Li, Y., Li, H., & Lee, T. (2019). "When morality opposes the law: an fMRI investigation into punishment judgments for crimes with good intentions," *Neuropsychologia*, 127, pp.195–203.

Young, L., Camprodon, J.A., Hauser, M., Pascual-Leone, A. and Saxe, R. (2010) "Disruption of the right temporoparietal junction with transcranial magnetic stimulation reduces the role of beliefs in moral judgments," *Proceedings of the National Academy of Sciences of the United States of America*, 107(15), pp.6753–6758.

21
BEHAVIORAL GENETICS AND SENTENCING

Allan McCay

Should criminal courts reduce punishment where an offender advances evidence that suggests they are genetically predisposed to commit criminal offences? How should the courts punish those who, through no fault of their own, have what has been colloquially referred as the "the warrior gene"[1] or, in respect of whom, some other genetic cause of behavior is pointed to in mitigation?

In this chapter I will primarily focus on the prospects for a plea in mitigation at sentencing that claims that the offender has a genetic predisposition to engage in certain forms of behavior, which should be taken account of by a judge or jury, who is deliberating about the nature and/or severity of a sentence in respect of an offence that the offender has either been found guilty of, or pled guilty to. An example of such a plea might occur in a situation where an offender claims they deserve a reduced punishment for their crime, relative to other offenders who have been convicted of otherwise similar offences, because their genetic predisposition (perhaps in combination with a childhood of maltreatment by their family members) increased the difficulty of compliance with the criminal law relative to the difficulty faced by those other offenders.

While it is possible that the defence or prosecution might use evidence derived from behavioral genetics in other ways, it is not possible here to survey the whole range of possibilities and I will primarily address the desert-based claim as it raises some important theoretical considerations relating to the philosophy of science and punishment. Another reason for this focus is that it appears to have some relationship to the way that behavioral genetics has been used in the relatively small number or cases that have been discussed in the scholarly literature.

While, as will be seen, in the past legal arguments have been made based primarily on genetics rather than gene/environment interaction, on the basis of current science it may well be that that an offender would argue that the *interaction* of their genetic predisposition and their formative social environment led to their offending, and the sentencing judge or jury should take note of that interaction and its effects, and as a consequence, reduce the sentence. Whether based solely on genetics, or the interaction of genes and social environment, I will refer to such pleas as behavioral genetics-based pleas in mitigation (BGBPIMs) and my aim is to critically examine them, drawing attention to related ethical, legal and psychological issues. As will be noted later a major study on behavioral genetics as used in the US justice system found no cases where the prosecution introduced the evidence and so my primary focus will be on the use of behavioral genetics in attempt to mitigate punishment.

I will start by outlining what is meant by the terms "behavioral genetics" and "sentencing" before considering how behavioral genetics might be used in a plea in mitigation and then consider various concerns about such pleas. After noting that BGBPIMs might be treated differently depending on the nature of the offence (or offences) committed, and are likely to be subject to considerable regional variation, I will use the example of an Australian jurisdiction as case study to consider the issues raised by the kind of plea under consideration.[2] In relation to this jurisdiction, I will consider relevant legal authorities in order to consider how a plea could be put to the court.

After outlining various epistemic, ethical and legal problems, some psychological hurdles pertaining to attempts to persuade a sentencing decision-maker that less punishment is merited, and some ethical support for a BGBPIM, I will examine the way that some courts have actually responded. Finally, I will very briefly consider the future of this kind of plea.

What Is Meant By Behavioral Genetics and What Is Sentencing?

Behavioral genetics is the field of study that considers the way that genes and environment interact to exert influence over people's behavior. It is a discipline pursued by scientists who work with a very different set of concepts than those that are found in the criminal law. Despite the conceptual mismatch, legal arguments advanced by defendants in criminal matters have sometimes required judges and juries to respond to evidence derived from behavioral genetics. Before examining the way that developments in science have elicited, or ought to elicit, a response from the courts in the context of sentencing, it is worth saying something about the scope of the chapter and its focus on *sentencing*. I will do this by contrasting sentencing with some other stages in the criminal process.

Sentencing is not the only stage in the criminal process in which evidence derived from behavioral genetics might be used. A defendant is only sentenced if they are found guilty of an offence (or have pled guilty), and an example of an earlier stage in the criminal process in which behavioral genetics might be used is the stage in which guilt is contested.

In a criminal matter, the prosecution must show that the defendant engaged in prohibited conduct which is most usually an act and sometimes an omission. This is known as the actus reus.[3] At least in respect of serious offences the prosecution must show the defendant acted with the requisite mens rea (guilty mind). Different offences require different forms of mens rea such as intention, recklessness or negligence. Before considering sentencing, it is useful to point out that evidence derived from behavioral genetics might conceivably feature (in conjunction with other evidence) in an argument about mens rea.

Even if the defendant has performed the actus reus with the requisite mens rea, they may have a defence. Thus, the insanity defence (which in some jurisdictions is referred to as the mental illness defence) might be available to a defendant who did not know the nature and quality of what they did, or if they did, they did not know it was wrong. In some jurisdictions this defence might also be available to a defendant who was acting under an irresistible impulse. Behavioral genetics might be used (again in conjunction with other evidence) to support a defence to a criminal charge such as the insanity defence. So perhaps if a genetic predisposition to schizophrenia could be demonstrated, it might be additional confirmation that the defendant was not feigning mental illness. While perhaps raising some similar issues to sentencing, a consideration of the use of behavioral genetics to argue that a defendant is not guilty is outside the scope of this chapter as the focus is on *sentencing.*

Sentencing is the process by which a legal decision-maker (a judge or sometimes and in some jurisdictions, a jury) decides on the nature and severity of the punishment that is to be imposed. In a sentencing hearing, an offender has already been convicted of one or more offences so there is no longer any question about whether they are criminally responsible for what they did. The question is just what kind of punishment is merited and how severe should it be. In the hearing an offender has the opportunity to present a plea in mitigation that may use evidence derived from the field of behavioral genetics.

It is also worth contrasting sentencing with decisions about parole. In many jurisdictions, offenders might be paroled – that is, released from jail early subject to some conditions in order to serve the remainder of their sentence in the community. This might happen where their prospects of recidivism are thought to be low. It seems possible that a parole decision-maker might be interested in whether an offender has a genetic predisposition that is likely to lead to recidivism, but while this clearly relates to the degree of punishment, it is not a sentencing decision and is outside the scope of this chapter. Thus, in a volume about the philosophy and science and punishment, it is worth bearing in mind that for the criminal law, decisions about the *degree* of punishment go beyond decisions about sentencing and include other contexts.

What Kind of Pleas Are Under Consideration?

In order to outline one form of plea that has been put to some courts it is necessary to briefly say something about the scientific background to the plea. While behavioral geneticists have considered genetic influences on a wide variety of human conditions that have a behavioral aspect and could potentially be referred to in a sentencing hearing, including depression, psychopathy, schizophrenia, post-traumatic stress disorder, alcoholism and many others, a significant number of the actual cases have focused on monoamine oxidase A and its link with crime. Because of its significance in the sentencing cases and in scholarly literature, I will use this to illustrate how a BGBPIM might be made.

Monoamine oxidase A is an enzyme (a chemical in the brain) which is linked to impulsivity and aggression. Genetic variations in people result in the level of MAOA activity varying from nothing to high levels in different people. Early research focused on a group of males who produced none of the enzyme and who engaged in conduct ranging from arson to exhibitionism and attempted rape (Brunner et al 1993). The production of none of the enzyme turned out to be rare and later research became more biosocial in orientation, focusing on the interaction of genes and social environments. An influential paper published by Caspi et al. (2002) suggested that for males, the combination of having a low-activity MAOA gene with the experience of maltreatment was strongly predisposing toward impulsivity and aggression. Most of the research has focused on MAOA in the context of the antisocial behavior of males but there is also research which focuses on the antisocial behavior of females (e.g. Ducci et al. 2008).

One way that behavioral genetic research might find its way into a courtroom at sentencing is where an offender, most likely through their legal representative, engages an expert witness who gives evidence suggesting that a male offender who has committed a crime of impulsive aggression has a low-activity MAOA gene, and has also been maltreated during childhood. The expert might suggest that the interaction of gene and formative social environment has led to the act of impulsive aggression for which the offender is now being sentenced. The offender's legal representative might then use this evidence in a plea in mitigation to support the contention that he is deserving of less punishment (more on this shortly) perhaps by suggesting that it supports a claim that he is less morally culpable for what he did. Another approach to the use of behavioral genetics in a plea in mitigation focuses on the identification of a family history of a particular trait in order to suggest that the offender has that trait.

Before considering how pleas might be made it is important to note that one must be mindful of issues of time and place when considering such pleas. Approaches to sentencing vary over time and one can see this in the way the aims of punishment have ebbed and flowed over the decades (Tonry 2011). Sentencing can often have a significant political dimension and it is important to bear in mind that a high-profile behavioral genetics case might one day elicit a rapid political response from a legislature that is disconnected from matters of legal or moral principle. Of course, the various different jurisdictions around the world may take very different approaches to behavioral genetics-based pleas in mitigation. For these reasons it is difficult to generalize about the way "the law" responds to behavioral genetics in a sentencing matter.

Making a Plea

In order to consider the merits of BGBPIMs, it is useful to consider more precisely how such a plea could be made. In particular it seems important to understand the *legal basis* for a mitigation argument – that is to say how legislation and/or cases might be used to support a legal argument. Given the significance of the plea in mitigation for the sentencing decision-maker's response to behavioral genetics, it is perhaps unfortunate that in the scholarly literature such a plea-based approach is uncommon. Furthermore, as will be seen, at a theoretical level, the examination of the legal basis for the plea highlights the way that at least one legal system attends to both the *capacities* of the offender, and concerns about the *origins* of criminal behavior.

Mindful of the variation between legal systems around the world and across time, I will focus on an Australian jurisdiction – the state of New South Wales – a state which has a great deal in common with other Australian jurisdictions and a significant similarity with many common law jurisdictions around the world. I will use a case study in order to consider some more general themes that may be prevalent in a number of other jurisdictions.[4]

In making a plea in mitigation it is important to consider the aims of punishment. New South Wales like many other systems has a number of aims and sentencing judges[5] have to consider both retributive and consequentialist aims. Thus judges must consider what an offender deserves for their crime but they must also consider whether the offender can be rehabilitated, deterred or needs to be incapacitated in order to protect the community. They must also consider the likely deterrent effect of the sentence on others.[6]

At their sentencing hearing the offender has an opportunity to make a plea in mitigation which is often made on their behalf by their legal representative. This plea may draw attention to factors which make the offence less serious relative to other offences of a similar kind and is done in the hope the judge will impose a lesser punishment relative to that imposed for those other offences.

Many factors are of possible relevance to such pleas including remorse, difficult formative circumstances, good character, age, health, mental condition and the likelihood of reoffending. Sometimes there may be expert evidence provided by a mental health professional in support of the plea in mitigation. In relation to behavioral genetics as a factor at sentencing a forensic psychiatrist might well be thought of as a suitable expert to provide such evidence to the court. In any particular case it is very unlikely that the plea would solely address the behavioral genetics issue and most likely the forensic psychiatrist's evidence would be presented to the court along with one or more other purportedly mitigating factors. The prosecution may also wish to draw attention to aggravating factors (factors tending to a longer sentence) such as the vulnerability of a victim (if there was an identifiable victim) and perhaps also emphasize the risk of recidivism. After the hearing the judge then imposes a sentence and gives reasons for the decision. Even if a judge were to mention the significance of any evidence derived from behavioral genetics in their remarks on sentence, it may be hard to assess the impact of the evidence on the sentence relative to other factors that were also referred to.

With that general background in mind, I will now consider how a BGBPIM might be made. There are a variety of ways that this could be done and using the research on MAOA, I will consider one possible way. As noted earlier, in Australia judges are permitted to mitigate punishment where an offender has come from an extremely difficult set of formative circumstances relative to other offenders. Judges do not have to mitigate – there maybe countervailing considerations of dangerousness that a judge could take into account and decide, all things considered, not to mitigate. There is a weighty authority that could support an argument for formative circumstance mitigation – the High Court decision in *Bugmy v R* (2013). In this the case, which concerned a very serious assault committed by an Aboriginal offender, the High Court made it clear that sentencing judges must take note of the difficult formative circumstances of an offender, even when some time has passed since their childhood. Perhaps a male, low-activity MAOA offender who had been convicted of a crime of impulsive aggression, who had also been maltreated in childhood could argue that they had a genetic vulnerability which exacerbated the impact of their difficult formative circumstances and as a result are *especially* deserving of mitigation given the *Bugmy* precedent.[7] It could be argued that it would be perverse for a court to allow mitigation for those who have encountered difficult formative circumstances and yet deny further mitigation to those who, through no fault of their own are particularly susceptible to the adverse effects of the maltreatment. Such a mitigation strategy might thus support a narrative of adversity and vulnerability and thus recognize "the importance of behavioral genetics evidence to telling a defendant's story" (Denno 2011: 988).

It must be acknowledged that, as such a plea has not yet been considered by an Australian court, one cannot be sure of how a judge would respond. An argument like this would be likely to have greater force if concerns on the part of the judge about reoffending could somehow be neutralized. Perhaps if it seemed to the court that the offender had, between offending and sentencing, engaged in a successful anger management program (or other intervention such as some form of neurointervention) that had now diminished their tendency to impulsive aggression, a judge would be able to put the issue of community protection to one side and focus primarily on the mitigating effects of the offender's gene/environment interaction and thereby reduce punishment.

It may also be that the offender would refer to authority that enables a judge to take account of their mental condition at the time of the offence as a sentencing factor which diminishes their moral culpability. The range of mental issues that are relevant to sentencing are far wider than those relevant at the criminal responsibility stage and the case *R v Verdins* (2007), an often-cited and important Victorian[8] Court of Appeal case which sets out principles relating to mitigation in respect of the offender's mental conditions, may be argued to permit the judge to mitigate punishment as a result of the offender's MAOA-related impulsivity. In respect of this line of authority the behavioral genetics evidence might be thought of as buttressing a claim that an offender has diagnosable impulse control issues – that is to say it makes it more probable that a claim of agential impairment based on other behavioral evidence, and amounting in law to a relevant mental condition is true.[9] It remains to be seen whether a court would deem that MAOA-related issues fell within the scope of the conditions they are prepared to accept, and again such a plea would have greater force if the issue of community protection had been neutralized (perhaps by way of some form of intervention on the offender's agential issues).

Of these two elements to the plea the latter case (*Verdins*) emphasizes the agent's diminished *capacities* at the time of the offence (the impulsivity) and the former *(Bugmy)* is historical in nature and focuses to a greater extent on the *origins* of conduct (in an unfortunate combination of biological constitution and events in the past). It seems possible that that the effect of one or quite possibly both of these lines of authority might successfully support a claim for mitigation, especially if the offender was not seen by the judge to be likely to reoffend.

It is important to emphasize that any plea would need to be orientated toward something of legal relevance. In the example under discussion, I have focused on lines of authority relating to offenders' formative circumstances and their mental conditions. Various other factors of legal significance might conceivably be addressed in a BGBPIM including the offender's good character, their moral culpability, their prospects for rehabilitation, any remorse shown, and the likely degree of suffering in jail (if jail was a possible sentencing option). Different types of behavioral genetic evidence will require consideration of how they may or may not support a plea in mitigation. Thus, even if it were possible to find some support for a claim that the interaction of the offender's genes and environment predisposed them to psychopathy, this may have no overall mitigating effect as it may raise countervailing concerns about bad character and increased prospect of recidivism (with little chance of the risk being successfully reduced by some form of intervention). It is also worth noting that mitigating factors only need to be proved on the balance of probabilities. Thus, the standard of proof is not particularly high.

Concerns about BGBPIMs

With an understanding of how a BGPBPIM might be made, in at least one jurisdiction, it is now time to consider the sentencing response. Whether in New South Wales or some other jurisdiction are there any reasons to be concerned about the possibility of a favourable response?

To continue with the MAOA example, while some research has suggested that the cumulative effect of the interaction between low-activity MAOA and experience of maltreatment during childhood is strongly correlated with impulsivity and aggression (Caspi et al 2002) other research has called this into question.[10] It may be that at least in respect of BGBPIMs, the sentencing decision-maker might have reason to be concerned that the research was not sufficiently consistent to even consider whether much could be inferred that was of legal relevance in a sentencing matter. In any case, to the extent that the evidence was purported to explain some agential issue with respect to the crime(s) that the offender had been convicted of (rather than say to support a claim about excessive suffering in prison) it would need to be orientated toward the offence(s) for which the offender was being sentenced. Evidence relating to a genetic predisposition to impulsivity would be of little relevance in the sentencing of an offender for a premeditated crime and at least in some cases there might be reason to be concerned about whether the evidence was sufficiently connected to the offence.

But are there also reasons to be concerned about the prospect of the courts responding favourably to mitigation strategies involving credible evidence that is appropriately related to the offences under consideration? I will now consider some concerns appearing in the theoretical literature which are not supportive of a favourable response, and which suggest that there may be moral and other downsides to mitigation of punishment in response to a BGBPIM.

One concern is the potential for stigmatization (Rothenberg and Wang 2009). Perhaps if sentencing decision-makers were to accept behavioral-genetics based pleas as having mitigating effects they might have a role in stigmatising the offender by formally endorsing a view of them as somehow biologically problematic. However, it is not clear that this is any worse than the stigma of conviction. Furthermore, courts may already stigmatize offenders by endorsing the view that their social circumstances have made them problematic – one might interpret the *Bugmy* precedent as having this effect.

One should also be mindful of "criminology's darkest hour" (Rafter 2008:76) and biocriminology's association with Nazi policies. It would be of concern if the legitimization of biocriminology through sentencing practices could somehow be used to lend support to those who wish to taint a racial group with biological inferiority. While outside of the context of sentencing, research into MAOA may have already been distorted in a racial context (Lea and Chambers 2007). Perhaps the courts should be mindful of this and at least in jurisdictions where judges issue reasons for judgment, take it into account when giving reasons.

Another concern is that if the courts were to accept BGBPIMs, this might lead some (perhaps low-activity MAOA males who have been maltreated) to view themselves as less responsible for what they do. In an interview, one Australian judge worried that: "it's got the potential to allow people to behave anti-socially because they have a particular genetic makeup without being required to exercise free will and self-control" (McCay 2013: 87). However, this concern perhaps assumes that potential offenders are more aware of the mitigation practices of the courts than is actually the case.

If the courts were to recognize a biosocial form of mitigation it might be seen by some to shift blame towards female victims of male crime. For example, it may be that a female victim of male violence might be blamed for provoking a man who is known to be impulsive (Radford 2004:145). However, to the extent that victim blaming attitudes are prevalent in society it may be that they can be successfully addressed otherwise than through moderating approaches to biosocial mitigation.

One might also worry that if the courts recognize genetic mitigation in sentencing, it would lend support to a more general view which locates responsibility for crime in faulty individuals rather than acknowledging the responsibility of society to deal with crimogenic social conditions. Biological explanations may be politically convenient by getting society off the hook (Taylor, Walton and Young 1973:40). However, it is not clear that the gene/environment example used in this chapter absolves society. Much contemporary research is biosocial in orientation and does not downplay the significance of the social environment.

Relatedly one might consider the merits of the social response that takes place when legal systems are faced with certain forms of conduct they aim to prevent. Many jurisdictions around the world have in the past criminalized and some still do criminalize, consensual sex between adults of the same sex. If we assume that gene/environment interactions have a role in one's sexual orientation, to say that those whose gene/environment interactions have resulted in same-sex attraction are "predisposed to crime" seems to ignore the contingency involved in questions of criminalization. It seems to ignore the fact that the criminal law may be grossly unjust and to criminalize conduct which ought not to be criminalized. Perhaps the acceptance of BGBPIMs might be seen as forming part of a conservative approach to crime that problematizes only individuals and turns a blind eye to the sometimes problematic nature of the criminal law that individuals may find themselves subject to.[11] However this does not seem to be a special problem for behavioral genetics as a mitigating factor– this concern seems to apply to many approaches to mitigation.

A final and significant concern relates to victims of crime. It may be distressing for a victim of a very serious crime to have their victimization explained away in scientific terminology and the offender's culpability thereby partly excused. However, victims of crime may also be distressed by other forms of mitigation and so again, this does not seem to be a special issue for behavioral genetics.

Some concerns perhaps can be addressed but some are harder to dismiss as they raise more general issues about mitigation. What about countervailing considerations in favor of mitigation?

Ethical Support for BGBPIMs

Although there are some reasons to be concerned about a positive response to a BGBPIM, there are also compelling ethical reasons to doubt whether it is right to dismiss such a plea. As noted earlier there is a retributive element to sentencing in New South Wales– an element which is shared with many, perhaps all jurisdictions around the world. For retributivism the degree of blameworthiness of the offender and the harm done are often thought to be significant in determining how much punishment is deserved (Duff 2001:135, Von Hirsch 1993:29).

It is plausibly the case that the degree of *difficulty* that an offender faced in complying with a norm is relevant to the assessment of blameworthiness (Nelkin 2016). According to this view, the more difficult it was to comply with a norm, the less blameworthy one is for failing to comply. Difficulty has also been seen as central to mitigation of sentence by perhaps the most influential legal philosopher of the 20th century, HLA Hart (2008:15).[12] It has been argued that the difficulty of complying with the criminal law is diachronic in nature and includes difficulties faced around the time of the offence (including for example the cognitive[13] difficulty of appreciating the full degree of wrongfulness of a criminal act), and historical[14] difficulties (for example, the difficulty of forming a self that would be more motivated to comply with the criminal law given adverse formative circumstances encountered early in life), or the difficulty of structuring one's life around one's antisocial predispositions so that one does not find oneself in a situation in which one is likely to act in a way that does not comply with the criminal law (McCay 2019).[15]

It seems that for low-activity MAOA males who have been maltreated, the genetic predisposition may make it more difficult to overcome their adverse formative social environments and form more prosocial adult selves that would be more likely to comply with the criminal law. With such a problematic start in life derived from the social environment, and exacerbated by the genetic vulnerability, the self-formative task required would be larger and more challenging for these males than for other offenders who do not need to take such self-formative steps to address the effects of the particular form of adverse gene-environment interaction under consideration here. Furthermore, in the immediate run-up to the offending, the impulsivity resulting from the gene-environment interaction may have made it more difficult to refrain from the criminal act that they have been convicted of. The effects of the gene-environment interaction may also have made it more difficult for them to structure their lives in order ensure that they do not find themselves in a situation that that leads them to act impulsively, by increasing the range of potential situations (relative to other offenders) that may lead them to act badly and thus must be avoided in order to comply with the criminal law. In short, the gene environment interaction and its effects may, in a variety of ways, have made it more difficult for them to have refrained from what they did relative to an otherwise similar offender who was not a maltreated, low-activity MAOA male. All other things being equal, this increased difficulty leaves them less blameworthy and deserving of less retributive punishment than that other "normal" offender. As sentencing is at least in part a retributive enterprise it must take note of the blameworthiness issue and to fail to do this would be unfair to the offender.

While there are some legitimate concerns about BGBPIMs, arguably they are not sufficient to trump the reduced blameworthiness argument, particularly if one takes the view that it is unjust to punish an offender to a greater extent than deserved. It thus seems that a compelling ethical case for mitigation can be made using the concept of difficulty. A major question in legal theory focuses on the link between ethics and law and a significant perspective, that of Dworkin, maintains that ethics and law are not so distinct, and that an ethical argument might have a role in interpreting the law.[16] If that were true, then the ethical argument presented here might have a role in interpreting the concept of difficulty into subsequent legal analysis of the precedents mentioned earlier – with *Bugmy* addressing self-formative difficulties given one's starting point in life, and *Verdins* addressing difficulties present at the time of the offence resulting from one's mental condition. While Morse has argued against some theoretical approaches to BGBPIMs that he maintains cannot as a matter of law support mitigation (2015) perhaps the concept of difficulty, a concept that he does not address in relation to behavioral genetics, can have some role in legal approaches to mitigation, at least in New South Wales and similar jurisdictions.

Impediments to Behavioral Genetics-Pleas in Mitigation

Now that the way that a plea might be put to the court has been considered and some concerns about acceptance and rejection of the plea have been canvassed, before moving on to consider how courts have actually responded it is useful to consider some impediments to acceptance of BGBPIMs. These impediments are legal and psychological.

The first thing to note is that that there are some matters which leave no scope to make a plea in mitigation based on behavioral genetics. Sometimes the sentencing decision-maker's discretion is limited or eliminated by a system of mandatory sentencing. This is a legal impediment to a plea in mitigation. The psychology of the decision-maker may also be an impediment to the positive reception of a behavioral- genetics based plea in mitigation. For example, it may be that people generally (presumably including at least some sentencing decision-makers) have conflicting intuitions about the mitigation which cancel each other out. Perhaps on the one hand, they see the plea as failing to show that the offender is deserving of mitigation because the genetic predisposition has supposedly revealed their true self to be intrinsically bad, but on the other hand, supporting mitigation by drawing into question their capacity to do otherwise. It may also be that the desire to punish, or the belief that people cannot be genetically predisposed to crime because people are thought to be fundamentally good, may lead to rejection of the behavioral genetic evidence and thus of the BGBPIM.[17]

But how have the courts actually responded?

The Cases

Criminal cases in involving behavioral genetics are often thought to form part of a broader area of study that has become known of as "neurolaw". This broader area of study includes analysis of neuroscientific evidence concerning many agential issues such as brain tumors and dementias. It is notable that relative to some other areas of neurolaw there have not been large numbers of behavioral genetics cases. Thus, at the time of writing, while there are large numbers of cases discussing dementias in the Australian Neurolaw Database,[18] there are no cases in which MAOA is discussed, despite its inclusion in the scope of the database.

However, there are cases in other jurisdictions including USA and Italy (McSwiggan et al. 2017), and the Netherlands (de Kogel and Westgeet 2016). An early, and unsuccessful, argument for mitigation in an American death penalty case that was not biosocial in orientation (focusing narrowly on a genetic predisposition rather than a gene/environment interaction) was made on behalf of a male who had been convicted of murder. The defendant, Stephen Mobley, argued that his MAOA levels should be tested but the court was not receptive to his arguments and he was ultimately executed (McSwiggan et al. 2017). In a major study which looked at 33 more recent US behavioral genetics and crime cases Denno noted that behavioral genetics has been advanced almost exclusively in cases in which the offender faced the death penalty for the crime of murder. According to her, the behavioral genetic evidence was discussed primarily in two ways. One is in relation to a claim about ineffective assistance of counsel and the other is to buttress a claim about impaired mental condition. In relation to ineffective assistance of counsel, defendants have argued that their legal representatives failed to advance potentially mitigating behavioral genetic evidence. In relation to the buttressing approach to mitigation, the argument in support of mitigation draws on the behavioral genetic evidence to support a claim about a mitigating mental impairment of some sort.

While Denno's research suggest that US courts in death penalty cases generally admit behavioral genetics-based evidence, it also suggests that there is little evidence that it has great impact. She says that:

> at the very least behavioral genetics evidence has no decipherable impact on a defendant's case or, at most, it becomes an effective tool along with a range of other kinds of variables in rendering a defendant ineligible for the death penalty.
>
> *(Denno 2011: 1028)*

Denno uncovered no cases where the prosecution introduced the evidence or where it appeared to have an aggravating effect on sentence. Earlier in the chapter when discussing the way that a plea might be constructed in New South Wales, I suggested that those making a plea in mitigation might wish to take steps to try to neutralize any concerns about dangerousness on the part of the decision-maker. From Denno's research the extent to which this neutralization has been attempted by the defendant is not apparent and it is not clear whether such strategies explain the lack of cases in which aggravation is apparent.

Bearing in mind what has been argued earlier in relation to the construction of a plea in mitigation in New South Wales, the difference between jurisdictions is interesting to consider. I argued that the High Court decision in *Bugmy* could assist with a BGBPIM in New South Wales. This kind of argument is not referred to by Denno and it may be that it is more difficult to make an argument analogous to the one presented earlier in some jurisdictions. It seems likely that BGBPIMs may be constructed differently around the world and over time contingent on the special features of the jurisdictions they are presented to.

The Future

The future of BGPIMs is contingent on a number of variables. One may be the interest of expert witnesses in this kind of evidence (McCay 2016). If experts do not include the evidence in their reports, then lawyers won't make legal arguments and there won't be any cases. Another is the strategic decisions of legal representatives. If the evidence is not seen to be of great assistance, perhaps due to the underwhelming response of the courts, there may be little enthusiasm for BGBPIMs (Scurich and Appelbaum 2017). Questions of cost and availability may have an impact and perhaps the relevant tests may become more widely available in the future.

Much may depend on the science. If developments in behavioral genetics lead to explanations of criminal behavior that can be addressed to sentencing considerations of the kind mentioned earlier, then there may be an increase in BGBPIMs. Beaver et al. (2018) have argued that behavioral genetics may have a role in approaches to rehabilitation both in identifying the risk level of those who might be rehabilitated, and in individualizing treatment in light of knowledge about offenders' genetic predispositions. So perhaps behavioral genetics may one day be discussed to a greater extent in relation to sentencing's rehabilitative aim.

The impact of developments in genetic engineering is harder to speculate on. And if one day, BGBPIMs were seen to be too widely made, one cannot discount the possibility of a hardening of attitudes and a backlash against them (McCay and Kennett 2019). For the moment it seems that behavioral genetics, while raising some concerns that are worthy of consideration, may also have significant ethical force. In practice such pleas only sometimes benefit a defendant, in some jurisdictions, and the impact does not appear to be substantial.

Notes

1 See Lea and Chambers (2007).
2 The justification for this choice will be discussed later.
3 Occasionally it is status, such as being a member of a terrorist organisation.
4 This case study to some extent draws on work outlined in (McCay 2012)
5 Unlike some US jurisdictions, juries are never involved in sentencing in Australia.
6 Section 3A of the *Crimes (Sentencing Procedure) Act 1999* (NSW), and the High Court decision *Veen v R* (1988) outline these aims.
7 A related argument is advanced in respect of another legal authority prior to the decision in *Bugmy v R* (2013) in McCay (2012).
8 Although from another Australian state this authority could be referred to in a New South Wales plea in mitigation.
9 For a discussion of the role of neuroscientific evidence in buttressing claims about psychological conditions see Jones (2016).
10 For a recent overview of relevant research see Beaver et al. (2018). In light of this overview these authors are supportive of the view that the interaction *is* related to antisocial behavior.
11 Biosocial approaches might be thought of as part of the positivist tradition in criminology which locates the causes of crime in the individual and takes scientific orientation to the study of the phenomenon. As Taylor, Walton, and Young have noted, the social reaction in the positivist model is not seen to be a problem (1973: 28).
12 Hart was focussing on English law but his views may have applicability to other common law systems.
13 This relates to the agents capacities and a legal analog would seem to be the *Verdins* form of mitigation.
14 A legal analog to this would seem to be the *Bugmy* form of mitigation that focusses to a greater extent on the origins of criminal behavior. The case has also been argued to raise issues of self-formation. See McCay 2019.
15 This diachronic view of mitigation makes it very difficult to assess how blameworthy people are for their wrongs because of the complexity of blame-assessment task. If one wholeheartedly embraced the view one might think that many retributive practices are somewhat reckless give sentencing decision-maker's lack of knowledge of salient facts about the offender and the cognitive difficulty of accurately assessing blameworthiness (McCay 2019).
16 For an overview of Dworkin's view see Postema (2011:401–456).
17 For an overview of these psychological factors see Tabb et al. (2019).
18 The Australian Neurolaw Database is publicly accessible resource which aims to identify Australian cases in which there is a significant discussion neuroscience. See here: https://neurolaw.edu.au.

References

Beaver, K.M., Connolly, E.J., Nedelec, J.L. and Schwartz, J.A., (2018) "On the Genetic and Genomic Basis of Aggression, Violence, and Antisocial Behavior" in Hopcroft, R. L. (Ed.), *The Oxford Handbook of Evolution, Biology, and Society*, p.265.

Brunner, H.G., Nelen, M., Breakefield, X.O., Ropers, H.H., van Oost, B.A. (1993) "Abnormal Behavior Associated with a Point Mutation in the Structural Gene for Monoamine Oxidase A," *Science* 262: 578–580.

Caspi, A., McClay, J., Moffitt, T.E., Mill, J., Martin, J., Craig, I.W., Taylor, A. and Poulton, R. (2002) "Role of Genotype in the Cycle ofViolence in Maltreated Children," *Science 297*: 851–854.

De Kogel, C.H. and Westgeest, E.J.M.C. (2016) "Neuroscientific and behavioral genetic information in criminal cases in the Netherlands." *Journal of Law and the Biosciences 2*(3): 580–605.

Denno, D. (2011) "Courts' Increasing Consideration of Behavioral Genetics Evidence in Criminal Cases: Results of a Longitudinal Study," *Michigan State Law Review* 2011: 967–1047.

Ducci, F, Enoch, M.A., Hodgkinson, C., Xu, K., Catena, M., Robin, R.W. and Goldman, D. (2008) "Interaction between a Functional MAOA Locus and Childhood Sexual Abuse Predicts Alcoholism and Antisocial Personality Disorder in Adult women," *Molecular Psychiatry* 13: 334–347.

Duff, R.A. (2001) *Punishment, Communication and Community*, Oxford: Oxford University Press.

Hart, H.L.A. (2008) *Punishment and Responsibility: Essays in Philosophy of Law* (Second Edition), Oxford: Oxford University Press.

Jones, O.D. (2016) Keynote: Law and the Brain Past, Present, and Future. *Arizona State Law Journal* 48(4): 917–34.

Lea, R. and Chambers, G. (2007) "Monoamine Oxidase, Addiction, and the Warrior gene hypothesis," *New Zealand Medical Journal* 120: 1250.

McCay, A. (2012) "The Fernando Principles and Genetic Vulnerabilities to the Criminogenic Effects of Social Environments," *Indigenous Law Bulletin* 8(6): 9–13.

McCay, A. (2013) "Behavioral genetics, moral agency and retributive sentencing: the case for mitigation," University of Sydney Library: PhD dissertation.

McCay, A. (2016) "Genetics, Crime and Justice by Debra Wilson," *Current Issues in Criminal Justice* 28 (2): 249–252.

McCay, A. (2019) "Mitigation is Difficult: A Moral Evaluation of a Mitigation Practice at Sentencing" in A. McCay and M. Sevel (eds.) *Free Will and the Law: New Perspectives*, London and New York: Routledge.

McCay, A. and Kennett, J. (2019, online first) "Neuroscience and Punishment: From Theory to Practice," *Neuroethics*: 1–12.

McSwiggan, S., Elger, B. and Appelbaum, P.S. (2017) "The Forensic Use of Behavioral Genetics in Criminal Proceedings: Case of the MAOA-L Genotype," *International Journal of Law and Psychiatry* 50: 17–23.

Morse, S.J. (2015) "Genetics and Criminal Justice," in *The Oxford Handbook of Molecular Psychology*, Oxford: Oxford University Press, p.409.

Nelkin, D.K. (2016) "Difficulty and Degrees of Moral Praiseworthiness and Blameworthiness," *Noûs* 50(2): 356–378.

Postema, G. (2011) *A Treatise of Legal Philosophy and General Jurisprudence: Legal Philosophy in the Twentieth Century: The Common Law World. Vol.* 11, Heidelberg, London and New York: Springer Science & Business Media.

Radford, L. (2004) "Programmed or Licensed to Kill? The New Biology of Femicide," in Rees, D. and Jones, S. (eds) *The New Brain Sciences: Perils and Prospects*, Cambridge: Cambridge University Press.

Rafter, N. (2008) *The Criminal Brain: Understanding Biological Theories of Crime*, New York: New York University Press.

Rothenberg, K. and Wang, A. (2009) "The Scarlet Gene: Behavioral Genetics, Criminal Law, and Racial and Ethnic Stigma in Farahany," in Nita A. (ed), *The Impact of Behavioral Sciences on the Criminal Law*, Oxford: Oxford University Press.

Scurich, N. and Appelbaum, P.S. (2017) "Behavioral genetics in criminal court," *Nature Human Behavior* 1(11): 772.

Tabb, K., Lebowitz, M.S. and Appelbaum, P.S. (2019) "Behavioral genetics and attributions of moral responsibility," *Behavior Genetics* 49(2): 128–135.

Taylor, I, Walton, P. and Young, J. (1973) *The New Criminology: For a Social Theory of Deviance,* London: Routledge.

Tonry, M.H. (2011) "Thinking About Punishment" in M. Tonry (ed) *Why Punish? How Much? A Reader on Punishment,* Oxford: Oxford University Press.

Von Hirsch, A. (1993) *Censure and Sanctions*, Oxford: Oxford University Press.

Cases and legislation

Crimes (Sentencing Procedure) Act 1999 (NSW).
Bugmy v The Queen [2013] HCA 37.
Veen v R (No 2) [1988] HCA 14.
R v Verdins (2007) 16 VR 269

22

PREDICTION, SCREENING AND EARLY INTERVENTION

A Critical Analysis

Dorothee Horstkötter

Actually, you are playing with someone's life. Because one is getting a label and all. … If then one has given someone a label he does not deserve, that is the same as sentencing someone who is innocent.

(Tom, 16 years, admitted to Judicial Youth Care)

Introduction

Reduction of antisocial behavior (ASB) is typically considered an important social and political aim. The past decades, however, have shown a significant paradigm shift in this regard from mere reactive punishments to emphasizing the early identification of children at risk and the implementation of early preventive interventions. Accompanying continuous trends in (mental) health care (e.g., Arango et al. 2018; Jacka & Reavley 2014; Ozonoff 2015), the credo "prevention is better than sanction" is also influencing criminology (Beauchaine, Neuhaus, Brenner, & Gatzke-Kopp 2008; Farrington & Welsh 2007), linking it directly to both youth care work and the youth mental health care system. From a scientific and policy point of view, the question is no longer whether prevention is sensible and feasible, but rather which kind of screening method and which preventive and interventional measurements are most effective (Farrington & Welsh 2007; Sherman et al. 1996). The term "early" is thereby taken very seriously. The target group of early intervention is not merely young offenders or those with overt behavioral disturbances, but is also aimed at very young children, still in their infancy if not even prenatally; and preferably before the onset of observable behavioral troubles (Loeber, Slot, Van der Laan, & Hoeve 2008; Tremblay 2010; van Goozen & Fairchild 2008). Traditionally, prediction and prevention concern the assessment of a series of social and psychological risk-factors – for example, showing low attainment and empathy, living in a disrupted family and experiencing poor and inconsistent parenting, and growing up in a deprived area (Farrington & Coid 2003) – in order to decide on and make the appropriate intervention. More recently, this early-prevention paradigm has been given a particular boost by research done in the life sciences, particularly genomics, neurobiology and neurophysiology (Beauchaine et al. 2008; Fishbein 2000; van Goozen & Fairchild 2008). These contemporary approaches aim to identify biomarkers that indicate a risk of developing antisocial behaviors and have therefore triggered great hopes and expectations for the development of more accurate screening methods and more effective means of early ASB-prevention and intervention. Against this background, the following assumption has come to dominate the field: improved prediction, screening and early intervention brings about a win-win situation in which all concerned are better off. Children and juveniles at-risk can enjoy a better future: a future with improved mental health, less engagement in delinquent behavior, and therefore fewer sanctions or punishments in the form of fines, community services, or admission to closed or judicial youth care facilities. At the same time, public safety will increase, society will be better protected and fewer people will be victimized.

There are, however, reasons to temper this enthusiasm. Screening, prediction and early prevention are not a panacea in crime prevention, and more seriously, they might come to lead a life of their own with unintended and questionable implications and side-effects. Even proponents of prevention programs cautioned *ab initio* that the way to prevention will be rocky and paved with false predictions, warn that:

> Caution is... required. In particular, any notion that better screening can enable policy makers to identify the young children destined to join the 5 percent of offenders responsible for 50–60 percent of crime is fanciful. ... This demonstrates the danger of assuming that antisocial five-year-olds are the criminals ... of tomorrow.
>
> *(Sutton, Utting, & Farrington 2004: 5)*

But there is more than limited predictive validity and the lack of crystal balls. There are concrete concerns about what happens with those young children, and their families, who become participants in early prevention efforts. The quotation at the start of this chapter expresses this worry. It comes from my interview with Tom (fictive name, to protect his privacy), a juvenile delinquent whom I asked to think through the personal impact of early identification and prevention (Horstkötter, Berghmans, de Ruiter, Krumeich, & De Wert 2012). Tom was rightly concerned that prevention can be a form of sanction, and even worse, a sanction of the innocent. This very possibility calls on anybody involved in research and practice to reconsider the very relationship of prevention and sanction from an ethical point of view. It also adds up to a whole series of questions and concerns regarding the ethical and social implications of early ASB-prevention elaborated on in criminological (Gatti, 1998), youth mental health (Singh & Rose 2009; Sterzer 2010), sociological (Case 2006; Stephen & Squires 2004) and bioethical (Horstkötter, Berghmans, & De Wert 2014; Horstkötter & De Wert 2013; Walsh 2014) literature.

Against this background, the current chapter critically analyzes common assumptions about the value of prediction and early intervention from an ethical point of view. The relationship of prevention and sanction or punishment might not be a one-way straightforward road but instead involves detours and oncoming traffic. Before I dig into the details, some remarks should be made. So far, I have used the terms of "antisocial behavior," "delinquency," "wrongdoing," or "offending" in a rather loose and synonymous way. This will continue throughout the chapter. By doing so, I fully realize that these terms are notoriously difficult to define and distinguish. In the following, a broad understanding of this conglomerate will be invoked and the discussion will be taken to cover (potential) behaviors that inflict significant harm on self or others (for example violence, truancy, or burglary) as well as (potential) personality traits that render such behaviors more likely (for example, aggressiveness, impulsivity, or low empathy). The chapter will be informed by the scientific and applied ethical literature at hand. In addition, it will revert to the views and experiences of stakeholders (juveniles and parents) as I have elicited them in two qualitative interview studies (Horstkötter et al. 2012; Horstkötter, Berghmans, Feron, & De Wert 2014; Horstkötter, Dondorp, & de Wert under review). I will refer to these voices to provide checks and balances on the academic discourse.

The chapter will proceed in four steps. First, I will briefly present the state of art in screening, prediction and early ASB-prevention (Horstkötter, Berghmans, & De Wert 2014). Second, I will focus on the implications for individual children concerned. Third, given that early prevention targets rather young children, I will also discuss what ASB-prevention might entail for their parents and families. Finally, I will show how early ASB-prevention can lead to tensions between child well-being and public safety and I will discuss the implications of any conflicts of interest.

Prediction, Screening and Early Prevention Across Disciplines, a Digest

Over the years, research has tried to identify risk-factors that might characterize children and juveniles who behave antisocially, commit offences or are likely to do so. Traditionally, this covers psychological and social factors, but more recently, findings from neuroscience and genomics aim to complement the overall picture by identifying a series of biomarkers (Beauchaine 2009; van Goozen & Fairchild 2008). On that basis, various prevention and intervention measurements have been implemented and evaluated (Farrington & Coid 2003; Farrington & Welsh 2007; Loeber et al. 2008; Sherman et al. 1996) and there is great interest in how biomedical findings can enhance these initiatives (Beauchaine et al. 2008; van Goozen & Fairchild 2008). The following discussion will provide a brief overview of features considered important in the context of ASB risk, as well as interventions implemented to attenuate them.

Potential risk-factors not only include individual characteristics, but also familial and social features. On the individual level both psychological and biomedical aspects have been emphasized. From a psychological perspective, low attainment and intelligence, but also little empathy or high impulsiveness have been considered important (Farrington & Welsh 2007). From a biomedical perspective, genetic polymorphisms, structural and functional deviations in the brain and aberrations of psychophysiological responses to stress have been referred to as underlying the behavior of those who behave antisocially and engage in crime (Hodgins, Viding, & Plodowski 2009).

It has long been established that various kinds of risk factor do interact with each other and with protective factors, contributing to resilience, or potentially increasing vulnerability (depending on the specific set of risk and protective factors). In their early work, Viding and colleagues noted a difference in the likely etiology of different kinds of aggressive behavior. The so-called callous-unemotional traits of children who show instrumentally aggressive behavior seem closely related to shared genetic features, whereas reactive forms of aggression are influenced by children's shared – adverse – environment (Viding, Jones, Frick, Moffitt, & Plomin 2008). Even though the idea of "genes for crime" has been debunked, the gene that codes for the enzyme Monoamine Oxidase A (MAOA) has attracted much attention in this context. Caspi and colleagues showed that people with a short version of that gene have increased levels of arrest and police contacts, but only if they had also experienced severe maltreatment during childhood; otherwise their behavior was unremarkable (Caspi et al. 2002). This seminal research provided strong evidence for the now widely established idea that it is not genes or environments alone that impact any individual's risk, but instead complex interactions between these factors (Moffitt 2005). Something similar holds for neurobiological and neurophysiological features. Altered brain function in brain areas responsible for, among others, emotion regulation, processing of social information and inhibitory control have been emphasized (Shirtcliff et al. 2009; Sterzer & Stadler 2009). In addition, divergent neurophysiological reactions, for example lower resting heart rates and skin conductance (Ortiz & Raine 2004) and deviations in neuroendocrinological systems are considered to contribute to aberrant stress reactions, reduced fear experience and increased risks of ASB engagements (McCrory, De Brito, & Viding 2010; van Goozen & Fairchild 2009). Again, these features are not considered in isolation, but instead in the context of children's familial and environmental circumstances. Potentially, this adds to the understanding of well-known familial and environmental risk factors. Living in a disrupted family, having a single teenage parent, or experiencing poor, affectionless, or inconsistent parenting have for a long time been thought to contribute to children's risk of developing ASB. It is now presumed that adverse childhood experiences can disturb children's brain development and contribute to a divergent regulation of the stress system and to low self-regulation capacities. Something similar seems to hold for social risk-factors like growing up in deprived areas or attending a school with high delinquency. Aberration in brain structure and function and in stress systems and executive functions are at first adaptions to adverse circumstances, rendering children better able to cope; but later render them more likely to perform behaviors that are particularly risky, disadvantageous or harmful to others.

The question is: how can we make use of these insights into risk-factors to prevent children from engaging in harmful behavior? Overview articles and reviews present and discuss what works in youth crime prevention and which interventions yield good results or are promising (de Vries, Hoeve, Assink, Stams, & Asscher 2015; Loeber et al. 2008; Sherman et al. 1996). Such programs can operate universally and aim at all children and families living in certain areas or attending specific schools (Coid 2003; Hawkins & Herrenkohl 2003) or they can be set up in a targeted fashion and intervene in the lives of only those children and families who had been identified individually through screening. To that purpose, standardized assessment instruments like the Strengths and Difficulties Questionnaire (Goodman 1997) and the Child Behavior Checklist (Achenbach 1991; ASEBA 2011) have been developed to gather information about children's emotions, behaviors and relationships. More recently, hopes have been raised that life science findings on genomics, brain structure or neurophysiology and neuroendocrinology might lead to improvements in risk assessments and might, in the foreseeable future, contribute to more accurate predictions (van Goozen, Fairchild, Snoek, & Harold 2007).

Today's prevention programs are largely based upon psychosocial findings and interventions typically aim to ameliorate the familial and social conditions under which children grow up. ASB-prevention during infancy largely consists of mentoring and coaching parents and of giving advice on parenthood, care for young children and positive parent-child relationships (Olds et al. 2004). Additional programs are offered to children of elementary school age that enhance children's cognitive development, or provide environmental enrichments (Parks 2000; Webster-Stratton, Kolpacoff, & Hollinsworth 1988). School-based programs aim to reinforce the development of pro-social behaviors and to teach emotional and social interaction skills. (Hawkins & Herrenkohl 2003; Kellam et al. 2011).

It is noteworthy that while these programs are currently deployed in the context of ASB-risk prediction and prevention, initially they had different purposes. Their goal was to enhance cognitive and social skills at the individual and familial level, reduce emerging disruptive behaviors, and thereby support child and family well-being. These programs were not only successful in this regard, but also reduced delinquency and antisocial behavior when children grew older (Tremblay & Japel 2003). This finding then led to a shift in perspective, such that currently what started in the context of youth care and family well-being is now being implemented in the context of crime prevention and public safety. I will later discuss the potential implications of this shift and the new focus, particularly in situations where the interests of individuals or families and the wider community conflict.

Presently, findings in the biomedical sciences have hardly been implemented in actual screening and prevention practices. Still, there are clear indications of how this could occur. First, insights into neurobiological and neurophysiological effects of children's familial and environmental conditions as well as into gene/brain-environment interactions both contribute to the reaffirmation of the worth of well-known psychosocial interventions that try to improve these conditions (Viding, Larsson, & Jones 2009). A recent report from the Dutch Research Office of the Ministry of Justice on the usage of neuroscience findings presented almost exclusively a series of such psychosocial means, covering environmental enrichment, self-regulation training, family interventions, dietary supplements, mindfulness training, and psychophysiological feedback (Cornet, Bootsma, Alberda, & De Kogel 2016) as neuroscience-based applications.

Second, it has been argued that insights into differences among children's neurobiological functioning might be used to further specify the early identification of children at risk. Biomedical measurements could contribute to the establishment of subgroups of children whose stress-systems have or do not have aberrations (Beauchaine et al. 2008; Frick & Petitclerc 2009). A more stable distinction could be drawn between children with so-called callous-unemotional and psychopathic traits and those who instead show reactive aggression (Viding 2012; Blair 2013). Potentially, ratings could be made to decide which children to prioritize (van Goozen & Fairchild 2008). Based on children's neurobiological profile, so the argument goes, therapists might then invoke different and more tailored treatment approaches. For some it might suffice to provide psychotherapy or any of the above mentioned psychosocial interventions, while for others additional, more specialized treatments might be necessary, such as psychopharmacology or other direct means of neuromodulation (De Brito & Hodgins 2009). In an ideal scenario, neuroscience findings together with their psychosocial companions can be invoked to further mental health literacy among professionals, parents and juveniles and thereby support them in learning to deal autonomously with the features that apparently characterize specific individuals (de Kogel 2018).

Children at Risk

The above seems to present a rather clear picture. There is a series of risk-factors, covering psychological, social and neurobiological/genetic features that render young children and juveniles more likely to engage in ASB, that allow for the early identification of these children and that give guidance on how to set up and further improve prevention and intervention. At first glance, this focus on adverse features and circumstances that seem to characterize children at risk has many advantages over mainly normative ways of understanding antisocial behavior that condemn these behaviors from a moral point of view and aim to consolidate and justify a punitive response. By contrast, if adverse circumstances rather than – mainly – bad intent triggers children's and juveniles' antisocial behavior, punishment seems inapt and therapeutic approaches and attempts to change social and familial circumstances are more appropriate. This is not the place to discuss the philosophical justification of punishment in greater detail, but the following will critically discuss the basic assumption that a preventive and interventional approach would, almost by definition, avoid punishment and solely do good for the children concerned.

Since their onset, risk-based approaches to ASB in general (Case 2006; Gatti 1998; Wright 2017), and those based on the life sciences more recently (Horstkötter, Berghmans, & De Wert 2014; Singh & Rose 2009; Walsh 2014), have been met with a plethora of questions and concerns. While benefits are sensible, pitfalls and drawbacks lurk as well and the science of screening, prediction and early prevention faces a dual-use dilemma. That is, while in theory it could contribute to increased human well-being and the flourishing of children growing up, it can likewise be invoked to make life even more difficult when people are required to meet various demands inherent in these practices.

First, screening and other means engaged to predict who is or isn't at-risk can be rather intrusive. Genetic screening for possible vulnerabilities has the potential to undermine children's "right not to know" and their future autonomy. This right is considered particularly important in situations in which it is not in children's direct interest to be screened (Bortolotti & Widdows 2011; Tarini, Tercyak, & Wilfond 2011), for example, in case no therapy or intervention is available that could mediate the condition looked for; or in which the screening outcome is likely inconclusive because genetic influences can be mitigated by other factors. This is likely to hold in the context of ASB-prevention and intervention, where gene-environment interactions prevail, but where there is also broad consensus that a specific gene that would provoke antisocial behavior does not exist (Viding et al. 2009). Still, one might want to advocate for the screening of children with early symptoms in order to determine who will or will not respond to therapeutic treatments or to identify those who are most vulnerable to developing ASB because of their genetic profile. Van Goozen & Fairchild (2008) have argued that screening should occur in order to determine which children deserve priority in treatment programs, such as children with the short version of the MAOA gene who are also being maltreated. While such an approach might lead to better clinical results, it has serious consequences, particularly for maltreated children who have the long version of the MAOA gene. Their "positive" genetic screening outcome might result in a situation where they are placed at the back of the row because they are considered not at risk to translate their dreadful personal situations into social adversities. In that scenario, screening might have particularly negative consequences for those children who seem rather resilient from an ASB and a public safety perspective, but still have low individual well-being.

In addition, screening – particularly diagnostic differentiation – might better identify those children who are likely to be "treatment resistant", and will not, or barely, respond to existing interventions. This might hold, for example, for children with so-called callous-unemotional (CU) traits: children who exhibit behavior with a persistent disregard of others, lack of empathy and a generally deficient affect (Viding, Fontaine, & McCrory 2012). While on the one hand differentiation between children with and without CU traits has triggered new initiatives for the development of interventions for these hard-to-reach children (Dadds & Rhodes 2009), the risk of this differential approach is an increased tendency to write off these children and instead focus on the easier cases. A different problem arises with the way particularly hard-to-reach or hard-to-change children are sometimes described. A subtype of children with severe forms of conduct disorders are presented as children who exhibit *psychopathic traits* (Blair 2013; Rutter 2012). The terminology of "psychopathy", however, almost by definition triggers a whole set of very negative associations and the question arises whether this term could ever be justified in the case of children and juveniles. *The New York Times* posed the question "Can you call a 9-year old a psychopath?" (Kahn 2012). This is not mainly a question about the diagnostic possibility or reliability. Instead, a moral question has been posed on whether it can ever be morally justified to label a child in such a stigmatic way. The moral criticism here is that creating this subtype of children has the potential to take away any hope that these children could ever change and take a different path in life. This labeling undermines the very idea of childhood and what one might be entitled to as a child: an educational perspective and a focus on one's developmental potential (Horstkötter & De Wert 2013; Stephen & Squires 2004).

A different but related issue is the risk that children who are identified as being at risk of developing ASB will therefore be labeled, stigmatized or discriminated against in education, leisure time activities and maybe even inside their families (Nuffield Council on Bioethics 2002; Rose 2000; Sterzer 2010). In this sense, screening procedures that try to determine individual children's risk status run the danger of singling out certain children and portraying them as being essentially different from their peers. For children who show no behavioral disturbance this is particularly problematic, because they might receive negative attention almost "out of the blue". But also children who show initial behavioral disturbances run the risk of being further singled out and treated differently than their peers when being considered at risk of developing ASB. This initially theoretical concern has been largely confirmed by a group of juvenile offenders who have been interviewed about their views on early prediction and prevention (Horstkötter et al. 2012; Horstkötter, Berghmans, Feron et al. 2014). Juveniles view screening and early prevention efforts with skepticism for two reasons. First, they fear that this will lead to "selective perception" or "prejudice about these people" (Horstkötter et al. 2012: 294). Secondly, they fear that these practices might lead to a situation in which those identified are no longer viewed as "normal" children, and the juveniles greatly feared being labelled abnormal (Wright 2017). As one juvenile put it: "And I know that I am just a normal boy [...] We are also normal humans, you know?" (Horstkötter et al. 2012: 292)

Issues of personal identity have formed a further cluster of concerns. It has been argued that not only biomedical but also psychosocial risk-factors might be perceived as largely stable (Levitt & Manson 2007; Singh & Rose 2009) and that children who early in life come to know that others perceive them in these ways might adopt a personal identity that fits such findings. That is, they might develop low self-esteem, feelings of worthlessness or of being a hopeless case, or actively come to adapt their behavior to their announced risk status, giving rise to a self-fulfilling prophecy. To date, empirical proof of these concerns is largely lacking. Our own studies with delinquent juveniles and with juveniles diagnosed with severe behavioral disorders point in an opposite direction. It is not only that juvenile delinquents perceive themselves as normal human beings (cf. above); for juveniles with serious behavioral disturbances, whose normalcy is challenged, (re)gaining "normalcy" even is an important motivator to engage in specialized mental health treatment (Horstkötter et al. under review). Moreover, the juveniles concerned emphasize their capacity to make personal choices rather than to be determined by some risk-factor that others attributed to them. Maybe some of their choices have been bad, but still they see themselves as choice-makers, rather than as mere performers of some adverse bodily, psychological, or social factors (Horstkötter, Berghmans, Feron, et al. 2014).

So far, concerns about prediction and early ASB intervention have mainly related to the *indirect* implications of screening, identification and intervention – that is, pitfalls and drawbacks that occur because, for example, the identification of an at-risk child brings about stigmatization or discrimination. But the means that might be employed to tackle any risks and bring about behavior change can also entail *direct* troubles. The most prominent concern in this context regards the risk that findings from the biomedical sciences could lead to increased prescriptions of psychopharmacological drugs and to subjecting children to intrusive medical investigations and interventions. Potentially, these could entail general attacks on children's bodily, and maybe also their mental, integrity (Singh & Rose 2009). Moreover, the greater plasticity of children's brains, as compared to adults', renders young people not only more likely to experience long-term effects, but also to face long-term undesired side-effects. Because of this particular danger, it has been suggested that psychopharmacologically based behavior change should only be applied to the most severe cases of established antisocial behavior and preferably on a voluntary basis only (Glannon 2007). Obviously, this excludes preventive applications, particularly in very young and in asymptomatic children. While this advice seems sensible, the reality is likely to be more complex. Apparently, no psychopharmacological intervention against antisocial behavior as such currently exists. But psychiatric conditions have been identified that may eventually contribute to children's engagement in ASB. In this sense, Lichtenstein and colleagues' study on ADHD, medication and criminality (2012) is noteworthy. Here the authors showed that children with ADHD who used medications showed less criminal behavior later in life, compared with their peers who did not take medicines. The authors accompanied their findings with clear warnings against possible misuse and with requests for due care. However, such findings seem to easily find their way into more widely read newspapers, to attract public attention and to risk further stigmatizing children with ADHD who, for whatever reason, prefer not to be treated psychopharmacologically. Their fear of long-term side effects might be perceived to be less relevant than increased public safety, putting additional pressure on a group of children who are struggling already. Again, this raises questions about the main goal of screening, prediction and prevention and about how to balance conflicting individual and public safety interests.

Parents of Children at Risk

Screening, prediction and early ASB-prevention in young children is different from similar efforts in adults, and it is also different from efforts to prevent any worsening of existing behavioral disturbances or of recidivism. Targeting young children not only involves the individuals concerned, but also those surrounding them, most notably their parents. Parents might be affected by similar kinds of stigmatization or discrimination to those that their children are confronted with and so the labeling and treatment cover whole families rather than single members only. The following paragraphs will provide a critical analysis of screening, prediction and early ASB-prevention from the perspective of parents and discuss what these efforts entail for them.

Most prominent are concerns about increased social control and the surveillance of parents of children considered at risk. Critical sociologists and criminologists have frequently emphasized the danger that early intervention programs may not only have pronounced positive outcomes and provide support to vulnerable families, but also increase such families' marginalization and social exclusion (Case 2006; Kelly 2000; Muncie, Hughes, & McLaughlin 2002). This danger is particularly pressing, in so far as early ASB-intervention programs apparently target already marginalized, working class families who are likely to experience additional stigmatization and exclusion from wider social communities when they are included in any ASB-prevention program. In their critical appraisal of early prediction and screening, Munthe and Radovic (2015) warn that social exclusion and the restriction of individuals' freedom might even become the premeditated goals of such measures, rather than "merely" their unintended side-effect. This might occur particularly if screening practices develop more rapidly than therapeutic means to change troublesome behaviors. The danger discussed above – the possibility of "hard cases" being written off earlier and more easily – will not only affect the children themselves, but will also have a negative impact on their parents and wider family. Moreover, adverse inferences about the behavior of parents might be drawn from screening findings and these findings might be invoked to evidence poor parenting (Walsh 2011).

A second concern relates to the respective roles and positions of parents and professionals. According to current ethical standards for the care of children, parents decide whether and when to involve their children in screening and treatment endeavors. Parents ought to be fully informed about such possibilities and then allowed, or even expected, to make decisions on their children's behalf and with their best interests in mind (BMA Ethics Department 2004). Asking parents to have their children screened and then, if appropriate, interventions made to detect and reduce any behavioral disturbances and ASB risk is well in line with these general requirements and preserves parental autonomy. However, given that juvenile delinquency triggers social concerns, the worry is that screening efforts might be extended to all children, reducing parents' say about these matters. Refusing to have one's children screened or even treated by professionals for the sake of ASB-prevention might then be considered an act of irresponsible parenting and render parents suspect, rather than their refusal being seen as an expression of parental autonomy and authority. This, however, raises the question of how to ensure that children and families indeed participate in the programs considered effective in terms of ASB-prevention and intervention. From a policy point of view, one might want to ensure participation by outright pressure and coercion. This was the case in the UK, for example, with *Acceptable Behavior Contracts* (ABCs) that can be imposed on young people aged 10–18 who show behaviors deemed antisocial, and which oblige them to desist (Stephen & Squires 2004). While these contracts are not legally binding, breaches can have severe consequences including legally binding Antisocial Behavior Orders (ASBO's) and possession orders against themselves or their parents if living in social housing. This is not the place to discuss in detail the ethical implications of these particular measures. However, regarding the involvement of very young and asymptomatic children, pressure or coercion to involve participants is highly problematic. Attempts to render prevention programs more attractive to parents and efforts to motivate participation might avoid these problems and still safeguard enrollment. As pointed out before, most ASB-prevention programs were initially developed in the context of family support. Strikingly, ASB-prevention is still frequently presented in that same context of care and support for children and their families. Titles of such programs are rather "user-friendly" (Kemshall 2007), avoid explicit references to crime prevention, and instead make use of terms that emphasize child development and family well-being. On the one hand, such approaches have the potential to facilitate voluntary participation, while avoiding coercion and the labeling and stigmatization of participants. However, at the same time, the question arises whether and to what extent parents indeed give their *informed* consent and are informed about the primary goal of the program in which they, and their children, are participating. If the aim of ASB-prevention is not an explicit part of the information process, parental consent remains uninformed and parental autonomy is undermined.

In a series of interviews we conducted with juvenile delinquents (Horstkötter et al. 2012) and with parents of children with serious behavioral disturbances residing in intramural mental health care (Horstkötter et al. under review), participants voiced fundamental concern about early intervention in general. For parents and juveniles, the main question is the role of parents versus professionals, not whether any practice works or is efficient. Parents clearly indicated that it is central to their role as parents to first have the chance to look for solutions themselves, even in difficult times, rather than immediately being preempted by some professional or outside intervention. Therefore, regardless of how well parents are informed about the primary goal of any preventive measure, the very idea of prediction and early intervention has the potential to undermine the value of parenthood and the special relationship that parents, rather than professionals, can have with their children. Moreover, particularly in situations where interventions are proposed before or at the very beginning of upcoming problems, parents have pointed towards clear counterproductive effects. As one father put it forcefully: "A child must be able to develop. If one already very early, before someone falls, picks him up already, I would say than he never learns to pick up himself" (Horstkötter et al. under review). By their very intent and design, early interventions can deny children and their families the possibility to make mistakes, go through difficult times, encounter problems and then come to learn from these experiences, manage to deal with problems and rise again on their own. In this sense, early intervention might not only undermine parental autonomy, but more seriously inhibit the natural development of children and the coping and problem-solving capacities of parents. In addition, early intervention can entail the danger that uniform pre-given social formats on what counts as a "good child" and a "good parent" get imposed, potentially hindering the development of individual unique features. Opponents of ASB-prevention programs argue that the behaviors causing concern are not necessarily bad or undesirable, but can in fact have a social function and worth of their own (Horstkötter et al. 2012: 292; Horstkötter et al. under review), and trying to take these away might also be undesirable.

Society and Children at Risk

To date, scientists and professionals easily assume that screening, prediction and early ASB-prevention brings about a win-win situation and benefits the development of children concerned, as well as acting as a safeguard and increasing public safety. Put differently, scientists and professionals take these practices to contribute to population health, that is, to the wellbeing and mental health of the child population; and, in addition, to public health, that is, to the health of the broader public, because fewer victims of ASB are to be expected (Horstkötter 2015; Welsh, Braga, & Sullivan 2012; Wilson 2009). But proponents of this alleged win-win situation apparently ignore the various ways in which the interests of children, and also of their parents, can be endangered rather than served when getting involved in ASB-prevention. Therefore, conflicts of interest between child well-being and public safety are likely to arise. Conflicts of interests, however, require us to reflect carefully on whose interest should be favored and why, and hence to reflect on what ought to be the primary goal of screening, prediction and early prevention.

Public health policies tend to prioritize public interests above individual interests. Criminal law policies uphold high standards of proof to justify any infringement of individual interests; public health policies, however, are less strict about this and operate on only moderate standards of evidence and proof. It is this specific combination of affecting individual interests and inflicting some burden or harm on individual children and parents while accepting relatively low levels of evidence that has given rise to far-ranging concerns about preemptive screenings with a primarily forensic aim (Munthe & Radovic 2015). Findings about risk-factors are always on a group level, but do not necessarily allow for conclusions about specific individuals, who can be false positives. In addition, protective factors can compensate for risk-factors: children who experience behavioral troubles early in life might outgrow them, supported by informal care and education provided by parents, teachers or other significant third persons. Finally, children who are identified by an ASB screening device while no therapeutic or preventive approach is available might face social exclusion, potentially together with their whole family (Munthe & Radovic 2015). The Dutch Centre for Crime Prevention and Safety once clearly warned that "a society in which the precautionary principle predominates comes dangerously close to an authoritarian state" (CCV 2010: 146, translation DH).

Inspired by research in brain development, today there is increasing reciprocal interest and cooperation between educational or youth care approaches, (forensic) youth mental health care, and judicial youth care perspectives. This can be a particularly laudable development, because it allows bridges to be built between sectors that have operated separately for decades (cf. the Dutch initiatives *Brain and Cognition* and the more recent *Neurolab.nl*). Cooperation can be mutually fruitful and give each domain insight into the promises and perils of the other domain. That is, the judicial perspective that traditionally focuses exclusively on transgressions can learn to understand and take better account of the possible individual underpinnings of these behaviors, while those working from an educational or youth care perspective gain further insights into the wider social and social-safety implications of their work. However, in cases of conflict, for example when parents reject the screening of their child or refuse participation in some preventive ASB-intervention for an apparently high-risk child, mixing up judicial and childcare contexts can become problematic. Here the question about the primary versus the secondary goal of screening, prediction and early ASB-prevention becomes particularly pressing.

Psychosocial intervention measures that are now presented in the context of early ASB- and crime- prevention were initially developed for the sake of child well-being and family support. While the original aim of these interventions was to support vulnerable children and families, it turned out that children who took part in these interventions also developed less antisocial behavior (Tremblay & Japel 2003). That is, prevention of ASB and increased social safety appeared as long-term positive side-effects. From a forensic perspective, social safety and the protection of potential victims of ASB prevail above individual well-being, potentially justifying individual drawbacks or infringements on parental autonomy. From a youth care perspective, however, this justification does not hold: any burdens or drawbacks inflicted upon an individual child can be justifiable only if they are somehow unavoidable and if the intervention or therapy applied is likely to result in an improved individual outcome in the long run.

The participation in any preventive or therapeutic interventions is likely to be burdensome to some extent. It requires, at the very least, additional time-investment, attention to the advice given and effortful behavior change. As long as the primary aim of such measures is increased individual well-being this need not be a problem and interventions can be proportionate. However, when the primary aim is social safety, possible individual drawbacks do not need to be outweighed by individual benefits. For this reason, typical forensic situations request high individual proof of, for example, offending. However, in the context of screening, prediction and early ASB-prevention there is no such certainty, because the main focus is on asymptomatic or merely mildly disturbed children. For these children merely considered "at risk" it remains uncertain whether they might ever benefit personally or instead would only experience the various possible drawbacks of screening, prediction and early preventive intervention.

The same train of thought seems to apply to children and juveniles who have serious behavioral troubles but express these – so far – in a non criminal way. In our study with parents of children in intramural orthopsychiatric care, many parents expressed very serious concerns about potential future violent and criminal behaviors of their children. Still, their main motivation and primary justification for exposing their child, and themselves as parents, to the troubles of treatment and clinical admission was their hope for their child's better mental health and increased overall well-being and for building up their prospects for a good future. In the words of two mothers: "that he will be healthy again, just that" and "that he learns to survive in this society. [...] that had been our biggest goal to provide him a bit of a future in our society" (Horstkötter et al. under review). In this sense, the moral justification of screening, prediction and early intervention is not to be found in the potential reduction of crime or ASB-rates, but must be looked for in the positive impact such actions can have on the individuals concerned. This requires taking seriously any negative impacts that might result and weighing these appropriately. This also requires focusing on crime or ASB-prevention not in a direct way, but by facilitating individual and social circumstances that improve the situations of those considered at risk, thereby rendering such behaviors less likely and indirectly contributing to better public safety.

Conclusion

Screening, prediction and early ASB intervention are potentially powerful means to support individual child and family well-being and to safeguard public security. However, this alleged win-win situation is not self-evident. Relevant practices entail the danger of serious drawbacks and pitfalls for the children and families that are identified and treated. Insofar as very young and asymptomatic children are the preferred primary target group, while an increase in public safety constitutes the main goal of ASB-prevention, this is a problematic situation. Forensic aims in non-offender populations are hard to justify, are almost by definition disproportionate, and could even be taken to constitute a form of punishment in themselves. Therefore, ethically good practice should consist in attempts to primarily serve individual and familial interests in well-being and good mental health. ASB-prevention might then in the long run also result. However, that would be a positive side-effect of screening, prediction and early intervention, rather than their main goal.

References

Achenbach, T. M. (1991). *Manual for the Child Behavior Checklist / 4–18 and 1991 Profile*. Burlington, VT: University of Vermont Department of Psychiatry.

Arango, C., Díaz-Caneja, C. M., McGorry, P. D., Rapoport, J., Sommer, I. E., Vorstman, J. A., … Carpenter, W. (2018) "Preventive strategies for mental health," *The Lancet Psychiatry 5* 7 591–604. doi:10.1016/S2215-0366(18)30057–9

ASEBA. (2011) "Achenbach System of Empirically Based Assessment ASEBA". Retrieved from: www.aseba.com

Beauchaine, T. P. (2009) "Role of biomarkers and endophenotypes in prevention and treatment of psychopathological disorders," *Biomarkers in Medicine 3* 1 1–3. doi:10.2217/17520363.3.1.1

Beauchaine, T. P., Neuhaus, E., Brenner, S. L., & Gatzke-Kopp, L. (2008) "Ten good reasons to consider biological processes in prevention and intervention research," *Development and Psychopathology 20* 3 745–774. doi:doi:10.1017/S0954579408000369

Blair, R. J. R. (2013) "The neurobiology of psychopathic traits in youths," *Nature 14* 786–799. doi:10.1038/nrn3577

Bortolotti, L., & Widdows, H. (2011) "The right not to know: the case of psychiatric disorders," *Journal of Medical Ethics 37* 11 673–676. doi:10.1136/jme.2010.041111

British Medical Association (BMA) Ethics Department. (2004). *Medical Ethics Today, The BMA's Handbook of Ethics and Law*. London: BMJ.

Case, S. (2006) "Young people 'at-risk' of what? Challenging risk-focused early intervention as crime prevention," *Youth Justice 6* 3 171–179. doi:10.1177/1473225406069491

Caspi, A., McClay, J., Moffitt, T. E., Mill, J., Martin, J., Craig, I. W., … Poulton, R. (2002) "Role of genotype in the cycle of violence in maltreated children," *Science 297* 5582 851–853. doi:10.1126/science.1072290

Centrum voor Criminaliteitspreventie en Veiligheid (CCV). (2010) *Trendsignalement 2010, Ontwikkelingen in maatschappelijke veiligheid,* [Developments in social security] Utrecht, NL.

Coid, J. W. (2003) "Formulating strategies for the primary prevention of adult antisocial behaviour: 'high risk' or 'population' strategies?" In D. P. Farrington & J. W. Coid (Eds.), *Early Prevention of Adult Antisocial Behaviour* (pp. 32–78). Cambridge: Cambridge University Press.

Cornet, L. J., Bootsma, F., Alberda, D., & De Kogel, C. H. (2016) *Neurowetenschappelijke toepassingen in de jeugdstrafketen, Inventarisatie instrumenten, preventie en interventie.* [Neuroscientific applications in the juvenile criminal justice system. An inventory of measurement instruments, prevention and intervention methods] Meppel, NL: Boom.

Dadds, M. R., & Rhodes, T. (2009) "Aggression in young children with concurrent callous-unemotional traits: Can the neurosciences inform progress and innovation in treatment approaches?" In S. Hodgins, E. Viding, & A. Plodowski (Eds.), *The Neurobiological Basis of Violence: Science and Rehabilitation* (pp. 85–99). Oxford: Oxford University Press.

De Brito, S. A., & Hodgins, S. (2009) "Executive functions of persistent violent offenders: A critical review of the literature," In S. Hodgins, E. Viding, & A. Plodowski (Eds.), *The Neurobiological Basis of Violence: Science and Rehabilitation* (pp. 167–199). Oxford: Oxford University Press.

de Kogel, C. H. (2018). "More Autonomous or more Fenced-in? Neuroscientific Instruments and Intervention in Criminal Justice," *Neuroethics*. doi:10.1007/s12152-018-9384-5

de Vries, S. L., Hoeve, M., Assink, M., Stams, G. J. J., & Asscher, J. J. (2015) "Practitioner Review: effective ingredients of prevention programs for youth at risk of persistent juvenile delinquency - recommendations for clinical practice," *Journal of Child Psychology and Psychiatry 56* 2 108–121. doi:doi:10.1111/jcpp.12320

Farrington, D. P., & Coid, J. W. (Eds.). (2003). *Early Prevention of Adult Antisocial Behaviour*. Cambridge: Cambridge University Press.

Farrington, D. P., & Welsh, B. C. (2007). *Saving children from a life of crime, Early risk-factors and effective interventions.* Oxford: Oxford University Press.

Fishbein, D. H. (2000) "How can neurobiological research inform prevention strategies?" In D. H. Fishbein (Ed.), *The science, treatment, and prevention of antisocial behaviors: Application to the criminal justice system* (pp. 25–30). Kingston, NJ: Civic Research Institute.

Frick, P. J., & Petitclerc, A. (2009) "The use of callous-unemotional traits to define important subtypes of antisocial and violent youth," In S. Hodgins, E. Viding, & A. Plodowski (Eds.), *The Neurobiological Basis of Violence: Science and Rehabilitation* (pp. 65–83). Oxford: Oxford University Press.

Gatti, U. (1998) "Ethical issues raised when early intervention is used to prevent crime," *European Journal on Criminal Policy and Research 6* 113–132.

Glannon, W. (2007) *Bioethics and the brain.* Oxford: Oxford University Press.

Goodman, R. (1997) "The Strengths and Difficulties Questionnaire: A research note," *The Journal of Child Psychology and Psychiatry 38* 5 581–586.

Hawkins, J. D., & Herrenkohl, T. I. (2003) "Prevention in the school years," In D. P. Farrington & J. W. Coid (Eds.), *Early Prevention of Adult Antisocial Behavior* (pp. 265–291). Cambridge: Cambridge University Press.

Hodgins, S., Viding, E., & Plodowski, A. (2009). *The Neurobiological Basis of Violence.* Oxford: Oxford University Press.

Horstkötter, D. (2015) "Forensic screening and prevention in children and adolescents: Public health ethical aspects," *Public Health Ethics 8* 3 266–269. doi:10.1093/phe/phv027

Horstkötter, D., Berghmans, R., de Ruiter, C., Krumeich, A., & De Wert, G. (2012) "'We are also normal humans, you know?' Views and attitudes of juvenile delinquents on antisocial behaviour, neurobiology and prevention," *International Journal of Law and Psychiatry 35* 4 289–297. doi:10.1016/j.ijlp.2012.04.006

Horstkötter, D., Berghmans, R., & De Wert, G. (2014) "Early prevention of antisocial behavior (ASB): A comparative ethical analysis of psychosocial and biomedical approaches," *BioSocieties 9* 1 60–83. doi:10.1057/biosoc.2013.36

Horstkötter, D., Berghmans, R., Feron, F., & De Wert, G. (2014). "'One can always say no' Enriching the bioethical debate on antisocial behaviour, neurobiology and prevention: Views of juvenile delinquents," *Bioethics, 28* 5 225–234. doi:10.1111/j.1467-8519.2012.01997.x

Horstkötter, D., & De Wert, G. (2013) "The prevention of psychopathy: what we owe to young people," *American Journal of Bioethics Neuroscience, 4* 2 19-20. doi:10.1080/21507740.2013.782921

Horstkötter, D., Dondorp, W., & de Wert, G. (under review). *'You have to let someone take a fall before they can stand on their own' Parents and children in residential mental health care on the provision of care and the prospects of early crime prevention: a qualitative pilot study,* Maastricht University.

Jacka, F. N., & Reavley, N. J. (2014) "Prevention of mental disorders: evidence, challenges and opportunities," *BMC Medicine 12 1* 75. doi:10.1186/1741-7015-12-75

Kahn, J. (13th May 2012) "Can you call a 9-year-old a psychopath?" *New York Times Magazine.* Retrieved from www.nytimes.com/2012/05/13/magazine/can-you-call-a-9-year-old-a-psychopath.html?pagewanted=all.

Kellam, S. G., Mackenzie, A. C., Brown, C. H., Poduska, J. M., Wang, W., Petras, H., & Wilcox, H. C. (2011) "The Good Behavior Game and the future of prevention and treatment," *Addiction Science and Clinical Practice* 6 1 73–84.

Kelly, P. (2000) "The dangerousness of youth-at-risk: the possibilities of surveillance and intervention in uncertain times," *Journal of Adolescence 23* 4 463–476. doi:10.1006/jado.2000.0331

Kemshall, H. (2007) "Risk assessment and risk management: the right approach?" In M. Blyth, E. Solomon, & K. Baker (Eds.), *Young People and 'Risk'* (pp. 7–23). Bristol: Policy Press.

Levitt, M., & Manson, N. C. (2007) "My genes made me do it? The implications of behavioural genetics for responsibility and blame," *Health Care Analysis 15* 1 33–40. doi:10.1007/s10728-006-0038-0

Lichtenstein, P., Halldner, L., Zetterqvist, J., Sjölander, A., Serlachius, E., Fazel, S., ... Larsson, H. (2012) "Medication for attention deficit–hyperactivity disorder and criminality," *New England Journal of Medicine 367* 21 2006–2014. doi:10.1056/NEJMoa1203241

Loeber, R., Slot, N. W., Van der Laan, P., & Hoeve, M. (Eds.). (2008) *Tomorrow's Criminals. The Development of Child Delinquency and Effective Interventions.* Farnham: Ashgate.

McCrory, E., De Brito, S. A., & Viding, E. (2010) "Research Review: The neurobiology and genetics of maltreatment and adversity" *Journal of Child Psychology and Psychiatry 51* 10 1079–1095. doi:10.1111/j.1469-7610.2010.02271.x

Moffitt, T. E. (2005) "The new look of behavioral genetics in developmental psychopathology: Gene-environment interplay in antisocial behavior," *Psychological Bulletin 131* 4 533–554. doi:10.1037/0033-2909.131.4.533

Muncie, J., Hughes, G., & McLaughlin, E. (Eds.). (2002) *Youth Justice, Critical Readings.* London: Sage.

Munthe, C., & Radovic, S. (2015) "The return of Lombroso? Ethical aspects of (visions of) preventive forensic screening," *Public Health Ethics 8* 3 270–283. doi:10.1093/phe/phu048

Nuffield Council on Bioethics. (2002) *Genetics and Human Behaviour: The Ethical Context*. London: Nuffield Council on Bioethics.

Olds, D. L., Kitzman, H. R. N., Cole, R., Robinson, J., Sidora, K., Luckey, D. W., … Holmberg, J. (2004) "Effects of nurse home-visiting on maternal life course and child development: Age 6 follow-up results of a randomized trial," *Pediatrics 114* 6 1550–1559. doi:10.1542/peds.2004-0962

Ortiz, J., & Raine, A. (2004) "Heart rate level and antisocial behavior in children and adolescents: A meta-analysis," *Journal of the American Academy of Child and Adolescent Psychiatry, 43* 2 154–162. doi:10.1097/01.chi.0000101373.03068.5c

Ozonoff, S. (2015) "Early detection of mental health and neurodevelopmental disorders: the ethical challenges of a field in its infancy," *Journal of Child Psychology and Psychiatry 56* 9 933–935. doi:10.1111/jcpp.12452

Parks, G. (2000) "The High/Scope Perry Preschool program," *Juvenile Justice Bulletin of the Office of Juvenile Justice and Delinquency Prevention* October 1–8.

Rose, N. (2000) "The biology of culpability: Pathological identity and crime control in a biological culture," *Theoretical Criminology 4* 1 5–34. doi:10.1177/1362480600004001001

Rutter, M. (2012) "Psychopathy in childhood: Is it a meaningful diagnosis?" *British Journal of Psychiatry 200* 175–176. doi:10.1192/bjp.bp.111.092072

Sherman, L. W., Gottfredson, D., MacKenzie, D., Eck, J., Reuter, P., & Bushway, S. (1996) *Preventing crime: What Works, What Doesn't Work, What Is Promising. A Report to the United States Congress*. Maryland, VS: Department of Criminology and Criminal Justice

Shirtcliff, E. A., Vitacco, M. J., Graf, A. R., Gostisha, A. J., Merz, J. L., & Zahn-Waxler, C. (2009) "Neurobiology of empathy and callousness: Implications for the development of antisocial behavior," *Behavioral Sciences and the Law 27* 2 137–171. doi:10.1002/bsl.862

Singh, I., & Rose, N. (2009) "Biomarkers in psychiatry," *Nature 460* 202–207.

Stephen, D. E., & Squires, P. (2004) "'They're still children and entitled to be children': problematising the institutionalised mistrust of marginalised youth in Britain" *Journal of Youth Studies* 7 3 351–369. doi:10.1080/1367626042000268962

Sterzer, P. (2010) "Born to be criminal? What to make of early biological risk-factors for criminal behavior," *American Journal of Psychiatry 167* 1 1–3.

Sterzer, P., & Stadler, C. (2009) "Neuroimaging of aggressive and violent behaviour in children and adolescents," *Frontiers in Behavioral Neuroscience 3* 1–8. doi:10.1176/appi.ajp.2009.09111601

Sutton, C., Utting, D., & Farrington, D. P. (2004) "*Support From the Start: Working With Young Children and Their Families to Reduce the Risks of Crime and Antisocial Behaviour*" London: UK government Department of Education.

Tarini, B. A., Tercyak, K. P., & Wilfond, B. S. (2011) "Commentary: Children and predictive genomic testing: Disease prevention, research protection, and our future," *Journal of Pediatric Psychology, 36* 10 1113–1121. doi:10.1093/jpepsy/jsr040

Tremblay, R. E. (2010) "Developmental origins of disruptive behaviour problems: the 'original sin' hypothesis, epigenetics and their consequences for prevention," *Journal of Child Psychology and Psychiatry 51* 4 341–367. doi:10.1111/j.1469-7610.2010.02211.x

Tremblay, R. E., & Japel, C. (2003) "Prevention during pregnancy, infancy, and the preschool years," In D. P. Farrington & J. W. Coid (Eds.), *Early Prevention of Adult Antisocial Behaviour* (pp. 205–242). Cambridge: Cambridge University Press.

van Goozen, S. H. M., & Fairchild, G. (2008) "How can the study of biological processes help designing new interventions for children with severe antisocial behavior?" *Development and Psychopathology 20* 3 941–973. doi:10.1017/S095457940800045X

van Goozen, S. H. M., & Fairchild, G. (2009) "The neuroendocrinology of antisocial behaviour," In S. Hodgins, E. Viding, & A. Plodowski (Eds.), *The Neurobiological Basis of Violence: Science and Rehabilitation* (pp. 201–221). Oxford: Oxford University Press.

van Goozen, S. H. M., Fairchild, G., Snoek, H., & Harold, G. T. (2007) "The evidence for a neurobiological model of childhood antisocial behavior," *Psychological Bulletin 133* 1 149–182. doi:10.1037/0033-2909.133.1.149

Viding, E., Fontaine, N. M. G., & McCrory, E. (2012) "Antisocial behaviour in children with and without callous-unemotional traits" *Journal of the Royal Society of Medicine 105* 5 195–200. doi:10.1258/jrsm.2011.110223

Viding, E., Jones, A. P., Frick, P. J., Moffitt, T. E., & Plomin, R. (2008) "Heritability of antisocial behaviour at 9: do callous-unemotional traits matter?" *Developmental Science 11* 1 17–22. doi:10.1111/j.1467-7687.2007.00648.x

Viding, E., Larsson, H., & Jones, A. P. (2009) "Quantitative genetic studies of antisocial behaviour," In S. Hodgins, E. Viding, & A. Plodowski (Eds.), *The Neurobiological Basis of Violence: Science and Rehabilitation* (pp. 251–264). Oxford: Oxford University Press.

Walsh, C. (2011) "Youth Justice and neuroscience," *British Journal of Criminology 51* 21–39. doi:10.1093/bjc/azq061

Walsh, C. (2014) "Bioprediction in youth justice," In I. Singh, W. Sinnott-Armstrong, & J. Savulescu (Eds.), *Bioprediction, Biomarkers and Bad Behavior* (pp. 42–56). Oxford: Oxford University Press.

Webster-Stratton, C., Kolpacoff, M., & Hollinsworth, T. (1988) "Self-administered videotape therapy for families with conduct-problem children: Comparison with two cost-effective treatments and a control group," *Journal of Consulting and Clinical Psychology 56* 558–566.

Welsh, B. C., Braga, A. A., & Sullivan, C. J. (2012) "Serious Youth Violence and Innovative Prevention: On the Emerging Link Between Public Health and Criminology," *Justice Quarterly 31* 3 500–523. doi:10.1080/07418825.2012.690441

Wilson, J. (2009) "Towards a normative framework for public health ethics and policy, *Public Health Ethics 2* 2 184–194. doi:10.1093/phe/php012

Wright, K. (2017). "Inventing the 'normal' child: Psychology, delinquency, and the promise of early intervention," *History of the Human Sciences 30* 5 46–67. doi:10.1177/0952695117737209s

23

COMPARISON OF SOCIO-AFFECTIVE PROCESSING ACROSS SUBTYPES OF ANTISOCIAL PSYCHOPATHOLOGY

Scott Tillem, Shou-An Ariel Chang, and Arielle Baskin-Sommers

Antisocial behavior is characterized by a wide variety of actions that violate social norms. These actions range from relatively minor behaviors, such as lying or intimidating others, to more disruptive behaviors, such as selling drugs or physically assaulting others. Individuals chronically engaging in antisocial behaviors are at risk for a variety of adverse life outcomes, such as suicide, school dropout, unemployment, psychopathology, substance abuse, and incarceration (Caspi et al. 1998; Fergusson et al. 2005). Moreover, estimates of the financial impact of antisocial behavior (e.g., the cost of law enforcement, incarceration, property damage, loss of wages, healthcare) on society exceeds $2 trillion annually in the United States alone (Kiehl and Hoffman 2011). Given the profound personal, economic, and social impacts of antisocial behavior, determining which individuals are at the greatest risk for chronic engagement in these behaviors is essential.

Of note, research has demonstrated that there are two clinically meaningful subtypes of individuals engaging in high levels of antisocial behavior (Hyde et al. 2013; Viding et al. 2012; Drislane and Patrick 2013; Brennan et al. 2017). The first subtype we term "psychopathy"; these individuals are infamous for their prolific antisocial behavior and their ability to be interpersonally manipulative and charming. They engage in elaborate cons, callously assault others, impulsively look for adventures, and chronically commit antisocial acts in order to obtain their goals (e.g., money, power, thrills). For adults, in both clinical and research settings, the gold standard assessment of psychopathy is Hare's Psychopathy Checklist-Revised (PCL-R; Hare 2003), an interview-based measure of the four characteristics (interpersonal, affective, impulsive, and antisocial) of this disorder. The PCL-R rates individuals on 20 different items that cut across these four characteristics on a scale from 0 to 2 for each item. In the United States, individuals with a score of 30 or above are diagnosed with psychopathy. Notably, psychopathy impacts approximately 15–25% of incarcerated adult, male offenders, but only 1% of the general population (Hare 2006; Hare and Neumann 2008; Hare 2003).

Moreover, there is a growing body of research demonstrating that the interpersonal, affective, and behavioral characteristics of psychopathy emerge during childhood and often persist throughout development (Raine et al. 2010; Blair et al. 2006; Gao et al., 2009). Researchers theorize that, in youth, the presence of callous-unemotional traits (CU; e.g., callous use of others, a lack of remorse or guilt, and an absence of empathy; in DSM-5 a specifier of conduct disorder called "limited prosocial emotions"), grandiose narcissism, and impulsive-antisocial traits, increase risk of developing psychopathy (Frick et al. 2014; Frick and White 2008; Frogner et al. 2016; Viding et al. 2012; Viding et al.

2009; Viding and McCrory 2015; Viding and McCrory 2018). Similar to adults with psychopathy, CU traits are present in, on average, 9–25% of youth offenders (Frick et al. 2014; Frick and White 2008; Frogner et al. 2016).

The second subtype, which we term "antisocial-only," are defined by their chronic impulsive, irresponsible, reactively aggressive, and antisocial behavior. Individuals in this subtype are typically assessed using formal diagnostic criteria or through personality trait models. First, individuals in this subtype can be identified diagnostically by assessing children for conduct disorder (CD; in the absence of CU) or adults for antisocial personality disorder (APD; in the absence of psychopathy) using the diagnostic criteria put forth by the DSM. According to the DSM-5, youth with CD are characterized by a chronic pattern of behaviors that violate the rights of others or societal norms in several ways (e.g., aggression to people or animals, destruction of property, theft, rule violations). APD is a continuation of CD, requiring this pattern of impulsive, irresponsible, and antisocial behaviors that began in childhood to persist into adulthood (American Psychiatric Association 2013). Second, individuals in this subtype can be identified as individuals high on a measure of latent trait externalizing. Externalizing is conceptualized as a continuous, heritable predisposition to engage in maladaptive, disinhibitory behaviors (e.g., crimes, substance abuse; Gorenstein and Newman 1980; Iacono et al. 2008). Assessments of latent trait externalizing typically either tap the common variance associated with symptoms of CD, APD, and substance use disorders (Iacono et al. 2008), or use personality/temperament measures to assess predisposing personality traits (e.g., constraint, impulsivity, negative emotionality; Krueger et al. 2007; Patrick et al. 2002). In terms of prevalence, estimates suggest that between 50–66% of male prisoners meet criteria for APD, more than double the prevalence of psychopathy (Moran 1999; Fazel and Danesh, 2002).

Both of these subtypes of individuals are known to act on impulse and engage in antisocial behaviors. Perhaps, though, one aspect of their behavior that distinguishes them from other antisocial individuals is the presence of significant interpersonal difficulties (e.g., callousness, hostility, affective idiosyncrasies) that impedes their ability to form and maintain, meaningful, long-term relationships. The combination of chronic antisocial behavior and interpersonal dysfunction produces suffering, for the individual, for their family members, for their community, and for society at large. Interestingly, despite similarities in behavior, a growing body of research suggests that the underlying neurocognitive processes contributing to these behavioral and interpersonal difficulties are relatively distinct (Hyde et al. 2013; Viding et al. 2012; Drislane and Patrick 2013; Brennan et al. 2017; Moffitt 2017; Lobbestael et al. 2013; Schönenberg and Jusyte 2014; Baskin-Sommers and Newman 2013; Estrada et al. 2018). Accordingly, a closer examination of the underlying processes could tell us *why* a particular individual continues to engage in these behaviors and have interpersonal difficulties despite the persistence of suffering.

The primary goal of this chapter is to review neurocognitive processes, specifically socio-affective processes, which contribute to the behavioral and interpersonal difficulties in these antisocial subtypes. To this end, we (1) briefly describe the specific components of socio-affective processing that will be examined in this chapter; (2) review existing literature examining these components of socio-affective processing within each antisocial subtype; and (3) discuss the limitations of the current research and potential future directions.

Socio-Affective Processing

Socio-affective processes encompass a set of interrelated, yet distinct, neurocognitive processes that support intra- and inter-personal functioning. They can vary from basic facial recognition (i.e., recognizing and identifying a familiar face) to judging another agent's beliefs, goals, or intentions (e.g., theory of mind). Within antisocial populations, research primarily has been limited to two specific domains of socio-affective processes, which we will refer to as emotion recognition and theory of mind.

Emotion recognition is a set of processes involved in assessing an agent's emotional state based upon an affectively valenced cue displayed by the agent. These cues can be facial cues (e.g., facial expression) or non-facial cues (e.g., body language, vocal pitch, prosody, or intonation).

Emotion recognition can be assessed in two ways: explicitly or implicitly. On the one hand, explicit emotion recognition, an individual's ability to explicitly identify, or label, another agent's emotional state when directly asked to do so, is often assessed behaviorally using facial affect recognition tasks (Munoz 2009; Sharp et al. 2015; Stevens et al. 2001; Fairchild et al. 2009). These tasks involve presenting participants with an image of a face displaying an emotional expression (e.g., happiness, anger, fear) and asking the participant to identify the expression being displayed. On the other hand, implicit emotion recognition, an individual's ability and/or inclination to automatically attend to, evaluate, and respond to another's emotional state without being instructed, is assessed using physiological or behavioral responses during tasks where affective cues are presented but do not form the basis of evaluation for the required task. In the former context, affective cues are displayed, and often participants are asked to passively view those cues while physiological responses are recorded. Differentiation between types of affective cues based on physiological measures are inferred to reflect implicit recognition of those cues (Vuilleumier et al. 2001). In the latter context, affectively valenced cues (e.g., fearful face cues) are presented peripherally to other goal-relevant information (e.g., press one button for eyes looking left and one for eyes looking right) and may inform performance but are not explicitly evaluated (e.g., participants are not instructed to name the emotion) during the task (Baskin-Sommers and Newman 2014).

Measurement of neural activity during implicit or explicit emotion recognition tasks also informs our understanding of the neurocognitive underpinnings of emotion recognition. The amygdala is central to understanding emotion recognition, as it is important for the detection of affectively salient information (Sergerie et al. 2008; Cunningham and Brosch 2012). Additionally, frontal regions including the medial prefrontal cortex (mPFC), specifically the ventromedial prefrontal cortex (vmPFC), and orbital frontal cortex (OFC) are implicated in both implicit and explicit emotion recognition (Sabatinelli et al. 2011). Together, these form key neural regions that support emotion recognition.

Emotion recognition, whether explicit or implicit, is critical to everyday social interactions. These processes allow individuals to understand and predict how others are feeling in order to respond to others appropriately and adapt their own behavior accordingly.

Theory of Mind (ToM) is a set of socio-affective processes involved in assessing another agent's emotions, beliefs, goals, or intentions within a given situational context. During ToM tasks, participants are presented with scenarios or scenes, and are asked to use and integrate information about the situational context of a scene and/or the agent's actions to evaluate the agent's feelings or thoughts (e.g., Character A just told Character B s/he could not have a piece of candy; how does Character B feel?).

Much like emotion recognition, ToM can be assessed explicitly or implicitly. Tasks explicitly evaluating ToM typically expose participants to a scenario (either by having them read a vignette, view a cartoon image or photograph, or watch a film clip), then ask participants about different characters' feelings (i.e., affective ToM), or ask participants about the characters' beliefs, goals, or intentions (i.e., cognitive ToM; e.g., Sally-Ann type false belief task; Leslie et al. 2004; Shamay-Tsoory and Aharon-Peretz 2007). In contrast, tasks implicitly evaluating ToM assess the degree to which an individual automatically assesses another agent's feelings, beliefs, goals, or intentions during an apparently unrelated task (e.g., see Samson et al. 2010).

Additionally, during all types of ToM tasks, affective or cognitive ToM judgments can vary in their level of complexity, depending upon the number of "minds" (i.e., different individuals/agents) the participant needs to represent and track. For example, a first-order judgement is when an individual evaluates another agent's thoughts or feelings, only requiring that the individual represents one other agent's feelings or thoughts (e.g., evaluate if Character A likes Object X). A second-order judgement, however, is when an individual judges what another agent thinks about a third agent's thoughts or feelings, requiring the individual to simultaneously represent two other agent's feelings or thoughts (e.g., evaluate if Character A thinks Character B likes object X).

At a neurobiological level, both affective and cognitive ToM rely on dynamic integration of information between a variety of cortical structures. Specifically, the mPFC, precuneus, and right temporoparietal junction are implicated in an individual's ability to judge another agent's feelings, beliefs, goals, or intentions (Spreng and Grady 2010; Spreng et al. 2009; Jack et al. 2013).

ToM is crucial for human development. Perspective-taking allows individuals to both understand and predict how other agents will respond in social situations. It provides a foundation for the formation and maintenance of social relationships that are mutually constructive.

Psychopathy and CU/PP

Generally, individuals with psychopathic traits display deficits in their implicit and explicit assessment of facial, vocal, and bodily affective information, particularly when that information is reflecting distress (e.g., fear or sadness; Dawel et al. 2012; Wilson et al. 2011; Marsh and Blair 2008). More specifically, there is clear support for emotion recognition problems in psychopathic individuals throughout developmental stages. Starting as young as 2 to 5 years old, youth with CU traits exhibited blunted implicit neural detection of fearful prosody (as measured by mismatch negativity; Hoyniak et al. 2018). Pre-adolescents and adolescents with CU traits, and adults with psychopathy, were slower and less accurate at explicitly identifying emotions displayed by other agents (e.g., displayed in faces, voices; Blair and Coles 2000; Blair et al. 2001; Munoz 2009; Sharp et al. 2015; Stevens et al. 2001; Dadds et al. 2018; Fairchild et al. 2009; Jusyte et al. 2015; Rehder et al. 2017; Woodworth and Waschbusch 2008; Sharp and Vanwoerden 2014; Blair et al. 2005; Bagley et al. 2009; Blair et al. 2004; Blair et al. 2002; Dolan and Fullam 2006; Eisenbarth et al. 2008; Hastings et al. 2008; Kosson et al. 2002; Montagne et al. 2005; Sandvik et al. 2014; Stanković et al. 2015). Additionally, youth with CU traits and adults with psychopathy showed diminished amygdala responses during implicit emotion recognition (e.g., when assessing the gender of a face; Marsh et al. 2008; White et al. 2012; Decety et al. 2014; Hyde et al. 2014; Deeley et al. 2006). Further, in support of these findings, multiple meta-analyses have reported small, but significant, effect sizes for the relationship between CU traits and psychopathy with difficulties in emotion recognition (Dawel et al. 2012; Wilson et al. 2011).

While there is good support for psychopathy-related impairments in emotion recognition, there are some inconsistencies across studies. Several studies reported that adults with psychopathy compared to those without do not exhibit significant differences in either response speed or accuracy during explicit facial emotion recognition tasks (Richell et al. 2005; Glass and Newman 2006; Mowle et al. 2018; Kunecke et al. 2018; Dolan and Fullam 2004). Additionally, psychopathy-related difficulties in emotion recognition may not reflect a specific deficit in emotion recognition *per se*, but rather a more general deficit in attention that impedes their ability to spontaneously attend to affectively relevant information (Gillespie et al. 2015; Dargis et al. 2018; Boll and Gamer 2016; Luckhurst et al. 2017; Olderbak et al. 2018; Dawel et al. 2015; Dadds et al. 2008; Bedford et al. 2017; Dadds et al. 2006).

For example, the eye region of the face provides the most relevant information for evaluating emotional distress cues (e.g., fear cues; Adolphs, 2008, Johnson, 2005). However, eye tracking research suggests that youth with CU and adults with psychopathy did not attend to the eyes when viewing another's face (Gillespie et al., 2015, Dargis et al., 2018, Boll and Gamer, 2016, Bedford et al., 2017, Dadds et al., 2008, Dadds et al., 2006), even when explicitly instructed to evaluate another agent's overall facial expression (Dadds et al., 2008, Dadds et al., 2006). Instead, youth with CU and adults with psychopathy attended to other parts of the face, such as the mouth, which do not convey as much affective information (Gillespie et al., 2015, Dargis et al., 2018, Boll and Gamer, 2016, Bedford et al., 2017, Dadds et al., 2008, Dadds et al., 2006). However, when their attention was drawn to the eyes (e.g., by explicitly instructing them to attend to the eyes), both youth with CU traits and adults with psychopathy did not differ from controls during emotion recognition tasks (Dadds et al., 2008, Dadds et al., 2006, Richell et al., 2005). Similarly, if psychopathic individuals were instructed to physically mimic facial expressions displayed prior to evaluating the facial cue, they were able to accurately recognize others' emotional expressions (Luckhurst et al., 2017). Together, these findings suggest that individuals with psychopathy, regardless of developmental stage, have difficulty implicitly evaluating others' emotions, or spontaneously attending to the most relevant information. However, they appear capable of emotion recognition when their attention is drawn to very specific (e.g., eyes), salient affective cues. It seems that while individuals with psychopathy are able to recognize emotions, their natural ability to do so is inadequate. Ultimately, this may result in inaccuracies in recognizing how others feel or failing to fully appreciate the complex emotional expression being displayed by others. The fact, though, that individuals with psychopathy are able to recognize emotions, with deliberate supports, also highlights a potential target for intervention.

Research examining ToM in psychopathy produces a divergent pattern of results for cognitive and affective ToM. Across studies, neither youth with CU nor adults with psychopathy showed neural differences or behavioral deficits in cognitive ToM, suggesting intact cognitive ToM in psychopathy (Sebastian et al. 2012; Jones et al. 2010; O'Nions et al. 2014; Sommer et al. 2010; Blair et al. 1996; Dolan and Fullam 2004; Sharp and Vanwoerden 2014; Shamay-Tsoory et al. 2010). By contrast, the evidence regarding the relationship between affective ToM and psychopathy is more mixed.

To date, three studies reported that individuals with psychopathy were able to successfully assess another agent's affective state during affective ToM tasks (Sebastian et al. 2012; O'Nions et al. 2014; Sommer et al. 2010), suggesting that psychopathic individuals did not display deficits in affective ToM. In contrast, two other studies reported psychopathy-related behavioral abnormalities during affective ToM tasks. First, Sharp and Vanwoerden (2014) demonstrated that, after viewing a 15-minute long video clip depicting a dinner party, adolescents high on CU were significantly worse than adolescents low on CU at evaluating what the characters in the film were feeling. Second, Shamay-Tsoory et al. (2010) showed that after viewing a static cartoon image, adults with psychopathy were able to successfully make simple, first-order affective evaluations (e.g., Character A loves X object), but exhibited difficulty completing more complex, second-order affective evaluations (e.g., Character A loves the same object that Character B loves).

At first glance, these two studies appear to contradict the studies suggesting that individuals with psychopathy show intact affective ToM. However, it is possible that these apparently contradictory findings were actually the result of differences in task complexity. For example, Sharp and Vanwoerden (2014) used a video of a dinner party as their task stimulus, requiring participants to process and track various pieces of information over the 15-minute duration of the video. By contrast, other studies examining affective ToM in psychopathy used relatively simple, static cartoon images, requiring participants to process and track, at most, three frames of information (Sebastian et al. 2012; O'Nions et al. 2014; Sommer et al. 2010; Shamay-Tsoory et al. 2010). Similarly, Shamay-Tsoory et al. (2010) report that psychopathy-related difficulties in affective ToM were limited to complex, second-order judgements, which were not examined in any of the other studies. Collectively, these findings suggest that psychopathic individuals exhibit difficulties with affective ToM, but only when evaluating affective information that is embedded in a particularly complex stimulus (e.g., a movie), or when the judgment itself is highly complex or multilayered (e.g., second-order affective evaluations). This pattern of results suggests that when presented with more complex stimuli or scenarios, either the complexity of the scenario, the complexity of the affective judgments, and/or the amount of information they need to process and track, impairs psychopathic individuals' ability to successfully evaluate or predict other agents' affective states.

Neural examinations of affective ToM in psychopathy yield similarly mixed results. On the one hand, O'Nions et al. (2014) reported that youth with CU did not significantly differ from healthy controls, either behaviorally or neurally, during an affective ToM task. On the other hand, both Sebastian et al. (2012) and Sommer et al. (2010) reported that while individuals with psychopathy were able to successfully perform an affective ToM task (i.e., psychopathic individuals showed no behavioral differences compared to controls), they exhibited distinct neural abnormalities while performing the task. Sebastian et al. (2012) specifically found that adolescents with CD who were high on CU (CD+CU) showed blunted amygdala responses during an affective ToM task that required participants to view and evaluate a static cartoon image. However, in their analysis, Sebastian et al. (2012) examined amygdala reactivity across entire trials (i.e., during the initial presentation of the image and the judgement). This type of analysis made it difficult to determine what precise component of the trial was driving the blunted amygdala reactivity in adolescents with CD+CU. It is possible that the CD+CU-related blunting of the amygdala response was driven by neural differences when these youth initially saw (and affectively responded to) the cartoon images, rather than any CD+CU-related neural abnormalities in affective ToM (judgement).

Sommer et al. (2010) reported that, during an affective ToM task, adults with psychopathy showed blunted responses in cortical regions associated with action observation and execution (i.e., the bilateral supramarginal gyri and superior frontal gyrus; Van Overwalle and Baetens, 2009) and heightened responses in cortical regions generally associated with socio-affective processing, such as the orbitofrontal cortex, temporoparietal junction, and mPFC (Spreng and Grady 2010; Spreng et al. 2009; Jack et al. 2013). This finding suggests that while adults with psychopathy were able to engage in affective ToM, they required more (or at least different) socio-affective neural resources to do so (Sommer et al. 2010). While speculative, this need for additional neural resources to complete relatively simple (i.e., first-order) affective ToM judgments could potentially explain psychopathic individuals' apparent difficulties with more complex (i.e., second-order) affective evaluations (Shamay-Tsoory et al. 2010). More specifically, it is possible that psychopathic individuals are able to engage enough neurocognitive resources to compensate for psychopathy-related difficulties in affective ToM during relatively simple, first-order, affective ToM evaluations. However, the additional neural resources needed to compensate for affective ToM deficits during more complex, second-order, affective evaluations may exceed the available neurocognitive resources for psychopathic individuals.

Taken together, these findings suggest that individuals with psychopathy exhibit intact cognitive ToM and only exhibit difficulties in affective ToM during complex evaluations, or when another agent's affective state is embedded in a complex stimulus. However, these studies exclusively examine tasks which explicitly instruct participants to engage in ToM, and do not assess whether individuals with psychopathy spontaneously engage in ToM (i.e., they have not assessed whether these individuals implicitly evaluate other agents' feelings, beliefs, goals, or intentions, without being explicitly instructed to do so).

A recent study by Drayton and colleagues (2018) helped address this gap in the literature by examining the impact of psychopathy on an implicit measure of cognitive ToM in an incarcerated sample. In this study, Drayton and colleagues (2018) had inmates complete a cognitive ToM task (Samson et al. 2010). During this task, participants were presented with static scenes depicting a gender- and race-matched avatar in a room with varying numbers of dots on the walls. The dots appeared in front of the avatar (i.e., the avatar had complete information), behind the avatar (i.e., the avatar had no information), or both (i.e., the avatar had partial information); however, the participant always saw all of the dots on every trial (i.e., the participant always had complete information). On some trials, participants were asked to evaluate how many dots the avatar could see (other-trials) and on some trials participants were asked to evaluate how many dots they personally could see (self-trials). The other-trials provided a measure of explicit ToM: could the participant take the avatar's perspective? The self-trials provided a measure of implicit ToM: did the avatar's perspective automatically affect the participant's perspective? Consistent with previous research, inmates higher on psychopathy were able to engage in explicit ToM and performed similarly to inmates lower on psychopathy in the other-trials. However, inmates higher on psychopathy compared to inmates lower on psychopathy displayed significantly less interference on the self-trials (i.e., their reaction time was not affected by the information available to the avatar). These findings suggest that psychopathic individuals do not implicitly evaluate others' mental states (i.e., they do not implicitly engage cognitive ToM; Drayton et al. 2018), but can do so explicitly.

Another study examining pain perception in psychopathy suggests a similar pattern of psychopathy-related impairment in implicit affective ToM. Meffert et al. (2013) used fMRI to examine neural responses to hand pain in three different conditions: passive viewing of a clip of a hand being hurt (i.e., implicit affective ToM), imagining what the person in the clip might be experiencing (i.e., explicit affective ToM), and physically experiencing the actual scenarios depicted in the clips. Meffert et al. (2013) reported that, when adults with psychopathy passively viewed the pain clips, they did not exhibit significant neural overlap with their actual experience of pain (relative to controls), which the authors interpreted as evidence that adults with psychopathy did not implicitly engage in affective ToM. In contrast, however, Meffert et al. found that individuals with psychopathy showed similar overlap in neural responses to controls when instructed to imagine what the person was feeling (i.e., explicit affective ToM) and when physically experiencing the pain. These two findings suggest that adults with psychopathy are able to engage in affective ToM, but do not do so implicitly (i.e., without instruction).

While the purely neural nature of these findings makes this interpretation somewhat speculative, these findings and interpretations are consistent with both prior research demonstrating psychopathy-related neural abnormalities in pain perception in others (Decety et al. 2013), and Drayton et al.'s (2018) findings indicating that adults with psychopathy do not implicitly engage in cognitive ToM. Thus, the current literature examining ToM in psychopathy provides strong evidence that individuals with psychopathy largely are able to engage in ToM when instructed to do so, but do not do so implicitly. This is an important distinction because it helps in explaining why psychopathic individuals can so easily manipulate others' thoughts and feelings when conning them (as the act of conning someone explicitly requires ToM), yet have difficulty with more everyday social interactions, which may require more implicit ToM.

Overall, individuals with psychopathy exhibit clear deficits in both emotion identification, and certain types of affective ToM. However, in both instances, these deficits are limited to specific contexts. In the case of emotion identification, if attention is explicitly directed to relevant affective information, individuals with psychopathy are able to accurately recognize others' emotions based on socio-affective cues (Dadds et al. 2008; Dadds et al. 2006; Richell et al. 2005; Luckhurst et al. 2017). Similarly, when presented with relatively simple, first-order scenarios, individuals with psychopathy exhibit intact affective ToM (O'Nions et al. 2014; Sebastian et al. 2012; Sommer et al. 2010; Shamay-Tsoory et al. 2010). These findings suggest that individuals with psychopathy may not have a complete deficit in either of these socio-affective processes *per se*, but rather a more general impairment in processing and/or attending to relevant affective cues embedded in complex situations or stimuli. Moreover, a recurrent finding across various aspects of socio-affective processing in psychopathy is that, even if individuals with psychopathy are able to normatively engage various different socio-affective processes (in specific circumstances), they tend to only do so when instructed. The failure to implicitly attend to, and process, others' emotions or mental states may explain how psychopathic individuals are able to callously harm others during goal-pursuit, but also able to charm, con, and manipulate others when necessary.

Antisocial-Only

The research examining socio-affective processing in antisocial-only individuals is fairly limited, particularly in comparison to the extensive literature examining socio-affective processing in psychopathy. However, the existing literature generally shows that youth with CD (in absence of CU) and adults with APD may exhibit difficulties in explicit emotion recognition. Several studies have shown that youth with conduct problems, in general, or CD, in particular, are slower and/or less accurate at labeling facial expressions, particularly anger (Fairchild et al. 2010, Sharp 2000, Leist and Dadds 2009; Fairchild et al. 2009). Similarly, Schönenberg et al. (2013) and Dolan and Fullam (2004) both reported that adults with APD exhibit difficulties recognizing basic emotions (e.g., angry and sad) from facial cues. Taken together, these findings suggest that, much like individuals with psychopathy, antisocial-only individuals, regardless of developmental stage, exhibit difficulties explicitly recognizing others' emotions, particularly negative ones.

This apparent consistency between the research examining antisocial-only individuals and research examining psychopathy raises the possibility that deficits in explicitly identifying others' emotions may not be inherently related to either antisocial-only or psychopathic individuals, specifically. Rather, difficulty explicitly identifying others' emotions may index a more general risk factor for antisociality (Marsh and Blair 2008). In fact, several studies reported that more general measures of antisociality predict both behavioral and neural abnormalities in emotion identification, and that these relationships are not moderated by factors such as group status (e.g., antisocial-only vs. psychopathic individuals), or levels of CU traits (Pfabigan et al. 2015; Schönenberg et al. 2016; Hyde et al. 2016). Accordingly, difficulty explicitly assessing and labeling affective cues may reflect developmental or environmental risk-factors common to both antisocial subtypes, such as early maltreatment, or a poor social environment leading to minimal exposure to social cues early in development, either of which could impair early socio-affective development and produce long-lasting deficits in socio-affective functioning (Leist and Dadds 2009; Dadds et al. 2018).

Interestingly, however, while both antisocial-only and psychopathic individuals exhibit similar difficulties explicitly identifying others' emotions, unlike psychopathic individuals, antisocial-only individuals appear to implicitly recognize socio-affective cues. Baskin-Sommers and Newman (2014) found that, during a gaze cueing task, adult inmates high on externalizing (a latent trait associated with antisocial-only individuals) committed significantly more errors when asked to ignore affectively valenced faces (particularly fearful faces) compared to neutral faces, suggesting that they not only implicitly recognized the fear emotion in the stimuli, but over-responded to it. In line with this finding, Hyde et al. (2014) reported that, during an fMRI face-matching paradigm, adults higher on APD symptoms (controlling for CU traits) exhibited significantly enhanced amygdala reactivity to emotional faces. These two studies suggest that antisocial-only individuals implicitly recognize socio-affective cues, and seem to over-respond to these cues, both behaviorally and neurally (Hyde et al. 2014; Baskin-Sommers and Newman 2014). Thus, antisocial-only individuals' difficulties evaluating other agent's emotions do not appear to be due to a failure to implicitly attend to relevant affective content (as seems to be the case in psychopathy), but rather, may reflect a true impairment in explicitly recognizing socio-affective cues they are exposed to.

Research suggests that ToM is largely intact in antisocial-only individuals. When assessed behaviorally, several studies demonstrated that antisocial-only individuals, across all developmental stages, exhibit intact cognitive and affective ToM (Woodworth and Waschbusch 2008; Jones et al. 2010; Sebastian et al. 2012). However, one study partially contradicts this set of findings.

Dolan and Fullam (2004) reported that, while antisocial individuals (regardless of whether they had APD or psychopathy) were able to successfully complete traditional false belief tasks and identify subtle violations of social norms (e.g., identify when someone accidentally said something that should not have been said; i.e., social faux pas), they exhibited difficulties with affective ToM within the context of these subtle norm violations. More specifically, both adults with APD and adults with psychopathy displayed difficulties assessing characters' affective states after a subtle norm violation. The singular nature of this finding within the antisocial-only subtype makes it hard to reconcile with the various other studies showing that antisocial-only individuals exhibit intact affective ToM. However, if replicated, this result can be viewed as consistent with the affective ToM patterns in psychopathy showing that psychopathic individuals exhibit intact affective ToM, unless presented with more complex stimuli or scenarios. Collectively, these studies seem to suggest that, if antisocial-only individuals exhibit any deficits in affective ToM, it is limited to the context of complex social situations.

Beyond these studies examining potential behavioral issues with ToM in antisocial-only individuals, only one study examined neural differences in these individuals during a ToM paradigm. Sebastian et al. (2012) reported that, during an affective ToM fMRI paradigm, CD symptomology (controlling for CU traits) in adolescents, was unrelated to behavioral task performance. However, in contrast to CU traits (which were associated with diminished amygdala reactivity during this task), CD symptomology (controlling for CU traits) was associated with increased amygdala reactivity (Sebastian et al. 2012). However, as with the CU findings reported above, the fact that Sebastian et al. (2012) examined the amygdala response across entire trials (rather than specifically during the affective ToM judgment), makes it unclear whether the CD-related increase in amygdala activity is truly the result of neural abnormalities in affective ToM, or simply the product of increased amygdala reactivity when initially seeing (and affectively responding to) the affectively valenced scenes. Regardless of the specific interpretation, however, the existing research examining ToM in antisocial-only individuals suggests that these individuals exhibit largely intact cognitive and affective ToM, albeit with potentially atypical neural responses during affective ToM judgments[1].

Generally, research examining socio-affective processing in antisocial-only individuals shows that these individuals exhibit deficits in explicitly recognizing others' emotions based upon socio-affective cues, but generally intact ToM and intact implicit recognition of others' emotions. Specifically, unlike psychopathic individuals, antisocial-only individuals appear to spontaneously attend to and process socio-affective cues and even potentially over-respond to these cues, both behaviorally and neurally (Hyde et al. 2014; Sebastian et al. 2012; Baskin-Sommers and Newman 2014; Baskin-Sommers and Newman 2013). However, antisocial-only individuals display a specific deficit in explicitly recognizing others' emotions. This specific difficulty explicitly recognizing others' facial expressions, in combination with their tendency to over-respond to affective content, may partially explain the hostile interpersonal interactions characteristic of antisocial-only individuals. It is possible that antisocial-only individuals' difficulties recognizing facial expressions may lead them to label faces as negatively valenced or hostile, even when they are not. Subsequently, these individuals may then affectively over-respond to this perceived hostile facial expression and act in a hostile manner in return (Lobbestael et al. 2013; Schönenberg and Jusyte 2014).

Considerations for Future Research and Conclusions

There is both clinical and empirical support for socio-affective disruptions in psychopathic and antisocial-only individuals. However, close examination of the available data suggests that the specific types of dysfunction vary between subtypes of individuals. Psychopathic individuals appear capable of socio-affective processes, such as emotion recognition and cognitive ToM, but they do not engage these processes automatically. Instead, psychopathic individuals seem to require instructions to explicitly draw their attention to relevant socio-affective cues in order to respond normatively. By contrast, antisocial-only individuals' socio-affective difficulties appear limited to a specific deficit in explicitly recognizing socio-affective cues (e.g., facial expressions). Overall, it seems that the neurocognitive processes underlying socio-affective dysfunction in these two subtypes of individuals are distinct.

While there is quite a bit of research examining certain socio-affective processes, such as emotion recognition and ToM in antisocial subtypes, other socio-affective processes receive little attention. Socio-affective functioning spans a wide array of neurocognitive processes, including basic facial recognition (i.e., recognizing and identifying a familiar face), impression formation (e.g., how trustworthy is a given individual), social status evaluation (e.g., how important is this individual to others/society), and social valuation (e.g., how important is this person to me). Given the profound interpersonal difficulties exhibited by individuals who engage in chronic antisocial behavior, having a more holistic understanding of the various potential socio-affective dysfunctions present in these individuals, and the relationships among these dysfunctions, may be critical to fully understanding how aberrant socio-affective functioning may be contributing to their antisocial psychopathology.

For example, psychopathic and/or antisocial-only individuals' difficulties initially forming meaningful relationships may reflect a fundamental issue during initial impression formation; however, research on this topic is exceptionally limited. More specifically, it is possible that neurocognitive abnormalities lead these individuals to initially view others as inherently untrustworthy and avoid them, reducing opportunities for psychopathic or antisocial-only individuals to interact with others and form new relationships. Alternatively, if psychopathic and/or antisocial-only individuals do not have impairments in impression formation, but rather social valuation, it is possible that their difficulties maintaining meaningful relationships are due to an inability to represent the value of these relationships. Understanding not only if such deficits in impression formation or social valuation exist in antisocial subtypes, but also the specific neurocognitive underpinnings of each deficit within each antisocial subtype, would greatly advance our understanding of the socio-affective dysfunctions displayed across antisocial subtypes.

Beyond specific neurocognitive processes supporting socio-affective functioning, little research in this domain accounts for the contribution of environmental risk factors that are related to both the quality of socio-affective functioning and expression of antisocial psychopathology. For example, early childhood deprivation, maltreatment, and poverty occur at high rates among individuals who chronically engage in antisocial behavior (Braga et al. 2017; Cicchetti et al. 2012). Outside of research on antisocial psychopathology, early childhood maltreatment and other environmental factors, such as concentrated disadvantage, are known to negatively impact socio-affective functioning and development (Cicchetti et al. 2003; Pears and Fisher 2005; Drukker et al. 2003). For example, maltreated children experience substantial deficits and delays in both emotion recognition and ToM (Cicchetti et al. 2003; Pears and Fisher 2005). Accordingly, it is possible that some of the socio-affective deficits associated with antisocial psychopathology, particularly those deficits which span antisocial subtypes, are promoted by certain environmental experiences. However, research examining the intersection of antisocial psychopathology, early environment, and socio-affective processing is limited, making this possibility hard to evaluate, but an exciting endeavor for future research.

The current literature examining socio-affective processing and antisocial psychopathology suggests different antisocial subtypes exhibit distinct patterns of socio-affective disruptions. Moreover, the patterns of socio-affective dysfunction found in each subtype may promote antisocial behaviors in unique ways. For example, psychopathic individuals' failure to implicitly recognize emotion or implicitly engage in ToM may explain why they are able to callously harm others during goal-pursuit, while their intact ability to engage in ToM when explicitly required to do so allows them to also con and manipulate others when necessary. In contrast, antisocial-only individuals' difficulties explicitly recognizing emotion combined with their general hypersensitivity to affective content may lead these individuals to over-react, potentially violently, to misperceived socio-affective cues. Advancing our understanding of the links between socio-affective processing disruptions and antisocial subtypes is crucial to providing unique insight into the development and maintenance of the chronic, disruptive, and costly behaviors exhibited by these antisocial psychopathologies.

Note

1 To date, no studies have examined implicit ToM in antisocial-only individuals.

References

Adolphs, R. 2008. Fear, faces, and the human amygdala. *Current Opinion in Neurobiology*, 18, 166–172.

American Psychiatric Association 2013. *Diagnostic and statistical manual of mental disorders (DSM-5®)*, Washington, DC, American Psychiatric Pub.

Bagley, A. D., Abramowitz, C. S. & Kosson, D. S. 2009. Vocal affect recognition and psychopathy: Converging findings across traditional and cluster analytic approaches to assessing the construct. *Journal of Abnormal Psychology*, 118, 388–398.

Baskin-Sommers, A. R. & Newman, J. P. 2013. Differentiating the cognition-emotion interactions that characterize psychopathy versus externalizing. *Cognition and Emotion*. New York: Guilford Press.

Baskin-Sommers, A. R. & Newman, J. P. 2014. Psychopathic and externalizing offenders display dissociable dysfunctions when responding to facial affect. *Personality Disorders: Theory, Research, and Treatment*, 5, 369–379.

Bedford, R., Wagner, N. J., Rehder, P. D., Propper, C., Willoughby, M. T. & Mills-Koonce, R. W. 2017. The role of infants' mother-directed gaze, maternal sensitivity, and emotion recognition in childhood callous unemotional behaviours. *European Child & Adolescent Psychiatry*, 26, 947–956.

Blair, J., Budhani, S., Colledge, E. & Scott, S. K. 2005. Deafness to fear in boys with psychopathic tendencies. *Journal of Child Psychology and Psychiatry*, 46, 327–336.

Blair, J. & Coles, M. 2000. Expression recognition and behavioural problems in early adolescence. *Cognitive Development*, 15, 421–434.

Blair, J., Colledge, E., Murray, L. & Mitchell, D. G. V. 2001. A selective impairment in the processing of sad and fearful expressions in children with psychopathic tendencies. *Journal of Abnormal Child Psychology*, 29, 491–498.

Blair, J., Mitchell, D. G. V., Peschardt, K. S., Colledge, E., Leonard, R. A., Shine, J. H., Murray, L. K. & Perrett, D. I. 2004. Reduced sensitivity to others' fearful expressions in psychopathic individuals. *Personality and Individual Differences*, 37, 1111–1122.

Blair, J., Mitchell, D. G. V., Richell, R. A., Kelly, S., Leonard, A., Newman, C. & Scott, S. K. 2002. Turning a deaf ear to fear: Impaired recognition of vocal affect in psychopathic individuals. *Journal of Abnormal Psychology*, 111, 682–686.

Blair, J., Peschardt, K. S., Budhani, S., Mitchell, D. G. V. & Pine, D. S. 2006. The development of psychopathy. *Journal of Child Psychology and Psychiatry*, 47, 262–276.

Blair, J., Sellars, C., Strickland, I., Clark, F., Williams, A., Smith, M. & Jones, L. 1996. Theory of mind in the psychopath. *Journal of Forensic Psychiatry*, 7, 15–25.

Boll, S. & Gamer, M. 2016. Psychopathic traits affect the visual exploration of facial expressions. *Biological Psychology*, 117, 194–201.

Braga, T., Gonçalves, L. C., Basto-Pereira, M. & Maia, A. 2017. Unraveling the link between maltreatment and juvenile antisocial behavior: A meta-analysis of prospective longitudinal studies. *Aggression and Violent Behavior*, 33, 37–50.

Brennan, G. M., Hyde, L. W. & Baskin-Sommers, A. R. 2017. Antisocial pathways associated with substance use disorders: Characterizing etiological underpinnings and implications for treatment. *Current Opinion in Behavioral Sciences*, 13, 124–129.

Caspi, A., Wright, B. R. E., Moffitt, T. E. & Silva, P. A. 1998. Early failure in the labor market: Childhood and adolescent predictors of unemployment in the transition to adulthood. *American Sociological Review*, 424–451.

Cicchetti, D., Rogosch, F. A., Maughan, A., Toth, S. L. & Bruce, J. 2003. False belief understanding in maltreated children. *Development and Psychopathology*, 15, 1067–1091.

Cicchetti, D., Rogosch, F. A. & Thibodeau, E. L. 2012. The effects of child maltreatment on early signs of antisocial behavior: genetic moderation by tryptophan hydroxylase, serotonin transporter, and monoamine oxidase A genes. *Development and Psychopathology*, 24, 907–928.

Cunningham, W. A. & Brosch, T. 2012. Motivational salience: Amygdala tuning from traits, needs, values, and goals. *Current Directions in Psychological Science*, 21, 54–59.

Dadds, M. R., El Masry, Y., Wimalaweera, S. & Guastella, A. J. 2008. Reduced eye gaze explains "fear blindness" in childhood psychopathic traits. *Journal of the American Academy of Child and Adolescent Psychiatry*, 47, 455–463.

Dadds, M. R., Kimonis, E. R., Schollar-Root, O., Moul, C. & Hawes, D. J. 2018. Are impairments in emotion recognition a core feature of callous-unemotional traits? Testing the primary versus secondary variants model in children. *Development and Psychopathology*, 30, 67–77.

Dadds, M. R., Perry, Y., Hawes, D. J., Merz, S., Riddell, A. C., Haines, D. J., Solak, E. & Abeygunawardane, A. I. 2006. Attention to the eyes and fear-recognition deficits in child psychopathy. *British Journal of Psychiatry*, 189, 280–281.

Dargis, M., Wolf, R. C. & Koenigs, M. 2018. Psychopathic traits are associated with reduced fixations to the eye region of fearful faces. *Journal of Abnormal Psychology*, 127, 43–50.

Dawel, A., Mckone, E., O'kearney, R., Sellbom, M., Irons, J. & Palermo, R. 2015. Elevated levels of callous unemotional traits are associated with reduced attentional cueing, with no specificity for fear or eyes. *Personality Disorders: Theory, Research, and Treatment*, 6, 216–228.

Dawel, A., O'Kearney, R., Mckone, E. & Palermo, R. 2012. Not just fear and sadness: meta-analytic evidence of pervasive emotion recognition deficits for facial and vocal expressions in psychopathy. *Neuroscience & Biobehavioral Reviews*, 36, 2288–2304.

Decety, J., Skelly, L., Yoder, K. J. & Kiehl, K. A. 2014. Neural processing of dynamic emotional facial expressions in psychopaths. *Social Neuroscience*, 9, 36–49.

Decety, J., Skelly, L. R. & Kiehl, K. A. 2013. Brain response to empathy-eliciting scenarios involving pain in incarcerated individuals with psychopathy. *JAMA Psychiatry*, 70, 638–645.

Deeley, Q., Daly, E., Surguladze, S., Tunstall, N., Mezey, G., Beer, D., Ambikapathy, A., Robertson, D., Giampietro, V. & Brammer, M. J. 2006. Facial emotion processing in criminal psychopathy: Preliminary functional magnetic resonance imaging study. *British Journal of Psychiatry*, 189, 533–539.

Dolan, M. & Fullam, R. 2004. Theory of mind and mentalizing ability in antisocial personality disorders with and without psychopathy. *Psychological Medicine*, 34, 1093–1102.

Dolan, M. & Fullam, R. 2006. Face affect recognition deficits in personality-disordered offenders: Association with psychopathy. *Psychological Medicine*, 36, 1563–1569.

Drayton, L. A., Santos, L. R. & Baskin-Sommers, A. R. 2018. Psychopaths fail to automatically take the perspective of others. *PNAS*, 115, 3302–3307.

Drislane, L. E. & Patrick, C. J. 2013. Psychopathy and antisocial personality disorder. In: Shally-Jensen, M. (ed.) *Mental Health Care Issues in America: An Encyclopedia*. ABC-CLIO.

Drukker, M., Kaplan, C., Feron, F. & Van Os, J. 2003. Children's health-related quality of life, neighbourhood socio-economic deprivation and social capital. A contextual analysis. *Social Science & Medicine*, 57, 825–841.

Eisenbarth, H., Alpers, G. W., Segre, D., Calogero, A. & Angrilli, A. 2008. Categorization and evaluation of emotional faces in psychopathic women. *Psychiatry Research*, 159, 189–195.

Estrada, S., Tillem, S., Stuppy-Sullivan, A. & Baskin-Sommers, A. R. 2018. Specifying the connection between reward processing and antisocial psychopathology across development: Review, integration, and future directions. *In:* Gruber, J. (ed.) *Oxford Handbook of Positive Emotion and Psychopathology*. New York: Oxford University Press.

Fairchild, G., Stobbe, Y., Van Goozen, S. H., Calder, A. J. & Goodyer, I. M. 2010. Facial expression recognition, fear conditioning, and startle modulation in female subjects with conduct disorder. *Biological Psychiatry*, 68, 272–279.

Fairchild, G., Van Goozen, S. H., Calder, A. J., Stollery, S. J. & Goodyer, I. M. 2009. Deficits in facial expression recognition in male adolescents with early-onset or adolescence-onset conduct disorder. *Journal of Child Psychology and Psychiatry*, 50, 627–636.

Fazel, S. & Danesh, J. 2002. Serious mental disorder in 23 000 prisoners: A systematic review of 62 surveys. *Lancet*, 359, 545–550.

Fergusson, D. M., Horwood, L. J. & Ridder, E. M. 2005. Show me the child at seven: The consequences of conduct problems in childhood for psychosocial functioning in adulthood. *Journal of Child Psychology and Psychiatry*, 46, 837–849.

Frick, P. J., Ray, J. V., Thornton, L. C. & Kahn, R. E. 2014. Can callous-unemotional traits enhance the understanding, diagnosis, and treatment of serious conduct problems in children and adolescents? A comprehensive review. *Psychological Bulletin*, 140, 1–57.

Frick, P. J. & White, S. F. 2008. Research review: The importance of callous-unemotional traits for developmental models of aggressive and antisocial behavior. *Journal of Child Psychology and Psychiatry*, 49, 359–375.

Frogner, L., Gibson, C. L., Andershed, A. K. & Andershed, H. 2016. Childhood psychopathic personality and callous–unemotional traits in the prediction of conduct problems. *American Journal of Orthopsychiatry*, 88, 211–225.

Gao, Y., Glenn, A. L., Schug, R. A., Yang, Y. & Raine, A. 2009. The neurobiology of psychopathy: A neurodevelopmental perspective. *Canadian Journal of Psychiatry*, 54, 813–823.

Gillespie, S. M., Rotshtein, P., Wells, L. J., Beech, A. R. & Mitchell, I. J. 2015. Psychopathic traits are associated with reduced attention to the eyes of emotional faces among adult male non-offenders. *Frontiers in Human Neuroscience*, 9, 552.

Glass, S. J. & Newman, J. P. 2006. Recognition of facial affect in psychopathic offenders. *Journal of Abnormal Psychology*, 115, 815.

Gorenstein, E. E. & Newman, J. P. 1980. Disinhibitory psychopathology: A new perspective and a model for research. *Psychological Review*, 87, 301.

Hare, R. D. 2003. *Manual for the Revised Psychopathy Checklist,* Toronto, Ontario, Canada, Multi-Health Systems.

Hare, R. D. 2006. Psychopathy: A clinical and forensic overview. *Psychiatric Clinics of North America*, 29, 709–724.

Hare, R. D. & Neumann, C. S. 2008. Psychopathy as a clinical and empirical construct. *Annual Review of Clinical Psychology*, 4, 217–246.

Hastings, M. E., Tangney, J. P. & Stuewig, J. 2008. Psychopathy and identification of facial expressions of emotion. *Personality and Individual Differences*, 44, 1474–1483.

Hoyniak, C. P., Bates, J. E., Petersen, I. T., Yang, C. L., Darcy, I. & Fontaine, N. M. G. 2018. Reduced neural responses to vocal fear: a potential biomarker for callous-uncaring traits in early childhood. *Developmental Science*, 21, e12608.

Hyde, L. W., Byrd, A. L., Votruba-Drzal, E., Hariri, A. R. & Manuck, S. B. 2014. Amygdala reactivity and negative emotionality: divergent correlates of antisocial personality and psychopathy traits in a community sample. *Journal of Abnormal Psychology*, 123, 214–224.

Hyde, L. W., Shaw, D. S. & Hariri, A. R. 2013. Understanding youth antisocial behavior using neuroscience through a developmental psychopathology lens: Review, integration, and directions for research. *Developmental Review*, 33, 168–223.

Hyde, L. W., Shaw, D. S., Murray, L., Gard, A., Hariri, A. R. & Forbes, E. E. 2016. Dissecting the role of amygdala reactivity in antisocial behavior in a sample of young, low-income, urban men. *Clinical Psychological Science*, 4, 527–544.

Iacono, W. G., Malone, S. M. & McGue, M. 2008. Behavioral disinhibition and the development of early-onset addiction: Common and specific influences. *Annual Review of Clinical Psychology*, 4, 325–348.

Jack, A. I., Dawson, A. J., Begany, K. L., Leckie, R. L., Barry, K. P., Ciccia, A. H. & Snyder, A. Z. 2013. fMRI reveals reciprocal inhibition between social and physical cognitive domains. *NeuroImage*, 66, 385–401.

Johnson, M. H. 2005. Subcortical face processing. *Nature Reviews Neuroscience*, 6, 766.

Jones, A. P., Happe, F. G., Gilbert, F., Burnett, S. & Viding, E. 2010. Feeling, caring, knowing: Different types of empathy deficit in boys with psychopathic tendencies and autism spectrum disorder. *Journal of Child Psychology and Psychiatry*, 51, 1188–1197.

Jusyte, A., Mayer, S. V., Kunzel, E., Hautzinger, M. & Schonenberg, M. 2015. Unemotional traits predict early processing deficit for fearful expressions in young violent offenders: An investigation using continuous flash suppression. *Psychological Medicine*, 45, 285–297.

Kiehl, K. A. & Hoffman, M. B. 2011. The criminal psychopath: History, neuroscience, treatment, and economics. *Jurimetrics*, 51, 355.

Kosson, D. S., Suchy, Y., Mayer, A. R. & Libby, J. 2002. Facial affect recognition in criminal psychopaths. *Emotion*, 2, 398–411.

Krueger, R. F., Markon, K. E., Patrick, C. J., Benning, S. D. & Kramer, M. D. 2007. Linking antisocial behavior, substance use, and personality: An integrative quantitative model of the adult externalizing spectrum. *Journal of Abnormal Psychology*, 116, 645.

Kunecke, J., Mokros, A., Olderbak, S. & Wilhelm, O. 2018. Facial responsiveness of psychopaths to the emotional expressions of others. *PLoS One*, 13, e0190714.

Leist, T. & Dadds, M. R. 2009. Adolescents' ability to read different emotional faces relates to their history of maltreatment and type of psychopathology. *Clinical Child Psychology and Psychiatry*, 14, 237–250.

Leslie, A. M., Friedman, O. & German, T. P. 2004. Core mechanisms in 'theory of mind'. *Trends in Cognitive Sciences*, 8, 528–533.

Lobbestael, J., Cima, M. & Arntz, A. 2013. The relationship between adult reactive and proactive aggression, hostile interpretation bias, and antisocial personality disorder. *Journal of Personality Disorders*, 27, 53–66.

Luckhurst, C., Hatfield, E. & Gelvin-Smith, C. 2017. Capacity for empathy and emotional contagion in those with psychopathic personalities. *Interpersona*, 11, 70–91.

Marsh, A. A. & Blair, J. 2008. Deficits in facial affect recognition among antisocial populations: A meta-analysis. *Neuroscience & Biobehavioral Reviews*, 32, 454–465.

Marsh, A. A., Finger, E. C., Mitchell, D. G. V., Reid, M. E., Sims, C., Kosson, D. S., Towbin, K. E., Leibenluft, E., Pine, D. S. & Blair, J. 2008. Reduced amygdala response to fearful expressions in children and adolescents with callous-unemotional traits and disruptive behavior disorders. *American Journal of Psychiatry*, 165, 712–720.

Meffert, H., Gazzola, V., Den Boer, J. A., Bartels, A. A. & Keysers, C. 2013. Reduced spontaneous but relatively normal deliberate vicarious representations in psychopathy. *Brain*, 136, 2550–2562.

Moffitt, T. E. 2017. Adolescence-limited and life-course-persistent antisocial behavior: A developmental taxonomy. In: Beaver, K. & Walsh, A. (eds.) *Biosocial Theories of Crime*. London: Routledge.

Montagne, B., Van Honk, J., Kessels, R. P. C., Frigerio, E., Burt, M., Van Zandvoort, M. J. E., Perrett, D. I. & De Haan, E. H. F. 2005. Reduced efficiency in recognising fear in subjects scoring high on psychopathic personality characteristics. *Personality and Individual Differences*, 38, 5–11.

Moran, P. 1999. The epidemiology of antisocial personality disorder. *Social Psychiatry and Psychiatric Epidemiology*, 34, 231–242.

Mowle, E. N., Edens, J. F., Ruchensky, J. R. & Penson, B. N. 2018. Triarchic psychopathy and deficits in facial affect recognition. *Journal of Personality*, 87, 240.

Munoz, L. C. 2009. Callous-unemotional traits are related to combined deficits in recognizing afraid faces and body poses. *Journal of the American Academy of Child and Adolescent Psychiatry*, 48, 554–62.

O'Nions, E., Sebastian, C. L., Mccrory, E., Chantiluke, K., Happe, F. & Viding, E. 2014. Neural bases of Theory of Mind in children with autism spectrum disorders and children with conduct problems and callous-unemotional traits. *Developmental Science*, 17, 786–796.

Olderbak, S. G., Mokros, A., Nitschke, J., Habermeyer, E. & Wilhelm, O. 2018. Psychopathic men: Deficits in general mental ability, not emotion perception. *Journal of Abnormal Psychology*, 127, 294–304.

Patrick, C. J., Curtin, J. J. & Tellegen, A. 2002. Development and validation of a brief form of the Multidimensional Personality Questionnaire. *Psychological Assessment*, 14, 150.

Pears, K. C. & Fisher, P. A. 2005. Emotion understanding and theory of mind among maltreated children in foster care: Evidence of deficits. *Development and Psychopathology*, 17, 47–65.

Pfabigan, D. M., Seidel, E. M., Wucherer, A. M., Keckeis, K., Derntl, B. & Lamm, C. 2015. Affective empathy differs in male violent offenders with high-and low-trait psychopathy. *Journal of Personality Disorders*, 29, 42–61.

Raine, A., Lee, L., Yang, Y. & Colletti, P. 2010. Neurodevelopmental marker for limbic maldevelopment in antisocial personality disorder and psychopathy. *British Journal of Psychiatry*, 197, 186–192.

Rehder, P. D., Mills-Koonce, W. R., Willoughby, M. T., Garrett-Peters, P. & Wagner, N. J. 2017. Emotion recognition deficits among children with conduct problems and callous-unemotional behaviors. *Early Childhood Research Quarterly*, 41, 174–183.

Richell, R. A., Mitchell, D. G. V., Peschardt, K. S., Winston, J. S., Leonard, A., Dolan, R. J. & Blair, J. 2005. Trust and distrust: The perception of trustworthiness of faces in psychopathic and non-psychopathic offenders. *Personality and Individual Differences*, 38, 1735–1744.

Sabatinelli, D., Fortune, E. E., Li, Q., Siddiqui, A., Krafft, C., Oliver, W. T., Beck, S. & Jeffries, J. 2011. Emotional perception: Meta-analyses of face and natural scene processing. *Neuroimage*, 54, 2524–2533.

Samson, D., Apperly, I. A., Braithwaite, J. J., Andrews, B. J. & Bodley Scott, S. E. 2010. Seeing it their way: Evidence for rapid and involuntary computation of what other people see. *Journal of Experimental Psychology: Human Perception and Performance*, 36, 1255.

Sandvik, A. M., Hansen, A. L., Johnsen, B. H. & Laberg, J. C. 2014. Psychopathy and the ability to read the "language of the eyes": Divergence in the psychopathy construct. *Scandinavian Journal of Psychology*, 55, 585–592.

Schönenberg, M. & Jusyte, A. 2014. Investigation of the hostile attribution bias toward ambiguous facial cues in antisocial violent offenders. *European Archives of Psychiatry and Clinical Neuroscience*, 264, 61–69.

Schönenberg, M., Louis, K., Mayer, S.V. & Jusyte, A. 2013. Impaired identification of threat-related social information in male delinquents with antisocial personality disorder. *Journal of Personality Disorders*, 27, 496–505.

Schönenberg, M., Mayer, S.V., Christian, S., Louis, K. & Jusyte, A. 2016. Facial affect recognition in violent and nonviolent antisocial behavior subtypes. *Journal of Personality Disorders*, 30, 708–719.

Sebastian, C. L., Mccrory, E. J. P., Cecil, C. A. M., Lockwood, P. L., De Brito, S. A., Fontaine, N. M. G. & Viding, E. 2012. Neural responses to affective and cognitive theory of mind in children with conduct problems and varying levels of callous-unemotional traits. *Archives of General Psychiatry*, 69, 814–822.

Sergerie, K., Chochol, C. & Armony, J. L. 2008. The role of the amygdala in emotional processing: A quantitative meta-analysis of functional neuroimaging studies. *Neuroscience & Biobehavioral Reviews*, 32, 811–830.

Shamay-Tsoory, S. G. & Aharon-Peretz, J. 2007. Dissociable prefrontal networks for cognitive and affective theory of mind: A lesion study. *Neuropsychologia*, 45, 3054–3067.

Shamay-Tsoory, S. G., Harari, H., Aharon-Peretz, J. & Levkovitz, Y. 2010. The role of the orbitofrontal cortex in affective theory of mind deficits in criminal offenders with psychopathic tendencies. *Cortex*, 46, 668–677.

Sharp, C. 2008. Theory of Mind and conduct problems in children: Deficits in reading the "emotions of the eyes". *Cognition & Emotion*, 22, 1149–1158.

Sharp, C. & Vanwoerden, S. 2014. Social cognition: Empirical contribution: The developmental building blocks of psychopathic traits: Revisiting the role of theory of mind. *Journal of Personality Disorders*, 28, 78–95.

Sharp, C., Vanwoerden, S., Van Baardewijk, Y., Tackett, J. L. & Stegge, H. 2015. Callous-unemotional traits are associated with deficits in recognizing complex emotions in preadolescent children. *Journal of Personality Disorders*, 29, 347–359.

Sommer, M., Sodian, B., Dohnel, K., Schwerdtner, J., Meinhardt, J. & Hajak, G. 2010. In psychopathic patients emotion attribution modulates activity in outcome-related brain areas. *Psychiatry Research*, 182, 88–95.

Spreng, R. N. & Grady, C. L. 2010. Patterns of brain activity supporting autobiographical memory, prospection, and theory of mind, and their relationship to the default mode network. *Journal of Cognitive Neuroscience*, 22, 1112–1123.

Spreng, R. N., Mar, R. A. & Kim, A. S. N. 2009. The common neural basis of autobiographical memory, prospection, navigation, theory of mind, and the default mode: A quantitative meta-analysis. *Journal of Cognitive Neuroscience*, 21, 489–510.

Stanković, M., Nešić, M., Obrenović, J., Stojanović, D. & Milošević, V. 2015. Recognition of facial expressions of emotions in criminal and non-criminal psychopaths: Valence-specific hypothesis. *Personality and Individual Differences*, 82, 242–247.

Stevens, D., Charman, T. & Blair, J. 2001. Recognition of emotion in facial expressions and vocal tones in children with psychopathic tendencies. *Journal of Genetic Psychology*, 162, 201–211.

Van Overwalle, F. & Baetens, K. 2009. Understanding others' actions and goals by mirror and mentalizing systems: A meta-analysis. *Neuroimage*, 48, 564–584.

Viding, E., Fontaine, N. M. G. & Mccrory, E. J. 2012. Antisocial behaviour in children with and without callous-unemotional traits. *Journal of the Royal Society of Medicine*, 105, 195–200.

Viding, E., Fontaine, N. M. G., Oliver, B. R. & Plomin, R. 2009. Negative parental discipline, conduct problems and callous–unemotional traits: monozygotic twin differences study. *British Journal of Psychiatry*, 195, 414–419.
Viding, E. & Mccrory, E. 2015. Developmental risk for psychopathy. In: Thapar, A., Pine, D., Leckman, J. F., Scott, S., Snowling, M. J. & Taylor, E. A. (eds.) *Rutter's Child and Adolescent Psychiatry*. John Wiley & Sons, Ltd.
Viding, E. & Mccrory, E. J. 2018. Understanding the development of psychopathy: Progress and challenges. *Psychological Medicine*, 48, 566–577.
Vuilleumier, P., Armony, J. L., Driver, J. & Dolan, R. J. 2001. Effects of attention and emotion on face processing in the human brain: An event-related fMRI study. *Neuron*, 30, 829–841.
White, S. F., Marsh, A. A., Fowler, K. A., Schechter, J. C., Adalio, C., Pope, K., Sinclair, S., Pine, D. S. & Blair, J. 2012. Reduced amygdala response in youths with disruptive behavior disorders and psychopathic traits: Decreased emotional response versus increased top-down attention to nonemotional features. *American Journal of Psychiatry*, 169, 750–758.
Wilson, K., Juodis, M. & Porter, S. 2011. Fear and loathing in psychopaths: A meta-analytic investigation of the facial affect recognition deficit. *Criminal Justice and Behavior*, 38, 659–668.
Woodworth, M. & Waschbusch, D. 2008. Emotional processing in children with conduct problems and callous/unemotional traits. *Child: Care, Health and Development*, 34, 234–244.

24
FORENSIC MENTAL HEALTH TREATMENT AND RECIDIVISM

Daniel Whiting, Howard Ryland and Seena Fazel

Introduction

Forensic mental health services are provided typically for people with severe mental illnesses who have committed violent offences, and tend to refer to secure hospitals which treat and manage individuals who are transferred from court or prison. In the UK, these services are described by those commissioning them as being for "individuals who have a mental disorder and pose or have posed risks to others" (JCPMH, 2013). There is typically a link between the mental disorder and that risk.

Such individuals are commonly located in hospitals, usually specialized secure units, but also in prisons or in the community under supervision. Forensic mental health services work collaboratively with a wide range of other health and justice professionals and services (Eastman et al. 2012a).

The International Context

There are significant variations worldwide in the availability, structure and function of forensic mental health services. This is a result of a complex interplay between a wide range of factors, including funding, the legal context and the structure of healthcare services (Nedopil 2009; Abdalla-Filho and Bertolote 2006; Arboleda-Florez 2006).

Firstly, the total level of funding available for all mental health services varies significantly between countries. According to the World Health Organization, the global median expenditure on mental health is 2.5 USD per head per year. In many lower income countries, mental health services receive a smaller proportion of the overall health budget, which can result in very low levels of funding assigned to mental health services. Consequently, the services provided in lower income countries may be limited in nature, with little provision for more specialized services, such as forensic mental health. Most mentally ill individuals in such countries who commit offences are likely to be dealt with by the criminal justice system. Forensic hospital services that do exist may in practice be extensions of prisons (Njenga 2006). At the same time, in resource-poor settings, mentally disordered individuals who behave in a violent manner may be more likely to come to the attention of mental health services, due to the disruptive nature of their behavior. In higher income countries, there may be substantial resources ring-fenced for forensic mental health services (Wilson et al. 2011). The European region spends 20 times as much per capita on mental health as Africa or South East Asia (WHO 2018). This can facilitate the provision of a sophisticated range of specialized services, specifically for mentally disordered persons who have committed serious offences (Arboleda-Florez 2006).

Secondly, criminal law varies significantly between jurisdictions, with consequences for the provision of forensic mental health services (Edworthy et al. 2016). Most countries worldwide now have a specific mental health act, with 111 countries reporting that they have stand-alone mental health legislation in 2017, which represents 57% of World Health Organization member countries (WHO 2018). Despite these advances, a sizeable minority of countries still do not have such legislation, while in other jurisdictions the legislation may be outdated (Zhang et al. 2015). Only certain countries have dedicated provision within their legal framework that governs the judicial management and medical treatment of mentally ill individuals who come into contact with the criminal justice system. Frameworks vary in a number of respects, such as whether prisoners can be involuntarily given psychiatric medications, which has an impact on the way forensic mental health services are organized (Eastman et al. 2012b). There is also considerable variation in the public perception of mentally ill individuals who offend, which relates to the perceived degree of culpability for crimes committed when unwell. This can have an impact on the legal outcome from the courts for mentally ill individuals and transitions between the criminal justice and mental health systems (Meynen and Oei 2011). Due to the lengthy process required to create and modify statute law in many jurisdictions, the legal situation can often lag behind contemporary practical and ethical norms (Simpson 2015).

Finally, the structure and funding of the healthcare and criminal justice system shows considerable variation between countries and even within countries. This can have a sizeable impact on the way that services are provided for mentally ill individuals who pose a risk to others. In some countries, forensic mental health services may be exclusively provided and paid for by the state, while in others a range of providers may be allowed to compete for business, which may be wholly or partly commissioned by the state (Abdalla-Filho and Bertolote 2006).

Given the complex differences between forensic mental health services worldwide, it is not possible to provide a comprehensive description of all such services in this chapter. We will therefore use the example of how services are provided in England. This provides an illustration of how such services can be organized within a high-income setting, and English services have acted as a model for service development in other countries.

Overall Structure of Forensic Mental Health Services in England

Forensic mental health services in England are highly developed and receive around £1.3 billion funding each year, which is equivalent to around 19% of the entire national mental health budget (Wilson et al. 2011).

The backbone of these services are the secure hospitals, which provide inpatient care within the healthcare system. Many regions now have some form of specialized forensic community mental health team to manage individuals discharged from secure hospitals. Within the criminal justice system, there is also increasing provision of liaison services (between the courts and community mental health teams) for individuals with mental illness. In addition, prisons will usually have some form of mental health provision. There are also an expanding range of services that provide liaison with earlier stages of the criminal justice system, including police stations and criminal courts (Durcan et al. 2011).

Secure Hospitals

England has a long history of providing inpatient forensic mental health care, starting in 1863 with the establishment of the Broadmoor Criminal Lunatic Asylum. This was established as a humane alternative to the prison system for the "criminally insane," which could provide some measure of treatment, as well as containment (Stevens 2013). Over the subsequent century other "special hospitals" were also opened to manage increased numbers of individuals. Reforms initiated in the 1960s led to the creation of lower tiers of security and further expansion of capacity from the 1970s onwards (Seppänen et al. 2018).

Currently there are around 6000 inpatient beds available in secure hospital services across England (JCPMH 2013). These are arranged over three levels of security, namely high, medium and low, with the majority of individuals located in the lower two. Services are commissioned nationally as part of specialized commissioning at NHS England, which receives funding directly from the Department of Health. The delivery of services is performed by a range of providers, including the National Health Service, charitable hospital organizations and private companies (Hare Duke et al. 2018).

There are currently three high secure hospitals in England, namely Broadmoor, Rampton and Ashworth Hospitals. These cater for the highest risk individuals who pose a serious and immediate danger to the public. Security measures resemble those at a prison, with high walls, airport-style screening and high staffing levels. Medium and low security hospitals offer progressively lower levels of security, but usually still require that all patients be detained under the Mental Health Act (Durcan et al. 2011). These have security in the form of physical, procedural and relational measures, such as perimeter fencing, searching of patients returning from leave and the development of a therapeutic relationship between patients and a named member of staff (Chester et al. 2017).

Patient admissions are usually lengthy, typically lasting two to ten years (Hare Duke et al. 2018). A recent study found that 20% of patients in high and medium security stayed for more than 20 years (Völlm et al. 2018). Individuals will enter the system from different routes. Many will have treatment mandated by a court as an alternative to a prison sentence. Others will be transferred from prison, either before or after conviction. Less commonly some patients will be transferred from general psychiatric services, due to unmanageable levels of aggression.

Treatment within secure services is multidisciplinary and includes optimization of pharmacological management, psychotherapeutic interventions, occupational therapy and a range of other therapeutic activities. Patients will usually receive progressively more leave from the hospital. Initially they will be escorted by staff and, if this is judged to be successful, will be given unescorted leave, in preparation for discharge (Eastman et al. 2012c).

Community Forensic Mental Health Teams

Complementing these inpatient services, there are clinical teams that provide specialized services to patients who have been discharged from secure care. These are currently varied in their structure, function and funding, although there are moves to create greater standardization in the model of provision. Responsibility for care may be shared with adult community services. The majority of patients will be discharged in a highly structured way, so that they are required to live in some form of supported accommodation, with regular review by mental health and other professionals, with provision for returning them to hospital if concerns are raised about increasing risk or deteriorating mental health (Natarajan et al. 2018).

Prison Mental Health Services

Rates of mental illness in prison are high, with around one in seven prisoners suffering from a psychotic illness or major depressive disorder (Fazel et al. 2016a). A recent survey in England and Wales found that almost all prisons will have some specialized mental healthcare provision, although 13% of prisons had no such services (Forrester et al. 2013). The study concluded that services can be highly variable in their structure and the level of support offered. Some prisons will have a dedicated healthcare area, where prisoners with advanced needs can be more closely monitored and treated. The majority of mental illness is treated within the prison context; however, in England, the Mental Health Act does not sanction the use of involuntary medication in prison. If a prisoner becomes mentally unwell and refuses treatment, then they can be referred for a transfer to a hospital, under the Mental Health Act (Bradshaw et al. 2017).

Liaison and Diversion Services

A relatively recent addition to national forensic mental health services are mental health professionals, usually nurses, who provide brief assessments at police stations and courts. These liaison and diversion services were a policy priority arising from the Bradley review, a government-sponsored inquiry to examine the extent to which offenders with mental health problems, or learning disabilities, could be diverted to other services and the barriers to such diversion. The resultant recommendations emphasized prevention and early intervention (Bradley 2009). Liaison services in police stations are used to screen people following arrest who are known to have, or appear to be suffering from, mental illness. Additionally, police officers have the power under the Mental Health Act to take people to a place of safety for assessment by mental health professionals.

Liaison services in courts are usually focused on Magistrates' Courts, which are the lower criminal courts in England, and deal with less serious offences. Referrals to such teams can come from prisons, custody officers, probation officers or a range of other sources. Liaison services aim to assist the criminal justice process, advise courts on appropriate disposal, signpost individuals to relevant services and divert those requiring assessment or treatment to the relevant healthcare services (Birmingham et al. 2017).

A recent evaluation of ten pilot sites implementing the new national service model concluded that such services led to better identification of individuals with vulnerabilities and an improved provision of timely, relevant information to the police, courts and partner organizations. There were statistically significant increases in the average number of cases for which appointments were offered for learning disability, which increased from 0.39 to 1.22 ($p=0.001$) and for financial appointments, which increased from 0.12 to 0.92 ($p=0.012$). The authors identify limitations to the data available for analysis and conclude that the qualitative information collected from stakeholders is the main strength of the evaluation (Disley et al. 2016).

Recidivism in Forensic Mental Health Services

One of the main aims of forensic mental health services in England is to reduce reoffending in those discharged from secure care. Other important outcomes are preventing early mortality, especially from suicide, and the need for rehospitalization.

A systematic review and meta-analysis examined patient outcomes following discharge from secure hospitals and specifically reported on reoffending, all-cause mortality, suicide and readmission (Fazel et al. 2016a). This review identified 35 papers that met the inclusion criteria, of which 30 studies provided information about reoffending. The crude reoffending rate for forensic patients ranged from 0 to 24,244 per 100,000 person-years. The pooled estimate was 4,484 per 100,000 person-years (with a 95% confidence interval of 3,679–5,287). The review also compared this rate with other potentially comparable groups, such as released prisoners of similar age, and individuals who have committed crimes with personality disorder or mental illness. In these studies, the rates of reoffending varied from 4,535 to 36,964 per 100,000 person-years. The group with the highest rate of reoffending was prisoners who were released on probation. Fifteen studies identified specifically reported violent reoffending for patients in forensic mental health services, which was a pooled rate of 3,902 per 100,000. Prevalence ratios were calculated comparing reoffending in forensic patients with prisoners, matched on factors such as country and age. In the UK, the prevalence ratios ranged from 1.4 to 7.7 and in the USA from 2.7 to 5.0.

This review concluded that, based on the information available in the literature, rates of reoffending appeared to be lower in forensic patients than those in comparable groups such as prisoners. However, there are a number of challenges in comparing these two populations, especially as forensic patients tend to have committed more serious offences and have a longer time in hospital. Several possible explanations may help to account for the observed differences (Fazel et al. 2016a). Patients accepted for inpatient forensic psychiatric treatment are usually carefully selected, often on the basis of perceived treatability, which contrasts to the unfiltered prison population. Forensic patients also differ in the profile of crimes committed, with higher rates of more serious, violent crimes than the equivalent prison populations. Perpetrators of acquisitive crimes, drug offences and minor violent crimes are more likely to reoffend, and these make up the majority of prisoners. In addition, forensic patients may have committed their offence when acutely unwell, which is associated with a low risk of reoffending, especially if receiving regular follow up and ongoing treatment in the community.

Assessing Risk of Recidivism

A period of admission within a forensic mental health service has a range of goals. These include optimizing a patient's mental and physical wellbeing, and improving function across broad social and occupational domains. A fundamental task, however, is developing a clear understanding of an individual's risks of reoffending. This in part guides treatment decisions, and ultimately the timing and nature of reintegration into community settings. Indeed, one major rationale for any court to transfer a convicted individual to a secure hospital is the expectation that such a pathway is the most suitable to address future risk. In the main part, it is the risk of future violent offending that is of concern, and the majority of secure psychiatric patients have a history of violent offending (Fazel et al. 2016b).

Risk assessment is a dynamic process that is repeated and updated throughout an individual's contact with forensic mental health services. It is a core part of progress reviews and planning meetings. All members of the multi-disciplinary team of clinicians may contribute. Typically this team will include doctors, nurses, psychologists, occupational therapists and social workers, each of whom may provide information regarding different relevant factors. Whilst approaches vary, all assessments to some extent combine different factors and observations associated with future offending to formulate an overall estimation of risk. Such assessments may also seek to predict the nature that any offending may take, and the circumstances in which it may occur. Factors considered may be "static" or historical, such as a past offence, or "dynamic", changing over time and potentially modifiable such as substance misuse.

To guide risk assessments, clinicians in secure hospital settings often utilize structured assessment tools (Khiroya et al. 2009). In antisocial personality disorder, the use of such a tool is recommended in guidelines produced by the National Institute for Health and Care Excellence in England (NICE 2009), and their use is also a performance indicator for forensic units in some countries, such as England. Tools generally involve either an actuarial approach of using weighted or unweighted factors to generate a probabilistic estimate of future violence, or "structured clinical judgement" in which clinicians use the presence or absence of certain factors as a basis for their risk stratification. The latter approach is more common in secure hospital settings, as it can potentially guide treatment planning. However, the accuracy of currently used structured instruments for such management decisions has been questioned (Coid et al. 2015a), and other limitations include requiring significant time, money and training (Singh et al. 2011), and the presence of authorship bias in validation studies (Singh et al. 2013). Whilst these tools can more accurately assign low-risk status, their positive predictive ability is not such that they should be relied on in isolation for decisions around sentencing or discharge (Fazel et al. 2012).

Factors Associated with Recidivism

A Swedish longitudinal study examined the rate of conviction for violent offences for a cohort of 2,248 patients discharged from secure psychiatric hospitals into community settings between 1992 and 2013 (Wolf et al. 2018). Linking of several national data registers provided information on risk factors, and violent conviction data was collected for up to 24-months following discharge. The strongest predictors of violent offending were previous violent crime (hazard ratio 3.2, 95% confidence interval 2.3 to 4.5) and sex (female vs. male hazard ratio 0.4, 95% confidence interval 0.3 to 0.6). Lifetime drug use disorder was also associated with future violent offending (hazard ratio 2.2, 95% confidence interval 1.7 to 2.9). The importance of substance use disorder comorbidity for risk of violent offending is also clearly demonstrated in broader psychiatric populations (Fazel et al. 2009), and recent substance use has been identified as a dynamic risk factor for perpetration of a violent offence (Witt et al. 2013). Assessing an individual's substance use and its relevance to past offending is therefore a key part of addressing risk in secure settings.

This Swedish study also found a length of inpatient stay of 12 months or more to be associated with a lower risk of violent offending on release, as was a history of five or more previous inpatient episodes (Wolf et al. 2018). This may be related to post-discharge supervision, and the extent to which services are able to develop knowledge of a patient over time. When compared with *no* history of violent crime, a previous history of *serious* violent crime (defined as homicide, aggravated assault, aggravated robbery, rape, sexual coercion or sexual exploitation) was associated with a lower increased risk of recidivism than history of *any* violent crime. Low rates of recidivism for grave crimes such as homicide when associated with mental illness have elsewhere been demonstrated (Golenkov et al. 2014). This may reflect the effectiveness of long-term treatment and supervision for such individuals in areas where forensic psychiatric services are established.

Psychiatric diagnosis is also associated with recidivism. Rates of post-discharge violent offending in different diagnostic groups were examined in a cohort of 6,505 patients discharged from forensic psychiatric hospitals in Sweden (Fazel et al. 2016b). Over a mean follow-up of 9.4 years, a primary diagnosis of personality disorder (characterized by pervasive and impairing patterns of behavior and modes of relating to oneself and others) was associated with the highest rates of violent offending (hazard ratio relative to reference category of schizophrenia-spectrum disorders 1.73, 95% confidence interval 1.57 to 1.92). Relative to schizophrenia-spectrum disorders, substance use disorder and bipolar disorder were also associated with increased hazards of post-discharge violent offending, but unipolar depression was not. Personality disorder was also associated with the highest rates of reoffending in 1,344 patients who were discharged from medium secure psychiatric settings in England and Wales and followed up for an average of six years (Coid et al. 2015b).

In clinical practice, judgements around recidivism risk are also informed by more qualitative observations of a patient's clinical course, therapeutic engagement, interpersonal functioning and patterns of behavior. Whilst such parameters have been less robustly epidemiologically linked to future violent offending, few clinicians would omit such complementary knowledge from their assessments. Developing this in-depth individualized knowledge assists in understanding and managing risk both in the short to medium term on a secure unit, and in the longer term in supervised community settings. Of these types of observation, factors including lack of insight or noncompliance, impulsivity, negative attitudes and hostility are among the more strongly associated with recidivism in released male prisoners (Coid et al. 2011) and with violence outcomes in a meta-analysis of 45,533 individuals with psychotic illness (Witt et al. 2013).

Treatment in Forensic Mental Health Care

Where there is a link between offending and mental illness, forensic services assume that evidence-based treatment of the underlying mental disorder will result in a reduction of criminal behavior. Such treatment is usually initiated in hospital and may include a number of components (Howner et al. 2018). In practice, typically in the first months of a hospital admission, the presence of mental illness in the acute phase requires a largely medication-based approach, before entering a more multi-faceted rehabilitation phase of treatment with the longer-term goals of maintaining stability and reducing recidivism.

Medication

Almost all patients in forensic mental health services will receive some form of long-term psychopharmacotherapy. Evidence in support of pharmacotherapy to reduce violent behavior comes from both randomized controlled trials (Leucht et al. 2012) and observational studies (Chang et al. 2016; Fazel et al. 2014). An inpatient admission provides an intensively supported healthcare environment, and an opportunity to either commence a trial of medication, restart previously effective medication, or optimize a patient's medication regimen. This includes identifying which medication or combination of medications is most effective at controlling symptoms of mental illness. In some cases, the nature of an individual's presentation may necessitate coercive use of medication under the framework of relevant mental health law as a last resort, when a collaborative approach has failed. The side-effect profile of medications is important, ensuring that these are tolerable for the individual and weighing longer term potential harms against benefits. The route of administration is also often relevant, for example considering a long-acting depot injection for antipsychotic medication, which can be more easily monitored and can ensure improved adherence. The main challenges arise following discharge, where much lower levels of supervision may mean that patients stop taking their medications, resulting in relapse and potentially an increased risk of aggression.

In terms of classes of medication, antipsychotic medication was shown to reduce violent crime by 45% in a within-individual observational study of 82,647 individuals in Sweden, and a reduction was also seen of 24% with mood-stabilizing medication (Fazel et al. 2014). When separated by diagnosis, mood-stabilizing medication was associated with a reduction in violent offending only in those with a diagnosis of bipolar disorder. These data also demonstrated the association of long-acting depot injection formulations with reduced offending. It did not, however, support the addition of mood stabilizers to antipsychotic medication to reduce offending, an important finding that should support initiatives to reduce the use of polypharmacy for this purpose. A particular antipsychotic medication, clozapine, used in treatment-resistant schizophrenia, was associated with reductions in arrest rates (although the investigation was underpowered to test its association with conviction). Other work suggests that clozapine may have superior anti-aggressive effects (Topiwala and Fazel 2011), that are not explained by better psychotic symptom control or sedation alone (Frogley et al. 2012).

Medication to treat attention deficit hyperactivity disorder (ADHD) has also been shown to reduce offending when time periods for an individual being on- and off-medication were compared for 25,656 individuals with ADHD (Lichtenstein et al. 2012), and also in an observational study of released prisoners (Chang et al. 2016). Whilst a disorder like ADHD would not be a primary reason for admission into forensic mental health services, identification and treatment of such important comorbidities are a potential advantage of a more intensive assessment that can be provided in forensic psychiatry.

Substance Misuse

Substance misuse is common in people under the care of forensic mental health services and has been shown to significantly increase a number of adverse outcomes, including repeat offending. Treatment of substance misuse is therefore a priority for those affected, and many secure units will provide programs targeting it. Mandatory drug testing may form part of both the procedural security of a unit and supervised community follow-up after discharge. Opioid substitution medications, methadone and buprenorphine, were shown to specifically reduce arrests for violent crime in a total population cohort study (Molero et al. 2018), and observational data has also shown pharmacological treatment of substance use disorders to be associated with substantially lower rates of violent reoffending in individuals with comorbid schizophrenia spectrum disorders or bipolar disorder (Chang et al. 2016).

Psychological Therapies

Most patients will be expected to engage with psychotherapeutic interventions in preparation for release. The emphasis placed on psychological intervention varies between patients, often depending on diagnosis. The purpose of therapy can be wide ranging, but can focus on management of anger, increasing tolerance of frustration, gaining insight into the index offence and triggers for a relapse of symptoms. Patients are often encouraged to make some form of relapse prevention plan, and clinicians may use an individual's ability to engage in such a piece of work as a guide to readiness for less restrictive settings. Psychotherapy broadly aims to equip patients with longer-term tools to sustain general wellbeing and avoid interpersonal conflicts.

Individuals with a primary diagnosis of personality disorder may receive a form of psychotherapy as their primary treatment. In England, national guidelines for the treatment of individuals with antisocial personality disorder and a history of offending recommend offering group-based cognitive and behavioral interventions with a focus on reducing offending and other antisocial behavior (NICE 2009). Impulsivity and interpersonal difficulties may be targets for treatment. Overall, however, good quality evidence for the efficacy of particular psychological interventions to reduce aggression or reoffending in antisocial personality disorder is somewhat limited (Gibbon et al. 2010), and is a research priority going forward.

Occupational Therapy

Many admitted to secure services lack basic skills in self-management. This may be because they have either never learned such skills, or these have been lost due to prolonged illness or institutionalization. Admission aims to maximize functioning and independence. The ability to structure time appropriately is fundamental for long-term rehabilitation. Occupational therapy is considered important to achieving this and focuses on supporting the development of essential practical skills and fostering creativity. Although the specific contribution of occupational therapy to reducing recidivism has yet to be empirically demonstrated, it is undertaken as part of a multidisciplinary approach to improve wellbeing and reduce risk. Themes of volitional realignment towards prosocial goals and experiences, increasing protective factors and community integration have been identified as relevant to this goal (Connell 2016).

Other factors that are important in ensuring patients have stability on discharge include the identification of suitably supportive accommodation, links with primary medical services, and the support of family.

Pooled Evidence for Interventions

A recent umbrella review demonstrated that in both general and forensic psychiatric settings, high-level evidence for targeted interventions to reduce the risk of violent offending is limited (Wolf et al. 2017). Ten databases were searched for systematic reviews of violence prevention interventions within general psychiatry, forensic psychiatry, and individuals with mental disorders who had offended. Umbrella reviews such as this incorporate existing systematic reviews and meta-analyses to allow comparison of multiple interventions, and identify areas deficient in evidence. Three systematic reviews and two meta-analyses including a total of 8,876 patients were identified. However, none specifically included forensic psychiatric populations. Any conclusions drawn will therefore be extrapolated from evidence in other populations.

The strongest evidence was a meta-analysis of moderate quality that examined interventions to prevent relapse into criminality, drug use or both for individuals in the justice system with mental disorder and comorbid substance use (Perry et al. 2015). This meta-analysis included eight trials with diverse interventions in the United States justice system, from case management to interpersonal psychotherapy. The only positive evidence was for therapeutic community treatment long term, structured daily activity programs with a group-based approach used widely in the treatment of substance use disorders. Of three randomized studies that examined this type of intervention (n = 636), two found a significant reduction in re-incarceration. One was a 12-month program for prisoners that consisted of psychoeducational classes, cognitive-behavioral methods, medication and group therapy followed by aftercare of counselling, medication, psychiatric services and basic skills (relative risk [RR] 0.3, 95% confidence interval [CI] 0.1–0.6). The second examined a 6-month residential program undertaken alongside working in the community, in which participants had incremental responsibility in the group and attended various psychoeducational classes and counselling (RR 0.5, 95% CI 0.3–0.9). A third randomized study of a therapeutic community program found no superiority to cognitive-behavioral intervention. Another review also found that a modified therapeutic community approach that focused on treating substance abuse, mental illness and criminal thinking and behavior reduced re-incarceration in individuals with antisocial personality disorder (Wilson 2014).

Lower quality evidence was also found for other approaches to individuals with mental disorder within the criminal justice system. One meta-analysis found an overall effect on violent crime for six different interventions (n = 7,677), with a pooled effect size of 0.2 (95% CI 0.03–0.5) (Martin et al. 2012). The interventions were correctional programs, psychiatric treatment, use of a mental health court, forensic psychiatric aftercare, a maximum security therapeutic community for individuals with psychopathy, and intensive community treatment. The effects were not broken down by individual intervention, so it is not possible to identify the therapeutic ingredients with the clearest effects.

Individual trials have shown the potential for interventions more widely evaluated in forensic groups without mental illness to translate to forensic psychiatric populations. A randomized controlled trial in medium secure units in the UK examined the effectiveness of a cognitive skills program targeting problem-solving skills and thinking styles (Cullen et al. 2012). Individuals who completed the program showed a reduction in inpatient violence during treatment, though only effects on verbal aggression and substance use were maintained at 12-month follow-up. There is a need for evaluation and development of such targeted treatments.

The process alone of structured risk assessment embedded in shared decision-making between clinician and patient has been shown to be insufficient to reduce recidivism in a cluster randomized controlled trial including 632 forensic psychiatric outpatients (Troquete et al. 2013). One hypothesis for the lack of reduction in recidivism in this trial was that the shared care-planning approach shifted focus away from factors predictive of future offending and towards quality-of-life needs. Whilst, as has been discussed, a range of outcomes are important in forensic mental health services, it may be that in order to address recidivism, the process of risk assessment needs to be more explicitly linked to specific interventions that have been shown to effectively target those modifiable risk factors related to future offending. For example, the current evidence would place symptoms of mental illness and substance misuse as two such core modifiable factors, and one role of risk assessment should be to inform decisions about the level of assertiveness and supervision that is proportionate to longitudinally address these factors for an individual patient. Due to less than perfect accuracy of risk assessment, those targeted interventions should be non-harmful (such as adding psychosocial treatments for substance misuse, rather than, for example, detention in hospital).

Summary

Forensic mental health services have been developed to meet the diverse needs of individuals with mental illness within the criminal justice system, and to provide a specialist approach to assessing and managing the risk of reoffending in this population. Such provision typically involves significant resource and a multi-disciplinary team of mental health clinicians working in secure hospitals, prisons and the community. There is a need for high-quality treatment research in forensic psychiatric populations, ideally using standardized and objective measures of recidivism. However, emerging research suggests that complex interventions targeted at mental health needs, substance misuse, and criminal behavior can reduce recidivism even in individuals with comorbidities.

References

Abdalla-Filho, E. and Bertolote, J. M. (2006). Forensic psychiatric systems in the world. *Revista Brasileira de Psiquiatria,* 28**,** 56–61.

Arboleda-Florez, J. (2006). Forensic psychiatry: Contemporary scope, challenges and controversies. *World Psychiatry,* 5**,** 87–91.

Birmingham, L., Awonogun, L. and Ryland, H. (2017). Diversion from custody: An update. *BJPsych Advances,* 23**,** 375–384.

Bradley, K. (2009). *Lord Bradley's Review of People with Mental Health Problems or Learning Disabilities in the Criminal Justice System.* London, UK: House of Lords.

Bradshaw, R., Pordes, B. A., Trippier, H., Kosky, N., Pilling, S. and O'Brien, F. (2017). The health of prisoners: Summary of NICE guidance. *British Medical Journal,* 356**,** j1378.

Chang, Z., Lichtenstein, P., Långström, N., Larsson, H. and Fazel, S. (2016). Association between prescription of major psychotropic medications and violent reoffending after prison release. *Journal of the American Medical Association,* 316**,** 1798–1807.

Chester, V., Alexander, R. T. and Morgan, W. (2017). Measuring relational security in forensic mental health services. *Psychiatric Bulletin,* 41**,** 358–363.

Coid, J. W., Kallis, C., Doyle, M., Shaw, J. and Ullrich, S. (2015a). Identifying causal risk factors for violence among discharged patients. *PLOS ONE,* 10**,** e0142493.

Coid, J. W., Yang, M., Ullrich, S., Hickey, N., Kahtan, N. and Freestone, M. (2015b). Psychiatric diagnosis and differential risks of offending following discharge. *International Journal of Law and Psychiatry,* 38**,** 68–74.

Coid, J. W., Yang, M., Ullrich, S., Zhang, T., Sizmur, S., Farrington, D. and Rogers, R. (2011). Most items in structured risk assessment instruments do not predict violence. *The Journal of Forensic Psychiatry and Psychology,* 22**,** 3–21.

Connell, C. (2016). Forensic occupational therapy to reduce risk of reoffending: A survey of practice in the United Kingdom. *The Journal of Forensic Psychiatry and Psychology,* 27**,** 907–928.

Cullen, A. E., Clarke, A. Y., Kuipers, E., Hodgins, S., Dean, K. and Fahy, T. (2012). A multisite randomized trial of a cognitive skills program for male mentally disordered offenders: Violence and antisocial behavior outcomes. *Journal of Consulting and Clinical Psychology,* 80**,** 1114–20.

Disley, E., Taylor, C., Kruithof, K., Winpenny, E., Liddle, M., Sutherland, A., Lilford, R., Wright, S., McAteer, L. and Francis, V. (2016). *Evaluation of the offender liaison and diversion trials.* Santa Monica, CA: RAND Corporation. www.rand.org/pubs/research_reports/RR1283.html.

Durcan, G., Hoare, T. and Cumming, I. (2011). *Pathways to Unlocking Secure Mental Health Care.* London, UK: Centre for Mental Health.

Eastman, N., Adshead, G., Fox, S., Latham, R. and Whyte, S. (2012a). Forensic Psychiatric Services. *In:* Eastman, N., Adshead, G., Fox, S., Latham, R. and Whyte, S. (eds.) *Oxford Specialist Handbooks on Forensic Psychiatry.* Oxford, UK: Oxford University Press.

Eastman, N., Adshead, G., Fox, S., Latham, R. and Whyte, S. (2012b). Legal Systems. In: Eastman, N., Adshead, G., Fox, S., Latham, R. and Whyte, S. (eds.) *Oxford Specialist Handbooks on Forensic Psychiatry.* Oxford: Oxford University Press.

Eastman, N., Adshead, G., Fox, S., Latham, R. and Whyte, S. (2012c). Treatment. In: Eastman, N., Adshead, G., Fox, S., Latham, R. and Whyte, S. (eds.) *Oxford Specialist Handbooks on Forensic Psychiatry.* Oxford: Oxford university Press.

Edworthy, R., Sampson, S. and Völlm, B. (2016). Inpatient forensic-psychiatric care: Legal frameworks and service provision in three European countries. *International Journal of Law and Psychiatry,* 47**,** 18–27.

Fazel, S., Fiminska, Z., Cocks, C. and Coid, J. (2016a). Patient outcomes following discharge from secure psychiatric hospitals: Systematic review and meta-analysis. *British Journal of Psychiatry,* 208**,** 17–25.

Fazel, S., Gulati, G., Linsell, L., Geddes, J. R. and Grann, M. (2009). Schizophrenia and violence: Systematic review and meta-analysis. *PLoS Med,* 6**,** e1000120.

Fazel, S., Singh, J. P., Doll, H. and Grann, M. (2012). Use of risk assessment instruments to predict violence and antisocial behavior in 73 samples involving 24 827 people: systematic review and meta-analysis. *British Medical Journal,* 345**,** e4692.

Fazel, S., Wolf, A., Fimińska, Z. & Larsson, H. (2016b). Mortality, rehospitalisation and violent crime in forensic psychiatric patients discharged from hospital: Rates and risk factors. *PLoS One,* 11**,** e0155906.

Fazel, S., Zetterqvist, J., Larsson, H., Langstrom, N. and Lichtenstein, P. (2014). Antipsychotics, mood stabilisers, and risk of violent crime. *Lancet,* 384, 1206–14.

Forrester, A., Exworthy, T., Olumoroti, O., Sessay, M., Parrott, J., Spencer, S. J. and Whyte, S. (2013). Variations in prison mental health services in England and Wales. *International Journal of Law and Psychiatry,* 36, 326–32.

Frogley, C., Taylor, D., Dickens, G. and Picchioni, M. (2012). A systematic review of the evidence of clozapine's anti-aggressive effects. *International Journal of Neuropsychopharmacology,* 15, 1351–71.

Gibbon, S., Duggan, C., Stoffers, J., Huband, N., Völlm, B. A., Ferriter, M. and Lieb, K. (2010). Psychological interventions for antisocial personality disorder. *Cochrane Database of Systematic Reviews,* 16(6), Cd007668.

Golenkov, A., Nielssen, O. and Large, M. (2014). Systematic review and meta-analysis of homicide recidivism and schizophrenia. *BMC Psychiatry,* 14, 46.

Hare Duke, L., Furtado, V., Guo, B. and Vollm, B. A. (2018). Long-stay in forensic-psychiatric care in the UK. *Social Psychiatry and Psychiatric Epidemiology,* 53, 313–321.

Howner, K., Andiné, P., Bertilsson, G., Hultcrantz, M., Lindström, E., Mowafi, F., Snellman, A. and Hofvander, B. (2018). Mapping systematic reviews on forensic psychiatric care: A systematic review identifying knowledge gaps. *Frontiers in Psychiatry,* 25, 452.

JCPMH. (2013). Guidance for commissioners of forensic mental health services. Joint Commissioning Panel for Mental Health. www.jcpmh.info/resource/guidance-for-commissioners-of-forensic-mental-health-services/

Khiroya, R., Weaver, T. and Maden, T. (2009). Use and perceived utility of structured violence risk assessments in English medium secure forensic units. *Psychiatric Bulletin,* 33, 129–132.

Leucht, S., Tardy, M., Komossa, K., Heres, S., Kissling, W., Salanti, G. and Davis, J. M. (2012). Antipsychotic drugs versus placebo for relapse prevention in schizophrenia: A systematic review and meta-analysis. *Lancet,* 379, 2063–71.

Lichtenstein, P., Halldner, L., Zetterqvist, J., Sjolander, A., Serlachius, E., Fazel, S., Langstrom, N. and Larsson, H. (2012). Medication for attention deficit-hyperactivity disorder and criminality. *New England Journal of Medicine,* 367, 2006–14.

Martin, M. S., Dorken, S. K., Wamboldt, A. D. and Wootten, S. E. (2012). Stopping the revolving door: A meta-analysis on the effectiveness of interventions for criminally involved individuals with major mental disorders. *Law and Human Behavior,* 36, 1–12.

Meynen, G. and Oei, K. (2011). Internationalizing forensic assessments of criminal responsibility. *Medical Law Review,* 30, 529–534.

Molero, Y., Zetterqvist, J., Binswanger, I. A., Hellner, C., Larsson, H. and Fazel, S. (2018). Medications for alcohol and opioid use disorders and risk of suicidal behavior, accidental overdoses, and crime. *American Journal of Psychiatry,* 175, 970–978.

Natarajan, M., Srinivas, J., Briscoe, G. and Forsyth, S. (2018). Community forensic psychiatry and the forensic mental health liaison model. *Advances in Psychiatric Treatment,* 18, 408–415.

Nedopil, N. (2009). The role of forensic psychiatry in mental health systems in Europe. *Criminal Behavior and Mental Health,* 19, 224–234.

NICE. (2009). *National Institute for Health and Care Excellence. Antisocial personality disorder: prevention and management [CG77].* London, UK: NICE. www.nice.org.uk/guidance/cg77

Njenga, F. G. (2006). Forensic psychiatry: The African experience. *World Psychiatry,* 5, 97.

Perry, A. E., Neilson, M., Martyn-St James, M., Glanville, J. M., Woodhouse, R., Godfrey, C. and Hewitt, C. (2015). Interventions for drug-using offenders with co-occurring mental illness. *Cochrane Database of Systematic Reviews,* 6, Cd010901.

Seppänen, A., Törmänen, I., Shaw, C. and Kennedy, H. (2018). Modern forensic psychiatric hospital design: Clinical, legal and structural aspects. *International Journal of Mental Health Systems,* 12, 1–12.

Simpson, A. I. (2015). Commentary: Civil commitment and its reform. *Journal of the American Academy of Psychiatry and the Law,* 43, 48–51.

Singh, J. P., Grann, M. and Fazel, S. (2013). Authorship bias in violence risk assessment? A systematic review and meta-analysis. *PLoS One,* 8, e72484.

Singh, J. P., Serper, M., Reinharth, J. and Fazel, S. (2011). Structured assessment of violence risk in schizophrenia and other psychiatric disorders: A systematic review of the validity, reliability, and item content of 10 available instruments. *Schizophrenia Bulletin,* 37, 899–912.

Stevens, M. (2013). *Broadmoor revealed: Victorian Crime and the Lunatic Asylum.* Barnsley, Yorkshire, UK: Pen and Sword Social History.

Topiwala, A. and Fazel, S. (2011). The pharmacological management of violence in schizophrenia: A structured review. *Expert Review of Neurotherapeutics,* 11, 53–63.

Troquete, N. A. C., Van Den Brink, R. H. S., Beintema, H., Mulder, T., Van Os, T. W. D. P., Schoevers, R. A. and Wiersma, D. (2013). Risk assessment and shared care planning in out-patient forensic psychiatry: Cluster randomised controlled trial. *British Journal of Psychiatry,* 202, 365–371.

Völlm, B. A., Edworthy, R., Huband, N., Talbot, E., Majid, S., Holley, J., Furtado, V., Weaver, T., McDonald, R. and Duggan, C. (2018). Characteristics and pathways of long-stay patients in high and medium secure settings in England; a secondary publication from a large mixed-methods study. *Frontiers in Psychiatry,* 9, 140-140.

WHO. (2018). Mental Health Atlas 2017. Geneva, Switzerland: World Health Organization. www.who.int/mental_health/evidence/atlas/mental_health_atlas_2017/en/

Wilson, H. A. (2014). Can antisocial personality disorder be treated? A meta-analysis examining the effectiveness of treatment in reducing recidivism for individuals diagnosed with ASPD. *International Journal of Forensic Mental Health,* 13, 36–46.

Wilson, S., James, D. and Forrester, A. (2011). The medium-secure project and criminal justice mental health. *Lancet,* 378, 110–111.

Witt, K., Van Dorn, R. and Fazel, S. (2013). Risk factors for violence in psychosis: Systematic review and meta-regression analysis of 110 studies. *PLoS One,* 8, e55942.

Wolf, A., Fanshawe, T. R., Sariaslan, A., Cornish, R., Larsson, H. and Fazel, S. (2018). Prediction of violent crime on discharge from secure psychiatric hospitals: A clinical prediction rule (FoVOx). *European Psychiatry,* 47, 88–93.

Wolf, A., Whiting, D. and Fazel, S. (2017). Violence prevention in psychiatry: An umbrella review of interventions in general and forensic psychiatry. *Journal of Forensic Psychiatry and Psychology,* 28, 659–673.

Zhang, S., Mellsop, G., Brink, J. and Wang, X. (2015). Involuntary admission and treatment of patients with mental disorder. *Neuroscience Bulletin,* 31, 99–112.

25

RECOVERY OF PERSONS LABELED "NOT CRIMINALLY RESPONSIBLE"

Recommendations Grounded in Lived Experiences

Natalie Aga, Freya Vander Laenen and Wouter Vanderplasschen

Theoretical Background

Not Criminally Responsible: Security and Treatment Intertwined

Persons with mental illness or disabilities are entitled to support and assistance based on international standards for example, access to services and inclusion in the community (UN 2006; WHO 2018). However, when these individuals commit an offense, they instantly become part of a dual discourse (Adshead and Sarkar 2005; Niveau and Welle 2018; Ward 2014). The prevailing approach is not to convict these people because of their psychiatric, cognitive or developmental condition and thus not to hold them responsible for their actions. On the other hand, they are seen as a danger to society, which leads to their confinement and exclusion, aimed at protecting society. Faced with this dichotomy, most criminal justice systems give priority to the latter approach, in which "dangerousness" and "protection of society" justify legal interventions (Brown and Pratt 2000; Lamb et al. 1999). Consequently, these persons are legally labeled "not criminally responsible" (NCR) and often end up in environments where the application of the above-mentioned standards is problematic (ECHR 2016; Salize et al. 2007; Zinkler and Priebe 2002).

Under Belgian law, people who are considered NCR for an offense they committed due to a "mental disorder" or a disability are subjected to what is known as an "internment" measure (Vandevelde et al. 2011). This measure has a twofold goal: on the one hand it focuses on the protection of society and on the other it involves the provision of appropriate treatment and care for the persons concerned (Heimans et al. 2015). Individuals who are subject to an "internment" are assigned to various systems of support and care in penitentiary centers or in secure or general mental health care settings (inpatient as well as outpatient), depending on the support and degree of protection needed. Protective measures are classified as low, medium or high risk (Rowaert 2018) and refer to both physical security measures to meet the estimated level of dangerousness, as well as to the risk of recidivism. Theoretically, persons assessed as "low risk" are assigned to mandatory treatment and support provided by general inpatient and outpatient services (e.g., a day care center of a general psychiatric hospital or sheltered housing). When a person is categorized as "medium risk", treatment can be provided within a medium-security care network, accommodated within inpatient and outpatient facilities. In such settings, the focus on risk reduction is addressed more explicitly. Persons who are considered "high risk" are admitted to high-security or correctional settings, where physical security and specific precautions are prominent to prevent escape and with a clear focus on risk reduction in treatment protocols (De Clercq 2006).

Currently, policy stakeholders plan to develop forensic care networks, in line with the ongoing tendency of deinstitutionalization of care in favor of community-based support in general mental health care. This should facilitate the outflow of persons labeled NCR from correctional services, as well as optimize the transfer between different treatment and support types and between different security levels (Lauwaert et al. 2014) for example, from forensic-psychiatric units to general mental health services. Additionally, two high-security forensic-psychiatric centers have been built in Belgium and have been operational since 2014 and 2017. These centers are seen as a missing link in the Belgian forensic-psychiatric care continuum.

Recovery: a Paradigm Shift in Mental Health Care

The recovery approach originated from patient movements in the '60s and '70s and a growing adherence to psychosocial support within psychiatric rehabilitation and substance abuse treatment (Dekkers et al. 2017; Pouncey and Lukens 2010). The concept of "recovery" has recently gained considerable support in the psychiatric field, with "giving voice to the persons concerned" as one of its most salient features (Oades et al. 2005; Slade 2010). Transformations embedded in the recovery paradigm are currently prioritized by practice and policy initiatives (Castillo et al. 2018; Compagni et al. 2006). In Western welfare states, this new frame of reference in general mental health care is accompanied by a deinstitutionalization of inpatient care (Gordon and Lindqvist 2007). Deinstitutionalization aims at downsizing psychiatric beds service capacity by re-allocating state subsidies (Sisti et al. 2018) in favor of community-based services. It strongly promotes participation and full acceptance of persons with a mental illness in the community (Vandevelde et al. 2017). As a result, mental health care has undergone profound transformations: from residential care to support at home, from medical expertise to support by experts-by-experience, from service-based to patient-driven support (Director of Mental Health 2010; Vandeurzen 2017; Mental Health Review Tribunal 2010). In addition, participation of family members and the social and informal network in the recovery process is increasingly encouraged. This shift implies an evolution away from paternalistic, institutional care and from the idea that the course of a disease is invariably linear: from experiencing symptoms to "being in treatment" to "being cured". Recovery highlights a more multidimensional approach, focusing on different life domains (e.g., relationships, housing, work, leisure activities) and putting well-being, self-management and social support central in care provision (Ralph and Corrigan 2005; Repper and Perkins 2003).

Within the recovery literature, three recovery dimensions are usually distinguished: the clinical, social and personal (Aga and Vanderplasschen 2016). Clinical recovery is based on objectivity, and aims at sustained symptom reduction and restoration of former functioning by means of rehabilitation (Slade et al. 2008). The clinical recovery approach is characterized by professional and expert imperatives and is traditionally practiced in specialist biomedical and/or psychiatric settings. The second dimension, social recovery, emphasizes the presence of social opportunities, agency and resources to achieve social goals (Slade 2009). The presence of contexts that enable participation is crucial (Hopper 2007; Ware et al. 2007) for example, by working on cordiality in society for persons with a psychiatric background (Kal 2001). This social dimension adds nuance to the individualistic view of the disease model and recognizes societal responsibilities as vital in the transition toward inclusive citizenship. The third dimension, personal recovery, is shaped by subjective and self-determined accounts of how a person can lead a valued life despite the presence of symptoms and difficulties caused by a psychiatric illness (Brown and Kandirikirira 2007; Roberts and Boardman 2013; Roberts and Wolfson 2004). This strategy is generally considered as a strengths-based approach for persons in mental health care (Farkas 2007; Gagne et al. 2007; Laudet 2008; Vandevelde et al. 2017). Researchers have differentiated this form of recovery by working toward ownership and agency, optimizing quality of life with a focus on developing meaningful relationships and competencies, and by searching for positive elements that add value for the individual (Bonney and Stickley 2008; Drennan and Alred 2012; Gudjonsson et al. 2010; Simpson and Penney 2011).

The personal recovery approach refers to a long process in which individuals work toward the realization of a dignified and satisfying life by addressing a wide range of problems in different life domains, such as work, relationships, and housing (McLellan 2002; Mead and Copeland 2000). According to experts-by-experience, personal recovery is supported by narratives of lived experiences (e.g., Brown and Kandirikirira 2007), so-called "recovery-stories", written by persons with a mental illness and shared with peers. Another method of shaping the recovery process is known as "shared decision-making", constituting an essential part of the partnership between professionals and patients (Deegan and Drake 2006). Also peer-support and self-help groups are essential in providing potential for recovery (Mead et al. 2001) and add to traditional care provision by reinforcing a non-patient identity.

Initiating, promoting and maintaining recovery is not a static result of professional interventions (Slade et al. 2012), but rather a dynamic process directed by personal responsibilities and support from an individual's wider social network (van Gestel-Timmermans 2011). Because recovery is a highly individual and subjective process (NIMHE 2005), aiming for uniformity in the elements that constitute recovery would be both undesirable and artificial (Simpson and Penney 2011).

(In)compatibility: Recovery and Persons Labeled "Not Criminally Responsible"

As the recovery paradigm is amplified in government policies and mental health care practices, research on recovery and mental illness is simultaneously expanding (Bradstreet and McBrierty 2012; Perkins and Slade 2012). By contrast, correctional and forensic-mental health research primarily focuses on criminogenic needs and risk reduction (e.g., Andrews and Bonta 2010). The widespread Risk-Needs-Responsivity model (RNR) of Andrews and Bonta (2010) is a theoretical framework that starts from a risk-oriented approach. Criminogenic needs are needs an offender wants to meet through deviant and criminal conduct. These dynamic needs correlate with recidivism and can be assessed and targeted for change in treatment programs (Latessa and Lowenkamp 2005). This is a risk approach that does not focus on well-being and long-term needs of persons who offended, even though optimizing these non-criminogenic aspects could reduce the risk of recidivism (Bouman et al. 2009). In summary, this rehabilitation model delineates both central causes of continued criminal behavior and defines broad principles for reducing involvement in future criminal activities (Polaschek 2012). Although this framework is based on general and cognitive social learning perspectives (Busch and Vandevelde, 2015) and does not start from a retributive stance, risk management is predominant. At the same time, it is criticized for omitting the offenders' welfare and neglecting specific treatment needs (Bauwens and Snacken 2010; van Swaaningen 2001).

Various scholars have pointed at several incompatibilities in relation to recovery in forensic-psychiatric contexts (Andrews and Bonta 2010; Dorkins and Adshead 2011; Henagulph et al. 2012; Mezey et al. 2010; Pouncey and Lukens 2010; Simpson and Penney 2011; Viljoen et al. 2011). This section summarizes the main findings.

First, the judicial status hinders recovery because it rigidly controls the provision of mental health support and treatment programs of forensic-psychiatric patients. These programs are primarily based on the assessed security level and are characterized by containment, coercion and detention.

Second, the unawareness of significant aspects of recovery by persons labeled NCR themselves plays a crucial role in impeding recovery (Dorkins and Adshead 2011). In a qualitative study, O'Sullivan and colleagues (2013) found that these persons are not conscious of the transitional and temporary identity they have as a forensic service user and of the identity they need to (re)build after the judicial measure was adjourned. Additionally, these persons tend to be harsh on themselves, as they are legally sanctioned and limited in agency and personal choices (Ferrito et al. 2012). Furthermore, their perception of the recovery process is limited to taking medication, having good relationships with staff members or other patients and residing in secure wards (Mezey et al. 2010).

Third, features of inpatient settings are found to be obstacles for recovery. These settings and treatment protocols prioritize safety, control and confrontation, rather than providing a context for optimistic and hopeful approaches, such as *positive risk taking* (see 'Forensic Recovery as an Omnipresent Lived Experience' below; Corlett and Miles 2010; Mezey et al. 2010).

Fourth, recovery dynamics are hampered by a high level of social prejudice toward persons with aberrant behavior and identities (Casey et al. 2007; Young et al. 2010). The experienced public stigma together with self-abasement, both related to a clinical as well as legal label, have been shown to increase the burden of disease (Davidson et al. 2005; LeBel 2012; Slade et al. 2008; Tew et al. 2012). Focquaert (2018) affirms stigmatization is a possible consequence of "being labeled" and of being an at-risk patient. She states that its internalization and consequently self-blame may result in the development of maladaptive cognitions and narratives. In turn, these types of stigma lead to discrimination against individuals in employment, housing, medical care and social relationships (Pescosolido et al. 2010). This underscores the fact that in addition to the individual objectives of recovery, societally directed phenomena are omnipresent, especially within forensic-psychiatric contexts. The outside world sets the expectation that persons labeled NCR must learn to behave better and their psychiatric condition be sufficiently improved before the measure is abrogated. However, Mezey and Eastman (2009) indicate that persons who are allowed a transfer to less secure conditions have rarely "improved", but are rather deemed to be sufficiently stable to handle a minimal degree of autonomy. Yet, their intrinsic "offender identity" remains (Mezey and Eastman 2009).

A last impediment for recovery is the complexity of the criminal justice system in which a person labeled NCR is placed. Different disciplines, coming from a psychological, social or legal background, aim at different objectives within each individual "case" (Barnao and Ward 2015; McNeill 2012; Vandevelde et al. 2017). Consequently, offending behavior and mental health problems are addressed from a blended approach to psychopathology, security and risk in daily practice (Vandevelde et al. 2017).

In considering these impediments, several authors emphasize the importance of approaching the recovery paradigm differently in specific judiciary contexts and conditions (Corlett and Miles 2010; Dorkins and Adshead 2011; Drennan and Alred 2012; Ferrito et al. 2012). The overall tension between recovery and forensics is embedded in "recovering from a mental illness" and "being subjected to law enforcement and mandatory treatment" (Simpson and Penney 2011), owing to the societal responsibility to reduce risks (Shepherd et al. 2015). This dichotomy is described as "dual recovery" or "secure recovery" (e.g., Corlett and Miles 2010; Drennan and Alred 2012; Green et al. 2011) and is complemented with "offender recovery" (Drennan and Alred, 2012). Offender recovery is defined as "the subjective experience of coming to terms with having offended, perceiving the need to change the personal qualities that resulted in past offending – which also creates the future risk of reoffending – and accepting the social and personal consequences of having offended" (Drennan and Alred, 2012: 15). These specific subprocesses are seen as major challenges when implementing recovery-oriented support with persons who have offended (Corlett and Miles 2010).

In this introductory section, we explored the (in)compatibility of recovery and legal practices and attempted to link "the recovery agenda (which looks for the best in people) and the forensic agenda (which must consider the worst in people)" (Dorkins and Adshead 2011: 178). We conclude that, in forensic and correctional contexts, the recovery approach is often overlooked and/or insufficiently employed for supporting persons labeled NCR. Given the enormous complexity of the legal framework and the subjective, multi-layered concept of recovery, recovery is challenged, but remains all the more relevant.

Exploring Recovery of Persons Labeled "Not Criminally Responsible" Grounded in Lived Experiences

To unfold the outlines and essential elements of recovery of persons labeled NCR, we conducted a study that explored what aspects initiate, promote and maintain the recovery process, grounded in lived experiences. Ninety-four in-depth interviews were conducted with persons currently or formerly labeled NCR. These interviews showed us how recovery is conceptualized and allowed us to determine "forensic recovery" as an additional, interrelated recovery process, besides the well-known clinical, social and personal dimensions (Aga and Vanderplasschen 2016; Aga et al. 2017; Aga 2018). The narratives also enabled us to enhance our understanding of the needs of the population under study.

The study sample (n = 94) was selected in Flanders (Belgium) and involved individuals labeled NCR for at least a six-month period and individuals whose internment measure was abrogated at least six months prior to the interview. Participants were recruited across inpatient and outpatient treatment facilities and across all security levels (low, medium, high) (Table 25.1), including a variety of approaches (e.g., criminal justice system, social welfare and mental health services, and services for individuals with intellectual disabilities). Persons who lived independently were also contacted. In total 94 participants were interviewed, of whom 14 were female. Their ages ranged between 19 and 68, with an average of 42. Sixty-eight persons suffered from a psychiatric disorder and 26 participants were persons with intellectual disabilities. Twelve of these 26 persons resided in or were supported by specialized care for persons with disabilities.

To contribute to our understanding of recovery as an individual mental health phenomenon that is influenced by a range of conditions, perspectives and contexts, a qualitative research design is most appropriate (Jenkins et al. 2005). A descriptive phenomenological approach was adopted throughout this research to maximize the resonance of the lived experiences (Osborne 1990; Van Manen 1990). As the lived experiences of recovery of persons (formerly) labeled NCR were the central focus of this study, a phenomenological approach enabled a fuller understanding of the phenomenon "recovery"

Table 25.1 Sample characteristics of the study participants (n = 94)

Sex		Male	79
		Female	15
Age		18–20	1
		21–30	10
		31–40	28
		41–50	35
		51–60	15
		61–70	5
Security level –	High	Prison	15
Treatment facilities	Medium	Forensic psychiatric center	12
	Low	Forensic inpatient	19
		Forensic outpatient	14
		General inpatient	10
		General outpatient	13
		Formerly interned	11
Experiences of incarceration		Yes	86
		No	7
		Unknown	1

and allowed the researchers to provide reflections on the uniqueness of the experiences of the study participants.

In-depth interviews were conducted, guided by a topic list used to elicit the respondents' narratives (Kvale 1983; Kvale 1994; Kvale and Brinkmann 2009; Josselson 2013; Spector-Mersel and Knaifel 2017). This topic list consisted of open-ended questions inspired by a review of the literature on recovery in general and forensic mental health care in particular (e.g., Leamy et al. 2011; Tew et al. 2012). The sequence of the questions was not fixed, and the interviews were minimally structured. The interview generally started with questions concerning the actual situation of the participant, such as "How are you?" and "What makes a day a *good* day?" (Giorgio 2009) to establish an informal, comfortable atmosphere. Other questions dealt with the major factors contributing to a feeling of progress or well-being in life as well as with future aspirations (Francis 2014).

Because this research was exploratory, we considered a thematic analysis to be most suitable. Braun and Clarke (2006) stated that thematic analysis can be used as a constructionist method, investigating how societal dynamics relate to factual as well as subjective actions, meanings and experiences. To enhance the rigor of this type of analysis, the principal researcher (NA) developed the topic list, administered the interviews, and read the transcriptions of all interviews.

The coding practices are described in four separate studies of which this chapter is a synthesis (Aga et al. 2017; Aga et al. 2018; Aga et al. accepted; Aga et al. submitted).

Forensic Recovery as an Omnipresent Lived Experience

This study shows that understanding recovery as a concept and an ongoing process is significant for persons labeled NCR. Results highlight the following three discernible categories: clinical, personal and social recovery. The findings are similar to research in recovery of persons in general mental health care (Leamy et al. 2011; Ralph and Corrigan, 2005; Repper and Perkins, 2003; Resnick et al. 2005). Additionally, our research points at facilitators of recovery, by indicating needs and resources that should be addressed in the process of regaining a sense of well-being and recovery (e.g., authenticity in supportive professional relationships). It has previously been argued that a broader understanding of both needs and resources can be a means to shape sustained recovery experiences (Shepherd et al. 2008; Slade et al. 2014). Yet, while exploring separate ingredients and discerning subprocesses, the overarching finding was that these subprocesses are interrelated and affect each other mutually and in a continuous way. The most pronounced finding was that clinical and personal dimensions were continuously affected by the social dimension of recovery. Moreover, the personal recovery dimension includes values and conditions that have no foundation without social recovery mechanisms. Generally, we argue that no single recovery subprocess is sufficient *as such*: all dimensions are mutually supportive of one another. This is illustrated by a woman who stated that "the sum of the people I met and the events in my life I was involved in, that's me" (Participant 2, residing in prison). Consequently, discerning these subprocesses serves the goal of enhancing knowledge, but it cannot serve as a guideline for practice. Without a holistic stance and an understanding of recovery as an all-encompassing process, we devalue the overall process and reduce it to traditional clinical approaches or fragmented services (Rose et al. 1998; Tondora and Davidson 2006).

Besides mapping interrelated facets, we observed that recovery elements and resources are strongly influenced by and embedded in an individual's personal story and life history: how recovery is constituted and how it is layered is determined individually. Nevertheless, the results show a clear common aspect: an overall emphasis on the quality of meaningful elements. For example, "proper housing" is often described as very meaningful, but the same house or room can bring about a feeling of "being placed" or a sense of belonging in different persons. This indicates that recovery is only adequate if the quality of the various aspects of recovery is attuned to a person experiencing something as meaningful. Approaching recovery first and foremost as a personal journey requires a mind shift and attitudinal changes in supporting persons labeled NCR. It implies that a professional cannot enable recovery without an attitude of collaborating and maximally engaging with the individuals concerned (Davidson et al. 2005; Rose et al. 1998; Tondora et al. 2014).

In the narratives, respondents paid substantial attention to the impact of the legal label. Besides its possible positive effects on recovery for example, compelling them to access treatment and to adhere to it, the findings show that the recovery process is jeopardized by judicial constrictions and supervision. This confirms the results of a parallel study on desistance by Van Roeyen and colleagues (2016; Van Roeyen 2018). Judicial control and incapacitation are experienced as ambivalent during the implementation phase of the legal measure, being described as "lifesaving" as well as "hard to bear". As time passes by, persons describe its damaging and traumatizing effects. Barriers to recovery are mainly the indefiniteness of the measure and the continuous feeling of being supervised. The latter is experienced as a restraint on one's agency and choice, which are often identified as active ingredients of recovery (Brown 2018; Whitley and Campbell 2014). Since these findings are directly linked to the nature of criminal justice interventions, we argue that a clear distinction between a recovery approach in general and in forensic mental health care in particular is essential (Aga and Vanderplasschen 2016; Aga et al. 2017; Corlett and Miles, 2010; Dorkins and Adshead 2011; Drennan and Alred, 2012; Ferrito et al. 2012). This is supported by the following quote: "I have a bit the impression that [...] lots of family members have another view upon me since I have been interned. And it seems like they are a bit more cautious in their words [...]. Like they have the image that I will punch them in the face or so" (Participant 9, forensic residential treatment). Based on these findings, forensic recovery was added as an additional recovery dimension. It implies "the ambiguous experiences related to features of the judicial trajectory. This can be seen as an additional mechanism, besides more established recovery dimensions" (Aga et al. 2017: 1). This ambiguous experience is unique to persons labeled NCR and illustrates the presence of another typifying dynamic: the impact of having offended and the accompanying distressing effect of the legal label, which simultaneously reveals the possible absence of preconditions for recovery. For example, some participants were unaware of the dual ground of their legal label and presumed they were in treatment as a punitive consequence of their offense. Considering the importance of clinical recovery and – for some persons – the need to recognize their diagnosis to enable their recovery process, we wonder how recovery can "occur" if persons are not aware of their mental health diagnosis and can only refer to the offense. We argue that to initiate recovery it is of great importance that a person acknowledge and recognize what he or she should recover "*into*" and not "*from*" (Davidson and Roe 2007). At the same time forensic recovery also highlights that particular *forensic* elements and dynamics *can* enable recovery for example, a judicial measure can contribute to personal development when it enhances educational opportunities.

Based on our findings, forensic recovery may include but does not necessarily imply offender recovery (Drennan and Alred 2012). In fact, we are of the opinion that "offender recovery" (Drennan and Alred 2012) potentially describes a newly imposed, legally constructed identity which is mainly centered around the index crime, rather than representing individual pathways. Caution is needed to avoid these additional burdens if and when the recovery approach is employed in the criminal justice system. In summary, the need for forensic recovery can be considered as a consequence of persons labeled NCR being positioned between care and justice systems (Prior 2007).

Due to the negative impact of the judicial constrictions and supervision accompanying an internment measure, it was perceived that personal change usually only starts when the judicial measure stops (Figure 25.1). In most of the interviews, persons mentioned being diagnosed with a psychiatric disorder or being assessed with an intellectual disability for a considerable period of time preceding the implementation of the legal label. Also, some participants were already involved in treatment or in other services prior to committing an offense. When the offense took place, the implementation of the measure helped to compel treatment that had often already been part of the individual's life to some extent. Nevertheless, the negative impact of being judicially labeled was observed in most

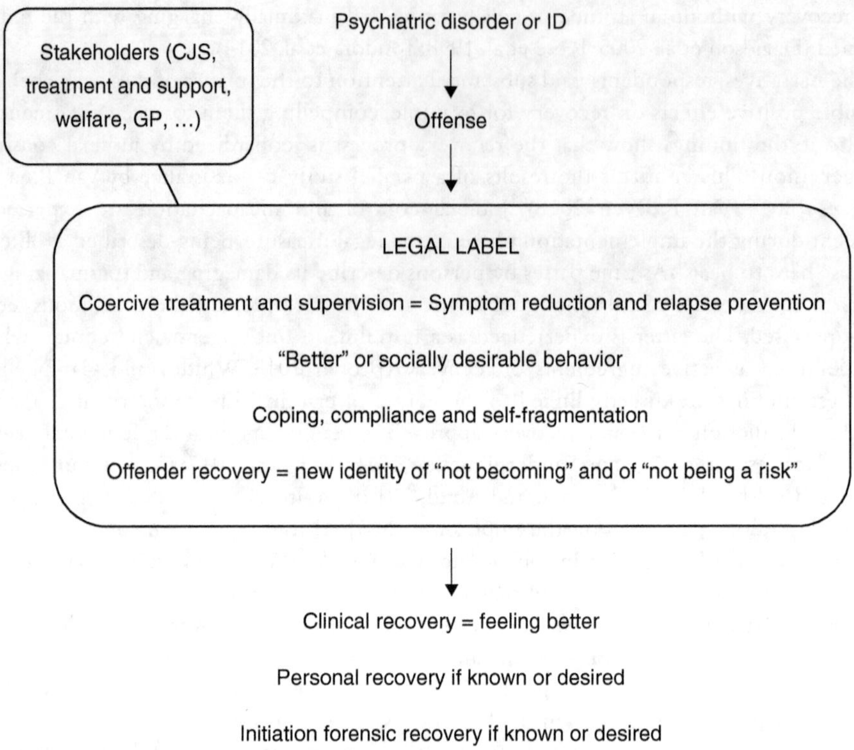

Figure 25.1 The course of transitions when labeled NCR.

narratives and was tangible, transcending all types of support, settings and physical security measures (low, medium, high). In general, persons described the legal process as their future/life being put "on hold" or encapsulated, which isolated them from real life. This "encapsulation" seems to be the overall experience of interventions that target criminogenic needs and aim to reduce recidivism instead of promoting resilience and strengths.

Looking at being legally labeled as a transitional process (Figure 25.1), we observed experiences strictly limited to coercive treatment and supervision, resulting in symptom reduction and relapse prevention. This finding seems to render socially desirable behavior that is perceived as "better" by evaluators. Within a forensic context, personal recovery efforts are frequently limited to coping and complying, with self-fragmentation as a result. Moreover, offender recovery (Drennan and Alred 2012) can lead to new identities of "not becoming" and of "not being a risk" in the case of our interviewees. What hinders respondents in "becoming" is for example, not addressing trauma or developing additional trauma through coercive interventions. These are themes identified as hindering individual recovery processes (Covington 2007). Also, the narratives revealed that the number of professionals involved in one trajectory mounts quickly: criminal justice staff members, lawyers, welfare and treatment providers (e.g., for therapy, housing, work, education). Each of these stakeholders addresses – from their own distinct perspective – complex social, behavioral and health issues. This makes an attuned engagement of professional stakeholders to the personality and the context of their clients or patients very complicated. Unclear expectations from and toward professionals can compromise the recovery journey and encourage learned helplessness among the persons involved (Roberts and Wolfson 2004). We summarize the above with the quote: "What I would do if the measure would stop tomorrow? Then it would truly start..." (Participant 11, forensic outpatient treatment), illustrating that these persons are cocooned within their legal label and merely learn how to live through it rather than actively engaging in their personal recovery (Aaltola et al. 2016; Coffey 2011; Reynolds et al. 2014).

To overcome the observed hegemony of risk orientation over care, we suggest linking rehabilitation and treatment for persons labeled NCR to their personal needs. In this respect, the Good Lives Model (GLM) of offender rehabilitation offers a promising new perspective (Maruna et al. 2004). The GLM is a strengths-based approach that assists individuals who offended in developing internal and external resources/capacities to build a fulfilling and prosocial life (Ward and Maruna 2007; Ward and Stewart 2003; Ward et al. 2007). It focuses on an individual's capacities and positive characteristics rather than on shortcomings and risks (Farrall and Maruna 2004; Saleebey 2005). So far, research in a forensic context linking recovery-oriented programs to mental health outcomes is non-existent. Nevertheless, an evolution toward strengths-based approaches can be observed, promoting models that reinforce individuals' recovery journeys even when a criminal justice intervention is required.

Practice and Policy Recommendations Based on Participants' Lived Experiences

In this final section, we formulate policy and practice recommendations derived directly or indirectly from the lived experiences of persons labeled NCR.

Addressing Individual Support Needs

The recognition of victimization and a therapeutic focus on trauma are deemed to be necessary but are frequently indicated as absent. Trans-institutionalization, abuse, neglect and trauma due to committing an offense were identified throughout the stories as significant life events (Prins 2011; Richards et al. 2000). Addressing these obstacles can have positive outcomes on well-being, in turn reducing the likelihood of relapse. Also, narratives show that the trajectories of the studied population depend on multiple clinical evaluations often emphasizing an interdictory perspective and focusing on what the person "should not be", namely "a risk", rather than focusing on possibilities and capacities. Such an approach coheres with being judged as "a potential danger". By framing "risk" and "risk taking" as situations that can evolve positively, this could imply that estimations can also be guided by trust and belief, values that are indicated by the participants as helpful (Stickley and Felton, 2006). In order to further meet the needs of persons labeled NCR, the professional network should be unconditionally supportive and genuinely engaged. The majority of involved professionals have to evaluate the behavior and "actual situation" of the central persons for criminal justice purposes. For the patients, this often leads to distress and a feeling of being pressured to perform. This professional role is described as a conflicting ethic and is experienced as "dual" by professionals themselves (Ward et al. 2015; Ward 2014). To overcome this tension for example, the number of persons who are involved in formal practices could be limited. Also, non-evaluative contacts can be increased. In relation to the latter, former personal mentors and animals are referred to as helping relationships. Former personal mentors are deemed to be non-judgmental, because of their dissociation from the criminal justice trajectory. Animals may contribute through specific animal-assisted interventions, but above all, through companionship and instigating a mutual bond.

Integrating Stagnation in Care Pathways

Persons labeled NCR are often subject to pathways in which professionals expect and evaluate progress. Both clinical and legal routes are focused on better conduct and the exclusion of deviant behavior. Places and relationships where stagnation is allowed, where persons can just "*be*", are described as helpful. This could lead to positive outcomes in relation to both legal and recovery pathways.

Increasing Awareness of the Social Recovery Dimension

This study showed that the need for social recovery has a dominant presence in all narratives, while at the same time being the most difficult dimension to initiate and maintain. Throughout the research project, it became clear that this dimension intersects with both clinical and personal recovery. It is therefore important to increase professionals' awareness of this aspect of recovery. A chat with the person who administers medication or a silent cleaning lady are examples of "hidden" relationships that are described by the respondents as meaningful. In addition to personal relations, society also plays a leading role (Cullen et al. 2017; Mezzina et al. 2006a, 2006b; Price-Robertson et al. 2017). This societal dimension requires a collaborative approach, which should promote the acceptance and social participation of the population under study and of vulnerable populations in general (Freire 1970).

Using a Common Language

The broader criminological and forensic-psychiatric discourse pays little attention to a patient's perspective (Livingston et al. 2016; Livingston 2018; To et al. 2015; Youngs and Canter 2012). Taking this view seriously is an indispensable condition to implement recovery. The accessibility of language and the way in which language is used in this power-imbalanced context is an important prerequisite. This recommendation urges that the use of language be reviewed in a creative manner, aiming at providing clear and comprehensible information between services and service users.

Tackling Practical Barriers

Recovery stories from persons labeled NCR show that tackling practical obstacles is an important element in facilitating the recovery process. This is about reconsidering certain measures and procedures for example, limited access to the internet, withdrawal of one's driver's license, correspondence in an inaccessible language, lack of information on one's own (legal and support) pathway, large distances to family and supportive persons and lack of a clear financial overview. Participants indicate that these obstructions lead to isolation. If these practical obstacles are not addressed, they will continue to hinder the individual's change processes (McNeill 2012).

Including Space and Time to Sustain Recovery

Respondents strongly emphasize the role of the environment on their well-being and recovery. "Environment" includes time as well as spatial features. Spending time in nature, tranquility, privacy and a comfortable room are mentioned as important determinants to sustain recovery. The ownership over "filling in time" is a similar area, that enhances a sense of recovery. Individuals' stories show that both elements allow people to build resilience (De Ruysscher 2016; Fullilove 1996; Hagerty et al. 1992). These environmental aspects are underexposed within the current debate on the implementation of recovery.

Adjusting Professionals' Training Programs

Persons labeled NCR strive to lead ordinary lives. Therefore, participants indicate a need for relating to professionals as role models, assuming that professionals can rely on a robust personal and conventional framework (Jas and Wieling 2018). This study also found that professionals are appreciated as persons in themselves, over and above their formal role. We argue for the integration of these findings into professionals' training programs, making a shift away from a merely "professional training" toward promoting "holistic growth as a human being".

Implementing Policies that Enable Continuity in Relationships

Currently, we observe that professional organizations and sectors exclude individuals labeled NCR because their needs are assessed as too complex and because they do not meet services' eligibility criteria. This issue reflects national policy domains (WHO 2018) that have a direct influence on creating or restricting opportunities and can tackle debilitating institutional and structural obstacles. Mental health policies encourage deinstitutionalization by the implementation of community-based initiatives and the construction of integrated care networks. Recovery is seen as a guiding concept within these initiatives (Amering and Schmolke 2007; Scott and Wilson 2011). Under Belgian Law, this development is initiated by a clause of the Act on hospital legislation, the so-called "Article 107". This is a statutory provision allowing the re-allocation of state subsidies for residential care into community-based support (See 1.2.). Due to this impulse, integrated care networks have been set up to offer "stepped care": from high-security to low-security treatment in forensic-psychiatric settings (Lauwaert et al. 2014). However, when listening to the stories of persons labeled NCR, we perceived trajectories characterized by fragmentation (Hörberg et al. 2012; Schaftenaar 2018), despite recent political efforts. For practice and policy, continuity means seamless and integrated transitions between different services. For persons labeled NCR, continuity of care is about experiencing continuous relationships with ongoing support from practitioners. Care systems should facilitate this continuity in their managerial thinking.

Debating Tensions

At present, security-and-cure hybridity results in the reinforcement of the legal framework. The influence of the indefiniteness of the measure's duration, as well as the stress and stigma generated by the judicial label are legal factors that affect individuals' well-being enormously. To meet this mixture of tensions, there are no ready-made solutions. Nevertheless, at this cutting edge, there must always be room for constructive debate, instead of further polarizing care-control ideologies. Just as the legal measure itself, the person labeled NCR seems stuck in between two mindsets. Besides a care-control duality, normativity will always be guiding systems of support for this population. Discrepancies between societal and judicial expectations and what the persons labeled NCR really expect/want/desire are omnipresent (Ward and Maruna, 2007). "Oscillating between the status of patient and offender, their management still seems to be dominated by a managerial, risk-reduction logic that threatens their reintegration within the society" (Cartuyvels and Cliquennois 2015: 18). The questions here concern who determines and imposes these norms and what bounds the imposition of normativity. At present, it is "lawful behavior" that seems to be the guiding frame of reference.

Conclusion

As outlined throughout this chapter, the recovery approach is challenged within the criminal justice system, but is not incompatible with it. This statement is consistent with earlier research, pointing at the care-control ambivalence in forensic care pathways (Henagulph et al. 2012; Mezey et al. 2010; Stuart et al. 2017; Viljoen et al. 2011). Elements such as "growth", an important aspect of recovery according to the lived experiences, clashes fundamentally with a legal framework of fixed prescriptions. Any sense of growth and progress can be undermined by the obligation to "perform and conform" (To et al. 2015). Yet, based on the lived experiences explored in this study, we argue that recovery is possible, on the condition that compulsory care is carefully reconsidered. A cultural transformation in favor of the recovery paradigm embedded in lived experiences is championed and requires a shift from an individualistic, punitive approach toward a rhetoric of shared responsibility on a relational, organizational and policy level.

References

Adshead, G., and Sarkar, S. P. (2005) "Justice and welfare: Two ethical paradigms in forensic psychiatry," *Australian and New Zealand Journal of Psychiatry* 39: 1011–17.

Aga, N. (2018) "Recovery of persons labeled as not criminally responsible: a qualitative study grounded in lived experiences" (unpublished doctoral dissertation), Ghent University, Ghent, Belgium.

Aga, N., and Vanderplasschen, W. (2016) "De Schone en het Beest: persoonlijk herstel in een forensische context," in T. Vander Beken et al. (eds), *Sterktes van mensen. Sterktegerichte strategieën voor het ondersteunen van mensen met een psychiatrische problematiek die strafbare feiten* pleegden, Antwerpen: Maklu: 149–68.

Aga, N., Vander Laenen, F., Vandevelde, S., Vermeersch, E., and Vanderplasschen, W. (2017) "Recovery of offenders formerly labeled as not criminally responsible: Uncovering the ambiguity from first-person narratives," *International Journal of Offender Therapy and Comparative Criminology* 1–21.

Aga, N., De Landtsheer, I., Vander Laenen F., and Vanderplasschen, W. (2018) "Herstel in een forensische context: een exploratieve studie naar doorleefde ervaringen van geïnterneerde personen in een ambulant, regulier ondersteuningstraject," *Orthopedagogiek: Onderzoek en Praktijk* 57: 245–59.

Aga, N., Vander Laenen, F., Vandevelde, S., and Vanderplasschen, W. (accepted). "A Qualitative Inquiry on Recovery Needs and Resources of Individuals with Intellectual Disabilities Labelled Not Criminally Responsible," *International Journal of Applied Research in Intellectual Disabilities.*

Aga, N., Rowaert, S., Vander Laenen, F., Vandevelde, S., Vander Beken, T., Audenaert, K., and Vanderplasschen, W. (submitted) "Connectedness in Recovery Narratives of Persons Labeled Not Criminally Responsible: a Qualitative Study," *International Journal of Forensic Mental Health.*

Andrews, D. A., and Bonta, J. (2010) *The Psychology of Criminal Conduct. 5th edition,* Elsevier Science.

Amering, M., and Schmolke, M. (2007) *Recovery. Das Ende der Unheilbarkeit,* Bonn: Psychiatrie Verlag.

Askola, R. A., Nikkonen, M., Paavilainen, E., Soininen, P., Putkonen, H., and Louheranta, O. (2016) "Forensic psychiatric patients' perspectives on their care: A narrative view," *Perspectives in Psychiatric Care* 54: 64–73.

Barnao, M., and Ward, T. (2015) "Sailing uncharted seas without a compass: A review of interventions in forensic mental health," *Aggression and Violent Behavior* 22: 77–86.

Bauwens, A., and Snacken, S. (2010) "Modellen van daderbegeleiding: op weg naar een geïntegreerd model?," *Panopticon* 31: 42–56.

Bradstreet, S., and McBrierty, R. (2012) "Recovery in Scotland: Beyond service development," *International Review of Psychiatry* 24: 64–69

Braun, V. and Clarke, V. (2006) "Using thematic analysis in psychology," *Qualitative Research in Psychology* 3: 77–101.

Bonney, S., and Stickley, T. (2008) "Recovery and mental health: A review of the British Literature," *Journal of Psychiatric and Mental Health Nursing* 15: 140–53.

Bouman, H. A. Y., de Ruiter, C., and Schene, A.H. (2009) "Recent life events and subjective well-being of personality disordered forensic outpatients," *International Journal of Law and Psychiatry* 32: 348–54.

Brown, J. (2018) "Parents' experiences of their adolescent's mental health treatment: Helplessness or agency-based hope," *Clinical Child Psychology and Psychiatry.*

Brown, W., and Kandirikirira, N. (2007) *Recovering Mental Health in Scotland: Report on Narrative Investigation of Mental Health Recovery,* Glasgow, Scotland: Scottish Recovery Network.

Brown, M., and Pratt, J. (eds.) (2000) *Dangerous Offenders: Punishment and Social Order,* London/New York: Routledge Press.

Busch, C., and Vandevelde, S. (2015) "De rehabilitatie van daders: Naar een integratie van het Risk-Need - Responsivity-Model en het Good Lives Model?" in C. Wittouck et al. (eds.) *Handboek Forensische Gedragswetenschappen,* Antwerpen, Apeldoorn: Maklu.

Cartuyvels, Y., and Cliquennois, G. (2015) "La défense sociale pour les aliénés délinquants en Belgique: Le soin comme légitimation d'un dispositif de contrôle?" *Champ Penal,* 12.

Casey, S., Day, A., Howells, K., and Ward, T. (2007) "Assessing suitability for offender rehabilitation: Development and validation of the Treatment Readiness Questionnaire," *Criminal Justice and Behavior* 34: 1427–40.

Castillo, E. G., Chung, B., Bromley, E., Kataoka, S. H., Braslow, J. T., Essock, S. M., ... and Wells, K. B. (2018) "Community, public policy, and recovery from mental illness: Emerging research and initiatives," *Harvard Review of Psychiatry* 26: 70–81.

Coffey, M. (2011) "Resistance and challenge: Competing accounts in aftercare monitoring," *Sociology of Health & Illness* 33: 748–60.

Compagni, A., Adams, N., and Daniels, A. (2006) International *Pathways* to *Mental Health System Transformation*: Strategies and *Challenges,* Sacramento: California Institute for Mental Health.

Corlett, H., and Miles, H. (2010) "An evaluation of the implementation of the recovery philosophy in a secure forensic service," *British Journal of Forensic Practice* 12: 14–25.

Cullen, B. A., Mojtabai, R., Bordbar, E., Everett, A., Nugent, K. L., and Eaton, W. W. (2017) "Social network, recovery attitudes and internal stigma among those with serious mental illness," *International Journal of Social Psychiatry* 63: 448–58.
Covington, S. (2007) "Women and the criminal justice system," *Women's Health Issues,* 17: 180–82.
Davidson, L., O'Connell, M. J., Tondora, J., Lawless, M., and Evans, A. C. (2005) "Recovery in serious mental illness: A new wine or just a new bottle?" *Professional Psychology: Research & Practice* 36: 480–87.
Davidson, L., and Roe, D. (2007) "Recovery from versus recovery in serious mental illness: One strategy for lessening confusion plaguing recovery," *Journal of Mental Health* 16: 459–70.
De Clercq, M. (2006). "Uitdagingen in de forensische psychiatrie vanuit een mediumriskbehandelingsperspect ief," *De Orde van de Dag*, 34: 29–32.
De Ruysscher, C. (2016) "A place to be (me)." [Lecture] The Desistance and Recovery Academy Launch, Sheffield, UK, 14th December.
Deegan, P. E., and Drake, R. E. (2006) "Shared decision making and medication management in the recovery process," *Psychiatric services* 57: 1636–39.
Dekkers, A., Aga, N., and Vanderplasschen W. (2017) "Herstel van verslaving: achtergrond en situering," in W. Vanderplasschen and F. Vander Laenen (eds) Naar *een herstelondersteunende verslavingszorg, Praktijk en beleid.* Leuven/Den Haag: ACCO: 45–66.
Director of Mental Health (2010) Annual Report 2009, Wellington: Ministry of Health.
Dorkins, E., and Adshead, G. (2011) "Working with offenders: Challenges to the recovery agenda," *Advances in Psychiatric Treatment* 17: 178–87.
Drennan, G., and Alred, D. (2012) *Secure Recovery: Approaches to recovery in forensic mental health settings*, London: Routledge.
European Court of Human Rights (ECHR) (2016) *Affaire W.D. contre Belgique.*
Farrall, S., and Maruna, S. (2004) "Desistance-focussed criminal justice policy research: Introduction to a special issue on desistance from crime and public policy," *The Howard Journal of Criminal Justice* 43: 358–67.
Farkas, M. (2007) "The vision of recovery today: What it is and what it means for services," *World Psychiatry* 6: 68–74.
Ferrito, M., Vetere, A., Adshead, G., and Moore, E. (2012) "Life after homicide: Accounts of recovery and redemption of offender patients in a high security hospital – A qualitative study," *Journal of Forensic Psychiatry & Psychology* 23: 327–44.
Focquaert, F. (2018) "Neurobiology and crime: A neuro-ethical perspective," *Journal of Criminal Justice* 65. doi.org/10.1016/j.jcrimjus.2018.01.001
Francis, A. (2014) "Strengths-based assessments and recovery in mental health: Reflections from practice," *International Journal of Social Work and Human Service Practice* 2: 264–71.
Freire, P. (1970) *Pedagogy of the Oppressed*, New York: Continuum.
Fullilove, M. T. (1996) "Psychiatric implications of displacement: Contributions from the psychology of place," *The American Journal of Psychiatry* 153: 1516–23.
Gagne, C., White, W., and Anthony, W. A. (2007) "Recovery: A common vision for the fields of mental health and addictions," *Psychiatric Rehabilitation Journal* 31: 32.
Giorgio, G. (2009) "Traumatic truths and the gift of telling," *Qualitative Inquiry* 15: 149–167.
Gordon, H., and Lindqvist, P. (2007) "Forensic psychiatry in Europe," *Psychiatric Bulletin* 31: 421–24.
Gudjonsson, G., Webster, G., and Green, T. (2010) "The recovery approach to care in psychiatric services: Staff attitudes before and after training," *Psychiatric Bulletin* 34: 326–29.
Green, T., Batson, A., and Gudjonsson, G. (2011) "The development and initial validation of a service-user led measure for recovery of mentally disordered offenders," *Journal of Forensic Psychiatry & Psychology* 22: 252–65.
Hagerty, M. K., Lynch-Sauer, J., Patusky, K. L., Bouwsema, M., and Collier, P. (1992) "Sense of belonging: A vital mental health concept," *Archives of Psychiatric Nursing*, 6: 172–77
Heimans, H., Vander Beken, T., and Schipaanboord, E. A. (2015) "Eindelijk een echte nieuwe en goede wet op de internering? Deel 1: De gerechtelijke fase," *Rechtskundig Weekblad* 79: 1043–64.
Henagulph, S., McIvor, R., and Clarke, A. (2012) "Risk and recovery group for offenders with mental disorders," *Psychiatric Services* 63: 94–95.
Hopper, K. (2007) "Rethinking social recovery in schizophrenia: What a capabilities approach might offer," *Social Science & Medicine* 65: 868–79.
Hörberg, U., Sjögren, R., and Dahlberg, K. (2012) "To be strategically struggling against resignation: The lived experience of being cared for in forensic psychiatric care," *Issues in Mental Health Nursing* 33, 743–51.
Jas, E., and Wieling, M. (2018) "Providers' competencies positively affect personal recovery of involuntarily admitted patients with severe mental illness: A prospective observational study," *International Journal of Social Psychiatry* 64: 145–55.

Jenkins, J. H., Strauss, M. E., Carpenter, E. A., Miller, D., Floersch, J., and Sajatovic, M. (2005) "Subjective experience of recovery from schizophrenia-related disorders and atypical antipsychotics," *International Journal of Social Psychiatry* 51: 211–27.

Josselson, R. (2013) *Interviewing for Qualitative Inquiry: A relational Approach*, London-New York: Guilford Press.

Kal, D. (2001) *Quarter-making: Clearing the way for people with a psychiatric background*, Amsterdam, The Netherlands: Boom.

Kvale, S. (1983) "The qualitative research interview: A phenomenological and a hermeneutical mode of understanding," *Journal of Phenomenological Psychology* 14: 171–96.

Kvale, S. (1994) "Ten standard objections to qualitative research interviews," *Journal of Phenomenological Psychology* 25: 147–73.

Kvale, S., and Brinkmann, S. (2009) *Learning the craft of qualitative research interviewing* Thousand Oaks, CA: Sage Publications.

Lamb, H. R., Weinberger, L. E., and Gross, B. H. (1999) "Community treatment of severely mentally ill offenders under the jurisdiction of the criminal justice system: A review," *Psychiatric Services* 50: 907–13.

Latessa, E. J., and Lowenkamp, C. (2005) "What works in reducing recidivism," *U. St. Thomas LJ* 3: 521.

Laudet, A. B. (2008) "The road to recovery: Where are we going and how do we get there? Empirically driven conclusions and future directions for service development and research," *Substance Use & Misuse*, 43: 2001–20.

Lauwaert, F., Mattheeuws, K., and De Deygere, M. (2014) "Het schakelteam internering: Naar een completer en dynamisch zorglandschap voor geïnterneerden," *Panopticon* 35: 237–41.

LeBel, T. P. (2012) "Invisible strips? Formerly incarcerated persons' perceptions of stigma," *Deviant Behavior* 33: 89–107.

Leamy, M., Bird, V., Le Boutillier, C., Williams, J., and Slade, M. (2011) "Conceptual framework for personal recovery in mental health: Systematic review and narrative synthesis," *The British Journal of Psychiatry*, 199: 445–52.

Livingston, J. D. (2018) "What does success look like in the forensic mental health system? Perspectives of service users and service providers," *International Journal of Offender Therapy and Comparative Criminology* 1: 1–21.

Livingston, J. D., Crocker, A. G., Nicholls, T. L., and Seto, M. C. (2016) "Forensic mental health tribunals: A qualitative study of participants' experiences and views," *Psychology, Public Policy, and Law* 22: 173.

Maruna, S., Immarigeon, R., and LeBel, T. (2004) "Ex-offender reintegration: Theory and practice," in S. Maruna and R. Immarigeon (eds) *After crime and punishment*, Cullompton, UK: Willan: 3–27.

McLellan, A. T. (2002) "Have we evaluated addiction treatment correctly? Implications from a chronic care perspective," *Addiction* 97: 249–52.

McNeill, F. (2012) "Four forms of 'offender' rehabilitation: Towards an interdisciplinary perspective," *Legal and Criminological Psychology* 17: 18–36.

Mead, S., and Copeland, M. E. (2000) "What recovery means to us: Consumers' perspectives," *Community Mental Health Journal* 36: 315–28.

Mead, S., Hilton, D., and Curtis, L. (2001) "Peer support: A theoretical perspective," *Psychiatric Rehabilitation Journal* 25: 134–41.

Mental Health Review Tribunal (2010) *Annual Report of the Mental Health Review Tribunal*, Sydney: Mental Health Review Tribunal.

Mezey, G. C., and Eastman, N. (2009) "Choice and social inclusion in forensic psychiatry: Acknowledging mixed messages and double think," *The Journal of Forensic Psychiatry and Psychology* 21: 683–96.

Mezey, G. C., Kavuma, M., Turton, P., Demetriou, A., and Wright, C. (2010) "Perceptions, experiences and meanings of recovery in forensic psychiatric patients," *The Journal of Forensic Psychiatry & Psychology* 21: 683–96.

Mezzina, R., Davidson, L., Borg, M., Marin, I., Topor, A., and Sells, D. (2006a) "The social nature of recovery: discussion and implications for practice," *American Journal of Psychiatric Rehabilitation* 9: 63–80.

Mezzina, R., Borg, M., Marin, I., Sells, D., Topor, A., and Davidson, L. (2006b) "From participation to citizenship: How to regain a role, a status, and a life in the process of recovery," *American Journal of Psychiatric Rehabilitation* 9: 39–61.

National Institute for Mental Health in England (NIMHE) (2005) NIMHE guiding statement on *recovery*. https://docplayer.net/16612492-Nimhe-guiding-statement-on-recovery.html

Niveau, G., and Welle, I. (2018) "Forensic psychiatry, one subspecialty with two ethics? A systematic review," *BMC Medical Ethics*, 19: 1–10.

Oades, L., Deane, F., Crowe, T., Lambert, G. W., Kavanagh, D., and Lloyd, C. (2005) "Collaborative recovery: An integrative model for working with individuals who experience chronic and recurring mental illness," *Australasian Psychiatry*, 13: 279–284.

O'Sullivan, M., Boulter, S., and Black, G. (2013) "Lived experiences of recalled mentally disordered offenders with dual diagnosis: A qualitative phenomenological study," *Journal of Forensic Psychiatry & Psychology* 24: 403–20.

Osborne, J. W. (1990) "Some basic existential-phenomenological research methodology for counsellors," *Canadian Journal of Counselling and Psychotherapy* 24: 2.

Perkins, R., and Slade, M. (2012) "Recovery in England: Transforming statutory services?" *International Review of Psychiatry* 24: 29–39.

Pescosolido, B. A., Martin, J. K., Long, J. S., Medina, T. R., Phelan, J. C., and Link, B. G. (2010). "'A disease like any other'? A decade of change in public reactions to schizophrenia, depression, and alcohol dependence," *American Journal of Psychiatry,* 167: 1321–30.

Polaschek, D. L. (2012) "An appraisal of the risk–need–responsivity (RNR) model of offender rehabilitation and its application in correctional treatment," *Legal and Criminological Psychology* 17: 1–17.

Pouncey, C. L., and Lukens, J. M. (2010) "Madness versus badness: The ethical tension between the recovery movement and forensic psychiatry," *Theoretical Medicine and Bioethics* 31: 93–105.

Price-Robertson, R., Obradovic, A., and Morgan, B. (2017) "Relational recovery: Beyond individualism in the recovery approach," *Advances in Mental Health,* 15: 108–20.

Prins, S. J. (2011) "Does transinstitutionalization explain the overrepresentation of people with serious mental illnesses in the criminal justice system," *Community Mental Health Journal,* 47: 716–22.

Prior, P. M. (2007) "Mentally disordered offenders and the European Court of Human Rights," *International Journal of Law and Psychiatry* 30: 546–57.

Ralph, R. O., and Corrigan, P. W. (2005) *Recovery in mental illness: Broadening our understanding of wellness,* Washington: American Psychological Association.

Repper, J., and Perkins, R. (2003) *Social inclusion and recovery: A model for mental health practice,* London: Baillière Tindall.

Resnick, S. G., Fontana, A., Lehman, A. F., and Rosenheck, R. A. (2005) "An empirical conceptualization of the recovery orientation," *Schizophrenia Research* 75: 119–28.

Reynolds, L. M., Jones, J. C., Davies, J. P., Freeth, D., and Heyman, B. (2014) "Playing the game: Service users' management of risk status in a UK medium secure forensic mental health service," *Health, Risk & Society,* 16: 199–209.

Richards, J. M., Beal, W. E., Seagal, J. D., and Pennebaker, J. W. (2000) "Effects of disclosure of traumatic events on illness behavior among psychiatric prison inmates," *Journal of Abnormal Psychology,* 109: 156.

Roberts, G., and Boardman, J. (2013) "Understanding 'recovery'," *Advances in Psychiatric Treatment,* 19: 400–409.

Roberts, G., and Wolfson, P. (2004) "The rediscovery of recovery: Open to all," *Advances in Psychiatric Treatment,* 10: 37–48.

Rose, D., Ford, R., Lindley, P., and Gawith, L. (1998) *In Our Experience: User Focused Monitoring of Mental Health Services,* London: Sainsbury Centre for Mental Health.

Rowaert, S. (2018) *Supporting Family Members of Mentally Ill Offenders. A Strengths-Based Approach,* Gent: Orthopedagogische reeks.

Saleebey, D. (2005) *The Strengths Perspective in Social Work Practice (4th Ed.),* Boston: Pearson Education, Inc.

Salize, H. J., Dreβing, H., and Kief, C. (2007) *Mentally Disordered Persons in European Prison Systems.* Needs, *Programmes* and *Outcomes,* (EUPRIS), European Commission.

Schaftenaar, P. (2018) *Contact gezocht. Relationeel werken en het al.ledaagse als werkzame principes in de klinische forensische zorg.* Amsterdam: SWP.

Scott, A., and Wilson, L. (2011) "Valued identities and deficit identities: Wellness Recovery Action Planning and self-management in mental health," *Nursing Inquiry* 18: 40–49.

Shepherd, G., Boardman, J., and Slade, M. (2008) *Making Recovery a Reality.* London: Sainsbury Centre for Mental Health.

Shepherd, A., Doyle, M., Sanders, C., and Shaw, J. (2015) "Personal recovery within forensic settings: Systematic review and meta-synthesis of qualitative methods studies," *Criminal Behaviour and Mental Health* 26: 59–75.

Simpson, A. I. F., and Penney, S. R. (2011) "The recovery paradigm in forensic mental health services," *Criminal Behaviour and Mental Health,* 21: 299–306.

Sisti, D. A., Sinclair, E. A., and Sharfstein, S. S. (2018) "Bedless Psychiatry—Rebuilding Behavioral Health Service Capacity," *JAMA psychiatry,* 75: 417–18.

Slade, M. (2009) *Personal Recovery And Mental Illness. A Guide For Mental Health Professionals,* Cambridge: Cambridge University Press.

Slade, M. (2010) "Mental illness and well-being: The central importance of positive psychology and recovery approaches," *Health Services Research,* 10: 26.

Slade, M., Amering, M., Farkas, M., Hamilton, B., O'Hagan, M., Panther, G., ... and Whitley, R. (2014) "Uses and abuses of recovery: implementing recovery-oriented practices in mental health systems," *World Psychiatry* 13: 12–20.

Slade, M., Amering, M., and Oades, L. (2008) "Recovery: An international perspective," *Epidemiologia e Psichiatria Sociale* 17: 128–137.

Slade, M., Williams, J., Bird, V., Leamy, M., and Le Boutillier, C. (2012) "Recovery grows up," *Journal of Mental Health,* 21: 99–104.

Spector-Mersel, G., and Knaifel, E. (2017) "Narrative research on mental health recovery: Two sister paradigms," *Journal of Mental Health* 1–9.

Stickley, T., and Felton, A. (2006) "Promoting recovery through therapeutic risk taking,". *Mental Health Practice* 9: 26–31.

Stuart, S. R., Tansey, L., and Quayle, E. (2017) "What are the barriers to recovery perceived by people discharged from a medium-secure forensic mental health unit? An interpretative phenomenological analysis," *Journal of Theoretical & Philosophical Criminology* 9(1): 1–31

Tew, J., Ramon, S., Slade, M., Bird, V., Melton, J., and Le Boutillier, C. (2012) "Social factors and recovery from mental health difficulties: A review of evidence," *British Journal of Social Work* 42: 443–60.

To, W. T., Vanheule, S., De Smet, S., and Vandevelde, S. (2015) "The treatment perspectives of mentally ill offenders in medium-and high-secure forensic settings in Flanders," *International Journal of Offender Therapy and Comparative Criminology* 59: 1605–22.

Tondora, J., and Davidson, L. (2006) *Practice Guidelines for Recovery-Oriented Behavioral Health Care,* Connecticut: Connecticut Department of Mental Health and Addiction Services.

Tondora, J., Miller, R., Slade, M., and Davidson, L. (2014) *Partnering for Recovery in Mental Health: A Practical Guide to Person-centered Planning*, Hoboken-Oxford: John Wiley & Sons.

United Nations (UN) (2006) *Convention on the Rights of Persons with Disabilities* [A/RES/61/106].

van Gestel-Timmermans, J. A. W. M. (2011) *Recovery Is Up to You. Evaluation of a Peer-run Course*, Ridderprint: Ridderkerk.

Van Manen, M. (1990) *Researching Lived Experience: Human Science for an Action Sensitive Pedagogy*, London: Althouse.

Van Roeyen, S. (2018) "Een ander leven. Een belevingsonderzoek rond desistance bij personen met een psychiatrische problematiek die strafbare feiten plegen." Doctoral dissertation, Ghent University.

Van Roeyen, S., Van Audenhove, S., Vanderplasschen, W., and Vander Laenen, F. (2016) "Het desistance proces van wetsovertreders met een psychiatrische problematiek gehypothekeerd door de internering" in T. Vander Beken et al. (eds) *Sterktes van mensen. Sterktegerichte strategieën voor het ondersteunen van mensen met een psychiatrische problematiek die strafbare feiten pleegden*, Antwerpen, Belgium: Maklu: 123–48.

van Swaaningen, R. (2001) "Criminaliteitsbeleid en risicobeheersing," in E. Lissenberg et al. (eds) *Tegen de regels IV: een inleiding in de criminologie,* Nijmegen: Ars Aequi Libri: 277–92.

Vandevelde, S., Vander Laenen, F., Van Damme, L., Vanderplasschen, W., Audenaert, K., Broekaert, E., … and Vander Beken, T. (2017) "Dilemmas in applying strengths-based approaches in working with offenders with mental illness: A critical multidisciplinary review," *Aggression and Violent Behavior* 32: 71–79.

Vandevelde, S., Soyez, V., Vander Beken, T., De Smet, S., Boers, A., and Broekaert, E. (2011) "Mentally ill offenders in prison: The Belgian case," *International Journal of Law and Psychiatry* 34: 71–78.

Viljoen, S., Nicholls, T., Greaves, C., de Ruiter, C., and Brink, J. (2011) "Resilience and successful community integration among female forensic psychiatric patients: A preliminary investigation," *Behavioral Sciences and the Law*, 29: 752–70.

Vandeurzen, J. (2017) *Vlaams Actieplan Geestelijke Gezondheid, Strategisch plan 2017–2019.*

Ward, T. (2014) "The dual relationship problem in forensic and correctional practice: Community protection or offender welfare?" *Legal and Criminological Psychology* 19: 35–39.

Ward, T., Gannon, T. A., and Fortune, C. A. (2015) "Restorative justice-informed moral acquaintance: Resolving the dual role problem in correctional and forensic practice," *Criminal Justice and Behavior* 42: 45–57.

Ward, T., and Stewart, C. A. (2003) "The treatment of sex offenders: Risk management and good lives," *Professional Psychology: Research and Practice* 34: 353.

Ward, T., Mann, R. E., and Gannon, T. A. (2007) "The good lives model of offender rehabilitation: Clinical implications," *Aggression and Violent Behavior* 12: 87–107.

Ward, T., and Maruna, S. (2007) *Rehabilitation,* London and New York: Routledge.

Ware, N. C., Hopper, K., Tugenberg, T., Dickey, B., and Fisher, D. (2007) "Connectedness and citizenship: Redefining social integration," *Psychiatric Services* 58: 469–74.

Whitley, R., and Campbell, R. D. (2014) "Stigma, agency and recovery amongst people with severe mental illness," *Social Science & Medicine* 107: 1–8.

World Health Organization (WHO) Regional Office for Europe (2018) European Health Report 2018. *More than numbers – evidence for all. Highlights.*

Young, S., Chick, K., and Gudjonsson, G. (2010) "A preliminary evaluation of reasoning and rehabilitation 2 in mentally disordered offenders (R&R2M) across two secure forensic settings in the United Kingdom," *The Journal of Forensic Psychiatry & Psychology* 21: 336–49.

Youngs, D., and Canter, D.V. (2012) "Narrative roles in criminal action: An integrative framework for differentiating offenders," *Legal and Criminological Psychology* 17: 233–49.

Zinkler, M., and Priebe, S. (2002) "Detention of the mentally ill in Europe – a review," *Acta Psychiatrica Scandinavica* 106: 3–8.

PART IV

Alternatives to Current Punishment Practices

26
PUNISHMENT AND ITS ALTERNATIVES

William R. Kelly

In this chapter, I trace the evolution of tough on crime policies, tally what it has cost and what it accomplished, discuss why punishment does not effectively change behavior and reduce recidivism, and outline why American criminal justice policy should emphasize alternatives to punishment in order to effectively reduce crime, recidivism, victimization and cost.

America Embraces Tough on Crime

America's penchant for punishment has been the centerpiece of criminal justice policy for 50 years. It was born out of concern about historically high crime rates, Vietnam War protests, the increasingly common presence of drugs in cities and college campuses, and massive civil disorders during the 1960s and 1970s. By any realistic account, there was a palpable lack of law and order. The violent crime rate was 160 per 100,000 in 1960. In eight short years, it had increased to 300. By 1980, it was 600. An unprecedented wave of violent race riots began in 1965 in the Watts neighborhood of Los Angles. By the time they wound down in 1969, there had been 750 separate riots, 230 deaths, 12,700 injuries, 70,000 arrests and hundreds of billions of dollars in property damage in today's dollars. Protests over the Vietnam War occurred on countless college campuses and urban areas during this same period. The proliferation of drugs in the inner cities and on college campuses was another element in the bigger picture of crime and disorder.

Richard Nixon, the Republican candidate for president in the 1968 election, was the first national figure to leverage the crime and disorder problem. He painted an explicit picture on the campaign trail – bad people doing bad things. He also made ample use of fear of crime in many of his campaign ads. Nixon argued that judicial liberalism was a very important contributor to the problem. He explicitly targeted the U.S. Supreme Court of the 1960s under Chief Justice Earl Warren and a series of cases such as *Mapp v Ohio, Escobedo v. Illinois, Miranda v. Arizona, and Gideon v. Wainwright*. Among other things, these cases provided for the exclusion of evidence that was searched and seized in violation of the Fourth Amendment (*Mapp*), identified the way to ensure one's Fifth Amendment protection against self-incrimination (*Escobedo and Miranda*), and clarified that every indigent defendant in a felony case is entitled to defense counsel provided by the state (*Gideon*). While many saw these decisions as providing meaning and substance to basic protections and guarantees in the Bill of Rights, Nixon claimed they simply are technicalities that get criminals off – "…the cumulative impact of these decisions has been to set free patently guilty individuals on the basis of legal technicalities."[1]

Nixon's remedy for all of this was to get tough on crime, meaning more punishment for more people. The 1968 presidential election was the beginning of this 50-year punishment binge.

Thus began the extensive transformation of criminal justice policy in the United States that among other things fundamentally changed our thinking about crime and punishment. Crime was seen in very simple terms of bad people, making bad decisions, and hanging around with the wrong crowd. That simplicity was a good fit with an equally simple, intuitive solution. How better to encourage law-abiding decision making than punishment? It makes sense, it is intuitive, and rings true with our personal experiences. More on this later.

The new tough on crime agenda not only changed our thinking, it also dramatically increased our capacity to punish by expanding prisons, jails and other forms of correctional supervision and control. There was a 430 percent increase in prison capacity between 1980 and today, and a subsequent 400 percent increase in the prison population over the same time period. Jails expanded on a similar scale. State legislatures and Congress invested billions of dollars in building state and federal prisons. Counties spent hundreds of millions in expanding local jails.

Today the United States has the highest incarceration rate in the world. We also have the highest rate of correctional control and supervision in the world (this includes the four primary components of correctional control – prison, jail, probation, and parole).

The transition to punishment also required fundamental changes to how we sentence convicted offenders. This involved changing state and federal sentencing laws by moving away from what is called indeterminate sentencing to determinate and mandatory sentencing. Indeterminate sentencing, which characterized criminal sentencing in the United States prior to the tough on crime era, typically provides broad minimum and maximum ranges of punishment for a particular conviction offense. The idea behind indeterminate sentencing is that offenders, their crimes, and their circumstances differ, so judges should be given the opportunity to consider an array of evidence at the sentencing hearing in order to determine the appropriate sentence. Some of the evidence may be what is called aggravating evidence, negative information that would indicate a harsher sentence. On the other hand, mitigating evidence could lead to less punishment. For example, mental illness or neurodevelopmental impairment may be viewed as mitigating by a judge who in turn imposes a lighter sentence. In effect, indeterminate sentencing was designed to allow for sentencing the offense and the offender.

Indeterminate sentencing provides judges with considerable discretion or latitude in handing down sentences. Therein lies what many considered the problem. When judges have so much discretion, two things can happen: (1) judicial bias enters into the decision making, resulting in sentencing disparity (similar offenders getting different sentences), or in the extreme, sentencing discrimination; and/or (2) judges tend to be too lenient. Both of the problems (whether real or imagined) share a common solution, which is reducing judicial discretion.

"Sentencing reform" is the label that was given to the sweeping changes to sentencing laws at the federal level and among all 50 states. While there is considerable variation in sentencing schemes across jurisdictions, the end result is a movement away from indeterminate sentencing to determinate or fixed sentencing. Determinate sentences place legislators in the key role of determining what punishment is appropriate for each offense, which in turn is codified in the sentencing law. One result is substantially reduced judicial discretion in sentencing. Another consequence of this is considerably enhanced punishment, either in the determinate sentences reflected in the penal code, or in mandatory sentences, mandatory minimum sentences, and habitual offender sentences like three strikes.

In the end, sentencing reform has played a fundamental role in enhancing punishment. Absent these sentencing changes, it is fair to say we would not have seen such a dramatic increase in incarceration rates and prison populations.

Overcriminalization is the term applied to the increasing reliance on the criminal law for solving a variety of society's problems. It involves the expansion of federal and state criminal codes, making more acts and behaviors illegal, and in turn attaching criminal liability and punishment for example, using the criminal law to manage the increasing mentally ill population and homeless population, both of which are a result of inadequate public health resources and a lack of affordable housing. Regardless of the reasons for it, the expansion of the criminal code has significantly increased the numbers of individuals coming in the front door of the criminal justice system.

Another very important element in understanding the tough on crime agenda is the protracted war on drugs. The primary agenda of the war on drugs has been supply control, meaning attempting to control what is grown in other nations, what crosses our borders, what is distributed and/or grown and manufactured within our borders, and what is sold on street corners. The vast bulk of the effort has been the use of the criminal justice system as the primary mechanism for trying to reduce supply. Obviously absent from the formula is any significant role for demand and harm reduction. Demand reduction involves things like addiction treatment, while harm reduction involves needle exchange programs, drug substitution (like methadone for heroin addiction), and safe injections sites, among others.

Absent reductions in demand, there is a large supply of drug users at risk of ending up in the justice system. Thus, what the war on drugs has done, among other things, is contributed substantially to the increase in correctional control. The prison population has increased roughly 400 percent since 1980. However, the incarceration of drug offenders increased at a rate three times that of the overall prison population. The sheer numbers of drug offenders help create the unprecedented increase in incarceration and correctional control more broadly.

That this transition to tough on crime was remarkable is an understatement. It included the federal system, all 50 state systems, and most of the 3,242 counties in the United States, each of which comprises a criminal justice system. While there was variation by states and by counties, as well as the federal system, a fair overall observation is that tough on crime affected the policies, procedures, laws, cultures, and budgets of essentially all of these federal, state and local jurisdictions. It rendered punishment the defining characteristic of American criminal justice policy over the last 50 years.

What Did Tough on Crime Cost?

Monetizing tough on crime policy invariably results in estimates. Nevertheless, here is what we know. The federal, state and local governments have spent approximately $1 trillion over the past 50 years in direct criminal justice costs. The war on drugs has consumed another $1 trillion (Kelly, Pitman, and Streusand 2017).

A broader way of looking at cost involves the criminal justice costs combined with the social, economic, crime, and victimization costs. Recent estimates put that total at $1 trillion per year.

What Did Tough on Crime Accomplish?

Presumably, criminal justice policies were intended to reduce crime and recidivism (reoffending). Unfortunately, there is no record of policy makers or elected officials specifying how much crime and recidivism would be reduced. Nevertheless, here is what we know.

A glance at a chart that plots incarceration and crime rates over time will appear to show a strong relationship. Incarceration has continued to increase unabated over most of the past 50 years. Crime rates increased through the 1960 and 1970s, declined a bit in the early 1980s, then increased again until 1993, when crime rates declined dramatically until today. The quick and dirty interpretation is that locking up more and more offenders caused the great crime decline. Many political candidates have made that claim and taken credit for it. Unfortunately, the reality is that Canada and most Western European nations had very similar crime declines without the incarceration policies of the United States. Various researchers have estimated the statistical effect of punitive policies on crime declines and the consensus is that around 10 percent to 15 percent of the crime decline in the United States is due to tough criminal justice policies.

Another common metric of criminal justice policies is recidivism. The news is not any better here. Very recent data provided by the Bureau of Justice Statistics, U.S. Department of Justice is that 83 percent of offenders released from prison are rearrested within nine years of release. Seventy-nine percent are rearrested within six years of release. However, these are official statistics of those who have been caught. The actual percentage is higher than the official figure since over one-half of crimes are never reported to the police. Unreported crimes cannot lead to an arrest.

Whether it is the minimal impact of punitive policies in accounting for the crime declines since the 1990s or the nearly 85 percent recidivism rate, it is hard to imagine that anyone could, with a straight face, claim that this anything remotely resembling success.

To add to the pessimism is the lack of evidence of success of the war on drugs. All else equal, as the supply of drugs is reduced, the street price of drugs should increase. We have seen precisely the opposite.

While the track record for tough on crime policies has been dismal, there have been political benefits. The transformation of United States criminal justice policy was greatly facilitated by leveraging fear, whether that fear is of predatory crime like violent assault, robbery and burglary during the 1980s and 1990s, or fear of terrorism as we saw subsequent to September 11, 2001, or today, the Trump administration's labeling illegal immigrants as rapists, drug dealers and murderers. Fear is a significant motivator and elected officials at all levels of government have used it to their political benefit. Few candidates have lost elections because they were tough on crime.

As alternative Smart on Crime policies have emerged in recent years, some of the political leverage from punishment has been lost. Nevertheless, Donald Trump ran as the law and order candidate and his Attorney General Jeff Sessions has ordered his United States Attorneys to charge the maximum offense in federal prosecutions, has declared that the federal government will pursue marijuana possession cases in states where possession is legal (rescinding a policy that the Attorney General's Office under the Obama Administration put in place), and is threatening federal prosecution of cities that have set up medically supervised safe injection sites for IV drug users. Tough on crime seems alive and well at least in the White House.

The Functions of Punishment

Punishment has three primary purposes in the context of criminal justice policy, retribution, incapacitation, and deterrence. Retribution or an eye for an eye is supposed to involve a harm-based system where the punishment is somehow equivalent to the harm perpetrated on the victim. While retribution is well ingrained in our culture and Christian belief, it is important to point out that it has little utility in terms of crime and recidivism. There is nothing about a retributive sentence that accomplishes the purported goals of criminal justice.

Incapacitation involves removing or reducing criminal opportunity. One goal of correctional control and supervision is to prevent an offender from reoffending. Incarceration is one version of incapacitation, but so are probation and parole where the individual is supervised and is supposed to comply with conditions of supervision. While it is logical to presume that incapacitation can effectively prevent reoffending, in turn reducing crime and recidivism, the reality is not quite so simple. There are many situations where incarceration removes the offender from the community but does not remove the crime. For example, convicting and incarcerating a drug dealer in all likelihood does not eliminate the drug dealing. There is a replacement effect, whereby someone else fills the vacancy. The replacement effect likely is in play in many organized (gang related) criminal activities.

Deterrence has been the primary rationale for punishment over the course of our tough on crime initiative. Once again, the logic is simple – when someone makes a bad decision and commits a crime, the way to keep them from doing that again is severe punishment. That is specific deterrence. General deterrence is the idea that non-offenders are aware of the consequences of a criminal act, thus the threat of punishment keeps them from engaging in crime.

Deterrence theory argues that punishment has three dimensions: the certainty of punishment, the swiftness of punishment, and the severity of punishment. The only dimension that United States criminal justice policy has pursued is severity. The evidence is clear that neither specific deterrence (experiencing punishment) nor general deterrence (the threat of punishment) effectively prevent crime or reduce reoffending (Nagin 2013; Nagin, Cullen, and Jonson 2009)

Why Punishment Does Not Reduce Crime and Recidivism

As mentioned earlier, punishment as the means to achieve law-abiding behavior makes sense, it is intuitive, and it rings true to our personal experiences. What this logic fails to appreciate is that criminal offenders enter the criminal justice system with an array of chronic and acute disorders, impairments, and deficits. They also largely come from poverty and disadvantage, which present additional challenges.

Mental illness is common among the prison and jail population. Nearly three-quarters of female and 55 percent of male state prison inmates have a mental health problem. The prevalence is a bit higher in local jails – 75 percent of female and 63 percent of male jail inmates have a mental illness. The majority of those with a mental health problem have had prior criminal convictions (James and Glaze 2006).

Substance use disorders (abuse, dependence and addiction) are also quite common among the incarcerated population, affecting over one-half of those in prison or jail. Comorbidity, or the co-occurrence of disorders is also common. Three-quarters of those prison and jail inmates who have a mental health problem also have a substance use disorder.

Neuroscience has been playing an increasingly important role in understanding criminal offending. For example, the age-crime curve affirms common sense that younger individuals have a substantially higher likelihood of engaging in crime. The high-risk age range is roughly 14 to 20. We understand that risk in part is due to neurodevelopmental deficiencies in juveniles. The frontal lobe of the brain, which controls executive functioning, things like impulse control, decision making, delayed gratification, working memory, and planning, is not fully developed until the early to mid-20s. Moreover, there are a variety of influences in the environment that can impact cognitive functioning throughout the life cycle. Research has shown that growing up in an environment of poverty and all of the associated stresses and adverse experiences can impede brain development, especially the volume of gray matter in the frontal lobe. That in turn has implications for cognitive functioning, which can persist into adulthood.

Neurocognitive impairment is common among individuals in the criminal justice system. About one-half have had at least one traumatic brain injury, which often causes neurocognitive problems. Since the majority of criminal offenders come from environments of poverty and disadvantage, we have to appreciate the potential for neurocognitive impairments such as executive dysfunction.

There is nothing about punishment that improves mental health. Abstinence from drugs and/or alcohol while in prison or jail is not remotely the same thing as substance abuse treatment. The same reasoning applies to neurodevelopmental and neurocognitive impairments.

Part of the problem is that prisons and jails are generally not in the business of providing treatment for mental illness, substance use disorders, and cognitive problems. Only one-third of mentally ill state prison inmates, one-quarter of mentally ill federal prison inmates, and one in six mentally ill jail inmates receive <u>any</u> treatment (James and Glaze 2006). In addition, there are questions of quality of treatment, intensity and duration of treatment, and whether appropriate medications are used. This is true for substance use treatment while incarcerated. What passes for treatment when any intervention is provided is highly problematic. It is often a 12-step approach modeled after Alcoholics Anonymous, which is not evidence-based treatment. I am not aware of any concerted, evidence-based efforts to assess and treat inmates' cognitive problems.

There is a bigger picture regarding punishment and reoffending. The evidence indicates that not only does punishment not reduce reoffending, it seems to actually increase the likelihood of recidivism (Nagin 2013; Nagin, Cullen and Jonson 2009; Kelly 2016; Kelly, Pitman and Streusand 2017). That may be related to factors such as the length of incarceration, how offenders are treated while incarcerated, and the barriers that released offenders face in terms of housing, employment, social services, and education, among others.

Let me be clear. I am not excusing bad behavior. This is not "get out of jail free." Criminal offenders do bad things. They hurt people physically, financially, emotionally, and psychologically.

But think about the reality of American criminal justice. What we are doing in terms of punishment is not working. In fact, it is counter-productive. Crime statistics indicate that there will be approximately 6 million violent crimes and 16 million property crimes in the United States this year. This means there will be 6 million violent crime victims and 16 million property crime victims. Many of those victimizations are avoidable if our efforts at recidivism reduction were successful.

Spend a little time in a felony or misdemeanor courtroom in any metropolitan jurisdiction and you will see another consequence of extraordinarily high recidivism. Courts are crowded. Judges' dockets are unmanageable, as are prosecutors' and public defenders' caseloads. By way of example, every year in Travis County (Austin) Texas, the felony courts have roughly 25,000 cases that have to be carried over to the next year. These are cases that do not get resolved because of too many offenders and too few resources. The situation is more dire at the misdemeanor level where upwards of 80,000 cases go unresolved every year. The irony is that at least two-thirds to three-quarters of the cases in these courtrooms have been in the system before. They are recidivists. We create our own problems.

The 1 trillion dollars we will spend on crime, criminal justice and the associated collateral social, economic and victim costs could be considerably reduced, and taxpayers could save substantial sums of money, if our criminal justice system was effective at reducing recidivism.

Where Do We Go From Here?

It seems that the two primary goals of criminal justice should be: (1) to preserve public safety by managing the risk of offenders while in custody of the justice system; and (2) to reduce the likelihood of reoffending once offenders have been released or discharged. We should strike a balance between the short-term goal of risk management while in the system – in jail, on probation, in prison, or on parole, and the longer-term goal of behavioral change and recidivism reduction. A cursory glance at the justice system indicates that the vast majority of effort and resources have been devoted to punishment and risk management. That must change.

A more equal balance of risk management and behavioral change, resulting in dramatically expanded efforts at recidivism reduction using evidence-based procedures and practices requires reallocation of resources, changes to law and procedure, a change in the culture of the criminal justice system, and, importantly, better decision making.

Prosecutors have always had considerable discretion in making key decisions such as who to prosecute, what charges to bring, what evidence to use, what to indict someone for, what to offer in a plea deal, and either what sentence to agree to in a plea deal or what sentence to recommend to the court at the sentencing hearing. However, that discretion has expanded greatly due to changes in sentencing laws such as the creation of mandatory sentences and fixed or determinate sentences, which dramatically reduce the latitude or discretion of judges in sentencing. The sentence is determined by the conviction charge. The conviction charge is decided by the prosecutor.

Today, over 95 percent of criminal convictions are determined by a plea negotiation. A plea deal is essentially a confession by a defendant, an admission of guilt to an agreed upon charge or charges, in exchange for lesser punishment. Plea bargaining exists because of the tremendous pressure on court dockets, and prosecutor and public defender caseloads. Defendants benefit by receiving reduced punishment. The government benefits by avoiding a criminal trial.

There are many problems and concerns regarding plea negotiation (see Kelly, Pitman and Streusand 2017; and Kelly and Pitman 2018). I focus on one in particular here, which is that plea bargaining puts the prosecutor in the position of being judge, jury and sentencer in most criminal prosecutions. They make all of the key decisions and judges largely take a back seat. Prosecutorial decision making is largely done behind closed doors with relatively little oversight. Prosecutors are, without question, the most powerful actors in the American criminal justice system.

Moreover, punishment is the currency of the plea bargaining process. It is what is negotiated. It is what prosecutors understand. That is one of the primary reasons that we have been and continue to be on this path of punishment. Uninterrupted, there is little reason to expect prosecutors to change how they discharge their responsibilities.

Plea bargaining is not going away and there is little reason to expect a significant reduction in plea deals. Thus, the question is: how can we implement significant changes to criminal justice policy and procedure within the context of plea bargaining and the fact that prosecutors are the key decision makers?

A key component of fundamental reform is related to the earlier discussion of the characteristics of criminal offenders. What I described earlier – mental illness, substance use disorders, neurocognitive impairment, comorbidities of these conditions, and many more deficits and disadvantages – leads to an obvious conclusion that many offenders enter the criminal justice system with very complex situations. These are disorders and impairments that require clinical expertise to screen, assess and diagnose, as well as develop an appropriate, evidence-based treatment plan. The three sets of individuals who play the primary roles in criminal prosecution – prosecutors, judges and defense attorneys – are lawyers, not clinicians. They do not have the experience or expertise to effectively deal with individuals with these circumstances.

Another challenge is revealed in the results of interviews we conducted with prosecutors in our recent book *Confronting Underground Justice: Reinventing Plea Bargaining for Effective Criminal Justice Reform*. We asked prosecutors what their role is regarding recidivism reduction. The most common answer was that it is not their responsibility. They said, "Not my job" or "I don't see that as my responsibility." The few who said that it is their responsibility indicated that punishment is the mechanism they use to reduce recidivism.

This focus on prosecutors certainly does not mean judges have no role in criminal justice reform. Judges have without question played a fundamental role in our penchant for punishment. Judges' sentencing decisions have reliably delivered maximum punishment over the 50-year course of our crime control efforts. Moreover, most state judges in the United States are elected, and tough on crime has been extraordinarily effective in electoral politics.

Judges, like prosecutors, are lawyers and do not have the expertise to appreciate the role that mental illness or substance use disorders or neurocognitive impairment play in criminal offending, nor do they have the expertise regarding evidence-based treatment or intervention strategies that can effectively reduce recidivism. We also asked judges what they believe is their role in terms of recidivism. The interview results were surprising, especially if one assumes that judges consider recidivism when they make sentencing decisions. However, judges were all over the map on this issue. A few said they play no role. A couple said that it is up to individual judges. Some indicated that they try to consider recidivism in sentencing, and a couple of judges said that probation is the appropriate venue for addressing recidivism.

While there is plenty of responsibility to go around for the failed state of United States criminal justice, my focus is principally on: (1) prosecutors and judges and their decision making, especially regarding the circumstances, disorders, deficits and impairments of offenders; (2) prosecutors and judges accepting primary responsibility for recidivism reduction; and (3) diversion from traditional criminal prosecution and punishment for perhaps the majority of offenders, depending on risk and circumstances (mental health, etc.).

Prosecutorial and Judicial Decision Making

In a 2017 book, we proposed the concept of independent, expert panels of clinicians (psychiatrists, psychiatric nurse practitioners, psychologists, clinical social workers) who are responsible for screening and assessing everyone who comes into the criminal justice system using evidence-based practices (Kelly, Pitman and Streusand 2017).

The concept of the expert panel is justified by the importance of the decisions that prosecutors and judges make regarding things like pre-trial detention and post-conviction incarceration. It is also based on the obvious conclusion that the key actors in the criminal justice system do not have the necessary expertise to make the best decisions. It is important that the panels are independent, not simply an arm of the prosecutor's office. The purpose of this is to determine the presence and severity of a variety of mental, cognitive, substance-related, and intellectual disorders. The goal is to diagnose disorders and impairments, and identify the degree of associated dysfunction, in order to understand the role of any disorders and dysfunctions in offending behavior. The panels are also responsible for assessing the risk of reoffending, especially violent reoffending, in order to help prosecutors and judges make more informed decisions about pre-trial custody or supervision. The panels also recommend evidence-based treatment plans to effectively treat identified conditions. The panels' responsibility also involves making recommendation about diversion or incarceration.

The interviews I discussed earlier also included proposing the expert panel concept to prosecutors and judges. Nearly universally, they embraced the idea, saying things like:

"I'm not a psychiatrist"
"We need all the help we can get"
"Most definitely. I didn't go to medical school…if there's independent experts, third parties not working for either side, then I think their input would be invaluable to me."
"I think that would be ideal. This would be a great system if we could get there. I'm all for it."

Having these independent experts could change the dynamics of decision making by helping prosecutors and judges, as well as defense counsel, make informed decisions that reflect the reality of the situations they confront. Saying it is one thing. Implementing it requires some fundamental changes to local criminal justice systems.

Making Recidivism Reduction a Priority

One would be hard pressed to find anyone in the criminal justice system that will accept responsibility for recidivism reduction. Certainly not law enforcement. We have seen from interviews that most prosecutors and judges largely do not see it as their responsibility. I suspect that corrections officials will indicate that they are just doing what they have been told to do. Even legislators would probably avoid accepting responsibility beyond acknowledging that punishment is the primary tool for reducing recidivism. Therein lies one of the great ironies. No one is in charge. That must change.

While many aspects of criminal justice are ripe for reform, I believe that the most important starting point is the pre-trial system. I suggest that the decisions that are made then largely determine everything downstream (Kelly and Pitman 2018). That takes us back to the fundamental role of the prosecutor.

Convincing prosecutors and judges to accept recidivism reduction as one of their primary responsibilities requires providing them with the tools to make informed decisions about alternatives to punishment that have a higher likelihood of reducing reoffending. Addressing criminogenic circumstances, those circumstances, disorders, impairments and deficits that are found to be related to one's involvement in the criminal justice system is key.

Also key is showing prosecutors and judges why this focus is in their interest, aside from the public good served by reducing crime. It is probably safe to conclude that nearly every prosecutor and every criminal court judge is overwhelmed by caseloads and dockets. That is why most of what they do day-to-day is move cases. The only way to reduce these caseloads and dockets (absent hiring substantially more judges and prosecutors) is to reduce reoffending.

We are beginning to see District Attorneys (the chief prosecutors, most of whom are elected to office in local elections) positioning themselves as progressive or reform oriented. Perhaps two-dozen are currently in office and many more ran for election in the 2018 midterm election. The platforms differ in substance, but they seem to share the common theme of doing business in a different way, including being "smart on crime" or addressing police shootings of minorities or ending mass incarceration. We will see how these play out. We must remember that this is electoral politics, so what is promised may not always see the light of day.

The culture of criminal prosecution and sentencing, which has placed a premium on punishment, often without regard to longer-term outcomes, may be starting to change in some jurisdictions. However, there is much that can be done to help prosecutors and judges make better decisions, decisions that have reducing reoffending as the primary goal.

Diversion is Key

Diversion comes in a variety of forms and can occur at a variety of points in the processing of criminal defendants. At the very front end, law enforcement officers in many jurisdictions have the ability to divert individuals with mental health problems to psychiatric facilities rather than the typical response, which is to book them into jail. Jail diversion, as it is called, is often reserved for individuals in a mental health crisis. This type of diversion is typically used in conjunction with specially trained law enforcement officers, called crisis intervention teams (CIT) or mental health units. The goal is not so much treatment as it is stabilization. Thus, jail diversion is short term. In most cases, once the individual is properly medicated and stable, they are returned to the justice system for processing.

Pre-trial diversion is premised on the idea that one can avoid a criminal conviction if they successfully complete the requirements of the diversion. Deferred adjudication or deferred prosecution is an example of an alternative disposition that sets aside determinations of innocence or guilt in lieu of the individual serving a form of conditional community supervision. This is essentially probation, whereby the individual is expected to comply with a variety of conditions including supervision. Often, the participant is expected to perform community service and/or pay restitution, in addition to the other requirements. Participation in deferred prosecution is largely at the discretion of the prosecutor, although eligibility criteria are often set by policy or statute.

There are many other forms of pre-trial diversion that are often managed by pre-trial services, the agencies that are responsible for managing offenders who are not detained in jail prior to processing. This pre-trial phase is an opportune time to provide services to individuals awaiting case disposition. Unfortunately, in many jurisdictions, it is an opportunity that is not pursued. Surveys of pre-trial diversion indicate that in those limited jurisdictions where such programs exist, the focus includes substance use disorders, mental health, counseling, employment training, as well as performing community service and paying restitution to victims.

Problem solving courts or diversion courts or specialty courts (all are terms that apply to the same concept) are a common form of diversion from traditional punishment. These diversion courts accept participants at various stages of criminal processing. Some are pre-indictment or pre-conviction, and others are post-conviction, typically involving a guilty plea. These courts tend to focus on a particular problem or criminogenic circumstance like drug abuse. They are designed to balance offender risk and therapeutic intervention, or supervision, control and accountability on the one hand and treatment on the other.

Drug courts are the most common form of problem solving court. There are over 3,200 adult drugs courts in the United States today. The first appeared in Miami Florida in 1989, a product of some creative problem solving by several local stakeholders who recognized that what they had been doing to address the drug problem in South Florida was not working. They observed that punishment as usual was producing unmanageably high recidivism. In response, they created the first problem solving court. The model has been applied to a wide variety of other issues and includes Mental Health Courts, DWI Courts, Veterans Courts, Domestic Violence Courts, Reentry Courts, Community Courts, Truancy Courts, Prostitution Courts, Homelessness Courts, Sex Offender Courts, and Juvenile Drug Courts, just to name a few.

A good bit of evaluation research has been conducted on these diversion courts, primarily on drug courts. The evidence indicates that when properly constructed and operated, drug courts can be considerably effective at reducing relapse and recidivism. While the concept is quite viable, there is substantial variation in design and operation of these courts, which render some less effective than others. The other problem is that even though there are over 3,100 drug courts in operation, they have the capacity to address about 10 percent of the need (Kelly 2016, Kelly, Pitman and Streusand 2017).

Probation or conditional, supervised release to the community is a post-conviction sentence that is diversion from incarceration. It is by far the most common form of diversion. The original intent of probation was to avoid the negative consequences of incarceration and provide individuals with programs and services in the community to reduce the likelihood of reoffending. There is a safety net in the sense that if a probationer violates the conditions of their release, they are subject to revocation, which means they are ordered to prison if they were on felony probation or jail if they were on misdemeanor probation.

Over the course of tough on crime policies, probation seems to have focused more on supervision, control and risk management, with relatively less attention paid to recidivism reduction. In many respects, probation today is a lost opportunity for addressing criminogenic circumstances. Only 60 percent successfully complete probation (40 percent are revoked, abscond or have an unsuccessful discharge). The vast majority of probationers will reoffend at some point (Kelly 2016). This poor track record is in part a result of extraordinarily high caseloads for probation officers, lack of resources for adequate screening and assessment of offenders, and lack of treatment resources in the justice system and in the community.

Conclusion

Criminal justice is arguably the greatest public policy failure in American history. Over the course of the past 50 years, we have created a near-perfect recidivism machine, needlessly flooding the justice system with recidivists, exposing the public to the risk of criminal victimization, and wasting hundreds of billions of taxpayer dollars.

Today, we have the evidence-based tools, the means to turn this thing around. We can develop strategies to help the key decision makers in the criminal justice system make the best decisions possible regarding who needs to be incarcerated and thus separated from society, and who should be diverted to alternatives to punishment, in turn, reducing the likelihood of reoffending.

However, we face tremendous challenges. Crime is local and so are its solutions. That requires that true, meaningful criminal justice reform originates in the 3,200 plus counties in the United States, each of which constitutes a criminal justice system. That requires changes to policy, procedure, law, resources, and perhaps most importantly, how we think about crime and punishment. I believe that the two greatest challenges going forward are political and cultural. We still seem to lack the political will to fundamentally change criminal justice, and we still seem entrenched in thinking that punishing bad behavior is the way to accomplish public safety.

Note

1 Quoted in Genovese, *Richard Nixon and the Politicization of Justice*, 76.

References

Genovese, Michael A. "Richard M. Nixon and the Politicization of Justice." (1992) In Leon Friedman and William F. Levantrosser (eds) *Watergate and Afterward: The Legacy of Richard M. Nixon*, Westport, CT: Greenwood Press.

James, Doris and Lauren Glaze. (2006). *Mental Health Problems of Prison and Jail Inmates.* Washington, DC. United States Department of Justice, Bureau of Justice Statistics.

Kelly, William R. (2016). *The Future of Crime and Punishment: Smart Policies for Reducing Crime and Saving Money.* Lanham, MD: Rowman and Littlefield.

Kelly, William R., Robert Pitman and William Streusand. (2017) *From Retribution to Public Safety: Disruptive Innovation of American Criminal Justice.* Lanham, MD: Rowman and Littlefield

Kelly, William R. and Robert Pitman. (2018) *Confronting Underground Justice: Reinventing Plea Bargaining for Effective Criminal Justice Reform.* Lanham, MD: Rowman and Littlefield.

Nagin, Daniel. (2013). *Deterrence in the Twenty-first Century: A Review of the Evidence.* Carnegie Mellon University, Heinz College Research, retrieved from http://repository.cmu.edu/heinzworks.

Nagin, Daniel, Francis Cullen, and Cheryl Jonson. (2009). Imprisonment and Reoffending, in M. Tonry (ed), *Crime and Justice: A Review of Research, Vol. 38*, Chicago, IL: University of Chicago Press.

27

PRE-TRIAL DETENTION AND THE SUPPLANTING OF OUR ADVERSARIAL SYSTEM

A Case for Abolition

Justine Olderman

In the United States today, there are approximately half a million people being held in our country's jails who have not been convicted of a crime (Minton & Zeng 2015: 1–2). People held pre-trial are presumed innocent and most are there because they can't afford to pay their bail. People held in jail pre-trial account for 95 percent of the growth in our country's jail population (Minton & Zeng 2015: 1). Today, there is growing consensus that this system of pre-trial mass incarceration penalizes the poor, discriminates against people of color, and is in desperate need of reform. Absent from the reform movement, however, is a nuanced discussion about the role of pre-trial detention in our adversarial system and a deeper questioning of the root causes of our current crisis. What is the impact on case outcomes of jailing someone pre-trial? How does pre-trial detention relate to post-conviction punishment? In what ways do conditions of confinement differ pre and post-conviction? Why are so many judges setting bail beyond a person's financial ability to pay? Engaging in these issues and questions is critical to the success of any reform effort. If we don't fully understand the drivers of pre-trial incarceration, we risk creating new systems that don't address the underlying problem and simply deepen existing harms.

This chapter pulls back the curtain and explores these questions through the lens of public defenders and the clients they serve. The Bronx Defenders is a public defender non-profit that is radically changing the way that low-income people are represented in the legal system and, in doing so, transforming the system itself. We represent 24,000 people each year in Bronx Criminal Court in New York City. We are on the frontlines in the fight for justice and have been working to advance reform of our bail system for the better part of a decade. Drawing on the lived experiences of both practitioners and clients, this chapter uses our expertise and proximity to the problem to elucidate the often hidden ways in which being held in jail pre-trial causes people to be punished before they have been found guilty and drives guilty pleas in ways that eviscerate the fundamental rights on which our justice system stands: the presumption of innocence, the burden of proof, and the right to trial. Our vantage point as practitioners, operating within the criminal justice system rather than as advocates outside of it, allows for a more insightful and intimate analysis of judicial motivations for imposing pre-trial detention and their complicity in perpetuating injustice. While this chapter focuses on the pre-trial detention system in New York, the observations made and conclusions drawn are not unique to any one jurisdiction but rather shed light on the inner workings of pre-trial detention more generally.

The first part of this chapter argues that our system of pre-trial detention supplants our adversarial system for adjudicating guilt and imposing punishment. Part two posits that the supplanting of our adversarial system is not an accidental byproduct of a "broken" pre-trial detention system but rather is an unacknowledged goal of that system. The chapter concludes that no set of reforms can fix our pre-trial detention system since it is not, in fact, broken. It is working exactly as it is supposed to. The only reform that can alleviate our current crisis is abolishing pre-trial jailing altogether.

Pre-Trial Detention: The Supplanting of our Adversarial System for Adjudicating Guilt and Imposing Punishment

While pre-trial detention in New York is simply supposed to ensure a person's return to court so our adversarial system can adjudicate guilt and, where necessary, impose punishment, the decision to hold someone in jail pending resolution of his case effectively eviscerates that adversarial system. Moreover, detaining someone before she has been found guilty of a crime turns the natural sequence of conviction and punishment on its head. The act of detaining someone pre-trial separates him from his life and loved ones and subjects him to harsh conditions of confinement in ways that are indistinguishable from punishment imposed post-conviction. Conviction then follows as a natural byproduct of this pre-trial punishment. People detained pre-trial regularly abandon their right to an adversarial process and plead guilty to avoid the Kafka-esque world in which they find themselves, resulting in high conviction rates for those detained pre-trial. To make matters worse, being detained pre-trial not only increases the likelihood of conviction but it also increases the severity of the charge and the length of the sentence the accused will receive. More than the nature of the charges, the strength of the evidence, or the number of witnesses, pre-trial detention is what determines guilt. It is also the system that imposes punishment and it does so both before and after conviction. When understood in these terms, a picture emerges of a pre-trial detention system that is not only doing the work of our adversarial one by convicting and sentencing the accused through the act of detaining but it eviscerates our adversarial system and supplants it under the guise of simply ensuring a person's return to court.

At The Bronx Defenders, we meet our clients for the first time at their first appearance in court or their arraignment. Many clients charged with low-level, non-violent misdemeanor offenses will be offered a plea bargain at their first appearance in exchange for giving up their right to trial and presumption of innocence. For those who wish to fight their case or are charged with a more serious offense, the judge must decide whether to release them on their own recognizance, release them with the condition that they report to supervised release, impose bail, or remand them. As public defenders, we know that the decision to release someone on her own recognizance or to hold her in jail, either by setting bail too high for her to make or on remand, is the single most important decision made in a criminal case. The reason it plays such an outsized role starts with the impact that it has on our clients' lives.

The vast majority of our clients jailed pre-trial in New York City are sent to the notorious Rikers Island. Approximately 200 people are sent to Rikers every day and there are approximately 8,900 people housed in eight jails on Rikers Island at any one time (NYC Department of Corrections 2018). The vast majority of them, 85 percent, have not been convicted of a crime (Schwirtz 2017). In 2015, there were 1,500 people incarcerated in New York City for more than a year and 400 who had been incarcerated for more than two years without being convicted of a crime (Mathias 2015).

Many of our clients' lives hang in a precarious balance – where two, three, five days in jail can lead to the loss of their jobs, housing, and medical care, in addition to having an equally devastating impact on their loved ones who depend on them. In 2015, over a five-week period, The Bronx Defenders conducted a survey of our clients charged with misdemeanors and held in on bail to measure the impact that even a few days of detention has on a client's life. The majority of the 50 clients we interviewed were low-income African-American or Latino men between 18 and 56 years old (average 33 years old). The clients we interviewed had been detained on average 4.5 days. They were held in jail because neither they nor anyone else they knew could scrape together the $500 to $3,000 necessary to pay bail, and therefore were trapped in Rikers Island.

Being held in jail pre-trial destabilizes families, separating parents from children – and husbands from wives – for days, weeks, months, even years waiting for a resolution to their case. Half of the clients we interviewed reported having families and loved ones who relied on them for financial and non-financial assistance. Thirty-two percent reported that they were parents with either full or shared custody of their children. For many, even while sitting in a jail cell, their greatest concern was the well-being of their children. For our clients and their families, being held in pre-trial detention meant finding someone they could trust to care for their young children, which often put a strain on already burdened extended families. In their absence, children missed school and had their daily routines interrupted.

One of the most devastating consequences of being held in on bail is that hardworking people lose their jobs. For most people, missing one, two, five, ten days of work while they are locked up trying to get bail money together – or trying to work out a plea bargain so they can get out of jail – is not an option. Fifty-two percent of clients reported being employed at the time of their arrest. They delivered food, sold water on the side of the road, and fixed cars. They worked in construction, in restaurants, in bakeries, and in IT departments. Nearly all of the clients we interviewed were unsalaried and were paid only for the days they worked. Many of our clients held in on bail were also employees responsible for supporting themselves and others.

Eighty-five percent of the 26 employed clients reported missing work as a result of being held in on bail, resulting in a collective loss of 91 days of work and $7,634 in lost wages. Not only was this income vital to our clients and their loved ones, but missing work for a few days often resulted in our clients losing their jobs. Approximately 41 percent of clients who were employed at the time of their arrest reported that they were either fired, suspended, or were unsure whether their job would still be there when they got out. Considering that approximately 57 percent of employed clients financially support someone else, the impact of a lost job spirals beyond the individual client, to the entire family. For people with few financial resources, losing a job can mean losing everything – their homes, their belongings, their access to healthcare, the pride and stability that comes from waking up each morning and earning that day's pay.

Eviction is another common consequence of a judge's decision to set bail. Our clients' homes are put at risk when they are arrested and detained. Approximately, 44 percent of our clients interviewed lived in private housing and 26 percent lived in public housing or subsidized housing. For some clients, posting bail meant not paying rent. Even when they had the financial resources, our clients' physical absence meant that they could not pay that month's rent on time or missed a critical housing appointment, both of which could result in losing their homes and belongings. Considering that many of our clients share their homes with relatives, significant others, and children, a client's eviction can lead to those connected to the client becoming homeless. Additionally, 12 percent of clients interviewed reported living in shelters and 8 percent reported living in supportive housing. For these clients, being detained for just one night put their housing at risk. Five of the six clients living in shelters reported losing their bed at the shelter because they were held in on bail. When these clients were eventually be released, they had nowhere to go and lost their belongings, since most shelters will only hold onto a person's belongings for one week.

Being held in on bail also causes people to lose their government benefits, which can take months to get back even after they are released from pre-trial detention. It can cause the Administration for Children's Services to start a neglect proceeding against a parent who has nobody to look after her child while in jail. But the real trauma of being held in jail, the experiences that leave enduring scars, often cannot be measured with quantifiable metrics such as lost wages, housing displacement, or termination of government benefits.

Repeatedly, the clients we interviewed discussed how their pre-trial detention was derailing their lives. They talked about their dreams of getting their degree, finding work, obtaining their drivers' licenses, having the financial ability to move into their own apartments, and being able to take custody of their children. One father discussed his desire to pull his life together and become the father that he never had. Being held in on bail was like "going back to square one." One client described being disappointed that the judge did not have enough faith in him to return to court. Clients reiterated this idea of trying to do everything right, trying to be better people, being held in on bail, and simply becoming disillusioned with the criminal system and their ability to ever escape it, improve their lives and fulfill their dreams.

While this study focused exclusively on clients charged with misdemeanors and the immediate impact detention had on their lives, the consequences of pre-trial detention are similar in nature for clients charged with felonies. In fact, these consequences are magnified as clients charged with felonies are detained for longer periods of time than their misdemeanor counterparts while their cases are pending (Chauhan et al., 2017).

When understood in terms of the impact on people's lives, it appears that pre-trial detention punishes people in many of the same ways that traditional sentencing does by separating them from their loved ones and unraveling the fabric of their lives. Looking at the conditions of pre-trial confinement confirms that our pre-trial detention system is imposing punishment in much the same way that our adversarial system does with one major caveat. Those held pre-trial are being punished without having been convicted of a crime.

If our pre-trial system is not supposed to be punitive, and is intended simply to ensure a person's return to court, one would expect conditions of pre-trial confinement to look entirely different from the conditions of facilities that house people who have been convicted and sentenced. People would be housed close to their families and communities. They would be able to visit their loved ones frequently, with ease, and without barriers. The facility where they are housed would be well maintained, safe and secure. There would be freedom of movement within the facility and opportunities for continued education and employment. And there would be consistent access to healthcare, treatment and medications. Yet conditions of confinement for those who have and have not been found guilty look shockingly similar.

An important marker of incarceration for those who are convicted and receive an incarcerative sentence is physical isolation; carceral facilities have been designed to completely segregate people our criminal legal system identifies as guilty. However, our clients who are in jail because they cannot afford to pay bail are similarly isolated. Rikers Island is situated on a remote piece of land in the middle of the East River. It is accessible by a single bridge that can only be traversed by visitors on a special bus. Isolation from family and friends is another marker of post-adjudication incarceration.

Visits are critical to the well-being of incarcerated people. They have been shown to reduce recidivism, improve re-entry upon release, maintain important family relationships, and prevent health problems (NYC Jails Action Coalition 2018: 7–8). However, our clients detained at Rikers Island have a difficult time staying connected to their families and friends. They are only allowed 3 hour-long visits per week. Visits can only be on certain days and at specified times (NYC Department of Corrections 2018a, 2018b). Most New Yorkers must take multiple forms of transportation to reach Rikers Island after which they must register, store their personal belongings, be subjected to scans and searches, and wait sometimes for hours to visit with their loved one. Once through the process, visitors must sit at long tables separated from their family members and friends by a plexiglass partition thwarting any meaningful human connection. Visiting a loved one in Rikers can take an entire day, causing people to miss work and make costly childcare and transportation arrangements. Many visitors describe not only the practical difficulty of visiting Rikers but also the harassment, humiliation, and abuse they must suffer. Both pre-trial and post-conviction incarceration bring families into secondary contact with the criminal legal system. In trying to remain connected with their loved ones on the outside, families and friends experience secondary contact with incarceration, resulting in relationships that are surveilled, policed, and strained.

Like so many carceral facilities, Rikers Island has a growing list of structural hazards that deeply impact those being held because they cannot afford bail. The problems go beyond rotting floors and malfunctioning heating and cooling systems. There are broken pipes, sewage backups, and leaking roofs in these overcrowded and unventilated facilities. Severe weather only worsens these already extremely poor confinement conditions. When there are storms outside, the inside of the jail frequently floods, further damaging the facility and the health and safety of those incarcerated inside. Media coverage has recently demonstrated how city and statewide evacuations due to weather conditions often exclude those incarcerated in structurally vulnerable and unsafe jails.

Recent reports recommending the closing of Rikers Island have noted that the physical isolation of Rikers is a gateway for the violence, neglect, and dehumanization experienced by those entrapped in both pre-trial and post-adversarial incarceration (Independent Commission on New York City Criminal Justice and Incarceration Reform 2017). Indeed, independent reports have found a deep-seated "culture of violence" on Rikers Island (Olivares 2017). One study from 2017 found that in the first half of the year, there were a total of 2,243 instances of use of force by corrections officers against the people housed at Rikers (*Nunez* Independent Monitor 2017: 22, 31).

Our clients detained pre-trial also have their freedom of movement and autonomy severely restricted. They are told when to wake, eat, bathe, and sleep. There are limited opportunities to work, exercise, or engage in educational programming. One client reported that the only regular programming available was church. And there is little freedom to move around on one's own. Movements are heavily monitored and guarded. There is also little privacy. While some of our clients are placed in closed in cells with another person, others are held in dormitory style rooms. There are no walls separating people. There are no doors one can close. There are no partitions. There is no privacy. Even the bathing isn't private. One woman describes the lack of privacy this way:

> There is a big open shower in the dorm. .... In the dorm, the guard desk, what they call a bubble, is right next to it. You could look straight into the bathroom from the bubble, and there was always male officers in that bubble. Officers could see the women showering. They pretended not to look, but you know they do.
>
> *(Chammah et al., 2015)*

In addition, strip searches are a daily part of life as a pre-trial detainee. One female client reported being forced to undress repeatedly in front of corrections officers for health screenings and searches. She had been molested as a child and being forced to continually undress revived the trauma.

Conditions of confinement also result in lack of adequate medical care and deteriorating medical conditions. Many held on Rikers Island have injuries, illnesses, mental health needs, and addictions. Fourteen percent of clients interviewed for our internal survey reported receiving Supplemental Security Income due to a disability. Nearly everyone with a reported illness, mental health need, or injury reported receiving inadequate care from the jail infirmary. Forty-six percent of clients reported adverse health consequences from their detention. Many received no medical care at all. In some instances, medical staff were aware of clients' medical conditions and refused to treat them.

Individuals with mental health conditions also face greater violence from correction officers. In a study by the Department of Health and Mental Hygiene, "over an 11-month period last year, 129 inmates suffered 'serious injuries' – ones beyond the capacity of doctors at the jail's clinics to treat – in altercations with correction department staff members" (Schwirtz and Winerip 2014). This study also found that 77 percent of those seriously injured had a diagnosed mental illness. In five of these 129 occurrences, these serious injuries were inflicted on people after they had attempted suicide (Schwirtz & Winerip 2014).

It is often the conditions of confinement in pre-trial detention that deter people from fighting their cases from the inside and inflict enough trauma to drive people further into the criminal legal system. In 2014, Mr Ewers spent a year in Rikers where the absence of privacy and self-determination made him a target for brutal violence. While in Rikers, he was attacked, causing him to go blind in one eye, have multiple seizures, and render him physically unable to control his bowels. Traumatizing cannot even begin to describe Mr Ewers' experience in pre-trial detention, which left him permanently disabled. Prior to being held in pre-trial detention, Mr. Ewers was motivated to prove his innocence at trial. His defense attorney even remarked that his chances of winning his case were high. However, after a year in pre-trial detention at Rikers, compounded by the likelihood of experiencing even worse conditions of confinement due to his poor health, Mr Ewers, chose to accept a plea, rather than wait for trial behind bars. He agreed to serve time at a prison in upstate New York, an outcome he never imagined himself settling for until pre-trial detention in Rikers "broke [him]" (Marsh, Pagones, & Whitehouse 2017).

For those who are held in on bail too high to post, which represents the vast majority of our clients detained pre-trial in NYC, the fastest path to "freedom" is often a guilty plea. While a detained person technically has the same right to trial as someone who is at liberty, it often takes months if not years for the accused to get his day in court. Our clients will do anything to get out of jail, return to their loved ones, their homes, and their jobs even if it means pleading guilty to something they didn't do. But as Mr Ewers' case shows, being detained pre-trial causes people to give up their right to trial and plead guilty even when doing so does not lead to their immediate freedom. Data confirms what practitioners and clients alike already know: that pre-trial detention determines who is convicted and who is not, as well as the severity of that conviction.

According to a 2012 study by the Criminal Justice Agency (CJA), 59 percent of people in New York charged with a felony offense and released at their first court appearance were ultimately convicted of a crime (Philips 2012: 115–117). That number rose to 85 percent for those who were held in on bail too high for them to post (Philips 2012: 115–117). For those facing non-felony charges (misdemeanors, violations, and infractions) and released at first appearance, their conviction rate was 50 percent. That number jumped to a staggering 92 percent for those held in on bail (Philips 2012: 115–117). Not only does bail impact the likelihood of a conviction but it also affects the severity of the charge. For those charged with a felony and released from arraignments, only 22 percent were ultimately convicted of a *felony* offense (Philips 2012: 115–117). For those similarly charged but detained for anywhere between eight and 60 days, that percentage rose to 53 percent (Philips 2012: 115–117). For people held longer, the felony conviction rate rose even further to 72 percent (Philips 2012: 115–117).

The simple fact of being detained pre-trial also exacerbates sentencing. There is a saying among criminal defense attorneys: "Once you are out, you stay out." While out, our clients can continue to go to work, care for their loved ones, get an education, get treatment, and improve their lives. Our clients' behavior and accomplishments are considered and weighed when determining sentencing. For people who are released at arraignments, only 20 percent of those charged with felonies ultimately receive an incarcerative sentence while 87 percent of those charged with felonies and detained pre-trial received a jail or prison sentence (Philips 2012: 119). Similarly, just 10 percent of those charged with non-felonies will be sentenced to jail or prison but for those detained, that percentage jumps to 84 percent (Philips 2012: 119). For the person languishing in jail for the duration of the case, she has little to bring to the court to convince the judge and the prosecutor that she should receive a non-incarceratory sentence - she cannot demonstrate her dedication to improving her life the same way someone can if she is already able to make progress outside of jail (Philips 2012: 119). The CJA reports that, "detention to disposition was the strongest *single* factor influencing a convicted defendant's likelihood of being sentenced to jail or prison for non-felony and felony cases alike (Philips 2012: 118)."

Pre-trial detention also increases the *length* of a jail or prison sentence. People charged with non-felonies who were detained for at least 60 days prior to their conviction were sentenced to 90 days in jail on average. By contrast, people who were similarly situated, but detained for one day or less, were only sentenced to five days in jail on average. These disparities are magnified in felony cases. People charged with felonies, detained for a day or less, and convicted, were sentenced to an average of 120 days in jail (Philips 2012: 120–121). Similarly situated people who were detained for over 60 days in jail were sentenced to an average of 730 days in prison (Philips

2012: 120–121). Detaining someone during the pendency of the criminal case – before proving they are guilty of anything – is the easiest and surest way to obtain a conviction and a lengthy sentence.

Whether a person is convicted of a crime, the severity of the charge, and the length of sentence are supposed to be determined through our adversarial system and should be based on the strength of the evidence, the credibility of the witnesses, and the viability of the defense. However, it is our pre-trial detention system that is dictating case outcomes, not our adversarial one. Pre-trial detention punishes the accused by separating him from his family and community resulting in hardship for his loved ones, job loss, eviction, and termination of benefits. It also imposes punitive conditions of confinement marked by lack of privacy and autonomy, extreme isolation, inadequate medical and mental health care, and a culture of violence. This pre-trial punishment causes people to give up their sacred rights and plead guilty which, in turn, results in worse charges and harsher sentences than for those at liberty. Our pre-trial detention system has all the hallmarks of our adversarial one. It determines guilt and imposes punishment. The only difference is that our pre-trial detention system is not supported by any of the hallmarks of a fair and just adversarial system: presumption of innocence, burden of proof, and right to trial.

Adjudication of Guilt and Imposition of Punishment: an Unacknowledged Goal of Pre-Trial Detention

A natural response to the realization that our pre-trial detention system is supplanting our adversarial one would be to reform our system of detention and mitigate these harms. However, such response is only rational if the true purpose of our pre-trial detention system is, indeed, to ensure a person's return to court rather than to convict and punish. But what if our pre-trial detention system is being used exactly as it is designed - to supplant our adversarial system? Indeed, our experience as public defenders strongly suggests that judges are detaining people not only fully understanding that such detention is tantamount to convicting and punishing them, but because of it. To test the validity of this theory, we must next examine whether the outcomes of judicial decision-making match the stated aim of our pre-trial detention system and, if not, what accounts for the discrepancy.

The most common mechanism for accomplishing the accused's return to court is release on recognizance or money bail. The theory behind our money bail system is that a person who is required to post money to secure his release will be incentivized to return so he can collect his collateral. The system only works if people who are not a flight risk are released without conditions or money bail and that those who are a flight risk have money bail set at an amount that they can afford yet significant enough to incentivize them to return. The question we must now turn to is whether, in fact, judges are making release determinations consistent with these assumptions. To answer that question, we must first look at whether, in fact, financial interest is what makes people come back to court.

In 2007, The Bronx Defenders launched The Bronx Freedom Fund, to post bail for those who are unable to do so on their own. The Fund does not require that an individual or his family contribute financially to the bail or provide collateral in exchange for being released. Nor does the Fund track down the accused or try to recoup the money should the person not return to court. In other words, those bailed out by the Fund have absolutely no financial stake in the transaction. Over a two-year period, the Fund posted bail for over 300 people. Even though they had not put up their own money and faced no financial consequence if they failed to appear, 97 percent of those bailed out returned for every single one of their court appearances, including some who had to come back to court 15 times or more before their case was resolved (Bronx Freedom Fund 2nd Annual Report 2015). By assuming the financial obligation of the accused, the Fund challenged the very assumption of our money bail system and proved its fallacy. Not only does the success of the Fund illustrate that money is not what makes people come back to court, but multiple studies have shown that simple reminders can significantly reduce "failure to appear" rates and that offering transportation, childcare, and flexible court hours could help reduce "failure to appear" rates even further.

Once it became clear that money does not, in fact, cause people to return to court and that they will return on their own without bail, one might expect that judges would simply have stopped requiring money as a condition of release. However, that is not what we have seen. Judges continue to require those presumed innocent to post bail to secure their freedom. If we assume that judges are simply unaware of the recent research, one would then expect that they would be setting bail in amounts that were affordable enough for the person to pay but significant enough to ensure his return to court. But they aren't. The vast majority of the clients we meet at arraignments are poor people of color from marginalized and under-resourced communities. And the vast majority of them cannot afford the price of their freedom. According to one local study, 88.7 percent of people in New York City who had bail set at $1,000 could not raise the money to pay that bail at their first court appearance and so, instead of being released, were sent to Rikers Island (Human Rights Watch 2010: 21). In 2009, at least half of the people sitting in New York City jails were there simply because they could not afford the price of their freedom (ibid.).

Not only has it been shown that people will return to court without a financial incentive to do so, but the fact that judges continue to set bail outside of our clients' ability to pay appears to be addressing a problem that doesn't truly exist. The vast majority of those facing criminal charges in New York City come back to court for all of their court dates. Even those who miss a court date almost always return within 30 days. Based on the most recent available data, those charged with felonies have an appearance rate of 96 percent and those charged with misdemeanors have an appearance rate of 93 percent, when returns within 30 days are included (New York City Criminal Justice Agency 2015: 35). Yet judges only release people on their own recognizance 70 percent of the time (NYC CJA 2015: 17).

If money is not what makes people come back to court, judges are setting bail in amounts that are far beyond what the accused can afford, and the vast majority of those accused are not a risk of flight – then why are judges holding so many people in jail who are presumed innocent? A common theory, and one that is being used in New York to advocate for adding risk to public safety as a consideration in release determinations, is that judges are setting bail in amounts too high for people to post because they are concerned that the person might be a danger to the community, not that he is in fact at risk for failing to appear. This theory suggests that people who are released pre-trial are committing new offenses at rates that require corrective action. However, a study by the Criminal Justice Agency reveals that only 17 percent of people released pre-trial on their own recognizance or on bail are re-arrested during the pendency of their case (Siddiqi 2009: 9–10). While 17 percent is not an insignificant figure, it includes arrests for minor offenses such as getting on the train without paying one's fare or driving with a suspended license. Presumably, when it comes to public safety, judges are more concerned with serious cases that involve acts of violence. Yet, according to the research, only 1.7 percent of people released on their own recognizance or on bail are re-arrested for a violent felony offense (ibid.).

Since New York does not explicitly allow judges to set bail because of a risk to public safety, it is hard to know whether judges are simply unaware that the risk of re-arrest for a violent felony is so small or are setting unattainable bail for another reason. Judges do not acknowledge publicly that they set bail because of perceived risks to public safety, because doing so violates state law. It follows that there are no studies showing how often judges detain someone because of that perceived risk. However, studies from other jurisdictions support the theory that judges are not detaining people who have a high likelihood of appearing in court and a low risk of getting re-arrested simply because they lack sufficient information to make an informed decision.

A study of Kentucky's pre-trial detention system illustrates the point (Stevenson 2018). In 2011, a law made the use of risk assessments, which purport to predict a person's risk for failure to appear and re-arrest, a mandatory part of detention decisions across the state. It also created a presumption of release for all low and moderate risk defendants. The goal of the new legislation was explicitly to reduce pre-trial detention. Nevertheless, a recent study shows that mandatory consideration of risk level and presumption of release for low and moderate risk defendants only led to a trivial increase in pre-trial release rates. Judges, the study found, ignored the release recommendations two-thirds of the time. More disturbingly, the study found that within a couple of years the release rates were lower than they had been before the law was passed.

As the Kentucky study and our own experience as public defenders strongly suggests, risk of flight and risk to public safety do not fully explain judges' detention decisions and greater knowledge of risk does not change judicial bail-setting practices. As most defenders will tell you, the more violent the crime and the more sympathetic the victim, the more likely it is that bail will be set too high for the client to make and that he will be held in jail regardless of risk. By way of illustration, judges will often release people on their own recognizance who are charged with low level drug offenses even when they have a lengthy criminal history and prior failures to appear in court. By contrast, the same judge will hold a person charged with a robbery of an elderly person on high bail that she cannot make, even if she has never been arrested before, has a job, stable residence and strong ties to the community. While it is hard to say without more research whether judges are using the nature of the charge and characteristics of the victim as a proxy for risk, a hypothetical helps illustrate the point. Consider a person accused of killing his wife. Assume that he is not a flight risk as he has strong ties to the community, a good job, and stable housing. Assume as well that he is not a danger to the community as he has never been arrested before and is a low risk for getting re-arrested while his case is pending. One would be hard-pressed to find a single judge that would be comfortable releasing such a person on their own recognizance.

Ensuring appearance in court and protecting the public surely explain some release decisions. But not all. Something else is driving the decision to detain. While human behavior is complex and motivation is hard to discern, judges who set bail are part of the broader adversarial process. They not only make detention decisions. They also oversee pre-trial litigation, the discovery process, plea bargaining, and trials. Through their proximity to the broader process of adjudicating guilt and imposing punishment, they are keenly aware of the impact that the decision to detain has on the accused. They see, first-hand, the difference between conviction rates for those at liberty and those who are held in jail because they are the ones accepting guilty pleas and presiding over the trials. They know from their own experience that people who are at liberty at the time of their conviction rarely receive an incarceratory sentence, and when they do their sentence length is less than their counterparts detained pre-trial. They learn about the impact of detention on people's homes, jobs, physical and mental health, and ability to care for their loved ones because defense attorneys use that information to seek release from jail. They see the trauma that pre-trial detention has on families because they watch the faces of family members in the courtroom who sit in anguish as their father, mother, sibling, or child is led away in handcuffs. And they read reports and articles that set forth in excruciating detail what Rikers Island is and what it does to the people who are confined there. In short, judges know very well the consequences of their decision to detain. They know that by remanding the accused or jailing him on bail too high to post, they are not just making a detention decision. They are deciding the outcome of that case. When asking what else explains judicial detention decisions other than risk of flight and risk to public safety, their knowledge of the consequences of their decisions cannot be ignored. More pointedly, it is evidence of the unacknowledged goal of pre-trial detention – the early and quick adjudication of guilt and imposition of punishment.

A Solution to Our Current Crisis: End all Pre-Trial Detention

As public defenders on the front lines in the fight for justice, we find ourselves at an exciting time. There is greater consensus than ever before that our criminal justice system in general, and our pre-trial detention system in particular, are in dire need of reform. These reform efforts are predicated upon widespread recognition that bail, or monetary conditions of release, unfairly punishes the poor and that structural racism and judicial bias in our pre-trial detention system result in discrimination against people of color. There is also recognition that our growing pre-trial detention population is a major contributor to our mass incarceration crisis and that the costs of detaining people at our current rate is prohibitive.

There is, however, little awareness that our system of pre-trial detention is not only acting as an adversarial one by determining guilt and imposing punishment, but has quietly supplanted our adversarial system and become the main mechanism by which we mete out justice. More importantly, there is little recognition that judges are detaining people pre-trial with a full understanding that in doing so they are effectively finding them guilty and punishing them. While there is no way to definitively determine why judges routinely incarcerate those who are not a flight risk or a danger to their community, there is plenty of evidence to suggest that the quick and early adjudication of guilt and imposition of punishment is at play. If one accepts the conclusions reached in this chapter, that our pre-trial detention system supplants our adversarial one, and does so purposefully, then it is clear that an adversarial system premised on the presumption of innocence, right to trial, and burden of proof cannot coexist with one that jails people pre-trial. It is also clear that reform will not come by eliminating money bail, by increasing the use of risk assessments, or by ensuring the release of those charged with certain categories of crimes. The only reform that can protect our adversarial system and the principles on which it stands is abolishing the pre-trial jailing of those presumed innocent altogether.

References

Chauhan, P., Hood, Q.O., Balazon, E.M., Cuevas, C., Lu, O., Tomascak, S. & Fera, A.G. (2017) *Trends in Custody*, New York City: New York City Department of Correction. From http://misdemeanorjustice.org/wp-content/uploads/2017/04/TrendsInCustody_FullReport.pdf

Bronx Freedom Fund, The (2015) *The Bronx Freedom Fund Report*

Chammah M., Goldstein D., Hager E., Santo A., Schwartzapfel B., Tabor N., Thompson C., & Weichselbaum S., (2015) "Rikers Island Population 9,790" *New York Magazine: Intelligencer.* from http://nymag.com/intelligencer/2015/06/inside-rikers-island-interviews.html

Human Rights Watch (2010), *The Price of Freedom*, Human Rights Watch, New York. from https://www.hrw.org/sites/default/files/reports/us1210webwcover_0.pdf

Independent Commission on New York City Criminal Justice and Incarceration Reform. (2017), *A More Just New York City*, The City of New York, New York. from https://static1.squarespace.com/static/5b6de4731aef1de914f43628/t/5b96c6f81ae6cf5e9c5f186d/1536607993842/Lippman%2BCommission%2BReport%2BFINAL%2BSingles.pdf

Marsh J., Pagones S., & Whitehouse K., (2017) "I Spent a Year at Rikers Island, and it's Hell on Earth" *New York Post*. from http://nyp.st/2mKEYJu

Mathias C., (2015) "1,500 Rikers Island Inmates Have Been Behind Bars More Than A Year Without Being Convicted" *Huffington Post.* From https://www.huffingtonpost.com/2015/04/14/rikers-island-de-blasio-justice-reboot_n_7065438.html

Minton, T.D. & Zeng Z. (2015) *Jail Inmates at Midyear 2014 – Statistical Tables.* NCJ 248629. Washington, DC: U.S. Department of Justice, Bureau of Justice Statistics. from https://www.bjs.gov/content/pub/pdf/jim14.pdf

New York City Criminal Justice Agency (2015) *Annual Report*, from www.nycja.org/publications/cja-annual-report-2015

New York City Department of Corrections. (2018a) *Facilities Overview*, Department of Corrections, New York City. from www1.nyc.gov/site/doc/about/facilities.page

New York City Department of Corrections. (2018b) *Visiting Schedule*, Department of Corrections, New York City. from www1.nyc.gov/site/doc/inmate-info/visit-schedule.page

New York City Jails Action Coalition (2018) *It Makes Me Want to Cry: Visiting Rikers Island*, NYC Jails Action Coalition. from http://nycjac.org/wp-content/uploads/2018/01/VISITING-RIKERS-ISLAND-JAILS-ACTION-COALITION-1.9.18.pdf. (An extensive report highlighting the importance of visits and the experience of visiting someone at Rikers)

Nunez Independent Monitor (2017) *Fourth Report of the Nunez Independent Monitor*, New York City Department of Correction. from https://assets.documentcloud.org/documents/4173501/Fourth-Monitor-Report-as-Filed-Nunez.pdf

Olivares J. (2017) "Despite Scrutiny, Rikers Island's 'Culture Of Violence' Persists, Report Says," *National Public Radio*. From www.npr.org/2017/11/30/559846083/despite-scrutiny-rikers-islands-culture-of-violence-persists-report-says

Philips M.T. (2012) *A Decade of Bail Research in New York City,* New York, NY: New York City Criminal Justice Agency

Schwirtz, M. (2017) "What is Rikers Island," *The New York Times*. From www.nytimes.com/2017/04/05/nyregion/rikers-island-prison-new-york.html

Schwirtz M., & Winerip W., (2014) "Rikers: Where Mental Illness Meets Brutality in Jail" *The New York Times*. from www.nytimes.com/2014/07/14/nyregion/rikers-study-finds-prisoners-injured-by-employees.html

Siddiqi Q., (2009) "Predicting the Likelihood of Pretrial Failure to Appear and/or Re-Arrest for a Violent Offense Among New York City Defendants: An Analysis of the 2001 Dataset" *N.Y.C. Crim. Justice Agency Res. Brief*

Stevenson, M. (2018), "Assessing Risk Assessment in Action" *Minnesota Law Review, Vol. 103,* from https://ssrn.com/abstract=3016088

Further Reading

Dobbie W., Goldin J., & Yang C.S. (2018) "The Effects of Pretrial Detention on Conviction, Future Crime, and Employment: Evidence from Randomly Assigned Judges." *American Economic Review*, 108 (2): 201–40. (An extensive analysis of the impacts of pre-trial detention on subsequent case and sentence outcomes)

Holsinger A., Lowenkamp C.T., & VanNostrand M. (2013) *Investigating the Impact of Pretrial Detention on Sentencing Outcomes*, Lauren and John Arnold Foundation. from www.arnoldfoundation.org/wp-content/uploads/2014/02/LJAF_Report_state-sentencing_FNL.pdf (A study that investigates the impact of pretrial detention on sentencing outcomes for both misdemeanors and felonies)

Olderman J. (2012) "Fixing New York's Broken Bail System" *City University of New York Law Review* 16, 1. from https://academicworks.cuny.edu/clr/vol16/iss1/3/. (Explains the history of bail in New York, the current bail statute, and the different provisions that provide tools for ensuring a fair and equitable bail system)

Stephanos B. (2004), "Plea Bargaining Outside the Shadow of Trial" *Faculty Scholarship at Penn Law*. 924. from https://scholarship.law.upenn.edu/cgi/viewcontent.cgi?article=1923&context=faculty_scholarship (How traditional notions of plea bargaining are distorted)

Stevenson, M. & and Mayson, S.G. (2017) "Bail Reform: New Directions for Pretrial Detention and Release". *Faculty Scholarship at Penn Law*. 1745. from https://scholarship.law.upenn.edu/faculty_scholarship/1745

28

A NON-PUNITIVE ALTERNATIVE TO RETRIBUTIVE PUNISHMENT

Gregg D. Caruso and Derk Pereboom

Punishment is the intentional imposition of a penalty upon a person or group of persons for conduct that is represented, either truly or falsely, as immoral or in violation of a law. Everyday examples include poker players excluding someone who has cheated from further play, and a teacher giving a group of pupils a "time out" for disrespectful behavior. *Legal punishment* is a specific sort of punishment; it is the intentional imposition of a penalty for conduct that is represented, either truly or falsely, as a violation of a law of the state, where the imposition of that penalty is sanctioned by the state's authority (Zimmerman 2011; Boonin 2008; Bedau and Kelly 2015).

One of the most prominent justifications of legal punishment, historically and currently, is *retributivism,* according to which wrongdoers *deserve* the imposition of a penalty solely for the backward-looking reason that they have knowingly done wrong. Michael S. Moore, a leading retributivist, highlights this purely backward-looking nature of retributivist justification:

> [R]etributivism is the view that we ought to punish offenders because, and only because, they deserve to be punished. Punishment is justified, for a retributivist, solely by the fact that those receiving it deserve it. Punishment may deter future crime, incapacitate dangerous persons, educate citizens in the behaviour required for a civilized society, reinforce social cohesion, prevent vigilante behaviour, make victims of crime feel better, or satisfy the vengeful desires of citizens who are not themselves crime victims. Yet for the retributivist these are a happy surplus that punishment produces and form no part of what makes punishment just: for a retributivist, deserving offenders should be punished even if the punishment produces none of these other, surplus good effects.
>
> *(2010: 153; see also 1987, 1993)*

Retributivism is also endorsed, for example, by Stephen Kershnar (2000, 2001), Douglas Husak (2000), and arguably by Immanuel Kant (1790). It's important to emphasize that the desert invoked in retributivism (in the classical or strict sense) is *basic* in the sense that it is not in turn grounded in forward-looking reasons such as securing the safety of society or the moral improvement of criminals, or, more broadly, in the value of consequences. Thus, for the retributivist, the claim that persons are morally responsible for their actions in the *basic desert* sense is crucial to the state's justification for giving them their *just deserts* in the form of punishment for violations of the state's laws. Retributivists typically also hold, in addition, that just punishments must be *proportional to wrongdoing*. Both the justificatory thesis and the proportionality requirement for punishments are reflected in Mitchell Berman's statement of retributivism:

> A person who unjustifiably and inexcusably causes or risks harm to others or to significant social interests deserves to suffer for that choice, and he deserves to suffer in proportion to the extent to which his regard or concern for others falls short of what is properly demanded of him.
>
> *(2008: 269)*

In the American criminal legal system, the retributivist justification of legal punishment and the attendant proportionality requirement are widely embraced. A number of sentencing guidelines in the US have adopted the retributivist conception of desert as their core principle,[1] and it is increasingly given deference in the "purposes" section of state criminal codes,[2] where it can be the guiding principle in the interpretation and application of the code's provisions.[3] Indeed, the American Law Institute recently revised the Model Penal Code so as to set desert as the officially dominant principle for sentencing.[4] American courts have identified desert as the guiding principle in a variety of contexts,[5] as with the Supreme Court's enthroning retributivism as the "primary justification for the death penalty"[6] (Robinson 2008: 145–146). But despite its prevalence in the criminal law, an important philosophical question remains: does retributivism as a theory of legal punishment withstand scrutiny? In particular, is state-sanctioned intentional imposition of penalties for violating the state's laws ever basically deserved?

Free Will Skepticism

One reason to think that no human agents ever basically deserve legal punishment, as retributivism presupposes, is that we lack the control in action, that is, the free will, required for moral responsibility in the *basic desert* sense, which we define as follows:

> For an agent to be morally responsible for an action in the basic desert *sense* is for it to belong to her in such a way that she would deserve blame if she understood that it was morally wrong, and she would deserve credit or perhaps praise if she understood that it was morally exemplary. The desert invoked here is *basic* in the sense that the agent, to be morally responsible, would deserve the blame or credit just because she has performed the action, given sensitivity to its moral status, and not by virtue of consequentialist or contractualist considerations.
>
> *(Pereboom 2001, 2014; cf. Feinberg 1970)*

Free will skeptics maintain that since what we do and the way we are is ultimately the result of factors beyond our control, we are never morally responsible for our actions in the basic desert sense (see, e.g., Pereboom 2001, 2014; Levy 2011; Caruso 2012). Free will skepticism accordingly presents a serious challenge to retributivism: if we never basically deserve blame just because we have knowingly done wrong, neither do we ever basically deserve punishment just because we have knowingly done wrong.

Free will skepticism, one might object, allows for non-basically deserved blaming and praising – for example, blaming that invokes desert grounded in consequentialist (e.g., Daniel Dennett 1984; Manuel Vargas 2013) or contractualist (e.g., Ben Vilhauer 2013) considerations. On one type of revisionary account, our practice of holding agents morally responsible in a desert sense should be retained, not because we are in fact morally responsible in this sense, but because doing so would have the best consequences relative to alternative practices. Daniel Dennett (1984) advocates a version of this position, as does Manuel Vargas (2013). But punishment justified in this way would not be genuinely retributivist, since its ultimate justification would be consequentialist, and this is incompatible with retributivism as it has traditionally been understood.

The case we favor for free will skepticism features distinct arguments that target three rival views, *event-causal libertarianism*, *agent-causal libertarianism*, and *compatibilism*, and then claims that the skeptical position is the only defensible position that remains standing. We begin by considering the libertarian positions. According to event-causal libertarianism, actions are caused solely by way of events, standardly conceived as objects having properties at times, and some type of indeterminacy in the production of actions by appropriate events is held to be a decisive requirement for moral responsibility (Balaguer 2009; Ekstrom 2000; Kane 1996).

According to agent-causal libertarianism, free will of the sort required for moral responsibility is accounted for by the existence of agents who possess a causal power to make choices without being causally determined to do so (Chisholm 1976; Clarke 2003; Griffith 2010; Kant 1781/1787/1987; O'Connor 2000; Reid 1788/1983; Taylor 1974). In this view, it is essential that the causation involved in an agent's making a free choice is not reducible to causation among events involving the agent, but is rather irreducibly an instance of the agent-as-substance causing a choice not by way of events. The agent, fundamentally as a substance, has the causal power to cause choices without being determined to do so.

Here, in brief, is the reason we reject event-causal libertarianism. For an agent to be morally responsible for a decision in the basic desert sense, she must exercise a certain type and degree of control in making that decision. In the event-causal libertarian picture, only events are causes, and free decisions are causally undetermined. The causally relevant events antecedent to a decision – most prominently agent-involving events – accordingly leave it open whether the decision occurs, and thus do not settle whether it occurs. Settling whether a decision occurs is a kind of control in action, and the event-causal libertarian is a causalist about control, specifying that control in action is a causal matter. But because on this view all causation is event-causation, the agent can have no role in settling whether a decision occurs beyond the role it plays in agent-involving events. Hence, given the indeterminism required for a free decision, the agent cannot settle whether the decision occurs. Therefore, in the event-causal libertarian picture an agent cannot have the control required for being morally responsible in the basic desert sense for a decision. Since the agent "disappears" at the crucial juncture in the production of the decision – when its occurrence is to be settled – Pereboom calls this the *disappearing agent argument* (Pereboom 2004, 2014, 2017a).

The agent-causal libertarian's response to this difficulty is to specify a way in which the agent might possess the required power to settle in indeterministic contexts. The solution on offer is to reintroduce the agent as a cause, this time not merely as involved in events, but rather fundamentally as a substance. The agent-causal libertarian proposes that we possess a distinctive causal power – a power for an agent, fundamentally as a substance, to cause a decision without being causally determined to do so, and thereby to settle whether it occurs (Clarke 2003; Chisholm 1976; Griffith 2010; Kant 1781/1787/1987; O'Connor 2000).

We don't think that the agent-causal libertarian picture is ruled out as incoherent. But it does face difficulties that undermine its credibility as a ground for a retributivist justification of punishment, in particular given the epistemic argument that we set out below. Immanuel Kant (1781/1787/1987) expresses a significant concern for this view, that it might not be reconcilable with what we would expect given our best empirical theories. He held that the physical world, as part of the world of appearance, is governed by deterministic laws, whereas the "transcendentally free" agent-cause would exist not as an appearance, but as a thing in itself. In his agent-causal picture, when an agent makes a free decision, she causes the decision without being causally determined to do so. On the route from this undetermined decision to its effects, changes in the physical world, for example, in the agent's brain or some other part of her body, are produced. However, it would seem that we would at these points encounter divergences from the deterministic laws, since the changes in the physical world that result from the undetermined decision would themselves not be causally determined. One might respond that it is possible that the physical alterations that result from free decisions just happen to dovetail with what could in principle be predicted on the basis of the deterministic laws, so nothing actually occurs that diverges from them. But this reconciliationist proposal would appear to involve coincidences too wild to be credible. Consequently, agent-causal libertarianism appears not to be reconcilable with a deterministic law-governed physical world. Pereboom (1995, 2001, 2014) also argues that similar sorts of wild coincidences would plague a view according to which agent-caused free choices would reconcile with indeterministic and probabilistic laws. If the libertarian agreed to these arguments from wild coincidences, she might propose that there are indeed departures from the probabilities that we would expect given the physical laws, thus abandoning the reconciliationist project. Roderick Chisholm (1964) proposes a solution of this sort. An objection to this proposal is that we would seem to lack any evidence that departures from the known physical laws occur in the brain when we make decisions.

The remaining and most popular alternative to skepticism about free will is compatibilism. One way to argue against compatibilism begins with the intuition that if an agent is causally determined to act by, for example, scientists who unbeknownst to her manipulate her brain, then she is not morally responsible for that action, even if she satisfies the prominent compatibilist conditions on moral responsibility (Ginet 1990; Kane 1996; Mele 1995, 2006; Pereboom 1995, 2001, 2014; Taylor 1974; van Inwagen 1983). The key subsequent step is that there are no differences between such manipulated agents and their ordinary deterministic counterparts that can justify the claim that the manipulated agents are not morally responsible while the determined agents are.

Pereboom's multiple-case version of such an argument first of all develops examples of an action that results from an appropriate sort of manipulation and in which the prominent compatibilist conditions on moral responsibility are satisfied (Pereboom 1995, 2001, 2014). In the setup, in each of the four cases the agent commits a crime, say homicide, for the sake of some personal advantage. The cases are designed so that the crime conforms to the prominent compatibilist conditions; for instance, the action meets the reasons-responsiveness condition proposed by John Fischer and Mark Ravizza (1998): his desires can be modified by, and some of them arise from, his rational consideration of the reasons, and if he understood that the bad consequences for himself that would result from the crime would be more severe than they are actually likely to be, he would have refrained for that reason. The individual manipulation cases featured in the argument, considered separately, indicate that it is possible for an agent not to be morally responsible in the basic desert sense even if these prominent compatibilist conditions are satisfied, and that these conditions are therefore insufficient. The argument acquires additional force by virtue of setting out three manipulation cases, each of which is progressively more like the fourth case, in which the action is causally determined in a natural way. The first case involves manipulation that is immediately causally determining – the neuroscientists directly control the agent's reasoning from moment to moment. The second is just like the first, except that it restricts the manipulation to a time at the beginning of the agent's life. The third case is also similar, except that the manipulation results from the strict upbringing on the part of his community. The fourth is the natural or ordinary deterministic case. The aim is to formulate these cases so that it is impossible to point to a difference between any two adjacent cases that would explain in a principled way why the agent would not be morally responsible in the basic desert sense in one but would be in the other. The conclusion is that the agent is not morally responsible in this sense in all four cases, and that the best explanation for this must be that he is causally determined by factors beyond his control in each of them. This result conflicts with the compatibilist's central claim.

Further Reasons to Reject Retributivism

Even if one is not convinced by the arguments against the sort of free will required for basic desert, there remains a strong *epistemic argument* against causing harm on retributivist grounds that is sufficient for the rejection of retributive legal punishment (see Caruso 2020). This is because the burden of proof lies on those who want to intentionally inflict harm on others to provide good justification for such harm. This means that retributivists who want to justify legal punishment on the assumption that agents are free and moral responsible (and hence *justly deserve* to suffer for the wrongs they have done) must justify that assumption in a way that meets a high epistemic standard of proof since the harms caused in the case of legal punishment are often quite severe. It is not enough to simply point to the mere possibility that agents possess libertarian or compatibilist free will. Nor is it enough to say that the skeptical arguments against free will and basic desert moral responsibility fail to be conclusive. Rather, a positive and convincing case must be made that agents are in fact morally responsible in the basic desert sense, since it is the backward-looking desert of agents that retributivists take to justify the harm caused by legal punishment.

The epistemic argument against retributive legal punishment can be summarized as follows (Caruso 2020):

(1) Legal punishment inflicts harms on individuals and the justification for such harms must meet a high epistemic standard. If it is significantly probable that one's justification for harming another is unsound, then, prima facie, that behavior is seriously wrong.
(2) The retributivist justification for legal punishment assumes that agents are morally responsible in the basic desert sense and hence justly deserve to suffer for the wrongs they have done in a backward-looking, non-consequentialist sense (appropriately qualified and under the constraint of proportionality).
(3) If the justification for the assumption that agents are morally responsible in the basic desert sense and hence justly deserve to suffer for the wrongs they have done does not meet the high epistemic standard specified in (1), then retributive legal punishment is prima facie seriously wrong.
(4) The justification for the claim that agents are morally responsible in the basic desert sense provided by both libertarians and compatibilists faces powerful and unresolved objections and as a result falls far short of the high epistemic bar needed to justify such harms.
(5) Hence, retributive legal punishment is unjustified and the harms it causes are prima facie seriously wrong.

This argument builds on previous work done by Double (2002), Vilhauer (2015), and Pereboom (2001, 2014), and has been more recently developed and defended by Caruso (2020), Corrado (2017), and Shaw (2014). We take our previous statements of the argument to be sufficient and have nothing new to add here other than to reiterate that all extant accounts of basic desert moral responsibility still fail to satisfy the high epistemic standard needed to justify retributive legal punishment.

Several additional considerations also count against retributivism. Retributivist sentiments may be grounded in vengeful desires, and therefore retribution has little more plausibility than vengeance as a morally sound policy for action. Acting on vengeful desires might be wrong for the following sort of reason. Although acting on such desires can bring about pleasure or satisfaction, no more of a moral case can be made for acting on them than can be made for acting on sadistic desires, for example. Acting on sadistic desires can bring about pleasure, but in both cases acting on the desire aims at the harm of the one to whom the action is directed, and in neither case does acting on the desire essentially aim at any good other than the pleasure of its satisfaction. But then, since retributivist motivations are disguised vengeful desires, acting for the sake of retribution is also morally wrong (Pereboom 2001, 2014).

Moreover, supposing that the requisite capacity for control is in place, and that basic desert could be secured as good or right, we can ask whether the state has the right to invoke it in justifying punishment. The legitimate functions of the state are generally held to include protecting its citizens from significant harm, and providing a framework for human interaction to proceed without significant impairment. These roles arguably underwrite justification that in the first instance appeals to prevention of crime. But these roles have no immediate connection to the aim of apportioning punishment in accord with basic desert. The concern can be made vivid by considering the proposal that the state set up a well-funded set of institutions designed to comprehensively and fairly distribute rewards on the grounds of basic desert (Pereboom 2014).

For these and other reasons (see, e.g., Boonin 2008; Zimmerman 2011; Caruso 2017, 2021, forthcoming), we conclude that retributivism as a justification of legal punishment should be rejected. We now turn to our non-retributive alternative for addressing criminal behavior – the *public health-quarantine model.*

The Public Health-Quarantine Model

The public health-quarantine model is based on an analogy with quarantine and draws on a comparison between treatment of dangerous criminals and treatment of carriers of dangerous diseases (see Pereboom 2001, 2014; Caruso 2016, 2017, 2021; Pereboom and Caruso 2018). In its simplest form, it can be stated as follows: (1) free will skepticism maintains that criminals are not morally responsible for their actions in the basic desert sense; (2) plainly, many carriers of dangerous diseases are not responsible in this or in any other sense for having contracted these diseases; (3) yet, we generally agree that it is sometimes permissible to quarantine them, and the justification for doing so is the right to self-protection and the prevention of harm to others; (4) for similar reasons, even if a dangerous criminal is not morally responsible for his crimes in the basic desert sense (perhaps because no one is ever in this way morally responsible) it could be *as* legitimate to preventatively detain him as to quarantine the non-responsible carrier of a serious communicable disease.

The first thing to note about the theory is that although one might justify quarantine (in the case of disease) and incapacitation (in the case of dangerous criminals) on purely utilitarian or consequentialist grounds, we want to resist this strategy (see Pereboom and Caruso 2018). Instead, our view maintains that incapacitation of the seriously dangerous is justified on the ground of the right to harm in self-defense and defense of others. That we have this right has broad appeal, much broader than utilitarianism or consequentialism has. In addition, this makes the view more resilient to a number of objections and provides a more resilient proposal for justifying criminal sanctions than other non-retributive options (see, e.g., Pereboom 2017b; Pereboom and Caruso 2018; Caruso forthcoming). One advantage it has, say, over consequentialist deterrence theories is that it has more restrictions placed on it with regard to using people merely as a means. For instance, as it is illegitimate to treat carriers of a disease more harmfully than is necessary to neutralize the danger they pose, treating those with violent criminal tendencies more harshly than is required to protect society will be illegitimate as well. In fact, in all our writings on the subject, we have always maintained the *principle of least infringement*, which holds that the least restrictive measures should be taken to protect public health and safety (Caruso 2016, 2017; Pereboom and Caruso 2018). This ensures that criminal sanctions will be proportionate to the danger posed by an individual, and any sanctions that exceed this upper bound will be unjustified.

Second, the quarantine model places several constraints on the treatment of criminals (see Pereboom 2001, 2014). First, as less dangerous diseases justify only preventative measures less restrictive than quarantine, so less dangerous criminal tendencies justify only more moderate restraints (Pereboom 2014: 156). We do not, for instance, quarantine people for the common cold even though it has the potential to cause you some harm. Rather, we restrict the use of quarantine to a narrowly prescribed set of cases. Analogously, on our model the use of incapacitation should be limited to only those cases where offenders are a serious threat to public safety and no less restrictive measures were available. In fact, for certain minor crimes perhaps only some degree of monitoring could be defended. Secondly, the incapacitation account that results from this analogy demands a degree of concern for the rehabilitation and well-being of the criminal that would alter much of current practice. Just as fairness recommends that we seek to cure the diseased we quarantine, so fairness would counsel that we attempt to rehabilitate the criminals we detain (Pereboom 2014: 156). Rehabilitation and reintegration would therefore replace punishment as the focus of the criminal justice system. Lastly, if a criminal cannot be rehabilitated and our safety requires his indefinite confinement, this account provides no justification for making his life more miserable than would be required to guard against the danger he poses (Pereboom 2014: 156).

In addition to these restrictions on harsh and unnecessary treatment, the model also advocates for a broader approach to criminal behavior that moves beyond the narrow focus on sanctions. As Caruso (2016, 2017, forthcoming) has proposed, and Pereboom has endorsed (Pereboom and Caruso 2018), we recommend placing the quarantine analogy within the broader justificatory framework of *public health ethics*. Public health ethics not only justifies quarantining carriers of infectious diseases on the grounds that it is necessary to protect public health, it also requires that we take active steps to *prevent* such outbreaks from occurring in the first place. Quarantine is only needed when the public health system fails in its primary function. Since no system is perfect, quarantine will likely be needed for the foreseeable future, but it should *not* be the primary means of dealing with public health. The analogous claim holds for incapacitation. Taking a public health approach to criminal behavior would allow us to justify the incapacitation of dangerous criminals when needed, but it would also make prevention a *primary function* of the criminal justice system. So instead of myopically focusing on punishment, the public health-quarantine model shifts the focus to identifying and addressing the systemic causes of crime, such as poverty, low social economic status, systematic disadvantage, mental illness, homelessness, educational inequity, exposure to abuse and violence, poor environmental health, and addiction (see Caruso 2017).

We maintain that since the *social determinants of health* and the *social determinants of criminal behavior* are broadly similar (Caruso 2017), the best way to protect public health and safety is to adopt a public health approach for identifying and taking action on these shared social determinants. Such an approach would require investigating how social inequities and systemic injustices affect health outcomes and criminal behavior, how poverty affects brain development, how offenders often have pre-existing medical conditions (especially mental health issues), how homelessness and education affects health and safety outcomes, how environmental health is important to both public health and safety, how involvement in the criminal justice system itself can lead to or worsen health and cognitive problems, and how a public health approach can be successfully applied within the criminal justice system. We contend that just as it is important to identify and take action on the social determinants of health if we want to improve health outcomes, it is equally important to identify and address the social determinants of criminal behavior.

Furthermore, our public health framework sees *social justice* as a foundational cornerstone to public health and safety (see Powers and Faden 2006; Caruso 2016, 2017). In public health ethics, a failure on the part of public health institutions to ensure the social conditions necessary to achieve a sufficient level of health is considered a grave injustice. An important task of public health ethics, then, is to identify which inequalities in health are the most egregious and thus which should be given the highest priority in public health policy and practice. The public health approach to criminal behavior likewise maintains that a core moral function of the criminal justice system is to identify and remedy social and economic inequalities responsible for crime. Just as public health is negatively affected by poverty, racism, and systematic inequality, so too is public safety. This broader approach to criminal justice therefore places issues of social justice at the forefront. It sees racism, sexism, poverty, and systemic disadvantage as serious threats to public safety and it prioritizes the reduction of such inequalities (see Caruso 2017).

The core of the public health-quarantine model, then, is that the right to harm in self-defense and defense of others justifies incapacitating the criminally dangerous with the minimum harm required for adequate protection. The resulting account would not justify the sort of criminal punishment whose legitimacy is most dubious, such as death or confinement in the most common kinds of prisons in our society. The model also specifies attention to the well-being of criminals, which would change much of current policy. Furthermore, the public health component of the theory prioritizes prevention and social justice and aims at identifying and taking action on the social determinants of health and criminal behavior. This combined approach to dealing with criminal behavior, we maintain, is sufficient for dealing with dangerous criminals, leads to a more humane and effective social policy, and is actually preferable to the harsh and often excessive forms of punishment that typically come with retributivism.

Implications

Since legal punishment requires the intentional imposition of a penalty for conduct that is represented as a violation of a law of the state, and since the public health-quarantine model does not involve punishment in this way, we consider it a non-punitive alternative to treatment of criminals. When we quarantine an individual with a communicable disease in order to protect people, we are not intentionally imposing a penalty for illegal conduct. The same is true when we incapacitate the criminally dangerous in order to protect people. The right of self-defense and protection of harm to others justifies the limiting or restricting of liberty, but it does not constitute punishment as standardly understood.

Given that the public health-quarantine model is a non-punitive approach to criminal behavior, a number of important implications follow. First, the model strongly suggests that we favor a *whole person* approach – one that understands that individuals are embedded in social systems, that criminal behavior is often the result of social determinants, and that prevention is always preferable to incapacitation. Second, after a criminal offense has occurred, courts would need to work with mental health experts, drug treatment professionals, and social service agencies to seek alternatives to incarceration. Lastly, for those who must be incapacitated, they would need to be housed in non-punitive environments designed with the purpose of rehabilitation and reintegration in mind.

Consider, for instance, the physical design of prisons.[7] With a growing number of exceptions, prisons are harsh, restrictive institutions, designed to enable maximum control over inmates' behavior at any time. As Lutham and Klippan write: "Their scale and appearance instill mistrust and anonymity…The ability to personalize space, have ownership and have personal control over one's situation is intentionally absent. Mostly, these are overtly punitive environments, unlike any other" (2016). These "cold" prison environments have an effect on the people inside them and they are typically not conducive to rehabilitation and reintegration. Consider the rates of suicide and self-harm in US prisons. According to the federal Bureau of Justice Statistics, suicides account for more deaths in state and federal prisons than drug and alcohol intoxication deaths, homicide, and accidents combined. Matters are worse in county jails where the suicide rate was 46 per 100,000 in 2013. Incidents of self-harm in England and Wales are also at an all-time high (Ministry of Justice 2016). Furthermore, US and UK prisons are also breeding grounds for violence (Bowker 1980; Irwin 1980; Johnson 1987; Ministry of Justice 2016), which is not surprising given that they typically confine large numbers of people in overcrowded quarters and in conditions characterized by material and social deprivation (Bowker 1980; Toch 1992; Toch and Adams 2002; Wolfgang and Ferracuti 1976; Wortley 2005).

In his book *Situational Prison Control* (2005), former prison psychologist Richard Wortley articulates strategies to reduce negative behavior in prison contexts, including through physical design. He suggests (a) setting positive expectations through domestic furnishings that confer trust; (b) reducing anonymity through small prison size; (c) personalizing victims through humane conditions; (d) enabling a positive sense of community through ownership and personalization of the space; and (e) reducing provocation and stress by designing in the capacity for inmates to enact control over environmental conditions and personal space. The current model of US correctional facilities represents the antithesis of each of these strategies. Lutham and Klippan correctly note, "When we create environments that fuel the negative behaviors we naturally associate with criminals, we are caught in a vicious cycle: harsh community and political attitudes toward prisons and prisoners are perpetuated, and overtly punitive prisons continue to be built" (2016).

Some good examples of innovating prison design include Halden Prison in Norway, Loobon in Australia, Enner Mark in Denmark, and the Norwegian prison island of Bastoy. These prisons are purposely designed to reduce crime. Lutham and Klippan explain:

> They do this by providing positive opportunities for inmates and building a greater sense of optimism for their future…These spaces are designed to more closely reflect environments in the outside community. The design treats these people not solely as "prisoners" but also as community members – with all the social, vocational and emotional responsibility that this entails.
>
> *(Lutham and Klippan 2016)*

Halden Prison in Norway, for example, features trees throughout its 75-acre site, whereas US prisons are usually devoid of vegetation in order to maximize visibility. In addition, to help inmates develop routines and to reduce the monotony of confinement, designers spread Halden's living quarters, work areas, and activity centers across the prison grounds. This provides offenders with some degree of autonomy and encourages interpersonal interactions – mirroring the kinds of conditions they will return to upon release. In fact, the Norwegian Correctional Services has officially adopted the *normality principle* – a principle we strongly endorse. The principle is that during the serving of a sentence "life inside [prisons] will resemble life outside as much as possible."[8] It further states that, "No one shall serve their sentence under stricter circumstances than necessary for the security of the community. Therefore offenders shall be placed in the lowest possible security regime." Lastly, it states that prison should be a restriction of liberty but nothing more, that is, "no other rights have been removed by the sentencing court." According to the normality principle, an offender should have all the same rights as other people living in Norway and life inside should resemble life outside as much as possible. All Norwegian prisoners, for example, have the right to study and they are all allowed to vote. Sentences are also kept short. On average they are no more than eight months long, and nearly 90% of sentences are for less than a year. Additionally, the longest sentence permitted by law is 21 years, but that can be extended in five-year increments if a prisoner is not rehabilitated and is considered a continued risk to society. Since most prisoners will eventually return to society, Norwegian prisons prepare inmates for reintegration by mimicking the outside world as much as possible.

Adopting the goals of rehabilitation and reintegration will lead not only to re-envisioning the physical design of prisons, but indeed to reconceiving all aspects of the criminal's experience while in custody. The entrenchment of purely punitive approaches to criminal behavior remains a stumbling block in the way of realizing these aims. We believe that in this domain, critical reflection on standard justifications for treatment of criminals is critical to progress.

Conclusion

We have argued that one of the most prominent justifications for legal punishment, retributivism, is inadequate and should be rejected. We began by exploring the retributive justification of legal punishment and explaining why it is inconsistent with free will skepticism. We then outlined our arguments in support of free will skepticism, concluding that it is the position to adopt. We further argued that even if one is not convinced by the arguments for free will skepticism, there are additional reasons for rejecting retributivism, such as the epistemic argument, and concerns about retributivism's dependence on vengeful sentiments. We then introduced a non-retributive and indeed non-punitive alternative for addressing criminal behavior, the public health-quarantine model, which draws on the public health framework and prioritizes prevention and social justice. We concluded with a discussion of some of the implications of this non-punitive approach for criminal justice, focusing on prison design as a case in point.

Notes

1 E.g., 204 Pa. Code Sect. 303.11 (2005); See also Tonry 2004.
2 E.g., Cal. Penal Code Sect. 1170(a)(1) (West 1985): "The legislature finds and declares that the purpose of imprisonment for crime is punishment."
3 E.g., Model Penal Code Sect. 1.02(2) (Official Draft 1962).
4 American Law Institute, Model Penal Code Sect. 1.02(2) adopted May 24, 2017.
5 See, for example, the US cases *Spaziano v. Florida*, 468 US 447, 462 (1984); *Gregg v. Georgia*, 428 US 153, 183–84 (1976); Cotton (2000).
6 *Spaziano v. Florida*, 468 US at 461.
7 The comments below on prison design where first made in Caruso (2017).
8 For more details, see the Norwegian Correctional Service's full document: www.kriminalomsorgen.no/informationin-english.265199.no.html

References

Balaguer, Mark. (2009). *Free Will As an Open Scientific Problem*, Cambridge, MA: MIT Press.

Bedau, Hugo Adam, and Erin Kelly. (2015). "Punishment," *Stanford Encylopedia of Philosophy*, first published on June 13, 2003; substantive revision on July 31, 2015. https://plato.stanford.edu/entries/punishment/

Berman, Mitchell. (2008). "Punishment and Justification," *Ethics* 18: 258–290.

Boonin, David. (2008). *The Problem of Punishment*, New York: Cambridge University Press.

Bowker, L. H. (1980). *Prison Victimization*, New York: Elsevier Science.

Caruso, Gregg D. (2012). *Free Will and Consciousness: A Determinist Account of the Illusion of Free Will*, Lanham, MD: Lexington Books.

Caruso, Gregg D. (2016). "Free Will Skepticism and Criminal Behavior: A Public Health-Quarantine Model," *Southwest Philosophical Review* 32(1): 25–48.

Caruso, Gregg D. (2017). *Public Health and Safety: The Social Determinants of Health and Criminal Behavior*, UK: ResearchLinks Books.

Caruso, Gregg D. (2020). "Justice Without Retribution: An Epistemic Argument Against Retributive Criminal Punishment," *Neuroethics* 13(1): 13–28. DOI:10.1007/s12152-018-9357-8.

Caruso, Gregg D. (2021). *Rejecting Retributivism: Free Will, Punishment, and Criminal Justice*. New York: Cambridge University Press.

Caruso, Gregg D. (forthcoming). "The Public Health-Quarantine Model," in Dana Nelkin and Derk Pereboom (eds.), *Oxford Handbook of Moral Responsibility*, New York: Oxford University Press.

Chisholm, Roderick. (1964). "Human Freedom and the Self," The Lindley Lecture, Department of Philosophy, University of Kansas; reprinted, in Gary Watson (ed.), *Free Will*, pp. 24–35, New York: Oxford University Press.

Chisholm, Roderick. (1976). *Person and Object*, La Salle IL: Open Court.

Clarke, Randolph. (2003). *Libertarian Theories of Free Will*, New York: Oxford University Press.

Corrado, Michael Louis (2017). "Punishment and the Burden of Proof," UNC legal studies research paper. Available at SSRN: https://ssrn.com/abstract=2997654 or https://doi.org/10.2139/ssrn.2997654

Cotton, Michele. (2000). "Back With a Vengeance: The Resilience of Retribution as an Articulated Purpose of Criminal Punishment," *American Criminal Law Review* 34(4): 1313–1357.

Dennett, Daniel C. (1984). *Elbow Room*, Cambridge, MA: MIT Press.

Double, Richard. 2002. "The Moral Hardness of Libertarianism," *Philo* 5: 226–234.

Ekstrom, Laura W. (2000). *Free Will: A Philosophical Study*, Boulder, CO: Westview.

Feinberg, Joel. (1970). "Justice and Personal Desert," in Feinberg (ed.) *Doing and Deserving*, Princeton: Princeton University Press.

Fischer, John Martin, and Mark Ravizza. (1998). *Responsibility and Control: A Theory of Moral Responsibility*, New York: Cambridge University Press.

Ginet, Carl. (1990). *On Action*, Cambridge: Cambridge University Press.

Griffith, Meghan. (2010). "Why Agent-Caused Actions Are Not Lucky," *American Philosophical Quarterly* 47: 43–56.

Husak, D. (2000) "Holistic Retributivism," *California Law Review* 88: 991–1000.

Irwin, John. (1980). *Prisons in Turmoil*, Boston: Little, Brown, and Company.

Johnson, Robert. (1987). *Hard Times: Understanding and Reforming the Prison*, New York: Wadsworth Publishing.

Kane, Robert. (1996). *The Significance of Free Will*, New York: Oxford University Press.

Kant, Immanuel. (1781/1787/1987). *Critique of Pure Reason*, Translated by Paul Guyer and Allen Wood, Cambridge, MA: Cambridge University Press.

Kant, Immanuel. (1790). *The Metaphysics of Morals*, Translated by W. Hastie.

Kershnar, Stephen. (2000). "A Defense of Retributivism," *International Journal of Applied Philosophy* 14(1): 97–117.

Kershnar, Stephen. (2001). *Desert, Retribution, and Torture*, Lanham, MD: University Press of America.

Levy, Neil. (2011). *Hard Luck: How Luck Undermines Free Will and Moral Responsibility*, New York: Oxford University Press.

Lutham, R., and L. Klippan. (2016). "From Expected Reoffender to Trusted Neighbor: Why We Should Rethink Prisons," *The Conversation*, 14 August: http://theconversation.com/from- expected-reoffender-to-trusted-neighbour-why-we-should- rethink-our-prisons-60114

Mele, Alfred. (1995). *Autonomous Agents*, New York: Oxford University Press.

Mele, Alfred. (2006). *Free Will and Luck*, New York: Oxford University Press.

Ministry of Justice. (2016). "Safety in custody statistics bulletin: England and Wales," www.gov.uk/government/statistics/safety-in-custody-quarterly-update-to-june-2016

Moore, Michael S. (1987). "The Moral Worth of Retribution," in Jeffrie G. Murphy (ed.), *Punishment and Rehabilitation*, 3rd Ed., pp.94–130, Belmont, California: Wadsworth Publishing Company.

Moore, Michael S. (1993). *Act and Crime; The Philosophy of Action and Its Implications for Criminal Law*, New York: Oxford University Press.

Moore, Michael S. (2010). *Placing Blame*, New York: Oxford University Press.

O'Connor, Timothy. (2000). *Persons and Causes*, New York: Oxford University Press.

Pereboom, Derk. (1995). "Determinism *al dente*," *Noûs* 29: 21–45.

Pereboom, Derk. (2001). *Living Without Free Will*, Cambridge: Cambridge University Press.

Pereboom, Derk. (2004). "Is Our Conception of Agent Causation Coherent?," *Philosophical Topics* 32: 275–86.

Pereboom, Derk. (2014). *Free Will, Agency, and Meaning in Life*, Oxford: Oxford University Press.

Pereboom, Derk. (2017a). "Responsibility, Agency, and the Disappearing Agent Objection," in Jean-Baptiste Guillon (ed.), *Le Libre-Arbitre, approches contemporaines*, pp. 1–18, Paris: Collège de France.

Pereboom, Derk. (2017b). "A Defense of Free Will Skepticism: Replies to Commentaries by Victor Tadros, Saul Smilansky, Michael McKenna, and Alfred R. Mele on *Free Will, Agency, and Meaning in Life*," *Criminal Law and Philosophy* 11 (3): 617–636.

Pereboom, Derk, and Gregg D. Caruso (2018). "Hard-Incompatibilist Existentialism: Neuroscience, Punishment, and Meaning in Life," in Gregg D. Caruso and Owen Flanagan (eds.), *Neuroexistentialism: Meaning, Morals, and Purpose in the Age of Neuroscience*, pp.1–22, New York: Oxford University Press.

Powers, Madison, and Ruth Faden. (2006). *Social Justice: The Moral Foundations of Public Health and Health Policy*, New York: Oxford University Press.

Reid, Thomas. (1788/1983). "Essays on the Active Powers of Man," in Sir William Hamilton (ed.), *The Works of Thomas Reid, D.D.*, Hildesheim: G. Olms Verslagsbuchhandlung, 1983 511–680.

Robinson, Paul H. (2008). *Distributive Principles of Criminal Law: Who Should be Punished How Much*, New York: Oxford University Press.

Shaw, Elizabeth. (2014). "Free Will, Punishment, and Criminal Responsibility," Dissertation, University of Edinburgh, available at: www.era.lib.ed.ac.uk/bitstream/handle/1842/9590/Shaw2014.pdf?sequence=2&isAllowed=y

Taylor, Richard. (1974). *Metaphysics*, Englewood Cliffs: Prentice Hall.

Toch, Hans. (1992). *Living in Prison: The Ecology of Survival*, revised edition, New York: The Free Press.

Toch, Han, and K. Adams. (2002). *Acting Out: Maladaptive Behavior in Confinement*, Washington, DC: American Psychological Association, APA Books.

Tonry, M. (2004). *U.S. Sentencing Systems Fragmenting*, in M. Tonry (ed.), *Penal Reform in Overcrowded Times*, pp.21 28. New York: Oxford University Press.

van Inwagen, Peter. (1983). *An Essay on Free Will*, Oxford: Oxford University Press.

Vargas, Manuel (2013). *Building Better Beings: A Theory of Moral Responsibility*, New York: Oxford University Press.

Vilhauer, Benjamin. (2013). "Persons, Punishment, and Free Will Skepticism," *Philosophical Studies* 162: 143–63.

Vilhauer, Benjamin. (2015). "Taking Free Will Skepticism Seriously," *Philosophical Quarterly* 62(149): 833–852

Wolfgang, M.E., and F. Ferracuti. (1976). *The Subculture of Violence*, London: Tavistock.

Wortley, Richard. (2005). *Situational Prison Control*, Cambridge, MA: Cambridge University Press.

Zimmerman, Michael. (2011). *The Immorality of Punishment*, New York: Broadview Press.

29

THE TAKINGS DOCTRINE AND THE PRINCIPLE OF LEGALITY

Michael Louis Corrado

> For the system which makes liability to the law's sanctions dependent upon a voluntary act not only maximizes the power of the individual to determine by his choice his future fate; it also maximizes his power to identify in advance the space which will be left open to him free from the law's interference.
>
> (Hart 1968: 181–182)

Introduction

The prohibitions of the criminal law promise an arena within which we may pursue our lives pretty much free of the fear of being preyed upon by our less scrupulous neighbors; but that arena of freedom can be threatened by the intrusions that the state makes use of to enforce those very prohibitions. The limits that keep the state from overstepping its bounds, traditionally thought to be called for by the notions of moral responsibility and desert, are instead called for by the promise itself of personal freedom made by the criminal law.

Section 1

States use force to control crime. They take away the personal freedom of some individuals who, they claim, threaten the safety and security of others. No individual can feel free under such control unless there are limits upon what the state may do in the name of crime control. Without enforcement the promise of personal freedom would be worth very little; but without the proper limits upon enforcement the promise is worth little as well.

The classical tradition of retributive punishment puts limits on the state's use of force, limits incorporated into what is known as the principle of legality. Beccaria's case for the principle guides most western legal systems today:

> Only the laws can decree the punishments for crimes, and this authority can only reside in the legislator, who represents society united in the social contract. No judge (who is part of society) can with justice impose [unlegislated] punishment on other members of the same society.
>
> *(Beccaria 1764/1963)*

The principle is made explicit in the constitutions, common law, and criminal codes of many nations.[1] There are two parts to it, and the best formulation of the two parts is (as often happens) in Latin: *Nullum crimen sine lege, nulla poena sine lege*. The only crimes are those specified in law; the only punishments are those specified in law. Beccaria makes clear the reason for these limits: without them, those who enforce the law would not be accountable. Not only must there be well-defined laws and well-defined punishments, they must be set down by the representatives of the people.

The movement for what is being called "criminal quarantine," that is, for a regime of crime control that is based on an analogy with medical quarantine, rejects both those limits. We saw the origins of this movement in the work of Italian positivists, among others, in the late nineteenth century. It had greater or lesser influence at different points through the twentieth century but never really succeeded in completely displacing the hold of the classical theory of punishment and of the principle of legality (Corrado 2016).

Today, armed with evidence from the field of neuroscience, prominent philosophers like Derk Pereboom have undertaken a new assault on the principle, one that means to uproot retributive punishment entirely (Pereboom 2001, 2014; Pereboom & Caruso 2018; Caruso 2016). Criminal quarantine aims not to punish those who violate the law but to remove the dangerous from society for as long as they remain dangerous. Punishment is justified only if *deserved*, and if the evidence from neuroscience is to be believed human beings cannot be held morally responsible for what they do, and so cannot be said to deserve punishment. Abandoning desert, the advocates would also abandon the limits imposed by desert, including the two constraints found in the principle of legality.

If we were to limit the state to acting against those who deserve punishment, then the state would be able to use force (in the name of crime control) only against those who have done something forbidden, namely those convicted of a crime. And if it were desert that authorized punishment, the amount of punishment would in some way have to be limited to the deserved amount – determined by the community through their representatives in the legislature. Not only are those limits unwarranted, according to quarantine advocates, they are downright foolish, obstructing the state's attempt to eliminate dangerous behavior. Confronted with the sure knowledge that a person is dangerous, are we obliged to sit by and wait until he actually injures someone? Confronted with the knowledge that the person we have detained is dangerous, are we obliged to release him before the danger has been eliminated? No, say the advocates of quarantine, on both counts.

I am one of those skeptical about the notion of desert, and not just because of the findings of neuroscience. And because I believe whether a person deserves suffering can never be established to the level required to justify punishment I am skeptical about punishment as well. But conceding (however unhappily) that the state must act to control crime, I am also skeptical about criminal quarantine. In particular I am skeptical about its ability to keep criminal justice from descending into a regime under which the decision whether or not to deprive someone of his freedom depends upon the case-by-case balancing of utilities.

Being skeptical about both punishment and quarantine, I suggest a regime of law enforcement modeled after the compromise in property law known as the "takings doctrine." In western law the state may move to seize private property but only within legal limits – the property taken must be taken for a reasonable public use, and only with compensation. These limits prevent the seizure from falling into a utilitarian trap, balancing costs to the community against benefits to the community, and at the same time prevent the individual property owner from holding his property hostage. It is a compromise with limits that are not negotiable, a line the state may not cross. It is a compromise that is fundamental to the very institution of private property (Brudner 2013; Michelman 1967).

In exactly the same way, the regime of enforcement that I would call "correction" aims at protecting what I referred to above as the *arena of personal liberty*. It permits the state to take away liberty, but only within limits that are non-negotiable. The limits imposed by correction are the principle of legality and the requirement of compensation. With von Liszt I would say that the limits embodied in the principle of legality are "the citizen's bulwark against the State's omnipotence; they protect the individual against the ruthless power of the majority, against Leviathan" (von Liszt 1893). The limits set by the principle – limits which cannot find their proper ground in moral responsibility and desert – can be justified as essential to protecting this arena of freedom within which the members of the community may determine their own life courses. And compensation, modest compensation, is both a mark of respect for the institution of personal liberty and a measure forcing the community to internalize a larger portion of the cost of crime control.

There may be other sets of non-negotiable limits that would work as well, but limits there must be: limits called for not by any innate right to autonomy, a nebulous line that is sometimes appealed to, but rather by the simple fact that a society organized around the institution of personal liberty – the arena meant to be protected by the system of criminal justice in the first place – is preferable to any society without it. Since I believe that compensation and the principle of legality are as important to constraining the state's enforcement of the boundaries of permissible behavior as a well-defined criminal code is to setting those boundaries, I think that the advocates of criminal quarantine, though well intentioned, are making a serious mistake: quarantine recognizes no limit upon the community's concern with avoiding danger.

There are two parts to my argument. The first thing to be shown is that abandoning any part of the principle of legality has led to disastrous results in the past. The second thing to be shown is why compensation – modest compensation – is essential when we seize the freedom of innocent individuals to enforce the criminal law.

Section 2

Here is Pereboom's description of the undertaking that is criminal quarantine:

> This theory draws an analogy between treatment of dangerous criminals and treatment of carriers of dangerous diseases … The free will skeptic claims that criminals are not morally responsible for their actions in the basic desert sense. Plainly, many carriers of dangerous diseases are not responsible in this or in any sense for have contracted these diseases. We generally agree that it is sometimes permissible to quarantine them nevertheless. But then, even if a dangerous criminal is not morally responsible for his crimes in the basic desert sense (perhaps because no one is ever in this way morally responsible) it could be as legitimate to preventatively detain him as to quarantine the non-responsible carrier of a serious communicable disease. Furthermore, as less dangerous diseases justify only preventative measures less restrictive than quarantine, so less dangerous criminal tendencies justify only more moderate restraints. In addition, the incapacitation account that results from this analogy demands a degree of concern for the rehabilitation and well-being of the criminal that would alter much of current practice. Just as fairness recommends that we seek to cure the diseased we quarantine, so fairness would counsel that we attempt to rehabilitate the criminals we detain …. If a criminal cannot be rehabilitated, and our safety requires his indefinite confinement, this account provides no justification for making his life more miserable than would be required to guard against the danger he poses. Finally, there are measures for preventing crime more generally, such as providing for adequate education and mental health care, which the free will skeptic can readily endorse.
>
> *(Pereboom 2014: 156)*

This account is elaborated in work Pereboom has done with Gregg Caruso. They make the rejection of any punishment-like limits explicit: for one thing, they reject any limit upon the length of detention of a dangerous person, any limit, that is, except the one imposed by dangerousness itself: when the person is no longer dangerous he may be released. And although they believe it *preferable* to restrict detention to those who have already committed a crime (but *why*?), they admit that the theory calls precisely for the state to take control of the dangerous person who has not yet committed a crime when lesser measures are not effective to prevent him from committing a crime (Pereboom and Caruso 2018).

Section 3

> [The National Socialist regime] … considered every violation of the goal of life which the community set up for itself to be a wrong per se, [so] that the act could be punished even though it was not contrary to existing "formal law".
>
> *(Jackson 1946: 86–87)*

Criminal quarantine is inconsistent with the principle of legality: that point hardly needs making. Under the regime of criminal quarantine three implications of the principle of legality would be abandoned, and we should fully understand what it will mean to abandon them before we let them go. There would be no need for a *conviction* for violation of a well-defined prohibition. Because there would be no need for a conviction, there would be no point in *well-defined prohibitions* at all, except perhaps as guideposts to the sorts of things the community wants to avoid. Finally, there would be no limit under the law upon the detention of dangerous persons, and so no point to a published list of well-defined *sentences* for crimes.

(1) Leave in place for now the requirements of a conviction and well-defined prohibitions and take the last point first: the mere absence of restrictions upon how much force the state may use – limits upon the length of detention – invites abuse. Certainly this is the case where the judges are biased against individuals or groups. But even where there is in fact good will on the part of the judges, consistency in the determination of seriousness is famously unreliable across judges, and therefore so is consistency in determining which wrongs will be similar to which crimes and therefore what the punishment must be for each wrong. Does the judge see assertive behavior on the part of women as dangerously similar to the crime of uttering a threat, while similar behavior on the part of men is not seen that way at all? If that is the prevailing view in society, even the most reasonable and well-intentioned judge might impose a penalty on a woman that would never be imposed on a man for the same behavior.

And we needn't rely on hypotheticals of that sort to make the point. The history of the law is replete with such examples. In Victorian England courts were free to determine what penalty should be attached to each crime. Radzinowicz and Hood lay out the scene for us in some detail:

> Complaints centered around two main issues. The first was "the reprehensible leniency with which so many offenses against the person are punished, and the needless, … absurd severity with which those against property are punished." … Some magistrates, said William Reade, "appear to think two or three pounds a heavy punishment for savage assault, while they adjudicate constantly on petty larceny by giving the full sentence of imprisonment under the Criminal Justice Act."
>
> A similar concern was voiced in Parliament, sometimes about the lenient sentences imposed for wife beating, sometimes about harsh sentences on housebreakers and petty thieves and lengthy terms of ten or twenty years for persistent thieves. The Home Secretary was asked to remit two sentences of ten years' penal servitude, one for stealing a purse containing two shillings and four pence, the other for stealing an overcoat. … Likewise, at Liverpool Assizes "persons charged with small offences [had] been sentenced to seven years' penal servitude for stealing a coat." In contrast, the Home Secretary was asked about a man named Lowe sentenced to twelve months' imprisonment "for brutally assaulting and stabbing and then robbing a lady walking in a field in the neighborhood of her residence … [S]he was seized by the throat, knocked down, and violently assaulted, and when she

> resisted, a knife was used, and after being seriously stabbed in two places, she was robbed of £4 or £5."
>
> *(Radzinowicz and Hood 1979: 1308–1309)*

There is no need to suppose any ill will on the part of the judges who made these decisions. The importance of property over the physical integrity of those most likely to be subject to physical attack must have seemed obvious and beyond question to them, but the injustice of the outcomes where there is so much discretion allowed to judges is clear. So too are the outcomes in cases in which prosecutors, with the best will in the world, are given discretion to determine where, in a hierarchy of crimes (for example, in the array of possible kinds of criminal homicide) a certain action falls. And so too will be the outcomes when the determination of dangerousness is in the hands of regulatory agencies schooled in the nature of dangerousness.

Certainly leaving the length of detention to the legislature is no guarantee of justice, but bringing the length of sentence under a universal legal prohibition, one that everyone is subject to, at least ensures some fairness. To leave the length of detention to a case-by-case determination by individuals who come to the enterprise armed with their own differing prejudices introduces a whole new level of injustice and undermines whatever certainty the criminal law was meant to provide.

The point of allowing discretion is to permit the period of confinement to be fitted to the needs of the individual offender – or, as the case may be, the dangerous individual. And some discretion there must be. But to leave the field wide open, to deny that there is any limit after which the prisoner must be let go, sets the stage for abuse. The answer to such abuses is to place some limits upon sentences; in many of the United States there has been a movement toward structured sentencing that limits severely the discretion of the sentencing agent.

(2) But these are abuses that may occur where there is a conviction under a well-defined prohibition. Suppose we go one step further and remove the requirement that the prohibitions of the criminal law be well-defined: what then?

Consider what can happen, even if a conviction is necessary, where the contours of the prohibitions are not well-defined. There are three well-known examples of nations that rejected the principle of legality and that made that rejection explicit by adopting what is known as "the principle of analogy:" if the trial court sees that the behavior of the defendant presents a danger to others or to society but cannot find a violation of any criminal statute, it may sentence him under any statute criminalizing behavior similar to the behavior that shows him to be dangerous.

In 1922, for example, the legislature of Soviet Russia, in line with the General Principles of the Criminal Law published by the Soviet Union (of which Russia was a member state), included the following statute in its criminal code:

> Article 10. In case of the absence in the Criminal Code of direct references to specific forms of crime, punishment and measures of social protection are applied in accordance with the articles of the Criminal Code that provide for the most similar crimes in terms of gravity and type, in compliance with the general part of the present Code.
>
> *(Raimundo 1963; Starosolsky 1950)*

The position of the Soviet republics was precarious in the early years, and the greatest danger was believed to be from those who opposed the communist government. Any behavior at all that threatened the rule of the Party had to be repressed at any cost, and repression could not be limited by the bounded ingenuity of the legislature in thinking up ways in which individuals might threaten the existence of the state.

There were still two lines, then, protecting the individual from the state: there was a list of crimes, and there had to be a conviction for a crime. But the crime the individual was convicted and sentenced for did not have to match the behavior for which he was being convicted and sentenced, and so in effect the behavior that was being forbidden was not announced in well defined prohibitions. If the court before whom the accused individual came believed that his behavior was dangerous to the state, the court was free to sentence him under any legal prohibition that criminalized behavior in some way or other like his. If for example he had accused a certain official of graft and no statute prohibited such accusations, he might be sentenced under a statute criminalizing propaganda against the state. The principle embodied in Article 10 is, of course, the principle of analogy.

In 1951 People's Republic of China enacted a similar statute, and for similar reasons. As revised in 1979 Article 79 of the Criminal Code of China read like this:

> Article 79. Crimes that are not expressly defined in the Specific Provisions of this Law may be determined and punished according to whichever article in the Specific Provisions of this Law that covers the most closely analogous crime, but the judgment shall be submitted to the Supreme People's Court for approval
>
> *(Chiu 1992)*

The wording of both the Russian and the Chinese provisions does not ask the court to determine whether there *is* a relevantly similar crime prohibited by the code, but only to punish the individual considered dangerous by the court under whatever crime may be the most similar.[2]

And in Section 2 of the 1935 Nationalist Socialist Penal Code of Germany, we find this:

> Section 2. Whoever commits an act which the law declares to be punishable or which is deserving of punishment according to the fundamental idea of penal law and the sound perception of the people shall be punished. If no determinate penal law is directly applicable to the act, it shall be punished according to that law, the basic idea of which fits best.
>
> *(Note,* Columbia Law Review *1947)*

In each of these three cases, all of them instances of the explicit introduction of the principle of analogy into the criminal code, the existence of a crime does not depend upon a prior declaration in a published rule. It depends only upon whether a court that was sympathetic to the "fundamental idea of penal law" embodied in the ideology of the ruling party would find the accused's actions to be in conflict with that idea and therefore dangerous.

Each of the three legal systems were quite reasonably considered to be monstrous, and each of them eventually abandoned analogy: Germany after the end of the war, the Soviet Union and Communist China after extensive criticism of their criminal justice systems.[3] But even where the state is not evil the looseness permitted by the principle of analogy can be abused with the best will in the world by judges who happen to have the prejudices of their element of society. Supposing the criminal laws ofVictorian England had set definite limits on the sentence for each crime, what would have kept judges (with a certain background and operating under a principle of analogy) from finding that a defendant's behavior should fall under a more lenient statute when others from a different background found it to be of the sort proscribed by a different, more severe statute? Or finding that the same behavior on the part of individuals from different segments of society should be judged under different sections of the code? Or finding behavior dangerous and worthy of bringing under a statute when a more reasonable view would be that it was not dangerous at all?

(3) The requirement of a conviction for the voluntary commission of a crime places an additional barrier between you and the state: unless being competent you *choose* to violate a law, you may not be used as an example to deter others and you may not be preventively detained to incapacitate you. The fundamental objection to a simple utilitarian theory of punishment is that it would justify the punishment of the innocent in the name of deterrence. But criminal quarantine (conceding, as it

does, that the offender is not responsible and so is innocent) would detain the innocent in the name of incapacitation.

Quarantine theory can see no reason for insisting upon a conviction before detention of a dangerous person, and calls precisely for the state to take control when lesser measures are not effective to prevent him from committing a crime, even if he has not yet violated any law. The argument in favor of this move depends upon a nightmare premise, a scenario in which an "undeterrable other," a lumbering *golem* bent upon devastation, is not responsive to the threats of punishment. Surely we should be able to act to prevent the harm he would inflict, the argument begins. But if we may act in advance in that case, why not in any case in which harm can be reliably predicted?[4]

We cannot close our eyes to this issue, what we may call "the problem of the third man:" the competent but undeterrable actor who stands between those who are insane and therefore not deterrable by criminal law, and those competent actors who are deterrable (Robinson 2001). Those who have written about it have been concerned with actual cases: psychopaths (Morse 1999; Slobogin 2003), for example, or terrorists (Walen 2011). But the answer to the problem does not lie in tearing down all barriers to state action, but rather in distinguishing those cases in which limited prohibitions may be enforced in a limited way from cases in which indefinite civil commitment may be appropriate.

So, for example, Alec Walen proposes what he calls "the Autonomy Respecting Model of detention," under which the distinction is based upon accountability: preventive detention would be appropriate not only for those who lack autonomous capacity, but also those who cannot be held accountable for violating the criminal law. Prisoners of war may be held in detention without evidence of a crime under this standard, since if they are released they can't be held accountable to the jurisdiction that detained them. And with some reluctance Walen concludes that in some cases suspected terrorists may be detained preventively as well.

> The problem is (1) that the detainees have no legal claim on the United States that it release them in its own territory and police them there, and (2) that where they do have a legal claim to be taken in, there is too large a chance that they would not be held accountable for any future acts of terror. As a result, they are effectively unaccountable and can be subjected to [long term preventive detention] without disrespecting them as autonomous people.
>
> *(Walen 2011: 923–924)*

Kim Ferzan distinguishes cases in which "punitive interference" is justified on the basis of intent: one who culpably and actively intends to violate a law or is willing to risk violating a law but has not yet done so (and so, on Ferzan's account, is not yet deserving of punishment) may be subject to state control, but only if he has committed an act in furtherance. But punitive interference is not intended as justification for the creation of attempt "crimes," precisely because where the crime is not complete punishment is not yet deserved. Punishment, with its traditional limits, is reserved for those who while competent violate the criminal law; punitive interference is reserved for those who by their own voluntary intent to cause harm and some act in furtherance of that intent awaken the state's right to preventive action. The act requirement is essential: "Allowing the state unfettered police power to intervene in lives based on mere intentions could certainly lead to abuse" (Ferzan 2014). She rejects entirely the idea of prediction-based interference: "what grounds prevention is not 'naked statistical evidence' but the actor's own choice and action."

These writers are attempting to justify moving certain apparently intractable cases across the line from criminal law to civil commitment; they take for granted the justice of using the criminal law, with its principle of legality, for the majority of cases. What is important for us to see here is that the question they are dealing with is how to deal with the "nightmare premise" without undermining the very structure of personal freedom.

If the limits on the power of the state are not justified by desert and moral responsibility, they are nevertheless called for by the very thing that justifies the criminal law in the first place, the preservation of the institution of personal freedom. For the threat to personal freedom under quarantine would not be felt only by those whose freedom is actually appropriated in the name of crime control. The value of personal freedom would be diminished for each of us. The inability to rely on fixed sentences under more or less precisely defined laws would create an area of ambiguity around each proclaimed type of danger, leading us to avoid activity that in any way seemed to border on that type of danger.

Even under an unjust system of criminal laws, as Hart has said, we are better off if the system of enforcement is just. How dreadful a legal system that punished homosexual activity would be, but how much more dreadful would a system be in which a *tendency* toward homosexual activity could all by itself result in detention for as long as the homosexual tendency persisted. We strive for a just system of criminal prohibitions; but we must strive for a just system of enforcement as well. That system can only be one with measured responses to violations of more or less precise prohibitions.

Section 4

> We must not allow optimism, or hope, or benevolence in these matters to carry us too far. We must not forget that when every material improvement has been effected in prisons, when the temperature has been rightly adjusted, when the proper food to maintain health and strength has been given, when the doctors, chaplains, and prison visitors have come and gone, the convict stands deprived of everything that a free man calls life.
>
> *(Winston Churchill, quoted in Radzinowicz & Hood 1979: 1348–1349)*

All of this is meant to show that however inefficient the principle of legality may be in protecting us against harm by other members of the community, its abandonment brings with it an even more undesirable consequence: a powerful and efficient state, armed with authority to subject the freedom of individuals to the needs of the state and determined to wipe out the danger that the freedom of self-determination must inevitably involve. The principle of legality, properly understood and properly implemented, is a compromise between the rights of the individual and the rights of the community. Much like the compromise represented by the doctrine of takings in property law, it permits the state to act in the interest of the community but draws a line beyond which the state cannot go. And much as the institution of private property would not have much meaning without a compromise of that sort, so the promise of personal liberty, that collection of rights whose boundaries are defined by the criminal law, would not have much meaning without the compromise that the principle of legality represents.

Even without the justification of retribution and desert, then, we should prefer something very much like classic punishment to something like quarantine. Accordingly, the proposed system of "correction" would limit the state in much the same way punishment does, permitting only those invasions sanctioned by the principle of legality. But the attributes of correction would not be exactly the same as the attributes of classical punishment. Correction must take into account the innocence of those whose freedom is to be taken away. In addition to imposing limits on the state, limitations required not by retribution but by the very liberty that criminal law sets out to protect, correction would require compensation.

Just as the takings doctrine insists on compensation for the appropriation of private property for public use, there should be some compensation for the appropriation of personal liberty for public use in deterring crimes. In neither case, of course, can compensation be compensation in full. There is no amount given in compensation in property law for the seized right to dispose of the property, but only what the individual property owner would have gotten on the market if he had disposed of the property himself. There are even more pressing reasons in the case of criminal justice why the state cannot muster full compensation for the taking of liberty: as Saul Smilansky has argued, the attempt to do that would bankrupt the state (Smilansky 2000).

But some compensation must be made, and there are the same two reasons for that in criminal justice as there are for compensation in property law. The first is that compensation would recognize the loss of liberty that the person detained must suffer in the cause of community welfare, a loss that he, not being morally responsible for the harm he has caused, does not deserve to suffer. It is a gesture made in the name of fairness, a reminder to all of the prisoner's contribution to the welfare of the community, to be publicized prominently, a reminder that what we do to him we do with regret.[5]

The second reason is to force the community to internalize a greater portion of the cost of criminal justice. So long as we believed that those who committed crimes deserved to suffer, we believed that we were justified in saddling them with the full cost of crime control – outside of the cost of maintaining the system itself. Their suffering and their loss of freedom, we thought, was deserved and the community had no obligation to share in the cost of it. The courts and the police have to be maintained, and the prisons must be paid for – the "overhead," so to speak. But where the community believes that those who are imprisoned deserve to suffer it can continue producing punishment in unwarranted amounts, satisfied that there is no unpaid debt to those who subsidize that production, that is, to those who lose their liberty to provide the "raw material" of enforcement. Should there be less expensive ways of preventing crime, less expensive, that is, than the tremendous cost to the lives of the prisoners and their families, there is no economic reason for the community to pursue those ways: letting prisoners bear the brunt of the cost, even if inefficient, is a windfall for the community.

Having given up the rationale of desert, we are left face to face with the enormous debt we owe those whose liberty we have appropriated in order to control crime. If those in prison are owed compensation in return for what they have given up, the community will have to bear some part of their loss. There will be two important consequences of requiring the community to bear part of the cost. Alternative ways of combatting crime – education, jobs, information – that were not serious contenders under a system in which penalties are liberally meted out on the basis of desert should immediately become more appealing. And there will be downward pressure on sentences, to keep them, and therefore the compensation for them, reasonable.

Section 5

The regime that I advocate, a regime for which the label punishment remains inappropriate, would adopt the principle of legality. In my book that principle owes its force not to some unmediated right to autonomy, but rather simply to the fact that a society that accepts that principle is by far preferable to a society in which either desert or danger controls the actions of the state and the community. The limitation to legality, though, still permits the community to largely externalize the cost of crime control onto those whose liberty is restricted in its name, and thus would permit us to impose such restrictions on the freedom of more people and for longer than is justified by the true cost of this method of crime control. Were criminals to deserve punishment this issue would not arise, but if we reject the notion of desert there will have to be some compensation for the sake of both fairness and efficiency.

Notes

1 In the United States it is generally considered to be part of the common law and it has been incorporated into the due process clauses of the Fifth and Fourteenth Amendments to the Constitution. A nice survey of the documents around the world wherein the principle is to be found is contained in "Rule 101: The Principle of Legality," on the page devoted to Customary International Humanitarian Law on the website of the International Committee of the Red Cross, https://ihl-databases.icrc.org/customary-ihl/eng/docs/v1_rul_rule101. The list comprises international covenants and conventions, including the Third and Fourth Geneva Conventions, the International Covenant on Civil and Political Rights, the Convention on the Rights of the Child, the Statute of the International Criminal Court; regional human rights conventions such as the European and American Conventions on Human Rights and the African Charter on Human and Peoples'

Rights; and many national constitutions and criminal codes ("The principle of legality is . . . part of most, if not all, national legal systems," Id.). It was set down in French Declaration of the Rights of Man and the Citizen (1789) and in the Universal Declaration of Human Rights (1948).

2 Those who are logically inclined may see this as the difference between saying, where "b" designates the behavior of the accused, "For all x, if x prohibits behavior similar to b, then sentence the accused under x," and "There is an x such that x prohibits behavior similar to b and you will sentence the accused under x."

3 The laws quoted above are no longer in effect: the Nazi and Soviet systems are gone, the Chinese provision was removed in 1997. According to Professor Li Yifei, Article 79 of the 1979 Code was replaced in 1997 by Article 3:

> For acts that are explicitly defined as criminal acts in law, the offenders shall be convicted and punished in accordance with law; otherwise, they shall not be convicted or punished.

(Personal communication on file with the author.)

4 Starting from a scenario in which an individual has ingested a drug which will cause him to inflict unacceptable harm on others within a few days, a scenario which we are expected to agree would justify preventive detention, Pereboom and Caruso move to the more general case:

> Now suppose that reliable neural screening reveals that an agent, if left in his normal environment, is virtually certain to engage in rape and murder in the near future. There is no known viable drug therapy, and mere monitoring would be ineffective. Should he be preventatively detained?
>
> *(Pereboom and Caruso 2018)*

The expectation is that seeing no relevant difference between this case and the original scenario we will agree that preventive detention is justified here and therefore wherever predictions of danger are reliable.

5 Bruce Waller has persuasively argued the unjustness and at the same time for the unavoidability of what we do in the name of criminal justice (Waller 2015). I'm not sure he would accept the idea of compensation.

References

Beccaria, Cesare, 1764/1963. *Of Crimes and Punishments.* (H. Paolucci trans. 1963).

Brudner, Alan, 2013. "Private Property and Public Welfare," in James Penner and Henry E. Smith (Eds.), *Philosophical Foundations of Property Law.* Oxford University Press.

Caruso, Gregg D., 2016. "Free Will Skepticism and Criminal Behavior: A Public Health-Quarantine Model." *Southwest Philosophy Review,* 32(1), https://philarchive.org/archive/CARFWS-3v9.

Chiu, Hungdah, 1992. "China's Criminal Justice System and the Trial of Pro-Democracy Dissidents." 24(3) *New York University Journal of International Law and Politics*, 1181–1202.

Corrado, Michael L., 2016. "Two Models of Criminal Justice," UNC Legal Studies Research Paper No. 2757078. Available at SSRN: https://ssrn.com/abstract=2757078.

Ferzan, Kimberly Kessler, 2014. "Moving Beyond Crime and Commitment," 13(2) *APA Newsletter on Philosophy and Law* 1–4.

Hart, H.L.A., 1968. "Punishment and the Elimination of Responsibility," in *Punishment and Responsibility: Essays in the Philosophy of Law*, Oxford: Oxford University Press, pp. 158–185.

Jackson, Robert H., 1946. "Closing Arguments for Conviction of Nazi War Criminals," 20(1) *Temple Law Quarterly*, 86–87 (quoted in Note, *Columbia Law Review* 1947, at p. 613).

Morse, Stephen J., 1999. "Neither Desert Nor Disease," 5 *Legal Theory*, 265–309.

Michelman, Frank I., 1967. "Property, Utility, and Fairness: Comments on the Ethical Foundations of 'Just Compensation' Law," 80 *Harvard Law Review*, 1165–1258.

Note, 1947. "The Use of Analogy in Criminal Law," 47 *Columbia Law Review*, 613–629.

Pereboom, Derk, 2001. *Living Without Free Will.* Cambridge: Cambridge University Press.

Pereboom, Derk, 2014. *Free Will, Agency, and Meaning in Life.* Oxford: Oxford University Press.

Pereboom, D., & Caruso, G., 2018. "Hard Incompatibilism Existentialism: Neuroscience, Punishment, and Meaning in Life." In G. Caruso & O. Flanagan (Eds.), *Neuroexistentialism: Meaning, Morals, and Purpose in the Age of Neuroscience*, pp. 193–222. New York: Oxford University Press.

Radzinowicz, Sir Leon, and Roger Hood, 1979. "Judicial Discretion and Sentencing Standards: Victorian Attempts to Solve a Perennial Problem," 127 *University of Pennsylvania Law Review*, 1288–1349.

Raimundo, Bernard, 1963. "Analogy Reincarnated: A Note on the Form and Substance of Soviet Legal Reform," 19 *Military Law Review*, 157.

Robinson, Paul, 2001. "Punishing Dangerousness: Cloaking Preventive Detention as Criminal Justice," 114 *Harvard Law Review* 1429–1456.

Slobogin, Christopher, 2003. "A Jurisprudence of Dangerousness," 98 *Northwestern University Law Review*, 1–62.

Smilansky, Saul, 2000. *Free Will and Illusion.* Oxford: Oxford University Press.

Starosolsky, George V., 1950. "Basic Principles of Soviet Criminal Law," 28 *University of North Carolina Law Review*, 359–374.
Von Liszt, Franz, 1893."Die deterministischen Gegner der Zweckstrafe" [Deterministic Opponents of Purposive Punishment], 13 *Die gesamte Strafrechtswissenschaft* (1893) 325–370, at 357–368. Translated in Fraser 2007.
Walen, Alec, 2011. "A Unified Theory of Detention, With Application to Preventive Detention for Suspected Terrorists," 70 *Maryland Law Review* 871–938.
Waller, Bruce, 2015. *The Stubborn System of Moral Responsibility*. Cambridge, MA: MIT Press.
Yung, Corey Rayburn, 2011."Sex Offender Exceptionalism and Preventative Detention," 101 *Journal of Criminal Law and Criminology*, 969–1004.

30

HOW TO TRANSFORM A STATIC SECURITY PRISON INTO A DYNAMIC ORGANISM FOR CHANGE AND GROWTH

Arne Kvernvik Nilsen and Ekaterina Bagreeva

Introduction

Contemporary European research clearly shows that prisons are ineffective as a tool to reduce recidivism, with some 70% of people committing further crime within two years after release. At the same time, sciences like genetics deliver numerous arguments for a bio-social concept of criminal behavior which raises questions of locus of control, free will and its management. Increased international mobility as a result of migration is also presenting socio-cultural challenges within the penal system. Furthermore, the current socio-economic situation defies the laws of retributive justice and requires a different approach to the question of "crime and punishment."

In this chapter we suggest a model for radical penal reform. It is presented in the form of 12 principles united as metaphorical spokes in a "Wheel of Dynamic Change" (see Figure 30.1). These principles can help to transform a static security prison into a dynamic organism (for more on this, see Principle 12, on page 385). The thinking behind our approach is influenced by existentialist philosophy,[1] as well as an understanding of human ecology,[2] Gestalt therapy,[3] field theory,[4] phenomenology[5] and Makarenko pedagogy.[6]

A good understanding and positive implementation of all 12 principles across a penal system can improve the inmates' chance of socio-cultural rehabilitation and raise levels of public security – to mention just two of many positive outcomes. During Arne's years as governor of the Norwegian open/medium security Bastøy prison, he developed and implemented some of the 12 principles, and others were already implemented. A study of Norwegian prisons (Kristoffersen 2013)[7] showed an average recidivism rate of 21% during the two-year period after release; the recidivism rate from Bastøy prison for the same period was 16 %.

Principle 1 – The Prison Sentence Must Be Limited to Deprivation of Liberty. Full Stop!

Although international agreements such as the European Prison Rules (COE, 2006)[8] state that no punishment given to a prisoner should inflict more strain than strictly necessary and that a prison sentence must be limited to deprivation of liberty, the reality is quite different. The voices of former inmates tell the story that the loss of freedom is not always the worst element of the

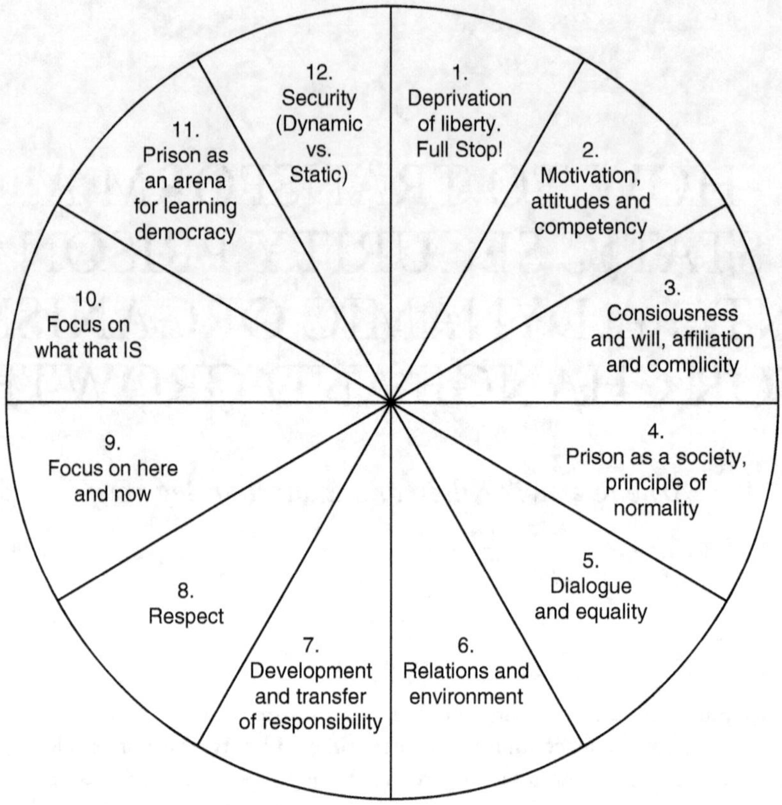

Figure 30.1 Transforming a static system into a dynamic organism: the 12 principles in the Wheel of Dynamic Change.
Source: The authors.

punishment. Many unintended elements, such as living in toxic and negative surroundings, or the injury of isolation, have severe undesirable consequences. Many inmates develop social anxiety and depression, and they leave prison in a worse psychological condition than when they arrived. Criminals are often people who to some extent have failed to integrate socio-culturally into society. If they are to have another chance to integrate successfully, then prison needs to be a platform for acquiring and practicing the skills required rather than serving as an incubator for the most disintegrated members of the community who on release will present an even greater danger to others.

The Norwegian penitentiary system has experienced an increase in the use of objective requirements, external standards and scorecards during the last few years. Yet the principle that prison punishment should be limited to the loss of freedom is still stated only as an executive principle rather than a firm requirement. If this is due to the complex nature of making the measurements, the voices of former inmates, their opinions, can provide an excellent source of information. Loss of freedom during a prison punishment is an important principle also because it is connected to the primary need for revenge among the wider population, well hidden under the statement *the public sense of justice*. In addition to this, stereotypes, lack of personal experience, as well as political and ideological attitudes are all obstacles to the process of humanizing our prisons. Thus, the limitation to deprivation of liberty is a postulated principle rather than the reality of today. However, if a prison and its entire staff were constantly focused on practicing this principle as a kind of quality barometer, there would be massive positive consequences both for inmates and employees. Conversely, if the opposite practice is true, then inmates are exposed to unintended psychological harm that can make their socio-cultural integration even more problematic, resulting in a larger security challenge for society at large.

Principle 2 – Prison Staff Motivation, Attitudes and Competencies

All 12 principles are strongly dependent on the quality and standard which each of them measures. Of all the resources in prison that have either positive or negative consequences for inmates and affect the recidivism rate, the *quality of human capital*, the prison staff, is by far the most important. The prison staff by definition covers *all* people working within the prison at different levels and carrying out a variety of tasks. In performing their tasks, it is the individual rather than the precise role or quantity of people that matters.

The quality of prison staff starts with the motivation behind their choice of career and is further affected by attitudes towards prisoners and colleagues, as well as the continued development of competencies. It is important to foster an awareness of the vulnerability of prison organism due to its specific nature, and that each person will inevitably influence its dynamics for good or bad, and is *never* neutral.

The personality and competency requirements for the individuals who opt to work in prison are diverse. On the one hand, they will need empathic skills, the ability to build a dialogical relationship, while on the other, they must be able to set boundaries, as well as resist attempts at and avoid being manipulated, and at the same time controlling the wish to defend themselves; this is the balance that they must master. But personal motivation and overall attitude are just as vital as having the necessary skills. Their absence will create a negative environment in the prison, and in time bring about a variety of psychological issues for those working there.

To acquire a better understanding of someone's personal motivation for working in a prison, the following topics should be raised in an interview: working with people in a difficult situation in life and the wish to contribute to safe socio-cultural reintegration; facing challenges with some risk involved; ability to manage a position of power; maintaining a daily dialogue and wanting to care. In screening applicants, one should be particularly wary of those motivated by a desire to use force and enjoy a position of authority over others. The personal attitudes of prison staff play a crucial role in the prison organism, and their behavior will either facilitate dynamic security, or result in a need for static security, isolation and force. For this reason, it is advisable during recruitment, training and employment always to challenge the development of negative attitudes.

In Norway, training for prison officers takes two years. The courses' focus should be adjusted so as to follow developments in human ecological reasoning and foster a holistic understanding of the prison organism. Within this framework, knowledge about the damage that isolation can cause, dynamic rather than static security, the use of dialogue, relationships and motivational skills should be core subjects. In addition, critical attention should be paid to how prison staff are influenced over time by inmates' culture, their behavior and attitudes, and the fact that they are spending hours, days and years side by side with criminals: people who suffer from the loss of freedom and possibly have problems with antisocial behavior, drug abuse and poor self-image. It is worth noting that there are numerous research reports on inmates, but very few studies have been made of prison staff within the prison and cohesion within the prison environment.

Principle 3 – Consciousness and Will, On Affiliation and Complicity

When asked the question "Who are you?" many people will reply with a job title. Working as a member of the prison staff is a position of great impact and power. For this reason, the individuals selected to work within the prison environment should be asked if they are aware of the power they represent, *why* they want to possess it, and *how* they intend to manage it.

There are at least two types of power: formal power resulting from a title and role in the prison, and an informal power which it is more difficult to be conscious of and recognize the potential of. It is therefore particularly important to identify and acknowledge the difference between one's position and role versus the situation in which one is acting. Regardless of their role in the prison organism, it is vital for prison staff to remember that they first of all hold a position of great power that must not be abused. Secondly and regardless of type of crime, background or personality, inmates are in a vulnerable situation due to their loss of freedom, even though their behavior and attitude from time to time can radiate misleading signals.

Working in a prison is thus a balancing act between a genuine wish to understand "who am I and how am I managing my power-position?," the desire to be an active part of the prison environment, and a conscious choice to take and delegate responsibility. However, it seems that avoidance is a "21st century disease": escaping responsibility, not taking sides, lying low, denying one's influence on the case at hand – these all seem to be hallmarks of an emerging lifestyle for many people. The reason for such an approach may appear to be a lack of knowledge and understanding that some cases and situations in fact *require* our conscious decision to execute change and that this constitutes a responsibility that cannot be left to either circumstance or another person.

One of the many challenges for people working in prison is consciously assuming responsibility for the way they manage their power: their behavior, their choices in creating and maintaining a dialogue, their ways of relating to and communicating with other prison staff and inmates, and handling their own reactions as well as feelings of frustration, anger and fear. Another challenge is to know oneself to the point of being aware of one's abilities in conducting a dialogue, as well as being able to provide the necessary support and guidance to inmates through difficult circumstances. A prison where the conscious use of one's power and participation in dynamic processes is not among the central principles of its staff will surely suffer from uncertainty, mistrust and poor dynamics, resulting in an environment that is detrimental to the functioning of the organization.

Principle 4 – Prison as a Society, cf. Principle of Normality

The concept of "normality" has through time been discussed within the sciences, and it seems to a great extent to be influenced by professional, political, cultural and religious beliefs. Thus, this concept can mostly be evaluated in relative, and not in absolute terms. "Normality" was introduced to the Norwegian penitentiary system as one of the most important concepts for prison punishment in the White Paper (2007–2008) entitled "Punishment that works – less crime – safer community." The principle of normality is considered one of the core values of the penitentiary system today. However, a better adjustment of prison conditions to embody this value would reduce the unintentional harm of the punishment and further improve the socio-cultural reintegration of inmates.

From one point of view, it is questionable if the word "normal" can be used at all in describing a prison environment; after all, there is no perfect community "out there." But by creating a prison as a small local community with its own problems and challenges, it is possible to expose inmates to the experiences they need in order to acquire essential life skills, communication, in particular. Thus, the inmates should not be overprotected from life's complexities, but rather be assigned responsibilities and have a platform for learning and practicing management of everyday challenges.

Best efforts should be made to create a prison community that as much as possible resembles communities in open society. If such work is not done, inmates will sorely lack reintegration training during their stay in prison with the result that those who have served long sentences there will at best return to open society in the same state as before. *Much more frequently, however, these persons will return to society representing an even greater threat than before they went to prison.*

It is a sad fact that politicians more often than not have chosen to prioritize escape security above ensuring that prison inmates present *less of a threat to society after their time in prison.* In evaluating this situation, many researchers have over time shown that the intimidating power of punishment is more myth than reality. In fact, it is quite possible to develop a prison that is very much like an ordinary local community with its challenges and daily routines.

An example of such a facility is Bastøy prison. The most important condition there is that inmates can spend their time in prison living in an environment as close to an open society as possible. They possess rights and have duties and responsibilities in organizing their everyday life within the framework of their incarceration. This includes the domains of housing, provision of food, work, school, leisure time activities, access to natural surroundings, freedom to move and public services. Besides these services, inmates should have commitments and be provided with opportunities to participate in forums influencing the administration of the community, its challenges and tasks.

Principle 5 – Dialogue and Equality

What might be a better prison? Consider a prison where inmates' punishment is limited only to the loss of freedom and the attitude of prison staff is to motivate career choices, as well as developing relevant skills and competencies. This would be an institution in *which employees are choosing to be an active part of the overall prison community along with the inmates.* The idea is that the totality of the prison body is functioning like a small local community inspired by the principle of normality. This is a modern and humane place to send individuals who, according to the court, should be punished for their crime with loss of freedom.

In an environment in which daily routines and institutional culture are often characterized by pressure, anxiety, anger and other, repressed emotions, it can be challenging for prison staff to maintain their focus on equality during episodes of rage from inmates. Many conflicts are rooted in the absence of dialogue and equality, as well as in the traditional opposition between the two main groups of people in prison: the inmates versus the prison staff.

What does dialogue and equality mean within the prison walls? *Dialogue is a communication between two persons in which the focus is not on their roles and statuses, but rather on where they intersect: what is happening in the middle and between the two.* Dialogue is much less a message or an order, but rather an exchange of opinions and reflections, understanding and experience in that moment. *It is one of dynamic energies exchanged, shared in the middle of the communication field at a particular moment.*

Dialogue is *only* possible if the participants understand and admit to being *equals.*

Dialogue should be a frequently used tool in prisons in order to reduce stress, misunderstanding and frustration, and strengthen the perception of being part of a community, as well as ensuring positive dynamics.

A prison in which the first four principles are implemented but dialogue and equality are not practiced as values and method is much more exposed to stress, with frustrated prison staff and aggressive prisoners, resulting in poor and even risky handling of conflicts.

Principle 6 – Relationships and Environment

All 12 principles must be well integrated in order to achieve the holistic effect of the prison organism which promotes the purpose and goal of the institution.

Environmental therapy is a well-known term in the penitentiary system of Norway. Unfortunately it is impossible to apply this principle unless awareness of and competence in the role, together with an awareness of and focus on the relationship, force and impact of each person within the prison organism is established. This is why *relationships and environment* is an important principle in the "wheel of change."

Prisons have always been an institution, or rather an organism, built on the use of force and focusing on differences, statuses and distance. The use of uniforms for prison staff is just one example of how to create a sharp separation between staff and inmates. One sad reality is that the more we distance ourselves from "the others" in prison and thereby create an excluding and exclusive environment, be it in the way we dress or communicate, the less reason we have to expect positive effects such as the successful reintegration of inmates into society after their prison stay and decreasing recidivism rates.

Unfortunately, interpersonal connections and relationships within this environment have rarely been considered a primary tool and method for achieving positive effects from incarceration, such as: security for everybody, absence of conflict and successful socio-cultural reintegration after release. Regardless of the methods used, extended research into modern psychotherapy shows that the key to success is a positive relationship between therapist and client. We believe that a similar focus on positive relations between prisoners and prison staff can constitute an important element in bringing beneficial changes in the behavior, thinking and attitude of prisoners.

Bastøy prison was declared a human ecological prison with the focus not on "Them versus us," but rather on creating a common communicative and behavioral field where inmates and prison staff can meet, interact and communicate through joint activities in both the internal and external environments. The unique setting of this prison – located on a picturesque island in a fjord – provides extra resources, giving the inmates an opportunity to be an integral part of this eco-environment. Daily routines include working side by side with the prison staff in everyday settings: in the stable, on the sports field, on the ferry, on the farm, in the fields, greenhouses and workshops. Such activities provide convincing experience of being an important part of the environment rather than being excluded from it. For this reason, it is also important that prison staff be provided with training in how to build and maintain positive relationships, as well as being made acutely aware of being a part of a particular group or environment.

Principle 7 – Development and Transfer of Responsibility

A typical misunderstanding in traditional reasoning about prison sentences is that we send criminals to prisons to *make* them responsible for their choices and behavior. It is difficult to name a place other than a nursery where people are given so little responsibility as in prison! In high security prisons it is the director and the prison staff who traditionally carry the 24-hour total responsibility for inmates. Prisoners are awakened, served food, shepherded to and from meetings, work, school and activities, all within the prison walls.

It is a provocative thought that the inmates' main task is in fact not to take any responsibility, but to adapt and follow the rules! Prison leaves very little room for decisions, responsibility and everyday dilemmas, as the majority of the daily needs of the population are already taken care of, up to the day they are released. Afterwards, when they are released, they will easily get frustrated, having *lost the ability to face the hardships of reality and responsibility for every step you make.* No wonder that many inmates feel that the punishment starts when they go back to open society, as the time spent in prison was a time in limbo without plans, goals or apparent meaning. Of all the mistakes made by and through a prison as an institution, removing responsibility from the inmates is one of the worst. It leads to an inability to live in an open society and increases recidivism! Unless there are objective reasons for such a course of action (age, illnesses, etc.), every inmate should be given a platform for development and be enabled to take responsibility for his actions and the decisions he makes during his time in prison.

In Bastøy prison, a large part of daily management is given to the inmates. It is *their responsibility* to get out of bed at the right time, to be on time when attending different meetings, to cook for themselves, buy food, arrange activities, provide for common well-being, take care of animals and different natural resources, etc. The majority of the people who served their prison sentence in Bastøy show positive behavioral changes, and express gratitude for these opportunities to succeed. In rare cases, however, prisoners have requested transfer to a traditional high security prison where every step is guarded and directed by prison staff, as they felt that the everyday responsibilities given to them in Bastøy were too much of a burden.

The sad fact is that, when politicians discuss the *principle of responsibility* being given to prisoners, they have a tendency to polarize the issue in the question: "Should we punish the criminals or should we send them to holiday camp?"Very few politicians have ever visited prison or possess an adequate understanding of its true functioning and the psychological aspects of a prison stay. Apparently, taking responsibility for your actions on a daily basis is hard in both open and closed society. Conversely, the question should rather be: should we provide people who have committed crimes with an opportunity to *take and master responsibility*, or merely set their lives on hold with no expectations of a positive behavioral change?

The simple fact is that the main task of a prison should be to do everything in its power to reduce the possibility of new crime after an inmate has been released. So, while Bastøy prison in Norway may look like a holiday camp from the outside, it is a rather tough regime on the inside, *designed for people to achieve integration into mainstream society through acceptance of responsibility for their own lives.* Even though a prison will always ensure that prisoners receive their sentence and punishment, it should also inculcate *a sense of responsibility for how* they are going to handle their time in prison and thereby prepare for a life in the outside world.

Principle 8 – Respect

It seems that a prerequisite for respect towards others is first and foremost a respect for oneself. Prison is a place where a lot of people struggle with this issue: respecting other people, their integrity and possessions. Some prisoners seem to have lost respect for themselves and others rather early in their lives; others never really understood what self-respect was. For many people, their first encounter with this issue was in prison: Once arrived, prisoners are informed that they are expected to show respect for the penitentiary regime, the prison staff, as well as laws and rules. Inmates have to demonstrate an appreciation of the "rules of the game" and prison staff, depending on the rank and amount of stars on the staff uniform.

In Bastøy, Arne implemented an *entrance routine* that included a conversation between the governor and each new inmate arriving on the island, where the main topics were *responsibilities and respect.* However, instead of focusing on the prison routines and rules, the newcomers were asked questions related to self-respect and self-esteem. Many inmates seemed to be surprised by this approach and found it difficult to talk about. Only as a second step, after discussing self-respect, were topics of reciprocal and equal respect towards fellow inmates, prison staff, animals and the environment naturally discussed.

At the end of their sentence in Bastøy, many prisoners reported that *their attitude towards self-respect* and self-acceptance had changed: "Earlier, I used to look at myself as a 'dirt bag,' but gradually, I discovered that I am an OK person." Such a positive development can only come when the prison staff are expected to treat and communicate with the inmates in the same way they are treating their colleagues. This was confirmed by many inmates on the day of their release. In such an environment, inmates gradually develop a natural respect for people and their surroundings, rather than merely unwillingly submitting to the rules in order to avoid punishments. For a dynamic and living organism such as a prison, there is hardly anything which is more provocative and destructive than condescending and rude behavior towards the inmates simply because they are prisoners. Any misuse of power has an extraordinarily devastating force, feeding a vicious circle as the lack of focus on developing the self-respect of the inmates in prison will result in prisoners' reduced respect toward the regime and prison staff!

> Respect yourself and others will respect you.
>
> *(Confucius, 551–479 bc)*

Principle 9 – Focus on Here and Now

It is difficult if not impossible to imagine how one would have reacted to and survived time in prison without actually having experienced it. Perhaps "exist" rather than "survive" would be a better choice of words? Some inmates *live in the past,* being burdened by traumatic memories and shame, and not in the present "here and now." Others are trapped in denial and anger, many suffering from deprivation of family and friends and *concerns about the future.*

People have the ability to remember, but also to dream, hope, fantasize and escape from the everyday reality of life with the help of thoughts. A lot can be said about the negative sides of such mental "escapes," but they allow us to deal with hurtful moments of our lives for some time: seconds, minutes, weeks. But if mental escapes from the reality become a chronic condition, *a person loses the opportunity to make decisions, experience choices and the feeling of being alive in the moment.* Life cannot be experienced in the past or in the future, but only here and now.

Prisoner societies in general and the penitentiary system of Norway in particular are to a great extent influenced by the dominating paradigm of "what is in" (i.e., the new big idea) and "what works." Previously, this meant that inmates were to explore how their pasts led to criminal behavior. The current paradigm, however, follows a different path: their futures. The Norwegian penitentiary system has for many years focused on measuring the number of inmates who were helped in developing a detailed plan for the future. *However, a long sought-after change in behavior is a day-to-day process, rather than an event you can just plan or wish to happen.* For this reason, the principle of "here and now" is a key platform for a positive change, as one cannot put life on hold and expect to blend into it later. Living in the moment, being able to reflect on and reason with one's steps *here and now* is a better way to prepare for the future.

Prison staff who lead activities connected to the future of inmates should have the proper skills and competencies to help prisoners discover, experience and research what is happening to oneself at this moment, this hour, day after day during the stay in prison. Getting lost in the world of painful memories or insecure futures without asking what is happening and can be changed here and now is a typical trap for prison staff in conversations with inmates. Furthermore, since it is impossible to change the past, the time in prison *should be focused on the awareness of one's personality and resources, and mastering life in its small moments.* A prison that does not have an understanding and methods to help inmates keep their focus on here and now will succumb to the role of an ice-box – where very little positive behavioral change can be expected.

Principle 10 – Focus on What IS

From time to time it seems necessary to remind ourselves of the obvious: A prisoner is more than his crime. Inmates are often stigmatized as a group of people who are different than the rest of the society, such as the prison staff. Criminals, prisoners, inmates and convicts are often spoken of as a homogeneous group of people: The belief that all people sent to prison belong to a particular group and those working in the penitentiary are a different type from the open society is far from reality. There is just as much variety in people in prison as in the rest of the population. Nevertheless, it is important to mention that among prison citizens in Norway more than 60% are suffering from serious social and health problems that often are among the reasons behind their crimes: addictions or psychological issues and often a combination of these two.

It is important to find and *see the person behind the sentence and his crime.* Prison staff should master an attitude towards the inmates focused on the human being, rather than his crime and its reasons. Such an attitude towards prisoners cannot be considered a guarantee that the reasons for crime will disappear, but can be *a platform on which to start a positive change, as well as reduce the psychological harm from the prison stay.* Our self-image is largely dependent upon the feedback on our behavior from people around us. When people start seeing our positive sides we are more likely to accept our better selves as well. Thus, empowerment of positive sides and discovery of a person's resources regardless of one's past *should be the main attitude towards inmates.* If the prison culture fails to produce positive focus and dialogical relations it risks causing a toxic negativity that spreads throughout the prison organism, creating dangers for both inmates and prison staff.

Principle 11 – Prison as an Arena for Learning Democracy

Spending weeks, months and even years behind bars, without responsibility for anything but your own behavior, with no opportunity to partake in and influence the surroundings or development, the community will gradually build up negativity and apathy in many people. Numerous inmates return from prison to an open society without having learned anything about contribution and without developing responsibility or an understanding of democracy. Often, self-proclaimed "representatives" of the inmates in the prison community are willing to present their demands and complaints but not accept any of the obligations that come with such a position.

To deal with issues of proper representation in Bastøy prison, Arne introduced an *Island Council* (Prison Council) in 2013. This council was established through a democratic election process based on the model of a municipal government. All the units in the prison were represented: both inmates and prison staff. These representatives were chosen by inmates and prison staff from their respective units. The Council was set up and governed based on enacted rules covering elections, council tenure, etc., and it processes and makes decisions about many aspects of life within the prison. In principle, there are only two areas in which the council is not allowed information or access: prison staff and prisoner issues, as these are both confidential and are governed according to external laws and regulations and in dedicated forums.

Following the creation of the Council, the list of complaints and demands from inmates was gradually reduced and the engagement and will to actively partake in a positive dynamic environment increased significantly. The Island Council was established in order for inmates to gradually contribute and assume their share of responsibility for their closest environment. The areas of learning and experience were numerous and essential, and inmates learned to represent others and not only present a personal opinion, learned how to manage a dialogue between representatives from both inmates and prison staff, learned about leadership, economy and total management, mastered staying loyal and defending decisions made. In that process they acquired an understanding of the basic principles of democracy.

If a prison is to function as a dynamic organism in an environment where both inmates and staff experience the surroundings as healthy, educational and progressive, an active participation and involvement is required. If there is a lack of democracy, humanity and collaboration, the slow degradation of the human psyche will at some point result in revolt.

Principle 12 – Security

All of the principles associated with the 12 spokes in *the wheel of a dynamic prison organism* are equally necessary and important. Mentioned last is *the principle of security*, which is obviously vital for a prison institution. The position in the sequence of this principle is due to the fact that *only when all other spokes are in place can the transformation from static to dynamic security in prison be made possible.*

Traditional widespread models to provide escape security, prison staff security, inmates' security and legal protection are based on static security: concrete walls, cameras, barbed wire, metal grids, alarms, as well as counting and other control measures. These measures are only at a very limited level based on the knowledge of human behavior, understanding of psychological factors or the consequences to the human psyche and personality. This is particularly apparent when considering recidivism rates and cases and the incidence of violent behavior in prisons. In fact, many of the security needs in prison *can* be resolved through dynamic security factors such as *people to people communication*, and common activities between prison staff and prisoners.

Bastøy prison is a unique example of how a dynamic versus static security regime influences the psychological condition of inmates, their behavior, management of life and skills development during their incarceration. This Norwegian prison located on an island has through the years experienced effective ways of prioritizing dynamic security. The prison has become known, not because of its unique and beautiful natural surroundings, but rather because of *an absence of violence and threats* even though this is a medium level security prison where the majority of the inmates have been convicted of murder, violence, or other serious crimes. Prisoners are left almost alone on the island at night and on the weekends with only four or five prison staff present.

A number of skeptics of this regime have tried to point out what terrible consequences might arise from such a security approach with regards to both inmates and prison staff. However, the plain truth is that none of these forecasts has materialized. Once they have become familiar with and gained experience in working in a dynamic security prison, the staff say that they would rather not return to a static security prison again. Furthermore, almost all inmates who transfer from high security prisons to Bastøy show a very strong positive change after spending time on the island. The absence of a static high security regime combined with extended freedom and responsibility for their own behavior, surroundings and daily routines, resulted in a decrease in stress, anger, fear and depression.

Implementation of the previously mentioned 11 principles combined with an elevation of the competence level of the prison staff in the mechanisms of dynamic security *will minimize the reasons and need for static security.* On the other hand, *when more priority is given to static security, more reasons and a greater need for such a model will accrue.*

A reduction or absence of good relations, contact and dialog with staff, loss of being a part of a positive and dynamic environment, loss of respect and responsibility and loss of a certain freedom to handle and live life day by day: these are some of many reasons why increased static security measures *have a negative impact* upon many inmates. Being locked up in the cell or subject to other static security measures will in many cases cause aggressive attitudes, threats and violence by inmates. The inmate's mental state and health might in many cases be worsened. *This happens because, as human beings, we are not equipped with skills to handle such treatment!* It is a frightening fact that after many centuries' use of static security prisons, we have not learned a lot. There should be no more need to explain the assertion "*when more priority is given to static security, more reasons and a greater need for such a model will accrue.*"

Closing Remarks

Our chapter focuses on the essential factors and tasks required to outline and establish a new model for prisons based on humanistic psychology and humane ecology. The principles presented are also founded on experience and practices in operational prisons.

A prison operated and characterized by the implementation of these 12 principles, values and methods is a prison requiring far greater effort and responsibility from each individual inmate: more work, more participation, clear feedback from staff if and when prisoners violate the terms and rules governing their incarceration. In addition to reactions and feedback from the staff, such a prison will encourage and spur reactions, requirements and expectations from other parts of the prison population as well. This is due to the fact that such a prison operates as a living organism in which all are involved – both prisoners and staff.

There will always be some inmates who, due to their personality or noticeable issues or problems – such as a prolonged and heavy exposure to drugs – will find it exceedingly difficult to function in such a prison. Regardless of this, there are numerous arguments in favor of such a reform – based both on humanistic as well as socio-economic perspectives.

A prison based on the 12 principles presented here will not be a "holiday camp for criminals," but rather a place where the convicted inmates are introduced to the demands and expectations that society has imposed on them as a reaction to the crime and damage they have committed. In addition to being a humane location for convicts to serve their sentences, this prison will also be a place which many victims of crime will consider an appropriate punishment for the offender. At the same time, many victims would probably benefit from visiting the facility to rid themselves of the myths and misconceptions that are prevalent in the wider society today. It is also important to stress that the need for closure and security that the victims of crimes may and often do feel have been clear in the minds of the authors and are incorporated into the model on a theoretical as well as a practical level.

Notes

1 Our existentialist influences are Søren Kierkegaard (1813–1855) and Martin Heidegger (1889–1976); see, in particular, *Væren og tid* (English: *Being and Time*), Martin Heidegger, State University of New York Press, 2010.
2 *Human Ecology – Basic Concepts for Sustainable Development*, Gerald G. Marten, Earthscan Publications, 2001.
3 *Gestalt Therapy.* Frederick Perls, Ralph F. Hefferline and Paul Goodman, Souvenir Press Ltd,1992; *The Healing Relationship in Gestalt Therapy*, Richard Hycner and Lynne Jacobs, Gestalt Journal Press, 1995.
4 *Field Theory in Social Science,* Kurt Lewin (edited by Dorwin Cartwright Lewin), American Psychological Association (APA), 1964
5 Edmund Husserl (1859–1938) is considered the founding father of phenemenology. See, for example, *The Philosophy of Edmund Husserl and Its Interpretation,* Joseph J. Kockelmans, Doubleday, 1967.
6 *The Basis of Legal Education,* Gennady Davidov, Pedagogic, 1976; *Return to Makarenko,* Elena Bagreeva, National Research Institute of the Penal system of the Russian Federation, 2006.
7 *Relapse Study in the Correctional Services of the Nordic Countries*, Ragnar Kristoffersen, Kriminalomsorgens utdanningssenter [The University College of Norwegian Correctional Service], 2013.
8 *European Prison Rules*, COE (Council of Europe), 2006.

31
TOWARDS A STRENGTHS-BASED FOCUS IN THE CRIMINAL JUSTICE SYSTEM FOR DRUG-USING OFFENDERS

Charlotte Colman and Eva Blomme

Although the exact nature of the relationship between drug use and offending is complex to understand, it is clear that a connection exists between these two phenomena. In fact, research on this topic stresses that not only do a substantial amount of drug users have experience with committing offences, but also that persons in the criminal justice system have higher rates of drug use (disorders) compared to the general population.

In this chapter we focus on criminal justice responses to offenders who come into contact with the criminal justice system because of committing drug-related offences. This applies to cases in which individuals violate specific drug laws (such as the possession of drugs), but mainly when they commit certain offences to finance their drug use (such as shoplifting or thefts), or when they commit an offence under the influence of drugs (Bennett and Holloway 2005). We focus specifically on those drug-using offenders whose offending is motivated by their drug use.

The relationship between drug use and offending has implications for the relationship between the processes of refraining from drug use, recovery, and refraining from offending, desistance. Consequently, desistance and recovery should be regarded as related processes that need to be considered jointly when developing criminal justice interventions targeting this group of drug-using offenders (Colman 2015).

A considerable body of research has highlighted that a strict repressive approach towards this group of drug-using offenders is not beneficial. After all, recidivism rates are higher with offenders who served prison sentences compared to drug-using offenders who received a non-custodial sentence (Andrews and Anderson 2006; Woldgabreal et al. 2014). Prison, in particular, may generate deprivation and criminogenic effects jeopardizing successful reintegration and long-term recovery and desistance (Spohn and Holleran 2002; Camp and Gaes 2005). Cloud and Granfield (2008), for example, have indicated that incarceration could represent a barrier to recovery and desistance due to the loss of personal and social resources, combined with discrimination and stigma from the public.

As a consequence, a growing group of policy makers are convinced that incarceration is not the right answer for these drug-using offenders. Moreover, treatment options in prisons are often limited, encouraging these authorities to divert drug-using offenders away from the criminal justice system.

The referral of these drug-using offenders from the criminal justice system to treatment programs relies on rehabilitative functions of punishment (Bean 2014; Bennett and Holloway 2005). Historically, however, the criminal justice system has struggled with finding a balance between punishment and protecting public safety on the one hand and offender rehabilitation on the other hand (Barton 2006).

Traditionally, the criminal justice system starts from deficit-based approaches mainly seeking to reduce risks and offence-related behaviors (Woldgabreal et al. 2014). Although these approaches are a well-documented starting point from which to develop individualized interventions, they are based on factors predicting criminal behavior, rather than factors predicting desistance or recovery (McNeill 2012). Rather than being defined in terms of "risk" and "need," drug-using offenders also possess personal and social strengths and resources enabling them to desist from offending and recover from drug use (McNeill 2012). A strengths-based client-empowering approach, influenced by the positive psychology movement, is suggested to complement older, risk-oriented approaches. Over the past decade, the emergence of this movement has influenced sentencing practices, striving to balance the traditional focus on risks and deficits with a renewing strengths-based approach integrating protective factors (Woldgabreal et al. 2014).

This chapter is organized into three sections. The first section will elaborate on the relationship between drug use and offending to clarify the relationship between these two phenomena. While this first section focuses on the onset of drug use and offending, the second section will highlight the processes of refraining from drug use and offending and thus elaborates on the link between recovery and desistance. These two sections provide an empirical basis for our third section in which we first examine the role of the criminal justice system in recovery and desistance and second, the reasons why we should apply more strengths-based principles within this system. Together, these three sections aim to contribute to the growing number of studies calling for a greater focus on holistic, desistance- and recovery- oriented practices in the criminal justice system for drug-using offenders.

The Complex Relationship between Drug Use and Offending

The relationship between drug use and offending has been widely studied (Bennett and Holloway 2005; Bean 2014; Bennett and Holloway 2009; MacCoun et al. 2003; Pierce et al. 2015; Stevens 2007). Two main assumptions could be drawn from this large evidence base. First, drug use seems to be more common among offenders. Studies have repeatedly shown that higher proportions of arrestees and inmates have used drugs (in a problematic way) compared to the general population (Fazel et al. 2006; Fazel et al. 2017; Hunt 2014; Bennett et al. 2004; Belenko and Peugh 2005). Drug use also appears to increase the intensity and frequency of criminal behavior (Chaiken and Chaiken 1990; Caulkins and Kleiman 2011). Second, a considerable number of clients in drug treatment programs report having committed offences (van der Zanden et al. 2007; Hayhurst et al. 2013).

There are different theories on how drug use and offending might be connected. In fact, four types of relationships can be broadly identified: (1) drug use leads to offending, (2) offending leads to drug use, (3) an external variable leads to drug use and offending and (4) drug use and offending have a bidirectional relationship (Bennett and Holloway 2005).

Theories on drug use leading to offending often rely on the tripartite framework of Goldstein (Goldstein 1985). This framework identifies three subcategories of drug-related offences: psycho-pharmacological offences, including offences committed under intoxication; economic-compulsive crime, involving offences committed to finance drug use; and systemic crime, in which certain aspects of the marketing of drugs (often linked with the illegal character of drug markets) cause offending (Caulkins and Kleiman 2011); these subcategories are often supplemented by a fourth – drug law violations (EMCDDA 2007). Another theory argues that offending leads to drug use, in which drug use is a part of a criminal lifestyle (Bennett and Holloway, 2005). Some refer to the subculture theory when explaining this theory. The subculture theory hypothesizes that offenders already circulate in an environment that is supportive of drug use, making access to drugs easier (Bean 2014). A third explanation refers to a common factor of both drug use and offending (Bean 2014; Bennett and Holloway

2005). This theory holds that a third variable (such as poor social support systems or deviant peers) leads to both drug use and crime. Lastly, some theories mention a bidirectional relationship between drug use and crime, in which drug use sometimes leads to crime and crime sometimes leads to drug use (Bean 2014; Bennett and Holloway 2005).

While it is clear that a connection exists between these two phenomena, the exact nature of this connection remains highly debated (Bennett and Holloway 2005; Bennett and Holloway 2009; Bean 2014; Stevens et al. 2003). That is to say, rather than a causal relationship between drug use and offending, a large body of literature merely confirms an association between both phenomena. The strength of this association *per contra* varies across type of drug, type and intensity of offending (Bennett et al. 2008; Best et al. 2001) and the characteristics of the individual or the setting (Bean 2014). For instance, MacDonald et al. (2008) report that participants in treatment programs who use alcohol and/or cocaine, are more often involved in violent offences, which was to a lesser extent the case for cannabis users. Moreover, MacDonald et al.'s research indicates that other variables such as lifestyle or one's attitude towards regulations seem to have an additional influence on the connection between drug use and offending (Macdonald et al. 2008). Similarly, Bennett, Holloway and Farrington (2008) have found that the odds for offending were 2.8 to 3.8 times higher for drug users compared to non-drug users. The odds for offending were particularly high for crack-users, followed by heroin users. Even recreational drug use was linked to offending, although the odds for offending were much lower compared to more problematic levels of drug use, which seems to confirm the variations in intensity of drug use. Additionally, the results vary among types of offences: the use of heroin, crack and cocaine enhances the odds of shoplifting and involvement in prostitution. Lastly, evidence suggests that there is variation in the drug-offending association when characteristics of the drug user (such as gender or age) were taken into account (Bennett et al. 2008).

Thus, the evidence clearly shows an association between drug (mis)use and offending, yet this does not necessarily mean this relationship is causal (Bean 2014; Colman and Vandam 2009). The latter would imply that all drugs users are criminally active, or that all criminals are drug users and that is – of course – not the reality (MacCoun et al. 2003). Studying causal relationships is also complicated and entails some methodological challenges, including the introduction of a comparison group of non-drug users. In practice, research on the drug-offending association often lacks this comparison group of non-drug users (Bennett et al. 2008), or suffers from selection bias due to the limited selection of respondents either from treatment facilities (with a high proportion of drug users) or from the criminal justice system (with a high proportion of offenders) (Bean 2014). Additionally, research seems to pay less attention to the socio-demographic features of the individuals involved in offending and drugs use, as well as to other circumstantial variables, although these might (partly) explain the differences in type of drug (mis)use and type of crime (Bean 2014; Stevens 2007).

The Relationship between Recovery and Desistance

The aforementioned relationship between drug use and offending as well as the common overlap in populations involved in the two activities (Bennett et al. 2004) has implications for the relationship between the process of refraining from drug use, recovery, and desistance, the process of refraining from offending.

The concepts of and explanations for recovery and desistance have varied over time and place. Some define recovery as "sobriety": "a voluntarily maintained lifestyle characterized by sobriety, personal health and citizenship" (Betty Ford Institute Consensus Panel 2007). A growing number of scholars, however, do not limit recovery to sobriety, but focus on the person's quality of life (Colman and Vander Laenen 2012; Valentine 2010), relating to their individual experience of recovery. In other words: people themselves defines when they are in recovery. It is clear that recovery emphasizes the experience of an improvement of quality of life and the feeling of empowerment throughout this process (Best and Laudet 2010). As a result, recovery also includes a sense of belonging in the community, meaning, purpose and hope. Recovery is mostly considered as a process rather than an abrupt event with an end state, as people in recovery engage in a process of personal and social transition (Best et al. 2016).

There is a strong rationale that recovery could be explained by (a combination of) three components. In this regard, a growing body of recovery research has been dedicated to the concept of "recovery capital" (Cloud and Granfield 2008; Best and Laudet 2010). Recovery capital (White 2008) consists of the range of personal, social and community resources that facilitate recovery. "Personal recovery capital" consists of physical capital such as health, as well as educational/vocational skills, self-esteem, sense of meaning and purpose in life. "Social recovery capital" includes supportive and prosocial relationships with family or friends. "Community recovery capital" refers to the attitude, policy and perception of the community related to recovery (-oriented initiatives). It encompasses initiatives to reduce recovery-related stigma and the availability of support and treatment in local communities (White 2008).

As with recovery, a growing number of scholars also point to desistance as a process. McNeill, Farrall, Lightowler and Maruna (2012: 2), for example, define it as "the long-term abstinence from criminal behavior among those for whom offending had become a pattern of behavior." Fairly recently, some desistance researchers made distinctions between phases in the desistance process. In this regard, Farrall and Maruna (2004) distinguished "primary" desistance, defined as an offence-free period, from "secondary desistance," entailing the successful orientation towards a (permanent) offence free life, including the construction of a (new or former) identity as a non-offender. A decade later, McNeill (2014) added "tertiary desistance" to Farrall and Maruna's dual framework focusing on the recognition of the offender's change by the community.

Desistance is also mostly understood in its interaction between internal and external elements such as changes in identity and informal social control (Giordano et al. 2002; Sampson and Laub 1995). In contrast to recovery, desistance mainly focuses on socially desirable outcomes – a reduction in offending – and less on client-reported outcomes. Still, over the past decade, criminologists have increasingly adopted aspects of the Good Lives Model (Ward and Stewart 2003), which could be considered as the counterpart of quality of life in recovery research (see above).

Although recovery originated as a central concept in mental health and addiction research, and desistance originated in criminal career criminology, researchers (Best et al. 2017) argue that desistance research and theory could learn from the emerging evidence base around recovery research and *vice versa*. As a result, our knowledge of both recovery and desistance could be enhanced. After all, theories on desistance and recovery share common ground: they are both transformational processes which are not linear but dynamic, gradual and subject to relapse. Moreover, similar internal and external components, including personal, social and community resources, seem to influence both processes of change (Colman 2015; Marsh 2011).

However, despite the focus on the link between the (onset) of drug use and offending, far less attention has been paid to the relationship between refraining from drug use and offending. The extrapolation of evidence from these two areas remains scant and few (empirical) studies assess the relationship between recovery and desistance. These few studies recognize a relationship between recovery and desistance and indicate that the road to recovery and desistance is different for the population involved in both drug use and offending (Best et al. 2017). One of these studies, elaborating on the recovery–desistance relationship in a population of drug-using offenders, shows that they perceive recovery as more important than desistance (Colman 2015; Colman and Vander Laenen 2012). Respondents indicated that their offending and drug use were related and that, to them, their desistance process is subordinate to their recovery process. Although the inclusion criteria of this study related to both drug use and offending, it became clear that most respondents viewed themselves mainly as recovering drug users rather than as desisting offenders. In this regard, most respondents were identified as primary drug users, who committed offences, rather than as primary offenders using drugs. Consequently, they acknowledged recovery as the first step to desistance (Colman and

Vander Laenen 2012). To the drug-using offenders included in the study, recovery was, however, not synonymous with sobriety: some respondents still used drugs, but in a significantly reduced way.

Sullivan and Hamilton (2007) highlight the need to focus on the reasons for developing and refraining from offending and drug use and to obtain a career perspective, rather than a sole focus on the onset of drug use and offending. Research conducted by Colman (2015; Colman and Vander Laenen 2012) confirms that not only recovery and desistance are related but that the relationship between drug use and offending has repercussions for the relationship between recovery and desistance. Similar results were found in other studies. Marsh (2011) indicates that sustaining desistance depends on sustaining recovery. Sullivan and Hamilton (2007) observe that although recovery is not sufficient for desistance, a decline in recovery and desistance often occur simultaneously. Likewise, other studies acknowledge the positive influence of recovery from drug use on desistance without discussing in detail the connection between desistance and recovery (Davis et al. 2013; Wooditch et al. 2014).

Recovery and Desistance in the Criminal Justice System

Because of the symbiotic relationship between drug use and offending, a large number of drug-using offenders could be found at different levels of the criminal justice system, from pre-trial stage to prison. They include both primary drug users who have committed drug-related offences and primary offenders who have used drugs. Research indicates that especially primary drug users, who have been using drugs or who have developed substance use disorders prior to their arrest, account for a substantial proportion of conviction and incarceration rates in many countries (Belenko et al. 2013). In this chapter, we focus on primary drug users whose offending is motivated by their drug use.

Taking into account the above-mentioned link between recovery and desistance and the fact that to most drug-using offenders recovery is equally or even more important than desistance (Colman 2015; Colman and Vander Laenen 2012), criminal justice actors should focus more on the drug-using problem instead of primarily or solely focusing on the offending. If adopting this focus, prison sentences should be avoided and other, non-custodial sentences should be favored. In practice however, we notice that many drug-using offenders end up in prison. Based on data from 74 countries worldwide, the United Nation Office on Drugs and Crime (UNODC) estimated that among convicted prisoners, drug-related personal consumption offences accounted for an estimated 18% of the global prison population (UNODC 2016).

However, custodial responses, in particular imprisonment, do not seem to achieve success in reducing drug-related offending (Stevens et al. 2003; Mitchell et al. 2017; Spohn and Holleran 2002) or improved psychosocial functioning (Massoglia 2008). Moreover, research shows that recidivism rates are higher with offenders who served prison sentences compared to offenders who received a non-custodial sentence provided in the community, especially within a sample of drug-using offenders (Andrews and Anderson 2006; Woldgabreal et al. 2014; Spohn and Holleran 2002). Spohn and Holleran (2002) speculate that the prison context may be criminogenic, as it weakens inmates' social bonds. Offenders sentenced to prison may therefore be less prepared to return to the community, making it more difficult to reintegrate after their sentence. This view is supported by Camp and Gaes (2005), who hypothesize that inmate culture and prison regime have a criminogenic effect. Non-custodial sentences, including the supervision of offenders in the community, may prevent people from experiencing these debilitating circumstances by letting them, amongst other things, maintain contact with the community (Woldgabreal et al. 2014).

In the following sections, we will focus on the diversion of drug-using offenders from the criminal justice system to treatment. This diversion relies on rehabilitative functions of punishment (Bean 2014; Bennett and Holloway 2005). As mentioned above, the criminal justice system has historically struggled to find a balance between punishment and protecting public safety on the one hand and offender rehabilitation on the other hand (Barton 2006). Recent changes, including improved screening and assessment, the promotion of strengths-based interventions, as well as the implementation of evidence-based treatment, have helped to find a balance between these competing demands (Barton 2006).

Treatment as One of the Pathways to Recovery

Recovery has many pathways that should ideally be tailored to fit the unique needs of each individual. While taking a repressive approach to drug-using offenders seems counter-effective, there is promising evidence of the beneficial effects of treatment on reducing drug use and related criminal behavior (Mears et al. 2003; Stevens et al. 2003). Therefore, there is a growing need to provide appropriate, individualized, evidence-based treatment for drug-using offenders. Imprisonment should be avoided and diversion to treatment should be available at earlier stages of the criminal justice system for those in need of it (UNODC/WHO 2016).

Although drug treatment will not be needed by everyone who seeks recovery, for some it may be one of the pathways to recovery. After all, drug treatment can be associated with reductions in drug use, the odds of offending and costs to society, as well as improved public safety and well-being for both the person and their direct environment (UNODC 2018; Holloway et al. 2006; Gossop et al. 2005).

These results are, however, not univocal for all types of treatment and it is clear that some treatment approaches may work better with some individuals than with others. Treatment should be based on scientific evidence and individualized to match the unique needs and coping style of each client. In general, positive results are found for a range of psychosocial interventions reducing drug use, drug-related problems and criminal activity (National Institute on Drug Abuse 2012; Dutra et al. 2008). Examples of these evidence-based approaches include contingency management (CM), motivational interviewing (MI), cognitive behavioral therapy (CBT) and therapeutic communities (TC) (NICE 2007). For psychostimulant misuse, for example, a systematic review of 52 randomized controlled trials (RCTs) found that psychosocial interventions (compared to no intervention) were effective in increasing recovery and reducing treatment dropout (Minozzi et al. 2016). Opioid substitution treatment (OST) programs have been identified as a key model for the treatment of opioid users (Mattick et al. 2009). Furthermore, a positive and supportive environment and the availability of a continuum of care including aftercare (recovery management) seem to gain better results (Joe et al. 1999; Mears et al. 2003). Also, treatment programs with an integrated and multi-methodological approach targeted at the participant's various social and mental health problems seem to be more promising than those programs that focus exclusively on the drug-using problem (Mears et al. 2003). When looking at the effectiveness of drug treatment programs in detail, research reveals that the characteristics of the participants (such as age, socio-economic background, mental and physical health) and psychosocial factors (such as motivation, family support) seem to have a meaningful influence on the outcome of a program, too (Bukten et al. 2012; Holloway et al. 2006). This implies that not all treatment programs are a good fit for every individual. Nevertheless, they could be effective for specific target populations and/or under some conditions (Holloway et al. 2006). It should, however, be noted that most evaluation studies focus on the short-term effectiveness of treatment interventions with a follow-up between one and two years. Thus, there is insufficient data about their long-term effectiveness on recovery, highlighting an urgent focus for further recovery studies (Laudet et al. 2002).

Generally, the above-mentioned evidence suggests that the criminal justice system may provide an opportunity for alternative (more effective and more humane) answers to drug use and associated criminal behavior in drug-using offenders (McCollister et al. 2004). Diversion from the criminal justice system to drug treatment programs as an alternative to more punitive sanctions could provide effective treatment to offenders with an underlying drug-using problem. Thus, the criminal justice system could be a window of opportunity and reach a group in need of treatment who might otherwise not receive it (Chandler et al. 2009).

Many countries therefore provide different linkages to a range of treatment programs at the different stages (ranging from pre-trial, trial and post-sentencing) of the criminal justice process. The promotion of these non-custodial measures is based on certain fundamental principles enshrined in various international legal documents.[1] At pre-trial stage, police and prosecuting authorities can exercise a degree of discretion to divert offenders to treatment programs instead of arresting or prosecuting them. At the sentencing stage, where most of the alternatives are situated, judges can opt to refer an offender to a treatment program instead of more severe punishment including a prison sentence. Some jurisdictions even have specialized drug treatment courts, where offenders are referred from the criminal justice system to drug treatment programs before being convicted (see below). At the post-sentencing stage, an offender can receive a conditional release when s/he has served a minimum term in prison. One of these conditions can be treatment for their drug-using problem (Belenko et al. 2013; UNODC/WHO 2018) and these non-custodial measures should be categorized in such a way that consistent sentencing remains possible. The type of alternative offered should depend on a thorough screening.

Criminal justice referral to treatment programs at each of these stages consists of a diverse range of treatment options. The type of treatment should depend on a thorough assessment conducted by treatment professionals (Tokyo Rules 1990). As mentioned before, treatment is not a one-size-fits-all. Drug users in the criminal justice system should also have access to the same level and quality of treatment and health care as the general population.[2] Treatment programs for criminal justice clients generally operate through various government agencies and private organizations within the community which means that services for criminal justice clients and voluntary patients are mostly overlapping.

Most offenders entering treatment after a diversion from the criminal justice system do this under legal coercion. This means that legal consequences may be deferred, reduced or even lifted when the offender participates in a treatment program. The decision whether or not to enter the treatment program remains with the person concerned. In other words, the offender still has a choice (i.e. s/he has to give her/his consent to be referred to drug treatment) (UNODC 2018; Seddon 2007).

This aspect in particular – the judicial coercion to enter a treatment program – is often criticized precisely because of this "coercion" component. Since motivation is recognized as an essential aspect in treatment participation and success, some authors argue that pressuring an offender into treatment contradicts this (Klag et al. 2005). They state that clients referred from the criminal justice system might not yet be ready to fully engage in treatment as they could lack internal motivation. Research has shown, however, that clients in drug treatment experience pressure from a number of sources and thus may experience coercion from informal sources such as friends, employer, parents and/or partner, if not from formal sources like the criminal justice system (Klag et al. 2005; Seddon 2007). Furthermore, Prendergast et al. (2009) show that offenders who are referred from the criminal justice system to treatment programs are more likely to believe that they chose to enter a treatment program than that they were forced into treatment; they are not necessarily unwilling clients. This illustrates that even for this target group of judicially coerced clients, treatment can still be useful.

Furthermore, research findings on the effectiveness of criminal justice referral to treatment in reducing drug use and offending in different populations and settings are mixed, yet promising, when compared to traditional jurisprudence (Lipsey and Cullen 2007; Mitchell et al. 2007). Regardless of some methodological constraints, studies that compare rehabilitative punishment (i.e. a diversion to treatment) to other sanctions, generally show lower recidivism rates for the offenders that received rehabilitation treatment (Lipsey and Cullen 2007). Additionally, research has indicated that treatment instead of punishment saves money. Even taking into account the preconditions and resources for the delivery of evidence-based treatment, the costs for treatment are lower than the indirect costs caused by untreated substance use disorders (e.g., prisons, unemployment, law enforcement, health consequences, etc.).

Several preconditions are needed, however, in order for this diversion to be effective. First, treatment interventions offered under judicial pressure need to be evidence-based and follow the same standards of good medical practice as voluntary treatment for them to be effective. Second, screening and assessment at the various stages of the criminal justice system are essential to identify offenders in need of treatment as well as to match the offender to the most adequate treatment trajectory. The intensity of the treatment program should be adjusted to the individual needs of the offenders (Mears et al. 2003). Offenders with low chances of recidivism do not respond well to intensive treatment programs (Andrews and Bonta 2010). The Risk, Need and Responsivity (RNR) model, also known as "What works," has become the dominant paradigm in risk and needs assessment in this context, connecting *an* offender's *level of risk* and *criminogenic needs* to the intensity of supervision and treatment. It therefore enables treatment providers to develop a treatment plan for individual offenders based on their assessed level of risk, areas of criminogenic need and personal learning style. Judicial-supervised treatment can use the RNR assessment at nearly all points of the criminal justice system to make decisions regarding the level of supervision and treatment an offender needs (Andrews and Bonta 2010).

Looking Beyond the Risks and Focusing on Empowerment

With the RNR model as a leading paradigm, it is clear that the criminal justice system generally suggests risk-driven criminal justice interventions involving the drug-using offender in a merely passive role. Traditionally, the criminal justice system starts from these deficit-based approaches, mainly seeking to reduce risk and offence-related behaviors (Woldgabreal et al. 2014). Although these approaches are an evidence-based starting point from which to develop individualized interventions, these interventions are based on factors predicting criminal behavior rather than factors predicting desistance (McNeill 2012). While risk factors such as anti-social attitudes and negative relationships are indeed associated with reoffending and as such are adequate predictors of offending behavior and judicial outcomes, targeting individual strengths could allow them to serve as protective factors (Woldgabreal et al. 2014).

Besides risks and needs, drug-using offenders also possess personal and social strengths and resources enabling them to desist from offending (McNeill 2012). More recently, the Good Lives Model (GLM) has been promoted as a complementary model to RNR. Willis and Ward (2010) argue that GLM has many links with desistance because of their similar theoretical concepts and their way of including the (social) context. Instead of primarily diagnosing weaknesses and focusing on recidivism risks and criminogenic needs, GLM recognizes the need to build on the strengths of offenders taking a client-empowering approach (Ward and Brown 2004). This strengths-based rehabilitation approach, influenced by the positive psychology movement, aims to complement the more traditional, risk-oriented approaches of which the RNR model is the best known. This alternative response to offending has emerged against the backdrop of prison overcrowding combined with increasing recidivism rates (Woldgabreal et al. 2014). Over the past decade, the emergence of this movement has influenced sentencing practices all over the world, striving for a balance between the historic focus on risks and deficits and a strengths-based approach integrating protective factors (Woldgabreal et al. 2014). So, while risk and needs- assessment remains important, the strengths of the offender must also play a part in sentencing practices.

In this regard, McNeill (2006) calls upon criminal justice actors to add a strengths-based and integrated approach to rehabilitation inspired by desistance research and practices. After all, desistance and rehabilitation are interlinked since desistance could be regarded as a core objective of rehabilitation (McNeill 2012). McNeill argues that offender management services, such as probation services, should see themselves as supporters of the desistance process, instead of mainly as providers of correctional services. The desistance and recovery process is owned by the offender him/herself, not by the providers. In this way, the professional intervention, including treatment, should be regarded as part of a broader process that belongs to the person undergoing desistance and recovery.

Consequently, the communication between the professional and the drug-using offender during an intervention is of vital importance (Weaver 2009). The content and the desired outcome of the intervention should be developed together with the client instead of being imposed on him or her. The drug-using offender should evolve from a passive actor (risk-approach) to an active actor (strengths-approach) during the intervention. They should be given a "voice" in their own desistance and recovery process by collaboratively defining the details of the intervention. The client should be empowered to take responsibility of her/his future by actively participating in the intervention and by being supported by professionals to strengthen their personal and social resources. Furthermore, the language used by professionals should focus on the future, rather than on past, their former criminal behavior, drug use and level of risk.

Example of a Promising Strengths-based Approach in the Criminal Justice System for Drug-using Offenders: the Drug (Treatment) Court

Strengths-based approaches could be integrated into all stages of the criminal justice system. Today we see an increasing number of criminal justice initiatives focusing on a balance between risk and strengths approaches, of which the drug (treatment) courts at sentencing level are exemplary.

Drug (treatment) courts were first introduced in the United States in 1989, and their popularity quickly rose in the following years (Wolfer 2006; Harrison and Scarpitti 2002). Other countries later introduced similar concepts, mostly based on the US model and adapted to their national (judicial) context (Harrison and Scarpitti 2002). Drug (treatment) courts, although varying greatly in eligibility criteria, procedure and treatment models, share the common goal to combine drug treatment with judicial supervision to move offenders towards long-term recovery and desistance (Mitchell et al. 2012). In general, during a drug (treatment) court trajectory the person and her/his treatment trajectory is emphasized rather than the criminal case itself. When treatment is deemed successful, the charges can either be dropped or the criminal case can be dismissed (Mitchell et al. 2012).

If implemented appropriately and taking into account the emerging evidence base regarding recovery and desistance, drug (treatment) courts hold considerable promise as a strengths-based alternative to traditional punishment. After all, drug (treatment) courts are different from traditional courts as they intend to be less punitive and actively cooperate in the rehabilitation process of a drug-using offender (Wolfer 2006; Goldkamp et al. 2001). Most drug (treatment) courts start from the client's needs and strengths and focus on increasing her/his empowerment, enabling the client to take responsibility for their successful trajectory (Dekkers et al. 2016). In general, drug (treatment) courts start from the broad definition of recovery, rather than the strict one focusing on abstinence alone. This is illustrated by the fact that relapse does not necessarily mean that the client is excluded from a drug (treatment) trajectory. Rather it indicates that adjustments in their treatment plan may be required. Additionally, these courts address impairment in other life domains (e.g., employment, financial situation, social network) too (Wolfer 2006), as problem drug use is often associated with problems within these other life domains (Laudet and White 2010). Previous studies have indicated that these additional interventions have beneficial outcomes regarding psychosocial functioning and criminal behavior (Leukefeld et al. 2007; Wittouck et al. 2013).

Life After Punishment: The Hard Work of Recovery and Desistance Happens in the Community

Recovery and desistance are individual processes happening in a social context rather than in a vacuum. Improving the offender's strength is not only required at an individual level, but also at a community level.

The importance of the role of the community has been acknowledged in both recovery and desistance research. In recovery research we see this reflected in the concept of community recovery capital (Cloud and Granfield 2008). Starting from this concept, Best and Savic (2014) developed the notion of "negative community recovery capital," describing the barriers to recovery and effective reintegration including discrimination, stigma and exclusion by the general public and professionals (Best et al. 2017). In desistance research, we already acknowledged the distinctions some scholars made between phases in the desistance process (Farrall and Maruna 2004; Nugent and Schinkel 2016). While much has been written about the role of personal transformation in desistance (see for example Paternoster and Bushway 2009), some have argued that personal change is not sufficient as the community must also accept this new identity of the person in desistance (Maruna 2001; Nugent and Schinkel 2016). As mentioned above, McNeill (2014) therefore added "tertiary desistance" to Farrall and Maruna's dual framework of "primary" and "secondary" desistance (2004) focusing on the recognition of change by the community and the fact that desistance is a social process as much as a personal journey.

The reality is such that many drug-using offenders will face significant structural barriers to community involvement. In practice, we find two main problems. First, criminal justice clients, including drug-using offenders, are not well-prepared to go back into society. Starting from desistance research, McNeill (2012) argues that the rehabilitation of offenders leading to desistance should include interplay between psychological, moral, legal and social elements. While research and practice have mainly focused on the psychological (internal) elements of rehabilitation such as identity, cognitive transformation, agency and self-control, Kewley argues that social, moral and legal elements need equal support in order to promote desistance and successful re-integration (Kewley 2016). The social element of rehabilitation should focus on intimate prosocial relationships with family and friends as well as the relationship with the wider community. After all, people often lack the resources and social relationships necessary to establish a new identity and promote/sustain desistance. The moral element refers to the fact that currently punishment offers limited opportunities for repair between the offender and the victim. Punishment mainly focuses on the offender, less on the conflict itself, the victim or the community. The legal element refers to the fact that the legal system, such as prosecution and incarceration rituals, might cause harm to the rehabilitation of the offender because the current legal processes support stigmatization and exclusion, jeopardizing the opportunities for an offender in desistance to return to the community as a prosocial member. In view of this, McNeill pleads for the development of a "more fully integrated and interdisciplinary theory and practice of rehabilitation" (McNeill 2012: 19), incorporating social, moral and legal elements besides the psychological elements in rehabilitative interventions.

Second, even when drug-using offenders have the necessary psychological and social resources to promote and sustain recovery and desistance, we notice that society is not always willing, or prepared, to accept these individuals back into the community (Cano, Best, Beckwith et al. 2019). While personal and social capital seem necessary to initiate desistance and recovery, the role of the (wider) community is crucial in providing opportunities to sustain the process (Best and Savic 2014). Effective community reintegration is an integral part of all successful desistance and recovery journeys: social structures, such as employment, housing and education, have to be configured so that the individual is afforded the necessary opportunities to complete the reintegration process (Best and Colman 2018).

However, the community is not always supportive towards persons who (problematically) use drugs and offend, not even towards those in recovery and desistance. On the one hand, there is considerable evidence highlighting the stigma people in both active addiction and in recovery are facing. In 2010, the United Kingdom Drug Policy Commission (UKDPC) commissioned a survey of 3000 adults living in private households across the UK (Jones et al. 2011). The findings indicated that people endorse the importance of supporting individuals in recovery and the need for them to reintegrate in the community. However, they do not want them as neighbors and are fearful of having treatment and support services in their neighborhoods. Nearly half of the respondents agreed that "people with a history of drug dependence are a burden to society" and over 40% agreed that "I would not want to live next door to someone who has been dependent on drugs" (Jones et al. 2011). In an earlier version of the survey (UKDPC 2008), almost two-thirds of employers who participated in a survey reported that they would not employ a former heroin or crack user even if they were fit for the job.

Additionally, criminal justice clients face stigma as well, both from the general public, the criminal justice actors and the criminal justice system. For example, in certain jurisdictions, a conviction includes an ineligibility to vote or disqualifications to participate in certain job activities, leading towards reduced citizenship (Lacey and Pickard 2015). Discrimination may also occur because of their criminal record impeding job opportunities, housing and relationships. Particularly the relationship between unemployment and offending has been widely documented, indicating that people are less likely to (re-)offend when they are employed. Employment also provides financial stability making reintegration easier (Sampson and Laub 1995). However, a study examining employers' attitudes towards hiring former offenders found that over 60% of employers would "probably not" or "definitely not" hire an individual with a criminal record (Holzer, Raphael and Stoll 2004: 7).

Furthermore, drug-using offenders face dual stigma considering the combination of their drug use and offending. Research indicates that the stigma associated with criminal offending also contributes to the stigma surrounding drug use (Pickard 2017). This becomes apparent also in the language the public is using towards them. Drug-using offenders are more likely to be labelled as "an addict" or "junkie" by the public, and negative adjectives are more often attached to these labels compared to people who only use drugs (without committing other offences) (UKDPC 2008).

These studies acknowledge the negative effects of stigma on drug-using offenders (Room 2005). The enduring stigma and discrimination may result in limited resources to attain full citizenship, creating obstacles to (sustaining) recovery and desistance (Uggen et al. 2004). After all, stigma and discrimination could impact several life domains, such as access to quality employment, housing and social relationships (Radcliffe and Stevens 2008). All these domains are vital components of recovery, desistance and community reintegration. What is also troubling, is that this stigma and discrimination did not markedly diminish when persons were described as being in recovery or desistance (instead of active addiction and offending), suggesting that, for many people, a substance use disorder and an offence leave an irreversible stain (Cano et al. 2019)(Philips and Shaw 2013). Such attitudes are central to the idea of "disintegrative shaming" (Braithwaite 1989) in which exclusion persists beyond official sanctions (Best and Colman 2018).

For the most part, the aversion among members in our community towards drug-using offenders, even when they are in recovery and desistance, is not based on personal experiences (Cano et al. 2019). Less negative attitudes have been found among those people who currently, or in the past, had lived, worked or were related to someone with a history of drug use or offending, compared to those who did not. This indicates that contact is generally associated with lower levels of stigmatizing behaviors and attitudes, suggesting that stigma could be tempered by increasing personal contact and experience (Batastini et al. 2014). Therefore, not only the person in desistance and recovery needs to be empowered (see above), the community needs this empowerment as well. In this regard, Weaver (2009: 24) indicates that citizens should be involved more in criminal justice decision-making or be actively engaged in restorative justice work.

In a recent publication, Best and Colman (2018) plead to promote the idea of building inclusive cities, an initiative to support the creation of Recovery-Oriented Systems of Care at city level (White 2008). The aim of Inclusive Cities is to make recovery visible, to celebrate it and to create a safe environment supportive to recovery. It actively engages all citizens in the recovery process. Some of the most promising examples of projects that fit within this idea of Inclusive Cities come from the restorative cities model (for example ACT Reform Advisory Committee 2017) where a range of governmental processes have been amended to increase inclusion and to reduce adversarial and discriminatory practices. Examples could be the organization of recovery weeks including recovery events where citizens can meet, or setting up a social enterprise to help people in recovery to learn a skill and thereby increase their job opportunities. The method and the outcomes of Inclusive Cities are predicated on improvements in connectedness, inclusion and civic participation, leading to greater bridging and bonding capital and stronger, more connected communities. Although the Inclusive Cities model starts from recovery to improve reintegration and social inclusion at city level, it aims to extend this model (in the near future) to other groups experiencing social exclusion, such as persons in the dual process of recovery and desistance.

Conclusion

The relationship between drug use and offending has implications for the relationship between the processes of abstaining from drug use (recovery) and offending (desistance). Research has indicated that recovery and desistance are related processes and that, especially in primary drug users, recovery is considered as the first step towards desistance. It is thus reasonable to consider that when developing criminal justice interventions for drug-using offenders equal attention should be paid to recovery and desistance.

There are many pathways leading to recovery and desistance. In this chapter we have focused on one particular pathway linked to the criminal justice system, namely a diversion to treatment. Drug treatment has proven its effectiveness in achieving recovery (including psychosocial improvements) and desistance. Treatment under judicial supervision seems to generate positive outcomes as well. Of course, not every drug-using offender will benefit from treatment and therefore it needs to be stressed that adequate and proper screening and assessment are essential in this process.

Up until today, the criminal justice system has been trying to balance punishment and the protection of public safety on the one hand and rehabilitation of the offender on the other hand. Starting from a health-oriented approach, dealing with drug-using offenders in the criminal justice system requires a flexible system of criminal justice interventions, allowing authorities to propose measures appropriate to each individual, including individualized diversion to treatment or other health care measures. This may in part be in response to the increase in prison overcrowding, including for drug-related offences, along with a recognition of significant shortcomings in prison systems when it comes to reducing drug use, reoffending or increasing possibilities for social reintegration.

Historically, most of these interventions are based on risk-driven approaches, considering the drug-using offender in a passive role. While risk factors such as anti-social attitudes and negative relationships are indeed associated with reoffending and as such are adequate predictors of offending behavior and judicial outcomes, drug-using offenders also possess personal and social strengths and resources enabling them to desist and recover. Instead of primarily diagnosing weaknesses and focusing on recidivism risks and criminogenic needs, there is a growing acknowledgement of the need to build on the strengths of offenders in an empowering, client-oriented approach. This strengths-based rehabilitation approach, influenced by the positive psychology movement, aims to complement more traditional, risk-oriented approaches.

In this chapter we have suggested that a strengths-based, client-oriented approach, starting from the emerging recovery and desistance evidence base, should be further expanded, implemented and promoted. The criminal justice system should focus on an integrated model promoting the use of more holistic, comprehensive approaches that are not solely based on risk factors. We propose that the effectiveness of interventions could be further improved if, besides psychological factors, equal attention was devoted to social and community factors promoting successful reintegration, recovery and desistance. Additionally, the drug-using offender should play an active role in this process and the community should also be empowered given its pivotal role in sustaining recovery and desistance.

Notes

1 Such as the United Nations Standard Minimum Rules for Non-custodial Measures (The Tokyo Rules), resolution 45/110 adopted by General Assembly on 14 December 1990
2 United Nations Standard Minimum Rules for the Treatment of Prisoners (the Nelson Mandela Rules), resolution 70/175 adopted by the General Assembly on 17 December 2015

References

ACT Reform Advisory Council (2017) *Canberra – becoming a restorative city. Issues Paper on legal and justice issues relating to restorative practices*, Canberra: ACT Law Reform Advisory Council.

Andrews, D. A. and Anderson, J. (2006) *The Psychology of Criminal Conduct*, Newark: Aufl. Anderson.

Andrews, D. A. and Bonta, J. (2010) 'Rehabilitating criminal justice policy and practice', *Psychology, Public Policy, and Law*, 16(1), 39.

Barton, W. (2006) 'Incorporating the strengths perspective into intensive juvenile aftercare', *Western Criminology Review*, 7(2), 48–61.

Batastini, A. B., Bolanos, A. D. and Morgan, R. D. (2014) 'Attitudes toward hiring applicants with mental illness and criminal justice involvement: The impact of education and experience', *International Journal of Law and Psychiatry*, 37(5), 524–533.

Bean, P. (2014) *Drugs and Crime,* Routledge.

Belenko, S., Hiller, M. and Hamilton, L. (2013) 'Treating substance use disorders in the criminal justice system', *Current Psychiatry Reports*, 15(11), 414.

Belenko, S. and Peugh, J. (2005) 'Estimating drug treatment needs among state prison inmates', *Drug and Alcohol Dependence*, 77(3), 269–281.

Bennett, T. and Holloway, K. (2005) *Understanding Drugs, Alcohol and Crime,* McGraw-Hill Education.

Bennett, T. and Holloway, K. (2009) 'The causal connection between drug misuse and crime', *British Journal of Criminology*, azp014.

Bennett, T., Holloway, K. and Byron, C. (2004) *Drug use and Offending: Summary Results of the First Two Years of the NEW-ADAM Programme,* Home Office Research, Development and Statistics Directorate.

Bennett, T., Holloway, K. and Farrington, D. (2008) 'The statistical association between drug misuse and crime: A meta-analysis', *Aggression and Violent Behavior*, 13(2), 107–118.

Best, D., Beckwith, M., Haslam, C., Alexander Haslam, S., Jetten, J., Mawson, E. and Lubman, D. I. (2016) 'Overcoming alcohol and other drug addiction as a process of social identity transition: the social identity model of recovery (SIMOR)', *Addiction Research & Theory*, 24(2), 111–123.

Best, D. and Colman, C. (2018) 'Let's celebrate recovery. Inclusive Cities working together to support social cohesion', *Addiction Research & Theory*, 1–10.

Best, D., Irving, J., Albertson, K. J. A. R. and Theory (2017) 'Recovery and desistance: what the emerging recovery movement in the alcohol and drug area can learn from models of desistance from offending', 25(1), 1–10.

Best, D. and Laudet, A. (2010) 'The potential of recovery capital', *RSA Paper London*.

Best, D., Man, L.-H., Gossop, M., Harris, J., Sidwell, C. and Strang, J. (2001) 'Understanding the developmental relationship between drug use and crime: Are drug users the best people to ask?', *Addiction Research & Theory*, 9(2), 151–164.

Best, D. and Savic, M. (2014) 'Substance abuse and offending: Pathways to recovery' in *Working within the Forensic Paradigm*, Routledge, 259–271.

Braithwaite, J. (1989) 'Criminological theory and organizational crime', *Justice Quarterly*, 6(3), 333–358.

Bukten, A., Skurtveit, S., Gossop, M., Waal, H., Stangeland, P., Havnes, I. and Clausen, T. (2012) 'Engagement with opioid maintenance treatment and reductions in crime: a longitudinal national cohort study', *Addiction*, 107(2), 393–399.

Camp, S. D. and Gaes, G. G. (2005) 'Criminogenic effects of the prison environment on inmate behavior: Some experimental evidence', *Crime & Delinquency*, 51(3), 425–442.

Cano, I., Best, D., Beckwith, M., Phillips, L. A., Hamilton, P., & Sloan, J. (2019) 'Stigma related to health conditions and offending behaviors: Social distance among students of health and social sciences', *Stigma and Health*, advance online publication: 1–15.

Cano, I., Best, D., Hamilton, P., Sloan, J., Beckwith, M. and Phillips, L. (in preparation) 'Overcoming stigma as a social problem: Health and social science students' social distance from offenders and substance users active, in desistance or in recovery', *Social Science and Medicine*.

Caulkins, J. P. and Kleiman, M. A. (2011) 'Drugs and crime' in *The Oxford Handbook of Crime and Criminal Justice*, New York: Oxford University Press, 275–320.

Chaiken, J. M. and Chaiken, M. R. (1990) 'Drugs and predatory crime', *Crime and Justice*, 13, 203–239.

Chandler, R. K., Fletcher, B. W. and Volkow, N. D. (2009) 'Treating drug abuse and addiction in the criminal justice system: Improving public health and safety', *JAMA*, 301(2), 183–190.
Cloud, W. and Granfield, R. (2008) 'Conceptualizing recovery capital: Expansion of a theoretical construct', *Substance Use & Misuse*, 43(12–13), 1971–1986.
Colman, C. (2015) *Stoppen met druggebruik en criminaliteit : een verhaal van vallen en opstaan, van rugzakjes en vangnetten,* Den Haag: Boom Lemma Uitgevers.
Colman, C. and Vandam, L. (2009) 'Drugs and crime: are they hand in glove?: A review of literature', *Contemporary Issues in the Empirical Study of Crime*, 21–48.
Colman, C. and Vander Laenen, F. (2012) '"Recovery came first": Desistance versus recovery in the criminal careers of drug-using offenders', *The Scientific World Journal*, 2012, 657–671.
Davis, C., Bahr, S. J., Ward, C. J. C. and Justice, C. (2013) 'The process of offender reintegration: Perceptions of what helps prisoners reenter society', *Criminology & Criminal Justice*, 13(4), 446–469.
Dekkers, A., Beerens, J., Wittouck, C. and Vanderplasschen, W. (2016) 'Recovery through the eyes of drug treatment court clients', *Cahiers Politiestudies*, 40, 191–210.
Dutra, L., Stathopoulou, G., Basden, S. L., Leyro, T. M., Powers, M. B. and Otto, M. W. (2008) 'A meta-analytic review of psychosocial interventions for substance use disorders', *American Journal of Psychiatry*, 165(2), 179–187.
EMCDDA (2007) *Drugs and Crime — A Complex Relationship*, Lisbon: European Monitoring Centre for Drug and Drug Addiction.
Farrall, S. and Maruna, S. (2004) 'Desistance-focused criminal justice policy research: Introduction to a special issue on desistance from crime and public policy', *The Howard Journal of Criminal Justice*, 43(4), 358–367.
Fazel, S., Bains, P. and Doll, H. (2006) 'Substance abuse and dependence in prisoners: a systematic review', *Addiction*, 101(2), 181–191.
Fazel, S., Yoon, I. A. and Hayes, A. J. (2017) 'Substance use disorders in prisoners: an updated systematic review and meta-regression analysis in recently incarcerated men and women', *Addiction*, 112(10), 1725–1739.
Giordano, P. C., Cernkovich, S. A. and Rudolph, J. L. (2002) 'Gender, crime, and desistance: Toward a theory of cognitive transformation', *American Journal of Sociology*, 107(4), 990–1064.
Goldkamp, J. S., White, M. D. and Robinson, J. B. (2001) 'Do drug courts work? Getting inside the drug court black box', *Journal of Drug Issues*, 31(1), 27–72.
Goldstein, P. J. (1985) 'The drugs/violence nexus: A tripartite conceptual framework', *Journal of Drug Issues*, 15(4), 493–506.
Gossop, M., Trakada, K., Stewart, D. and Witton, J. (2005) 'Reductions in criminal convictions after addiction treatment: 5-year follow-up', *Drug and Alcohol Dependence*, 79(3), 295–302.
Harrison, L. D. and Scarpitti, F. R. (2002) 'Introduction: Progress and issues in drug treatment courts', *Substance Use & Misuse*, 37(12–13), 1441–1467.
Hayhurst, K. P., Jones, A., Millar, T., Pierce, M., Davies, L., Weston, S. and Donmall, M. (2013) 'Drug spend and acquisitive offending by substance misusers', *Drug and Alcohol Dependence*, 130(1–3), 24–29.
Holloway, K. R., Bennett, T. H. and Farrington, D. P. (2006) 'The effectiveness of drug treatment programs in reducing criminal behavior: A meta-analysis', *Psicothema*, 18(3), 620–629.
Holzer, H., Raphael, S. and Stoll, M. (2004) 'Will employers hire ex-offenders?: Employer preferences, background checks, and their determinants' in Patillo, M. and Weiman, B., eds., *Imprisoning America: The Social Effects of Mass Incarceration*, New York: Russell Sage Foundation.
Hunt, D. (2014) 'Arrestee Drug Abuse Monitoring II in the United States, 2013 (Restricted Use)',
Joe, G. W., Simpson, D. D. and Broome, K. (1999) 'Retention and patient engagement models for different treatment modalities in DATOS', *Drug Alcohol Dependence*, 57(2), 113–125.
Jones, R. Simonson, P. and Singleton, N. (2011) *Getting Serious About Stigma in Scotland: The Problem with Stigmatising Drug Users.* London: UK Drug Policy Commission.
Kewley, S. (2016) 'Strength based approaches and protective factors from a criminological perspective', *Aggression and Violent Behavior*, 32, 11–18.
Klag, S., O'Callaghan, F. and Creed, P. (2005) 'The use of legal coercion in the treatment of substance abusers: An overview and critical analysis of thirty years of research', *Substance Use & Misuse*, 40(12), 1777–1795.
Lacey, N. and Pickard, H. (2015) 'To blame or to forgive? Reconciling punishment and forgiveness in criminal justice', *Oxford Journal of Legal Studies*, 35(4), 665–696.
Laudet, A. B., Savage, R. and Mahmood, D. (2002) 'Pathways to long-term recovery: A preliminary investigation', *Journal of Psychoactive Drugs*, 34(3), 305–311.
Laudet, A. B. and White, W. (2010) 'What are your priorities right now? Identifying service needs across recovery stages to inform service development', *Journal of Substance Abuse Treatment*, 38(1), 51–59.
Leukefeld, C., Webster, J. M., Staton-Tindall, M. and Duvall, J. (2007) 'Employment and work among drug court clients: 12-month outcomes', *Substance Use & Misuse*, 42(7), 1109–1126.

Lipsey, M. W. and Cullen, F. T. (2007) 'The effectiveness of correctional rehabilitation: A review of systematic reviews', *Annual Review of Law and Social Science*, 3, 297–320.

MacCoun, R., Kilmer, B. and Reuter, P. (2003) 'Research on drugs-crime linkages: The next generation', in Ashcroft, J., Daniels, D. and Hart, S. (eds.), *Toward a Drugs and Crime Research Agenda for the 21st Century*, Washington: National Institute of Justice, 65–95.

Macdonald, S., Erickson, P., Wells, S., Hathaway, A. and Pakula, B. (2008) 'Predicting violence among cocaine, cannabis, and alcohol treatment clients', *Addictive Behaviors*, 33(1), 201–205.

Marsh, B. (2011) 'Narrating Desistance: Identity change and the 12-step script', *Irish Probation Journal*, 8.

Maruna, S. (2001) *Making Good. How Ex-convicts Reform and Rebuild Their Lives*, Washington, DC: American Psychological Association.

Massoglia, M. (2008) 'Incarceration as exposure: The prison, infectious disease, and other stress-related illnesses', *Journal of Health and Social Behavior*, 49(1), 56–71.

Mattick, R. P., Breen, C., Kimber, J. and Davoli, M. (2009) 'Methadone maintenance therapy versus no opioid replacement therapy for opioid dependence', *Cochrane Database Of Systematic Reviews*, (3).

McCollister, K. E., French, M. T., Prendergast, M. L., Hall, E. and Sacks, S. (2004) 'Long-term cost effectiveness of addiction treatment for criminal offenders', *Justice Quarterly*, 21(3), 659–679.

McNeill, F. (2006) 'A desistance paradigm for offender management', *Criminology & Criminal Justice*, 6(1), 39–62.

McNeill, F. (2012) 'Four forms of "offender" rehabilitation: Towards an interdisciplinary perspective', *Legal and Criminological Psychology*, 17(1), 18–36.

McNeill, F. (2014) 'Three aspects of desistance.' Blog-post based on a short paper prepared for a University of Sheffield Centre for Criminological Research Knowledge Exchange Seminar at the British Academy in London on 15th May 2014, available at http://blogs.iriss.org.uk/discoveringdesistance/2014/05/23/three-aspects-of-desistance

McNeill, F., Farrall, S., Lightowler, C., and Maruna, S. (2012) *How and Why People Stop Offending: Discovering Desistance*. Insight 15. Institute for Research and Innovation in Social Services.

Mears, D. P., Winterfield, L. A., Hunsaker, J., Moore, G. E. and White, R. M. (2003) *Drug Treatment in the Criminal Justice System: The Current State of Knowledge*, Washington, DC: Urban Institute, Justice Policy Center.

Minozzi, S., Saulle, R., De Crescenzo, F. and Amato, L. (2016) 'Psychosocial interventions for psychostimulant misuse', *The Cochrane Library*.

Mitchell, O., Cochran, J. C., Mears, D. P. and Bales, W. D. (2017) 'The effectiveness of prison for reducing drug offender recidivism: A regression discontinuity analysis', *Journal of Experimental Criminology*, 13(1), 1–27.

Mitchell, O., Wilson, D. B., Eggers, A. and MacKenzie, D. L. (2012) 'Assessing the effectiveness of drug courts on recidivism: A meta-analytic review of traditional and non-traditional drug courts', *Journal of Criminal Justice*, 40(1), 60–71.

Mitchell, O., Wilson, D. B. and MacKenzie, D. L. (2007) 'Does incarceration-based drug treatment reduce recidivism? A meta-analytic synthesis of the research', *Journal of Experimental Criminology*, 3(4), 353–375.

National Institute on Drug Abuse (2012) *Principles of drug abuse treatment for criminal justice populations: A research-based guide*, National Institute on Drug Abuse.

NICE (2007) *Drug misuse in over 16s: psychosocial interventions Clinical guideline*.

Nugent, B. and Schinkel, M. (2016) 'The pains of desistance', *Criminology & Criminal Justice*, 16(5), 568–584.

Paternoster, R. and Bushway, S. (2009) 'Desistance and the "feared self": Toward an identity theory of criminal desistance', *The Journal of Criminal Law and Criminology*, 1103–1156.

Phillips, L. A. and Shaw, A. (2013) 'Substance use more stigmatized than smoking and obesity', *Journal of Substance Use*, 18(4), 247–253.

Pickard, H. (2017) 'Responsibility without blame for addiction', *Neuroethics*, 10(1), 169–180.

Pierce, M., Hayhurst, K., Bird, S. M., Hickman, M., Seddon, T., Dunn, G. and Millar, T. (2015) 'Quantifying crime associated with drug use among a large cohort of sanctioned offenders in England and Wales', *Drug and Alcohol Dependence*, 155, 52–59.

Prendergast, M., Greenwell, L., Farabee, D. and Hser, Y.-I. (2009) 'Influence of perceived coercion and motivation on treatment completion and re-arrest among substance-abusing offenders', *The Journal of Behavioral Health Services &Research*, 36(2), 159–176.

Radcliffe, P. and Stevens, A. (2008) 'Are drug treatment services only for 'thieving junkie scumbags'? Drug users and the management of stigmatised identities', *Social Science & Medicine*, 67(7), 1065–1073.

Room, R. (2005) 'Stigma, social inequality and alcohol and drug use', *Drug and alcohol review*, 24(2), 143–155.

Sampson, R. J. and Laub, J. H. (1995) Crime in the Making: Pathways and Turning Points through Life, Cambridge, Massachusetts: Harvard University Press.

Seddon, T. (2007) 'Coerced drug treatment in the criminal justice system: Conceptual, ethical and criminological issues', *Criminology & Criminal Justice*, 7(3), 269–286.

Spohn, C. and Holleran, D. (2002) 'The effect of imprisonment on recidivism rates of felony offenders: A focus on drug offenders', *Criminology*, 40(2), 329–358.

Stevens, A. (2007) 'When two dark figures collide: Evidence and discourse on drug related crime', *Critical Social Policy*, 27(1), 77–99.

Stevens, A., Berto, D., Kerschl, V., Oeuvray, K., van Ooyen, M., Steffan, E., Heckmann, W. and Uchtenhagen, A. (2003) 'Summary Literature Review: The international literature on drugs, crime and treatment', Canterbury: University of Kent, European Institute of Social Service.

Sullivan, C. J. and Hamilton, Z. K. (2007) 'Exploring careers in deviance: A joint trajectory analysis of criminal behavior and substance use in an offender population,' *Deviant Behavior*, 28(6), 497–523.

Sullivan, C. J., Veysey, B. M., Hamilton, Z. K. and Grillo, M. (2007) 'Reducing out-of-community placement and recidivism: Diversion of delinquent youth with mental health and substance use problems from the justice system', *International Journal of Offender Therapy and Comparative Criminology*, 51(5), 555–577.

The Betty Ford Institute Consensus Panel (2007) 'What is recovery? A working definition from the Betty Ford Institute', *Journal of Substance Abuse Treatment*, 33(3), 221–228.

Uggen, C., Manza, J. and Behrens, A. (2004) 'Less than the average citizen': Stigma, role transition and the civic reintegration of convicted felons' in Maruna, S. and Immarigeon, R., eds., *After Crime and Punishment: Pathways to Offender Reintegration*, Portland, Oregon: Willan Publishing, 258–290.

United Kingdom Drug Policy Commission (UKDPC) (2008) *Working Towards Recovery*, London: United Kingdom Drug Policy Commission.

UNODC (United Nations Office for Drugs and Crime) (2016) *World Drug Report*.

UNODC (2018) *World Drug Report*.

UNODC/WHO (World Health Organization) (2016) *International Standards for the Treatment of Drug Use Disorders*, Geneva, Switzerland: United Nations Office on Drugs and Crime.

UNODC/WHO (World Health Organization) (2018) *Treatment and care for people with drug use disorders in contact with the criminal justice system. Alternative to Conviction or Punishment*.

Valentine, P. (2010) 'Peer-based recovery support services within a recovery community organization: The CCAR experience' in *Addiction Recovery Management*, Springer, 259–279.

van der Zanden, B. P., Dijkgraaf, M. G. W., Blanken, P., van Ree, J. M. and van den Brink, W. (2007) 'Patterns of acquisitive crime during methadone maintenance treatment among patients eligible for heroin assisted treatment', *Drug and Alcohol Dependence*, 86(1), 84–90.

Ward, T. and Brown, M. (2004) 'The good lives model and conceptual issues in offender rehabilitation. Psychology', *Crime & Law*, 10(3), 243–257.

Ward, T. and Stewart, C. (2003) 'Criminogenic needs and human needs: A theoretical model. Psychology', *Crime & Law*, 9(2), 125–143.

Weaver, B. (2009) 'Communicative punishment as a penal approach to supporting desistance', *Theoretical Criminology*, 13(1), 9–29.

White, W. (2008) *Recovery Management and Recovery-Oriented Systems of Care,* Chicago: Great Lakes Addiction Technology Transfer Center, Northeast.

Willis, G. M. and Ward, T. (2010) 'Risk management versus the Good Lives Model: The construction of better lives and the reduction of harm', *Transnational Criminology Manual*, 3, 763–781.

Wittouck, C., Dekkers, A., De Ruyver, B., Vanderplasschen, W. and Vander Laenen, F. (2013) 'The impact of drug treatment courts on recovery: A systematic review', *The Scientific World Journal,* 2013.

Woldgabreal, Y., Day, A. and Ward, T. (2014) 'The community-based supervision of offenders from a positive psychology perspective', *Aggression and Violent Behavior*, 19(1), 32–41.

Wolfer, L. (2006) 'Graduates speak: A qualitative exploration of drug court graduates' views of the strengths and weaknesses of the program', *Contemporary Drug Problems*, 33(2), 303–320.

Wooditch, A., Tang, L. L. and Taxman, F. (2014) 'Which criminogenic need changes are most important in promoting desistance from crime and substance use?', *Criminal Justice Behavior*, 41(3), 276–299.

INDEX

Note: Page numbers in *italics* indicate figures and in **bold** indicate tables on the corresponding pages.

For Product Safety Concerns and Information please contact our EU representative GPSR@taylorandfrancis.com
Taylor & Francis Verlag GmbH, Kaufingerstraße 24, 80331 München, Germany

www.ingramcontent.com/pod-product-compliance
Lightning Source LLC
LaVergne TN
LVHW080011210926
848481LV00011B/2992
9780367553654